ROTH FAMILY FOUNDATION

Imprint in Music

Michael P. Roth

and Sukey Garcetti

have endowed this

imprint to honor the

memory of their parents,

Julia and Harry Roth,

whose deep love of music

they wish to share

with others.

THE PUBLISHER AND THE UNIVERSITY OF CALIFORNIA PRESS
FOUNDATION GRATEFULLY ACKNOWLEDGE THE GENEROUS
SUPPORT OF THE ROTH FAMILY FOUNDATION IMPRINT IN MUSIC,
ESTABLISHED BY A MAJOR GIFT FROM SUKEY AND GIL GARCETTI
AND MICHAEL P. ROTH.

THE PUBLISHER ALSO GRATEFULLY ACKNOWLEDGES THE GENEROUS
SUPPORT OF THE LLOYD HIBBERD ENDOWMENT OF THE AMERICAN
MUSICOLOGICAL SOCIETY, FUNDED IN PART BY THE NATIONAL
ENDOWMENT FOR THE HUMANITIES AND THE ANDREW W. MELLON
FOUNDATION.

STRAVINSKY IN THE AMERICAS

CALIFORNIA STUDIES IN 20TH-CENTURY MUSIC

Richard Taruskin, General Editor

STRAVINSKY IN THE AMERICAS

Transatlantic Tours and Domestic Excursions
from Wartime Los Angeles (1925–1945)

H. Colin Slim

Foreword by Richard Taruskin

UNIVERSITY OF CALIFORNIA PRESS

University of California Press, one of the most distinguished university presses in the United States, enriches lives around the world by advancing scholarship in the humanities, social sciences, and natural sciences. Its activities are supported by the UC Press Foundation and by philanthropic contributions from individuals and institutions. For more information, visit www.ucpress.edu.

University of California Press
Oakland, California

Library of Congress Cataloging-in-Publication Data

Names: Slim, H. Colin (Harry Colin), author. | Taruskin, Richard, writer of foreword.
Title: Stravinsky in the Americas : transatlantic tours and domestic excursions from wartime Los Angeles (1925–1945) / H. Colin Slim.
Description: Oakland, California : University of California Press, [2019] | Includes bibliographical references and index. |
Identifiers: LCCN 2018034901 (print) | LCCN 2018038153 (ebook) | ISBN 9780520971530 (epub and ePDF) | ISBN 9780520299924 (cloth : alk. paper)
Subjects: LCSH: Stravinsky, Igor, 1882–1971—Travel—United States. | Stravinsky, Igor, 1882–1971—Criticism and interpretation. | Music—United States—20th century—History and criticism.
Classification: LCC ML410.S932 (ebook) | LCC ML410.S932 S614 2019 (print) | DDC 780.92 [B]—dc23
LC record available at https://lccn.loc.gov/2018034901

Manufactured in the United States of America

26 25 24 23 22 21 20 19
10 9 8 7 6 5 4 3 2 1

In memoriam, beloved Canadian and US family members—
the greatest generation

ABBREVIATED CONTENTS

CONTENTS

   Two Veras in Paris · New York with secretary-valet, translator-blackmailer, Sabline · Piano and podium in eastern and midwestern cities: Paul Kochanski and Gershwin · Hoytie's party and Lester Donahue · Critics of Octet and Piano Concerto · Steinway's dinner and the inscribed, piano-shaped, chocolate cake · Greta Torpadie, chamber concerts, cropped photos · Roerig's interview and Schoenberg's delayed verdict · Pianola rolls and phonograph records · Thanks for eighteen Steinways · Consulting Dr. Garbat · Avoiding Soudeikine at the Met's Petrushka · *Antithetic reactions about the United States: Cincinnati (March) and home in Nice (May) · Kochanski's* Pulcinella Suite reassigned · *Enjoying the tour's profits with American expats and Picasso on the Riviera · Composer as conductor*

ILLUSTRATIONS

FIGURES

MUSIC EXAMPLES

FOREWORD

There has always been a white spot, as Russians say, in Stravinsky's biography. His early years in America, beginning with his stay at Harvard in 1939–40 and ending with the advent, in 1948, of his assistant Robert Craft, to whom we owe the hypervoluminous documentation of his last quarter-century, are the period of Stravinsky's least-played, least-esteemed compositions, and the period when least attention was paid to his comings and goings. Between the Symphony in C, begun in Paris and finished in Hollywood after Paris had fallen to the Germans, and the Symphony in Three Movements, composed in the hopeful and finally euphoric late phases of World War II, come a series of works known only to the most dedicated aficionados. Unless you can hum the Tango for piano, the *Danses concertantes*, the *Scènes de ballet*, the *Scherzo à la Russe*, the Ode, the *Circus Polka*, the cantata *Babel*, the *Four Norwegian Moods*, or the Sonata for Two Pianos, you are not among them.

Why the neglect? Among the reasons were the circumstances of their composition. They were written, either on commission or "on spec," by a composer getting his bearings in a new and unfamiliar environment, who needed money because his European royalties had been disrupted, and who sought the less than lofty affordances that popular performers (such as Paul Whiteman), Broadway producers (such as Billy Rose), local California conductors (such as Werner Janssen), or the Ringling Brothers Circus could provide—not to mention the Hollywood movie studios, with which Stravinsky haggled endlessly without ever reaching a meeting of minds, and for which he wrote a lot of music that ended up elsewhere, to his chagrin and occasional humiliation.

Once Craft was on the scene, moreover, he exerted a potent influence—not only on the music Stravinsky wrote, where it could seem that he managed to divert a mighty river in its course (and back toward high repute, to Stravinsky's lasting gratitude), but also on public knowledge of, and interest in, Stravinsky's daily life. To read Craft's diaries is to wonder whether Stravinsky knew anyone who wasn't famous. This was not only because Craft's account was skewed toward Craft's interests, or that Craft's interests eventually became Stravinsky's interests as well, but also because, partly thanks to Craft and the affordances he provided (especially on concert tours), Stravinsky's star-power grew appreciably, and his last decades were again glamorous, as they had been in Europe before the war.

In the early California years, the period we Stravinskians like to call BC (before Craft), Stravinsky's way of life was simpler and more modest than at any other time since his so-called Swiss period, coinciding with World War I. The reason was similar: he sought the peace and quiet of neutral territory (which the United States could provide until December 1941), and thereafter the second war isolated him. He lived in serenely uxorious domesticity with Vera Arturovna, his second wife, something he never achieved with Ekaterina Gavrilovna, his first, who had to put up with the restlessness of a young genius on the make. The Stravinskys lived among neighbors, at first in Massachusetts and then in California, who were far from A-list celebrities. They included some fellow émigrés, some local musicians, but also relatively regular Americans, whose names—McQuoid, Sample, Andersson—are as unfamiliar, even to most Stravinskians, as the sounds of *Babel.*

Now, with this book, H. Colin Slim has at last filled in the white spot. Always among the most distinguished of North American musicologists (and a past president of the American Musicological Society), this Canadian-born scholar was known in the wider world of learning as a specialist in sixteenth-century music, with an emphasis on sources and iconography. His first big achievement, the edition of *Musica Nova* (Venice, 1540), the earliest printed collection of instrumental part music, was issued by the University of Chicago Press in 1964 to inaugurate one of the most illustrious (and luxurious) series of American musicological publications, Monuments of Renaissance Music. There followed a steady stream of articles, editions, and monographs, including important studies of Francesco da Milano and Philippe Verdelot. His other signal achievement, with which his name will always be associated, was his role as *spiritus rector* to the nascent music department at the University of California at Irvine, where he spent practically his entire academic career, beginning in 1965 when the Irvine campus was founded and ending with his retirement in 1994.

Those who knew him, however, knew that Colin, a professionally trained pianist and conductor in his premusicological days, always nurtured a secret passion for Stravinsky, which until the end of the twentieth century found its outlet not in publication but in the assemblage, over many years, of an outstanding collection of Stravinskiana: letters, photos, documents, and memorabilia. This bug had bitten him early, and in the most personal possible way, during his student years at the University of British Columbia, when (according to his own testimony on the University of California Irvine Libraries website) his life "was touched directly by the renowned composer."

In 1952, as a young musician in the Department of Music at UBC, he took part in two Canadian premieres: the Concerto for Two Pianos and *Les Noces* (Cantata in Four Scenes), the latter of which he conducted. Six months later, he drove with Stravinsky to his final rehearsal with the Vancouver Symphony Orchestra. Slim again spoke with the aged but still vibrant composer backstage in Los Angeles in 1966, upon participating in two choral works under Stravinsky's direction.

Colin donated his collection to the UBC Library in 1999, and prepared a deeply researched and annotated catalogue for it, which the library published in 2002. This was the moment when his professional and avocational interests finally meshed, and he was welcomed into the ranks of Stravinsky scholars (a category that had not really existed in the musicology of his formative years). In retirement he has been living in Berkeley, a short drive from the campus where I worked from 1987 to 2014. He and I became Stravinsky pals, and I greatly enjoyed our many visits, always tactfully coinciding with my office hours (and only if he was not taking my pupils' time). "Hey, Prexy!" I would call out happily (recalling his stint at the helm of the AMS) whenever I saw him in my doorway, in anticipation of some rare and stimulating find. The Russian- (and in one memorable case, Yiddish-) language documents Colin had unearthed, and which he asked me to help translate, were always fascinating; and in their steady accumulation gave evidence that his interest in Stravinsky, postcollection, had only grown. Something, clearly, was cooking.

When in 2009 Colin published his magnificent eighty-page article, "Lessons with Stravinsky: The Notebook of Earnest Andersson (1878–1943)" in the *Journal of the American Musicological Society*, finally telling the story (one of countless tales the aging composer had resolutely forced down the memory hole) of Stravinsky's one long-term paying pupil and the "Futurama" Symphony he wrote with Stravinsky's help (or rather, that Stravinsky wrote in his presence and on his themes), it became common knowledge in the profession that Colin's hobby had become a serious, indeed major, research project, reflecting the sovereign forensic and interpretive skills one of our grandees had developed over the course of a long career. Buzz developed. A complicated sequence of negotiations, reminiscent of Stravinsky's with the "Hollywood boys" (as my old professor Paul Henry Lang, who had taken a few barbs along the way from the great man, liked to say), allowed the book to finally wend its way to the University of California Press and to my series, California Studies in 20th-Century Music. Thus, I became not only Colin's (somewhat) junior colleague and friend but also, and to my great delight, his editor.

So I have the honor of announcing to readers and scholars and fans of the Stravinsky literature that they have in store not only a narrative cornucopia but also a visual feast, reflecting Colin's lifelong devotion to the pictorial documentation of musical artifacts and events. The wonderfully variegated material is presented with compelling authority and is at all times thoroughly contextualized by a writer who has read more English-language documentation related to Stravinsky than anyone else had ever done before, as well as the whole Stravinsky literature in all the European languages except Russian (which is where I came in, together with my native-born pupil Olga Panteleeva, to whom I will add my thanks to Colin's). But at the same time, the writing communicates, in its warmth and wit, the deep relish that a hobbyist, such as the author had once been, enjoys. At once a Kenner and a Liebhaber, he has produced a kind of disciplined counterpart to the exuberant, unruly compendia that the uniquely privileged but spottily equipped Robert Craft got to issue in the decade or so between Stravinsky's death and the public availability of his *Nachlass*. Those who have burrowed in those books know what to expect from this one.

Richard Taruskin
El Cerrito, California
31 March 2018

PREFACE

Igor Stravinsky's compositional output during the first years of his immigration to the United States is sometimes considered a feeble and ineffective interlude between the two great symphonies—the one *In C,* the other *In Three Movements.* This is owing to what some consider a turn to commercialism, signaled by several of his commissions and by his efforts to compose Hollywood movie scores. I, however, regard these wartime works as eminently suitable, and often delightful, ways to come to terms with a radically new cultural and musical environment.

To fully understand, it is necessary to look back a little further, to Stravinsky's initial experiences on American shores before he resettled in the United States permanently in 1939. This book first tells the story of Stravinsky's transatlantic voyages to, and concert tours in, US and Canadian cities between 1925 and 1939 and one such voyage to South America in 1936. During his 1937 voyage to the United States, we can see, for example, insights into Stravinsky's past as he divulged some unexpected information during conversations with a Russian American friend living in Los Angeles. Their conversations, published here for the first time, tell us about Stravinsky's life circa 1904 in St. Petersburg with his esteemed composer-teacher, with a great entrepreneur, with a major painter, and with a great basso. The book then turns to concert excursions he made during World War II from Los Angeles to US, Mexican, and Canadian cities, this time as an émigré. It examines the effects these voyages and excursions had on him and he on a developing American modern music and art scene. I have determined not only to recount Stravinsky's voyages and excursions but also to gauge what effects they had on him and on those persons he met. Such persons include not only well-known international figures—Nadia Boulanger, Josef Hofmann, Serge Koussevitzky, Pierre Monteux, Victoria Ocampo, George Balanchine, Sir Ernest MacMillan, Dagmar Godowsky, Edward G. Robinson, Darius Milhaud, Feodor Chaliapin, Vladimir Serov, Walt Disney—but also the far less famous—for example, Dorothy and Edwin McQuoid, Earnest Andersson, James Sample, and Severin Kavenoki.

In accounting for his travel experiences and the reactions of others during them, the book contributes substantially to future studies about Stravinsky, particularly in countering the received wisdom on three points: that his voyages included extramarital affairs deserves mention as much as his other experiences on these shores; one might have thought that his mingling with so many musicians and plain citizens in North and South America would lessen his anti-Semitism, but alas, evidence from as late as 1948 shows otherwise; and because many of the works he composed in a wide variety of styles between 1925 and 1945 have been labeled *neoclassic*, a term he intensely disliked, I propose (in an appendix) an alternative, *ironical*, akin to present-day literary practice.

No systematic analysis of Stravinsky's works composed during the twenty-year period of his visits to and tours of the Americas appears here. Instead, brief comments are offered about the Violin Concerto, the close of Symphony in C, and the second and third movements of Symphony in Three Movements. I provide slightly more analysis on the lesser-studied works he completed before the Japanese surrender in August of 1945, such as his multiple "Star-Spangled Banner" arrangements, Ode, *Babel*, and *Scherzo à la Russe*. Thus, for example, the Mass is excluded: although its first two movements were written late in 1942, its other three were not finished until 1948. Similarly, the bewitching *Ebony Concerto* begun soon after hostilities ceased, was not completed until December of 1945. Consideration is also given to his contributions to the first movement of Earnest Andersson's *Futurama Symphony* and to several settings in English, made either on the spot for friends or offered later to them. Some settings employ his own music; others quote "The Star-Spangled Banner" or Tchaikovsky's "Little Russian" Symphony.

With the exception of the jazz-influenced *Praeludium* (1935–36), detailed analyses are restricted to the first wave of what Stephen Walsh calls "late neo-classical works."[1] Because such works are often burdened with the term *neoclassical,*[2] and because Stravinsky himself disavowed this term, it is avoided, in favor of the aforementioned concept involving "irony" (see Appendix).

By 1998, when I donated my 123-item Stravinsky collection to the University of British Columbia at its Point Grey campus in Vancouver (which published a catalogue in 2002), I had come to realize that, beyond the well-known resources of the Sacher Foundation, substantial documentation respecting Stravinsky's tours and excursions exists in US and Canadian institutions and in private collections, and that much was still passing through the hands of autograph dealers and auctioneers.[3] (Obviously, traces of such items are easily lost.)

Newspapers have been under-utilized as sources of information about the reception of Stravinsky's music in the Americas; as late as 2013, a call was sent out for "a new generation of scholars . . . to ransack the newspaper files of every city in which Stravinsky appeared as conductor, pianist, or duo-soloist with his son Soulima or the violinist Samuel Dushkin."[4] Although "scholars" should not "ransack," and although I am not part of that "new generation," I have spent many an enjoyable and profitable hour searching newspaper files for US, Canadian, and Mexican cities. Faintly palpable traces remain of an early subtitle for this book—"Dates, Plates, Details." Accuracy in dates is a desideratum. The severe review of errors in Eric White's 1966 biography should be warning enough.[5]

I offer corrections and emendations to Robert Craft's work where appropriate. Apropos Charles M. Joseph's fine chapter, "Boswellizing an Icon: Stravinsky, Craft, and the Historian's Dilemma," which examines Craft's several editorial roles, I have endeavored to follow the good advice in Professor Joseph's penultimate sentence: "go about the business of screening, evaluating, balancing, restoring, and assembling as accurate as we can a complete profile of Stravinsky."[6]

Plates are helpful, too. My long-standing interest in the iconography of music in paintings and other visual media has enabled a substantial visual documentation to accompany this narrative. Stravinsky's copious photographic *Nachlass* has sometimes misled biographers: I cite many examples of cropping (great and small), that can deceive the unwary reader.[7] Part 2 sanctions another kind of plate. It comes from that era's straightforward homonym for inevitable and ubiquitous periodontal interventions: during 1941–42 even a Stravinsky could not escape them.

In respect to the sheer number of details, the ones I have chosen from a sea of possibilities strike me as relevant[8] and, occasionally, revelatory. Gustave Charles Flaubert is reputed to have said, "God is in the details," and Stravinsky, an admirer of Flaubert, knew this saying well.[9] In our own century there is a variant that supplants the Deity: "the Devil is in the details," uttered, if not coined, by Mies van der Rohe.[10] And a current British novelist and Flaubert admirer observes, "All details, eventually, will be out of date. But their substance is universal. Without them, no account of real life can hope to outlive rust and larvae."[11] Relatively early in his acquaintance with Stravinsky, a Los Angeles critic took a related tack in respect to the several opinions of the composer held by his fellow scriveners. "Caught up in the argument about whether he [Stravinsky] is god or devil, many of us have forgotten to take his measure in his music, where he is, after all, a man like the rest of us."[12] More recently, the provocatively titled essay "Stravinsky as Devil" investigates a trio of censorious—and to many, baffling—essays by Theodor Adorno.[13] Stravinsky had profound beliefs in both God and the Evil One.

The present book relies on neither deity nor devil. Many details chosen for special examination concern visual images; others support or contest the hagiography now afforded the composer. Not every detail offered will be of equal interest to every reader. Yet, here and there, one or two may intrigue, and even delight, admirers of Stravinsky's works, if not always of the man. To appropriate a current cultural construct, Stravinsky was surely a figure of "complexity and contradiction."[14]

ACKNOWLEDGMENTS

In what turned out to be but a middle stage in this project, I owe much to Jann Pasler, who worked heroically with me over several years. Both readers' reports she solicited—even the error-strewn one closer to a harangue than a review—proved helpful, each in its own way.

Heartfelt thanks go to Beverly Wilcox. On grounds that she was learning about Stravinsky from me, this fine scholar of eighteenth-century musical France selflessly revised, edited, typed, computed, telephoned, communicated, wrote, assisted, and even motored countless times between Davis and Berkeley. Her unwavering support—material and moral—over several rather difficult years is profoundly appreciated.

To have attracted the attention of Richard Taruskin, who has kindly provided a foreword, is a great boon. From the publication in 1996 of his two-volume study of the Russian Stravinsky and his later contributions about the composer, I have admired his intellectual rigor, courage, and acute musical instincts. Going over my manuscript not once but twice and offering a great deal of wise counsel, he broadened my horizons and enabled me to avoid many a blunder.

Toward the close of this project, fortune smiled in the person of Desmond Sheehan. His abilities in computer usage shame my ignorance of and, indeed, timidity with and reservations about technology. Nor shall I omit thanking another young person, a family member, Janet Neary, newly tenured at Hunter College. Even while teaching there and completing her book, *Fugitive Testimony,* she more than once graciously undertook to examine the several literary sources concerning Stravinsky in the New York Public Library.

Here at UC Berkeley's Hargrove Music Library, John Shepard and his extraordinary and outstandingly obliging and helpful team—Allison, Manuel, Mat—never failed to come up with the needed information. I am also grateful to the following persons who aided me in diverse ways: Linda and George Bauer; Colonel (ret.) Edward Boggs; Leon Botstein; George Boziwick; Heather Briston; Charlotte Brown; Michael Bushnell; Jeanette L. Casey; Steven Chapman; Loring B. Conant; David Peter Coppen; Dorothy Crawford; Frank A. D'Accone; Rebecca Darby-Williams; Kristine K. Forney; David Gilbert; Michael Green; Daniel Heartz; Robert D. Heylmun; James A. Hijiya; Edward Hirschland; D. Kern Holoman; Rachel Howerton; Robert Hughes; Paul J. Jackson; Juliana Jenkins; Leonard W. Johnson; Robert Kosovsky; Steven La Coste; Marion Green LaRue; Kevin Madill; W. Gibson Mann; Lois Marcus; Ilene McKenna; Vera Micznik; James Neary; Del Nsumbu; Linda Ogden; Jessie Ann Owens; Olga Panteleeva; Michael Pettersen; Sigrid Piroch; William F. Prizer; Kate Rivers; Richard Rodda; Mary Rogers; William H. Rosar; Ezra Schebas; Nina Scolnik; Kay Shelemay; Lisa Shiota; Stanislav Shvabrin; Elaine Sisman; N. William Snedden; Elizabeth Valkenier; Pieter van den Toorn; Nancy van Deusen; Kate van Orden; Michael Walensky; Kirsten Walsh; Stephen Walsh; Kathryn Wayne; and James Westby.

INTRODUCTION

What distinguishes Stravinsky's initial North American tours from those of many other visiting composer-performers is the music-loving public's preconception of Stravinsky as a radical modernist, a notion sustained over many years. In 1925, for example, *Petrushka* was regarded in Philadelphia as "ultra-modern music,"[1] and the Piano Concerto reviewed in New York under the banner "Ultra-Modern Concerto Disgusts."[2] Chicago that year even considered him an "anarchist" and "diabolical."[3] The "modernist" label stemmed mostly from the initial reception in Paris of *The Rite of Spring* in 1913. Its worldwide notoriety continues even into our own epoch with, for example, Jan Kounen's 2009 film, *Coco Chanel et Igor Stravinsky*[4] and the 2013 centenary celebrations of the *Rite*'s premiere.[5] For many years the ignorance or laziness (often both) of North American critics, national and local, helped perpetuate this reputation of a "modernist" (Seattle, 1937, and Minneapolis, 1940),[6] even a "Prince of Modernists" (Toronto, 1937).[7] One clear proof lies in the shocked reaction as late as 1944 of US government officials to Stravinsky's arrangement of "The Star-Spangled Banner":[8] not the arranger's rather straightforward diatonic harmonization but his *name* and *reputation* that caused the outcry. Thus, in the early 1940s Stravinsky struggled to overcome his undeserved reputation as an extreme modernist. During 1940, his first year in Los Angeles, for example, only his *Firebird* was heard, and that in four performances only. His music was not played very often in his adopted hometown. A glance at the concert calendars for these years shows a paucity of concert engagements, and that was only partly due to wartime privations.

Notwithstanding his five transatlantic tours, this bugaboo about *The Rite*'s creator only began to dissipate in the excursions of the 1940s with the public's gradual acclimatization to Stravinsky's soundscape, and ironically, it came from a source Stravinsky hated: the "visualization" of *The Rite of Spring* in Walt Disney's *Fantasia*. The music was as mutilated as its performance, the images charmingly false. Stravinsky even lied to a Cincinnati reporter late in November of 1940 when he claimed that he had not yet seen it.[9] In fact, he and his new wife, Vera, had viewed *Fantasia* almost six weeks earlier in Disney's studio and were "horrified by the bad taste."[10] Confiding "somewhat anxiously" to the Cincinnati reporter that he thought Disney "should consult with me regarding *mes idées et l'effet général*,"[11] his fib served two purposes. First, it avoided giving his real opinion of *Fantasia*, and second, it kept open the possibility that this fib might serve him well with Disney during a "two-year contract to collaborate on film versions of some of his other ballets." Having signed such a contract on 28 October, he went on to inform this reporter that "America may yet see Mickey Mouse liberating the princess in the 'Fire Bird.'"[12]

When and how did Stravinsky become a great composer in the minds of the American musical public? It and the majority of Stravinsky's critics were slow to comprehend him as a composer who could even then be writing masterpieces (and a few minor gems as well). Late in 1939, the year Stravinsky settled in the United States, a poll in the weekly *Musical Courier* asked its readers "which living composers [might] still be in the active repertoire one hundred years from now."[13] Stravinsky ranked fourth, below Jean Sibelius, Richard Strauss, and Sergei Rachmaninoff. In January of 1940, a reviewer of an all-Stravinsky concert earlier that month with the New York Philharmonic observed that "it is dubious if the vital wine runs sufficiently strong in them (*Apollon, Petrushka, Jeu de cartes, Firebird*) to prolong their days much beyond their author's."[14] Vera's diary entry about the Symphony in C and its success in Los Angeles in February of 1941 was right on the mark: "very little [success]. The public prefers 'oldies.'"[15] Robert Craft, writing in 1982, thought that because of the first three great ballet scores—*Firebird, Petrushka*, and *Rite of Spring*—Stravinsky, had he died in 1913, "still would have ranked with Schoenberg as one of the century's two great composers," though adding that in the early 1950s his music was comparatively little performed in the States. In 1943 *Musical America* had polled its readers, asking which composers they regarded as "contemporary leaders"; Stravinsky placed only fifth, just after Sibelius. A year later, he ranked second, after Strauss, but by July 1945, he had slipped back three notches, giving pride of place to Strauss, ranking even below the long-deceased Debussy.[16] A normally supportive associate at Columbia Records, writing of the composer's concerts in January of 1944 with the Boston Symphony Orchestra when he led Symphony in C, *Pulcinella*, Four Norwegian Moods, and *Circus Polka*, had ruminated in a well-regarded journal on the fate of the composer's music: "It was also a little sad to realize that Stravinsky's later mode of making music, original and striking as it has been, is a dead end and is not going to survive him."[17]

A number of factors that built up gradually during the transatlantic tours and the later domestic excursions and their concerts led to Stravinsky's eventual success by the late

1950s. One was his immense adaptability to change. He had first exhibited this quality as a refugee in Switzerland, thereafter in France,[18] and above all in the United States. Two examples spring to mind: one, utilizing a first run-through of his Octet by DeLaMarter at the Chicago Arts Club in 1935 as an emergency rehearsal for his own performance of it there; and two, employing Dorothy Ellis McQuoid (whom he had previously coached) to replace the delayed Adele Marcus at his first Los Angeles Philharmonic rehearsal of Capriccio in 1941. Another factor stemmed from his Diaghilev collaborations, especially the famous premiere of *The Rite of Spring* in Paris. In addition to notoriety, music lovers thus associated his name with ballet, garnering an extra bounty of recognition by lovers of the terpsichorean art. And for better or worse, North and South Americans regarded prewar Paris, as they still do, as the epicenter of intellectual and artistic chic.[19]

By virtue of the territory traversed in the transatlantic tours and domestic excursions, the scope of his name-recognition in cities big and small was greatly expanded. At first, his reputation centered on his skill as a touring pianist, but it gradually shifted in favor of his increasing conductorial skills, more and more confined to his own music. Those two abilities equated to "authenticity" in the minds of his audiences and the record-buying public: they wanted, indeed, demanded active participation by the composer as his own executant. Bela Bartók, composer-pianist, was similarly rewarded, albeit to a lesser extent, and Rachmaninoff, composer-pianist-conductor, to a greater. Yet another factor, very necessary in Stravinsky's case because he hardly ever gave lessons, was the advocacy exerted by Nadia Boulanger.

A final factor, and the most problematic for some (but not for him), was Stravinsky's success in ventures bordering on commercialism, accompanied by great publicity, for example "The Star-Spangled Banner" "scandals" in St. Louis and Boston; having Paul Whiteman's band undertake a national broadcast of *Scherzo à la Russe;* and especially, the Ringling Brothers' commission of *Circus Polka* for its elephants, endorsed for US troops over the radio by Jack Benny on 4 February 1945.[20]

Beethoven purportedly said on his deathbed: "Vox populi, vox dei. I never believed it."[21] Whether Stravinsky knew this story or not, his disdainful remark uttered late in June 1956—"I have never attached much importance to the collective mind and collective opinion. . . . Music never was for the masses."[22]—still demands refutation. As shown here and elsewhere, Stravinsky *did* care what the masses thought of him and of his music.[23] This lifelong conflict between artistic sensibility and commercial considerations gives rise to additional reflection about his enduring and endlessly intriguing personal fallibility. Realist Lawrence Morton (who came to know Stravinsky well but in a different way than Robert Craft) had to remind his journalist colleagues early in 1944 that "he is, after all, a man like the rest of us."[24] His anti-Semitism, his adulteries—quaintly dubbed many years later as "marital augmentation"[25]—his concealment of musical sources, the misrepresentation of his contribution to Earnest Andersson's symphony, have become well known.

No widespread conception of Stravinsky as a composer of great works arose in the United States until the late 1940s, and that, partly from his own efforts. Even in 1948 a six-page laudatory essay in *Time* magazine still labeled him a "Master Mechanic."[26] Other factors included the special mystique of European composers, singers, instrumentalists, and especially conductors. A new generation of US composers (and eventually *their* students) admired him; so did a few of the most thoughtful critics; and ardent propagandists such as Nadia Boulanger indoctrinated their disciples with his latest scores.[27] Other European émigrés such as Arnold Schoenberg and Paul Hindemith were championed by their numerous US students; Stravinsky's disinclination to teach might have deprived him of such extensive support from the next generation of fledgling composers, had it not been for Boulanger and many of her followers. As Stravinsky's American assistant, Robert Craft's real influence on the musico-literary public began to be felt only in the late 1950s and was exerted through sharing conducting duties with the composer and through their many published conversation books. Without Craft's preparation and, in some instances, his participation, Stravinsky's late performances of his own music, c. 1956–66, would not have reached the high level they evince in the recordings.[28]

Robert Craft appeared in Stravinsky's life at a time of the gradual falling away of Stravinsky's close California "associates" during the latter years of World War II— Dagmar Godowsky, Earnest Andersson, the Samples, the McQuoids, and especially the decrepitude in 1948 of his longtime friend from old Russia, Dr. Alexis Kall. Craft first glimpsed Stravinsky in Carnegie Hall at a rehearsal preceding the concert on Thursday, 24 January 1946, when the composer led the New York Philharmonic in the world premiere of his Symphony in Three Movements, the so-called *Victory Symphony*.[29] On 8 February Craft witnessed the composer's last public appearance as pianist, in the *Duo concertant* with Joseph Szigeti, at a New York Philharmonic pension benefit. By 1 March 1947, however, the young man had introduced himself to Stravinsky in a very telling way: he wrote Stravinsky that he had discerned, in the Philharmonic rehearsals and performances of the new Symphony, "trouble with the clef in the cello part,"[30] that is, the tenor clef having been read as a bass clef at reh. 139 in the second movement.

As Craft himself later acknowledged, not long after his first face-to-face meeting with Stravinsky on 31 March 1948 in New York, "I was a factotum."[31] He was thus the last and by far the most competent successor to Kall and Earnest Andersson. Nicolas Nabokov correctly regarded Craft as a " '*Gottesgabe*' [godsend] to Stravinsky in his Hollywood isolation,"[32] even though Craft's and Nabokov's notion of the composer's isolation in movietown is an exaggeration. In truth Craft remained Stravinsky's longest, last, and certainly most loyal "associate" until death took the great composer on 6 April 1971. Even after Vera Stravinsky's death in 1982, Craft continued to write about both Stravinskys, and to record and promote Stravinsky's music, well into our new century and into his own extreme old age. Although illness prevented him from attending the Théâtre des Champs-Elysées for the one-hundredth anniversary of *The Rite*, he remained active, dying at ninety-two.[33]

World War II began in September 1939, three weeks before Stravinsky sailed from France for the last time. He had a temporary visa and return ticket for 1940, coinciding with the end of a series of lectures at Harvard University and a final Collegium Musicum. The war stranded him in the United States with his longtime Swedish-born Parisian mistress, Vera Soudeikina, who arrived in January of 1940 and whom he married two months later. The couple needed permanent rather than visitor visas to remain in the United States and apply for citizenship. Such visas could only be obtained in a foreign country. Hence the four concerts in Mexico City, arranged by composer-conductor Carlos Chavez.

Stravinsky's life in California during World War II, which concerns part 2 of this book, may be signaled by a series of domestic excursions and concerts in and around the United States. He and Vera settled in Southern California, at first as renters in Hollywood and Beverly Hills and then as homeowners in West Hollywood. His concert excursions, usually with Vera, were severely limited by wartime exigencies. On 18 April 1940 Vera noted plans for "a concert tour next season." This turned out to be a particularly extended one, spanning late May of 1940 to early December of 1941. There were performances in Chicago, Cincinnati, Minneapolis, Washington, Baltimore, Boston, New York, Los Angeles, San Diego, and St. Louis.[34] Trips to Mexico City in the summers of 1940 and 1941 count as domestic in two senses: they remained within the North American continent, and they included his second wife.[35]

These periods of wartime travel (here called "excursions") furnish sundry images and texts (some published for the first time here) concerning Stravinsky's adjustment to a new world. Roughly speaking, the completions of the Symphony in C (1938–40) and the Symphony in Three Movements (1942–45) frame the years of World War II. I have added a short coda about the January 1946 world premiere of Stravinsky's last symphony in New York, and his local premieres of it in Boston; San Francisco; and Washington, DC, and premieres led by others in Los Angeles and Oakland. This coda also takes up the vexed question of "programs" assigned to the symphony, perhaps by Stravinsky, certainly by others.

The over-the-border visits to Mexico in July of 1940 and August of 1941, and additional trips through December of 1941 are conceptualized as I believe the Stravinskys did: as his first domestic excursions rather than as the termination of his last international tour.[36] They occurred after the end of his obligations to Harvard, his move to California, and his decision to remain in the United States. After the Japanese attack on Pearl Harbor, only one other border-crossing occurred: for a Montreal concert in March of 1945. The Stravinskys became US citizens at the close of that year.

Many questions have arisen about Stravinsky's behavior during his travels: his performance abilities, his lessening interest in pianism, his growing interest in conducting, and his acquisition of suitable skills for that vocation. Assessments of such skills appear at the close of my accounts of each of the first four tours and near the close of the second half of the book, concerning the wartime period.[37] New light is also shed on his teaching activities from the last transatlantic tour through the end of the second domestic excursion: first at Harvard, and later in Los Angeles.

Throughout the book I address questions concerning Stravinsky's political, social, moral, personal, and amorous activities during his travels, when he was generally out of the public eye and free of family and friends. His relationships with women—his first wife, Catherine; Vera Janacopulos-Staal; Dagmar Godowsky—and with Jews—(Godowsky herself, half-Jewish), Monteux, Dushkin, Koussevitzky, Milhaud—were not uniformly gracious. Several pieces of evidence concerning these failings are examined here because they affected his compositions and performances and were, in turn, affected by his experiences in the Americas. To name two examples, Dagmar was probably not only his lover but also at times his tour promoter and business agent,[38] and he was a willing partner in travel and performances with Samuel Dushkin, a violinist of Jewish parentage, who remained close to him from late 1930 to the end of his days.[39]

Why did Stravinsky undertake these arduous tours beyond Europe, where he had lived continuously since the outbreak of World War I? The increasing number of transatlantic tours during the 1930s is partly—and sadly—explained by the need to support his tubercular and increasingly immobile first wife, Catherine; as early as 1932 he contemplated a South American tour with his then lover Vera. Another reason was a growing uncertainty about the future of his lucrative concertizing in Nazi Germany.[40]

"I like a lot of money," he famously exclaimed in mid-December 1939 to the same San Francisco reporter to whom he had confided just two years earlier that "[touring] is *bon business*."[41] He had never forgotten the monetary and artistic success of his initial US tour in 1925. Netting him the equivalent of nearly a half million dollars in late twentieth-century currency,[42] touring allowed him to partake of life's pleasures: good housing, fine food and wines, elegant clothes,[43] a car and chauffeur. Furthermore, people in France depended on him. He supported an aged mother, a tubercular wife, four children, a flock of impecunious in-laws, and, from 1922, a mistress in Paris. The result was a marked increase in the number of trips from 1935 onward.

Two other reasons developed during the course of these tours. One stemmed from a longtime Russian expatriate friend of his university student days (in 1901): Alexis Fyodorovich Kall, contacted during the 1935 tour. Dr. Kall, who lived in Los Angeles, urged Stravinsky to consider participating in the lucrative business of composing Hollywood movie scores. A second reason was his desire to increase the number of people who could experience and appreciate his music. By his piano performances—solo, with violinists, as a duo-pianist, and with orchestras—and by his own conducting, he hoped to show music lovers and professional musicians the proper way to perform his works. In Europe he had been giving duo-recitals with Dushkin from 1931 and with his pianist son Soulima from 1935. For concerts in the USA, he continued to perform with Dushkin and Szigeti, and also enlisted pianists Beveridge Webster, Adele Marcus (Kall's onetime student), Nadia Boulanger, Willard MacGregor, and Vincent Persichetti.

For his initial transatlantic tours Stravinsky had little control of his itinerary. Inexperience with the language, the terrain, and especially with US tour managers and their representatives allowed him little choice of cities and venues. After his return to France in 1925, he began to complain about his US bookings and Americans in general, voiced privately to his family and in correspondence. His disillusionment reverberates particularly strongly in a heavily annotated letter to Dushkin in 1936 that ends, "I can see nothing, nothing happening, and time is passing also."[44]

Among distinguished foreign touring composer-executants seeking their fortunes in the United States such as Bartók, Alfredo Casella, and Ravel, only Stravinsky's compatriot Rachmaninoff, who preceded him as a US citizen, offers a useful comparison. There are superficial similarities: both married their first cousins, both forsook their native country because of the Russian Revolution. Although both were world-famous by their thirties, their professional training greatly differed.

Studying law in St. Petersburg at his parents' behest, Stravinsky worked with Nikolai Rimsky-Korsakov (whose tutoring his countryman abjured). Stravinsky's piano training was private and haphazard, first with a governess, then with Alexandra Petrovna Snetkova—respecting neither one—although he allowed that his third teacher, a student of Anton Rubinstein, Leocadia Alexandrovna Kashperova, with whom he worked from 1899 to 1901, possessed "pianism of a high order."[45] Later, in Paris, he received some coaching from Isidore Phillip. Stravinsky's piano recitals were mostly confined to his own music. Nor did he aspire to be a virtuoso. Both Russians partnered occasionally with violinists: the elder with Fritz Kreisler, Stravinsky with Dushkin and later Szigeti and John Weicher. After his citizenship, Stravinsky rarely played in public.

Largely self-taught as a conductor, he had no advantage of the traditional broad training demanded of European and Russian conductors of the era. Undoubtedly, as a boy, he had watched Eduard Nápravník at the Maryinsky Theater, where his father, Fyodor Ignatievich, sang principal basso, and from 1903, he had watched Alexander Ziloti lead the St. Petersburg orchestra. In Paris he had seen Monteux conduct the premieres of *Petrushka* (1911) and *Rite of Spring* (1913), and in 1914 at Montreux he would have had some coaching from Ernest Ansermet when he rehearsed his Symphony in E-flat.[46] An unimpressed young American flautist, Otto Luening, recalled Stravinsky rehearsing the Zurich Tonhalle Orchestra between 1917 and 1920, "so nervous that he was not in control."[47] Monteux also had unhappy memories of Stravinsky rehearsing *Les Noces* in 1924.[48] But Stravinsky was soon leading the *Rite*, first in Amsterdam early in 1926. In 1929, competing commercial recordings of the *Rite* led by Monteux and Stravinsky caused the composer to give vent, privately, to jealous remarks about his rival, commencing with "this poor Jew."[49]

This was neither the first nor the last of his anti-Semitic rants, which most persons who have written about him have striven to mitigate.[50] They are surprising and ungracious, given what he had learned from many fine Jewish conductors, among them Fritz Reiner in Cincinnati and Otto Klemperer in Paris. Much later, Klemperer commented (privately) on Stravinsky's inability to get a certain passage right in 1928 at the composer's own premiere of *Oedipus Rex*.[51]

Late in life, Stravinsky may have resolved these deeply conflicted feelings. At Charles Munch's instigation in 1955, Stravinsky wrote a *Greeting Prelude* to celebrate Monteux's eightieth birthday: a forty-five-second orchestral work, elaborating an earlier two-voiced birthday canon.[52] A 1963 photograph shows the composer publicly applauding Monteux's fiftieth-anniversary performance of the *Rite* in London, although his body language seems to show little more than grudging approval, unlike the wholehearted pleasure he exhibited during a Monteux performance in Paris in 1952.[53] In respect to the 1963 performance, Stravinsky's longtime American assistant, the late Robert Craft[54]—in the uncropped photograph grim-faced behind the composer and not applauding— announced that Stravinsky had planned all along to avoid this particular performance, dreading the "inevitable" ovation that would follow.[55] But how often in his lifetime did Stravinsky dread ovations? Charitably, it could be assumed that Stravinsky's attitude in 1963 resulted from conductorial envy rather than anti-Semitism.[56]

Be that as it may, I was alerted to the composer's anti-Semitism only in 1999, when Richard Taruskin lectured at the University of California, Irvine, about Stravinsky's Cantata.[57] My *Annotated Catalogue*—written the following year—reveals me still sitting on the fence about Stravinsky's prejudice.[58] For this naiveté the present book affords an opportunity to offer correction.

Stravinsky (unlike Rachmaninoff) regularly conducted concert music by many composers.[59] Yet, unlike his fellow Russian, who trained early as an opera conductor, Stravinsky led no operas until *The Rake's Progress* in 1951. This inexperience manifested itself at the premiere, when he "remained completely glued to the score and failed to give the singers any of their cues."[60] Finally, it could be argued that Stravinsky learned how to conduct his very difficult and challenging late scores from observing his assistant, Craft, rehearsing and preparing them for concerts and recordings.

Stravinsky's encounter with his old St. Petersburg chum, Alexis Kall, during his second transatlantic tour, proved to be as consequential as was his first correspondence with Craft a decade later. Kall's Los Angeles home provided a peaceful respite from the endless hotels and receptions that Stravinsky and Dushkin endured, and it was Kall who introduced Stravinsky to the film star Edward G. Robinson. When this gave rise to the notion of writing movie scores, a meeting with MGM studio musicians was arranged, initiating efforts that persisted for almost twenty years. Kall's open garage door even served as a backdrop for twelve celebrated photographs of the composer by Edward Weston. Both Stravinskys remained close to Kall until his death in September of 1948,[61] shortly after Craft's first visit to their home.

Craft rightly believed that Stravinsky's early years in Hollywood are "the least known and least documented of his mature life."[62] During Stravinsky's transatlantic and domestic excursions, people far less known than the luminaries who populate Craft's narratives also touched the composer's life. Even in 1994, a close friend of Craft doubted that there was any "younger element" at all among Stravinsky's associates and acquaintances in those early years in Hollywood."[63] But there *was* a "younger element." Lest they disappear from the historical record, the ensuing chapters will introduce several thirtyish Los Angeles colleagues and friends, as well as some of their children. Although hardly any of them figure in studies of Stravinsky, several left written, oral, and even visual records of their encounters.

Dr. Kall was by no means Craft's only predecessor as a chronicler of Stravinsky's life, and I make no claim to have found them all. For example, there is the intriguing tale that in the summer of 1944 Stravinsky turned to Ingolf Dahl for aid in orchestrating portions of *Scènes de ballet*. Perhaps the unidentified student who told this story to Arnold Schoenberg in Los Angeles is still alive and could verify it or amplify the details.

Stravinsky exerted a strong influence on younger composers, above all on those to whom he actually gave lessons or less formal assistance. I have made a start at evaluating this influence here, but this is really a task for a new generation of scholars. Given the fragility of records and human life itself, I (though no composer), and other witnesses, have a duty to record our impressions, the sooner the better.[64] Among the fortunate young composers who worked briefly with Stravinsky were the Russian-born American, Alexei Haieff, introduced in 1939 at Cambridge, Massachusetts, by his teacher, Nadia Boulanger;[65] Robert M. Stevenson, introduced that same year; and Ingolf Dahl, Stravinsky's associate and sometime close collaborator during the first California years. Stravinsky's Harvard undergraduate students during his Norton Professorship (1939–40), included would-be-composers William Austin, Elliot Forbes, and Jan LaRue. The latter two kindly provided me with their recollections.

Stevenson, then enrolled at Yale, and later a distinguished scholar of Hispanic music, introduced himself to Stravinsky in the fall of 1939; twenty years later, he wrote him, recalling their private composition lessons in Cambridge, first at the Edward Forbes's home, and during the early spring at the Hemenway Hotel in Boston.[66] After retiring from UCLA, Professor Stevenson promised me a memoir (alas, never completed). What survives of this project appears in his "Comentario del autor," dated 27 January 2006.[67]

Stravinsky's pedagogic experiences were transitory with one exception: Earnest Andersson, a transplanted Minnesotan–New Yorker and retired inventor-industrialist, to whom Stravinsky taught composition and orchestration during 215 lessons in Hollywood in 1941–42. One of Andersson's works, the *Futurama Symphony,* is readily accessible, although Stravinsky's autograph contributions and sketches for it are much less so; nevertheless it and they are worth scrutinizing for Stravinsky's influence. *Futurama* is the sole document that reveals him ever *teaching* octatonicism. Andersson also kept a notebook in 1941 for the first few months of his lessons when they were jointly revising this symphony. Andersson's efforts must have met with Stravinsky's approval: twenty-five years later, and far from truthfully, he quipped: "*I composed it.*"[68]

Near the close of Charles M. Joseph's *Stravinsky Inside Out,* Joseph cautions his readers: "I never knew, met, or even saw Stravinsky."[69] I was luckier. As a young associate professor at the University of California at Irvine, I heard Stravinsky conduct several concerts; I sang under him, met him twice, and once even chatted with him. Such fleeting encounters with a great composer, however brief, are valuable but hardly unique: tales of many students and their mentors whom he rehearsed or merely encountered in California, Illinois, New Mexico, New York, Ohio, and Texas remain to be told.

My public initiation into Stravinsky's music occurred on 7 April 1952 in Vancouver at the University of British Columbia: playing his Concerto for Two Solo Pianos with the late John Brockington and conducting *Les Noces*—both were Canadian premieres.[70] Two days short of my twenty-third birthday, this was, to me, as daunting an occasion as was surely Craft's, who at nearly the same age conducted the Symphony in C in New York in April 1948 in Stravinsky's presence.[71] It was not as terrifying for me: although Stravinsky had been invited by my professor, violinist Harry Adaskin, he was not present.

The following 5 October (1952), I was thrilled to accept an invitation from the business manager of the Vancouver Symphony Orchestra to ride with the composer to his final rehearsal. This was especially thrilling because Stravinsky had banned visitors from rehearsals—even officers of the Symphony Society.[72] We were introduced by this manager at the entrance to the Hotel Vancouver; then Stravinsky sat next to the driver, and I sat in the backseat. Sensing that he was concentrating on the coming rehearsal, I dared not mention my performances of the Two-Piano Concerto and *Les Noces*. What might he have said?

That Sunday morning in the orchestra's home at the Orpheum Theatre, I watched him rehearse his own music and works by Glinka and Tchaikovsky. Some of my observations paralleled those noted by others in earlier years. A review of his account of Tchaikovsky's Second Symphony in 1945 with the New York Philharmonic had noted that it was "outlined by the conductor with such rhythmic clarity as to make its moments of lyrical expression even less prominent."[73] Craft, writing about Stravinsky's 1940 New York Philharmonic recording of the same work mentions that "the fleet-footed execution displays the neatest string—or, rather, off-the-string—staccato [i.e., spiccato] articulation"[74] and "the articulation, so clean and alive."[75] These observations paralleled my own. In addition, I remember him turning his back to the VSO strings during lyric, espressivo passages in the Tchaikovsky symphony and even when Glinka calls for vibrato in the cellos during *Ruslan and Lyudmila*.

With respect to Stravinsky's own music, my Kalmus reprint of his 1919 *Firebird Suite* has ever since that morning borne his spoken "*cédez*" directed to the string players during the "Introduction": it adds a subtle *rubato* just before rehearsal 4 (henceforth, reh. 4: −1). He also gave the "Ronde des princesses" a *ritardando* for pizzicato double basses (reh. 7: −1). Another (and equally expressive) *cédez* was directed to the second violins at their rising B-major arpeggio (reh. 13: −5).[76] I again heard him conduct in July of 1964 at Ravinia and in April of 1965 in Chicago.

To crown it all, under his direction in Los Angeles on 27 and 28 January 1966, I sang in the *Symphony of Psalms* and his arrangement of Bach's *Von Himmel hoch*.[77] Knowing Stravinsky's interest in early music, I made bold, during a break in our only rehearsal with Craft and Stravinsky (26 January), to present him a copy of my 1964 edition of *Musica nova* (Venice: Andrea Arrivabene, 1540). He immediately recognized the name of

Edward E. Lowinsky, general editor of the series of which *Musica Nova* was the inaugural volume: in 1959 he had given Professor Lowinsky a signed musical quotation from *Threni,* and in 1961 he had written a foreword to Lowinsky's *Tonality and Atonality in Sixteenth-Century Music* that concluded: "his method is the only kind of 'writing about music' that I value."[78] Stravinsky nodded at me and showed *Musica Nova* to Craft. Presumably it joined his library in his West Hollywood residence.[79]

After intermission the next evening, while Craft was conducting the Symphony in C, I wangled my way backstage in the Music Center and sat next to the composer. I managed to produce a few words of appreciation for his Symphony after Craft had conducted it magnificently. Stravinsky, as was his wont, clocked him all the while. The relevance of this act of timing becomes clear in an observation Craft had made four years previously. At Toronto in December of 1962, Craft noted that the composer "essentially follow[ed] my concert broadcast of it, but *slower.*"[80] Craft's differences lie chiefly in the outer movements, each shorter in his own recordings than the composer's by about 20 percent. There were occasional, but long-standing, creative differences between the two men; Craft was more than a musical amanuensis.

As late as January of 1966 the Symphony in C had still not conquered all hearts and minds. Trudging offstage that January toward the seated composer and me, a middle-aged violinist shook his head while muttering imprecations. But it was different for me: when I thanked Stravinsky for writing such a beautiful piece of music, he turned to me and said in his memorably deep, impossibly accented voice: "You zhnów, I like eet myzélf." Despite a recent claim that Stravinsky cried "every time he heard it performed live,"[81] I discerned no tears in 1966.

My last glimpse of Stravinsky was two years later at Sara Caldwell's thoroughly mod production of *The Rake's Progress* for the American Opera at the Los Angeles Music Center. At his opera's conclusion, Stravinsky, by this time disabled, acknowledged applause from his seat by raising his hat on his cane.[82]

As one of a rapidly dwindling group of persons who met Stravinsky, I feel a responsibility to recount these occasions. Undeniably, my face-to-face encounters, allied with studying, teaching, playing, conducting his music, and lecturing about him, plus thirty years as a Stravinsky collector, have shaped the ensuing narrative.

PART I

FIVE TRANSATLANTIC TOURS

(1925–1940)

1

TOUR I (1925)

CONCERT APPEARANCES

8–9 January: New York Philharmonic

15 January: New York charity, Vincent Astor Ballroom

23–24 January: Boston Symphony, and Piano Concerto soloist with Koussevitzky

25 January: New York, Aeolian Hall (chamber music) with Greta Torpadie

30–31 January: Philadelphia Orchestra

5–6 February: New York Philharmonic, and Piano Concerto soloist with Mengelberg

12–14 February: Cleveland Orchestra (half-concert with Sokoloff)

15 February: Philadelphia Orchestra, and Piano Concerto soloist with Reiner

20–21 February: Chicago Symphony (half-concert with Stock)

24 February [?]: Chicago Arts Club with Greta Torpadie

3 March: Detroit Symphony, and Piano Concerto soloist (half-concert with Kolar)

6–7 March: Cincinnati Orchestra, and Piano Concerto soloist with Reiner

Stravinsky's initial voyage to the New World was preceded by several failed attempts. In 1916, at Lausanne, he tried to attach himself to Diaghilev's and Nijinsky's first US tour of the Ballet Russes but was foiled by Romola Nijinsky's revision of her husband's cable to its sponsor, the Metropolitan Opera.[1] In 1919, while in New York, Nicolas Struve (director of Koussevitzky's music publishing firm) tried to arrange a Stravinsky tour of the United States.[2] When, in 1922, Stravinsky again contemplated a concert tour of the States, his letter from Biarritz on 4 February to Diaghilev seeks advice about whether he should write to America immediately or wait, because he must make up his mind quickly.[3] A further stimulus was surely a letter mailed from Cincinnati by his longtime close friend, composer-pianist-conductor Alfredo Casella: "a me amico carissimo,"[4] who wrote on 6 April 1923 of his own very successful second American tour, and even of his reengagement for "five similar tours."[5]

The first of Stravinsky's five transatlantic departures from France to the United States occurred in 1925, the next one in 1935; in 1936 he sailed with his pianist son to Brazil, Argentina, and Montevideo; in 1937 to the United States and Canada; and in 1939–40 to the United States, plus a train trip to Mexico. Reconstructing his travels has shed light on many aspects of his life.

"Igor's cabin is the best one, in the exact center, and with all conveniences. A piano has been installed."[6] On board ship for his initial transatlantic voyage in 1925, Igor Fyodorovich Stravinsky traveled, as always, in high style. Arriving in New York early that January for a two-and-a half-month tour of the United States, Stravinsky might well have reflected on the women he left behind in Paris. On the verge of this, his first transatlantic crossing, he was involved with four women living in the French capital: his long-widowed mother, Anna; his sickly wife, Catherine, mother of his four children; and two women named Vera. He was probably involved with one Vera only musically but with the other certainly amorously. He had invited Vera (Janacopoulos), a well-known Brazilian singer from whom he hoped to obtain financial support, to accompany him on the tour (fig. 1.1), but she had demurred. The other Vera (Soudeikina), a Russian émigré like himself, was his mistress whom he supported financially. He did not invite her at that time, although he tried doing so later for a projected 1932 tour. Midway through his last overseas tour, she finally voyaged to the States to join him, and became his second wife in March 1940.

Stravinsky's pretour correspondence with Vera, the singer, allows some notion of repertoire he planned for this initial transatlantic venture. Writing from Biarritz on 6 August 1924, he had asked the beautiful soprano Janacopoulos, then dwelling in Paris with her lawyer-husband, Alexey Fyodorovich Staal, to learn his 1906 orchestral-song cycle, *Faun and Shepherdess*.[7] During his first concert tour to the United States, he hoped that he and she would perform it together.[8] He had previously recommended it to her in 1923.[9] Performed only a few times since its 1907 premiere in St. Petersburg,[10] *Faun* was Stravinsky's first published work and his first to be reviewed abroad. Initially, his interest in Janacopoulos had perhaps been kindled by Sergey Prokofiev. In December 1919, she had given the US premiere of Stravinsky's *Pribaoutki* (1914) in New York. After attending both rehearsal and concert, Prokofiev wrote to Stravinsky, approving of the work and, equally, her performance.[11]

Was Stravinsky—married and with four children—simultaneously juggling one or even two married Vera's? Since 1921 he had been carrying on with Vera de Bosset-Lury-Shilling-Soudeikina.[12] She had never married Sergey Yuryevich Soudeikine, because he had never divorced his wife, Olga.[13] Stravinsky married Vera de Bosset in March 1940 in the United States, a year after the death of his first wife. This marriage was illegal if Stravinsky perjured himself before a judge in respect to Vera's nonmarriage to and non-divorce from Soudeikine.[14]

One writer believes that Janacopulos had a love affair with Stravinsky. These allegations are not convincing. But even if so, was this before or after she married Staal?[15] The precise date of the Janacopulos-Staal marriage is unclear. Prokofiev refers to her as "Mlle" in mid-February of 1919,[16] but Stravinsky's letters to her in 1923 and 1924 address her as "Madame," as does a Paris critic ca. 1925.[17] In contrast, Prokofiev, who knew Staal and Janacopulos very well from 1918 until a major quarrel in 1924, called them the "Stahls." Although he dearly loved gossip, he never penned a word about any such affair with Stravinsky.[18]

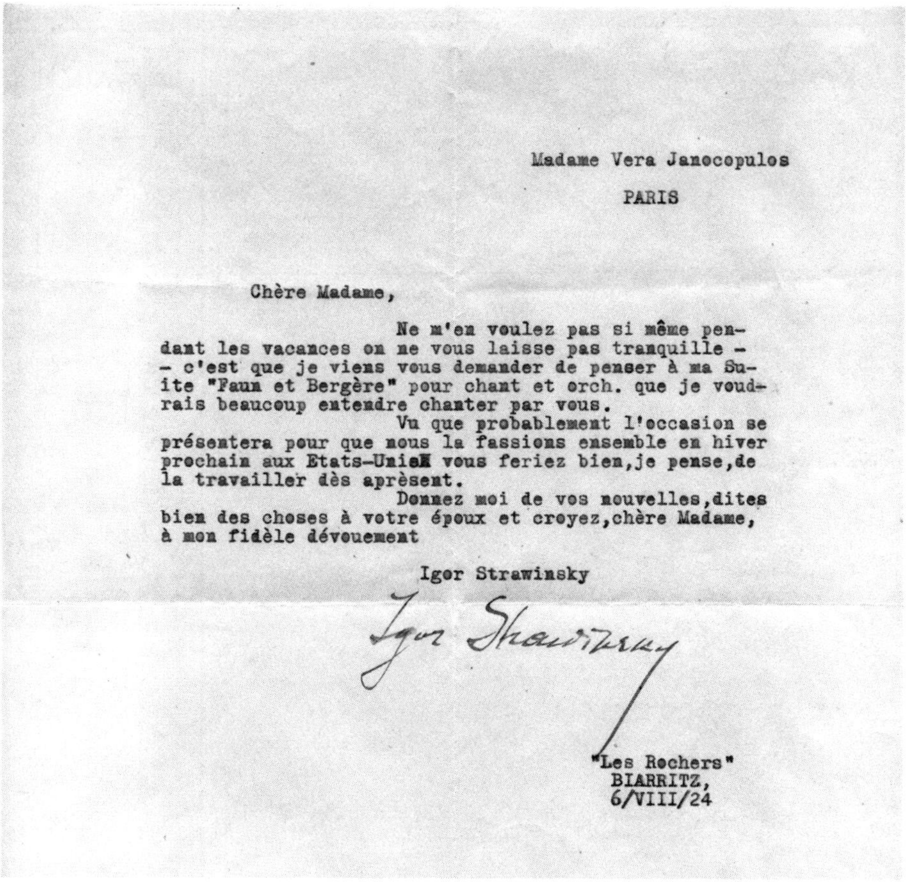

Madame Vera Janocopulos

PARIS

Chère Madame,

Ne m'en voulez pas si même pen-
dant les vacances on ne vous laisse pas tranquille -
- c'est que je viens vous demander de penser à ma Suite "Faun et Bergère" pour chant et orch. que je voud-
rais beaucoup entendre chanter par vous.
Vu que probablement l'occasion se
présentera pour que nous la fassions ensemble en hiver
prochain aux Etats-Unis vous feriez bien, je pense, de
la travailler dès aprèsent.
Donnez moi de vos nouvelles, dites
bien des choses à votre époux et croyez, chère Madame,
à mon fidèle dévouement

Igor Strawinsky

"Les Rochers"
BIARRITZ,
6/VIII/24

FIGURE 1.1
Stravinsky to "Madame Vera Janocopulos[-Staal]," 1924. UBC Stravinsky Collection, no. 27.

On 19 April 1923, Stravinsky had written Janacopulos—"Bien chère Madame"—
asking for a loan of four thousand francs (fig.1.2), with the implied threat that unless she
agreed, he would not accompany her at her Paris concert on 29 May. There she sang
several works of his, including *Tilimbom* (1917) accompanied by the pianola (a mechanical piano). Since he did not play for her, although he attended her concert, it seems that
she made him no loan and that she was not amorously involved with him.[19] In any event,
none of the four women crossed the Atlantic with him. It was just as well, because the
voyage was extremely turbulent.

THE VOYAGE AND ITS AFTERMATH

Sailing in utter comfort on the SS *Paris,* though "twelve hours overdue . . . because of
four days of rough weather . . . through blinding snow-storms,"[20] Stravinsky arrived in

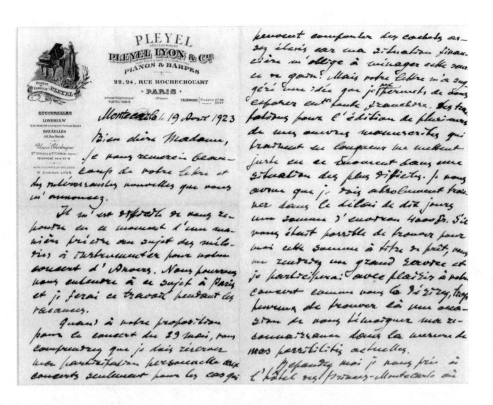

FIGURE 1.2a

Stravinsky to Vera Janacopoulos-Staal (front), 1923. UBC Stravinsky Collection, no. 23.

New York on 4 January 1925. He traveled with Alexis Mikhailovich Sabline, his valet, secretary, and English translator.[21] The very day of Stravinsky's arrival, the Sunday music section of the *New York World* welcomed him with a column, "Stravinsky Debut with Philharmonic." It also ran an illegibly signed drawing, counterfeiting a natty 1924 frontal photograph taken by the Studio Lipnitzki in Paris, that portrayed him with a dangling monocle, holding a cigarette in his left hand.[22]

In the words of a female observer on the Manhattan dock, it was a "flamboyant figure in black and orange who had walked down the gang plank."[23] The same reporter described his dapper attire at a press conference the next day: "Gold chain bracelets flanked a wrist watch. Rings with vari-colored stones covered his hands. With black patent-leather dancing pumps he wore grey bags, a striped shirt, a black tie with a pearl scarf-pin and a rose and taupe sweater." She noted his talking

> volubly and with precise phrasing and clever plays on words, now in French, now in German, lifting a monocle to emphasize his point and then screwing it into his eye with a determined gesture. . . . "I am not a modernist. I do not pretend to write the music of the future any more than I attempt to copy the music of the past. I am of today and I hope I am writing the music of today."

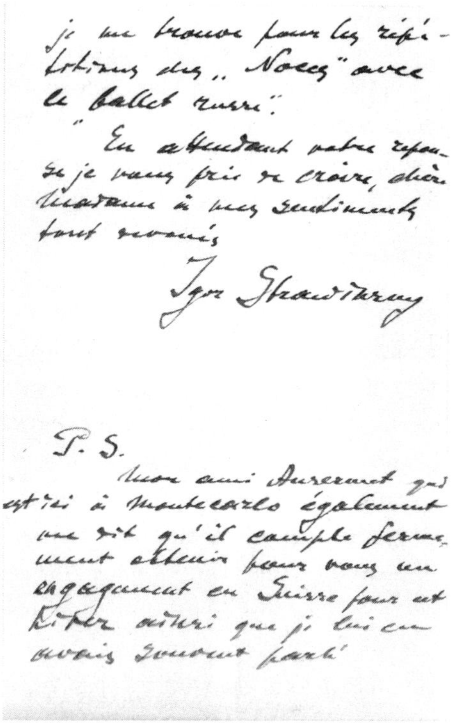

je me trouve pour les répétitions des „Noces" avec le ballet russe.

En attendant votre réponse je vous prie de croire, chère Madame, à mes sentiments tout dévoués

Igor Strawinsky

P. S.

Mon ami Ansermet qui est ici à Montecarlo également me dit qu'il compte fermement obtenir pour vous un engagement en Suisse pour cet hiver ainsi que je lui en avais souvent parlé

FIGURE 1.2b
Stravinsky to Vera Janacopoulos-Staal (back), 1923. UBC Stravinsky Collection, no. 23.

The reporter simultaneously observed that

> of all modern music Stravinsky is interested only in jazz. "There you have something," he says. "that is not the result of ostentatious theorizing. That almost sneaked in on us from an out-in-the-corner cabaret. We don't like to admit it, but real music has such simple origins. It comes from the soil." [*sic,* probably a misprint for "soul."][24]

His avowed interest in jazz lay dormant until the *Praeludium:* begun in France in late 1936, completed in New York in 1937, and thus his first work finished in the United States.[25]

Two weeks later, the same publication ran on its front page an equally elegant, but more arresting and arrogantly posed, photograph, also taken in 1924 by Studio Lipnitzki, right hand on hip and monocle again dangling.[26] He favored this image for a decade.

George Gershwin was apparently the sole US major American composer whom Stravinsky met in his initial visit to New York. They met at least three times between 7 and 9 January.[27] The first encounter took place at an evening reception held in Stravinsky's honor by Paul and Zosia Kochanski, mutual friends.[28] A Polish violinist, Paul Kochanski was then teaching at the Juilliard School. He had known Stravinsky since 1914, and met him when the SS *Paris* docked. Little is known about the interaction of Gershwin and Stravinsky: the former played piano and presumably gratified the latter's enthusiasm for jazz.

Gershwin's friend, the society hostess Mary Hoyt Wiborg (or Wyborg, familiarly known as "Hoytie"), arranged their second meeting for a soirée directly after Stravinsky's US conducting debut with the New York Philharmonic on 8 January.[29] She lived on lower Fifth Avenue, but for the occasion she borrowed an apartment on East Sixty-Ninth Street, closer to Carnegie Hall. It belonged to the banker and Philharmonic patron Arthur Sachs, who in 1924 had visited Stravinsky in France to negotiate the Philharmonic concerts; his generosity toward the composer continued for decades. Hoytie's party seems not to have been the same occasion in 1925 when Sachs himself hosted a dinner for Stravinsky, Leopold Auer, Fritz Kreisler, and Wilhelm Furtwängler.[30] Twenty years later, Sachs would commission the Symphony in Three Movements for the New York Philharmonic, and he hosted the Stravinskys often at his Featherhill Ranch in Montecito, California.

In any event, Sachs's New York apartment housed some kind of an electroacoustical piano linked to an organ, perhaps similar to the $50,000 Choralcelo then owned in New York by Stravinsky's future Los Angeles student Earnest Andersson.[31] Among Hoytie's guests was Lester Donahue,[32] a seasoned concert and "social" pianist (i.e., one bookable for parties). Another guest was John Hays Hammond Jr., of Hammond organ fame,[33] who would encounter Stravinsky once again later that month when Serge Koussevitzky escorted Stravinsky to the Hammond family home in Gloucester, Massachusetts.[34] Years after the party, Donahue recalled that Hoytie, determined to force Stravinsky and Gershwin—after just two evenings' casual acquaintance—to improvise four-hands, insisted on seating them at Sachs's piano. Realizing the acute discomfort of this unexpected and unwelcome ordeal, Hammond quietly flipped a switch and the instrument made not a sound.[35]

For the final New York meeting on 9 January, both Gershwin brothers arrived in the morning at Stravinsky's hotel room, along with young Jascha Heifetz and his older violinist friend Samuel Dushkin, former student of Leopold Auer and more recently of Fritz Kreisler. Forgetting their meeting in New York,[36] Stravinsky could not have foreseen that, following a second introduction to Dushkin late in 1930 in Germany,[37] he would invite the violinist to join him on his 1935 US concert tour. Stravinsky would also meet Gershwin again on this tour and once more in 1937.

During Gershwin's visit to Europe in 1928, they encountered each other in May at Kochanski's Paris apartment with composer Richard Hammond present.[38] Gershwin asked Stravinsky for lessons but was famously turned down, a story verified by Hammond. The earliest purveyor of this well-worn anecdote may have been New York critic Olin Downes in his memorial article, "Hail and Farewell," printed six days after Gershwin's death.[39] Downes averred he had it from an "American composer," presumably Hammond.

Stravinsky's antagonism toward Downes, said to have begun in "the mid 1940s,"[40] surely developed much earlier, long before the 1937 Gershwin memorial. However opinionated his first sentence, Downes's second one is especially daft and irrelevant:

We shall certainly expose ourselves to contumely when we say that we would prefer one of the representative Gershwin songs to many of the later compositions of Igor Stravinsky. This despite the fact that Stravinsky almost invariably succeeds in putting down on paper what he wants there, thus carrying out to the last tone his musical conception.[41]

This was far milder than his earlier attack, inaugurated on 1 February 1925:

[Stravinsky] has not originated a new score of major importance . . . in twelve years [i.e., since *Rite of Spring*] . . . [including] the rather lamentable *Octuor* for wind-players. . . . Every time he writes he is someone else, which is not the habit of great masters . . . precisely the opposite of a prophet of a new age; he seems to have succumbed utterly to the aimlessness, the superficialities and pretenses of this one.[42]

As for the 1923–24 Piano Concerto in its New York premiere on 5 February 1925 with Stravinsky as soloist, Downes claimed "in the melodic sense, there is not an original idea in the score." He described its opening as "called by courtesy a chorale . . . a rather cheap tune . . . an unlovely passage." Its slow movement was "a bad imitation of the slow movement of a violin sonata by Bach . . . a false melody." After conceding "the magnificent virtuosity of Mr. Stravinsky's performance," he added, "[he] is no conductor."[43] Yet, only two days later, even Downes had to hedge: "The concerto, heard a second time, . . . impressed the more by its masterly treatment of form and its quality of very sure and brilliant rhythmic development. But the concerto does not appear . . . to be of really authentic inspiration."[44] By "authentic inspiration" Downes referred back to his previous 6 February comments about "bad imitation" and "false melody," implying that Stravinsky's themes do not suffi- ciently resemble those of Bach, whose works Downes was so sure that Stravinsky was imitating.[45] Downes's tastes were mostly Franco-Germanic, and his criticisms mirrored those of British critics of the same period: Ernest Newman, Cecil Gray, and Constant Lam- bert.[46] Nor did Downes greatly favor music near his own time, except for Sibelius. In 1923 he successfully concealed his prejudices from Prokofiev in Paris, but in 1930 Prokofiev met him again in New York and realized Downes's hypocrisy. Although Stravinsky could not have known it, Prokofiev took care of Downes in a hilarious diary entry for 16 January 1930:

Seven years ago he fell out of an aeroplane and landed on his head, a circumstance that prompted the largest American newspaper to offer him the job of music critic. . . . To fall on one's head is not of itself a sufficient condition to begin to understand music.[47]

Among other New York critics in 1925, Deems Taylor, a minor composer himself, might be expected to have displayed a better understanding of the post-*Sacre* Stravinsky. Not always so. His first review on 9 January largely concerned Stravinsky's fame and physical appearance: "His whole personality is one of almost ferocious energy." Then on 6 February he lambasted the premiere of the Piano Concerto as the most fumbling, featureless work that we have ever heard from Stravinsky's pen. . . . The style, and the subject matter, are virtually anything you please. They are no Stravinsky that we have thus far met, and I am not sure that they are anybody at all. The audience . . . received the new work with the wildest enthusiasm, recalling the composer times without number.[48]

Just how wrong were Downes and Taylor about Stravinsky's new concerto and his audience is evident from Downes's grudging second review and the final sentence of Taylor's. New York audiences were much more receptive than their city's professional critics. By the time Stravinsky arrived, they had already heard the *Rite of Spring* conducted by Monteux in 1924 and by Koussevitzky in 1925, as well as *Firebird, Petrushka, Fireworks, Song of the Nightingale,* and *Pulcinella.*

Two days after Stravinsky led the New York Philharmonic, a good many fine musicians in the city embraced an opportunity to meet him in person at a dinner party.[49] The party was not really for Stravinsky but for the pianist Josef Hofmann. This surely unintended ambiguity may well have been the cause of an eruption more than a decade later in Brazil, when Hofmann lashed out against Stravinsky (see Tour III). Officially, the 1925 party had a dual purpose: it was a "reception in honor of Josef Hofmann" and a "farewell to old Steinway Hall" on Fourteenth Street, in anticipation of Steinway's new building, still found to this day on Fifty-Seventh Street.[50]

The several reproductions of a photograph taken that evening, 11 January 1925, by "Pach Bros. / New York" have sown much confusion. The best contemporaneous reproduction of this photograph appeared just four days after the party,[51] and strangely, the very few people identified in it do not include Stravinsky. His own personally mounted copy of the photograph (its right third cropped off) bears only the composer's annotation "Groupe du jubilé Steinway à New York / 1925."[52]

A slightly more accurate reference in 1982 to the photograph (without a reproduction) as the "Steinway birthday party" gives the correct date but omits its location.[53] A reproduction of Stravinsky's copy not only crops it more severely at the right and slightly at the left, but also omits the names of the two diners previously identified, dates it only to January, and again locates it at just Steinway Hall.[54] When reproduced in 1962 from the complete photograph supplied by Steinway and Sons, the image was slightly cropped at left, top, and bottom.[55]

These deficiencies do not appear in the foggy but more complete version of the photograph reissued in 1981.[56] It is correctly described as "Reception to Josef Hofmann" and assigned the proper date, but only the photograph in the paperback edition reveals (however dimly) honoree Hofmann's famous hands. Craft might better have criticized Walsh for not completely solving the muddle of date, occasion, and place that he himself had created. Although wrongly declaring Stravinsky the guest of honor (even if, unofficially, he was), Walsh correctly cites "a [chocolate] cake [in the form of] a grand piano with a score [on a music rack] and bearing Stravinsky's name on it."[57]

Craft identified eight musicians in the crowd of 172 diners. The name of every single guest is listed in *Musical America,*[58] yet, the majority of the men in the *Courier*'s "Flashlight" photograph—there were no women—still awaits identification. Kochanski, for example, is almost certainly the person seated far left, directly behind Walter Damrosch. There is no sign of Gershwin.

Precisely as Stravinsky recalled in 1962, his own countenance in the group photograph seems to say "I do not look happy,"[59] although he "must have been pleased to be speaking mother tongues" with some attendees.[60] Indeed, he is the only one in the entire group (including the famously dour-looking Rachmaninoff) to appear bored, even pained. This could well have resulted from his having to endure a program of chamber works composed by Anton Rubinstein, Benjamin Godard, and Moritz Moszkowski.

Nor could Stravinsky have then anticipated future ironies concerning four of his colleagues seated nearby: Furtwängler, Hofmann, Damrosch, and Rachmaninoff. In light of Koussevitzky's success the previous week with *The Rite of Spring* in New York, Stravinsky had wisely declined to lead the *Rite* that coming week himself,[61] but he was to advise the hapless Furtwängler how to do so.[62] Stravinsky's quarrel with a grossly inebriated Hofmann in Rio de Janeiro in 1936 has already been mentioned. Stravinsky was to decry Damrosch's 1917–18 harmonization of "The Star-Spangled Banner" in Los Angeles in 1941. And in the summer of 1942 he discovered in Rachmaninoff a shy but friendly Hollywood neighbor, whose death the following year shocked him while on tour.[63]

At the 15 January chamber concert in the ballroom of Vincent Astor's house, Stravinsky and the Swedish American soprano Greta Torpadie[64] performed *Faun and Shepherdess*. The composer was also at the piano for his trio arrangement of the suite from *Histoire du soldat*, repeated in Chicago six weeks later.[65] This New York afternoon concert was "for the benefit of the Mental Hygiene Committee of the State Charities Association." A photograph said to be taken in old Steinway Hall in January shows Stravinsky practicing the piano, perhaps for that very concert.[66] Another photograph, dated the same month by Stravinsky, shows him again at the piano, this time in Aeolian Hall, looking somewhat startled, perhaps by some intruder.[67]

On 25 January he was in Aeolian Hall, conducting American premieres of his *Octet* and *Ragtime* and a nonstaged concert performance of *Renard*, and once again accompanying Torpadie. At an afternoon rehearsal in Carnegie Hall for this chamber concert, Stravinsky was interviewed by, among others, Paul Rosenfeld, who offered the most sterling portrait of the composer at this period.[68]

An interview by one "N. Roerig" eventually reached Schoenberg in Berlin. A temptation to identify the author with the well-known artist, painter, and set designer Nicolai Konstantinovich Roerich, who was also in New York that year, must be resisted. Roerich, by then a long-time collaborator of Stravinsky (most famously in *Le Sacre*), would never have exhibited Roerig's overawed and subservient attitude. On the afternoon of 25 January Roerig observed and afterward interviewed Stravinsky in Carnegie Hall rehearsing his *Ragtime* (1917–18) for that evening's concert in Aeolian Hall. The interview was in English, presumably utilizing Alexis Sabline, Stravinsky's bilingual secretary-valet. Translated into German in 1927 for the *Blätter der Staatsoper und der Städtischen Oper*

FIGURE 1.3
Stravinsky at Aeolian Hall, New York, 1925. UBC Stravinsky Collection, no. 29.

Berlin, Roerig's interview caught the eye of Arnold Schoenberg, who was then living there and teaching at the Preussische Akademie der Künste, who clipped it. Five years later, he made several wry annotations.[69] At Roerig's (translated) quotation of Stravinsky's remark, "Ich ja auch alles, was ich fühle, hineinlege" (I certainly also put everything I feel into it [i.e., current composing]), Schoenberg wrote with considerable irony that "er fühlt—ah; hört nicht auf! / Ja darf man ihm leb?" (He feels—ah; don't stop! / Well, may one really do that?").

Schoenberg had no comment about Stravinsky's response to another query from Roerig about jazz: "the only music worthy of attention. It is not the result of dull theories. . . . True music always has the most simple origin. It comes from the soul [i.e., 'Seele']." Except for Roerig's "Seele," these comments are strikingly close to several, especially those by Henrietta Malkiel, except for her "soil" quoted above from the day after Stravinsky docked in New York. Either two weeks later Roerig was plagiarizing Malkiel's

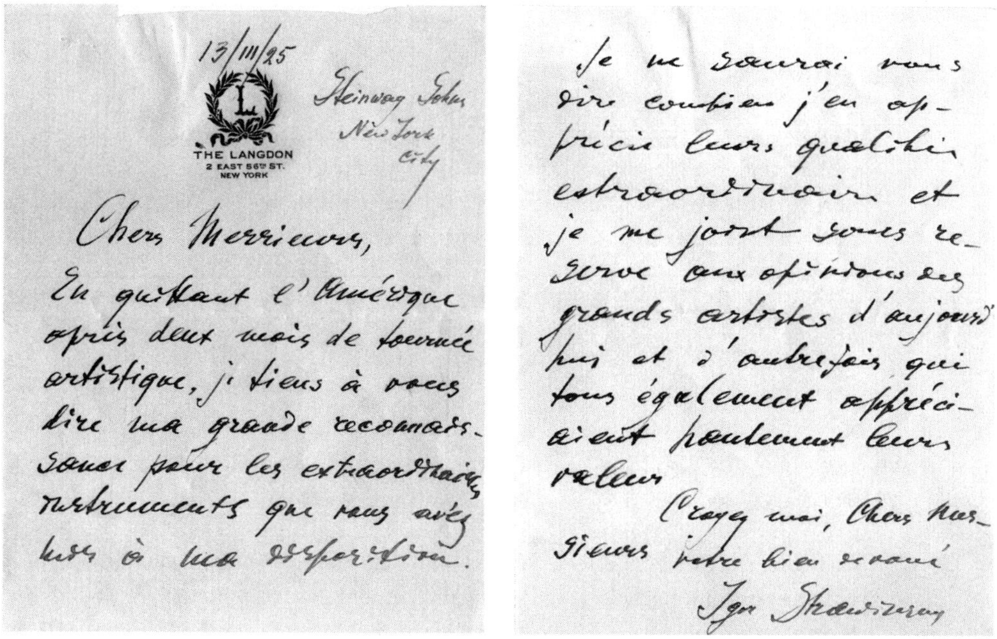
13/III/25

THE LANGDON
2 EAST 56th ST.
NEW YORK

Steinway Sohns
New York
City

Chers Messieurs,

En quittant l'Amérique après deux mois de tournée artistique, je tiens à vous dire ma grande reconnaissance pour les extraordinaires instruments que vous avez mis à ma disposition.

Je ne saurai vous dire combien j'en apprécie leurs qualités extraordinaires et je me joint sans réserve aux opinions des grands artistes d'aujourd'hui et d'autrefois qui tous également appréciaient pleinement leurs valeur

Croyez moi, Chers Messieurs votre bien dévoué

Igor Strawinsky

FIGURE 1.4
Stravinsky to Steinway and Sons, 1925 (front and back). UBC Stravinsky Collection, no. 31.

interview, or more plausibly, Stravinsky was uttering canned responses. The day after his Carnegie Hall concert, which also included excerpts from *The Nightingale,* New York critics considerably less well-disposed than Roerig reviewed this program savagely.[70]

Obviously, Stravinsky needed fine pianos for his New York concerts, as a soloist when touring, for making pianola rolls at the Aeolian Duo-Art Company in New York, and for making phonograph records for Brunswick.[71] Expressions of his gratitude to the providers survive.

On 9 February 1925, having recorded for Aeolian the first movement of his Piano Concerto and having given the New York premiere of the entire concerto on 5 and 6 February with Willem Mengelberg, he inscribed a splendid photograph of himself playing a Steinway in Aeolian Hall "To the Duo-Art Aeolian Organ / with best regards, Igor Strawinsky / New York, 9/II./25" (fig. 1.3). Taken by Horace Scandlin, who signed its mount, this image evidently pleased the composer. A duplicate (cropped a little at the right) is visible on his own piano at Nice, in a photograph taken in 1927.[72]

Slightly more than a month later, just before returning to Europe, he sent a warm note of appreciation in French on stationery of The Langdon, his New York hotel, to Steinway and Sons for fine instruments they had supplied as far west as Chicago (fig. 1.4).[73] He later told his niece that Steinway and Sons had allotted him eighteen different grand pianos.[74]

Steinway [and] Sons   New York
New York City   13 March 1925

Dear Sirs:

Upon leaving America after two months of concert touring, I must tell you of my great
gratitude for the extraordinary instruments you have placed at my disposal. I hardly
know how to tell you how much I appreciate their extraordinary qualities and I agree
entirely with the opinions of great artists of the present and the past who all likewise
esteem their worth.

Very sincerely yours,

Igor Strawinsky

Before departing for Chicago for concerts he led with its orchestra, he sent a message
on 6 February (the day of the New York premiere of his *Piano Concerto*) to the editor of
The New York Times. Two days later, it duly appeared, headed "Stravinsky Is Grateful":

Leaving New York for a Western tour, I am most desirous of expressing publicly the deep
gratitude which I feel toward the glorious Philharmonic Society of New York. The admirable orchestra of this brilliant organization, of which the superb ensemble has been forged
by the unique ability of Maestro Mengelberg, has permitted me to show to the New York
public my works in their best light.[75]

CHICAGO AND THE MIDWEST

The Chicago Symphony Orchestra concerts on 20 and 21 February had been sold out for
weeks. One critic had prepared music lovers there by describing Stravinsky's music a
little ambiguously as possessing "no beauty as we have known it heretofore," though
allowing that the composer "is modern in his psychology" with "a poetic imagination of
great power and scope."[76]

Just before entraining for the Midwest, Stravinsky had consulted a physician in New
York, one Abraham Leon Garbat.[77] Following an expedition to the Chicago stockyards
with composer John Alden Carpenter, and a journey to Detroit, he began to suffer from
a cold that greatly worsened at the beginning of March in Cincinnati.[78] Anticipating this
illness while still in Chicago, he must have again consulted Dr. Garbat, probably by telephone. On stationery of the Hotel Sherman (a fine Chicago building, since demolished),
he wrote in green ink, in French, to thank the doctor, who had been sufficiently concerned to send him a handwritten letter (fig. 1.5):

Dr. A. Garbat   Chicago
New York   25 February 1925

Deeply touched by your good letter, I send you, my dear Doctor, my best regards.

Yours very gratefully

Igor Strawinsky.

FIGURE 1.5
Stravinsky to Abraham Garbat, 1925.
UBC Stravinsky Collection, no. 30.

For at least the next twenty years, any time he visited New York, he consulted with Dr. Garbat. Just as some doctors now specialize in players of sports, Dr. Garbat may have specialized in musicians. The great Russian basso, Feodor Chaliapin, for example, was one of his patients, as were Mischa Elman, George Gershwin, and Yehudi Menuhin. For Chaliapin's fifty-fifth birthday on 15 February 1928, Garbat and his wife hosted a party, inviting such luminaries as Horowitz, Kochanski, Toscha Seidel, Rachmaninoff, and Giuseppe de Lucca.[79]

Evaluations of Stravinsky's ability as a conductor on this and other transatlantic tours will be found near the close of this and ensuing chapters. They show his progress in Europe in the years intervening, as well as the changes wrought by observing conductors in the United States. The tours were part of his schooling: except for his East Coast concerts in 1925 with the New York Philharmonic[80] and the Philadelphia Orchestra,[81] he generally shared the baton with each city's resident conductor. For example, on 20–21

February in Chicago, Frederick Stock began with Beethoven's Seventh Symphony; then Stravinsky led *Scherzo fantastique* and *The Firebird*.[82] One reviewer described the composer as "an anarchist blessed with occasional moments of sanity and possessing diabolical cleverness," but probably the "most interesting contemporary figure in the world of tone." Another stated that the Chicago Orchestra "responded to his desires with an artistic appreciation and technical skill that satisfied his highest hopes."[83] In mid-February concerts at Cleveland, Nikolai Sokoloff began with "a glowing performance of the Tchaikovsky 'Pathetic' [sic] Symphony."[84] And on 3 March in Detroit, Victor Kolar opened with the overture to *The Marriage of Figaro*.[85] As we will see, in subsequent tours this now rather rare practice persisted in 1937 with Sir Ernest MacMillan and the Toronto Symphony and up to 1945 with Otto Klemperer and the Los Angeles Philharmonic.[86] Late in life, of course, Stravinsky often split orchestral concerts with Robert Craft, but those concerts were normally devoted in full to his own music.

NEW YORK AGAIN

Back in New York and on the verge of sailing 14 March for France on the SS *Aquitania*, Stravinsky was surely relishing the previous evening's triumph of *Petrushka* performed at the Metropolitan Opera, led by Tullio Serafin, and with Adolf Bolm in the title role. He was equally aware of the irony of its stage sets being designed by Serge Soudeikine, whom he had displaced three years earlier in Vera's affection. And even Stravinsky's most savage critics had been forced to admit his worth. Oscar Thompson's long review titled "Stravinsky Lionized at Brilliant Revival of 'Petrushka'" noted that "the composer was present to enjoy and participate in the triumph of a work which will outlast all his later creations." In respect to the *Petrushka* performance, Thompson could not forgo noting, "For the moment, at least, it all but obliterated memories of the Octuor, the Piano Concerto and other recent experiments in glass-cut or stone-hewn counterpoint which had done so much in recent weeks to strip him of his last year's prestige." Nor did Thompson or Deems Taylor restrain themselves in praising Soudeikine. Thompson wrote, "If ever designs and colors have been used 'contrapuntally,' in a manner to correspond with music such as Stravinsky's, this has been achieved by Soudeikine."[87] And Taylor reported that "Mr. Soudeikine's scenery deserves a paragraph to itself" and proceeded to supply just that. Then he added, "Mr. Soudeikine and Mr. Serafin both took curtain calls, and Mr. Stravinsky, who was present, was called before the curtain to receive an overstuffed laurel wreath and shake hands with everybody."[88] Except Soudeikine! Apparently when Stravinsky saw the cuckolded artist coming toward him, he took a solo bow and rapidly retreated to the wings.[89]

HOMEWARD BOUND

Among Stravinsky's fellow passengers who boarded the SS *Aquitania* on 14 March was Mary Garden, Debussy's first Mélisande.[90] If they met on board, would they have discussed their recently deceased mutual friend? Perhaps they actually did meet, for she attended a New York concert on his 1935 tour.

A nice *da capo* frames the two Veras cited at the beginning of this first transatlantic tour. It unfolded directly after Stravinsky's return to France. Before joining his family in Nice, he traveled from Paris to Barcelona with Vera Soudeikina for three concerts beginning on 28 March 1925.[91] Then, journeying with his wife and children from Nice to Rome, on 24 April he led the Sala Accademica Conservatorio di Santa Cecilia in (among other orchestral and chamber works) "Song of the Fisherman" and the "Nightingale aria" (both from his opera, *Le Rossignol*), *Pribaoutki,* and the *Three Japanese Lyrics;* his soprano soloist was Vera Janacopulos.[92]

Back home at Nice in mid-May, Stravinsky began summing up his thoughts about his first tour of the United States and the Americans he had met. His publicly-expressed opinions were positive; for example, in Cincinnati on 4 March he said, "I Love America."[93] Later that month, while in Barcelona, he had reaffirmed to a reporter for *La Noche* that since leaving Europe (in January of 1925) it had been

> nothing but satisfying for me. . . . In North America, the successes have been resounding. . . . Artistic and also financial successes, since I earned a lot. . . . In Philadelphia, I was paid tribute . . . by two thousand old ladies! . . . They paraded by, one by one, kissing my hand.[94]

But from Leningrad, speaking in confidence to his niece Tanya, his private opinion differed markedly. On 14 May Tanya wrote from Nice to her family in Russia that "Uncle came to hate America and Americans, he says that he has never seen a more dull and boring people."[95] Perhaps after returning home to Nice, he had recalled one salutation at his arrival in the United States: "We hope that the stupidity of this country will not kill you."[96]

After his return to France, it was announced in New York, probably at Kochanski's instigation, that the two

> took advantage of the opportunity afforded by their sojourn in New York this season to renew the friendship which they have enjoyed for many years. Stravinsky was a frequent visitor at the Kochanski home, and as a mark of appreciation of the latter's art has promised to arrange a six-part suite from his ballet, *Pulchinella* [sic] for violin and piano.[97]

Once resettled in southern France, Stravinsky kept most of this promise, completing a five-movement suite from *Pulcinella* on 25 August 1925. But despite a "friendship . . . enjoyed for many years," he treated Kochanski rather shabbily even though Kochanski wrote him that he would "not be jealous if the suite is played by someone else."[98] When the wealthy Swiss Werner Reinhart offered a considerable sum of money to Stravinsky for a prior performance by Reinhart's protégée, attractive young Alma Moodie, he accepted.[99] Caught between an amorous patron and a loyal old friend, the awkward pickle in which Stravinsky found himself is best expressed in two letters of October 1925

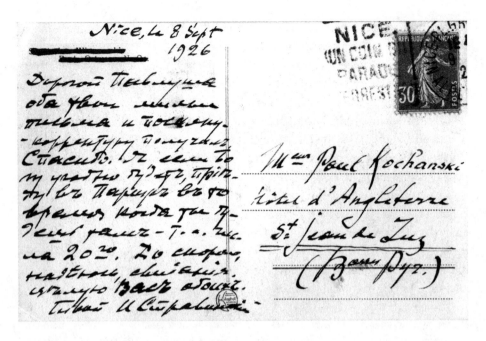

FIGURE 1.6
Stravinsky to Paul Kochanski, 1926 (postcard back). UBC Stravinsky Collection, no. 35.

to Reinhart.[100] Moodie, rather than Kochanski, premiered the arrangement privately on 12 November 1925 at Winterthur with Stravinsky at the piano, then publicly on 21 November in Berlin, poor Kochanski retaining but an American exclusivity.

Stravinsky had dedicated the suite to his friend Kochanski, and the violinist wrote to thank him on 14 September. After dealing with the galley proofs, Kochanski was given exclusivity, beginning 1 November 1926.

Mr. Paul Kochanski   Nice
Hôtel d'Angleterre   8 September 1926
St. Jean-de-Luz
Basses Pyr

Dear Pavlushka:
I received both of your nice letters and your package—galley proofs. Thank you. I, if God wills it, will arrive in Paris when you are there—i.e., on the 20th. So I hope soon to have a rendezvous. I kiss you both.

Thine, I Stravinsky.

When questioned on 16 May 1967 by a violinist in the Toronto Symphony Orchestra, Stravinsky replied that "I played [it] with Kochanski only once, many times with Dushkin."[101]

Even Kochanski's exclusivity was compromised a few years later by new suites from *Pulcinella,* resulting from Stravinsky's collaborations in 1932 with Gregor Piatigorsky and in 1933 with Samuel Dushkin.[102] Perhaps to soften the blow of *Pulcinella's* premiere by someone else, beginning on 1 November 1926 Stravinsky assembled another suite of three pieces, this time from *Firebird,* and at its publication in 1929 he dedicated it to Kochanski.[103] But despite Stravinsky's long friendship with Kochanski, it was Dushkin who premiered Stravinsky's new Violin Concerto in 1931 and accompanied the composer on his next tour of the United States. Stravinsky may have thought that the slightly younger violinist had already proved himself in the Concerto, was unmarried (until January of 1936), and free to travel, and could more easily adapt to Stravinsky's requirements.

The first tour netted Stravinsky a very tidy sum that derived more from his conducting engagements than from his piano performances. Not long after returning, he indulged himself in several ways. He bought a car and, on 21 July 1925, hired a chauffeur. Before long, he needed a new driver, and he sent a handwritten letter in French to unnamed friends (figs. 1.7a, 1.7b):

[Nice?]

Friday, 21 August 1925

My dear friends

Let me know if your chauffeur knows someone who could drive my car—my chauffeur quits in a week and I'm stuck here, which is extremely annoying.

I need someone perfectly reliable who could board and room across the street from me—my man can no longer work for me because he lives too far away from me at Nice, which means that for every meal he has to go home. I pay 800 [francs] net (I don't feed or house him)—if I leave for an entire day or for several days he gets 25 francs per day, and he himself takes care of his food and lodging.

We were extremely sorry at not finding you the other day. I thought the meeting was set for Picasso's place; it's you who gave me his address.

A thousand very sincere and friendly regards from your

Igor Stravinsky.

The "dear friends" were almost certainly his American acquaintances, the expat artists Gerald Murphy and his wife, Sara (sister of Hoytie Wiborg), who maintained their "Villa America" on the Riviera and were friends of Pablo Picasso.[104] Two years earlier, when Picasso was in love with Sara,[105] her husband had helped paint sets for *Svadebka* (*Les Noces*), and on 1 July 1923 this wealthy couple had given a party for Stravinsky on a converted barge in the Seine to celebrate the production of his ballet.[106] Among their guests were Jean Cocteau and Picasso. Stravinsky's letter regrets that they had not all met in July 1925 at "Picasso's place," referring to the painter's house at Juan-les-Pins.[107]

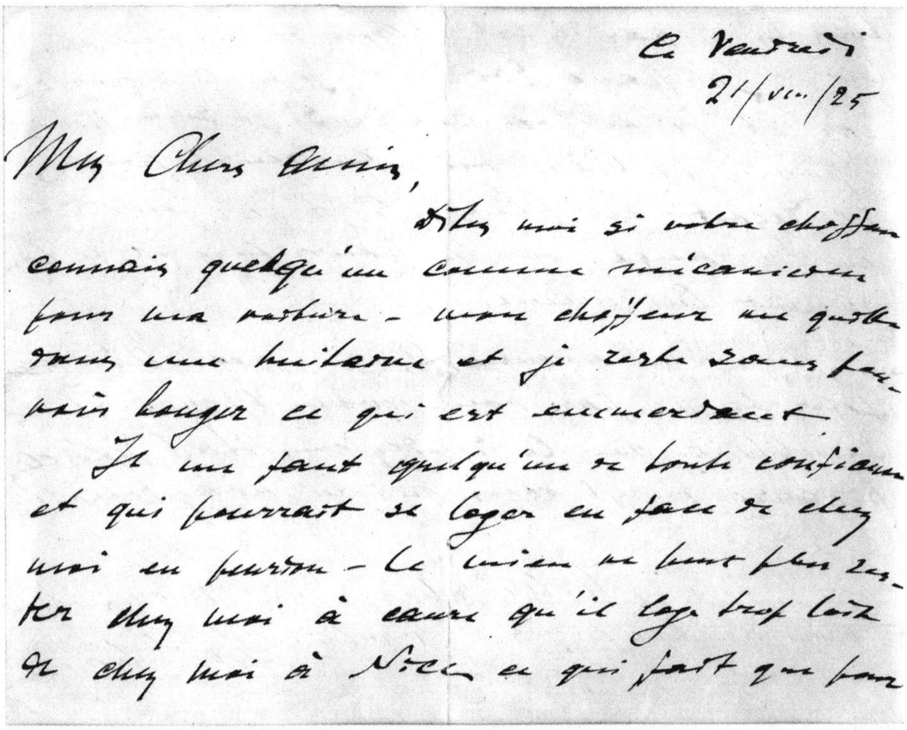
Ce Vendredi
21/VIII/25

Mes Chers Amis,

Dites moi si votre chauffeur connaît quelqu'un comme mécanicien pour ma voiture - mon chauffeur me quitte dans une huitaine et je reste sans pouvoir bouger ce qui est emmerdant.

Il me faut quelqu'un de toute confiance et qui pourrait se loger en face de chez moi en pension - Le mien ne peut plus rester chez moi à cause qu'il loge trop loin de chez moi à Nice ce qui fait que pour

FIGURE 1.7a
Stravinsky to "My dear friends," 1925. UBC Stravinsky Collection, no. 32.

STRAVINSKY AS CONDUCTOR

Stravinsky's diatribes against conductors of his music and, less often, of works by other composers, are well-known.[108] They began in 1921 with his raillery against Koussevitzky concerning the disastrous London premiere of Symphonies of Wind Instruments, continued in 1924 against Furtwängler at Berlin in respect to accompanying him in the Piano Concerto, peaked in 1937 with protests about unauthorized cuts made by Ansermet to *Jeu de cartes,* and continued in 1941 about Leopold Stokowski's interpretation of *Le Sacre* in the Disney film *Fantasia.*[109] Stravinsky's thoughts crystallized in 1962 in a London interview, "On Conductors and Conducting," published four years later.[110]

In light of these complaints, one might justly inquire about Stravinsky's own qualifications to lead his music. He first conducted an orchestra on 30 March 1914 at a morning rehearsal in the Kursaal at Montreux in one of the movements of his Symphony in E-flat and perhaps received some pointers from Ansermet. Late that year, Serge Diaghilev was sufficiently confident that he proposed that Stravinsky conduct *Scherzo fantastique, Fireworks,* and suites from *Petrushka* and *Firebird* in Rome on 3 January 1915, although Ansermet led the actual performances. In 1917 Stravinsky apparently conducted *Firebird,*

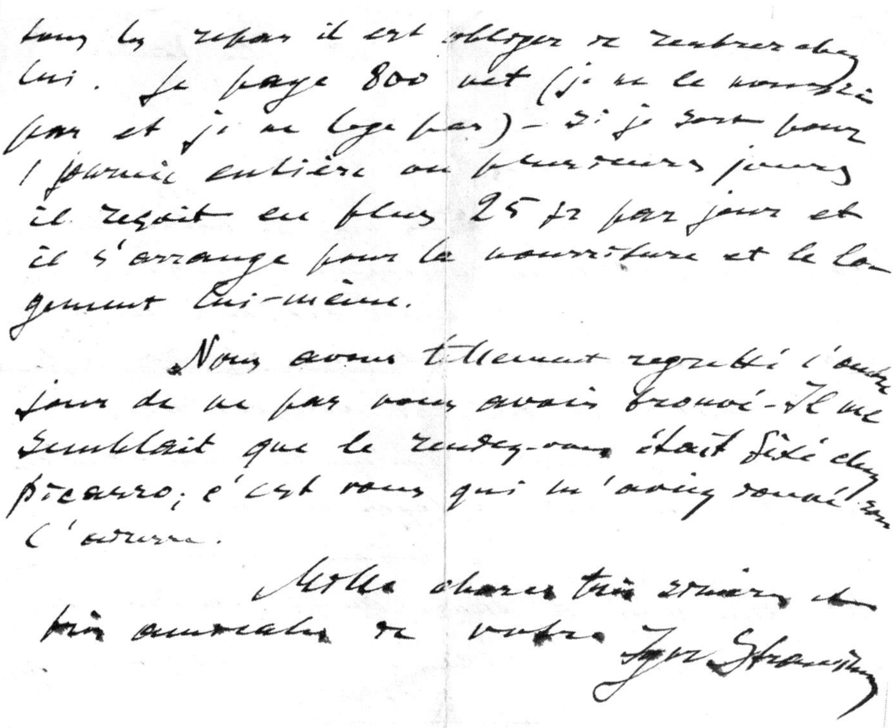

tous les repas il est obligé de rentrer chez lui. Je paye 800 net (je ne le nourris pas et je ne loge pas) – si je sors pour 1 journée entière ou plusieurs jours il reçoit en plus 25 fr par jour et il s'arrange pour la nourriture et le logement lui-même.

Nous avons tellement regretté l'autre jour de ne pas vous avoir trouvé – Il me semblait que le rendez-vous était fixé chez Picasso; c'est vous qui m'aviez donné l'autre.

Mille choses très sincères et bien amicales de nous. Igor Strawinsky

FIGURE 1.7b
Stravinsky to "My dear friends," 1925 (cont.). UBC Stravinsky Collection, no. 32.

Fireworks, and a suite from *Petrushka* at Rome; in 1922 in Paris, *Fireworks, Nightingale* excerpts, and *Firebird;* in 1923 there, his *Octet.*[111] Harvard-educated composer and choral conductor Virgil Thomson, who studied with Nadia Boulanger in Paris in 1921–22 and spent much of his time there until 1940, recalled that "like anyone who had not conducted very much . . . he was clumsy at it."[112]

Paul Rosenfeld's valuable essay, too long to quote here, offers the best account of Stravinsky's rehearsal techniques in New York in 1925.[113] An early evaluation of Stravinsky's first New York Philharmonic concert by Deems Taylor points to a still fairly primitive grasp of essentials:

> His conducting technique is what orchestra musicians sometimes call "an honest four-four"; that is, he beats the time in wide arcs that delineate the measures emphatically if not wholly gracefully. His interpretive indications are few and simple; his left hand usually accompanies his right, and an occasional turn of his body to indicate an entrance is about the only signal that he gives to players. . . . In the "Song of the Volga Boatmen" . . . he brought in every thud of the bass drum with a savage down-beat that nearly thrust him off the conductor's stand. . . . He conducted them [*Song of the Nightingale,* suites from *Pulcinella*

and *Firebird*] capably, but not, it must be confessed, as well as several other conductors have done. The orchestra, furthermore, did not rally to his support with any particular brilliance. The men sounded tired and a bit listless, and individual players made several technical slips during the evening.[114]

Lawrence Gilman noted that his conducting "in finesse and clarity, in tonal balance, in nuance, left something to be desired."[115] But even then, some awarded kudos for his emphasis on rhythm. In a cleverly titled essay, H. O. Osgood mused, "All [of Stravinsky's works] have had better performances. He is not a great conductor—and why should he be? He has done very little conducting. . . . His beat is perfectly clear, doubtless easy to follow.[116] In a more extensive review, Oscar Thompson, a critic who was to become one of Stravinsky's adversaries,[117] allowed that his "conducting was adequate and served to make his compositions intelligible and enjoyable" and that it "possessed dynamic and emotional force, but lacked abandon." Not realizing that "abandon" was thoroughly alien to Stravinsky's nature, he went on to complain—rather graphically—that the conducting "sometimes took on a nose-in-the-score meticulousness that militated against orchestral élan. There was no lack of lively gestures, these being supplemented by a Jack-in-the Box spring from a position not far from a crouch."[118]

One New York music-loving layman whose interests centered on stage design and who had just heard *Petrushka,* "conducted by [Stravinsky] himself," deplored talk that Stravinsky did not conduct his own music as well as others did: "This is not true for me. In this music he achieved a molten fire, a silvery radiance, a pearl-like sweetness, and a fearful barbaric storm that no one else has ever before gathered out of an orchestra with the same vividness."[119] A Boston critic, regretting that Stravinsky appeared solely as a pianist in his initial concerts with Koussevitzky and the Boston Symphony, and affording no opportunity to judge his skills in conducting, nevertheless made a trenchant observation about the centrality of rhythm at the US premiere of his Piano Concerto: "under his fingers, he exploits to the uttermost the percussive effects of the piano."[120] For Stravinsky's concerts a week later with the Philadelphia Orchestra, a reviewer wrote, "Mr. Stravinsky is surely a live-wire and conducts with spirit and particular attention to rhythm."[121] Still another Philadelphia writer observed that he

revealed something decidedly novel in the way of conducting, concentrating his powers chiefly upon the development and maintenance of rhythm in highly effective interpretive methods . . . less individualized instrumental clarity [than Stokowski, but] greater surge and sweep of pulsating tone. . . . His technic [*sic*] of conducting appeared to be almost as original as his scores.[122]

Perhaps the final sentence refers to the "Jack-in-the Box spring."

With the Cleveland Orchestra on 12 February, Stravinsky "led the players . . . with a minimum of flourishes and with a decisive beat, easily followed."[123] Later that month

(20 February) in Chicago, a critic similarly admired "the nervous vitality of Stravinsky's conducting, and his incessant emphasis upon the rhythmic energy of his music did much to define in the mind of his local audiences the proper approach to an understanding and evaluation of his music."[124]

Despite telling the Detroit press that he did not like to play the piano and conduct in the same concert, on 28 February he did just that. He played his Piano Concerto there (led by Victor Kolar) and conducted *Petrushka, Scherzo Fantastique, Fireworks,* and his arrangement for winds and timpani of *Volga Boatmen.* Although the Concerto elicited "gasps and giggles" from the audience, at the concert's close "the orchestra saluted Mr. Stravinsky with a fanfare."[125]

Incapacitated by a heavy cold on 4 March upon arrival in Cincinnati, Stravinsky greatly profited from Fritz Reiner—a superb conductor whom he admired—taking the first orchestral rehearsal. At the concert the orchestra "responded with precision and virtuosity and thrilling enthusiasm," earning Stravinsky "a ravishing ovation."[126]

Whatever reservations critics may have had early in 1925 about his conducting, his experience leading major US orchestras clearly improved his technique. Although the fine conductor Hermann Scherchen found Stravinsky's conducting "stiff and of little merit" in April at Rome,[127] Prokofiev (whose diaries reveal that he and Stravinsky were close but wary of each other) observed on 12 and 13 June 1925 in Paris that "Stravinsky . . . is getting much better at conducting: [but] he did not conduct *Ragtime* so much as dance it," allowing that he "has made strides not only as a conductor but as a pianist."[128] Two years later, however, following the premiere of *Oedipus Rex,* Prokofiev recorded in his diary for 2 June an evening gathering during which "Koussevitzky and [Arthur] Rubinstein, foaming at the mouth, tore into both *Oedipe* and Stravinsky's abominable conducting."[129] Klemperer commented (privately) that year on Stravinsky's failure to get a certain passage right.[130]

Although presumably unaware of these criticisms, in the decade between this tour and the next, Stravinsky did not hesitate to express himself to the European press about his conductorial ideals, namely, to remain true to the score and the composer's wishes.[131]

2

TOUR II (1935)

CONCERT APPEARANCES

7 January: Town Hall chamber music concert honoring composer Stravinsky

10 January: New York Plaza Hotel Ballroom, "Morning Musical," with Dushkin

13 January: Chicago Arts Club, with Dushkin

14 January: Milwaukee, with Chicago Symphony

17–18 January: Chicago Symphony

21 January: Minneapolis, Cyrus Northrop Auditorium, with Dushkin

22 January: Chicago Symphony

23 January: Toledo, Museum of Art, with Dushkin

25 January: Pittsburgh, Carnegie Music Hall, with Dushkin

27 January: Indianapolis, English Theatre, with Dushkin

3 February: New York, General Motors Symphony (radio broadcast)

10 February: St. Louis Symphony, Municipal Auditorium, plus duos with Dushkin

13 February: San Francisco Opera House, with Dushkin

14 February: Palo Alto, Stanford University, with Dushkin

16 February: Carmel, Sunset School, with Dushkin

21–22 February: Los Angeles Philharmonic

28 February: Los Angeles Auditorium, with Dushkin

3 March: Colorado Springs, Hotel Broadmoor, with Dushkin

4 March: Denver, Broadway Theatre, with Dushkin

6 March: Fort Worth, Central High School auditorium, with Dushkin

14 March: Cambridge, Boston Symphony

15–16 March: Boston Symphony

24 March: Washington, DC, National Theatre, with Dushkin

27 March: Winnetka, School of Musical Arts and Crafts, with Dushkin

[29 March: Chicago, Orchestra Hall, with Dushkin: cancelled]

9 April: Washington, DC, Library of Congress, with Dushkin

The decade between Stravinsky's first two tours to the United States saw the composer completing and premiering a wide variety of works, most of them now standard repertoire: two orchestral scores for ballets: *Apollon* (1927–28) and *The Fairy's Kiss* (1928); two works for speaker, vocal soloists, chorus, and orchestra: *Oedipus Rex* (1926–27) and *Perséphone* (1933–34); one work for chorus and orchestra: *Symphony of Psalms* (1930); three unaccompanied sacred choruses in Slavonic: *Pater Noster* (1926), *Credo* (1932), and *Ave Maria* (1934); arrangements of earlier works: Four Studies (1928–29), Divertimento for large orchestra (1934), and Suite No. 1 for small orchestra (1925); Serenade in A (1925) for solo piano; Capriccio (1928–29) for piano and orchestra; Concerto in D (1931) for violin and orchestra; *Duo concertant* (1932) for violin and piano; arrangements of earlier works for violin and piano, *Suite italienne* (1922, arr. 1932) and Divertimento (1934); and *Suite italienne* (1932) for cello and piano.

Almost as if Stravinsky's sour remarks to his niece about America had somehow leaked to the US press, midway through the tour he told *Los Angeles Times* reporter Isabel Morse Jones that "his attitude toward music and toward America has changed utterly since his visit ten years ago. He finds in America the eagerness and the vitality, the growth of mind he anticipated." This change may have been as much owing to his experiences with Samuel Dushkin, the young American violinist traveling with him, as to the tour itself. Stravinsky, speaking to Jones of his growing absorption in violin repertoire after the 1918 *Histoire du soldat,* regarded it "as the culmination of his condensation principles—his 'musical hygienics' program of shrinking musical forms into small, clear-cut, concentrated patterns with a high density," and he considered his colleague Dushkin "the perfect exponent of his music."[1] This absorption, and the association with Dushkin, begun in 1930, was the genesis of all the works for the violin listed above.

During the second tour, Stravinsky not only performed works with Dushkin but also employed him as translator. Although Stravinsky had begun a pocket dictionary of English the previous year, assigning many common words their French, German, and Russian equivalents,[2] he made few notes about pronunciation, bearing out his admission in 1925 to a reporter that "I would mispronounce English if I tried to speak it."[3] Because he spoke Russian with Dushkin (though he corresponded with him in French), Stravinsky had had little opportunity to practice his English, and even in Britain, his upper-class admirers probably spoke French with him.

The second tour was much more wide-ranging but less lucrative than the previous one.[4] When interviewed near its close in Washington, DC, with translators Dushkin and their concert agent's assistant, Severin E. Kavenoki, Stravinsky opined: "There was only one thing he had not liked about his journey. That was the cost. He said that in tips, he had given to the Pullman porters alone what amounted to [fees for] one concert. Except for the expense, America he dearly loved."[5]

Kavenoki worked for Alexander Bernardovich Merovitch. After briefly serving in 1930 as vice president and director for Arthur Judson's New York firm, Concert Management,

Merovitch founded his own concert agency, Musical Art Management. Merovitch began planning Stravinsky's 1935 tour in 1933.[6] It was to be their first, last, and only project: Merovitch was committed in mid-November 1935 for some months to an asylum for the criminally insane.[7] He booked many more cities than Stravinsky had visited the previous decade, and they were widely separated ones, often necessitating considerable backtracking. Rather than hugging the Eastern Seaboard, their concert itinerary emphasized the Midwest and the West Coast. By mid-February it brought both composer and violinist to the San Francisco Bay area and then on to Los Angeles, the abode of an old-time friend from St. Petersburg. In less than a decade and for almost the remainder of Stravinsky's life, that Southern California city was to be his home.

Stravinsky had been introduced to Dushkin during his first tour, and he was reintroduced to him in Europe. They had been giving recitals since 1931, and Dushkin had premiered Stravinsky's Violin Concerto in Berlin, so Dushkin, then unmarried and of an affable disposition, was a logical choice to travel with Stravinsky.[8] Probably owing to the composer's wishes, Dushkin participated in almost none of the better-paying orchestral and chamber concerts led by Stravinsky. Obliged to bear Dushkin's travel expenses, the composer netted less for himself than he had in his one-man tour a decade earlier.

NEW YORK

Stravinsky and Dushkin arrived in New York on the SS *Rex* on 3 January 1935, together with many other musicians: pianists Joseph Hofmann and Ignaz Friedman, and cellist Gregor Piatigorsky. Also disembarking was violinist Nathan Milstein, who later came to dislike Dushkin's transcriptions of Stravinsky works. Milstein amusingly described the composer's terror during the stormy voyage and Stravinsky's on-board reediting for cello with Piatigorsky of the final movement in Dushkin's 1932 arrangement of *Suite italienne*.[9] Stravinsky and Dushkin stayed in New York until 11 January before setting off for the Midwest.[10] They gave at least sixteen duo-recitals across the country.[11]

Just four days after arriving in New York, Stravinsky was honored by a concert of his music given by the League of Composers at the Town Hall Club. Nicholas Slonimsky was president of the League, and Claire R. Reis its executive chair. A previous concert led by Slonimsky at the Hollywood Bowl on 16 July 1933, including what was mysteriously entitled Stravinsky's *Fanfare for a Liturgy*,[12] probably helped Slonimsky and Reis two years later in convincing the League to put on an all-Stravinsky concert. The Town Hall Club was "packed."[13] Perhaps owing to the lukewarm reception in 1925 of then-recent works such as the Octet and the Piano Concerto, every work heard that evening in 1935 was decidedly retrospective in nature: Three Pieces for String Quartet (1914), a group of songs (composed 1908–18), an aria from *Mavra* (1922), the *Serenade* (1925), and the Concertino for String Quartet (1920).

Appropriately enough, given the compositional divide suggested by the dates of these works, an announcement for this concert featured a photograph taken by the

FIGURE 2.1
Portrait by Lipnitzki. Igor Strawinsky
Collection, Paul Sacher Foundation, Basel.

Studio Lipnitzki and already run in 1925 by *Musical America*. The image effectively sliced Stravinsky in two. Using only the upper half of the photograph, it omits the portion of the portrait that shows an elegant dangling monocle, a trademark during that decade (fig. 2.1).[14] Just six weeks later in California, he was to inscribe a copy of the same but full Lipnitzki portrait to Herbert Stothart, the general music director of MGM Studios.[15]

Apropos of this concert, the young Alexander Steinert, then conductor of the Russian Opera Company of New York, related three years later:

> [It was] merely by chance that I happened to be at a reception in honor of Stravinsky, given by the League of Composers at the Town Hall in New York during the winter of 1935. A slight tap of the shoulder caused me to turn around. It was George Gershwin.[16]

Steinert landed the job of coaching singers for the forthcoming production in October of *Porgy and Bess*. Because Gershwin attended this Town Hall concert, Stravinsky probably encountered him there; if so, it was their third meeting: the first had been in 1925 in New York, and the second in 1928 when Gershwin visited Paris.

One recent biographer implies that both Stravinsky and Dushkin performed at the League of Composers concert.[17] Neither did, although Dushkin probably also attended it. The concert received a devastating review, signed with the initials of a prolific but minor composer and longtime editor-in-chief for *Musical America*: A. Walter Kramer.[18] Kramer complained of

> the utter sterility of [Stravinsky's] lesser music in the light of today. . . . Something of a tragedy it is to observe the impotence, the dryness, and the willful, wayward, cerebral direction of a musician of cultivation and considerable technical skill. There was not a single phrase of thematic material in all the works performed worthy of a post-graduate student. As for the terror which this music once aroused, it was no longer in evidence. Nothing but its arrant ugliness has remained. Mr. Stravinsky was present, bowed, and at the close of the evening was introduced to many who told him how much they enjoyed his music. There were also many who did not.[19]

Neither critic nor composer then knew how much influence Kramer would have on Stravinsky's finances only five years hence.[20]

Three days later, on a program shared with several others for a "Morning Musical," held on 10 January in the ballroom of the Plaza Hotel, Stravinsky and Dushkin first performed together in New York. Despite the completion in 1932 of the great *Duo concertant*, their share in this program consisted exclusively of transcriptions and arrangements. Among such works was a genuine novelty, the Divertimento, comprising excerpts arranged from *Le Baiser de la fée*, an arrangement that they had just premiered the previous month in Strasbourg.[21] A reviewer of this "3rd Artistic Morning in the Hotel Plaza" who praised "Stravinsky's pianism . . . exact and fluent" also observed that "Mary Garden was in the audience."[22] In its orchestral garb, his Divertimento was to figure in this tour, in the 1936 one to South America, and in both trips to Mexico in 1940 and 1941.

At some point after he and Dushkin arrived in New York, although perhaps not during their first busy week there, the dapper Stravinsky sat—apparently more than once—for a drawing by Aline Fruhauf (fig. 2.2). Commissioned by *Musical America*, it appeared in the April issue.[23] Not only her drawing but also her perceptive recollection of their meeting deserve reproduction here:

> He was a small man with broad shoulders, a slim waist and a propulsive profile. At first his long, ovoid head suggested an Aztec carving; then it became a blanched almond. . . . At the first meeting, Stravinsky's hair was brownish and beautifully groomed, I was sure, with a pair of military brushes. He was well turned out in gray flannels, a chocolate-brown

FIGURE 2.2
Cartoon by Aline Fruhauf, 1935.
UBC Stravinsky Collection, no. 39.

cardigan, a gray striped shirt with a white collar, and a brown foulard tie with copper dots. And his image was punctuated by a large onyx ring on his right hand, pointed black shoes, and a cigarette in a long black holder.[24]

As Fruhauf related, when she "went to the office to pick up [the original] after it had been published, I found that one of my anonymous collectors had gotten there first." Who stole the drawing is not known, but one owner's initials, "D B W," were stamped on her drawing before it was acquired sixty years later by the New York dealer from whom I purchased it.

THE MIDWEST

Stravinsky and Dushkin started their tour westward on 12 January. The following day, the first concert at the Chicago Arts Club, which included the Octet for wind instruments and double bass, had no need for Dushkin. But something curious happened. The Octet was performed twice: led first by Eric DeLamarter, assistant conductor of the Chicago Symphony Orchestra, and then by Stravinsky himself,[25] the sole instance reported of this strange, and perhaps unique, instance of two different conductors—one directly after the other—leading the same work! The explanation probably lies in Stravinsky's hectic travel schedule, allowing him very little or perhaps even no rehearsal time at all. Thus DeLamarter essentially prepared the work for the composer's own performance (presaging Craft's rehearsals three decades later for the elderly Stravinsky's concerts and recordings).

Although the reporter of the above concert did not compare the two conductors, Stravinsky proved in Chicago that with a great orchestra and sufficient rehearsal time, he could inspire its players to considerable heights. Initially, he led the Chicago Symphony on 14 January at Milwaukee, introducing his recently assembled orchestral suite, called there "Divertimento, from *Le Baiser de la fée*." He repeated this work in Chicago on 17 and 18 January under a variant title, "FRAGMENTS from the Ballet *The Fairy's Kiss*." One reviewer wrote:

> Stravinsky knows what he wants and his wishes were so well expressed that the orchestra responded minutely to all his demands. His beat is easy to follow. . . . Rhythm and tone color . . . were brought out in bold relief by the orchestra under his skillful guidance. . . . The orchestra gave him a fanfare.[26]

Even Albert Goldberg—future bête noire at the *Los Angeles Times*—described the concert in the *Chicago Herald and Examiner* as "a triumph for orchestra, composer, and conductor . . . with the audience at the end venting its excitement in shouts and cheers."[27] A third reviewer summed up: "Critics differed as to whether Stravinsky's eccentricities in conducting were legitimate musical devices, but there was no doubt as to the effectiveness of his direction."[28]

Between these Chicago concerts, Stravinsky received a letter forwarded from New York. Postmarked Los Angeles, 15 January 1935 (though absent-mindedly dated 1934 inside), it contained an invitation for reacquaintance and for housing there. Stravinsky responded four days later from Chicago.[29] The letter writer was his old St. Petersburg friend Dr. Alexis Kall, living since 1920 in Los Angeles.

This friend may well have heard the 1907 world premiere (two movements only) at St. Petersburg of the next orchestral composition that Stravinsky programmed for Chicago, on 22 January 1935: his early Symphony in E flat (1905–7). The previous 6 December, Frederick Stock might have believed that he had scooped every conductor in the country by leading this work with the Chicago Symphony.[30] If so, he was mistaken. On 28 January 1919, Modest Altschuler had beaten both Stock and Stravinsky to it with the Russian Symphony Orchestra of New York in Carnegie Hall.[31] And in August 1927 Altschuler repeated it at the Hollywood Bowl, a concert that Kall, friend of Altschuler, would not have missed.[32]

Stravinsky's Chicago performance on 22 January closed, as had his concerts the previous week, with the "same large audience, almost the same amount of enthusiastic applause, [and] the same exultant fanfare by the orchestra when the concert was ended." Even though Chicago had recently heard the greatly revered Stock's "first time" performance of the E-flat Symphony, "Stravinsky's performance was greatly liked."[33]

The latter part of January was particularly hectic with duo recitals every two days beginning on 21 January in Minneapolis,[34] then Toledo on the twenty-third, Pittsburgh on the twenty-fifth, and Indianapolis on the twenty-seventh. Stravinsky confessed to his tour-weariness in an interview following his Pittsburgh concert; with Dushkin interpreting his rapid French, he explained: "It grieves me to have to say 'I can't come to your party, Madam.' But what else can I do? I arrive the night before, perhaps. I need a good night's sleep. I rest. I play. And then there is a train to catch at 9:27 or 11:15."[35]

The duo sometimes split a concert with another performing group, a practice unique to this tour. For example, the 23 January program in Toledo was shared with the Paris Instrumental Quartet,[36] and the 27 January one in Indianapolis, with the Glazounoff Russian String Quartet.[37]

Back in New York by 28 January and ensconced in the Ansonia Hotel at Broadway and Seventy-Third Street, Stravinsky then helped Columbia records and his German publisher, through its representative G. Schirmer, as well as his own royalties, with a book- and record-signing, announced in the *New York Times:* "Igor Stravinsky will personally autograph a limited number of phonograph recordings and printed copies of his works, at 11:30 a.m. on Friday February 1, 1935 at G. Schirmer, Inc. East 43rd St." A short essay appeared above the advertisement:

> Of the composers to whom the gramophone has been available as a means of issuing authorized versions of their works, Igor Stravinsky has made most use of it, . . . which leaves little remaining to be done and represents a greater proportion of [his] entire output recorded than any other composer living or dead. . . . Records of his music will be played. He will probably speak and souvenirs of the occasion, in the form of autographed sets and records will be available.[38]

A couple of weeks previously, on 19 January, artist René Auberjonois (Stravinsky's Swiss colleague in the 1918 production of *Histoire du soldat*) had urged Fernand, his twenty-four-year-old son then living in New York, to contact Stravinsky. Fernand replied that Stravinsky had asked him to go to the Schirmer book-signing with him, perhaps as a translator. He did so and observed that the composer "during the entire matinee . . . attended to this task, grudgingly paying attention."[39]

Two days later, *The New York Times* noted that Stravinsky, "making his only appearance [tonight] as conductor here at the Center Theatre, [will lead] the orchestra of N.B.C.'s sponsored broadcast in the fifth program of its present series. The Russian composer will present familiar works of Glinka and Tschaikovsky [sic]."[40]

The *Times* failed to mention a milestone: Stravinsky began the concert with a "sixty-eight word speech in English,"[41] so far as known, his first English words uttered in public. The program was unusual in other ways, as well: he not only split it with mezzo-soprano Gladys Swarthout, accompanied by another conductor, Hans Lange, but he somehow evaded restrictions imposed by the series, underwritten by General Motors, on a conductor leading his own music. Thus, he was able to broadcast excerpts from *Petrushka* and his 1917 *Song of the Volga Boatmen,* the earliest of his three patriotic arrangements (the others being "La Marseillaise" and "The Star-Spangled Banner"): "Mr. Stravinsky had great success with the attendant audience. The Glinka was particularly well done and the Tchaikovsky *Nutcracker* was much applauded."[42]

After the music and record-jacket signing on 1 February, Carl Engel, then president of G. Schirmer and well-known to Stravinsky since 1927 because of the commissioning of *Apollon Musagète,*[43] hosted a big reception in Stravinsky's honor.[44] Years later the former silent-screen star Dagmar Godowsky wrote that she and her father, the celebrated Polish-born pianist Leopold Godowsky, were among those invited to Engel's reception. After her mother's death in 1933, the beautiful Dagmar, a gifted pianist herself, was then living with her father on Riverside Drive and was probably invited in order to assist him; five years earlier he had suffered a severe stroke that ended his concert career.

In Dagmar's memoir she recalls that, upon being introduced to Stravinsky by Engel, and fascinated by the composer, she promptly invited him and several other musicians to tea "Tuesday next" at "my house,"[45] meaning the Godowsky Riverside Drive apartment. She was incorrect about both date and place. The approximate date can be determined from her guest list, the exact date and location from the *New York Times.* Among the musicians she invited were Otto Klemperer, Mischa Elman, and Artur Schnabel. Schnabel was in New York from 11 January, Elman from 16 January. Although guest-conducting the Philadelphia Orchestra on 4 and 25 January in its hometown, Klemperer led the same orchestra on 29 January and 19 February in New York. Between his Philadelphia and New York engagements, he was in New York on at least two other occasions.

On Tuesday evening, 5 February, Stravinsky, Leopold Godowsky, Klemperer, Elman, and Schnabel all attended the sole Metropolitan Opera House performance of Shostakovich's *Lady Macbeth of the Mtsensk District* (1932), conducted by Artur Rodzinski.[46] Dagmar is now said to have been there with Stravinsky.[47] This may be correct: living with her handicapped father, she would probably have accompanied him to the Metropolitan Opera, as she had several days earlier to Engel's reception. At the opera Stravinsky perhaps sat with the Godowskys and the other invitees at her upcoming tea party. But unless she gave two teas, her memory betrayed her. According to a recently uncovered newspaper clipping, she held it on Thursday, 7 February at the Park Central Hotel.[48]

A strenuous schedule for Stravinsky: the book-signing (1 February), Engel's receptions, the opera (5 February), and Dagmar's tea (7 February), all took place within seven days during which he also rehearsed and conducted the General Motors Symphony and made a radio address in English.[49]

The 15 January 1935 letter that Stravinsky had received in Chicago (the one forwarded from New York) was from his old friend of prerevolutionary Russia, the fifty-six-year-old Dr. Alexis Kall (sometimes spelled Kahl or Kal). Dr. Kall invited the composer and Dushkin to stay with him six weeks hence when their tour reached Los Angeles. Their reunion was to have a profound influence: Kall, a friend of the actor Edward G. Robinson, probably ignited Stravinsky's desire to write Hollywood movie scores. Stravinsky had known him since at least the summer of 1901 in St. Petersburg and perhaps even earlier.[50] The two friends were observed together at the home of Nikolai Andreyevich Rimsky-Korsakov on 9 November 1903 by Rimsky's indefatigable chronicler, V. V. Yastrebtsev.[51] This was the period, 1903–4, when Rimsky occasionally worked with Stravinsky, followed by formal weekly lessons from the fall of 1905 until Rimsky's death.[52] Stravinsky and Kall may even have shared the same piano teacher in St. Petersburg: Leocadia Alexandrovna Kashperova, Anton Rubinstein's pupil. She had taught Stravinsky for a while from December of 1899,[53] and Kall is also said to have studied with a pupil of Rubinstein. Kall probably knew Rimsky even before 1903.

After writing his dissertation, "Die Philosophie der Music nach Aristoteles" at the University of Leipzig in 1902, Kall became a professor of music history at the University of St. Petersburg. As early as 1913, he was also acquainted with the young Sergey Prokofiev, and when visiting Paris in June and July of 1913, Kall perhaps caught one of the four performances there of *Le Sacre du printemps*. Fleeing Russia forever at summer's end in 1917, he traveled via Tokyo to settle in Los Angeles, where he taught piano. Early in the 1940s two of his numerous young female pupils would enter Stravinsky's orbit.

When Prokofiev concertized on 21 December 1920 in Los Angeles, he not only reestablished an acquaintance with Kall that went back to Debussy's appearance at St. Petersburg in 1913,[54] but he also introduced Kall to Dagmar Godowsky. Prokofiev had first encountered her in 1919 at her father's house in New York, his diary noting her as "very pretty, but a terrible flirt. People say 'Poor Godowsky, to have such a wild daughter.'" Although there is no record of Stravinsky's initial reaction in February of 1935, he had surely been attracted to her.

On his way West, Stravinsky assumed two roles during a concert on 10 February with the St. Louis Symphony Orchestra: orchestra conductor and chamber music player. After leading the orchestra, he played piano in "five selections" with Dushkin, joined by some of the orchestral players.[55] This was nothing new for them: a year earlier in England, on 22 February 1934, the pair had pulled off a more elaborate chamber and orchestral feat with the Hallé Orchestra. There they mixed the Violin Concerto; purely orchestral works; the Pastorale for violin, wind quartet, and piano; and various violin and piano transcriptions.[56]

Stravinsky's arrival in San Francisco and his concert on 13 February with Dushkin were, of course, well publicized. Among the best-informed and most progressive of the

West Coast critics was Alfred Frankenstein, trained at the University of Chicago, who regularly reviewed for the *San Francisco Chronicle*. He wrote a substantial introductory essay of welcome, playfully entitled "Prince Igor," and illustrated with one of Picasso's portraits of the composer.[57] It touched briefly on most of the composer's works from *Firebird* through the 1931 *Duo concertant*. Perhaps because Frankenstein omitted mentioning *Mavra*, he considered the Symphonies of Wind Instruments and the Octet as progenitors of the "simple melodious clarity" exemplified in the *Duo concertant*, a work that he had studied from Stravinsky's and Dushkin's recent (1933) recording. Frankenstein's high-minded sense of a critic's responsibility persisted through later encounters with Stravinsky's music: in 1942 with the composer himself, and in 1957 when reviewing *Canticum sacrum* and *Agon*.[58] Not until the emergence in the 1930s and early 1940s of critical voices such as José Rodriguez, Lawrence Morton, and Ingolf Dahl is a similar seriousness and depth of critical response encountered in Southern California.

San Francisco's Russian-language newspaper, *Novaya zarya* (New dawn), ran articles and essays about the composer four times during that month. The first of these (7 February), entitled "Igor Stravinsky in the American West," featured a publicity photograph of Dushkin holding his violin and leaning on Stravinsky's shoulder while both men study music held by the composer. It also gave a schedule of their forthcoming concerts southward. For example, the 23 February issue noted their concert in Los Angeles and depicted Dushkin playing for a cigarette-smoking Stravinsky, who is holding an opened piece of music.[59]

The 7 February photograph, together with an essay by Alexander Fried claiming that Stravinsky "has had as much influence on latter-day music as all other contemporary composers put together," appeared on 10 February in the *San Francisco Examiner*.[60] Fried's views typified most critics' responses (aside from Frankenstein's): the article was headed "Stravinsky's Music Needs an Orchestra." Even the one work that did not, *Duo concertant*, failed to please; incredibly, he opined that "until the oddly vivacious 'Gigue,' the piece was inarticulate."[61] A Pittsburgh reviewer had perceived it much the same way three weeks earlier: "The *Duo concertant* seemed to this reviewer unimportant and uninteresting . . . [a] cleverly constructed work, typical of the miraculous craftsmanship of Stravinsky yet naught can mitigate the long vast stretches of dullness that strike upon the ear."[62] Time has shown that only Frankenstein understood its true significance: "a most ponderable and important composition, full of exquisite, restrained feeling and fascinating harmonic color. It is surely one of Stravinsky's greater contributions to the literature of chamber music."[63]

THE "EXPRESSION" CONTROVERSY

The year 1935 saw the export to the New World of Stravinsky's contentious phrase "music is, by its very nature, powerless to *express* anything at all." This concept was to dog him for the remainder of his days. Just before the San Francisco concert, the *Oakland Tribune* had run a piece by Jack Mason called "Inspiration Is Myth, Says Igor Stravinsky." Disclosing some of what he called Stravinsky's "astonishing views," Mason demonstrated that the composer had not been idle in promoting the first volume of his new (and ghost-written) autobiography, *Chroniques de ma vie,* more than two months before its publication in Paris on 14 March and well before its English translation published the ensuing year.[64] Mason's piece was a thirdhand report, relying on what a *Milwaukee Journal* reporter had labeled in January as "Queer Ideas . . . Voiced by Russian,"[65] ideas Stravinsky had vouch-safed to an Associated Press reporter in New York.[66]

Mason correctly stated that while in New York, Stravinsky had imparted to a group of reporters what was to become his most notorious pronouncement in *Chroniques:* " 'I consider music in its essence,' he began, 'to be incapable of expressing any sentiment, any attitude, any psychological condition or any phenomenon of nature.' " Although shortened a trifle by Mason, this is a nice translation of the passage forthcoming in *Chroniques,* and it may have motivated Stravinsky's remarks in 1936 about its translation into English. On 24 February 1935, Isabel Morse Jones in Los Angeles heard him say something similar about " 'pure music': it has no recourse to sources outside of music."[67] The germ of all this—Stravinsky's discussion of the prelude to *Le Sacre du printemps,* and with its related topic of "facile expression"—grew out of the self-provoked uproar surrounding the ballet's riotous premiere in 1913. The fuss resulted from remarks he had submitted to French and Russian journals (29 May and early August 1913, respectively). Years later, scholars carefully researched, studied, and labeled these remarks as *l'affaire Montjoie!*[68] and revisited them as recently as 2013.[69]

Espressivo, an instruction to be "expressive," appears in Italian or French in more than a quarter of Stravinsky's works: 47 of his approximately 160 compositions.[70] Some were added, however, when revising scores during the 1940s: Stravinsky "added numerous markings of *espressivo.*"[71] His aims are hardly consistent. For example, his ultrachic 1923 Octet for Wind Instruments—in his own words that year, "a musical object . . . not an 'emotive' work," from which he excluded "all sorts of nuances"[72]—still retains its 1923 *espressivo* in its 1952 revision (for flute at reh. 66). With this caveat in mind, a few broad generalizations can be offered: (1) the term does not appear in his arrangements of other composers' music; (2) it is not in works of mourning, except in Symphonies of Wind Instruments;[73] (3) nor is it in most choral music (except for *Symphony of Psalms* and the Mass); (4) Stravinsky occasionally uses *espressivo* for solo voices; (5) it pops up in his jazz-related works; (6) it occurs in *Agon,* but is mostly absent in late serial compositions from *Threni* onward, and only rarely appears in Movements, Sermon, *Flood,* and *Requiem Canticles.*

Possibly as early as his 1925 tour, he had a colorful exchange with Serge Koussevitzky. During a rehearsal by Boston Symphony musicians in an unnamed "neoclassic" work by Stravinsky, he interrupted from his seat in the hall with "Please, no expression!" If this anecdote concerns his first tour, it might refer to a sole passage marked *espr[essivo]* that he was to perform: a phrase for two French horns in his 1923–24 Piano Concerto (at reh. 60 in the 1950 revised score). Koussevitzky responded, "But there is expression," and soldiered on.[74]

This incident resembles another early in 1940 in New York: Stravinsky's bilingual request to Kall's former student Adele Marcus during their rehearsal of the Two-Piano Concerto to perform "ohne espressione."[75] This was surely prompted by her personal style; one obituary describes her as having an "almost religiously Romantic approach to the piano"[76]—hardly congenial to Stravinsky's music.

Sometime between 1947 and 1957, Stravinsky urged orchestral musicians to play his music "secco, non vibrato, senza 'espressivo.'"[77] Later, a leading scholar quipped that "this is no less an 'effect' than molto espressivo."[78] Nevertheless, New York Philharmonic woodwind players rehearsing the premiere of the middle movement of the Symphony in Three Movements under the composer in January of 1946 encountered the word espress[ivo] printed in their parts no less than seventeen times![79]

On 15 December 1945, just after the close of World War II, Stravinsky replied to a letter from a certain J. Nizon in France (who, to judge from this vague response, was probably not a musician). Although its particular wording was unknown to Charles Joseph, he accurately characterized its general tenor as marred (like so many similar statements) by the composer's circular verbiage (fig. 2.3). How much assistance Stravinsky's reply gave poor M. Nizon remains unknown. Its essence is this: "[Music] is not a language related to the one which uses words. . . . Music expresses nothing other than itself. It is itself both the subject and the object of expression, its end and its means."[80]

Six months later, in Mexico City, when responding to a reporter's query on 25 July, Stravinsky uttered his clearest and most succinct formulation: "Music expresses nothing. It is expressive in and of itself, but it does not express [ideas or feelings]."[81] Doth the composer protest too much?

This belief obviously resided deep in Stravinsky's psyche. A surviving fragment of a love letter that he sent to Vera Soudeikina in 1921—long before he and Walter Nouvel formulated this credo for the first volume of Chroniques—offers several insights (fig. 2.4). It stands out among the many statements he made about musical expression because the deeply personal nature of this early love letter reveals him thoroughly off guard for a moment: it may well be his most cogent and truthful statement on the subject. He confesses his inability to state in words the strength of his feelings for Vera: "music is more anonymous and for this reason I am less strongly ashamed to express myself in it. . . . Perhaps music is something completely different."[82] Decades later, in 1963 on the SS Bremen bound for Hamburg, Vera responded to a Canadian reporter's question about her husband that "he does not want to show he has emotions."[83] And in a letter of 23 September 1939 to Kall (cited below), written just before the last transatlantic tour, he refuses to make an emotive spectacle of himself during coming performances in the United States.

FIGURE 2.3

Stravinsky to J. Nizon, 1945 (mailer and letter). UBC Stravinsky Collection, no. 83.

These comments suggest that Stravinsky might well have endorsed a recent statement by the Polish poetess and Nobel Prize winner, Wislawa Szymborska. Preferring the singing style of Ella Fitzgerald, "who always kept a little distance from the text," to that of Billy Holiday, "who poured her heart, soul, and various other organs into her song," Szymborska warns that "expressive singing is a slippery slope; once you're on it it's hard to get off."[84]

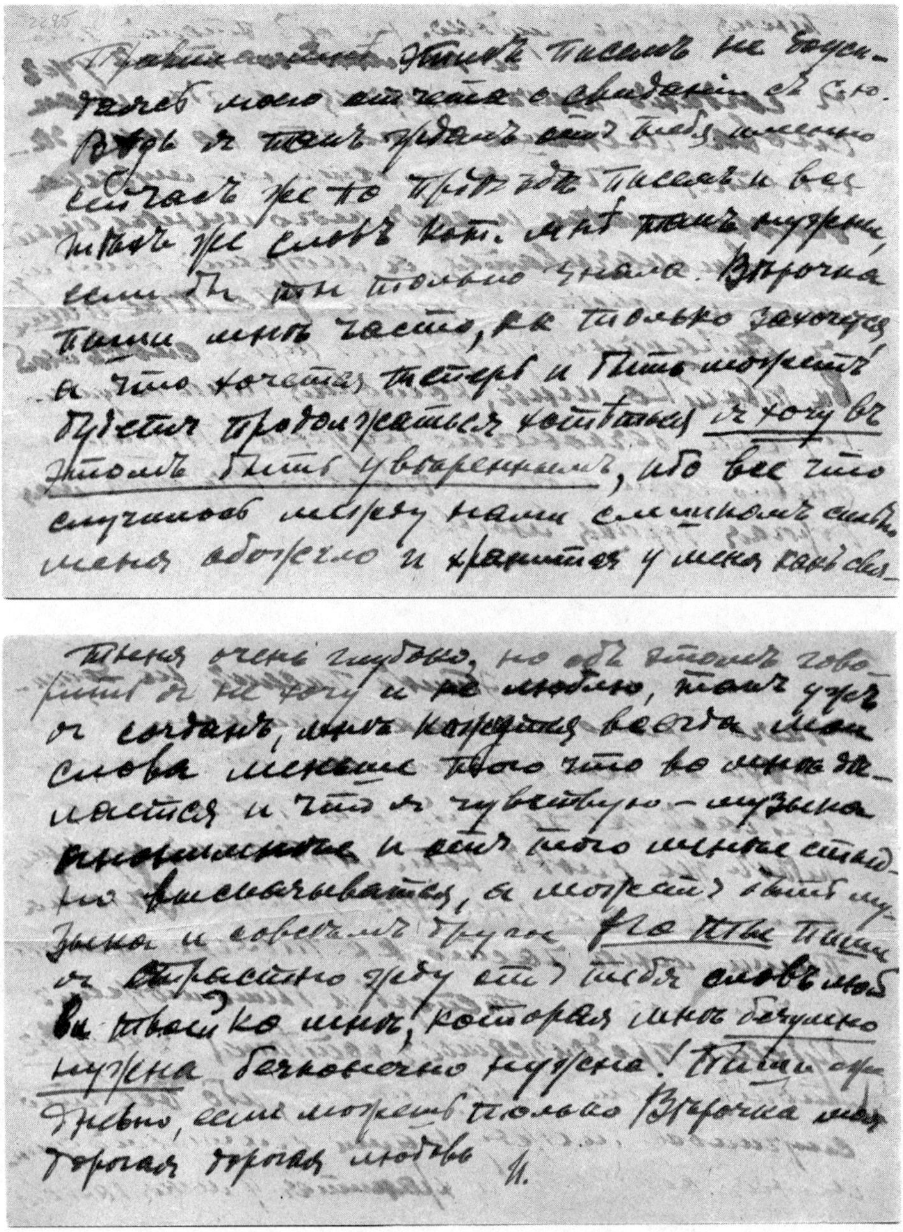

FIGURE 2.4

Stravinsky to Vera Soudeikina, 1921 (front and back). UBC Stravinsky Collection, no. 18.

During Stravinsky's long 1935 tour, he and Severin Kavenoki (then Merovitch's assistant) were also occupied with the business side of the English translation of the first volume of *Chroniques* and with the translation of its still-unfinished second volume. Half a dozen letters from the well-known New York publishing company Simon and Schuster to Kavenoki are extant in the New York Public Library for the Performing Arts.[85] The writers were Richard L. Simon, one of the founders of the firm; Leon Shimkin, a legal adviser; and Emil Hilb, the firm's music editor. Kavenoki clearly discussed at least one letter from Simon (17 January) and another from Shimkin (2 April) with Stravinsky while he was still in the States.

On the previous 9 December (1934), author and literary critic Clifton Fadiman had written Stravinsky in France on behalf of Simon and Schuster, indicating the firm's interest in publishing an English translation of the *Chroniques*.[86] Richard Simon's letter of 17 January 1935 to Kavenoki noted Fadiman's approval for publication, though Simon wanted both volumes published together rather than in succession, implying that Kavenoki should discuss this with Stravinsky, who was then in Chicago with Dushkin. Simon also wanted to talk to the composer "when he returns to New York" and enclosed a contract. The next letter, 2 April, is from Shimkin to Kavenoki. It must have included copies of agreements that had already been discussed with Stravinsky ("at your [i.e., Kavenoki's] last conference") and a contract ready to be signed by Stravinsky. Shimkin stated that a check for five hundred dollars for Kavenoki "will be forwarded promptly." At the top of Shimkin's letter Kavenoki scribbled, seemingly in great haste to judge by its garbled words, "As [a?]bove, all [want to?] publish / if they all advise and agree."

Notes by Kavenoki on the reverse side of this letter also hint at what he and Stravinsky had discussed: "copyright—taxes-able / cheap editions—10% / 6% does not refer / to the advance. / Canada." Below this, Kavenoki wrote in a careless Russian "Parisian" (masculine singular) preceding something that he then thoroughly obliterated. After the composer signed the contract, as an aid for future correspondence Kavenoki wrote on the face of the Shimkin envelope: "25 rue de la F[au]b[ourg] St. Honoré." This was Stravinsky's recent address in Paris. On the back side of this same envelope Kavenoki scribbled "Cartenet Hotel / 23rd [then in Chelsea at 208 W. Twenty-Third Street between:] 7th-8th Avenues] / [room?] 501 / Pyt [i.e., Polish for "five" or "question"] 6:30." It is unknown whether this scribble related to Kavenoki's business dealings with Stravinsky or some other client. Only nine days after Shimkin posted his letter, Stravinsky set sail for France.

An undated photograph of Kavenoki and Stravinsky shows them conferring (fig. 2.5).[87] Depicting Kavenoki seemingly in his late thirties, it might document a discussion in New York at the early stages of this publication project. The correspondence with Kavenoki continued after Stravinsky's return to Europe. A letter of 10 September 1935 from Simon to Kavenoki wonders whether Stravinsky really is working on the second volume of his *Chroniques* and requests a progress report (he finished it that

November). On 1 October Simon again wrote to Kavenoki, who had apparently been away during September. By the time of Simon's next letter of 10 October, Kavenoki had responded with such encouraging news that Simon announced that the translation of the "complete Stravinsky autobiography" would be published in the autumn of 1936.

Indeed, already on 21 January 1936, Stravinsky, not entirely at ease with the English translation offered by his London publisher Victor Gollancz, had shown it to Dushkin in France and then sent it to a young Englishman in Paris, a student of Nadia Boulanger and "a very serious person."[88] Stravinsky thanked him for his advice, penning a note dated Paris, 5 February 1936, in French on the title page of the first volume of the French edition (fig. 2.6):

> For Mr. David Ponsonby, a token of sincere gratitude for his very valuable assistance with the numerous difficulties in the English translation of these Chroniques,
>   the very grateful author,
>   I. Strawinsky.[89]

The final letter to Kavenoki (3 June 1936) shows that the optimism of Simon's 10 October letter had dissipated. Perhaps owing to the nature of its contents, it did not come from Simon himself but from music editor Emil Hilb, typed on the letterhead from Simon and Schuster's Music Division. Hilb told Kavenoki that Simon had refused to advance any more money for publication and demanded the creation of a musical appendix to help sell the book. Hilb had previously asked Stravinsky to write "a musical guide through his compositions in chronological order, telling the contents, the sources and presenting the musical themes of his works."[90]

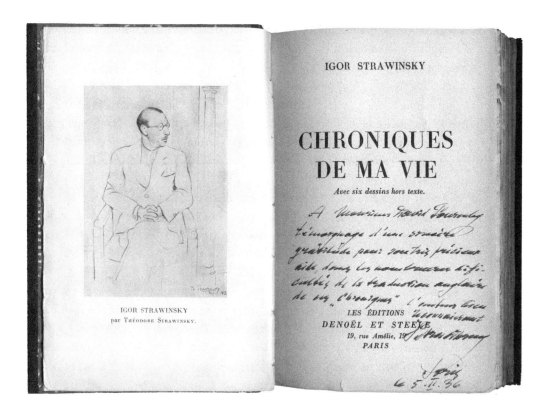

FIGURE 2.6

Chroniques de ma vie, inscribed to David Ponsonby, UBC Stravinsky Collection, no. 43.

The composer did not welcome this. A month later, on 6 July, Stravinsky wrote Simon and Schuster that they "must abandon this project" as "unessential" and that "understanding my music would require a new book."[91] Abandon it they did, and in the fall of 1936 the translation by Norman Collins of both volumes of *Chroniques de ma vie* came out by Simon and Shuster as one volume in the United States, entitled simply *Igor Stravinsky: An Autobiography*.

THE WEST COAST

Jack Mason's column in the 1935 *Oakland Tribune* alerted the East Bay to Stravinsky. Mason noted that on 11 February composer Charles Cushing, a music instructor at the University of California, would give in Berkeley an "illustrated lecture on the music of Stravinsky," one not attended by the composer. Cushing had "made a thorough study of the Stravinsky idiom and will shed light on that composer's art."[92] He had been a student of Nadia Boulanger in 1929; she probably introduced him to Stravinsky. The men remained friends until Stravinsky's death. Many performances of Stravinsky's music and the presence of his manuscripts, printed music, and letters in the Berkeley music library on campus are at least partly owing to their long acquaintance.[93] Cushing's son possesses a valuable letter of 9 October 1959 to his father from Stravinsky in Venice, refusing a commission from the University of California at Berkeley for a solo or concerted work for organ (the least Stravinsky-favored of all instruments), and in May 1968 the *San Francisco Examiner* published a photograph of Vera and the two men "exchanging ideas" on 21 May 1968 during the time of Stravinsky's final appearances at Berkeley.[94] A companion photograph taken on the same occasion evidently cropped out Cushing across the table at the far right.[95]

Sherman Clay and Co., San Francisco's best-known music firm, had a plan for Stravinsky to repeat his New York promotional signing. On the day before he arrived, it ran an advertisement on the front page of the morning paper, *San Francisco Chronicle*, and on an inner page of the *San Francisco Examiner*: if purchased that same day, Stravinsky would autograph his Columbia record albums.[96]

Arriving on the thirteenth, and ensconced at the Fairmont Hotel, perhaps Stravinsky preautographed some record albums, but more probably he inscribed them on the spot. The *Chronicle* ran a second notice: "This afternoon Stravinsky will be the guest of honor at an informal reception at the White House [a department store formerly on Market Street] at 3 o'clock, at which he will autograph a number of Columbia records of his works."[97] Apparently unaware of these advertisements, Craft stated that on Stravinsky's arrival by rail from Chicago, a crowd of autograph hunters awaited him at the train station: "He signed 100 record jackets but refused to be taken to meet a crowd gathered at one of San Francisco's shopping centers."[98] This apparent mean-spiritedness corresponds to young Auberjonois's description of the composer's *mauvaise grâce* two weeks earlier in New York. The incident is sufficiently telling to merit a more complete account from the Russian-language newspaper:

> The conversation with the renowned conductor [and] pianist took place yesterday after Stravinsky had signed almost one hundred record albums which had been bought by admirers of Stravinsky's talent. Judging from appearances, it was clear that this activity was rather tiring for the composer. As is the case with all talented people, he avoids contact with the broad masses. And now he had to sit in front of a large audience and sign autographs. In addition, this time Stravinsky's fervent admirers were overdoing it. The organizers of the "hour of autographs" wanted to present a great world-class figure to the public gathered in the hall of one of San Francisco's department stores [i.e., the White House]. Naturally, Stravinsky refuses such an acquaintance, just as he does shaking hands with all and sundry. "Autographs I'll sign"—said Stravinsky—"but to stand [around] on stage [in full view] and greet [everyone], that's too much."[99]

After a joint recital with Dushkin in the San Francisco Opera House on 13 February, one in Palo Alto at Stanford University, and one in Carmel, where they met the celebrated California photographer Edward Weston,[100] the weary musicians detrained in Los Angeles on

17 February and settled into Kall's house on South Gramercy Place. The next day, Stravinsky began rehearsing the Los Angeles Philharmonic for concerts on 21 and 22 February.

In the program booklet for these concerts, two pictorial notices appeared (pp. 238 and 234). One placed by Birkel Music Co., the sole Los Angeles agent for Steinway pianos—and reminiscent of Stravinsky's 1925 letter to Steinway cited above—probably netted him some emolument. Pictured with the (cropped) c. 1924 Lipnitzki photograph (right hand on hip and dangling monocle), the composer was quoted: "Steinway & Sons' matchless instruments have inspired and aided me by their gorgeously rich and responsive qualities." The other notice—recalling his recent New York and San Francisco signings—was placed by Barker Brothers, a music store on Hollywood Boulevard. It announced record-jacket signings, on 27 February, from 3 to 4:30 p.m.

ACTION AND FORMAL PHOTOGRAPHS

Two radically different sets of photographs were taken during Stravinsky's 1935 visit to Los Angeles. One set of at least six of him conducting was shot by an unknown newspaper photographer during a rehearsal with the Los Angeles Philharmonic; the other, a set of a dozen formal poses, was taken in Kall's garage around the same time by a famous photographer.

On 21 February, the *Los Angeles Illustrated Daily News* published in half lengths three of its six photographs taken of Stravinsky rehearsing *Petrushka* with the Philharmonic.[101] His rehearsal clothes were a dark-colored sweater over a tieless shirt and drab light-colored slacks. The newspaper identified its employee solely as "the photographer [who] sneaked in" and snapped "the first pictures ever taken of Igor Stravinsky at rehearsal" (referring, of course, only to Los Angeles). Three others from the same six appeared a year later but in full length—and neither cropped nor inscribed—in Merle Armitage's *Igor Strawinsky*, designed and published by him and the first book about the composer published in English.[102]

Stravinsky inscribed at least two of these half-dozen anonymous newspaper photographs. One of them (cropped at the left) he dedicated on 27 February 1935 to Sol Babitz.[103] A first violinist (third desk, inside), well-known then and later for his interest and expertise in early music, and also a figure during the 1940s in Stravinsky life, Babitz eventually replaced Dushkin concerning violin editorial matters. Two days later, Stravinsky inscribed the same image as Babitz's (even more cropped at the left) to Armitage.[104] He wrote: "To Merle Armitage / my wonderful art / ist mamager / in gratitude / I Stravinsky / Los Angeles / 29 II 35."

Three decades later, Armitage characterized this set of newspaper photographs, although he modified his reading of one of them:

> On a trip to Paris in 1937 . . . no longer his manager, . . . I had brought him some photographs taken of him in action in orchestra rehearsals in America, sweat shirt, baggy pants,

and all. When I left, Stravinsky presented one of them to me, autographed: "To my wonderful artist-manager, from his warmly appreciative, Igor Strawinsky."[105]

Clearly the same photograph, a discrepancy in Armitage's transcriptions of its inscription exists. Did Stravinsky inscribe the copy of this photograph that he gave to Armitage in 1935 or 1937? Stravinsky was indeed in Paris, off and on, from mid-May 1937 until Armitage left Europe late that June. Perhaps Armitage was relying in 1964 on his recollection rather than reading from the dated inscription, since the wording varies in only minor ways. Or perhaps Stravinsky, in Paris in 1937, backdated his inscription to 1935 to mark the period when Armitage was still his Los Angeles agent. If so, Stravinsky was also relying on his recollection since the date of the joint Stravinsky-Dushkin concert sponsored by Armitage in Los Angeles was *28* February.

Of these half-dozen newspaper photographs of Stravinsky conducting, the one that Stravinsky inscribed for Babitz and the same (but cropped) one he inscribed for Armitage best illustrate the rhythmic life that he demanded and got from his players. Captions below the three photographs reproduced from the *Illustrated Daily News* afford additional insights (all too obviously unproofread) about his conducting manners.

In addition to its four anonymous *Illustrated Daily News* photographs, Armitage's 1936 book included eight of twelve portraits of Stravinsky, commissioned from Edward Weston.[106] Here Stravinsky is impeccably dressed: striped blazer, striped shirt, and striped tie, wearing dark-rimmed glasses in two portraits, and holding or wearing clear-rimmed glasses in the remaining six. Craft, however, identified the anonymous newspaper photographer (and thus, this photographer's other five photographs) as Weston.[107] I disagree. None of the newspaper photographs is in his style. Neither Weston, his assistant, nor any of the numerous books and studies about the great photographer so much as mention newspaper images. Weston's photographs (nos. 6, 8, and 10–12 in box 2.1) magnificently capture the physical and spiritual power of Stravinsky's eyes, as well as the extraordinary and compelling forces residing in the composer's hands (nos. 1, 3–6, and 12).

Weston's dozen portraits were all signed. Eight of them were reproduced and credited specifically to him in Armitage's 1936 book (A1–A8 in the box). In 1950 Stravinsky inscribed and donated a copy of one Weston photograph (A1): "To the Memorial / Library of Music / Stanford University / Igor Stravinsky / Sept / 50."[108] Four of Weston's studies were reproduced in a 1984 catalogue of a Stravinsky exhibition in Basel[109] (Basel 1–4 in the box). The same four were displayed and reproduced in 2007 at Salzburg, celebrating the 125th anniversary of his birth[110] (Salzburg 1–4). Craft included five of them (nos. 6, 8, 10–12) in his 1985 edition of Vera's diary.[111]

Craft complained that the four Weston photographs exhibited at Basel—nos. 2, 5, 7, and 9—together with portraits by some other photographers, have Stravinsky "overposed" and that they "disastrously, avert the composer's eyes."[112] I do not know what Craft meant by "overposed." With respect to the composer's gaze, in two or three of the four Weston photographs at Basel, the eyes are indeed averted, but within the full set of a dozen, his eyes are a powerful force in all but two (nos. 7 and 9). Craft later included some of them in his edition of Vera Stravinsky's diary (nos. 6, 8, and 10–12).

The conditions under which Weston operated and Stravinsky's esteem for the photographer's art are also of interest. Having traveled from Carmel to Los Angeles in 1935, Weston himself reported a little in October 1939 on the circumstances of these portraits: "Heads of Stravinsky . . . were made in direct sunlight. . . . The portrait [no. 7 above] was made in a backyard; the background is the shadowed interior of a garage.[113] The garage was Kall's on South Gramercy; Kall had just moved there in January. Many years after Weston's death, his assistant, Charis Wilson, offered further details:

> [Weston] was not keen on celebrity sittings, which usually gave him a limited amount of time, often in difficult surroundings. Stravinsky, for example, was staying in a Hollywood bungalow [Kall's house] and was on his way to an orchestra rehearsal. Edward spotted the open garage door as we drove up, and that solved his background problem. He had Stravinsky stand in the sunlit driveway in front of the door, and although the garage was full of the usual clutter; there was not enough time to register anything but black in the brief exposures. The whole sitting took less than fifteen minutes, and thereafter, whenever Edward had to photograph someone in a bad setting, he immediately looked for an open garage door.[114]

Weston's daughter-in-law, Dody Weston Thompson, had already made known the photographer's instruction that the size of photographs he first printed should not be altered, a prohibition too often now disregarded. She also recorded Stravinsky's pleasure in them: "sharply focused, glossy prints in black and white, a mere 8 × 10 inches in size (since he would not enlarge) and uniformly mounted on chaste white board. . . . Igor Stravinsky sent a note [12 April 1935], "Mille meilleurs remercies, cher Monsieur Weston, pour ces splendides photographies."[115]

Early the next year, Stravinsky again praised Weston's portraits. On 12 February 1936 Stravinsky wrote from Paris to Simon and Schuster, about including illustrations by

Picasso, Ramuz, and by his own son Théodore, in the translation of *Chroniques:* "In addition, I would like to call your attention to the existence of an excellent series of photographs of me made by Edward Weston, Carmel (California), from which you could pick one or two to complete the illustrations.[116]

Unfortunately, none of Weston's twelve portraits appeared either in British or in American editions of Stravinsky's *Autobiography.* One of them, however—no. 3—showed up twice in *Musical America,* at years' ends of 1939 and 1941.[117] Because the composer was living in Boston in 1939, the photograph might even have been supplied to the magazine by the composer himself or his agent, Kavenoki.

ARMITAGE AS SPONSOR

Merle Armitage's role in Stravinsky's Los Angeles appearances should not be underestimated, but it got off to a rocky start when Stravinsky and Dushkin first arrived in Los Angeles from Carmel. Music critic Isabel Morse Jones alerted music lovers that they planned to play the violin-and-piano reduction of the 1931 Violin Concerto at a duo recital in Philharmonic Auditorium, which Armitage had scheduled for 28 February. But in the event, it was not played.[118] A newspaper columnist later revealed why:

> When Merle Armitage booked Stravinsky[,] the Philharmonic Orchestra [also] wished him to conduct. Although that made it necessary for Stravinsky to appear with the orchestra before he appeared in [duo-] concert, Armitage felt that the orchestra had the right to pay that tribute to the famous visitor, and gracefully agreed.[119]

Fatigue or insufficient practice time may have played a part in the decision to omit the Violin Concerto from the duo recital. As Stravinsky later explained to his pupil Andersson, his reduction of the concerto required "special fingering of his own" on the piano part because it was "really a concerto for violin and piano,"[120] thus implying equal difficulty for both performers.

Their duo recital on 28 February had a somewhat tepid reception. José Rodriguez, a well-respected composer, concert pianist, critic, and radio annotator,[121] praised by Jones for "conveying to his readers the most untranslatable Stravinsky,"[122] castigated his city's parochialism:

> The house was just as crowded [as for Stravinsky's orchestra concerts,] but the results were comically different. . . . Those who heard Mr. Stravinsky's essays in chamber music were puzzled, wary and even alarmed. The applause was tentative and reserved.
>
> The reason is obvious. The violin-and-piano Stravinsky is more advanced, more radical, more experimental [i.e., the *Duo concertant*] than the ballet-music Stravinsky; his idiom is more terse, daring and mature. [There is] the supreme mastery over problems of sonority, rhythm and contrapuntal structure. No adventure of Stravinsky's into the frontiers of idiom can obscure the compactness, the control and the ingenuity he proves everywhere in his music. Local

audiences are a little anemic from lack of vitamins that are particularly strong in Stravinsky; we have been softened by stale sentimentality, by sterile intellectualism. Whether we find Mr. Stravinsky's fare savory or not, we cannot doubt its tonic and nutritive value.[123]

A Los Angeles journal also observed "Stravinsky's piano playing is that of a composer rather than that of a virtuoso; but who would have it otherwise?"[124]

FIRST HOLLYWOOD ENCOUNTERS AND THE FILM INDUSTRY

Staying with Kall in the second half of February, Stravinsky fell in love with Southern California's climate. It was probably then he decided that he would one day live there. Writing to Kall from Colorado Springs on 2 March, he mentioned "a friendship . . . ripening 12 days in the California sun,"[125] and four months later in Paris he proclaimed to an interviewer, "Que la Californie est appétissante!"[126]

Stravinsky also fell in love with the film industry. Kall had written to him in Russian on 30 January, urging him, while in California to explore it "strictly for business" (this phrase in English).[127] Less than a month later, on 25 February, he paid a visit to MGM, accompanied by his New York agent, Merovitch, and Kall. Still unsure of his English, he addressed the twenty-nine assembled composers there in German, rather than French—perhaps because of the prevalence of exiled German Jews in the industry?[128] He quickly grasped Hollywood's piecemeal, assembly-line methods for producing film scores. He recalled (not quite correctly) the "forty salaried composers, all working from morning to night to produce music."[129]

Although film star Edward G. Robinson (then under contract to Warner Bros.) was not involved in this excursion, it was probably Kall who had introduced Stravinsky to him at their initial meeting on 20 February. A highly cultured émigré Romanian Jew, Robinson (and Gladys, his Protestant first wife) became friends with Stravinsky, though Robinson, never an intimate, always addressed him as "Mr. Stravinsky." Robinson saw Stravinsky and Kall on at least two more occasions. At one of these, the Robinsons hosted Charles "Charlie" Chaplin.[130] The Robinsons and Stravinsky were to meet again in late December of 1936, when they crossed the Atlantic together on the SS *Normandie*. With Stravinsky, Samuel Dushkin, and his wife also on board, this was the beginning of a fourth transatlantic tour.

Stravinsky's relations with Robinson and Chaplin and his unsuccessful attempts to write movie scores as late as 1966 may now be outlined. At the Robinson dinner party in 1935, Chaplin proposed collaborating on a movie about a Passion Play set in a nightclub. Although the subject was repugnant to Stravinsky on religious grounds, he nevertheless pursued Chaplin for several years to work on a movie with him. During Stravinsky's next US tour, Robinson gave a second dinner party in March of 1937 for Stravinsky; the guest list included, among others, Chaplin, Paulette Goddard, Douglas Fairbanks, Marlene Dietrich, Frank Capra, the Dushkins, and George Gershwin.[131] Later that month, Chaplin invited Stravinsky to have lunch in Beverly Hills, and the widely read *Life* magazine ran three photographs of the pair engaged in a game of rolling hoops.[132] That fall, returning to France, Stravinsky wrote Dushkin in New York thanking him for seeking Robinson's aid in recontacting Chaplin. To Stravinsky's great disappointment, Chaplin eventually disavowed any collaboration.[133]

As for Robinson, after Stravinsky settled in Hollywood in the early 1940s, they often entertained each other at dinner parties or socialized at parties given by other celebrities, many (if not all) recorded in Vera's published diary. In mid-May of 1945 Robinson gave a patriotic address at an "American-Russian Friendship Concert" at the Shrine Auditorium, the conducting duties shared by Klemperer and Stravinsky. At the close of that year, on 28 December, Robinson stood as a witness for the naturalization of the Stravinskys,[134] and the next day they celebrated with both Robinsons (among many others).[135] The friendship seems to have dwindled in the ensuing years, probably as a result of rumors that Robinson was a communist. Charges were made in 1950 by the House Committee on Un-American Activities, but Robinson was soon cleared.

Notwithstanding Stravinsky's 1935 visit to MGM, his friendship with Robinson, his efforts with Chaplin, a fresh attempt in 1937 with Boris Morros of Paramount Pictures (a longer tale, set out below), he had no success in the movie industry during his transatlantic tours. Even after he had settled in Hollywood in the 1940s, his refusals to adapt to the requirements of the industry blocked any progress but at least netted him some scores, which he recycled and put to good use.

The old compulsion "strictly for business," set in motion in 1935 by Dr. Kall to tap into the Hollywood pot of gold, did not finally exhaust itself until the mid-1960s: on 27 April 1964 Stravinsky had agreed to provide "services as composer and conductor of music in the motion picture [by] Dino de Laurentiis Cinematografica, SPA . . . entitled 'The Bible.'"[136] He planned to sell music that was, by then, in public domain for a huge fee to de Laurentiis and then conduct it for him. But on 8 August Stravinsky wrote his English publisher's agent, saying that he had turned down the film project on grounds that it held for him "more trouble, unpleasantness, and musical affliction than interest." De Laurentiis remained enthusiastic, so negotiations dragged on—fruitlessly—until November of 1964.[137] Nostalgia lingers in a phrase written before February of 1966 by Stravinsky for program notes for the Symphony in C. He wrote: "the passage beginning at number 145 [in the fourth movement]—which, incidentally, is perfect movie music for a Hollywood traffic scene.[138]

INSCRIBING ROBINSON'S PIANO

When Stravinsky first visited Robinson at his Beverly Hills home on 20 February 1935, he added his own name to those of several other musicians inscribed on the upper frame above the soundboard of Robinson's Steinway grand piano (fig. 2.7).[139] The earliest of these names (1 September 1933) was that of the celebrated, but by then seriously disabled,

FIGURE 2.7
Autographed soundboard of E. G.
Robinson's piano. From Robinson and
Spigelgass, *All My Yesterdays*, 152–53.

pianist Leopold Godowsky. When Toscanini visited in December of 1939, there was talk of him signing the piano and also of Stravinsky's approaching visit. Asked his opinion of Stravinsky, Toscanini replied, "He doesn't like Beethoven."[140] If he had signed Robinson's Steinway, Toscanini would have seen that Stravinsky had preceded him. The Italian maestro's signature does not appear in the only published photograph of the soundboard's frame that Stravinsky and so many others had inscribed.

Missing from among the names on Robinson's Steinway is Arnold Schoenberg, but the latest signature (1950) is that of the distinguished Canadian violinist Adolph Koldofsky (all too briefly my mentor in 1946 and associated with Schoenberg thereafter). He perhaps never met Stravinsky,[141] although the composer and Craft were to hear him play *violino piccolo* in Bach's First Brandenburg Concerto, conducted by Klemperer at the University of Southern California on 29 October 1950.[142] Two late Schoenberg works were probably known to Stravinsky. The 1946 String Trio, which premiered on the West Coast in May of 1948, was recorded there by Koldofsky.[143] But because Stravinsky attended a farewell dinner on 13 September 1949 for his Hollywood friend Eugène (Genia) Lourié,[144] he likely missed that evening's premiere of Schoenberg's Phantasy for violin and piano,[145] commissioned by Koldofsky and then recorded by him just before his tragically early death, a few months before Schoenberg's.[146]

Returning to February 1935: for its latter part Kall's diary is most informative, disclosing his wide acquaintance among Los Angeles notables and perhaps also signaling who introduced Stravinsky to Chaplin. For example, on 23 February Kall absent-mindedly entered "Chaliapin: [*recte* Chaplin]: 'Merrily we roll along.' "[147] That very day, the *Los Angeles Times* ran a story about and a picture of Dorothy Wilson, an attractive actress in the cast of the drama *Merrily We Roll Along* by George S. Kaufman and Moss Hart, then playing at the Belasco Theatre.[148] Kall's entry refers perhaps to attendance at the play or perhaps to a recommendation from Charlie Chaplin to Kall about it. It was, however, neither Kall nor Robinson, but Armitage, who took credit for introducing Chaplin to Stravinsky. Years later, Armitage told a television interviewer that "Charlie used to call me because I was always bringing these big celebrities to town and he wanted to meet Stravinsky."[149] Kall's diary also records that Edward G. Robinson held a reception on 26 February 1935 for Stravinsky (not to be confused with the party two years later, cited above, that included George Gershwin). On 28 February Kall noted another reception honoring Stravinsky and Dushkin, this time in Pasadena at the home of Mrs. Robert Woods Bliss, future copatron of the *Dumbarton Oaks Concerto* and, with Mrs. John Alden Carpenter, of the Symphony in C.

A LUTE QUARTET

On 25 February 1935 Kall entered "Aguilar!" in his diary. This entry, and four photographs from Stravinsky's residence at Kall's house, link Stravinsky—if only momentarily, and tangentially—to the Aguilar Lute Quartet:[150] Elisa Aguilar and her three brothers, Ezequiel, Francisco, and José Maria. They made their US debut in mid-September of 1929 in New York, returning there in November of 1930. The quartet also performed in 1930 and 1931 in Berkeley for its "Musical Association," and from 1933 to 1935 in Los Angeles.[151] A photograph and cartoon of its four members "now fulfilling engagements in California" appeared in 1934 and 1935.[152]

The undated photograph of the Aguilar Quartet with Stravinsky, Kall, and Dushkin was published in *Musical America* (fig. 2.8). Tantalizingly, its caption informed readers that "Mr. Stravinsky has promised to write a composition especially for this lute ensemble." If he ever seriously considered doing so, no trace of it remains. It would surely have provoked "early-music" buffs.

Kall owned three other photographs taken at this occasion.[153] One (fig. 2.9) shows the same persons plus the diminutive, hatted Edward G. Robinson, carefully posed so as to look even shorter than Stravinsky. Perhaps Kall or Robinson introduced the quartet to Stravinsky. The second (fig. 2.10) features Elisa Aguilar linking arms with Stravinsky and smiling broadly. The third (fig. 2.11) shows the lutenists and Dushkin close to Stravinsky. With Kall (far right) peeking over his shoulder, the composer and Elisa Aguilar are intently examining what might well be music in lute tablature.

Stravinsky and the Aguilar Quartet do not seem to have met again. They may have previously met in Europe, since the quartet was based in Madrid, during the composer's visits in 1916, 1921, and 1925 or in Barcelona in 1928. The presence of Kall and Robinson in the photographs suggests that one or the other introduced Stravinsky to the Quartet.

Two related photographs were taken on or about 1 March on the verge of Stravinsky's and Dushkin's departure for points east. Kall's diary is helpful for dating them. An entry

FIGURE 2.8 (Top left)
"Artists Seen on Tour and in Leisure Hours." *Musical America*, 25 March 1935, 13. *Left to right:* Samuel Dushkin, Igor Stravinsky, Alexis Kall, Elisa Aguilar, and the Aguilar Quartet.

FIGURE 2.9 (Top right)
Left to right: Alexis Kall, Stravinsky, Samuel Dushkin, Aguilar Quartet, and E. G. Robinson (2nd from right, front). Kall Papers, UCLA.

FIGURE 2.10 (Middle left)
Elisa Aguilar and Stravinsky. Kall Papers, UCLA.

FIGURE 2.11 (Middle right)
Aguilar Quartet, Stravinsky, Kall, and Dushkin. Kall Papers, UCLA.

FIGURE 2.12 (Bottom left)
Left to right: Alexis Kall, Igor Stravinsky, Edward G. Robinson. Kall Papers, UCLA.

for 1 March 1935 reads "Zab. [visit by] Robinson."[154] One of these photographs was reproduced in 1972, captioned "With Edward G. Robinson, Hollywood, March, 1935."[155] It has
Stravinsky linking arms with the actor. Because Kall owned its negative, he probably took
the picture himself. The other photograph had Stravinsky in the middle between Robinson and Kall (fig. 2.12). When first published in 1962, it was not only cropped, excluding
Kall, but also misdated to May,[156] by which time, of course, Stravinsky was back in
Europe.

BACK TO THE EAST COAST

After leaving Los Angeles on 2 March, Stravinsky and Dushkin slowly returned to New
York. They gave duo recitals in Colorado—Stravinsky venturing his second public speech
in English at their Denver concert and dating a facsimile of this speech "4 III 35"[157]—and
in Fort Worth, Texas. Back in New York on the evening of 10 March, Stravinsky visited
the American Ballet and afterward met with its supporters, Lincoln Kirstein and
Edward Warburg, who (then or shortly thereafter) broached "the idea of commissioning
a ballet for Balanchine's new company," into which negotiations Nicolas Nabokov, who
had known Stravinsky and Balanchine from October 1927 in Paris, tried in vain in 1933
to insert himself.[158] The eventual result was *Jeu de cartes*, which premiered in New York
late in Stravinsky's third transatlantic tour. Then on 14, 15, and 16 March, Stravinsky led
performances of *Perséphone* in Boston. One reviewer criticized "the good taste of the
composer. The tenor part and the choral sections are little more than declamation; the
orchestral accompaniment is austere and we found the work dull and regressive. . . . It
is a matter of record, however, that the performance was greatly applauded."[159]

At a Thursday matinee on 21 March in New York, Stravinsky is said—surely
incorrectly—to have conducted his first staged performance of *Firebird* in the United
States.[160] Apparently, he merely attended it, thus reserving that high distinction for the
Hollywood Bowl late in August of 1941, during the first excursion. He and Dushkin went
on to Washington, DC, where they gave concerts on 24 March and 9 April 1935 at the
National Theatre and the Library of Congress. Between these two concerts they squeezed
in a visit to Dushkin's brother in Winnetka, Illinois, performing there on 27 March. They
were forced to cancel a recital scheduled for 29 March in Chicago's Orchestra Hall, owing
to a Stravinskyian so-called severe cold—its harshness had increased ominously. They
intended to postpone the recital "from Friday night until next season," but there was
no 1936 season in North America for either of them. Nor did any Chicago concert
take place during the fourth transatlantic tour, even though they played two concerts in
nearby Winnetka.[161] One month later Stravinsky was diagnosed with a return of active
tuberculosis.

On 24 March 1935, the day of their first Washington recital, Stravinsky was interviewed at the Hotel Mayflower.[162] He and Dushkin signed an exemplar of its program
(figs. 2.13a, 2.13b), and its unknown owner (needlessly) added the year with the same pen.

This pair of concerts was reviewed, the second none too favorably.[163] The two Washington programs typify the repertoire that the duo offered audiences across the country during their preceding three months of travel.

With due caution for Dagmar Godowsky's waywardness with chronology and facts, her memoirs show that she met Stravinsky "some days later," after her 7 February tea. Yet he and Dushkin left New York on 8 February for St. Louis. In reality their meeting was on 9 April—at his second appearance at "the Elizabeth Sprague Coolidge Festival of Music" in Washington. She traveled to Washington and returned with him by train the next day (10 April) to New York. She states—correctly at last—that she and her father "saw him off to Paris" on 13 April. Her observation during their return trip from Washington that Stravinsky "had not [yet] fallen under my spell"[164] must be accepted at face value.

Stravinsky sailed home on the SS *Ile de France*, arriving at Le Havre on the nineteenth. Dushkin stayed in the United States to marry Louise Rorimer in January of 1936, returning later that year with her to France. Recently discovered and published, Mrs. Dushkin's startling observations about Stravinsky's Violin Concerto were probably made, not during this tour or the next, from which the Dushkins were absent, but rather during the 1937 tour when she traveled with both men.

STRAVINSKY AND ANTI-SEMITISM

The 1935 tour affords an opportunity to consider more intensively the composer's relationship with this young American violinist. Stravinsky's choice is surprising, not because of Dushkin's youth (a decade younger), his different national origin (born in Poland, then part of Russia), or his previous concertizing in Europe with Stravinsky (since 1931) but because his heritage presents the anomaly of an anti-Semite's close association and prolonged travel with a Jew.

Finished several months after his tour with Dushkin had ended, the second volume of Stravinsky's *Chroniques de ma vie* was printed 12 December 1935 in Paris and contained the following:

> A Jew, like the great majority of his colleagues, Dushkin possesses all those innate gifts which make representatives of that race the unquestionable masters of the violin. The greatest names among these virtuosi have in fact a Jewish sound. (Les plus grands noms de ces virtuoses sont, en effet, à consonance juive.)

His essentializing did not stop with this erroneous view of Jews as a "race," or of certain names as Jewish-sounding, or what "Jewish sound" on a violin might be or signify; he went on to ask why "the greatest names among these virtuosi" persisted in using Russian diminutives for their first names: "foreigners can have no idea of how such a lack of taste jars."[165] The translation by Norman Collins accurately conveys the whiff of anti-Semitism.

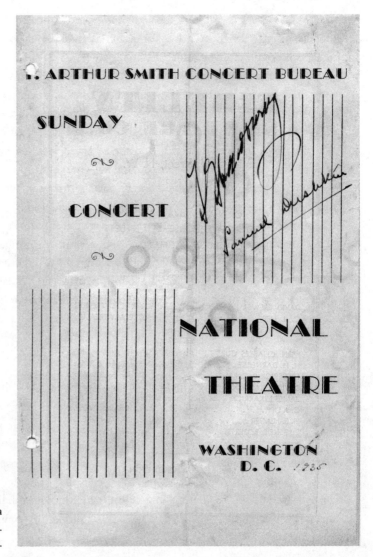

FIGURE 2.13a
Inscribed recital program, 1935 (cover).
UBC Stravinsky Collection, no. 41.

Despite this, Stravinsky displayed obvious and genuine affection for Dushkin, already evident in a photograph from the 1930s, that was manifest not only during this 1935 tour, the previous tours in Europe, and the next transatlantic one but also in their many friendly letters; indeed, it continued until the composer's death.[166] How can all these be reconciled with Stravinsky's noxious—if normally concealed, and perhaps unconscious—anti-Semitism? On 2 November 1935 he closes an amicable letter in French to Dushkin with some phrases of endearment in English (not entirely appropriate in a language he was just beginning to read) such as "my sweet heart" and "my darling."[167] These phrases are direct translations from the Russian, similar to those he had used the

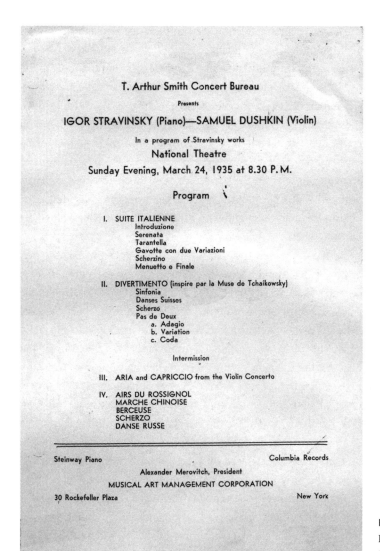

FIGURE 2.13b
Inscribed recital program, 1935 (cont.).
UBC Stravinsky Collection, no. 41.

previous March in a letter to his non-Jewish friend Kall.[168] A similarly paradoxical situation obtained in the long relationship Stravinsky enjoyed from the time of the *Rite* with a Jewish convert to Christianity, critic-composer Roland-Manuel (Roland Alexis Manuel Lévy); my former collection contains three affectionate notes of June and November 1920 and of June 1939 from Stravinsky to him.[169]

No evidence has surfaced for any anti-Semitic remarks from Stravinsky directed either at Roland-Manuel or Dushkin,[170] perhaps because most anti-Semites denigrate the group but exempt individuals. What might have transpired, if Dushkin, for example, had not been so affable, so amusing, so pliant, so comforting and reassuring, and above all, so useful? In these two instances at least, affection slew intolerance, for, as Stravinsky's compositions multiplied, so did his anti-Semitism.

During the decade separating transatlantic tours I and II, Europe (and indeed, the entire world) experienced the Great Depression, the rise of fascism under Benito Mussolini (1922) and Adolf Hitler (Reichschancellor from January 1933), and the Third Reich's truculent anti-Semitism. Stravinsky's own brand of anti-Semitism predates both dictators' regimes. It continued throughout the 1930s and, to some lesser extent, during the years he lived in the United States.[171] For example, following a rehearsal on 12 December 1930 of *Symphony of Psalms* in Brussels, Prokofiev lunched with Stravinsky. Afterward, Prokofiev entered in his diary: "Stravinsky never ceases to abuse Jews, the chief object of his ire being Milhaud. Einstein is [to Stravinsky] 'a veritable synagogue yid.'"[172]

Another prewar outburst, suppressed by Craft in his edition of Stravinsky's correspondence, was first brought to general attention by Taruskin and then amplified by Walsh. It appeared in a typed thank you letter of 27 March 1930 to a Swiss patron of the arts, Werner Reinhart, in Winterthur. Some additional details still need airing. Obviously during 18–20 March when Stravinsky visited with him, they discussed extreme right-wing politics. In the letter, Stravinsky wrote of his "genuine pleasure" at learning about Reinhart's "campaign against the freemasons": "I didn't realize that you were not indifferent to these Antichrists, and this with your disgust, as conscious as it is (I hope) natural, for universal Jewry (of which the freemasons are merely the servants): all this overwhelms me with joy!"[173] Reinhart responded on 9 April, thanking Stravinsky for his letter.

This "Jewish-Masonic link" has been traced by Taruskin back to the infamous and "venerable Tsarist forgery." The purported "link" was alive and well, not only in Switzerland but in Stravinsky's France during the 1920s and 1930s. It is one of the sources used in the fanatic writings of the later Vichyite, Gestapo agent, and French traitor, Bernard Faÿ, a devout Catholic ultra-right-wing conservative to whose views Stravinsky's own were akin.[174]

From 1933 onwards, Stravinsky toadied to the Nazis in the interest of his German concert fees.[175] Even so, it has been reported, citing unidentified and undated scrapbooks in which he ridiculed Himmler and Goering on unspecified dates, that he "loathed the Nazis."[176]

In a joust between Craft and Taruskin over the matter of Stravinsky's anti-Semitism, neither combatant discussed two relevant Stravinsky letters.[177] Writing in French on 14 August 1922 to Ernest Ansermet, Stravinsky mentions meeting "a young gentile German, full of talent,"[178] Paul Hindemith. The translator's choice of "gentile" was a bowdlerization. The original reads: "un jeune Allemand, *pas juif*, plein de talent."[179] And writing a letter of recommendation on 21 September 1936 for the distinguished Hans Rosbaud, conductor 1927–37 of the Frankfurt *Rundfunk* and no Nazi, Stravinsky chose to extol Rosbaud by means of a favorite Nazi code-phrase: "a pure-blooded musician,"[180] meaning, of course, one "untainted" by Jewish blood. A later chapter will continue this examination of Stravinsky's anti-Semitism from the early 1920s well into the 1960s with the case of his fellow Russian American, the conductor and Jewish convert to Christianity, Serge Koussevitzky.[181]

STRAVINSKY AS CONDUCTOR

After Stravinsky conducted the premiere of his Violin Concerto on 23 October 1931, Hindemith "bravely bawled out the Berlin Radio Orchestra after its bad playing."[182] Taken in conjunction with Hindemith's 1937 observation about Stravinsky's bad conducting in New York (discussed below), this suggests that Stravinsky (fluent in German) was at least partly responsible for the radio orchestra's poor performance. But over the course of the 1935 tour, critics in cities with major symphony orchestras began to reconsider the evaluations of his conducting they had made a decade earlier. They noted an improvement in his skills, and they continued to praise his attention to rhythmic articulation. A secondhand report that Vera Soudeikina received in Paris about his "great success" and his "abilities as a conductor finally having been recognized"[183] must have proceeded from reviews of his engagements in Chicago, such as this one, even though there his rehearsal instructions were in French:

> Stravinsky knows what he wants and his wishes were so well expressed that the orchestra responded minutely to all his demands. His beat is easy to follow. . . . Rhythm and tone color . . . were brought out in bold relief by the orchestra under his skillful guidance. . . . The orchestra gave him a fanfare.[184]

That particular fanfare was given "in honor of the man who has brought more hard work to symphonic players—and more dignity too than any other living composer."[185] When the same orchestra then played in nearby Milwaukee, a local critic summed up his own opinion and those of fellow scriveners that "critics differed as to whether Stravinsky's eccentricities in conducting were legitimate musical devices, but there was no doubt as to the effectiveness of his direction."[186]

But another writer, reviewing his 10 January concert in St. Louis, was more censorious, his last sentence recalling Stravinsky's jack-in-the-box lunges of a decade earlier:

> His beat is unmistakably clear, but unconventional. In some moments he is a graceful figure. But there are others, as he calls forth some abrupt phrase, or some cranky rhythm, when his body assumes a curious awkwardness as though he, himself, were the puppet Petrouchka. There were times he seemed lackadaisical in the listless movement of his arm. There were others when he bowed his back, as it were, in defence of the impact of tone about to crash upon his head; times when he literally danced to a lilting rhythm, and again when it seemed in his enthusiasm he would hurl himself across the conductor's desk.[187]

With the Los Angeles Philharmonic late in February 1935, according to that city's best-informed and most incisive writer:

> As a conductor, Stravinsky is an alert, fastidious and energetic general. He likes angular effects, sharp definitions of rhythm, exactitude in detail. He is not concerned with horizontal line and his command of the orchestra does not extend to the building of compact [sound] masses. Like his writing, his conducting is fundamentally episodic.[188]

This review should be read in the context of the splendid photographs of him rehearsing the orchestra in *Petrushka,* reproduced by Armitage (1936).

After *Perséphone* was slammed as "dull and regressive" at its US premiere,[189] another critic there, after a glowing account of this same score, added, "Stravinsky surprised everyone hereabouts by the authority, confidence and precision in his direction."[190] Still another Bostonian offered a ten-year comparison: "Stravinsky, a few years ago, was, as a conductor, less than negligible. Today he has a clear and alluring beat and a dynamism which is [as] inspiring as it is unaffected."[191] Most surprising of all were favorable remarks from Stravinsky's New York adversary, who had traveled to Boston. Of *Firebird:*

> He conducted . . . it in an entirely unromantic manner. He played it purely as ballet music; as music for dancing . . . all accent and rhythm, with little nuance, with no expansion of lyrical and dramatic episodes . . . with precise observance of tempo marks, and without emotional exhibitionism. . . . He had very clear and precise intentions, and was capable of getting just what he wanted.[192]

As a follow-up, that summer in Europe, a reporter's essay about migraine in a Copenhagen newspaper for 16 July stated: "Stravinsky once told me that he always has migraine pain the day he conducts a big concert. While conducting, the pain sometimes disappears, but afterwards, as a rule, it returns again."[193] Migraines or not, as a result of his successful performances in America, that October Stravinsky offered his credo about conducting to an interviewer in Paris: "A composer can be 'interpreted' by another conductor, but his music can be 'realized' faithfully only by himself."[194]

3

TOUR III (1936)

CONCERT APPEARANCES, WITH SOULIMA AND OCAMPO

28 April: Buenos Aires, Teatro Colón Orchestra, and Piano Concerto (Soulima)[1]

2 May: Buenos Aires, Colón Orchestra, Capriccio (Soulima)

7 May: Buenos Aires, Colón Orchestra, in pit for ballets, *Firebird, Petrushka*

9 May: Buenos Aires, Colón Orchestra, Capriccio and Concerto (Soulima), *Le Sacre*

10 May: Buenos Aires, repetition of 7 May

11 May: Buenos Aires, at Juan José Castro broadcast including Capriccio (Soulima)

12 May: Rosario, Teatro de la Opera, I.S. lecture and Two-Piano Concerto with Soulima

14 May: Buenos Aires, Colón Orchestra, in pit for ballets: *Firebird, Fairy's Kiss*

17 May: Buenos Aires, Colón Orchestra, in pit for *Apollon, Perséphone* (Ocampo)

18 May: Buenos Aires, Teatro Colón, I.S. lecture and Two-Piano Concerto with Soulima

22 May: Montevideo, Club Uruguay, Two-Piano Concerto with Soulima

23 May: Montevideo, Orquesta Sinfónica, Divertimento, Capriccio (Soulima)

5 June: Rio de Janeiro, Teatro Municipal Orchestra, *Firebird, Perséphone* (Ocampo)

12 June: Rio de Janeiro, Teatro Municipal Orchestra [program unknown; Ocampo absent]

Anticipating a US tour by Stravinsky and Dushkin during the first four months of 1936, Alexander Merovitch, president of Musical Art Management Corporation, placed a huge full-page advertisement in *Musical America* with a photograph of Dushkin and Stravinsky.[2] It alerted readers not only to the previous month's glowing reviews from Minneapolis, St. Paul, Toledo, Pittsburgh, and Indianapolis but also to the high praise Stravinsky had elicited when conducting in Chicago. Merovitch added that both musicians would "be returning to America January–April 1936" and that Stravinsky would appear as a concert pianist.

Events proved otherwise. A translation of a two-page typed letter about tours from Stravinsky to Dushkin of 8 January 1936, made from the composer's carbon copy, has been available for some time, although a misreading of "Janv.—Févr./37" as "January and February 1936"[3] sowed confusion. Relying solely on this carbon copy, the translator deprived himself of important information from marginalia in the composer's original letter, a document I acquired not long ago.[4]

A 1936 tour of the United States fell through because of Merovitch's confinement in November of 1935 to an asylum for the criminally insane. Thus, on 16 November 1935 Stravinsky wrote Dushkin, proposing a postponement until 1937 of the few engagements Merovitch had already secured. Even though Merovitch's secretary tried to salvage the tour, by 17 November 1935 Stravinsky had "decided to cancel my trip to America."[5] On 25 November 1935 Stravinsky then wrote choreographer George Balanchine in New York that "for various reasons, most of them of a personal, familiar nature, I have decided to cancel my trip to North America, especially since I will be going to Argentina in May."[6]

My newly obtained Stravinsky letter sent to Dushkin reveals that impresario Sol Hurok—probably learning of the difficulties at Merovitch's agency—had proposed a US tour for October and November of 1936 to Stravinsky. The composer declined this offer and on several grounds: that he had no confidence in Hurok, that "autumn was never a good period in the United States," and that he and Dushkin could do better in January to February of 1937 on their own hook. This letter, like an earlier one of 16 November 1935, reveals that, after Merovitch's institutionalization, Severin Kavenoki worked hand in hand with Dushkin to set up a US tour for 1937. This tour did, in fact, take place, extending into April.

The extensive marginalia on both sides of Stravinsky's 8 January 1936 letter to Dushkin are rather querulous:

> [verso:] Those gentlemen from the Sc[h]ola Cantorum sent me a cable to ask me to write for them an article of 200 words for the premiere of *Perséphone* which I myself so much wanted to perform in New York.[7] Even 200 dollars will not persuade me to write this article for them, and I throw their cable in the trash.

> When does [American pianist] Beveridge [Webster] arrive [in France]?

> [recto:] I am still waiting for a reply to my letters: one a recommendation of Balanchine for the Metropolitan [Opera], for which the ballet master [Balanchine] did not think it necessary to thank me, even though it was he who asked me for it (through [Gavrivil] Païchadze [in Paris]); the other [letter] about which I telegraphed you [is] on the subject of the commission of a ballet (also through Païchadze);[8] this second letter also requires a reply because it is also Balanchine who asked me to tell him what I think of it. I said nothing of the business side, I simply asked (while giving my acceptance in principle) *that they should enter into negotiations with me* if they want to have the ballet in the autumn of 1936. My letter left [here] in November [1935]—no reply! It is distressing. Keep all this to yourself and act discreetly if one can [so] act. I can see nothing, nothing happening, and time is passing also.

The ballet commission was for *Jeu de cartes* (1935–36) and the *"they"* was Lincoln Kirstein and Edward Warburg. The degree of anxiety evident in the final lines about the commission is understandable, but it may well be that Stravinsky hoped to appropriate any future intervening agent's fee. Although the proponents of this commission had discussed it during Stravinsky's 1935 US tour, and his earliest sketches for *Jeu de cartes* date from 2 December 1935, financial terms were not concluded until 2 August 1936.[9]

Several years earlier, on 18 February 1932, Stravinsky had written of his plans for a new production in Buenos Aires of *Le Sacre du printemps*. It was to have been staged at the Teatro Colón by dancer-choreographer Boris Romanoff, with costumes by Vera Soudeikina[10] and sets by the up-and-coming young Russian-French painter Eugene Lourié: "a young and extremely talented Russian painter. . . . I am at ease with Mr. Lourié, his art is fresh, he has a great deal of experience in set design, and he will execute the sets for *Le Sacre* according to my wishes and my intentions."[11]

Lourié remained a friend of Stravinsky's when, as a movie set-designer, he, too, lived in Hollywood.[12] The costumes were to have been by "Mme Vera Soudeikina . . . because it is with her that I intend to go to Buenos Aires." Only two days later he wrote his publisher in Germany that he awaited a definite reply from Buenos Aires and for him to inquire whether the administration of the SS *Cap Arcona* (a German ship departing on 20 May) "can be expected to make a fuss about Madame Soudeikina's accompanying me."[13] Although Romanoff did stage *Le Sacre* at the Colón in 1932,[14] Stravinsky was not there to take part in it. Nor did anything come of what has been called "a second, quite well-developed project in 1933."[15] Stravinsky's second transatlantic tour was not to occur until 1935.

TO SOUTH AMERICA

On 9 April 1936 Stravinsky and son Soulima embarked from Boulogne-sur-Mer on the *Cap Arcona,* their voyage first touching Rio de Janeiro and Montevideo and then reaching Buenos Aires on the twenty-fifth.[16] Among works that Stravinsky was to lead in Buenos Aires was the 1934 Divertimento, a suite drawn from his 1928 ballet, *Le Baiser de la fée*. With his son he played his Concerto for Two Solo Pianos twice in Argentina and once in Uruguay, a work they had premiered in Paris in November of 1935.[17]

Stravinsky's 1936 tour in South America was not only arranged but also largely under-written by his great friend, Victoria Ocampo, the wealthy Argentine author, editor, and publisher of the literary periodical *Sur*. It has been implied that Stravinsky first met her in 1925 in Paris, but in truth they met there in 1929 through their mutual friend, the Swiss conductor Ernest Ansermet; they met again in July of 1934 when Ocampo visited London.[18] Among the several purposes of Stravinsky's 1936 tour was to lead his melo-drama, *Perséphone,* with her as *diseuse,* and to conduct several of his ballet scores at the Teatro Colón in Buenos Aires. In addition to concerts with Soulima and concert perform-ances of his ballets in late April and early May at the Colón,[19] he led ballet performances staged there on 7, 10, and 14 May of *Firebird, Petrushka,* and *Le Baiser de la fée,* this last choreographed by Bronislava Nijinska. On the seventeenth he conducted *Perséphone* with Ocampo narrating, just before he and his son departed for Uruguay and, ultimately, Rio de Janeiro.[20] Among the many photographs of this tour that he and Ocampo preserved in albums are a group of him and his son on Ocampo's estate, revealing a zanier side of

FIGURE 3.1

Portrait by Sudak, inscribed for Aida Mastrazzi. UBC Stravinsky Collection, no. 44.

the composer. One photograph shows him lying prone at an outdoor party, pretending he is dying and attended by three women (one of whom is Ocampo);[21] apparently a favorite antic, he was to repeat a variant of it at Santa Barbara in 1941.

Several commentators have drawn attention to the nationwide political scandal that Stravinsky provoked on arriving in Buenos Aires. An interview on 25 April with the country's leading newspaper, *La Nación*, reveals his decidedly right-wing views: "I am neither royalist nor republican. But yes, I am anti-parliamentarian. That I can't stand, like a horse that can't put up with a camel.[22] *Critica*, an Argentine left-leaning journal, responded by scolding Stravinsky for his "imprudent inappropriateness."[23]

The Colón's official photographer, Lazaro Sudak of Buenos Aires, took several pictures of Stravinsky just before or after a rehearsal, one of them with choreographer Nijinska.[24] Another photograph features just a beautiful young woman, Aida Mastrazzi, who, under Nijinska's tutelage, was a member of the corps-de-ballet.[25] Stravinsky inscribed one of Sudak's photographs of himself with an unusually intimate inscription in French: "For the excellent artiste, Miss A Mastrazzi, a very grateful memento from I. Strawinsky Buenos Aires 17 May 1936" (fig. 3.1).

Having rehearsed with and danced in some or in all of the May 1936 ballets staged at the Colón, Mastrazzi would not have lost the opportunity to hear Ocampo narrate *Perséphone*, let alone experience Stravinsky's still relatively new ballet, *Apollon* (1928), both of which he led from the pit on the seventeenth. Mastrazzi's terpsichorean skills and her training in piano, theory, and solfège must also have caught his attention.

Just before embarking the following day with his son for Uruguay, Stravinsky also inscribed a single-leafed two-page orchestral fragment of his Divertimento, a suite drawn from his ballet *Le Baiser de la fée*,[26] for the conductor and composer Juan José Castro.[27] The inscription reads in translation "To J. Castro whom I admire, his friend, I. Strawinsky, B. Aires, 18 May 1936" (figs. 3.2a, 3.2b).

This was not the only time that Stravinsky inscribed a manuscript that had no foreseeable future as a profitable publication. The most famous example is his donation of his book of sketches for *The Rite of Spring* to Diaghilev in Paris in October of 1920.[28] On 11 June 1936 he gave the departing Victoria Ocampo an incomplete piano reduction, dated "Mai-Juin 1936," of *Perséphone*,[29] and early in July of 1941, he inscribed his piano draft of the orchestral arrangement of "The Star-Spangled Banner" to his Los Angeles student Earnest Andersson. On Christmas Day 1949 he dedicated an autograph copy of his 1933 compositional draft *Dialogue between Joy and Reason*, set for two voices and keyboard, to his young assistant Robert Craft.[30] At Christmas 1959 he gave the holograph (or perhaps its copy) of the two-page "Ricercar II" from his *Double Canon* to "Lilian [sic] Libman."[31] Revisiting Buenos Aires during August and September of 1960, he reinscribed for Ocampo the very same short score of *Perséphone* he had given her in 1936.[32]

An explanation for this 1936 gift to Castro is readily found. A week earlier, at an 11 May concert broadcast from the Teatro de la Comedia in Buenos Aires, Castro had led four orchestral works by Stravinsky, including Capriccio played by Soulima, a work he had repeatedly played with his father conducting.[33]

Deeply impressed by Castro's performance, Stravinsky sent a letter of commendation that very day to the editor of *La Nación*, a leading Buenos Aires newspaper. There he extolled Castro as a "brillant chef" and a "maître impeccable" of the baton.[34] Perhaps this letter to *La Nación* was also meant to ameliorate his earlier political gaffe. Even so, Castro, who was to be dismissed from his posts for more than a decade (1943–55) during the Juan Perón regime for his prodemocratic views,[35] must have been embarrassed at Stravinsky's outburst of antirepublicanism.

Stravinsky had conducted the Western Hemisphere premiere of his orchestral Divertimento with the Chicago Symphony Orchestra in mid-January 1935 at Milwaukee, judged there to be of "delicate loveliness."[36] Neither Castro nor Stravinsky led the Divertimento in the 1936 Buenos Aires concerts; instead, Stravinsky led its parent-ballet, *Le Baiser de la fée*, on 14 May. He then led the Divertimento on 23 May, at a concert in Montevideo, and again in Los Angeles in mid-February of 1937.

For some time the project of recording the Divertimento was jinxed. After programming it in Mexico City, Stravinsky attempted to record it with the Orquesta Sinfónica de México on 3 August 1940, but this failed because of extraneous noise. He rerecorded it

FIGURE 3.2a
Fragment of Divertimento, inscribed to Juan José Castro. UBC Stravinsky Collection, no. 45.

on 19 July 1941 with the same orchestra, but this session was ruined by a man shouting (at reh. 40). After all these years, the flawed 1941 recording has finally been issued.[37]

Not long after the premiere in 1929 of *Le Baiser de la fée* in Paris,[38] Stravinsky had begun excerpting various of its movements into a suite. He may have led some of these individual movements as early as 1931. Initially called "Fragments du ballet *Le Baiser de la fée*," the suite's official premiere took place in Paris on 4 December 1934, with its composer on the podium. Eight days later, with Dushkin in Strasbourg, he first performed their violin-piano arrangement of similar excerpts from *Le Baiser*. Printed that year, it was called Divertimento.

Tamara Levitz, unaware of my Stravinsky catalogue entry (no. 45) about the above-cited manuscript page of Divertimento and a longer essay about it published in 2004,[39] summarized her discussion of the Divertimento in an announcement for her lecture on 1 December 2011 at the University of California, Los Angeles. Two years later she followed this up with a substantial essay, although both times she missed the connection between Stravinsky and Castro afforded by the inscribed Divertimento fragment. She

FIGURE 3.2b
Fragment of Divertimento, inscribed to Juan José Castro (cont.). UBC Stravinsky Collection, no. 45.

also offers us multiple and delightful photographs as Stravinsky and son frolic with Victoria Ocampo on her estate.

In both her contributions Levitz calls Divertimento "a dance suite."[40] Yet, nothing suggests that the Divertimento / Suite Symphonique 1934 (Paris: Édition russe, 1938) was ever intended by Stravinsky to be danced. It comprises four selections from the ballet with a brief and newly reworked ending that he made in order for it to be played at concerts by an orchestra or by violin and piano. Having choreographed the entire *Baiser* for its US premiere in 1937, Balanchine shortly after the composer's death rechoreographed the Divertimento for the 1972 Stravinsky Festival in New York. Its success should not be gauged by Craft's report at the time that "Divertimento . . . is ruined by the peremptory ending." Even he had to admit that "Balanchine's excerpts, though weak in musical shape, were one of the festival's peaks."[41] These opinions have since been both strengthened and weakened by Joan Acocella, one of this country's finest dance critics. Writing about the 2012 Stravinsky/Balanchine festival, she observes that "Now the [Divertimento] ballet is all dancing, beautiful and sometimes . . . very strange."[42]

In Levitz's announcement for her December lecture (a prelude to observations she would subsequently make in her published article), she continued:

> Stravinsky's commodification of musical memories, affects, and emotions in the Divertimento reflect his experience as a migrant cosmopolitan and tourist operating within an increasingly globalized framework of capitalist music production and in dialogue with a transnational networks [*sic*] of friends and colleagues after 1917. The Divertimento resembles a collage of musical souvenirs that inspires nostalgia through the portrayal of a historical musical landscape.

In her published article she crystallizes these thoughts into two widely separated sentences:

> The Divertimento reflects the choices Stravinsky made in programming repertoire for his concerts around the world, and the subsequent transformation of his music from aesthetic object of modernist contemplation to cosmopolitan souvenir.

And:

> The auratic fragments in the Divertimento transform it into a souvenir shop—an aesthetic version of the marketplace of vernacular modernism.[43]

Her poetic, vivid, eminently ponderable proposals are slightly compromised by Stravinsky's pedestrian and practical, professional—almost mechanical—ways: when he gave away the opening twenty-four bars of his "Scherzo" (movement 3 from the Divertimento), it was only a relic, however precious to Castro. He had no need of it five days later when he conducted Divertimento in Montevideo with the Orquesta Sinfónica del Sodre at the Estudio Auditorio. The reason that not one other autograph page of the orchestral version of Divertimento survives is simple. Rather than make a "collage of musical souvenirs," Stravinsky coolly marked the passages he wanted in his autographed full score of the complete ballet and had them reassembled by professional copyists. This autographed score of *Le Baiser* (now in the Library of Congress) still has these cuts indicated by cloth tabs that he inserted into it. Only the rehearsal numbers differ. In these excerpts one looks in vain for the slightest change in musical content between *Le Baiser* and Divertimento, save for the latter's "peremptory ending," itself just a slight reworking from the former's "Coda" (rehs. 202–3).

The exact time that Stravinsky copied the above two-page fragment for Castro is unknown, but it surely precedes by several years the date that Stravinsky inscribed it for the Argentine maestro. Detailed examination suggests that the sheet is an abandoned attempt by the composer, perhaps as early as 1931, to bridge musical materials of the ballet's third scene in order to arrive smoothly at the "Scherzo" movement. Before the score was finished in 1934 and printed in 1938, he probably conducted from the ballet's full score (printed in 1928), where he had marked the desired excerpts with tabs.

Stravinsky's awareness of and sensitivity to the limitations of orchestral instruments is suggested by his omission in the Castro fragment of the low B-natural in the bassoon at the beginning of the third system ("Un poco più mosso"). His reason could well have been that at the first performance of the complete ballet in 1928–29, this low B, marked *piano* and *dolce,* was played neither softly nor sweetly: this pitch is always particularly treacherous to sound in dynamics and intonation and tends to be sharp. Moreover, low B may have had a special connotation for him. In all his works, he avoids a soft and unprepared low B unless it is covered by doubling with another instrument, with only three exceptions. Two of these, in *Oedipus Rex* and *The Rake's Progress,* concern death;[44] the third, in *Babel,* is about destruction.

However one may interpret Stravinsky's "very grateful memento" in Buenos Aires—his photograph inscribed to a young woman half his age—and his commitment since 1922 to his mistress Vera Soudeikina, near the end of his South American tour, there surfaced at Rio de Janeiro, in the company of Josef Hofmann and wife, none other than the great pianist's sometime agent, Dagmar Godowsky.[45] On 10 June, Dagmar, the Hofmanns, and Stravinsky *père et fils* all dined together. Stravinsky later (mis)remembered that this occasion followed a concert during which he had conducted his Capriccio with Soulima as soloist.[46] At this dinner an extremely inebriated Hofmann excoriated both Stravinsky and his music. Perhaps he harbored ill feelings toward Stravinsky since that 1925 banquet in New York's old Steinway Hall, when the elaborate chocolate cake in the shape of a piano honored not the piano virtuoso but the composer. On 13 June Stravinsky and his son departed Rio for France on board the SS *Cap Arcona.*[47] Dagmar recalled that while in Rio "we walked through the lush botanical gardens while Stravinsky quoted *Pique Dame* and told *us* [Soulima and Dagmar] how in his work he was struggling for order."[48]

Years later, Stravinsky described Dagmar to Ocampo in Rio as "a bad character."[49] Following his departure, Dagmar wrote him in June from Rio and that year twice more from New York, all three letters in German.[50] In correspondence with Kall, Stravinsky called her "the dangerous person,"[51] but by July of 1939, in another Stravinsky letter to Kall, she had become "cette brave Dagmar"[52] because of her business acumen.

STRAVINSKY AS CONDUCTOR

There are few evaluations of Stravinsky's conducting in South America. This lack is partly owing to the tour's brevity, partly to journalistic irritation at Stravinsky's clumsy political statements on his arrival in Buenos Aires, and partly to Castro's preeminent role in leading orchestras in Argentina but also because Stravinsky so often led his ballet scores from the pit. And in the pit conductors normally attract much less attention than dancers. Nevertheless, on 10 May, one reporter wrote of "a villainous composer, bad conductor, and worse pianist."[53]

4

TOUR IV (1937)

CONCERT APPEARANCES, MANY WITH DUSHKIN AND WIFE

5 January: Toronto, Toronto Symphony (half concert with Sir Ernest MacMillan)

8 January: Worcester with Dushkin

14, 15, 17 January: New York Philharmonic, soloist Beveridge Webster

21, 22, 23 January: New York Philharmonic

25 January: Montreal with Dushkin

27 January: New York with Dushkin

8, 9 February: Columbus with Dushkin

14 February: Detroit, General Motors Symphony

16 February: Brooklyn with Dushkin

18, 19, 20 February: touring with Cleveland Orchestra and Dushkin, Allentown, PA, and Princeton, NJ

24, 25, 27 February: Cleveland Orchestra, soloist Dushkin

3, 4 March: Winnetka with Dushkin and Beveridge Webster

12, 13 March: Los Angeles Philharmonic, in pit for *Petrushka*

16 March: Santa Barbara with Dushkin

23 March: San Francisco Symphony and Chorus (half concert with Gaetano Merola)

30 March: Tacoma with Dushkin

31 March: Seattle with Dushkin

27, 28 April: New York Metropolitan Opera Orchestra, in pit for three ballets

On Stravinsky's third North American tour were not only himself and Dushkin, but also the violinist's young wife, Louise. They arrived on Christmas Eve of 1936 in New York on the SS *Normandie*, with their friend Edward G. Robinson and his wife, Gladys. A photograph of Stravinsky seated, with his left arm affectionately over Dushkin's shoulder, was taken in the ship's lounge, possibly by Mrs. Dushkin in late December of 1936.[1] For the rest of December Stravinsky stayed with the Dushkins in New York at the Hotel Ansonia. Their tour was managed this time by the New York concert agency of Richard Copley, a firm that had been recommended to Stravinsky by Dushkin in 1935.[2]

Copley's full-time assistant in 1937 was the thirty-eight-year old Severin E. Kavenoki; Dagmar Godowsky apparently also worked for him part-time. Born in the Bronx,

Kavenoki had previously worked for Merovitch and had helped Stravinsky in Washington near the end of the second tour. After Merovitch's mental breakdown in mid-November of 1935, Kavenoki joined the Copley firm.[3] Late in November of 1936 he assisted with the US publication by Simon and Schuster of the single-volume, *Stravinsky: An Autobiography,*[4] an English translation of the composer's two-volume *Chroniques de ma vie.* In 1944, during World War II, Stravinsky wrote Kavenoki's first name on the initial page of an ozalid copy (similar to an architect's blueprint) made from the composer's original two-piano manuscript (1943–44) of the *Scherzo à la Russe.* By then, Kavenoki was in the US Army and at some point had shortened his family name to Kaven, a contraction probably unknown to and unused by Stravinsky.

This time, the tour would touch on eastern Canada. Just before Stravinsky returned to France in mid-April of 1935, Kavenoki had mentioned Canada to him. Among the earliest clear references to this junket is a notice in the *New York Times,*[5] probably arranged by Copley's firm and perhaps even placed by Kavenoki. In any event, on Wednesday, 30 December 1936, Sir Ernest MacMillan, conductor of the Toronto Symphony Orchestra, drafted a letter in French to Stravinsky in New York. He welcomed the composer's first-ever appearance in Canada "during the coming week," mentioned that he had contacted Copley "several months previously" about the specific edition of *Petrushka* needed, informed Stravinsky about the Toronto orchestra's strengths and weaknesses and its acquaintance with various sections of *Firebird* and *Petrushka,* and set a rehearsal for 9:30 a.m. on Monday, 4 January 1937.[6]

After detraining from a slightly delayed overnight coach from New York on the morning of 4 January, Stravinsky went straight to his first rehearsal for a concert the following evening, in which he and Sir Ernest were to share the podium. The concert was an extra, nonsubscription event. An announcement on 2 January 1937 in the *Toronto Globe and Mail,* featuring a headshot of Stravinsky made from one of the decade-old Lipnitzki photographs and captioned "Prince of Modernists," referred both chauvinistically and incorrectly to "his first appearance on this continent."[7]

Three days later, the same newspaper reported that Stravinsky had held

an interview yesterday . . . in the Palm Court of the Royal York Hotel. And because he speaks little English and his interpreter [probably Kavenoki] spoke no French, he looked as harassed as the interviewer felt uncomfortable throughout the brief ten minutes. . . . And, "Oh, no, no," not for any reason would he discuss Russia's present status in the musical world lest he trod [*sic*] on political grounds. What did he think of the radio? . . . The interpreter explained that there were 2 pages [in *Chroniques*] dealing with the radio. Asked about Hitler's recent edict prohibiting press criticism of music in Germany? This question was put to Stravinsky by the interpreter after being assured no political interest was contained therein. "No press criticism of any kind had ever had any effect on M. Stravinsky."[8]

A reporter for a rival newspaper, the *Toronto Daily Star,* garnered similar comments:

FIGURE 4.1

Left to right: Severin E. Kavenoki, Igor Stravinsky, and Sir Ernest MacMillan, 1937. Photograph courtesy of Colonel (ret.) Ed Boggs: from the Oscar W. Koch photograph collection (1944–45), no. 48905580, US Army Military Historical Institute, Carlisle, PA.

"All art is retarded by revolution," [Stravinsky] emphatically declared, dismissing modern Russian music as "not very interesting—nothing really new—very backward," . . . speaking chiefly in French because his English is poor. . . . Edward G. Robinson claims Stravinsky's highest admiration . . . one of the few stage actors who had had the "taste and conviction to transfer his art successfully to the cinema." . . . Screen music, however, he dismissed contemptuously. "It is in a very primitive stage—composers are asked merely to fill in empty spaces, a servile task," he said.[9]

This last remark may well have proceeded from his experience in 1935 at MGM.

Another Toronto interview, mostly in French, during which he repeated concepts from his recently published *Chroniques de ma vie,* demonstrates his precision of thought. When the reporter questioned him about his use of the word *change,* and then ventured to say that "you have since changed," Stravinsky responded:

"No"—and he repudiated the word he had before used—"it is not so much change as growth. You do not say the tree changes. It grows. It never stops being a tree, from the *moment* it is a seed until it dies. It is always a unity—its own unity, but it develops. *Pour vivre, il faut pousser.*"[10]

A winter photograph of Sir Ernest, Stravinsky, and Kavenoki, warmly dressed and posed on a lakeshore, is wrongly dated "1935" on its reverse side by an unknown hand; the location is identified as the "Toronto Country Club" (fig. 4.1).[11] Even though Kavenoki worked with Stravinsky in 1935, the hectic tour schedule allowed no opportunity for the pair to have visited Toronto that year. Thus, the photograph must really date from between 4 and 6 January 1937.

FIGURE 4.2
Stravinsky and Sir Ernest MacMillan.
From *Musical America*, 25 Jan 1937, 27.

Another photograph (fig. 4.2), taken 4 or 5 January 1937, pictures both conductors after a rehearsal in Massey Hall, the exiting orchestra players warmly dressed for the cold. At the concert Stravinsky led suites from his *Firebird* and *Petrushka*, first performances of these versions for Canada. Sir Ernest preceded them with Brahms's Fourth Symphony.[12] Stravinsky's effect on the orchestra and its audience is well conveyed by the reviews, such as one printed the following day:

> Our players rose splendidly to the occasion responding most sensitively and accurately to the composer's baton. . . . Stravinsky is a great and inspiring conductor. . . . After his first number the applause almost threatened to bring down the house, but even this demonstration was dwarfed by the final ovation when it seemed as if there would be no end to the recalls, the clapping and stamping and cheering and shouts of "Bravo!"[13]

The other was published ten days later:

> The incisiveness of his conducting brought out with clear, full color all the exotic charm and novelty of each work . . . [and] electrified the hearers into frenzies of applause. The alert yet ever cool brain of the composer-conductor maintained control of the difficult music and of the unfamiliar, however responsive orchestra. . . . The *tohu-bohu* after *Petrouchka* was extraordinary, bringing M. Stravinsky out many times; but the longer . . . *Firebird* . . . produced a stampede of acclaim such as has seldom resounded within those walls.[14]

Summing it all up on 9 January, a well-pleased critic nevertheless attributed Stravinsky's success in Toronto to the presence of a different type of audience from usual. This critic (correctly) perceived that a majority of attendees comprised younger—nonseason—subscribers. Ignoring the inconvenient age of *Firebird* and *Petrushka* (already more than a quarter-century old), he concluded that this more youthful audience came because they wanted to hear "a famous modern, Stravinsky, give them modern music in modern style."[15] Unsatisfactory as was this critic's thesis that those two 1910–11 scores were truly "modern," Toronto's vigorous applause endured until Stravinsky's conducting career ended there thirty years later, on 17 May 1967 in that same hall—conducting, "for the first time in his life, sitting down."[16]

He did not linger in Toronto after his 5 January concert. On the return trip to New York, presumably with Kavenoki, he visited Niagara Falls, which simultaneously awed and terrified him; then on 8 January he gave a duo recital with Dushkin in Worcester, Massachusetts. He spent the remainder of the month mostly in New York, leading the Philharmonic. The first concerts, on 14, 15, and 17 January, were with Beveridge Webster, substituting Capriccio for the Violin Concerto because Dushkin was ill.[17]

Immediately following a second round of Philharmonic concerts on 21, 22, and 24 January, Stravinsky and Dushkin gave a recital in Montreal on the evening of 25 January. It consisted of the *Suite italienne,* Divertimento, *Duo concertant,* "Air du Rossignol," and "Marche chinoise" from *Nightingale,* "Berceuse" and "Scherzo" from *Firebird,* and the "Danse russe" from *Petrushka.* Although one reviewer thought Stravinsky's piano playing attained "une divine indifférence," the city's most perceptive critic, Thomas Archer, said that he played the piano "with the utmost precision" and that "Dushkin is as sensitive to the composer's thoughts as a wire charged with electricity."[18]

By the twenty-seventh they were back in New York with still another joint recital at Town Hall. Downes's review of the *Duo concertant* revealed that, unlike Frankenstein two years previously, he had not done his homework. Downes's last five words exceed in pomposity and redundancy even the 1935 Pittsburgh review quoted above:

> The least familiar music in substance . . . was the "Duo concertant." It offers some problems characteristic of the later Stravinsky which may not be the easiest nut to crack at a first hearing. . . . It is a play of musical substances and is not an art primarily to evoke memories, experiences, emotions, or appeal particularly to sensuous or imaginative natures. . . . This was perhaps the least liked music of the program, which was probably instinctively right on the listener's part. It is not time to say that this music is immortal, or that it is intolerable if one is seeking living art. It is very arithmetical and geometrical. . . . But it has movement, development, form, and as it progresses, it grows.[19]

On 1 February Stravinsky visited Balanchine's dance studio at Fifty-Ninth Street and Madison Avenue "to oversee progress" of Balanchine's choreography for *Jeu de cartes.* He was very pleased, even though he liked neither the ballet's décor nor its costumes. Balanchine's rehearsal pianist, Leo Smit, vividly described Stravinsky's remarkable evocation on the piano of the entire score of *Jeu de cartes.*[20]

Such a strenuous winter itinerary could not but have exhausted Stravinsky. Even worse, a photograph of him resting between rehearsals in January with the New York

Philharmonic, bundled up in his fur-lined overcoat, shows him smoking a cigarette in his iconic holder,[21] a practice less than salubrious for a man about to be diagnosed, only three months later, with active tuberculosis.

GHOSTED ESSAYS AND US PUBLISHERS

"Dull and boring" as Stravinsky in 1925 had found America and Americans, he decried neither the country's wealth nor the riches still to be exploited within its citizens' pocketbooks. After the 1936 publishing success with Simon and Schuster for his autobiography, Stravinsky and Kavenoki began to focus on the US book market. During the second half of the 1930s, Kavenoki came into possession of English translations of two essays ghostwritten in France for Stravinsky, one of them on Pushkin, the other on Diaghilev.

Catherine Stravinsky wrote a letter to her husband on 3 January 1937, just after he arrived in New York. Their new son-in-law, the poet Yuri Mandelstamm, had "just written your article about Pushkin, and tomorrow is coming here to dictate it to Ira [Stravinsky's niece], who will type it on your machine as you asked."[22] The next day, the composer's daughter, Mika, also wrote to Stravinsky; her husband, Mandelstamm, added apologies for his typist's errors and noted that the letter and, presumably, the essay itself (in French) would travel by the SS *Aquitania*. The vessel sailed from Cherbourg on Wednesday 6 January but, delayed a day by storms, did not arrive in New York until Wednesday 12 January.[23]

Stravinsky certainly discussed this essay and possibly another one on Diaghilev—also ghosted—with Kavenoki. His papers include a six-page typescript in English entitled "CENTENARY OF PUSHKIN'S DEATH, February 10, 1837–February 10, 1937/by/IGOR STRAVINSKY."[24] It bears editorial annotations, and the title was altered in pencil to read "A Hundred Years after Pushkin." Also penciled at the upper right is "Sulgrave Hotel/Park av & 67th st./NY City/#" (i.e., lacking the hotel's room number). The Sulgrave was Stravinsky's usual abode when he stayed in New York. The *Aquitania*'s arrival on 12 January in New York still allowed sufficient time for whoever undertook the task of translating it into English. The typescript of this translation is accompanied by a rejection letter dated 16 February 1937 from the *Atlantic Monthly,* addressed to Mr. Severin Kavenoki at 133 East Seventy-Fourth Street in New York.

The translation in Kavenoki's typescript differs from the one in the essay's eventual publication in 1940 entitled "Pushkin, Poetry and Music," credited to Gregory Golubev, Alexis Kall's friend.[25] In 1941, Stravinsky received a payment of seventy-five dollars, presumably from Golubev's New York–Hollywood publisher, Harvey Taylor. Golubev's translation into English spawned, in turn, a Russian translation probably made during the Soviet era.[26]

The Diaghilev essay arrived later in New York and suffered a much lengthier delay in publication. The English translation consists of fourteen typewritten pages, headed "DIAGHILEFF—as I knew Him!/by/IGOR STRAVINSKY."[27] On 4 March Catherine Stravinsky had written her husband that it was being finished in Russian in Paris for

Stravinsky by Walter Nouvel, but it did not yet have "a sufficient number of anecdotes to please the American public."[28] Later that month it was translated into French. Though lacking clues as to when it came to New York, this essay could hardly have arrived earlier than April, and it is doubtful that it could have been translated into English before Stravinsky sailed home. It eventually made its way into print in November of 1953, in the *Atlantic Monthly* in a translation (presumably from the French) that differs from the one preserved in Kavenoki's papers. The new translation was made in 1946 by Stravinsky's friend Mercedes de Acosta, and it bore a different title: "The Diaghilev I Knew." Negotiations in the summer of 1953 and winter of 1954 with de Acosta for its publications in the United States and France reveal that she was as feisty about money matters as Stravinsky.[29]

COMPOSING FOR A JAZZ BAND

When Stravinsky first visited New York in 1925, Paul Whiteman, who had commissioned Gershwin's hugely successful *Rhapsody in Blue,* is said to have approached Stravinsky to write a jazz composition: the composer was apparently attracted to the project by a cimbalom player in the band.[30] Although nothing came of it, perhaps the experience planted an idea in his mind. He somehow found time to finish, early in February, a very brief work for jazz band and called it *Praeludium* (it has no cimbalom). Drafted late the preceding December in France,[31] he made fair copies in the Sulgrave Hotel, dating them 6 February 1937, New York.[32] On 17 February 1937 Galaxy Music Corporation sent a photostat of his completed orchestra score to the Register of Copyrights in Washington, DC; copyright was granted the next day.[33] At this time A. Walter Kramer had been in charge of Galaxy Music Corporation (the US agent of Édition russe) for some nine months. Perhaps his failure to publish the *Praeludium* immediately had something to do with his earlier opinion (cited above) about "the utter sterility of [Stravinsky's] lesser music." When finally published in 1968, it was titled *Praeludium for Jazz Ensemble.*

It is astonishing that Stravinsky could have even considered any additional work in December of 1936, while occupied with finishing *Jeu de cartes* (1935–36), but the fact is he did.[34] A photograph of him at the piano in his home in Paris is said to date from 1937 and to show him "playing from the manuscript of *Jeu de cartes.*"[35] Although the music in oblong format from which he is playing is unidentifiable in the photograph, another manuscript at the right, partly obscured behind the first manuscript, can be identified here for a first time. It is a reverse photostat (white staves on black) in tall format, with twenty-one preprinted staves: the first page of *Praeludium.* Accordingly, the photograph in his home must have been taken after his return to Paris in May of 1937, since the *Praeludium* photostat was created in February and *Jeu de cartes* premiered in April.

According to Stravinsky in 1949, *Praeludium* was composed for "a certain Reichman (jazz leader)."[36] Later, Lawrence Morton stated that it was intended for a radio orchestra. When it was finally premiered, on 19 October 1953 in Los Angeles by Robert Craft at an "Evening on the Roof" concert called "Stravinsky Jazz," the program note said that it was intended as a radio signature piece for a band prominent in 1937, the year of its composition [*sic*]. The composer has permitted this performance only for the sake of the performers' curiosity and because its instrumentation [the celesta excepted] was already provided for by other works on the program. The piece is of interest if only for the remarkable way in which the composer manages to show off each soloist and section of the band—the set problem of a signature piece—in so few bars.[37]

Stravinsky's holograph nine-page full score for *Praeludium,* in pencil and ink, signed and dated 1937, was preceded by several short-score drafts. One of these is a three-page short score dated 6 February 1937, the day before he and Dushkin left New York for Columbus, Ohio. Probably the same day, he copied his nine-page pencil draft of the full score, signed and dated New York, onto an arranger's custom-printed score-paper, printed as "Leo Reisman Score." This could mean that the score-paper came *from* Leo Reisman, or it may mean that Stravinsky's new score was *intended for* Reisman. Equally intriguing is Stravinsky's instrumentation list: it is written on one page of stationery from the Sulgrave Hotel, and another page lists some guitar chords.

His first work completed and inscribed on US soil thus deserves some attention, beginning with the question of whether its patron was Reichman or Reisman. If the patron was "Reichman," he would have been Joe Reichman (1898–1970), a jazz pianist known as "The Pagliacci of the Piano"; he was a "leader of popular hotel-styled orchestra[s] of [the] 30s and 40s," mostly active before World War II.[38] Reichman's band did indeed do radio broadcasts from New York, heard in 1934, for instance, on station KHJ in Los Angeles from the Hotel New Yorker, and in 1936 from the roof of the Pennsylvania Hotel; then he settled for a time in 1937–38 at the Coconut Grove in Los Angeles.[39] Stravinsky was never in California during 1934 or 1936, but while in New York in 1935, he could have heard Reichman's band, and Reichman could have contacted him then or later with the commission. No evidence has yet emerged that Reichman ever visited France.

Leo Reisman, the other contender for honors as commissioning patron, was better known, and seems the more likely candidate—and not just because his name appears in the holograph pencil draft. Born in Boston, Reisman studied violin at the New England Conservatory, joined the Baltimore Symphony at eighteen, and formed his own dance band the following year.[40] Soon established at the Casino in New York's Central Park, by 1931 his band was on radio shows, and then from 1934 regularly broadcast from the Hotel Waldorf-Astoria.[41] The Reisman Symphonic Orchestra of some thirty instruments has been described as "one of the premier tea-dance orchestras of the time, widely admired for its sophistication and refinement."[42] But because he broke his hip early in January of 1934 and was thus forced to cancel a January-February road tour of Gershwin's music, Reisman probably did not visit France in that year. By August of 1934, he and his band were broadcasting regularly on Tuesday evenings from New York on station WEAF. Stravinsky, during his short 1935 visit to the United States, could have heard Reisman's band in person at the Waldorf-Astoria in New York, or he may have heard its broadcasts while touring other US cities. No connection in France between the two men before the summer of 1937 has been established.[43]

Program notes for the 1953 "Evenings on the Roof" concert cite neither of these dance-band leaders.[44] Given Stravinsky's legendary parsimony in respect to utilizing paper,[45] it is conceivable that he would employ music paper from one band leader for a commission by another.

Stravinsky's 1949 identification of Reichman to Ralph Hawkes was most likely a lapse of memory; he could have been misremembering the name on the score paper or thinking of an earlier commission from Reisman, received when he returned to Paris from South America in June of 1936. The confusion of names is natural and reveals Stravinsky's continuing awareness of the US dance-band scene from the mid-1930s.[46]

Stravinsky scored this wispy, Webernesque *Praeludium*, totaling just thirty-five measures, for four saxophones (two altos, tenor, and baritone), three trumpets, two trombones, timpani, snare drum, double bass, guitar, celesta, and five string players.[47] Even with its unusual string players, one might argue that *Praeludium*, if not tailored to the normal resources of Reichman's band, shares certain family resemblances with it. Reichman's band usually employed four saxophones, three brass instruments, drums, double bass, and two pianos. A photograph from 1941–42 also reveals at least one trombone and a guitar.[48]

Resources available to Reisman, as demonstrated in his "Symphonic Orchestra" for its cancelled 1934 Gershwin tour, were somewhat greater and more varied. A photograph taken in the late 1930s or early 1940s in the Sert Room of the Waldorf-Astoria, reveals at its left edge a piano, a violinist, violist, guitarist, and double bass player, a percussionist with bass and snare drums (behind Reisman, who is taking a bow), and at its right side three clarinet-saxophonists, at least two trombones, and two trumpet players.[49]

Notable in such a tiny work is the incidence of the marking *espressivo* (despite Stravinsky's derogation in *Chroniques* of 1935) for saxophones (at reh. B, and at mm. 19–20). Unlike Walsh, who derided *Praeludium* as "a ragbag of things heard in Manhattan bars and clubs," I hear no echo in it, for example, of Jerome Kern's 1933 *Smoke Gets in Your Eyes*. Presumably, Walsh means Stravinsky's soulful melody (cited below as song X) set for alto saxophone (reh. B), and marked *cantabile espressivo*. This melody returns at the close (m. 30), distributed between trumpet I and viola-cello, where all three instruments are marked simply *cantabile*. Passed back to trumpet I just preceding reh. F, the melody cadences chromatically upward three times to the tonic E-flat, each a rhythmic diminution of its predecessor. To my ears, this melody seems closer to one that Edith Piaf was to compose for *La Vie en rose*, about a decade later.[50]

Rather than a "ragbag," the tiny *Praeludium*—in 1965 the composer recorded its thirty-five measures at one minute and twenty-four seconds—seems exoskeletal: a delicate, jeweled, and iridescent musical nano-insect that gradually sheds its appendages.[51] Nor do the snare drum and trumpet seem to be a "satiric military opening . . . that serves as an atmospheric deceptive-cadence," an allegation made in jacket notes for the composer's recording on 27 August 1965 in New York.[52] The trumpet flourish, built on octatonic Collection I (as is, mostly, the ensuing celesta variant), simply announces Stravinsky's long-standing favorite sonority: a simultaneous major-minor triad (here an arpeggiated E major-minor).[53]

As the structural diagram in box 4.1 implies, this miniature work embodies an introduction, a central thematic section and statement of materials, and then a rare procedure of combination and omission, concluding with dissolution. The opening roll on the snare drum, prolonged through the fifth measure, never occurs again. Even the several statements of the vamp (either introductory or accompanimental, but resolutely tonal and deploying harmonic resources common to demotic music of the 1930s) are varied. There are only two exact repetitions: the celesta with sustained muted second trumpet (mm. 6–8), recalling at mm. 27–29 the first trumpet's initial octatonic flourish at mm. 2–4 (save for a single pitch); and the beginning of song X (mm. 11–13) recalled at mm. 30–32. Although the ten-bar introduction constitutes almost a third of the entire work, elements of this introduction are suggested later by sustained muted trumpet and celesta arpeggios (mm. 6–8 and 27–29), and by the initial solo vamp (mm. 9–10) recurring several times as accompaniment (mm. 9–10, 14–15, 16–23, and 30–32). The effect of the cadential rhythmic diminutions in trumpet 1 (mm. 33–34 and the anacrusis to rehearsal F) is a narrowing and focusing on a single object, in this case, an E-flat-added-6th chord (the anacrusis to the last measure).

As usual with Stravinsky, the orchestration is ingenious. First, there is the harmonized reinterpretation (reh. A) by the celesta of the introductory solo trumpet flourish (eons remote from those "wanton celesta chords" so memorably characterized at the close of the G-major duet in the finale of *Der Rosenkavalier*).[54] Second, there is that subtle recoloration of the complete tune (reh. B) initially sounded by solo E-flat saxophone, achieved by passing it back and forth from trumpet to viola-cello (mm. 30–32); the composer finally allows it to cadence in successive rhythmic shortenings by the trumpet (mm. 33–35).

This brief work demonstrates how readily Stravinsky could jettison his well-advertised convictions about jazz and swing (or anything else!) when a commission was at hand. During a newspaper interview in Paris in December of 1933, he had stated that "jazz is not in itself an art. . . . Jazz is destined to disappear one day."[55] On 30 March 1935 a Chicago newspaper columnist had quoted him as saying that "music changes constantly. Jazz for instance is over. Something else will replace it. I don't know what. Personally, I love your Negro music best."[56] His admiration for black Americans and American music was fickle and not particularly well-informed. For example, returning to Paris from his second transatlantic tour, he had assured one reporter on 6 June 1935 that "Most of the *nègres* in the United States speak French."[57] After a visit to Harlem in December 1940, and after having declared swing as "American folk music," he exclaimed, "I love swings [*sic*]. I love all kinds of swings. It is appealing to me as a composer."[58] On 5 January 1941, interviewed by the *Washington Times Herald*, he indicated that swing's "present values are slight." By late January 1946 he could state "what [jazz] he has heard lately is of little interest."[59]

BOX 4.1. **STRUCTURE OF *PRAELUDIUM* FOR JAZZ BAND (1936–37; REVISED 1953)**

INTRODUCTION

1	2- - - - - - - - -4	5	6- - - - - - - - - - - -8	9- - - - - - - -10
snare	snare + tpt 1	snare	sustained muted tpt 2	tonic-dominant
drum	arpeggios	drum	+ celesta arpeggios	vamp

       E+/e–   E+/e–   E-flat+

SONG *X* plus 1 cadence   SONG *Y* plus 2 cadences

11- - - - - - - - - - - - - - -15	16- - - - -18	19- - - - - - - - - - - - - - - - - - - -26
alto sax solo (+ vamp on	tpt 1 + vamp	two alto saxes (sax 1 cadences at
tonic:14-15;	on tonic 7th	24-3, & 26-3)
sax cadences		
last note: 14)		

E-flat+   E-flat+   V of E-flat   E-flat+7

INTRODUCTION

27- - - - - - - - - - - -29
sustained muted tpt 2
+ celesta arpeggios

E+/e–

SONG *X* plus 3 cadences

30- - - - - -32	33- - - - - - - - - - - - - - -35
tpt 1, vla, vcl	tpt 1 cadences in rhythmic
(+ vamp on	diminutions above vamp at
tonic, 30-35)	33-3, 34-2, 34-4; all four
	brass close on E-flat+6.

E-flat+

In that second month of 1937 Stravinsky and Dushkin really racked up railway miles. On 8 and 9 February they performed in Columbus, Ohio. There, one critic, after quoting from the *Autobiography* about the association of Stravinsky and Dushkin, praised them both: "Mr. Dushkin is a well-schooled and sensitive player, able in spite of a limited volume of tone, to find expressiveness in formidable difficulties. As pianist, Mr. Stravinsky, always unobtrusive, was nimble and fluent and musicanly." Yet this critic was clearly impatient with the limited range of works that the duo offered, as well as with audience response in his provincial city:

> We were offered two movements from the Violin Concerto ["Aria" and "Capriccio"]. . . . Since all the works offered are adaptations and reductions from longer scores, it is almost as though we had seen small photographs of a half-dozen crowded and colorful canvases. But Columbus is not yet ripe for a full-sized Stravinsky Festival.[60]

Another critic felt similarly:

> The programs were well contrived to give a representative cross-section of the composer's work without resorting to his extreme later style. . . . Two movements from the violin concerto in D served to progressively prepare the ears of a none too sophisticated audience.[61]

By 11 February the pair were back in New York. That evening, Stravinsky, with "11,000" [*sic*] others, attended a "Benefit for the Flood Relief" at Radio City Music Hall. The equally celebrated Noël Coward noticed Stravinsky, together with "every star in New York."[62] Was the (by then, somewhat faded) "star" Dagmar Godowsky also there?

On 14 February Stravinsky and Dushkin played in Detroit, and two days later, in Brooklyn; then on 18–20 February they joined the Cleveland Orchestra on tour, where Stravinsky conducted in Allentown, Pennsylvania, and Princeton, New Jersey,[63] although Dushkin did not participate. At the university town, Stravinsky revealed that he had begun work on what would become the Symphony in C. By 22 February they had returned to Cleveland, where Stravinsky gave an interview in his hotel suite at Wade Park Manor. On 24, 25, and 27 February he conducted the orchestra at Severance Hall in three more concerts, joined by Dushkin for the last two.

Pairing Tchaikovsky's Pathétique with his own music in these concerts on tour almost certainly signaled his recollection of the concert in 1925 that he shared with Sokoloff and the Cleveland Orchestra, and was also intended to compete with Sokoloff's highly lauded, "glowing" performance of the Pathétique during their 1925 concert. Regrettably, Stravinsky never recorded the Pathétique, whose composer he had glimpsed in 1893 as an eleven-year-old and the premiere of whose final symphony he heard two weeks later, on 28 October.[64] Fortunately, a third-year Princeton undergraduate, Edward T. Cone, future professor there and scholar of Stravinsky, reviewed the 18 February 1937 concert, which took place in McCarter Hall:

Mr. Stravinsky's interpretation . . . stressed the purely musical aspects of the work rather than the emotional or sentimental ones. This does not mean that there was any lack of interpretation. On the contrary, the second theme of the first movement [Andante] was warm and moving and the march [third movement] was vivid and exciting. Nevertheless, in a few places the symphony seems to demand a more dramatic and fiery treatment than it received, as in portions of the development and recapitulation of the first movement. The advanced tempo of the second movement emphasized its dancelike qualities and minimized its nostalgia.[65]

Interviewed in Cleveland on 22 February by an anonymous and persistent reporter, Stravinsky overcame the aversion to discussing Russian politics that he had previously voiced in Toronto:

He dresses with a nattiness often characteristic of diminutive men—he is two inches under five feet—and carries a private stock of wine. . . . Was it true he had said he was "against Communism but in favor of Bolshevism?" Yes, replied Stravinsky, turning to Mrs. Dushkin for aid in expressing himself accurately in English. Communism as now practiced in his native Russia is in too narrow a groove, but Bolshevism, meaning the idealization of Communistic aims, he favored. But music, not politics, was his forte.[66]

Cleveland's critics had some difficulties with the musical aspects of the visit. One (Elwell, a Boulanger pupil) declared that the audience was "mystified" and that the Violin Concerto "will not make friends any more easily than did *The Firebird* or *The Rite of Spring.*"[67] Another still dimmer scrivener considered that splendid work (the Concerto) "hard and brittle, ingeniously contrived, expertly handled, impersonal and at times even repulsive."[68]

On 1 March, two days after his final orchestral concert in Cleveland, Stravinsky wrote a note of thanks to Clara Gehring Bickford from the Wade Park Manor (fig. 4.3), where he had been residing for several days:[69]

Dear Mrs. Bickford:
How to thank you for the kind reception that you accorded me and my music. I am deeply touched by this and send you all my gratitude.
Igor Stravinsky

A fine pianist, Mrs. Bickford was an influential member of the Board of Trustees of the orchestra's Women's Committee. According to her lawyer husband, around 1925 she had begun to collect music manuscripts, autographs, letters, and photographs of composers. Most, or all of these items she bequeathed to the Cleveland Institute of Music. Alas for the Institute, but happily for the University of British Columbia, the former auctioned off her bequest in 1997. Among many treasures she had collected over a span of fifty years—some 104 selected items had been exhibited in October of 1986 at the Cleveland Institute—were thirteen undated autograph musical quotations of Stravinsky's works

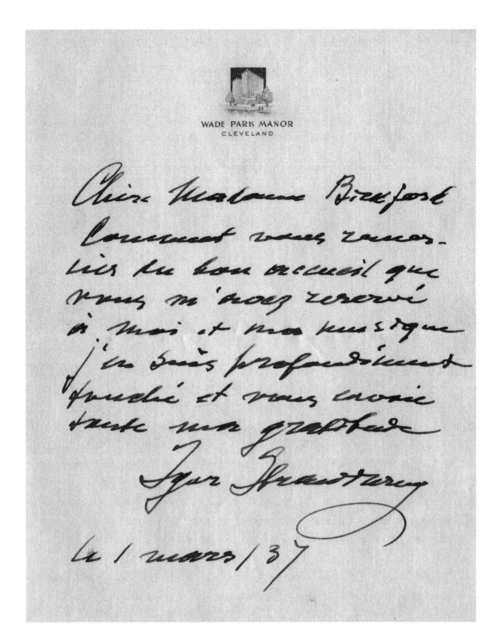

FIGURE 4.3
Stravinsky to Clara Gehring Bickford, 1937. UBC Stravinsky Collection, no. 47.

dating from *Firebird* to the Violin Concerto (see fig. 4.4). She had certainly heard Dushkin
play the latter, led by its composer on 25 and 27 February in Cleveland. Beautifully copied
and very carefully mounted by Stravinsky after he returned to France, these quotations
were thoughtful and considerate acts of kindness in respect to her hobby. They perfectly
answer his own query to her in the above-cited letter, "Comment vous remercier?"

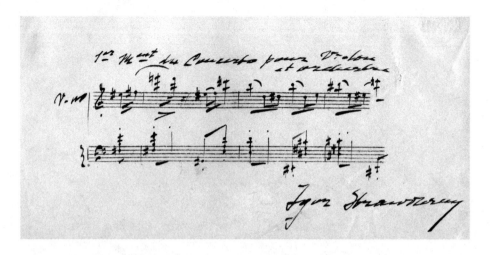

FIGURE 4.4

Incipit of Violin Concerto for Mrs. Bickford, 1937. UBC Stravinsky Collection, no. 60.

These thirteen musical inscriptions mask a subtext. Between the years 1916 (US premieres of *Firebird* in January at New York's Century Theatre and *Petrushka* in April at the Metropolitan Opera) and 1937 (the Violin Concerto at Cleveland), every work that he selected for her was one that he had conducted or played in the United States. These incipits are a spectrum of his compositions about which he was certain that an American connoisseur such as she would have knowledge. The subtext derives from Mrs. Bickford's considerable abilities at the piano. His exclusion of any work for that instrument (Sonata, Serenade, Capriccio, Concerto for Piano and Wind Orchestra, or his newest opus, Concerto for Two Solo Pianos) is noteworthy.

Most of these keyboard pieces required considerable practice-time on his part. Just the previous year (15 November 1936), he had written Alexis Kall: "long ago I told Klemperer [in Los Angeles] that I refused to participate as a soloist because I have not played my own concertos for two years, and I do not have time now to try to refresh my memory."[70] Back in France in 1937, he may already have been contemplating winding down his double career as traveling solo pianist and duo recitalist for what would ultimately prove to be a far more lucrative role: conductor and recording artist, chiefly of his own works. On 10 October 1937 he wrote Richard Copley, his US tour manager, that "for certain reasons, I would prefer not to appear in joint concerts." Whatever these reasons were— and money was certainly one of them—two weeks later he informed Dushkin that "I have renounced them [i.e., duo concerts]."[71] By the spring and summer of 1939 he was to have much more to say about public piano performance in letters to Kall sent from a French tuberculosis sanatorium at Sancellemoz, Sallanches, in the Haute Savoie, not far from Mount Blanc.

After a pair of concerts, 3–4 March 1937, with Dushkin in Winnetka, Illinois, during which Stravinsky and Beveridge Webster also gave the US premiere of his Concerto for Two Solo Pianos,[72] Stravinsky and the Dushkins boarded a train for Kall's house in Los Angeles. Renewed contact with Dr. Kall was to reveal Stravinsky's astonishing need (documented by Dr. Kall at the bottom of a loose page) this late in his career not only to be known as Rimsky-Korsakov's most gifted student but also to be deemed independent of his teacher. Arriving in Los Angeles on 8 March—Stravinsky, "impeccable in English tweeds, bowler and fawn-colored gloves"—they were met at Union Station by a small delegation. All—with the exception of Otto Klemperer—were Russian émigrés: Kall, choreographer Theodore Kosloff, conductor Modest Altschuler, and cellist and movie producer Boris Morros.[73]

Stravinsky had previously instructed Kosloff, in a letter to Kall of 15 November 1936, that he should prepare for the coming staged performances of *Petrushka* by using Stravinsky's own 1928 Columbia recording.[74] These instructions were scrupulously observed. Music critic Isabel Morse Jones reported: "Record and radio performances of Stravinsky's have been used for rehearsals and Dr. Alexis Kall, close friend of Stravinsky and a Russian musicologist of high standing, has aided Kosloff in the preparations."[75]

With the Los Angeles Philharmonic, on 12 March (evening) and 13 (afternoon) at the Shrine Auditorium, and financed (at least in part) by Merle Armitage, Stravinsky conducted two staged performances of *Petrushka* with an ensemble of 250 dancers. They were choreographed by Kosloff, who danced the title role.[76] The *Petrushka* performances were preceded by purely orchestral works: Divertimento and the *Firebird Suite*.

Local news media did not fail to exploit this occasion,[77] the first time that Stravinsky had conducted any of his own ballets in North America:

> Eyes of most fans and Stravinsky fans around the world have been focused on this event, and the twin program tomorrow afternoon, also at the Shrine, and the fact that the noted Russian has chosen Los Angeles for this presentation has occasioned comment both in the eastern press and over the coast-to-coast network of the air. Besides the presentation in the second half of the program of his most popular ballet, which will interest 250 dancers who have been trained for months under Theodore Kosloff, noted ballet master, with Kosloff to be seen in the main role, Stravinsky will give two of his most famous orchestral works in the first half of the evening: . . . ballet suite *The Fairy's Kiss* [i.e., Divertimento] and the suite from *The Firebird*.[78]

An unidentified but relatively friendly reviewer for the *Pacific Coast Musician* (a journal that, in the coming war years, proved venomously hostile to Stravinsky) described his conducting:

> Mr Strawinsky is a business-like, unobtrusive director. Though it was his own music in hand, he got less out of the orchestra than does its regular conductor, Otto Klemperer. At

least that was the impression of the writer, though this in part may have been due to the fact that the players were on the floor level, instead of on the stage—a location which in a measure dampened the tonal volume for those seated in the lower part of the auditorium.[79]

One young composer, Canadian-born Gerald Strang, then studying with Schoenberg and serving as his teaching assistant at the University of California, Los Angeles, was less forgiving:

> Stravinsky's appearances, March 12 and 13, at the Shrine Auditorium with the Philharmonic Orchestra . . . [were] marred by routine playing. . . . The ballet's version of *Petrouchka* proved amateurish and formless. . . . The affair unfortunately added nothing to Stravinsky's stature as composer or conductor.[80]

Even so, some of the city's most renowned musicians attended gala parties organized around these performances. One comprised mostly German-Jewish and Austrian-Jewish émigrés: "Dr. and Mrs. Otto Klemperer will entertain Mr. and Mrs. Arnold Schoenberg, Salka Viertel, Edward Steuermann, Mrs. Max Reinhardt, and Peter Lorre."[81] Most intriguingly, it was later claimed that "Klemperer escorted Schoenberg to hear Stravinsky conduct *The Firebird*" at one of these performances but that Schoenberg would not go backstage to congratulate Stravinsky.[82] Another party was largely of Russian exiles: "Theodore Kosloff, Prince and Princess A. V. Galitzin, Prince and Princess Lobanoff-Rostovsky, [and] conductors Nicolai Sokoloff, Modest Altschuler, Gastone Usigli."[83] Two of the last three conductors were Russians.

Whatever opinion critics held of Kosloff's staging of *Petrushka* in Los Angeles, the ballet was sufficiently welcomed by the public that Kosloff could repeat it on 2 September at the Hollywood Bowl with Efrem Kurtz conducting. Although this time, Kosloff did not himself dance the title role, he stated in the Bowl's program notes that he "knew that Stravinsky had never been happy over the way 'Petrouchka' was performed [meaning Fokine's previous staging]. . . . He [Kosloff] found that their ideas of the story coincided perfectly. 'Petrouchka' is a child's character, with the soul of a baby!"[84]

KALL'S FIRST PAGE OF PRIVATE NOTES

Apparently at the time of the two *Petrushka* performances at the Shrine, Dr. Kall took notes in Russian about discussions he had had with his houseguest. Dated 12 and 13 March (but lacking the year), Kall's notes appear on otherwise blank reverse sides of two identical flyers. The flyers announce a lecture and concert held a month earlier, on Friday 12 February 1937 at the Los Angeles Elks Club, honoring the centennial of the death of Pushkin. That same month, Kall had published an essay on Pushkin, "Glorious Poet," in the West Coast Russian-language newspaper *Novaya zarya*.[85] The principal speaker at the Elks Club was UCLA's professor of European affairs, Prince Andrei

Lobanoff-Rostovsky, with music organized by the soloist, soprano Nina Koshetz. Both were longtime friends of Kall.

His notes were most likely taken in 1937 in Los Angeles. The men were not together again until October 1939, and it seems implausible that Kall would carry two-year-old sheets all the way to New York and to Cambridge (where he lectured on 28 March 1940).[86]

Additional support for assigning the year 1937 to Kall's notes comes from the reference to "Berceuse" from *Firebird* in item 5. Stravinsky had rehearsed and conducted his second (1919) *Firebird Suite* to open the Los Angeles performance of the staged *Petrushka* ballet in 1937. Likewise, Stravinsky's request for *staccatissimo* in item 6 might well refer to a verbal demand he made during the same rehearsals. (Less probably, it could have concerned an upcoming performance of *Symphony of Psalms* in San Francisco.)

In any case, on a 12 March—presumably in 1937—Kall jotted down in Russian, in an exceedingly difficult hand to decipher,[87] the following items (fig. 4.5):

12 MARCH. FROM CONVERSATIONS WITH IGOR STRAVINSKY.

1. Creation is possible only when you love, when you are enamored of every measure you are creating. Only that is real.

2. Music and the erotic. Music is a pure, holy matter. It is a sin before the Lord to seek in music something else, personal, erotic.

3. Is it true that the trombone is your favorite instrument? "They are all my favorites."

4. An anecdote about [Valentin Alexandrovich] Serov, Chaliapin, and Diaghilev. Serov is in his studio, doing a portrait of Chaliapin—who is naked.[88] Diaghilev comes in, takes a look at Chaliapin: "How tiny yours is!" "Yes," answers Chaliapin: "I have a lady's one." That's for Diaghilev—the pederast.[89]

5. Some instrument played the theme from the Berceuse in the *Firebird* incorrectly. Stravinsky stops the orchestra. "By the way, you played that incorrectly [illegible]." The other [the player] shrugs his shoulders. Now that's impudence. If one were to excuse it, one would have to forgive everything. But these guys—you need to thrash them.

6. T......, plays timidly. "How polite he is! I want an insolent staccato. Staccatissimo.[90] But he's so affected."

Item 2 recalls Stravinsky's remarks quoted by a Los Angeles critic in February of 1935: "There is one thing in music I dislike even more than romanticism and this is eroticism, as found in the works of Scriabin, whose talents were in my opinion, very moderate." Even these were a warmed-over version of remarks that had appeared in an interview printed seven years earlier in a Russian émigré journal in Paris.[91]

Item 4 raises various questions, in addition, of course, to eyebrows. Stravinsky may have meant to denigrate Chaliapin. This is sometimes the way with men of small stature, and Stravinsky was four feet, ten inches tall,[92] whereas Chaliapin was well above six feet, a giant in those days. In a letter of 27 July 1901, for example, the nineteen-year-old Stravinsky wrote that "I cannot abide it when others look down on me from their superior

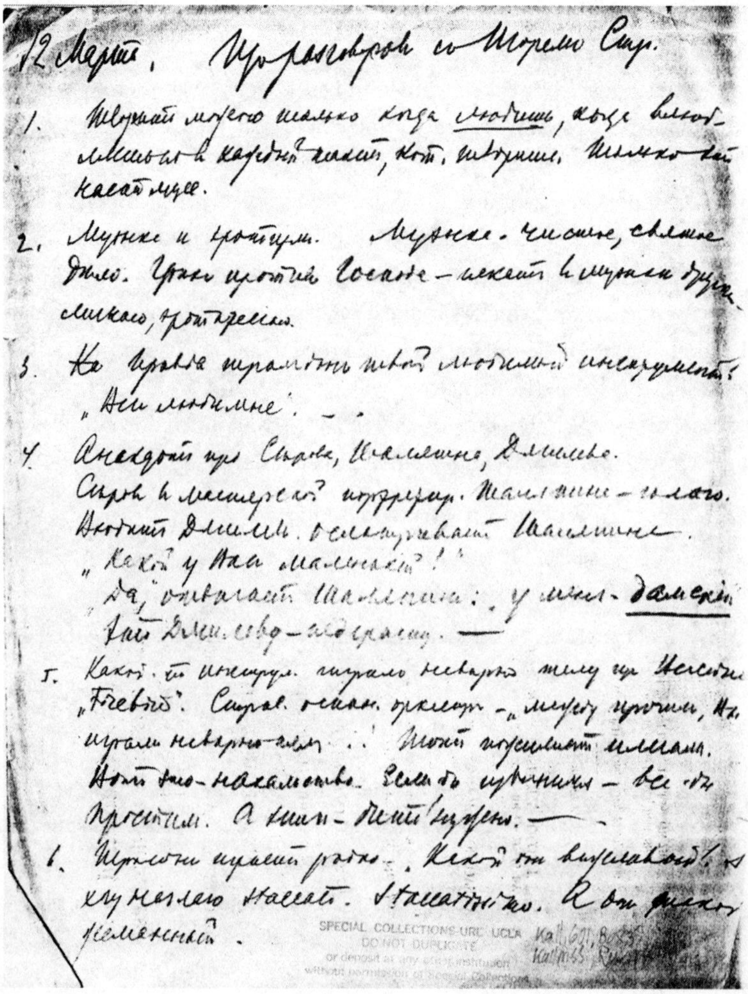

FIGURE 4.5
Kall's notes, 12 March 1937. Kall Papers, box 3, folder: MSS Russian, UCLA.

height." This was both a reference to the physical height of others as well as to their attitudes toward him "because of his diminutive height, a matter of supreme sensitivity for him."[93] As late as May of 1941, Earnest Andersson related a similar incident in his notebook (p. 25) "[Stravinsky] Weighs 145 [lbs.]. Would not tell [me] his height. Nearly a head shorter than my 6 ft."

Nor should we ignore the degree of flamboyance both men exhibited throughout their lives. Stravinsky's is well known from his notorious nude photograph of 1912. So carefully posed at his summer home in Ustilug (Ukraine), it even features a horse (a stallion?) in the background and was apparently sent only to a few male composer-friends in France, such as Maurice Delage.[94] There are also several other nude or near-nude photographs that Vera took in 1925 and 1930.[95] Even though Chaliapin's flamboyance is less well-documented, amusingly enough in 1899 Serov had already drawn him as the half-naked, incredibly long-waisted "Husband Chaliapin in the Form of a Centaur."[96] A more realist example is a photograph of him half-lying against a rock on a seashore, naked except for diaper-like bathing shorts. From this photograph at least,[97] it might be concluded that Chaliapin in the above-cited anecdote was merely being ironic about dimensions in a chilly studio. And if so, then in retelling this story, Stravinsky took the bait.

Kall's heading at the top of the page leaves no doubt that Stravinsky was the narrator; but who originated the anecdote? If not Stravinsky himself, then someone who told it to him. Who, when, and where? Surely not Diaghilev, the butt of the joke, and Chaliapin seems unlikely; it may well have been Serov himself. More than once, Diaghilev was present while Serov was painting portraits. In 1898 he even offered advice to the artist about the *Portrait of Princess Tenisheva*.[98]

Identifying Serov's portrait of Chaliapin "who is naked" is difficult but perhaps not impossible. Serov made between twenty and thirty sketches and paintings of the great singer. Those in various stages of undress occurred between 1897, when Serov first met Chaliapin in Moscow, and January 1911, when the two men broke off a profound friendship less than a year before the painter's death in Moscow.[99]

In the most likely image, one readily available in reproduction, Serov portrayed Chaliapin in watercolor, charcoal, and lacquer (cardboard, 47.9 cm × 34.1 cm.), signed it and dated it 1904.[100] First exhibited in December of 1904 through January of 1905 in St. Petersburg, at the second showing there of the Union of Russian Artists, it is now in that city's State Russian Museum, acquired from a Moscow dealer in 1911. Seated sideways, the half-naked Chaliapin holds a fur robe over one shoulder and across his chest, lower arm, buttocks and legs. Conceivably, the fur robe is more for warmth than for modesty because he had been, or soon would be, posing in the nude.

The peripatetic Serov lived in Moscow, but as one of Diaghilev's advisers for *Mir iskusstva* from 1898, he often visited St. Petersburg, the city of his birth, and maintained a studio there; it was an easy overnight train trip between the two cities. The 1904 itinerary of the great singer was hectic: Moscow, St. Petersburg, Milan, Rome, Moscow,[101] on 28 October to the Maryinsky Theatre in St. Petersburg, and on 11 December returning to Moscow.[102] As for Diaghilev, during much of 1904 he seems to have been in St. Petersburg. He knew Serov as early as 1896 and was with him in St. Petersburg on 7 June 1904 and shortly thereafter went to Moscow.[103] Serov portrayed Diaghilev that very year on a canvas that was never finished.[104] From this chronology, it appears that the only time in 1904 that Serov, Chaliapin, and Diaghilev were together was June in Moscow.

Stravinsky's feelings toward Chaliapin were contradictory and, in view of assistance Chaliapin rendered Stravinsky early in his career, boorish. Late in life, he disparaged Chaliapin as both singer and actor, "that idiot from every nonvocal point of view, and from some of these,"[105] but at the time of the 1904 portrait he would have been in awe of him. Indeed, in 1961 Stravinsky acknowledged that between 1903 and 1905 he "saw him frequently at Rimsky's and listened to his tales with much pleasure."[106] He surely saw Chaliapin on 4 January 1906 at Rimsky's home, where his younger brother, basso Gury Fyodorovich, sang that very evening.[107]

Unbeknownst to Stravinsky sojourning at his summer home in Ustilug in May of 1909, he should have thanked Chaliapin as the indirect (and the still anonymous) motivator for two commissions that came his way that month from pianist-conductor Alexander Ziloti, leader of the "Concert Series" in St. Petersburg.[108] His first commissions after those from Diaghilev, they were for orchestrations of settings by Beethoven and Mussorgsky of the "Song of the Flea" from Goethe's *Faust;* Stravinsky finished them on 21 August 1909.[109] At their premieres by Chaliapin on 10 December, both were praised by three local newspaper critics, as they were again early in the new year by two others, thus undercutting an observation that "Stravinsky earned no personal success."[110] Naturally, critical attention focused on Chaliapin, but such compliments from Russian critics as "delightful instrumentation," "superbly orchestrated," and "talented orchestration" can hardly account for Stravinsky's later discontent with the singer.[111] Moreover, in a letter to Maxim Gorky of mid-March 1912 esteeming Stravinsky (then in Switzerland) above Glazunov and Rachmaninoff, Chaliapin expressed his preference for "the lad." Proposing that Stravinsky consider setting a tale from Russian epic poetry, Chaliapin also told Gorky he would invite Stravinsky to visit him in Milan.[112]

Stravinsky had another emotional, though erroneous, connection with Chaliapin. Late in life, he recalled that his father, Fyodor Ignatievich Stravinsky, and Chaliapin had sung together in Borodin's *Prince Igor* at the Maryinsky Theater in St. Petersburg: his "father as the Drunkard [Skula], and Chaliapin as the Prince." Although he identified this particular occasion as his father's retirement in 1901 and the succession of Chaliapin as principal basso there,[113] he furnished no precise date; in point of fact, neither his father nor Chaliapin sang in *Prince Igor* at his father's retirement.[114] The Maryinsky held a benefit for Fyodor Stravinsky on 3 January 1901. At it, he sang Holofernes in *Judith* (1863), an opera by Alexander N. Serov,[115] father of the painter. Though Chaliapin, who often sang this role, was not there, he sent Fyodor a congratulatory telegram from Moscow the next day.[116]

Igor Stravinsky also recalled that in 1903, 1904, and 1905—that is, *after* his father's death on 4 December 1902—he often saw Chaliapin at Rimsky-Korsakov's house[117] and that "Chaliapin was also a gifted storyteller." This raises a possibility, however remote, that the good-natured, voluble, though self-centered Chaliapin was himself retelling the story of the portrait in Kall's item 4.

Less likely, young Stravinsky might have been present at the sitting. Perhaps the fledgling composer met the peripatetic Serov in St. Petersburg around 1902 at the Rimsky-Korsakovs, with whom Stravinsky seems also to have been close.[118] Serov drew portraits of Rimsky in 1898 and 1908.[119] In Stravinsky's first book of recollections he recalled that "Serov was the conscience of our whole circle [in St. Petersburg] and a very important friend to me in my youth; even Diaghilev feared him."[120] Stravinsky's choice of "conscience"—a guiding spirit, perhaps—recalls similar statements by Alexandre Benois and Mstislav Dobuzhinsky in their earlier memoirs.[121] Stravinsky's next joint book with Craft stated that:

> Serov was the conscience of the *Mir Isskustva* [*sic*] circle, but when Diaghilev referred to him as "la justice elle-même," he did so with regret, for Diaghilev wanted to sin. I knew Serov from the beginning of my association with Rimsky. Serov was a quiet type of man who was nevertheless full of sharp judgments, judgments that were not easily gainsaid.[122]

Just where and when Stravinsky heard the story about Chaliapin is difficult to say. Stravinsky surely would have attended the "spectacular premiere" in 1904 at the Maryinsky of Rimsky-Korsakov's most recently revised version of *Boris Godunov* during which Chaliapin sang the title role on 9 November and then several more times in November and early December.[123]

Possibly the artist himself originated the tale and conveyed it directly to Stravinsky. An optimal time for such a transmission would have been the final occasions on which they met: France or Italy in 1911. It would have been a good opportunity: neither Chaliapin nor Diaghilev was present. In mid-May during rehearsals in Rome for *Petrushka*, Stravinsky, Alexandre Benois and his wife, and Serov and his wife were all living in the same hotel, the Albergo d'Italia.[124] On that hotel's notepaper, Serov made a humorous drawing of Vera Nosenko[125] mock-whipping Stravinsky in his hotel room. Below, Stravinsky wrote in Russian, "caricature of me and Vera Nosenko who had promised to whip me if I did not obey her, because she is monitoring my health."[126] Even though this was a busy time for all concerned, Stravinsky, the Benoises, and the Serovs, sometimes joined by prima ballerina, Tamara Karsavina and her brother, all found time to sightsee in Rome together.[127]

During the final rehearsals for *Petrushka* and its first four performances, Stravinsky encountered Serov for the last time, in Paris in mid-June of 1911. In an undated letter from Serov to Benois, Stravinsky added a postscript, "Regards from the Stravinskys."[128] The painter died in Moscow on 22 November 1911.

Whether it was in March of 1937 in California, or another year or place, Dr. Kall surely relished the tale about Serov, Chaliapin, and Diaghilev in a long-vanished Old Russia. Kall's several sheets are important because they are among the very few records of Stravinsky's direct conversation in Russian with a compatriot of his own generation. They extend knowledge about Stravinsky's relationship with his teacher, Rimsky-Korsakov.

KALL'S SECOND PAGE OF PRIVATE NOTES

On 13 March (presumably in the same year, 1937), Kall headed the reverse side of his other copy of the 1937 Pushkin flyer, "Stravinsky." He followed this with three numbered entries, mostly in Russian, and a fourth entry that he left blank (fig. 4.6):

1. After the incident with Kastner, Strav. sends him a postcard [remainder in English:] "To . . . with professional ["friendship" lined out; replaced by:] "sympathy. Sincerely . . . I. Stravinsky."

2. Anecdote—"She is not indifferent towards you." So what should you do? Let it happen.

3. Anecdote about Stalin and Lunacharsky—"To you no longer."[129]

4.

The first item refers to some difficulty Stravinsky had at rehearsal with Viennese-born Alfred Kastner, principal harpist with the Los Angeles Philharmonic.[130] Kastner had joined the orchestra at its founding in 1919. Though he officially retired in 1936, rosters of the orchestra's personnel in 1937, 1939, and even 1941 still list him as principal harpist.[131] Even though Lunacharsky was executed in December of 1933, the *terminus ante quem* of 1937 on the printed side of the flyer could suggest the incident with *Petrushka* took place in 1937 rather than during Stravinsky's 1935 rehearsals.

Still another loose page in Kall's hand might as well be examined here.[132] It offers a half page in English, the other half in Russian, and is undated. Kall himself added the dots and the asterisk; his misspellings could be simply because he was translating on the spot (fig. 4.7).Perhaps this page embodied notes toward a future talk:[133]

COMPOS.

1. Music is not created to please . . .

2. . . . of no account, what pleases or what displeases.

3. . . . what pleases today, displeases tomorrow only what pleases *always*, goes through the centuries is the real thing.[134]

4. Beethoven how awquard* he was in his writing, but how true he is.[135]

    [below]

    *That is why once Rim[sky]-Korsak[ov] when I wrote something awquard angrily called me: "Beethoven."

[?5.] Music can be very pleasing, but—wrong can be very disagreeable, but—.

This page records observations probably uttered by Stravinsky. Although items 1–3 suggest he is the discussant, caution is needed respecting item 4: the "I" could refer to Kall, since he knew Rimsky-Korsakov and studied piano at the St. Petersburg Conservatory.[136]

In the lower half of this page (closed with four dots, the last one the heaviest and presumably a period), Kall wrote the following in Russian, in a hand exceedingly difficult to decipher:

Biog.[raphy?] At the Fren[ch] Dram[atic] Soc[iety], there was a meeting with Bel'sky, who has [had?] managed with difficulty to obtain an enormous sum for almost fifteen years. In gratitude, [he] sent out a letter from the Dram[atic Society], and reported that to his [Rimsky-

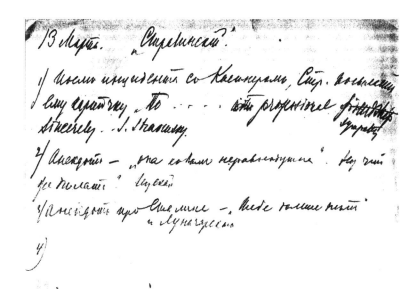

FIGURE 4.6
Kall's notes, 13 March 1939. Kall Papers, box 1, folder: Correspondence Russian, UCLA.

Korsakov's] very intimate friends like Bel'sky and [?] . . . R. K. [Rimsky-Korsakov] spoke of Stravinsky with exceptional enthusiasm—now remember—this is a real, enormous talent. You will be hearing about him. Care for him. Keep track of him. . . .[137]

Vladimir Ivanovich Bel'sky was Rimsky-Korsakov's friend and the librettist for five of his late operas, from *Sadko* (1895–96) through the never-completed *Sten'ka Razin* (1905) and the *Golden Cockerell* (1906–7).[138] Rimsky-Korsakov's chronicler, Yastrebtsev, documents many an encounter between Bel'sky and Stravinsky, chiefly at Rimsky's home,[139] even before young Stravinsky's working musical contacts around 1905 with Rimsky's opera on Bel'sky's libretto, *The Legend of the Invisible City of Kitesh* (1903–4).[140] According to Yastrebtsev, Stravinsky and Bel'sky met each other on 6 March 1903 at Rimsky's house during a celebration for his fifty-ninth birthday, and they saw each other there at least twenty-five more times through March of 1908.[141] Not long before Rimsky's death, Bel'sky also helped Stravinsky and his librettist on 9 March 1908 adapt H. C. Andersen's tale for Stravinsky's opera *The Nightingale* (1908–14). Knowing Bel'sky's "wonderful librettos for [Rimsky's] *Kitezh* and *Petushok*" and "very interested to meet him," the eighteen-year-old Prokofiev describes him in St. Petersburg on 23 October 1909 as "a quiet, taciturn gentleman with a big bump on his head."[142] By 1920 Bel'sky had emigrated to Yugoslavia, contacting Stravinsky from Belgrade in 1928.[143]

Years later, in 1963, Stravinsky observed that "when I try to associate the name [Yastrebtsev] with my memory of faces in Rimsky's group, I confuse it with the librettist, Bel'sky." Because in 1963 Stravinsky recalled meeting Bel'sky in Paris "30 years ago" and arranging

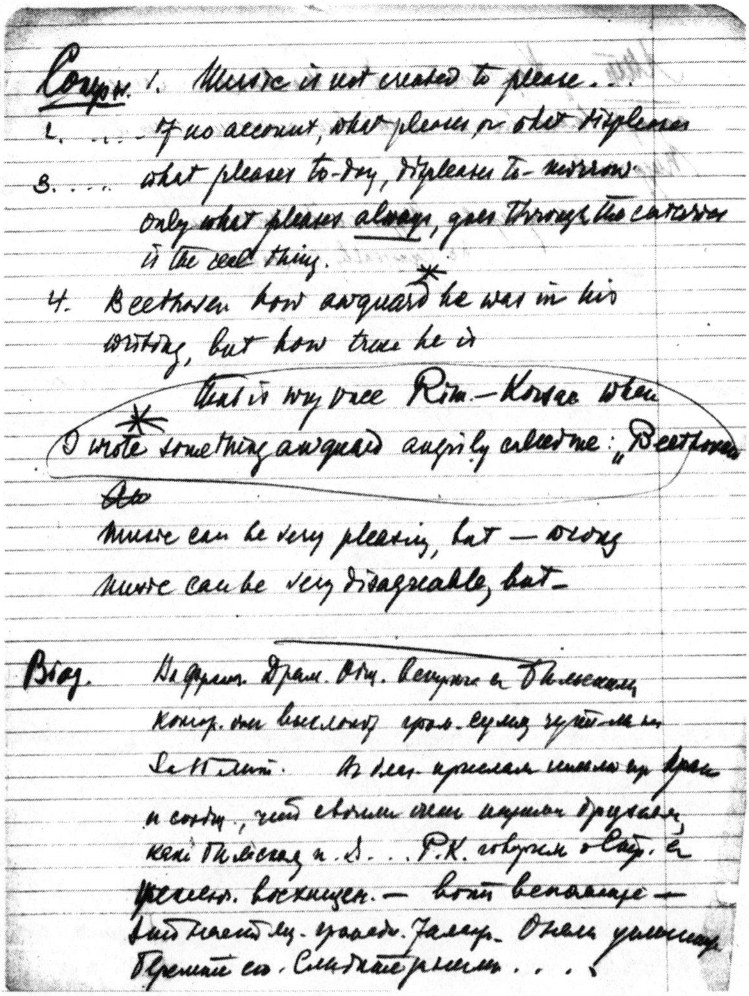
Compn. 1. Music is not created to please...
2. ... of no account, what pleases or what displeases
3. ... what pleases to-day, displeases to-morrow
only what pleases always, goes through the centuries
is the real thing.
4. Beethoven how avguard he was in his
writing, but how true he is
That is why once Rim.-Korsac. when
I wrote something avguard angrily called me: „Beethoven"
Ato
Music can be very pleasing, but — wrong
Music can be very disagreable, but—

FIGURE 4.7
Kall's notes, undated. Kall Papers, box 3, UCLA.

for payment to the Société Dramatique of Bel'sky's rights as Rimsky's librettist, Kall's loose page could be referring to Stravinsky's previous generosity.[144] Indeed, Bel'sky's letter of 15 November 1928 from Belgrade to Stravinsky in Paris, citing a meeting of the Society of Authors in Paris, mentions "my unforgettable friend Nikolai Andreyevich [Rimsky-Korsakov], who as you know, altogether doted on you. For all his stinginess with approval he absolutely recommended every new work of yours to me." In particular, Bel'sky also remembered that Rimsky once "emphatically" said, "Igor Stravinsky is perhaps a student, but he will not be a follower, neither mine nor anyone else's. Nor does he need to be, because his musical gift is uniquely enormous and original."[145] Obviously, Bel'sky and this letter made lasting impressions on the young, the middle-aged, and the elderly Stravinsky. Rimsky's declaration of his student's talent to Bel'sky should be deemed genuine, communicated in 1928 to Stravinsky, and ultimately communicated to Kall in 1937 by the beneficiary himself.

Stravinsky's final three and rather self-serving brief sentences to Kall at the bottom of this loose page (not appearing in Rimsky's remarks to Bel'sky but implicit in them) might have stemmed from remarks passed by Diaghilev during orchestral rehearsals for the premiere of *The Firebird* in May of 1910 in Paris. On the stage of the Opéra, pointing to Stravinsky, Diaghilev said: "Mark him well. . . . He is a man on the eve of celebrity."[146]

Rimsky's private remarks—in this case to Bel'sky—apropos of Stravinsky's gifts tally nicely with the composer's own recollections in 1959–60: "[Rimsky] never complimented me . . . very closemouthed and stingy in praising his pupils. . . . Friends after his death [told me] that he spoke with great praise of the *Scherzo fantastique* [1908–9]. He had many pupils and was always careful to avoid favoritism."[147] Taken together, Kall's undated loose page and Bel'sky's 1928 letter militate against Joseph's thesis that Stravinsky was "in the eyes of his teacher Rimsky-Korsakov, no more than another naive amateur."[148]

Kall himself arrived with Stravinsky chez Rimsky on 9 November 1903, an evening when Bel'sky was apparently absent.[149] Having studied classical philology and art history at the University of St. Petersburg, 1896–99,[150] and knowing Stravinsky from 1900, and Rimsky from the period when Stravinsky was beginning to work with him,[151] Kall was surely as much intrigued in 1937 by Rimsky's remark to Stravinsky about Beethoven as he was by Rimsky's remark to Bel'sky about Stravinsky's great talent. Rimsky venerated the German composer, although he once observed (26 December 1901) about his instrumental works, "I always like Beethoven, even though he could, I think, become boring."[152] Speaking with Rimsky again just before his death in 1908, Kall reported no negative evaluation of Beethoven by Rimsky, not surprisingly because Kall was discussing "Nationalism in Russian Music."[153] (Years later, on 11 June 1934, Kall lectured on Russian music in San Francisco. His topic was "the voice of Russia in song from Glinka to Prokofiev,"[154] and he probably lectured then and perhaps also later in Berkeley for the Slavic Department of the University of California—during the tenure of Professor Alexander Kaun.)[155]

ENTRAINING NORTHWARD

As noted above, just prior to their departure on 15 March 1937 for points north, Stravinsky's actor-friend Edward G. Robinson gave a party for Stravinsky and Dushkin. Among the guests was composer George Gershwin. In a letter to a friend Gershwin wrote, "Stravinsky was the guest of honor & was charming. He asked if he and Dushkin could play for the group. They played seven or eight pieces superbly. Stravinsky and my mother got on famously."[156] Gershwin informed another correspondent that Dushkin and Stravinsky played violin-piano pieces for the guests, "& very interesting too."[157] Stravinsky also autographed a copy of *Chroniques de ma vie* for Gershwin (this very copy offered for sale not long ago by a US dealer). Moreover, according to recent biographers, Gershwin's

> record collection reflected a great admiration for Stravinsky's music; so did a framed reproduction of a Picasso drawing [of Stravinsky] and some manuscript pages [i.e., inscribed] of

Stravinsky's autobiography that George prized. . . . In March [1937] he received inscribed copies (with a caricature portrait) of the composer's autobiography and of Merle Armitage's *Strawinsky*.[158]

Gershwin's admiration was reciprocated. Back in France and learning of the American composer's death on 11 July, Stravinsky wrote Dushkin on 8 August that not knowing the address of Gershwin's Russian-born mother with whom he had "got on famously," he wished to ask his current New York agent, Copley, to convey to her his "most sincere sympathies in her great sorrow."[159]

On 15 March 1937 Stravinsky, Kall, and both Dushkins headed north by train for their final Southern California engagement at Santa Barbara's Lobero Theatre. Stravinsky later wrote jocularly to Kall (by then back in Los Angeles), reminding him of their extremely naive reception:

> the kind of thing that you heard in Santa Barbara, you remember, when somebody said to you that he didn't understand a thing in the whole concert—*Pulcinella, The Fairy's Kiss,* "Scherzo" and "Lullaby" from *Bird* [*Firebird*], and "Russian Dance" from *Petrushka* (mind-bending music)—but he understood only that Stravinsky—the violinist—was a remarkable accompanist.[160]

Continuing north from Santa Barbara to San Francisco, Stravinsky was warmly received by its best music critic. Just as he had two years previously, Frankenstein educated his readers, this time with an intelligent comparison of the two sacred works to be performed: Stravinsky's *Symphony of Psalms* and Rossini's *Stabat mater*.[161] On 22 March Stravinsky rehearsed Monteux's well-trained orchestra for his half of the concert.[162] The same day, he managed to inform the *San Francisco Chronicle*'s readers about his politics: "I am opposed to the right, abhor the left and am altogether out of sympathy for the center," and to confirm that he planned to compose music for "a unique new kind of picture." The latter was by then thoroughly stale gossip.[163]

The next day, the composer led the West Coast premiere of his *Symphony of Psalms* "at Exposition Auditorium before an audience of eight thousand [and] when on the podium, [he] is as devoid of mannerisms as our own Pierre Monteux."[164] Probably during this brief stay in San Francisco, Stravinsky inscribed a copy of his *Autobiography* to Monteux's associate, Leonora Wood Armsby, president and managing director (1936–52) of the San Francisco Symphony Association: "Pour Madame / Leonora Wood Armsby / temoinage d'un très vive / sympathie." Below this he added an undecipherable musical quotation said to be from *L'Histoire d'un soldat*, signing between the two staves "Igor Stravinsky." Hers was apparently among the last two copies of the *Autobiography* available, so quickly had the 1936 Simon and Schuster edition sold out. At her death she was eulogized in the city as "Mrs. Music."[165]

In the afternoon following the sole orchestra rehearsal, Kall delivered a lecture, "Stravinsky as I Know Him," under the auspices of the Russian Music Society at the city's

FIGURE 4.8

Stravinsky (left) with Pierre Monteux, 1937. San Francisco Museum of Performance and Design.

Century Club.[166] The notes on the backs of his Pushkin flyers may well have been made for this purpose. Returning to Los Angeles shortly thereafter, he gave the same lecture, this time on Monday, 13 September 1937, at the California Arts Club.[167] Surely he wouldn't have recounted item 4 from his March 12 flyer in a public gathering!

It has been stated that Stravinsky and the Dushkins left San Francisco for New York by 24 March, but such was not the case.[168] A photograph, seemingly misdated in pencil as "NBC Photo 3/30/37" on its reverse side (perhaps the date when its negative was developed), depicts Stravinsky in the same heavy overcoat he wore in Toronto and New York at the beginning of the tour (fig. 4.8). He stands next to Pierre Monteux, the two men separated by a National Broadcasting Company microphone.[169] The occasion for this photograph was either "The Standard Hour" for the live NBC broadcast of Stravinsky's 1919 *Firebird Suite,* performed by Monteux and the San Francisco Symphony on Thursday evening, 25 March, or a rehearsal. On a half-sheet attached below the photograph, a penciled annotation reads almost as if it were destined for, or taken from a newspaper column:

That sharp-featured, keen-eyed gentleman who was an unobtrusive but watchful spectator at last Thursday night's Standard Symphony broadcast, has reason to look so interested when Pierre Monteux and the orchestra presented the Firebird Suite. . . . Unrecognized by the audience in which he sat so modestly was the famous composer, Igor Stravinsky, who later congratulated Maestro Monteux and NBC Producer John C. Ribbe on the performance.

Perhaps Stravinsky's traveling companions, the Dushkins and Alexis Kall (if he remained in San Francisco after his lecture), also went unrecognized by the audience.

Then came concerts in Tacoma at the First Baptist Church on the thirtieth (San Francisco to Tacoma is but twenty-four hours by rail),[170] and in Seattle on the thirty-first. The Seattle concert was first advertised on 28 March as by "Igor Stravinsky, modernist composer." On the day of the concert, a reader might have grimaced a little at the three errors in a single sentence in Seattle's self-identified "Quality Newspaper": "in 1931, when the eminent composer was thirty-one he had to face his first infuriated audience after a performance of his *La Sacre du printemps*.[171] The sole review the next day by one Dolly Madison, "Stravinsky and Dushkin Attract Large Audience," was, save for its heading, entirely devoted to naming member-attendees of the "Ladies Musical Club which presented these two great artists," and describing the gowns of each with photographs of three bedecked attendees. Just three husbands were named as attending this concert, although surely there were more.[172]

DEALING WITH DAGMAR

As Louise Dushkin disclosed in 1980, it might have been on this 1937 tour that she observed Stravinsky weeping during the third movement of the Violin Concerto; he told her that he had written one movement ("Aria II") as an apology—for his infidelities—to his wife, Catherine.[173] Whatever the occasion may have been, any remorse Stravinsky felt did not hinder a relationship with Dagmar Godowsky. Nathan Milstein, the composer's shipmate in 1935, recalled in his 1990 memoirs that

> Stravinsky . . . adored big women with voluptuous curves. . . . His onetime girlfriend Dagmar Godowsky . . . was plump, merry and aggressive. She spoke loudly and with temperament, cultivating a gypsyish style and [was] always making scenes. I can't imagine Stravinsky liked that, being basically quite bourgeois.[174]

And yet, she is a valuable witness to Stravinsky's ways,[175] now too frequently ignored, even censored, owing to a prudish quasi-Victorian sense of academic propriety.

HEALTH AND THE MOVIE INDUSTRY

Returning to New York from Seattle near the end of the first week in April, Stravinsky faced not only the world premiere of his staged ballet, *Jeu de cartes*, but also endured two misfortunes. A lesser man might have been floored by either: the discovery of a tuberculosis infection and the collapse of his negotiations to write a movie score.

A statement in Dagmar's memoir that "When next he [Stravinsky] came to New York ... at the [Hotel] Sulgrave ... and was put to bed for a long rest" accurately reflects doctor's orders in April of 1937 concerning his tuberculosis, which, she later noted, she was forbidden by lawyers even to mention![176] Goat's milk, rare those days in New York, was prescribed, and she obtained it from the farm of the Cleveland Orchestra conductor, Arthur Rodzinski. Stravinsky was not a cooperative patient. Ill as he was, "Pa and I took him to the New York premiere of *Amelia Goes to the Ball* at the New Amsterdam Theater," where her father and Stravinsky were "polite and slightly patronizing."[177] The New York premiere of this opera by Gian Carlo Menotti was on Easter Sunday, 11 April 1937, and was led by Fritz Reiner,[178] one of the few conductors whom Stravinsky esteemed. A photograph (taken before mid-April) shows Stravinsky holding a small vial of pills close to Reiner's nose.[179] How much of *Amelia's* newly translated English libretto Stravinsky would have understood in 1937 is open to question, but Stravinsky's exposure to Broadway was not.

Stravinsky had dated an unstamped postcard "San Francisco 25 III 37." He had probably purchased it in March in Albuquerque, New Mexico, while he and the Dushkins were en route via the Santa Fe Railroad to Los Angeles. He addressed it to a certain "Chère amie," none other than Dagmar Godowsky. For the sake of discretion, and lack of space for an address, he enclosed it in a (now lost) envelope before mailing it to her.

A translation from the French of his 1937 postcard to her follows:

San Francisco 25 III 37

Dear lady-friend,
A thousand best regards from your sincerely devoted I. Stravinsky. Morros will come to New York on 14 or 15 April with a libretto [i.e., a scenario] that is in the process of being prepared for me in Hollywood. If it suits me, we will conclude this matter which I hope will be profitable for me.

The "libretto" to be delivered by Boris Morros, head of the Music Department at Paramount Pictures, was, of course, the scenario for a film. Just before 8 March, when Stravinsky and the Dushkins had arrived in Los Angeles, Isabel Morse Jones announced in the *Los Angeles Times* a tidbit gained, perhaps, from her acquaintance with Kall: "It is strongly rumored about Hollywood that he [Stravinsky] is to stop a while and engage himself in creative work for the films."[180]

The rumor was correct. Dagmar, in New York, had been negotiating with Boris Morros on Stravinsky's behalf. Morros, also a pianist and cellist trained in the St. Petersburg Conservatory, was one of that delegation of several musicians who had met Stravinsky and the Dushkins upon their arrival in Los Angeles on 8 March. Shortly thereafter, Stravinsky, Morros, Dushkin and his wife, screen actors Claire Trevor and Akim Tamiroff, movie director and writer Robert Florey, and Dr. Sergei Bertensson—Mussorgsky scholar, friend of Kall, and ultimately his executor—had posed on the steps of a Los Angeles building (fig. 4.9; Kall's absence suggests he took the photograph).[181] Dagmar cabled on 10 March from New York that Morros should immediately sign up the composer. Just three days later, Morros invited Stravinsky to dinner. The two men drew up a contract "under which Paramount would supply Stravinsky with several scenarios, from which he would choose one to compose" for a fee of $25,000.[182] In 1937 this was a very large sum; the year before, the commission for his ballet *Jeu de cartes* had been only $5,000. Kall had been perfectly accurate about film scores when he had written to Stravinsky in 1935: "Even if [movie studios] ask you for just one scene (a ballet!), believe me, it pays more than conducting symphonies."[183]

Although Dagmar was acting as Stravinsky's agent, the idea of writing movie scores came from the visit to the MGM film studio with Kall in 1935. The idea was revived on 4 November 1936 when Stravinsky's American admirer, friend, and supporter the author and bookman Merle Armitage urged Stravinsky to consider writing a film with Morros, and probably again in 1937, when Armitage was managing Stravinsky and Dushkin's West Coast appearances.[184] At some point Stravinsky placed this matter in Dagmar's capable hands.

Interviewed in San Francisco, Stravinsky told two music critics about his composing for movies. One reported:

Yes, Igor Stravinsky likes the idea of writing music for the movies. No, if you please—he will NOT write a mere accompaniment score for someone else's story. . . . The famous Russ-Parisian composer has signed no contract. "I have left them my subject, . . . [and] they have given it to a noted writer. If I like what he does with it, I will then develop the story and music into an artistic unity."[185]

The other critic also quoted the composer, who had

been in the film capital for the past two weeks making plans and laying the groundwork for a unique new kind of picture. "I shall not compose music in accompaniment to a photoplay. . . . The story and the setting and all the rest will be written around the music, and the music will be composed in terms of the sound film. Thus the whole production will be conceived as a unit. I am not able at the present time to reveal the theme of the picture but it will not be a Russian folk story." This work will not be undertaken on a regular Hollywood contract. Stravinsky will write and Hollywood will take it or leave it.[186]

On 15 April, Stravinsky attended a Hindemith concert in Carnegie Hall; Hindemith mentions Dushkin with Stravinsky that night[187] but neither Dagmar nor her father, who had conservative musical tastes. Nor did Stravinsky's diagnosis prevent him from smoking while visiting Balanchine's dancers, or from rehearsing the orchestra for the coming Stravinsky Festival, with its world premiere of *Jeu de cartes* choreographed by Balanchine,

STRAVINSKY AT WORK

by FRANCIS STEEGMULLER

In 1967 there was published a volume called *Bravo Stravinsky*, consisting of photographs by Arnold Newman and text by Robert Craft* combined to depict in pictures and words an artist at work. At work the year before, in 1966, when he was eighty-four and happened to be composing, in California, the *Requiem Canticles*, commissioned by Princeton University, and a score for Edward Lear's great epithalamion *The Owl and the Pussycat* as a surprise for his beautiful wife, Vera, who loved the poem. To the sorrow of us all, those proved to be the artist's last works. The year 1966 was the last in which he was really well.

unemployed. *Petrushka* came next. Then, the composition in Russia and Switzerland of *The Rite of Spring*, its turbulent premiere in Paris, and its subsequent triumph would have kept them well occupied during what was left of La Belle Époque. (Indeed, it might be said that *The Rite* precipitated the fall of La Belle Époque.) And through two world wars and interludes of so-called peace, composing at pianos on two continents and directing in auditoriums on six, creating the songs and tollings of *Les Noces* ("The Wedding"), the grandeurs of *Oedipus Rex*, the adventures of *The Rake*, and all the rest, the same artist was continuously at work.

When Stravinsky was in his eighties, there was something uncanny in his superb ineligibility for the labels habitually pasted on eminent men of his span of years and of similarly glorious careers. It would have been a shrill mistake, like the scrape of chalk on a blackboard, to speak of Stravinsky as

that inspiration is less fluent in old age?" he said, "I suppose for you I am in old age. For me, I just happen to be in my eighties." And he said, grinning again, about one of his physical ailments: "I ask my doctor, 'How long does it last?' 'Not long,' he said, 'but all your life.'"

"All your life"! A common phrase—but not when Stravinsky used it.

For those who deal in words, there is a particular joy in the coming-to-life of a common phrase like that—the discovery of new meaning in words dulled by use in combination, their revitalizing into a thing of meaning and pleasure. Stravinsky was a prodigious provider of this kind of joy. Just as in his music he put life into many an unpromising sound, so his example recharged all the old clichés about time: "the fullness of time," "the richness of time," "time stands still," "time marches on," and the rest. And similarly with "all your life"; "*so much* life" was its Stravinskian sense.

So much life and so much time were concentrated in this delightful and formidable Stravinsky. Sitting in the Hollywood house where he lived in 1966, you were, as Robert Craft pointed out, only a few hundred yards from the grotesqueries of Sunset Strip; but the banal sensationalism down the road was colorless compared with the excitement that assailed you if you were of the historically impressionable type and found yourself reflecting—as a start—that your host had been Rimsky-Korsakov's pupil. That he had been Diaghilev's "discovery" ("Take a good look at him. He's a man about to be famous!"), admired by Debussy and Satie. And yet in the 1960s, as Craft put it, younger people were just learning to be his contemporaries. Today, many of his works are still to become familiar to the general public—his *Mavra*, for example, or his Symphony in C. In other words, his music still holds mysteries and reserves, is still "ahead of its time," in fact, beyond time. Cocteau was his librettist in 1925 and Auden in 1948, Picasso his portraitist in 1917 and Giacometti in 1957.

In the charming white-and-green living room of the house in Hollywood, or around the dinner table, reminiscence was far from being the chief climate, though it came forth richly if requested. "Nijinsky was a weak man —as weak as his muscles were strong"; "Yes, of course Nijinsky made love just to the nymph's scarf. What more would Diaghilev have allowed?"; "Cocteau's first libretto for *Oedipus Rex* was full of ideas. The second was still full of ideas. I told him, 'I want not ideas. I want words!'" But soon you found that your host was drawing *you*

—Culver

Stravinsky "a few hundred yards from the grotesqueries of Sunset Strip." Left to right: Boris Morros, Claire Trevor, Robert Florey, Mrs. Samuel Dushkin, Stravinsky, violinist Samuel Dushkin, Akim Tamiroff, and Dr. Serge Betrennsen (1937).

How many active years there had been! Had Messrs. Newman and Craft been photographing and writing more than half a century before 1966, they might have chronicled the same artist composing, in St. Petersburg, on commission from Serge Diaghilev, his first great score—one for a ballet, based on the Russian fable of the Firebird, which took Paris by storm in 1910. From then on, photographer and biographer need never have been

*And a foreword by Francis Steegmuller, of which this article is a variation. (Courtesy of the World Publishing Company.)

a "veteran," or as a "grand old man." Immense as the legend had become, it continued to be constantly replenished from its bubbling source. Stravinsky knew this to be a peculiarity of himself, and his references to the subject were apt to be humorous. "Yes, then I had hairs, now I have no hairs," he said, with a grin, to an interviewer who pointed to the drawing Picasso had made of him in 1917; and indeed the mere absence of "hairs" may be taken as properly symbolic of the irrelevance of aging in the case of Stravinsky. When a reporter who hadn't grasped this asked him, "Do you find

FIGURE 4.9

A page from the *Saturday Review*, May 1971.

and performances of his *Apollon* on the Metropolitan Opera's stage.[188] And on 27 April, Hindemith heard Stravinsky conduct *Apollon* and wrote to his wife: "the music struck me as very corpse-like: this must surely have been because the good Igor is a truly mediocre conductor and cunningly avoids any step in the direction of free and spontaneous music making."[189]

Stravinsky's letter of 13 April to Kall named one of the film projects with Morros as *The Knights of St. David*.[190] Another letter mailed around 19 April to Kall announced the return of tuberculosis and updated him on the status of the movie projects. The composer wrote once again from the Sulgrave Hotel, utilizing stationery purloined from the Hotel Hermoyne in Hollywood (where he is not known to have stayed):

> Morros and I agreed to abandon everything in Hollywood, and to go to New York on the 14th or 15th of April. And when these dates began to approach, Morros began to distance himself and did so to such an extent that I heard nothing more from him. The silly thing is that I took all this seriously and wasted time with people of so little interest to me.[191]

Loath to accept the defeat of his visionary but thoroughly impractical concepts for film music, he told an interviewer in Paris on 19 May: "Music must stop being the accompaniment to film. . . . I've suggested to our Hollywood friends that I provide them with the score for a film in the same way that one gives a ballet score to the scenarist."[192]

Despite Stravinsky's claims that film composers were being "asked merely to fill in empty spaces, a servile task" (Toronto in January) and that he had merely "wasted time" with Morros and Hollywood, the experience clearly rankled. Interviews in San Francisco newspapers during his final transatlantic tour (1939) confirm his continuing sour-grapes attitude: "Two years ago . . . he intended going to Hollywood to write a movie. . . . Hollywood, he [now] says, is interested only in making money and while he likes to make money also, he insists on maintaining artistic values." [193] And "Hollywood offered me lots of money. But it would not guarantee that I could do what I like. I like a lot of money. But I must also do what I like."[194] Yet this did not put an end to his interest in a movie project. Five years later, on 26 September 1942, the day after both Stravinskys dined with Jean Renoir at the Louriés', Vera reported in her diary that "Lourié comes with a scenario."[195]

Ultimately, Morros's disinclination to undertake Stravinsky's utopian cinematic schemes served the composer well. A fellow Russian émigré, Morros was enlisted in 1933 as a reluctant spy for Soviet Russia. Feeling himself threatened in the early 1940s, Morros went to the FBI and became a counterspy, active in Europe until late January 1957. Stravinsky was spy-plagued; his friend Pierre Souvtchinsky is also now said—by Sir Isaiah Berlin among others—to have been a Soviet spy in the 1930s.[196] Had Stravinsky associated with Morros, he might well have found himself also testifying before the House Un-American Activities Committee twenty-years later, the last kind of publicity he would have wanted.

Fourteen months before Hitler invaded Russia, Stravinsky voiced some lofty views when he was interviewed in Chicago:

Stravinsky does not like to be identified as a Russian composer, but his objections are not political, he says. He does not wish to be considered of the Russian school. . . . "I am international," says Stravinsky. "I was born in Russia, but I belong to the country of music."[197]

After the invasion of Russia in June of 1941 and during the remainder of World War II, it was quite another matter. As Craft exclaimed, "He was the proudest Russian in Hollywood." Composer Nabokov later described the majority of Americans at this period, ignorant of or forgetting Stalin's atrocities, as basking "in a state of Sovietophilic euphoria."[198]

Despite Hindemith's rather sour opinion in 1937 of *Apollon,* Stravinsky enjoyed a major success with it, with his American premiere of *Le Baiser de la fée,* and with his world premiere of *Jeu de cartes,* all three choreographed by George Balanchine and staged by the American Ballet, 27 and 28 April 1937, at the Metropolitan Opera House. Much of this success proceeded from his collaboration with Balanchine, for whom Stravinsky expressed deep admiration.[199] A great deal of publicity attended these performances, including some artfully-posed photographs by the Ermates-Maharadze firm that depicted Stravinsky, Balanchine, Edward Warburg, and five members of the troupe playing cards.[200] Fascinating information came to light about Stravinsky composing and adding new music on the spot for *Jeu de cartes* during its New York rehearsals.[201] The orchestra for these three ballets was not the Met's own; it was drawn from members of the New York Philharmonic, "who did a splendid job under Stravinsky's baton and as the hero of the evening, he was recalled to the stage time and again."[202] Leo Smit notes: "Years later I learned that Stravinsky had had an attack of stomach cramps the afternoon of the premiere. Luckily . . . his pain disappeared and he conducted perfectly."[203] Stravinsky's reward for this triumph, his tours, and his occasional radio broadcasts[204] was to be featured on the cover of *Musical America* for 10 May 1937.

Nonetheless, near the end of their 1937 tour, when by chance Stravinsky and Dushkin ran into a fellow Russian exile, Nicolas Nabokov, in a New York milk-bar, a weary Stravinsky said that he was "soon ready to go home ('thank God!')." He was not so weary, however, that it prevented him from inviting Nabokov to the Dushkins' residence for a rehearsal of the *Duo concertant.* This work "amazed" Nabokov, owing to Stravinsky's "constancy of imaginative power" and his Russianness "under whatever formal or stylistic garb he chose to disguise it."[205]

Among the observers at the ballet performances were not only Nabokov but Stravinsky's Los Angeles *Petrushka* choreographer, Theodore Kosloff. Stravinsky expressed regret to Kall: "It's a shame that I will see Kosloff instead of you."[206] Nevertheless, before long he was attempting, through Kall, to arrange performances with Kosloff's ballet company during his next US tour. Six days before he sailed back to France, his Easter letter to Kall of 2 May discloses that "my performances went very well (Kosloff will tell you—ask him), but despite all this I feel great irritability and dissatisfaction that I attribute partly to the ludicrous fiasco of all my plans for the next year."[207] The "fiasco" was a new transatlantic tour: Stravinsky and Kosloff corresponded during all the ensuing summer. Near the close of 1937, the composer wrote Kall: "On August 19 I replied to F[eodor] Kosloff's letter of 28 July and so far have not received any answer."[208] At least two now lost letters concerned future ballet performances with Stravinsky conducting.

Sailing 4 May 1937 on the SS *Paris* from New York to Le Havre (where it arrived on 11 May), Stravinsky was photographed shipboard with nine others enjoying themselves in first class: the Dushkins, the Koussevitzkys, Mrs. Koussevitzky's niece, a Mrs. Calling, the Arthur Rodzinskis, and the ship's purser. In August of 1937 *Musical America* printed the photograph, named the ship, and identified all the subjects under a jolly heading: "Conductors Enjoy Life Aboard Ship."[209] Still another memorable and often-reproduced photograph, taken topside on the same voyage, depicts Stravinsky and Nadia Boulanger, arm in arm. He holds a book; she clutches what appears to be a menu from the vessel's restaurant. He was later to inscribe this image for her in Russian: "To a dear friend Nadia Boulanger from Igor Stravinsky who is devoted to her / 1937."[210] He had good reason for such devotion: during the voyage, she told him that her visit the month before to Mr. and Mrs. Robert Woods Bliss in Washington, DC, had secured a $2,500 commission for what would become his *Dumbarton Oaks Concerto* (1937–38).[211]

Barely arrived back in Paris, he wrote Dagmar on 17 May, asking her to perform an errand in New York.[212] She was to have a prescription filled for him at a Madison Avenue pharmacy. His letter perhaps hints at their ongoing relationship: Dagmar is not to have the medication sent to his home address.

Late in the summer of 1937, Kavenoki made some proposals that Stravinsky write a ballet based on American folklore, dealing with themes in José Clemente Orosco's great mural, *The Epic of American Civilization*, painted 1932–34 in the Dartmouth College Library.[213] The substantial commission for *Dumbarton Oaks*, the prestige of its donors, and Stravinsky's declining interest in folklore probably explain his reason for not entertaining Kavenoki's proposal, despite their growing friendship.

STRAVINSKY AS CONDUCTOR

Hindemith had justified his baleful opinion in New York about Stravinsky's *Apollon* "because the good Igor is a truly mediocre conductor and cunningly avoids any step in the direction of free and spontaneous music making." Nevertheless, Stravinsky's reputation as a conductor continued to improve during the fourth tour, even if this report of a rehearsal still posits a rather primitive approach. Early that year, a music critic, privileged to attend both Stravinsky rehearsals on 4 and 5 January with the Toronto Symphony Orchestra, wrote of his impressions:

> The [orchestra] men say he is really a wonderful master of simplicity in technique at rehearsal. When I saw him for half an hour on Monday—for he came a day early to be sure of his job—his coat was off; in a grey guernsey he was smacking out the tempo on his score with the baton. [Whereas, at the concert:] he got his tremendously authentic effects with

masterly serenity. . . . At the second rehearsal he even changed many of the expression marks in the printed score [i.e., orchestra parts]. . . . A revelation of what a good orchestra can do on short notice under a genius conductor.[214]

By far the most precise and astute evaluation during this tour came from another distinguished composer, Elliott Carter. Reviewing the mid-January concerts with Beveridge Webster and the New York Philharmonic in Mozart's G-major Piano Concerto, later that spring Carter analyzed the "non-expressive" playing by the orchestra. Here he undoubtedly alludes to Stravinsky's notorious disdain for "expression." Carter wrote:

Actually, Stravinsky did a great deal of interpretation. . . . Rather than expressive playing and "golden sonorities," his method was to give strong upbeats, treat repeated accompaniment notes in heavy staccato, keep each part clear of the others, lend rhythmic independence to the bass, and play melodies in an even way over the strong unfluctuating rhythm so that tension, instead of dissipating itself at each rise and fall, piles up to burst out at the accents.[215]

This is as excellent an exposition as can be found of the manner in which Stravinsky conducted his own scores and avoided "expressive" playing.

One reviewer, identified only as "Q," wrote in a widely read national music journal:

As conductor, Stravinsky retains the attributes known in former years: the ability to secure from his players the manifestation of his wishes; a strong decisive beat; rhythmic security; an utter lack of mannerism; and an economy of gesture. . . . The performance [of *Petrushka*] was an astonishingly exciting one in view of Stravinsky's avowed dislike of "making effects" in conducting.[216]

Curiously enough, even in the face of such intelligent and perceptive evaluations as these, one anonymous New York writer felt a need to leap to Stravinsky's defense. After the composer's performances the following week on 21–22 January 1937 with the New York Philharmonic of *The Rite of Spring*, the 1919 *Firebird Suite*, and Tchaikovsky's Third Symphony, he wrote:

Stravinsky is an excellent conductor. The reviewer of this paper was the only New York publication to say so after the opening concerts directed by the composer last week. Other commentators appeared to accept the long-standing legend that Stravinsky is not adept with the baton. That opinion might have been justified in 1925 when he made his previous New York appearances at the head of the Philharmonic, but he has had wide experience since then, and now masters the craft completely. What misleads some of the listeners is that Stravinsky is a quiet figure on the platform, employs no violent gestures or theatrical posings, and having established his interpretations thoroughly at rehearsals, permits the music to speak for itself at the public concerts.[217]

Fortunately, composer Roger Sessions recalled how Stravinsky conducted Tchaikovsky's Pathétique with the Cleveland Orchestra at Princeton on 18 February: "Always on the toes, the upbeat, the accentuation, the great concern for phrasing, for attack, for release and very little concern about enormous effects of crescendo, etc." Sessions is said to have followed Stravinsky to various US cities in 1935 and 1937, partly to learn how Tchaikovsky's orchestral works should be played.[218]

The reader might also turn to the compelling series of photographs of Stravinsky taken in 1937 by Eric Schaal in New York. They aid substantially in conjuring up his rehearsal methods.[219]

And yet, strident voices lingered in the provinces. Gerald Strang's remark about "routine playing" by the Los Angeles Philharmonic has been quoted above. Another Los Angeles critic utterly failed to comprehend Stravinsky's aims: "He proved himself to be an uninteresting conductor, able enough to accompany the [staged] ballet [Petrushka], but not sufficiently capable to extract tonal balance or shading from the orchestra [in the Divertimento and Firebird]."[220]

Aside from the undoubtedly weaker orchestra Stravinsky had in Los Angeles (despite improvements effected through Klemperer's tenure), all such details would have been lost in the vastness and horrible acoustics of the Shrine Auditorium.

DAGMAR AND UNREALIZED TOURS

Seeing off her client-friends Josef Hofmann and wife aboard the SS *Britannic* on 14 April 1938 in New York, Dagmar managed to "miss" the departure announcement and disembarked at Southampton on 23 April with only her purse (and no passport).[221] According to her, Stravinsky then cabled from Paris: "Please come and see the Stravinskys," purportedly following this up with a phone call. Whether or not he did so, by 6 May she arrived in Paris where she installed herself in the Edouard VII. That day he wrote her a note in barely legible mixture of languages:

> Mein lieber Freund, Dagmar, unserer noch nicht ganz gesund. Hoffe Montag Sie zu sehen bei mir oder bei Ihren—cela depend de mon état. Ich bin von dieser dummer Grippe so schwach. Also bis Montag. (My dear friend, Dagmar, our [family is] not yet in full health. I hope to see you on Monday here or at your place—that depends on my condition. I am so weak from this stupid flu. So, until Monday.)

In the upper margin he complained about his poor treatment regarding business matters compared to Toscanini and Bruno Walter "and company."[222] Though (supposedly) invited to meet Stravinsky's wife, Dagmar declined. She did accept an invitation from a mutual woman friend to meet Vera Soudeikina for lunch, but—according to Dagmar herself—reneged the next day.[223]

The unreliability and sheer selectivity of Dagmar's memoir is again demonstrated by the facts. According to Vera's diary, Dagmar *did* meet her in Paris on *two* occasions: 21 and 23 May, 1938.[224] Meanwhile, Stravinsky had entrained on 16 May with Soulima for Brussels, where they concertized on the nineteenth. The day they departed, Dagmar wrote Stravinsky a moving letter about their relationship.[225]

None of the tours Stravinsky had contemplated outside Europe for 1938 materialized. One projected for January through March in the United States was discussed late in 1937 by correspondence with Copley in New York and would have included only symphonic engagements and excluded Dushkin.[226] Like his predecessor, Merovitch, in 1935, Copley jumped the gun by placing a full-page advertisement on the back cover of *Musical America*. It read "Preliminary List of Artists, Season 1938–1939 / Igor Stravinsky / Composer-Conductor / January to April 1939."[227] Stravinsky's correspondence reveals his ambivalence: "Copley even attempted to reschedule Stravinsky's concerts in 1938 to allow 'two or three weeks in California to keep in touch with the picture people.' "[228] This tour was to have been separated by some period of time from another, with son Soulima, to Australia. Planned by his London agent Wilfrid van Wyck, it would have followed the projected 1939 US tour.[229]

The death of Stravinsky's daughter Lyudmila on 30 November 1938, his wife's on 2 March 1939—both tuberculosis victims—his mother's on 7 June 1939, and a major recurrence of his own tuberculosis thwarted all such plans.[230] Unavoidable as these cancellations were, they had a deleterious effect on bookings for his final transatlantic tour.

5

TOUR V (OCTOBER 1939–LATE MAY 1940)

CONCERT APPEARANCES

28 November: Providence, Boston Symphony

1, 2 December: Boston Symphony

15, 16 December: San Francisco Orchestra

3, 4, 7 January 1940: New York Philharmonic

26, 28 January: Pittsburgh Symphony

22, 23, 27 February: Chicago Symphony

6 March: Boston, Women's Republican Club: Adele Marcus plus BSO Players

8 March: Cambridge: Marcus and BSO Chamber Players (recorded)

14 March: New York Town Hall, a matinee with Marcus and chamber works

17 March: Exeter with Marcus

28 March: Cambridge, Boston Symphony

29, 30 March: Boston Symphony

4 April: New York Philharmonic (recording)

5, 6, 7 April: New York Philharmonic

Quite unexpectedly, the last transatlantic tour was one-way, from Europe to North America. Fully confident of returning in May of 1940 to France,[1] Stravinsky planned to sail for home after the end of his appointment as the Charles Eliot Norton Lecturer at Harvard, but war intervened. As a result, Stravinsky remained in the United States, married again, and eventually became an American citizen.

On 27 March 1939 Professor Edward Waldo Forbes of Harvard's Fogg Museum and chair of the Norton Lectureship in Poetry, invited Stravinsky to fill the post for the academic year 1939–40,[2] and Stravinsky accepted on 11 April. Ten days later, he invited Kall to live with him, help out at Cambridge (serving as translator when needed), and assist with arrangements for concerts. On 5 June Stravinsky assured his old friend that "you will have your own cigar and beer and I will pay for your apartment in Los Angeles (of course)," and Kall quickly agreed to these arrangements.[3]

The terms of the Norton lectureship specified eight public lectures. In addition, Stravinsky was to teach composition students enrolled in the university's Music Depart-

THE POETRY OF MUSIC. Igor Stravinsky, who came to this country to accept a year's appointment as Professor of Poetry at Harvard, at work on his fourth symphony in Cambridge.

FIGURE 5.1
Stravinsky composing at Harvard, *New York Times,* 29 Oct. 1939.

ment. Harvard allowed him to concertize during the interstices of its academic terms. By 30 June, with Dagmar Godowsky's assistance (according to her), he had negotiated the public lectures down to six because of his composing commitments—"je puisse travailler la musique"—as he put it to Forbes.[4]

Contemporary accounts of Stravinsky's first Norton lecture the ensuing 18 October are often cited.[5] In a 1971 memoir, "My Saint Stravinsky," the Russian American émigré composer Vladimir Ussachevsky (who quickly bonded with Kall) recalled the lectures as having "the ceremonial aspect of the Russian Court. . . . Stravinsky wore tails. There were embraces, much bowing: suddenly the drafty academic hall was hushed and Stravinsky, the great cosmopolitan, was reading, somewhat earnestly, in French: excellent and unmistakably Russian."[6] Stravinsky told a different story in 1940, when he and Nabokov met on 31 December in New York: he had been asked to give ten lectures, but in the end offered five lectures for the $10,000 honorarium and one extra lecture as a kind of "encore."[7]

Whatever the truth of this latter tale, paramount among his commitments was the completion of his Symphony in C. A photograph of him working on it in October of 1939 at Harvard appeared late that month (fig. 5.1).[8] It depicts him at the keyboard with a piano draft for its third movement (October 1939–28 April 1940). This movement's G-major sections are clearly indicated by the F-sharps of the key signature on the partly-opened verso at the left side of the photograph. Read even from such a wretched image, all five

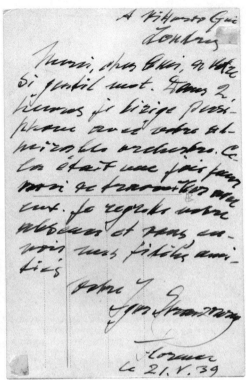

FIGURE 5.2
Stravinsky to Vittorio Gui (postcard front and back), 1939. UBC Stravinsky Collection, no. 63.

double staves on the partly opened verso (though in halved note values) appear to include materials he later assigned to wind instruments, though in doubled note values (as in the published score at reh. 103).

Beginning in mid-March 1939, and off and on during substantial portions of April, May, June, July, and August, Stravinsky had been an out-patient in a tuberculosis sanatorium at Sancellemoz.[9] Nineteen photographs of him, taken there by Roland-Manuel, were auctioned in March 2000, three of them still accessible.[10] A letter of 10 May 1939 describes the sanatorium and his rapidly improving condition in it.[11] Late in April, Stravinsky wrote Kall that his doctors advised his health was sufficiently recovered that he could conduct concerts in Milan and Florence and safely travel to the United States at the close of September.[12]

Indeed, he was well enough to conduct *Perséphone* on 21 May (with Victoria Ocampo as diseuse) at the Maggio Musicale in Florence, as this postcard (fig. 5.2)[13] to its regular conductor, Vittorio Gui, then in London, attests. Yet, thirty years later in Los Angeles and New York a diagnosis of tuberculosis was confirmed and listed on his death certificate.[14]

During those many months—more in than out of Sancellemoz—he collaborated with Roland-Manuel and Souvtchinsky in preparing his Norton lectures for Harvard. He had known Roland-Manuel in Paris since at least 1920, Souvtchinsky in Berlin since 1922.[15] Souvtchinsky played a much greater role in the Norton lectures than previously thought: essentially, he conceived the ideas, Stravinsky assimilated and developed them, and Roland-Manuel put them in order, amplifying and completing them through discussions with the composer.[16]

In 1984 a lengthy essay about this collaboration cited an important letter from Sancellemoz to Roland-Manuel of 24 June 1939 (fig. 5.3). Excerpted and published in a somewhat flawed translation from the French[17] before it arrived in my hands in 1998, the letter (now at UBC) concerns Stravinsky's lectures and the difficulties he was to experience in travel arrangements and preparations:

Mr. Roland-Manuel
42 rue de Bourgogne (and thus I cabled you [there] and not [to] 44)
Paris

Thanks for your letter, my dear Roland.

I have before me the letter from Victoria Ocampo of 31 May which speaks of Mr. [Jean] Marx. When I saw her two weeks ago in Paris, she did not mention him to me, and I did not think to ask her, being still too much affected by my recent sorrow. This is what she wrote me: "This note is to tell you that I had Marx to lunch today and that I spoke to him about your business. It's all set. You need only tell him when you will leave and give him the details yourself." What does the expression "It's all set" mean? What has been arranged? Knowing that Victoria was going to see Mr. Marx in Paris, I asked her in Florence [c. 21 May] to speak to him about my next trip to America and to see if it was possible for him *to help me with it* (in the sense of an official mission: diplomatic visas, introductions at frontiers; in sum, what was done, for example, for Nadia Boulanger, Alfred Cortot, etc.). Is free round trip to America what she means by her expression "It's all set"? This is what I want you to clarify in your conversation with the above-named Mr. Marx. You have guessed that it bothers me to write him and you are really kind to offer your intervention. I accept it gratefully. I know Mr. Marx, he is a combination of Jean Zay and [Jacques] Larmanjat [i.e., socialists], he is quite nice, very taken with his position (a legacy from the Popular Front, I think), and in any case from [Léon] Blum; he's not exactly pre-eminent. If I do have to write him a letter, you would be a love to send me a sample. What is his first name? I'm rather in a hurry to settle all this because I must respond to the [Compagnie] Transatlantique, whose letter of the fourteenth of this month you bring to my attention.

From what you write me about the typescript [for the Norton lectures] in five copies and the English translation of the summaries, I agree to the sum of about 500 francs.

I impatiently await the sixth lecture. When shall I have it? Soon? And Claude's [Roland-Manuel Levy's son's] graduation? No mention in your letter? Why?

Monsieur Roland Manuel

42 rue de Bourgogne

P A R I S VII

Mr.Roland Manuel
42 rue de Bourgogne(et c'est ainsi que je vous cablé et non 44)
P a r i s

Merci de votre lettre,mon cher Roland.

Je retrouve la lettre de Victoria Ocampo du 3I mai où elle
me parle de Mr.Marx. Lorsque je l'ai vu,il y a deux semaines à Paris,elle ne m'en a pas parlé et moi je n'ai pas pensé de la questio-
nner là-dessus étant encore trop sous le coup de mon recent deuil.
Voici ce qu'elle m'écrivait:"Ce mot pour vous dire que j'ai eu Marx
à déjeuner aujourd'hui et que je lui ai parlé de votre affaire.C'
est arrangé. Il faut seulement que vous lui disiez quand vous partez
et lui donniez vous même les détails". Que veut dire la phrase "C'est
arrangé"? Qu'est ce qui est arrangé? Sachant que Victoria va voir Mr
Marx à Paris je l'avais demandé à Florence de lui parler(à Mr Marx)de
mon prochain voyage en Amérique et de voir avec lui si cela était possible de me le faciliter(dans le sens d'une mission officielle:visas
diplomatiques,recommandations aux frontières;bref,ce que l'on fait pour
p.ex.Nadia Boulanger,Alfred Cortot etc.). Est-ce le passage gratuit
aller-retour en Amérique qu'elle entend dans la phrase "c'est arrangé"?
C'est ce que je vous demanderai d'éclaircir dans votre conversation avec
le nommé Mr.Marx. Vous avez deviné,cela m'ennui de lui écrire et vous
êtes vraiment gentil de me proposer votre médiation, je l'accepte avec
reconnaissance. Je le connais Mr.Marx,c'est un mélange de Jean Zay et de
Larmanjat,il est plustôt gentil,très impressionné de ma situation(hérita-
ge du front populaire,je crois,de Blum en tout cas),ce n'est pas une
excellence. S'il faut que je lui écrive une lettre vous serez un amour
de m'envoyer un échantillon. Quel est son prénom? Je suis un peu pressé
de mettre tout cela au clair puisque je dois répondre à la Transatlantique dont vous me fâite connaître la lettre du I4 cr.

Pour ce que vous m'écrivez au sujet de la dactylographie en cinq
exemplaires et la traduction anglaise des résumés - d'accord pour la som-
me d'environ 500 fr.

Attends avec impatience la 6-ème leçon. Quand l'aurai-je? Bientôt?

Et le bachot de Claud? Aucune trace dans votre lettre? Pourquoi?

Je m'em.... ici sans vous et ne prends plus d'Arquebuse à la ti-
sane de mente-tilleul.

Je vous ambrasse bien affectueusement. Mes respectueuses amitiés
à votre femme,je vous prie.

Sancellemoz
le 24 juin /39

I'm bored here without you and no longer take Arquebusse with linden-mint tea. Yours very affectionately. My kindest regards to your wife, please.

[signed] Your Stravinsky.

Sancellemoz

24 June / 39.

Securing concert dates in the United States from such an isolated place as Sancellemoz proved a real challenge. To that end, while recuperating at the sanatorium, he certainly enlisted Kall and Dagmar, even though at one point near the end of June 1939 he had to curb her enthusiasm with a telegram: "Regrette votre venue Europe impossible. Strawinsky."[18]

PLANNING THE TOUR

Much information is available about arrangements for this final prewar transatlantic tour, about Stravinsky's increasing disillusionment with one of his US concert managers, about his hardening attitude against performing his own solo and concerted piano music in public, and about his willingness to have Kall lecture about him. At least thirty letters in Russian, French, and English among Stravinsky, Kall, Kosloff, Monteux, Vera, Dagmar, Charles N. Drake (his agent after Copley's death on 28 February 1939), and Paul H. Stoes (his concert manager from 1940) are extant.[19] A few selections from them, supplementing information already at hand from other authorities, will illustrate the above points concerning repertoire, piano playing, and difficulties with Drake and occasionally with Kall. Although not all of this correspondence survives, what remains suffices to reconstruct a coherent account of four months of negotiations. In 1939, letters between France and Los Angeles took about a week in either direction. Not all of them reached their respective recipients in the order they were mailed.

During the spring and summer months of 1939, Stravinsky was adamant that he and Theodore Kosloff should repeat their 1937 Los Angeles staging of *Petrushka* when Stravinsky would be conducting that December in San Francisco. He knew that the 1937 ballet production had been artistically successful and had returned a quite unexpected profit to Merle Armitage.[20]

20 May 1939 Stravinsky to Kall, Russian.[21] Learning from Kall that Stravinsky would be coming to the United States for the Norton lectures, Theodore Kosloff wrote to the composer in Paris. He proposed to stage both *Jeu de cartes* and his 1937 version of *Petrushka,* thus making a double bill for Los Angeles in August or September. Stravinsky had initially nixed Kosloff's request on 28 July 1937 to rechoreograph *Jeu de cartes* on the

---

FIGURE 5.3

Stravinsky to Roland-Manuel, 1939 (cover and letter). UBC Stravinsky Collection, no. 64.

grounds that the American Ballet in New York had exclusivity with George Balanchine's choreography. These rights expired on 1 January 1938.[22]

5 June   Stravinsky to Kall, Russian.[23] Stravinsky wrote Kall, surprised that Kosloff wanted to perform in Los Angeles before Stravinsky could arrive in California. He told Kall to instruct Kosloff to use Stravinsky's own 1938 Telefunken recording of *Jeu de cartes* so as to establish proper tempos, just as he had instructed Kosloff in 1936 (again through Kall) to use his 1928 *Petrushka* recording (Columbia).[24] Stravinsky was annoyed about what he called "such an attitude on Kosloff's part," but he excused him on grounds that "perhaps he simply did not think of inviting me [to conduct]." In view of his denying Kosloff's 1937 request, Stravinsky might well have worried about the choreographer's "attitude." With some irony, he instructed Kall to suggest to Kosloff "this original and practical idea," of inviting Stravinsky to conduct his own score.

15 June   Kall to Stravinsky, Russian.[25] Kall replied that he had delayed answering Stravinsky's letter (now lost) of the previous day until he had a chance to talk with Kosloff. Teasingly, Kall chastised the composer for believing that he, Kall, would not already have thought about Stravinsky's "clever idea." Indeed, Kosloff (through Kall) had now invited Stravinsky to conduct ballet performances in Hollywood on 12 and 15 September. But this was still prior to the composer's now-planned arrival in the United States.

27 June   Stravinsky, French.[26] Stravinsky told Kall that a week earlier he had written Charles N. Drake, the new manager of Copley Concert Management.[27] "Is it really impossible to convince Kosloff to reschedule his performances to the time when I should be in California, as I hope, in January?" He warns Kall that in contacts with Drake: "Restrain yourself from informing him about our projects and in telling him that you will be with me [in Cambridge] so as to share my loneliness, etc." As for Drake, "He seems to be a nice man."

7 July   Moses Smith to Stravinsky, English.[28] At Dagmar's suggestion, Moses Smith of Columbia Records writes Stravinsky about recording (probably the *Rite of Spring* and *Petrushka*, in April of 1940).

11 July   Stravinsky to Kall, French.[29] Stravinsky has just received a delayed letter of 5 June from Kosloff, who had expressed his joy at seeing Stravinsky soon in America, although Kosloff avoids any of what he deems "useless" specifics in respect to possible dates for engagements.

11 July   Stravinsky to Kall (Russian?).[30] Stravinsky hopes that Steinway would provide Kall with a free piano in Boston, as it does for Dagmar, who may, however, be lying to Stravinsky "as she does about everything, this dear Dagmar."

13 July Kall to Stravinsky (Russian?).[31] Kall writes that Kosloff has agreed to reschedule his ballet performances for December of 1939.

14 July Drake to Kall, English.[32] Drake from Copley Concert Management advises Kall in Los Angeles that the agency is trying to arrange performances by the Kosloff Ballet on 8 and 9 December in Los Angeles or Hollywood. The fee for Stravinsky would be "at least [$]2500 for two evenings and a matinee." The Los Angeles Philharmonic is not interested in booking Stravinsky. Drake is arranging for him to conduct in December at San Francisco and in January at Pittsburgh. Chicago is already booked, as is the Boston Symphony Orchestra for the last week of March.

18 July Stravinsky to Kall, French.[33] At Aix-Les-Bains Stravinsky has visited Koussevitzky, who told him "about probable difficulties [at Cambridge] in finding a reliable maid and about the exceptionally high cost of labor in this charming country. . . . Have you [Kall] seen Kosloff and succeeded in convincing him to reschedule his performances to the ensuing winter (December–January, when I shall be free)?"

24 July Stravinsky to Kall, French.[34] Responding to Kall's letter of 13 July, Stravinsky congratulates him for arranging the Kosloff matter. Kall should conclude the Kosloff business for $3,000 for three performances, or $2,000 for two, because Drake, "who wants to seem courteous, from everything that I have been able to discern up to the present, is nevertheless a noodle [*un nouille*]." Stravinsky will need to spend at least a day upon arrival in New York before leaving for Cambridge because Dagmar Godowsky has arranged that he talk to Moses Smith of Columbia Records. Kall should also know that, except for Chicago, where Drake proposes that Stravinsky conduct its Symphony Orchestra with just one rehearsal, Stravinsky knows of no other engagements and "it is already the end of July! How can one deal with such a concert agent?"

30 July Kall to Stravinsky, Russian.[35] In a now-lost letter to Stravinsky, Kall had worried that appearances in California by the Monte Carlo Ballet Company might coincide with the proposed Kosloff project. This also bothers Stravinsky. He now asks Kall if he should propose that Kosloff postpone his ballet appearances until December or January, when the Kosloff company "*should come there* [to Los Angeles] *especially* [his emphases]. This is [now] the only thing left, [if I don't] want to lose this profitable engagement, only if the latter is not spoiled by Drake, about whom I have written to you with such high regard in my last letter of 24 July 1939."

8 August Stravinsky to Kall, French.[36] Replying to Kall's letter of 2 August, Stravinsky refers to a delayed Kall letter of 13 July in which he told Stravinsky that Kosloff had consented to reschedule his ballet performances to December of 1939, Drake having proposed 8 and 9 December to Kosloff for three appearances. Stravinsky quotes a letter from

Drake: "I have written him [Kosloff] asking a fee of $2500 for the three programs; he [Kosloff] was willing to pay $2000 for two programs if you [Stravinsky] came in September." Stravinsky then even goes on to badger poor Kall, "Why didn't you propose $3000?"

21 August   Stravinsky to Kall, French.[37] He asks Kall to find out from Monteux in San Francisco if last year's program remains the same; if so, Stravinsky will need to bring the individual parts to Tchaikovsky's Symphony No. 2 in C minor *(The Little Russian)* with him. In addition, Kall should tell Drake to take precautions to ensure that Kosloff really makes payments. Drake has established with Kosloff that Stravinsky's fee would be $2,500 for the three performances. Through Dagmar Stravinsky has just learned that there will be no bookings at Cleveland this season, and Drake has told him that Pittsburgh is not yet assured but that Drake has hopes (in fact Stravinsky conducted there late in January of 1940). Stravinsky closes with a droll "C'est gai!" ("This is just delightful!")

On 3 September 1939,[38] a Los Angeles newspaper columnist, apprised of Stravinsky's future conducting engagements in Boston, Chicago, and San Francisco, reported (in English): "it is proposed to bring him [Stravinsky] to Los Angeles to direct his ballets, *Jeu de cartes* and *Petrouschka*. Why not organize a ballet company under the famous choreographer, Adolph Bolm, and present these ballets in full?" Sadly enough, few of these wishes were realized. Although the composer had reservations about Bolm as a choreographer,[39] he and Stravinsky did collaborate on the 1919 *Firebird Suite* at the Hollywood Bowl in August of 1940 and again on *Petrushka* in 1943 in California and New York.

Circa 8 October 1939   Kall to Kosloff, Russian.[40] Still hoping for Stravinsky's engagements with the Kosloff ballet, Kall, then ill with a heavy cold and dwelling for a week in New York with the equally ill composer, drafted a letter (perhaps never sent) to inform Kosloff and to make a request of him:

> [Harvard] gives I[gor] F[edorovich] two months' vacation (December and January). During this period he will conduct in San Francisco on December 11–15, probably in St. Louis at the end of December, and [for] Columbia [Records] in New York in the second half of January and in Pittsburgh in the last week of January. Then we will return to Cambridge where we remain, February through April. I have communicated to I. F. the matter of our conversation about your intention to stage *Jeu de cartes* and *Petrushka* under his supervision. . . . This is very important for the final planning of his concert schedule. Therefore, we kindly ask you to reply immediately by Air Mail to Mr. I. Stravinsky (or to me), c/o Prof. E. Forbes, Cambridge, Massachusetts. I. F. sends you his warmest regards and trusts that you would not keep us waiting long for your response.

These elaborate proposals and tedious negotiations with Kosloff came to naught. Stravinsky grew annoyed with Drake as early as 30 July; perceiving that Drake was dragging his feet in negotiations, he held Drake responsible for the challenge posed by the arrival of the Monte Carlo Ballet in New York. Moreover, until late November Drake kept Stravinsky in the dark about some of the repertoire for San Francisco and rehearsal dates (see the composer's letter of 17 November 1939 to Monteux, below).

As easy as it is to blame Drake, we must sympathize with him as a businessman; he had written to Kall the previous 14 July: "Frankly, the cancellation [by Stravinsky] of last year's visit made all the orchestra managers quite hesitant about committing themselves to another possible cancellation or postponement."[41] Moreover, as the Stravinsky-Kall letters demonstrate, both men were bypassing the Copley Agency in order to avoid paying commissions. Sooner or later, such maneuvers must have come to Drake's attention and may explain his offhand attention to Stravinsky's interests.

An even more blatant example of bypassing the Copley Agency occurred in August. Kall had proposed a concert in Tucson; Stravinsky wrote to him about it twice from the Sancellemoz sanatorium. Kall's first letter, dated 2 August, has been lost, but on 8 August Stravinsky replied in French:

> I would like to accept the proposal [except that] I could not give them a piano recital (or concert), not having sufficient pianistic repertoire for that. (The Sonata and the Serenade are too austere for the public and not long enough, and fundamentally that is all that I have—let us not consider the *Piano Rag Music* which does not go with those two pieces.) I propose this: find me a good young pianist who could learn the first piano part of my Concerto for Two Solo Pianos (I prefer to play second piano, the two parts being of equal importance) and we could play for them in [Tucson] . . . [and] before its performance I would deliver a little lecture that would last about ten minutes. If this idea intrigues you, it could be exploited by finding other places to perform. Only I don't want this to go through the R. Copley firm since it would be unnecessarily dunned for commission. I propose the following: the 50 dollars for this commission thus spared, I would gladly give it to the young pianist; and your friend, the lady [in charge] from Tucson, could perhaps yet add a small sum for the pianist.[42]

After Kall's response on 16 September, Stravinsky replied in French on the twenty-third, probably from Bordeaux:

> You write me that the public prefers to hear the composer, not the pianist. My pianistic ability was always so fully professional that I would never want to make a spectacle of myself. Let others who do not possess the same performing gift (pianist or orchestral conductor) content themselves in displaying their own selves. As for me, I find this too stupid; I have never had any taste for that. With Dushkin, our programs were tailored to works for piano and violin and nothing was for solo piano. That is why I propose my Concerto for Two Solo Pianos. I am astonished that you don't know this concerto. $500 is the least I could accept for such an appearance. It could be very profitable if you could arrange similar appearances in San Diego and San Francisco during the California tour.[43]

In a lost letter to Stravinsky (probably sent the previous May), Kall must have indicated his own wish to lecture. Stravinsky replied in Russian on 5 June: "About your desire to give lectures in Boston, it will be possible to talk that over on the spot."[44] Either Stravinsky or Kall then communicated this desire to Drake. On 14 July Drake wrote Kall: "The lecture field is pretty well filled." Still, he requested Kall send him any "circulars" he might have and that Drake would try with "various heads of music departments."[45] Whether Drake succeeded in placing a lecture remains unknown, but Stravinsky did more than keep his word for his old friend. On 21 November 1939 he wrote in fluent English—surely with Kall's help—from Gerry's Landing in Cambridge to Mrs. Kathleen O'Donnell Hoover, Metropolitan Opera Guild, who had requested a lecture from Stravinsky: "I always recommend my friend, Dr. Alexis Kall, who is a professional lecturer and lives with me. He could give you a fine talk on any subject connected with Russian music, on Russian opera or ballet, or about myself: 'Igor Stravinsky. The Man, The Composer.'"[46] Kall did, in fact, lecture the ensuing March, though neither in New York nor in Boston proper.

SETTLING IN CAMBRIDGE

Sailing on 25 September 1939 from Bordeaux on the SS *Manhattan*, Stravinsky arrived on 30 September in New York. Kall and Dagmar met him dockside. Recovering from severe colds, both men hunkered down for a week in New York's Hotel Sulgrave on East Sixty-Seventh Street.[47]

After the 28 February death of Richard Copley (Stravinsky's former agent and her boss), Dagmar worked directly for Stravinsky and continued as his booking agent in New York well into 1940. Probably before leaving New York on 10 October 1939 with Kall for his first Norton lecture in Cambridge on 18 October, Stravinsky informed Dagmar about his plan to marry Vera Soudeikina as soon as she would arrive in the United States. This plan was fraught with difficulties owing not only to Vera's marital history cited above but also to her status as a stateless person.[48] Dagmar subsequently complained, "He was my great love. He was going to marry me. Then he got well and he married that other woman."[49] Craft believed that after 1 November Stravinsky had spent a few days at her New York hotel.[50]

Apparently without involving Dagmar, in a letter to Kall on 20 November 1939, Claire R. Reis, executive chair (1923–48) of the League of Composers, requested negotiations with Stravinsky to conduct the *Dumbarton Oaks Concerto* "gratis" in New York.[51] Notwithstanding the concert and generous reception that the League of Composers had tendered him at the outset of his second US tour, and despite Reis's notable services to contemporary American music,[52] a request to conduct "gratis" was, needless to say, predictably doomed.

Not long before, in late October, Dagmar had driven to Boston to bring Stravinsky some wine: although fine vintages were readily available in Massachusetts after the repeal in 1929 of the Eighteenth Amendment,[53] they were apparently not normally consumed chez Forbes at Gerry's Landing. She certainly dined with him, and two sources suggest they tried unsuccessfully to sleep together in Boston.[54] Then, at dinner with her in Boston on 4 November, Kall introduced Adele Marcus to Stravinsky. Kall's former piano student,[55] Marcus was exactly that "bon jeune pianist" whom Stravinsky had asked Kall to find the previous August, who could play first piano (the more difficult of the two, *pace* Stravinsky) in his Concerto for Two Solo Pianos. On 6 November Marcus wrote Kall from New York: "how delighted I was to be with you, Mr. Stravinsky[,] and Dagmar Godowsky last Saturday night. . . . You mentioned . . . the possibility of doing the two piano Concerto with Mr. Stravinsky. . . . Please tell him how happy I would be to learn it."[56]

Kall's nomination was brilliant. A pupil from 1921 of Josef Lhévinne at Juilliard, Marcus won the Naumburg Prize in 1928, made her New York debut in 1929, and studied in Berlin with Artur Schnabel. She went on to teach at Juilliard. Among her prize students was Bryon Janis, whom she taught from 1938 to 1944. He later reported:

> So at the age of ten, I was brought to Adele Marcus, who was not only an extraordinary pianist, but an extraordinary teacher as well. . . . [She] really laid the foundations of my musical technique and thought. Though she was extremely detailed in her remarks and criticisms of my work, I felt somehow that it was still I who was expressing myself. I was never put into any one style or method of playing. Through the normal trials of musical growth, her total belief in me was a powerful asset to my musical development.[57]

In 1937 Marcus had played Stravinsky's challenging early *Études*, opus 7 (1908) in New York, "with much fluency."[58] Stravinsky met Marcus just in the nick of time for her to learn the difficult concerto by early March. A notice in the 1 March 1940 issue of *Musical Courier*, with another picture of her, announced the event:

> Adele Marcus, American pianist, has been chosen to appear with him in four all-Stravinsky concerts. On all of the programs Miss Marcus and Stravinsky will play his concerto for two pianos. The dates of the concerts are March 6, Boston; 8, Cambridge; 14, Town Hall, New York; and 17, Exeter, N.H.[59]

Over the course of 1940 she played the two-piano concerto with Stravinsky no fewer than nine times, six of them within a three-week period.[60]

Sometimes, of course, Stravinsky's business matters were out of Dagmar's hands. One case in point: until late November he was still uncertain about rehearsal dates and repertoire for the San Francisco Orchestra, as this letter (fig. 5.4), which he dictated to Kall on 17 November from Gerry's Landing, so plainly reveals:

Mr. Pierre Monteux   November 17, 1939
Empire Hotel   Gerry's Landing
San Francisco   c/o Mr. Edward W. Forbes
                                                    Cambridge, Mass.

My dear Monteux:

Since Mr. Drake does not even trouble himself to inform me about days for the rehearsals in San Francisco, may I ask you kindly to request your secretary to send me the exact
dates for my rehearsals (indicating days and times) because I must know this in order to
settle my departure date from here.

Could I also ask you to reserve two rooms at your hotel for me and for Dr. Kall?

Very happy to see you again,

Yours faithfully, with kindest regards to Madame Monteux,

[signed, and remainder handwritten:] Igor Strawinsky

Who sends you this copy by airmail so as to have your reply the more quickly.

P.S. Have you received the orchestra parts for "The Card Game"? I'm directing it here on
1 and 2 December and if *Associated Music Publishers* (representing B. Schott) do not have
a second copy, it will be absolutely necessary for me to bring these parts. Let me know
what I should do, please.

[P.P.S.] I am bringing the Tchaikovsky Second Symphony with me.

That "P.P.S" masks a nifty little Stravinskian stratagem. In the spring of 1930 Stravinsky
had paid to have orchestra parts extracted in Paris from the full scores of Tchaikovsky's first
two symphonies. Whenever he programmed either one of them, he would *rent* these parts
to whichever orchestra he was then leading as a supplement to his conducting fees.[61] His
earlier letter in French to Kall of 21 August 1939 from Sancellemoz shows how far in advance
he planned this maneuver. Asking Kall to ascertain from Monteux if the San Francisco program would remain the same as planned, he added that "I need to know especially about the
Tchaikovsky Sym[phony No. 2] because I'm the one who will be carrying the parts."[62] On 19
October Vera Soudeikina wrote Stravinsky that the two Tchaikovsky symphonies were probably with her in Paris. As of 25 November she could find only one, but on 16 December she
wrote him: "Monsieur Munch will take the music with him by airplane."[63] Charles Munch,
with whom Stravinsky in 1934 had played his Capriccio in Paris ("a huge, fully warranted
success!"), expected to make his US conducting debut with concerts on 29–30 December in
St. Louis, but war conditions forced a cancellation.[64] Although Monteux informed Stravinsky
that the San Francisco Orchestra owned the necessary parts, Stravinsky's P.P.S. shows that
he probably brought his own parts—and collected his rental fee for them.

A QUICK TRIP OUT WEST

Kall and Stravinsky left Boston for New York on 5 December, stayed overnight, and
entrained for San Francisco. Arriving on Sunday morning, 10 December, the two men

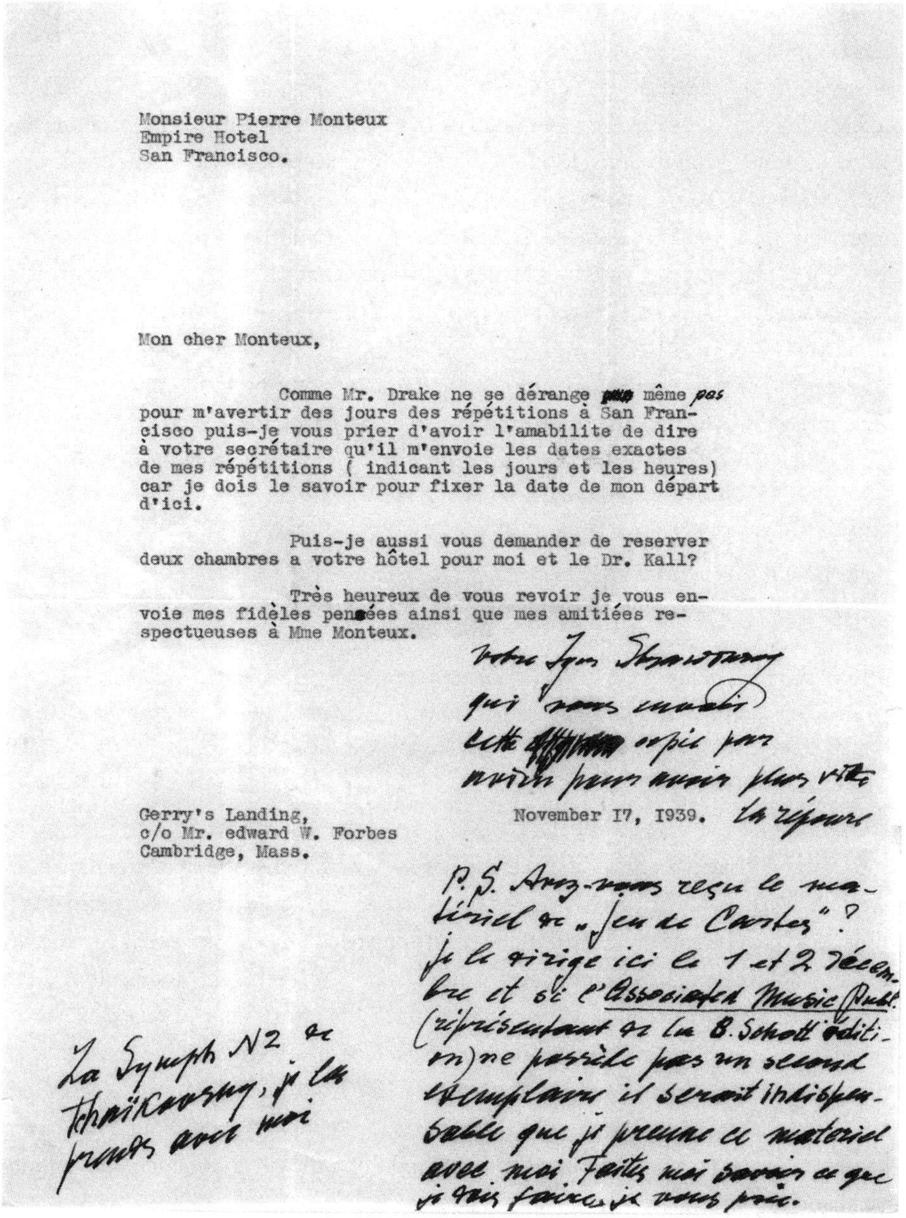

Monsieur Pierre Monteux
Empire Hotel
San Francisco.

Mon cher Monteux,

      Comme Mr. Drake ne se dérange ~~pas~~ même *pas*
pour m'avertir des jours des répétitions à San Francisco puis-je vous prier d'avoir l'amabilite de dire
à votre secrétaire qu'il m'envoie les dates exactes
de mes répétitions (indicant les jours et les heures)
car je dois le savoir pour fixer la date de mon départ
d'ici.

      Puis-je aussi vous demander de reserver
deux chambres a votre hôtel pour moi et le Dr. Kall?

      Très heureux de vous revoir je vous en-
voie mes fidèles pensées ainsi que mes amitiées respectueuses à Mme Monteux.

votre Igor Strawinsky
qui vous envoie
cette copie pour
avoir pour avoir plus vite
la réponse

Gerry's Landing,   November 17, 1939.
c/o Mr. edward W. Forbes
Cambridge, Mass.

P.S. Avez-vous reçu le ma-
tériel de « Jeu de Cartes » ?
je le dirige ici le 1 et 2 décem-
bre et si l'Associated Music Publ.
(représentant de la B. Schott éditi-
on) ne possède pas un second
exemplaire il serait indispen-
sable que je prenne ce matériel
avec moi. Faites moi savoir ce que
je dois faire, je vous prie.

La Symph N2 de
Tchaïkowsky, je la
prends avec moi

FIGURE 5.4

Stravinsky to Pierre Monteux,1939. UBC Stravinsky Collection, no. 65.

settled in the Empire Hotel on Sutter Street, since renamed Hotel Vertigo after Alfred Hitchcock's movie. Stravinsky rehearsed the orchestra several times between 10 and 14 December for his two concerts on 15 and 16 December. On a day off he once again honored Mrs. Armsby, the doyenne of the Orchestra Association, with an inscription, this time on a photograph of himself (probably taken in 1936 by Gar Vic in Buenos Aires): "To Mrs. Armsby / affectionately / Igor Strawinsky / San Francisco / Dec 11th [19]39." Later, perhaps in 1942, when he again led the San Francisco Orchestra, he gave her yet another photograph, this one taken by Edwin McQuoid in October of 1940.[65] He met Mrs. Armsby at least once more, at a supper on 25 October 1944, following his lecture at Mills College in Oakland.

On one of his free evenings, or after one or the other of the orchestra's performances, he dined at the Palace Hotel with Monteux and the well-known pianist, dance-band leader, and songwriter, Vincent Lopez, in town just then for an engagement, in the Rose Room of the Palace Hotel, 8–23 December.[66] A photograph made for the city's Yiddish-speaking community (with a legend printed in Yiddish) shows the three men in evening clothes, dining at the Palace. Translated, it reads:

> Three famous personalities of the music world at an intimate gathering in San Francisco. Seated on the right is Igor Stravinsky, Russian composer, guest conductor of the San Francisco Symphony Orchestra. In the center is Pierre Monteux, French musician, the permanent conductor of the aforementioned orchestra. On the left is Vincent Lopez, popular conductor of jazz orchestras.[67]

Lopez and Stravinsky had—and were to have—several rather unusual experiences in common. Each made arrangements of "The Star-Spangled Banner"—Lopez in 1938, Stravinsky in 1941. Each harmonization quickly provoked officialdom: Lopez's in the US House of Representatives, Stravinsky's from advisers to President Roosevelt and the governor of Massachusetts. Each was pilloried for his efforts: Lopez was picketed in Baltimore in 1938; Stravinsky was forbidden to lead his arrangement in St. Louis in 1941 and Boston in 1944. Conversation of the two men in 1939 would have been most intriguing. Beyond their mutual interests in swing, might Lopez have mentioned his trying experience in 1938 with the national anthem, and Stravinsky recommended his unpublished and unplayed 1937 *Praeludium* for jazz ensemble?

An avid collector of autographs,[68] Lopez may have obtained Stravinsky's in San Francisco that very December of 1939. A fragment of a letter—the entire document once in Lopez's possession—has Stravinsky's signature on one side, the long tail of his final *y* slightly cropped. The other side of the letter, dated "November 1939 / New Orleans," was written in succession by two female fans urging Lopez's quick return to New Orleans. His first admirer was a pianist and writer domiciled there; the other one remains unidentified,[69] partly owing to the cropping. Both women had probably heard Lopez and his dance band during a week's engagement in New Orleans, mid-February of 1939.[70] Dining with Stravinsky that December in San Francisco, Lopez probably made good use of the blank side of the letter his New Orleans fans had sent him the previous month.

On 16 December Stravinsky and Kall departed for Los Angeles. That the composer continued his relationship with Dagmar virtually up to Vera's arrival in New York in early 1940 may be inferred not only from postcards, letters, telegrams, and telephone calls exchanged between San Francisco and New York but also from a bill for a prescription filled in his absence (similar to the task she had undertaken in New York in 1937). On 11 December 1940 she wrote to him in San Francisco, in German:

> Dearest friend. Your cards made me very happy: . . . I would as lief hear from you with a letter. Will you please telephone me the evening of the 16th and if that fails, please telegraph me? Yes? Or an airmail letter? . . . I embrace you. Your Dagmar always.[71]

Four days later she received a prescription from J. Leon Lascoff and Son Pharmacists, 1209 Lexington Avenue. It was for "Mr. Igor Stravinsky / Hotel Navarro / 112 Central Park S / New York." At the bottom of the bill, in a different colored ink and in a different hand, someone in the pharmacy had written "Ordered by Miss Dagmar Godowsky."[72]

Dagmar's business relationships with Stravinsky are more easily dated. To quote Dagmar herself:

> When Richard Copley, who handled Igor's affairs, passed away [February of 1939], I became Igor's personal manager. Actually, I hired Paul Stoes for the detail work, and I acted as personal representative because of my musical knowledge and my many contacts. I had interfered in his professional life before and had been a help. Now I.S. made it official. I was stunned when he insisted that I accept ten percent of his earnings. But I accepted.[73]

Obviously, the operable word here is not her noun, *manager,* but her adjective, *personal.* That she "hired" Paul Stoes is manifestly untrue. It was the reverse because on 18 June and 3 September 1940 Stravinsky mentions "my manager, Mr. Paul H. Stoes."[74] Three months later, "Concert Management Paul H. Stoes, Inc.," affiliated with WGN Concerts, listed among its "distinguished attractions[:] Igor Stravinsky World renowned conductor and composer."[75] The agency announced that he would guest-conduct in Los Angeles, Indianapolis, Cincinnati, Boston, Minneapolis, and Baltimore.

Whatever Dagmar's precise relationship with Stoes, the following examples allow some idea of tasks she undertook on Stravinsky's behalf. On his instructions in May of 1939, she fixed the six dates with Edward Forbes for the Norton lectures at Harvard[76] and arranged a New York exhibition in January of 1940 for Stravinsky's painter son,

Théodore.[77] Godowsky's letter to the composer, dated "Monday 12" [March 1940], is particularly valuable—horrible handwriting, spelling, breathless run-on prose, and all.[78] It mentions that Moses Smith of Columbia Records plans to visit him in Boston;[79] that she will talk with Smith again to arrange "the radio hour" and the "price": Stravinsky's fee for it; and that she will talk to the *New York Herald-Tribune* about a proposed article and their objections to his price of $1,000: "they thought *much* to [sic] much." She also advises him about joining ASCAP; and she promises that she will see to both Drake and Simon and Schuster the next day. Her reference to the latter may concern royalties for the single-volume English translation of *Chroniques de ma vie*.[80]

Dagmar also negotiated contracts for New York Philharmonic recordings early in April of 1940. She even freed Stravinsky after he accidentally—appropriately enough, on April Fools' Day 1940—locked himself in a Carnegie Hall bathroom at his first rehearsal.[81] Perhaps knowledge of this comic incident fueled the ensuing mockery of the composer by Philharmonic musicians.[82] She also told Kall on 25 March:

> Am arranging for Zirato to buy 2nd performance of Stravinsky new symphony with Columbia doing recording at the same time next season!!!! Don't mention as yet to Zirato. The price must be exceptional. . . . Do arrange for Sunday interview [with the *New York Post*] and let me know about this *at once* so we can fix interview at once. Dear Woof—will *you* tell Drake that (*we* have discussed this long ago)[?] I ought to get the percentage on Philharmonic concerts April week. I did and am doing all the work for it—I never mentioned this to Drake myself![83]

Dagmar truly earned her money and was unafraid to demand it. The newly wed Stravinskys and Kall arrived a week later, on Easter Sunday, 31 March.[84]

In respect to recording Stravinsky's "new" (but still not finished) Symphony in C, Dagmar's efforts bore no fruit whatever. Nor did a proposal on 22 August 1940 by Moses Smith of Columbia Records to record it on 7 November with the Chicago Symphony Orchestra during the rehearsals for its world premiere there. The large number of mistakes in the orchestra parts, noted in Vera's diary for 5 November 1940, probably doomed that project.

RECALLING STRAVINSKY AND KALL AT HARVARD

Stravinsky felt a "family" relationship with the Boston Symphony Orchestra; he developed close friendships with three of its players and with some acquaintances in Cambridge.[85] By utilizing sources in the Harvard University Archives and in the Kall and Morton Papers in Los Angeles at the University of California, Stephen Walsh has admirably set out the history of 1939 to 1940 of both Stravinsky and Kall.

A few stories told to me in April and May of 1995 by the late Professor Elliot Forbes, a Harvard graduate (class of 1940; AB, 1941), and known affectionately to all as El,[86] plus some written recollections by his father, Edward Waldo Forbes, offer further insights about life with Stravinsky and Kall in Cambridge and at Harvard.[87] Some details concern their first months, October to December 1939, when both dwelt in the Forbes family home at Gerry's Landing; others deal with the latter half of the academic year.

Twenty-one-year-old El Forbes had been studying with Nadia Boulanger in France at Gargenville and, thus, already knew Stravinsky through her when his father arrived late in the summer of 1939 and met the composer for a first time. On 9 September El, his father, and his sister "Ros" (Rosamond) sailed home from Le Havre on the SS *President Harding*. On 4 October, the senior Forbes wrote from Cambridge to Stravinsky in New York:

> I telephoned to Dr. Kall yesterday, and he said that you were still in bed. . . . I hope that you and Dr. Kall will come to my house, which is known as Gerry's Landing to stay for a few days until we settle the question of exactly where you are going to live.[88]

Edward Forbes recalled in 1961 than when Stravinsky arrived in Cambridge, he came to dinner at Gerry's Landing and he and Kall were overnight guests. The next morning, after breakfast, Stravinsky asked if he and Kall could spend the winter there.[89] On 1 November Forbes wrote Jerome D. Green (presidential assistant to the House Committee of the Harvard Club, New York) that the composer's "comfort seems to depend on his always being accompanied by Dr. Kall. . . . We had also to provide for his *fidus Achates*."[90] On 11 December, while Stravinsky and Kall were away in San Francisco, the elder Forbes wrote Nadia Boulanger in France that "Kall was most devoted and kind to him [Stravinsky]."[91]

El remembered that Stravinsky established an immediate rapport with his mother Margaret ("Peg") and his sister Marla, even though his mother had no French; his father spoke and read that language but pronounced it poorly. El's father also remembered that Stravinsky "loved a poker game and would always ask us to let him know if we were going to play." Family members did not normally drink wine at table, but Stravinsky had to have his *Médoc*.[92] He had a favorite parlor trick. It was to vibrate the prongs of a fork and then to touch it to a glass, which would resonate as if the sound originated in it. This trick seemed to awe Kall, although El allowed that he might have been dissembling. At table, Kall was not a great talker, even though his English was adequate. El remembered this overweight scholar saying "Woof?" when requesting food and exclaiming "Woof!!"—breathing heavily—after climbing the stairs to the floor where the two men had their rooms. Neither El nor Craft was the first to be engaged by this mannerism. Already in 1935, Merle Armitage had observed it: "Stravinsky and I found this amusing and began to imitate him. . . . This teasing of Dr. Kall . . . signaled to both men a sort of fraternal greeting in a strange, if beloved land."[93]

In 1995 El could not recall whether Stravinsky persisted in wearing tails for the five remaining lectures as he had at his first Norton lecture in New Lecture Hall on

18 October 1939, all of which, of course, El attended.[94] Father Edward observed that Stravinsky "was extremely nervous the first time he addressed the students and asked me to sit behind him with a second copy of his notes in case he got mixed up, which never happened."[95] El recalled his father—troubled by his lack of knowledge of Stravinsky's music—coming to him early in the spring of 1940 and requesting help. El gave him an LP of *Petrushka*. The elder Forbes thought it seemed "as though someone were trying to hammer hot nails into my head!"—probably a reference to the loud repeated notes in the fourth tableau (rehs. 114–17).

Kall's constant presence as a linguistic aide was crucial. El remembered that in some sessions with student composers in rooms 1 and 3 of the music building (and not the more usual Eliot House) that Stravinsky spoke both French and English, probably more of the former. And at a San Francisco Orchestra rehearsal in mid-December, a reporter had observed that "he gets all tangled with the verbs and nouns of the English language."[96] El recalled Stravinsky in room 3 complaining that "Il me fait si chaud," whereupon windows would be opened, and then "Il me fait si froid," whereupon they would be closed. At one lesson fledgling composer El showed one of his juvenile songs to Stravinsky, which elicited little, if any, comment. Nevertheless, in an affectionate gesture, Stravinsky later inscribed a copy of Mercury's piano-vocal edition of his 1941 arrangement of "The Star-Spangled Banner" to El and his "beautiful wife I Str / 1942."

A Boston newspaper photograph taken on 21 November 1939 in Harvard's Eliot House shows three music students behind Stravinsky at the piano and the right shoulder and upper body of a fourth (far right). The accompanying narrative mentions four men: Jan LaRue (class of 1940), William Austin (class of 1939), and more advanced composers William Denny (then on his way to Rome, and in 1941 an instructor at Harvard); and Vladimir Ussachevsky.[97] The photograph fully depicts only three men; LaRue, the youngest, is on the far left. The middle fellow is William Austin.[98] Available (later) photographs do not suggest that the young man at the right is either Denny or Ussachevsky, but perhaps the far right shoulder belongs to one or the other. Just a week later, Ussachevsky traveled with the Boston Symphony Orchestra on tour to Providence, Rhode Island, where Stravinsky led it, the young man recalling that "in Providence, R.I., Stravinsky, [1st] trombonist [J.] Reichman [*recte:* Raichman], and [1st] trumpeter [G.] Mager, and I were having a beer.[99]

Raichman, "a pleasant and talkative Russian," queried Stravinsky about composing *Le Sacre;* he replied: "Well, yes, I did write it with an axe." Unexpected perhaps as is the notion of Stravinsky shooting the musical breeze with brass players over beers, Ussachevsky's memoir adds two more Boston Symphony musicians as Stravinsky's friends, though unlikely to the same degree of intimacy then enjoyed by the concertmaster, English horn player, and contrabassoonist,[100] the latter two having played in the premiere of *Le Sacre.*

LaRue kindly wrote me the following account in 2001, supplementing the Boston newspaper report.[101] Although his letter fleshes out the newspaper, it is to some degree contaminated by the latter, which he certainly read in 1939 and perhaps again later in life, for his widow recalls that he owned a copy of the newspaper's photograph. In any event, on 21 November 1939 young LaRue had brought along to a class held in the Eliot House his new composition: three short movements for clarinet. The newspaper reports that Stravinsky heard the piece to its end, and only *afterward* objected to an F-sharp "as out of place" and to that passage as "too difficult to play." LaRue, however, says that Stravinsky complained about the note even *before* the young clarinetist had played it. Here is his recollection in 2001:

> [Stravinsky] pointed with a long forefinger to a high F-sharp, saying: "Clarinet can't play that high in *piano*." That may be the conventional wisdom, but I'm a clarinet player, so greatly daring—really not so daring . . . he was extremely friendly, though formal—I said, "Maestro, I have practiced this passage quite a bit. May I play it for you?" He grunted, and after moistening my reed thoroughly, I played it fairly convincingly. . . . I don't think he asked me to play any more.

Recently, it has been claimed that Stravinsky "did not take his teaching duties seriously, perhaps because he had no need to take them seriously." Five years later this indictment was expanded to "Stravinsky did not take his teaching duties seriously, feeling he was neither talented for nor inclined to such a task."[102] To this latter evaluation must be added Stravinsky's own public remarks at Eastman in March of 1966 that "I have no pedagogical talent, not at all, I don't feel it. . . . I have no passion [for] teaching."[103] But just because one does not feel a vocation for something, it does not follow that one executes a required task poorly. In point of fact, neither El Forbes in 1995–96 nor Jan LaRue in 2001 ever criticized Stravinsky's diligence, seriousness, or effectiveness as a teacher during their lessons.

Nor did Stravinsky's student in Los Angeles, Earnest Andersson, perceive any slackness during instruction in 1941–42. Andersson found Stravinsky both diligent and generous with his time; two examples suffice. In April of 1941 he insisted on teaching, even though he had "had 8 teeth out of upper jaw and was ill. Got out of bed to work with me." The following May, Andersson noted that "I usually work with him from 11:30 [a.m.] to 1:30 [p.m.] though I am not supposed to get more than one hour."[104]

Stravinsky's view of LaRue's clarinet playing might well be compared to his reactions in May of 1943 when he was unavailable to coach a Mr. Polatschek, who was slated to perform Stravinsky's Three Pieces for Clarinet (1919) at Harvard. Stravinsky later told Professor Tillman Merritt that Polatschek's "apprehension concerning my clarinet pieces" was warranted: had Stravinsky "couched [*sic*] him for a short while," the clarinetist would "have availed himself perfectly."[105] Many years later, in April of 1965, he coached a Texas student and Benny Goodman on that same work.[106]

Near the end of November, El attended Stravinsky's rehearsal with the Boston Symphony Orchestra of *Jeu de cartes,* in preparation for concerts on 28 November in

FIGURE 5.5
Fragment from *Jeu de cartes* for Moses Eisenberg, 1939. UBC Stravinsky Collection, no. 66.

Providence and on 1 and 2 December in Boston. Afterward, Stravinsky told El that when a trombonist at the rehearsal missed an entrance, the composer "felt as if an ax had severed his arm." Owing to newspaper publicity and to the novelty of its title, the Boston premiere of *Jeu de cartes* evoked considerable interest in the city: El was hardly the only attendee at these rehearsals.

At one of them, Stravinsky dashed off three measures from *Jeu de cartes*'s "First Deal" for a Dr. Moses Joel Eisenberg, a research dentist in Boston.[107] Apparently he did so from memory and perhaps in a hurry, because his inscription (fig. 5.5) contains several pitch displacements and other errors.

Nor was this his only inscription from this tour containing musical notation. He also inscribed a placard said by Craft to have been "posted at Harvard" and to be his "first composition of the American period,"[108] although Stravinsky may have filched the placard from a restroom in San Francisco's Empire Hotel (fig. 5.6). Uncertainty stems from Stravinsky's ambiguous date. It can be read as either "6 XI 39" (6 November, when he was in Cambridge) or "16 XII 39" (the day of his final concert with the San Francisco Orchestra). Heading the placard, "Andante," Stravinsky wrote out on it his earliest-known musical setting of a text in English.[109] In C major, it is syllabic (save for the fifth word), "DO NOT / THROW / PAPER TOWELS / IN TOILETS." What has been called a "minor jewel" survives because Stravinsky gave it to Kall, remaining to this day in his papers at the University of California, Los Angeles. Considering its initial two pitches as an anacru-

FIGURE 5.6
Fragment "Do not
throw . . ."

sis allows a better scansion in English, although both rebarring and Stravinsky's notation stress "toilettes," as in French.

CHRISTMAS IN LOS ANGELES

On Sunday, 17 December, the two men arrived in Los Angeles by train from San Francisco. Despite Stravinsky's impending marriage to Vera (9 March 1940), his eye for pretty young women, married or not, rarely wavered.[110] Nor did it fail him years earlier in respect to the vivacious Dorothy Ellis McQuoid Hopper (she remarried after her first husband's premature death).[111] Among claims for her as a Stravinsky "associate" (Craft's useful term) is an unaddressed postcard he gave her with a photograph of himself (fig. 5.7). It bears on its reverse side a musical inscription dated 17 December 1939.

It is a little tune composed by Stravinsky and set on two staves to his own text of "Dorothy, o Dorothy / you are nice."[112] This, Stravinsky's second setting in English, was her reward for meeting him and Kall (her piano teacher of some years earlier) at Union Station when their train arrived that same day, 17 December. In October of 1994 Mrs. McQuoid Hopper told me that when Kall appeared, climbing up from the train station's lower platform, she, as usual, kissed her former teacher. She impulsively kissed Stravinsky, too; he was only a little taken aback. Then she drove both of them to Kall's house on South Gramercy where, he had arranged a Christmas party for Russian-speaking friends.

A fine new study subtitled Stravinsky's "Evolving Approach to Setting Text,"[113] can be supplemented with these earliest of the composer's English-text settings. Most native

FIGURE 5.7
Postcard with fragment "Dorothy, O Dorothy" (front and back). Photo, author's collection.

speakers would deliver the words of the declarative sentence as "Do nót / throw / paper tówels / in tóilets." But by setting it in $\frac{2}{4}$ meter, Stravinsky stresses it as follows, employing quarter notes, one melisma, and reiterating the highest note in the final measure (e′): "Do not / thrów / paper tówels / ín toiléts." His sole bar lines imply this kind of a performance (see ex. 5.1a).

This is not entirely unsatisfactory. Emphasizing *throw* by a quarter note on the supertonic surely proceeded from Stravinsky's observation that this word occupies, visually at least, a central position on the placard. His unfortunate stress on the E at *in* results from the tiny two-note melisma proceeding upward to the mediant (see ex. 5.1b).

Rebarring it helps only a little, dispelling some of the mediant stress at *in*, but failing to avoid the reversed stress of *toi-léts*, an accentuation certainly due to his habit of pronunciation *à la française*. These infelicities make it virtually certain that he had no help from linguist Kall, who, after almost twenty years in Los Angeles, would have known better.

But Kall's influence cannot be denied in the case of Stravinsky's second setting, the postcard for Mrs. McQuoid[114]—"Dorothy o Dorothy, you are nice" (see ex. 5.2). Stravinsky

EXAMPLE 5.1a

"Do not throw, etc."

Do not throw pa - per tow - els___ in toi - lets.

EXAMPLE 5.1b

"Do not throw, etc." rebarred.

Do not throw pa - per tow - els___ in toi - lets.

EXAMPLE 5.2

"Dorothy, o Dorothy etc."

Do - ro - thy, o Do - ro - thy you are nice.

ranges more boldly over his C-major scale than earlier. Encompassing a full octave from g to g′, he induces a modal feeling by opening on e′ and concluding on a sustained a. Normally this little encomium would be uttered as "Dórothy, o Dórothy you áre nice." Mrs. McQuoid Hopper once informed me that Kall always addressed her as "Dórothée," adding a very light stress on, and lisping, the third syllable of her name. Setting his greeting in $\frac{2}{4}$, but drawing bar lines instead of a time signature, Stravinsky reveals that he well understands both its normal stress and the particular stress that he had already learned that very afternoon at Union Station. His barring, choice of octave, and note lengths point to example 5.2.

The very next day, 18 December 1939, Dorothy added her younger son, Cary Ellis McQuoid (1934–97), to the list of Stravinsky's "associates." Heeding suggestions from her short-lived photographer husband, Edwin, she posed their five-year-old with the composer in front of Kall's house and took their picture (fig. 5.8). This image has been credited—incorrectly—to Edward G. Robinson, the writer (or his editor) heartlessly cropping out the little boy and the ambient neighborhood.[115]

THIS PHOTOGRAPH OF MY SON CARY ELLIS MCQUOID (BORN 29 SEPTEMBER 1934) AND IGOR STRAVINSKY WAS TAKEN BY ME, DOROTHY ELLIS MCQUOID HOPPER, ON 18 DECEMBER 1939 IN LOS ANGELES NEAR THE HOME OF ALEXIS KALL, MY TEACHER AND A LONGTIME FRIEND OF STRAVINSKY. THE PHOTOGRAPH WAS MADE WITH MY PERMISSION IN OCTOBER 1994 FROM THE ORIGINAL NEGATIVE IN MY POSSESSION.

FIGURE 5.8
Stravinsky with Cary Ellis McQuoid,
1939. UBC Stravinsky Collection, no. 67.

Just a week later, Stravinsky inscribed her copy of the 1933 Kalmus miniature score of *Petrushka* (figs. 5.9a, 5.9b)—the only time, according to her, that she sought his autograph. Having just purchased it for that very purpose, she well remembered having attended and been enchanted by the Stravinsky-Kosloff production in the Shrine Auditorium two years earlier. After duly warning her of the many errors in this reprint, he inscribed it "To Dorothy Ellis / very very sincerely, / I Strawinsky / Los Angeles / Christmas / 1939."

Stravinsky, Kall, and George Balanchine visited the Disney studios, perhaps on 17 December,[116] the very Sunday that Stravinsky and Kall arrived by train from San Francisco. *Fantasia* was being completed, and the visitors, seemingly delighted, were photographed several times with Disney and his colleagues. Only Walsh[117] reproduces a picture from this visit that so fully reveals Dr. Alexis Fyodorovitch Kall's bulky figure in all its glory, although an earlier photograph that shows a seated Kall, during Stravinsky's visit to the MGM studios on 25 February 1935, certainly justified the composer's admonition a year later: "Be healthy and do not lose that which by years and with such industry has accumulated."[118] These images, combined with others taken later at Gerry's Landing, allow glimpses of this "huge gentle Russian,"[119] whose papers in Los Angeles preserve so much information about this early part of Stravinsky's US exile.

BACK IN BOSTON

Kall's duties included writing and typing letters for Stravinsky. But occasionally, Stravinsky took matters into his own hands. Edward Forbes sent letters on 5 and 8 January 1940 from Gerry's Landing to Stravinsky at the Great Northern Hotel in New York: Stravinsky replied on 17 January from Pittsburgh, two days after arriving there with Kall and Vera Soudeikina, who had disembarked in New York on 12 January. Stravinsky's reply is handwritten in French on stationery of the Webster-Hall Hotel. It alludes to mild domestic tensions at Gerry's Landing and documents a rare defeat for the composer in any financial negotiation:

17 January 1940

Dear Mr. Forbes:

Finally freed from my [conducting] responsibilities in New York, I have arrived here, in Pittsburgh, to recuperate before my week of [in English:] guest-conducting. And it is only today that I have been able to respond to your friendly letters. I am really startled that you could believe the price increase for our room and board justifiable. If while looking over your statements in Cambridge (for last December), I had raised those questions, it was solely because of the amount of 250 dollars per month (that you had originally committed to, corresponding to your own expenditures) such as I recalled. And the increase that you had made surprised me the more because several times per week we did not take meals at your house and even still more that during November we were in New York for several days.

But, as I said latterly to Mrs. Forbes, I have complete trust in your calculations and do not wish to criticize.

Thus we are in perfect agreement and it is understood (otherwise you will inform me) that we (Dr. Kall and I) will incur a future monthly charge (300 dollars per month), *except for* our absences from Cambridge. . . .

Believe me, dear Mr. Forbes, your devoted servant,

Igor Strawinsky.[120]

Kall's diary for 1940, which served him as a reminder, and eventually, a memoir, occasionally supplements the many events and the composer's growing national prominence during the initial four months before Kall and the Stravinskys left Massachusetts for Southern California. For instance, at the beginning of 1940 the composer himself was once again a cover boy for a national music magazine, this time, the year's first issue of *Musical America*.[121]

KALMUS MINIATURE
ORCHESTRA SCORES

No. 79

IGOR
STRAVINSKY

PETROUSHKA

A Burlesque in four scenes

E. F. KALMUS ORCHESTRA
SCORES, INC.
NEW YORK CITY

FIGURE 5.9a.
Dorothy McQuoid's 1933
Kalmus miniature score of
Petrushka (front). UBC
Stravinsky Collection, no. 68.

The meagerness of Kall's diary and the gradual disintegration of his handwriting was perhaps owing to increasing inebriety, although, strangely enough, it reveals his passion for ice-skating at rinks in New York, Pittsburgh, and Chicago. Closely monitoring his deterioration, Vera deplored his forgetfulness, oversleeping, misaddressing of correspondence, and ineptness in business matters.[122]

Kall's entries begin in January, a few days before Vera arrived in New York on 12 January, and end with the notation "Pascha" (Easter), celebrated with Igor and Vera on 28 April.[123] Stravinsky's schedule for this period can be reconstructed by supplement-

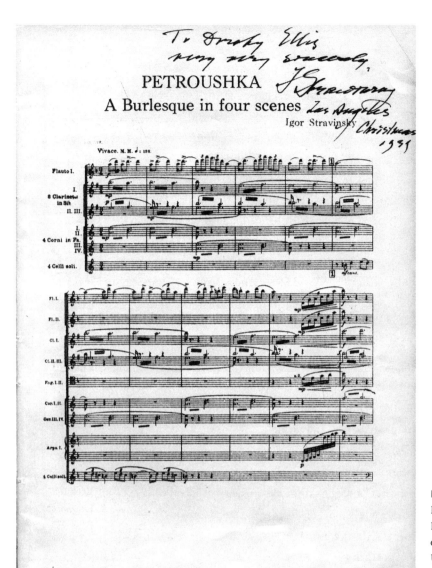

FIGURE 5.9b
Dorothy McQuoid's 1933
Kalmus miniature score
of *Petrushka* (inscribed).
UBC Stravinsky Collection,
no. 68.

ing Kall's laconic notes with information from Vera's diary. His entries are mostly in Russian; square brackets denote material supplied by me; his relatively few entries in English are italicized here.

1940 JANUARY

New Year's Eve: [in New York; Kall celebrates with Stravinsky(?)] at Dagmar's.

1: day at Sophia Alekseevna's

2: *Rehearsal* [for New York Philharmonic's all-Stravinsky concert, 4 January]

4: *Evening*

5: *Afternoon*

6: *Evening*

7: *Afternoon* /1000 / [Russian = P?] *income tax* 700 [Russian = ?]

8: *Wuthering Heights.*

9: Opening of the [New York] exhibition [of paintings by Théodore Stravinsky]

10: Illness / [cancelled:] Dinner with Carl Engel

11: Illness / Dinner at Kaufman's [probably pianist Harry Kaufman, who would later be Dushkin's accompanist for Tango in New York, March 1941]

12: Arrival [7 p.m.] of V[era] A[rturovna Soudeikina] on the *Rex* [Kall, Stravinsky, Dushkin, Bolm, and Bolm's daughter meet her dockside]

13: *Adele's* [Marcus] concert / Russian New Year

14: Ice rink ["Iceland"] on 52nd Street [and Broadway] / dinner at the Dushkins

15: Arrival in Pittsburgh / [Hotel] Webster[-]Hall

16: Ice rink

17: [Stravinsky interviewed];[124] Dinner at [Hotel] Webster.

19: Symphony concert [Josef] (Hofmann) [performs with Vladimir Bakaleinikov and the Pittsburgh Symphony] / *Concordia Club*

20: At the Bakaleinikovs' [Reiner's assistant conductor at Pittsburgh]

21: Down to the ice rink and ravine

22: 2 rehearsals [10 a.m. and 3 p.m.]

23: 2 rehearsals [of *Apollon* and *Jeu de cartes*]

26: 1st concert / hand-shaking at the Musicians Club[125]

28: 2nd concert [3–5 p.m.] / Dinner at the Bakaleinikovs'

29: Dinner at [Hotel] Webster

30: Dinner at Glick's

1940 FEBRUARY

2: Departure for New York

4: Arrival in Cambridge

9: *Boston Symphony* [in New York]

11: My birthday / Lunch at the Koussevitzkys' [in Boston]

12: Theater *"Candle Light"*[126]

13: Lots of work / *Meeting with* [Harvard] *students*

14: Snow[127]

15: Snow

16: 4 [p.m.] Igor has a dinner with Mrs Coolidge / cancelled

18: 7 a.m. Departure for Chicago

19: Arrival in Chicago at 4:45 p.m.

20: Rehearsal

21: Rehearsal

22: *Eve[ning] Chicago* rehearsal *[cancelled] Concert*

23: *Aft[ernoon] Chicago Concert*

25: Ice rink [plus a short, illegible Russian word in parentheses]

26: Rehearsal / ice rink

27: 2:15 *Con[c]ert* Chicago / Departure

28: Arrival in Cambridge

1940 MARCH

[1: On Stravinsky's behalf, Kall writes Carlos Chávez concerning the latter's invitation to conduct concerts in July 1940 in Mexico City][128]

2: Requiem service for E[katerina] T. S[travinskaya] / Arrival [in Boston of] Vera Art[urovna Soudeikina]

6: *Mrs. Forbes* birthday / [Kall and Vera heard: Stravinsky's] *Chamber Music* / in Boston.[129]

7: [Kall heard? Giovanni] Gabrieli [motets?—sung by the Harvard]—*Glee Club*

8: *Chamber music* / in *Cambridge* [Kall and Vera heard Stravinsky and Adele Marcus perform Concerto for Two Solo Pianos at Harvard's Sanders Theatre in Cambridge, where it was recorded]

9: 12:30 [p.m.] Wedding of Igor / and Vera Arturnovna[130] / lunch at Amalfi's [restaurant near Symphony Hall]

10: Dinner at the Koussevitzkys' / Eve[ning:] Subway [to] Cambridge

11: French consulate / At home

12: Lunch at Pickman's[131] / Cambridge / At night retreated to Andrey

13: Morning in Cambridge / [Stravinsky's] 4th Lecture / Departure for New York at 12 midnight

14: *New York* [matinee in Town Hall:] *Concert* [for French war relief].

15: Returned from NY.

17: Leave at 3 [p.m. by train from Back Bay; Stravinsky, Vera, Kall, and Marcus arrive at] / Exeter 6:45 [p.m. and stay at Exeter Inn. Stravinsky lectures and with] / Adele [Marcus they again play the Concerto for Two Solo Pianos]

20: 4:30 Rehearsal / 5th lecture

21: 7 p.m. Rehearsal Harvard [Glee Club]

24: [Easter Sunday / illegible Russian. Kall arrives too late to assist Vera, interviewed by the *Boston Post*]

25: 11/4 ? [= 1:25 p.m. rehearsal?]

26: Rehearsals [at] 12:30 [a.m.] / 10[a.m.] *Orchestra only* / 41/2 / *Orch. and Chorus at* / 5 [for *Oedipus Rex*]

27: 6:15 [dress rehearsal orchestra and Harvard Glee Club of *Oedipus Rex*]

28: [Russian = ?] / 10 -1 *no chorus* / *orchestra* / My *Colleg[ium] Mus[icum]* / 8. [p.m.] Cambridge [Kall lectures in Cambridge, while Stravinsky leads Boston Symphony in *Apollon* and *Oedipus Rex*.]

29: [3 p.m.] Stravinsky concert. *Boston* / *Symphony*.

30: [8 p.m.] Evening Stravinsky's concert *B[oston] Symp[hony]*

31: 12 [noon; both Stravinskys and Kall] leave for NY [with Kall in disgrace for having forgotten train tickets and then losing two suitcases and a pocketbook in New York.][132]

1940 APRIL

1: *Rehearsals* 10 [and] 2 [–3: Stravinsky's NY Philharmonic rehearsals of *Petrushka* and *Sacre*][133]

2: *Reh.* 10 [and] 2

3: *Reh.* 10 / *Concert* 8:45

4: 1:30 [p.m.] *Recording* [of above compositions]

5: [New York Philharmonic] *Concert* 2:30 Dinner at Mitchell's [with Fritz] (Kreisler)

6: 8:45 *Concert*

7: Last Concert / 3:00 [the first live Stravinsky program heard by Robert Craft] / Igor [and Vera] left for Washington, DC; Kall for New York] at 10 p.m.

8: [The Stravinskys in] Washington. / I'm in New York / lunch with Adele, D[a] gm[ar], I[?] & V[?] two hours

9: [Smudged, illegible erasure. Both Stravinskys left Washington for Boston at 9 p.m.] I arrive in Boston [from New York] at 10 p.m.

10: [6th Stravinsky] Lecture / Dinner and farewell tea at Forbes's[134]

11: [Smudged, illegible erasure]

23: Pitirim Sorokin [a Harvard University sociologist, his invitation cancelled by the Stravinskys in favor of a movie]

25: [Stravinsky speaks in Cambridge, followed by a] *Collegium Musicum*[135]

28: Pascha

Kall's diary was apparently meant to serve two purposes, neither well: a series of reminders (possibly entered first), and a haphazard record of events, probably testifying to growing alcoholism.

Traveling by train from Charleston, South Carolina, after a visit to friends Georgette and Pearce Bailey, Vera had arrived in Boston's Back Bay station at midnight on 2 March 1940 and was met there by Stravinsky and Kall, who took her to the Forbes house at Gerry's Landing. Whereas a mistress in Paris was no anomaly, there could be no thought of her sharing quarters with Stravinsky in proper Boston. Her initial comings and goings thus comport with El's guarded remark to me in 1997 that "when Vera first arrived in Cambridge, her presence was kept rather under wraps"; the well-known straitlaced Forbes family was uncomfortable with her illicit relationship with Stravinsky.[136] To obtain a marriage license, he and she drove the next day to Bedford, a respectable distance northwest of Boston, where she stayed until the wedding there on 9 March. After their marriage, the Stravinskys moved to Boston's Hemenway Hotel; presumably, Kall remained at Gerry's Landing.

Nevertheless, at the Women's Republican Club in fashionable Beacon Street, Vera, discreetly escorted by Kall, was present on 6 March to hear Stravinsky perform at 9 p.m. for the Chamber Music Club. He conducted his wind Octet, *Dumbarton Oaks Concerto*, and excerpts from *L'Histoire du soldat,* and he played his Concerto for Two Solo Pianos with Adele Marcus. He repeated the program on 8 March at Harvard, where years later, El Forbes noted that there was "such a demand for tickets that the site was shifted from Paine Hall to Sanders Theatre." Once again, Kall escorted Vera. Fortunately, the concert was recorded, a copy surviving in the Music Division of the Library of Congress.[137]

For their New York Town Hall concert on 14 March, sponsored jointly by Mrs. Bliss and the French embassy, Stravinsky and Marcus played the Concerto for Two Solo Pianos. One writer merely noted that they played it "brilliantly and colorfully," but another (with photographs of both pianists) was more discerning; in the last movement, "the fugue . . . [was] a veritable apotheosis of martellato playing."[138] The 8 March recording made at Sanders Theatre sustains this opinion. Marcus recalled Stravinsky applying "concoctive paste to the pads of his fingers . . . as a weighing agent." This was a reasonably common (if somewhat) bizarre practice of the time, also employed to prevent or to alleviate cracks in the skin from playing too forcefully.[139] Conceivably, Stravinsky's recourse to such a paste resulted from years and years of what one Boston critic had noted as early as January of 1925: "[exploiting] to the utmost the percussive effects of the piano." The terms *marcato, martelé,* and even *marcatissimo* are omnipresent in the Double Concerto and are evident in the way he had recorded it in mid-February of 1938 with his son in Paris. That grim performance is best described as "awe-inspiringly graceless and unyielding . . . [a] despotic reading of the Concerto."[140]

Stravinsky's Sunday afternoon broadcast concert of 7 April 1940 with the New York Philharmonic was the first one in which Craft heard the composer live on the radio (as opposed to a recording).[141] For concerts of that week Stravinsky preautographed "I Strawinsky" in black ink on at least four copies of the program for prospective admirers: there are several autographed—but undistributed—programs in Kall's papers. This practice of presigning harks back to the stunning photographs that George Hoyningen-Huené took in 1934, as shown by one he signed in 1941 without any dedication,[142] and probably to the mid-twenties, on a photograph taken by Studio Lipnitzki of Paris.[143] In later years Stravinsky continued this practice. There are examples in Boston for his symphony concerts, 14–15 January 1944,[144] and in Los Angeles on programs for 15 January 1952 at Royce Hall. Some of the latter are now held at Vancouver and Basel.[145] On 25 August 1964 he presigned one hundred programs while on a flight to New York.[146]

Kall's diary gives no hint of his own major achievement, the first English translation of *Poétique musicale,* a compilation of Stravinsky's Norton lectures. Nor has he ever received credit for it, which is strange because several scholars have shown interest,[147] Stravinsky having later put the translation to good use. On 27 March 1940 the frugal Professor Edward Forbes advised Harvard's treasurer that "most of the work of translating on Strawinsky's lectures has been at no expense to us." Not long thereafter, on 2 May, the New England professor requested payment for Kall by means of a voucher: "Dr. Kall has translated Mr. Stravinsky's book and resumés into English. Further work is being done by Mr. Forbes and Mr. [Irving] Fine [Harvard teaching fellow; Boston composer]."[148]

Modest though he was, Kall fully expected his translation would one day appear in print. His fourteen-page summary, "Stravinsky in the Chair of Poetry," published in July of 1940, states that "the lectures . . . have been translated by the writer from French into English and will be published by the Harvard press early in the autumn."[149] Although his translation never appeared in print, it survives in his handwritten pages, and the first lecture also in a typed version. Although Kall revised these documents,[150] and in 1942 Harvard published Stravinsky's Norton lectures in French, the English translation, when it appeared in 1947, was the work of two others. Stravinsky rather desperately needed Kall's translation later, in 1943.[151]

Five weeks after Kall stood as a witness to their wedding on 9 March 1940 at Bedford, Mr. and Mrs. Stravinsky went to a police station in Boston to have fingerprints and photographs taken so they could apply to renew their US visas and, ultimately, apply for citizenship.[152] The police photograph shows a placard across Stravinsky's chest that reads "14 April 1940." At the beginning of our new century, this photograph spawned several risible conclusions based on imaginary evidence. Rectification of these errors may appropriately be postponed until just before one of the perpetrators enters Stravinsky's life— and when the present narrative begins to wind down.

EXPRESSION, AGAIN

Béla Bartók gave a lecture-recital with his wife in Harvard's Paine Hall on 22 April 1940.[153] We do not know whether the Stravinskys attended, or were even aware of it: the published portion of Vera's diary has no entry for 22 April. Bartók might well not have invited his fellow composer: on 10 April 1922, writing privately about a conversation they had in Paris, Bartók described Stravinsky as "an egoistic and uninterested partner."[154] Stravinsky's public statements about Bartók were more positive: when interviewed during a concert tour at Budapest late in March of 1933, he commented that "I know the works of Béla Bartók and greatly admire them," and he even boasted to another reporter that "Béla Bartók is a personal friend of mine."[155] When in Hungary, act as Hungarians do: some of Stravinsky's remarks were verifiably hypocritical.

Bartók's discomfort extended beyond Stravinsky's personality to one aspect of his music. Seven years before the publication of *Chroniques*, Bartók's firmly entrenched position—"I cannot conceive of music that expresses absolutely nothing"—placed him squarely in opposition to what would become *Chroniques*' most notorious dictum.[156] Bartók's convictions date back to at least 1909, when he wrote to a friend: "It is possible to call contemporary composition realistic when it candidly and indiscriminately admits truly every human emotion within its expressive repertory.[157] Many years later, the terminally ill Bartók changed his mind after hearing Germain Prévost, its dedicatee, play Stravinsky's remarkable 1942 *Élégie* for solo viola. During his last days Bartók said to his physician, Dr. Lax, that "one of the most important things I learned from Stravinsky was daring."[158] Bartók's pleasure in the *Élégie* delighted Stravinsky.[159]

The hypocrisy of Stravinsky's 1933 comments in Budapest had long since been discovered: on 7 February 1945 in New York, Stravinsky declined an invitation to hear Bartók's magisterial *Fifth String Quartet,* and in a blunt letter the day after Bartók's death, he opined that "I never liked his music anyway."[160] One wonders what the two men might have thought of a remark passed about a decade later by a disinterested expert: Paul Hindemith. Hindemith told New York critic Howard Taubman that "there were only two composers in the last fifty years, whose music, in his view, would survive: Stravinsky and Bartók."[161]

FAREWELL TO GERRY'S LANDING

On 5 May 1940, just before the Stravinskys and Kall left Massachusetts for California, a group photograph was taken at Gerry's Landing (fig. 5.10).[162] In 1995 El Forbes, who appears in it, kindly identified everyone gathered to bid farewell to the three travelers. In respect to Marla Forbes (front row, far right), El told me that entries of "Zazy" and "Betsy" Forbes in Vera's published diary[163] are erroneous readings of "Basey," Marla's nickname.

During that day, there were also various games and pleasures, several of which El photographed. Two of the most charming moments involve Stravinsky with dogs—one fabricated, the other real. Though a well-known animal lover, Stravinsky's affection for dogs is not as well-documented as for cats. His fondness for the latter is displayed, for example, in the famous 1947 photograph by Henri Cartier-Bresson and in another one showing him in 1956 feeding feral felines in Venice.[164] Yet, as early as August of 1915 in a group photograph taken at the Villa Belle Rive at Ouchy (near Lausanne), he is shown with his long fingers caressing the neck of a small border collie. In 1926 at Biarritz, he strokes a German shepherd; in another picture taken in 1932 at Voreppe (near Grenoble) of the composer arm in arm with his mother, a sleek, black, and seemingly frightened dog (perhaps not belonging to the family) slinks away to his right.[165]

FIGURE 5.10
Forbes family, Gerry's Landing, 1940.
Back row, left to right: John M. Forbes
("Drig"), Elliot Forbes, William Bowers
("Bill"), Ruth Laighton (sister of "Peg").
Middle row: Gorg [*sic*] Street; Rosamond
F. Bowers ("Ros"), Alexis Kall, Igor
Stravinsky, Edward W. Forbes. *Seated:*
Margaret Laighton Forbes ("Peg"), Vera
Stravinsky, and Marla Forbes ("Basey").
Author's collection.

FIGURE 5.11
Stravinsky with Kall and toy dog,
1940. Author's collection.

FIGURE 5.12
Stravinsky attempts to befriend a
neighbor's dog, 1940. Elliot Forbes's
collection.

In May of 1940 at Gerry's Landing, the first of El's canine pictures shows Stravinsky
and Kall deep in some sort of conversation about a miniature stuffed animal (fig. 5.11).
Two closely related versions of this image survive from Mrs. McQuoid's collection (probably given to her by Kall), and the other from El's collection (omitting the table from the
right side). A different photograph by El shows a crouched Stravinsky doing his very best

to interest "Michael," a neighbor's wary police dog, with limited success (fig. 5.12). Yet another catches Michael lying quite amiably behind Stravinsky and Peg Forbes. As usual, the composer prevailed.

COMPOSER AS CONDUCTOR

Reviewing Stravinsky's concerts in mid-December of 1939 with the San Francisco Symphony, one critic remarked:

> The Card Game was extravagantly applauded by yesterday's audience, probably as much for the composer's superb handling of the orchestra as for its sardonic implications. . . . Stravinsky's conducting is a joy to watch as well as hear. His little figure, left hand on hip, bends with flexed knees, and he sways rhythmically as the baton lifts and lashes. He's dramatic without being "efforty" and poetic without pose. One feels his complete mastery of his conducting and his quiet self-confidence.[166]

By 1940, even New York critics usually acknowledged Stravinsky's improved conducting. A reviewer of Stravinsky's January concerts with the Philharmonic in Carnegie Hall noted:

> The composer has been heard before in New York under the same circumstances, when he was less efficient with the directorial stick. Since then, because of the many experiences as a guest leader all over the world, Stravinsky has acquired much technic in the handling of an orchestra, and now makes it play and interpret with excellent effect.[167]

But these reviews do not comport with the composer's recording of *Le Sacre* made on 4 April 1940 with the New York Philharmonic. It is flawed by several frantic insecurities in his conducting, as well as by the inadequate sonic reproduction of that era.

PART II

DOMESTIC EXCURSIONS FROM WARTIME LOS ANGELES

(1940–1946)

War conditions in Europe made it small wonder that as early as his wedding day on 9 March 1940, Stravinsky publicly announced that he planned to stay in the United States indefinitely.[1] Alexis Kall, residing for so many years in Los Angeles with his circle of Russian American friends, clearly influenced their choice of city. "But of course they will want to live in Los Angeles," said Dr. Kall in an interview printed in the *Boston Daily Globe* on 25 March. "That is where I live."[2] A month later, Stravinsky reported his departure on 15 May for California with his new bride, Kall, and Kall's friend Gregory Golubev via ship from New York to Galveston and thence by train—as well as his plans for a concert tour in 1940–41.[3]

Kall was in high disgrace for having forgotten the train tickets and losing two suitcases and a pocketbook in New York.[4] He further annoyed Vera shipboard by reciting Turgenev,[5] and presumably continued on with them by train from Houston to Los Angeles, where they were dismayed by the condition of Kall's house, which had been neglected during his absence.[6]

Two years later, after the attack on Pearl Harbor, and after almost a year in his newly purchased home on North Wetherly Drive in Hollywood, Stravinsky told his publisher that he would remain in California.[7] As Tamara Levitz has observed, "the dynamics of vernacular cosmopolitanism may explain why Stravinsky felt so at home in Los Angeles."[8] The Stravinskys did not become US citizens until 28 December 1945, after war's end. The event was documented for the *Los Angeles Times* by a photographer standing just outside the courtroom's double doors. He caught them smiling broadly, an image dubbed by the newspaper "Goal Reached."[9]

Valuable information about Stravinsky's wartime years in Los Angeles, and the music he composed and concerts he led during this period, is preserved in the holdings of the Sacher Foundation in Basel.[10] Among the most recent studies of these holdings, issued on the centennial of *Le Sacre du printemps* is David Schiff's witty and cleverly titled "Everyone's *Rite* (1939–1946)."[11]

Some writers (but neither Craft nor Cross) consider the five-year period between completing the Symphony in C (August 1940) and the Symphony in Three Movements (August 1945) as a relatively shallow one in Stravinsky's output, dismissing rather too readily—in my opinion—the compositions of those years: the Tango (1940–41), several arrangements of "The Star-Spangled Banner" (1941), *Danses concertantes* (1941), *Circus Polka* (1941–42), *Four Norwegian Moods* (1942), Ode (1943), Sonata for Two Pianos (1942–44), *Scherzo à la Russe* (1943–44), *Babel* (1944), *Scènes de ballet* (1944), and Élégie (1944). Paul Griffiths, for example, relegates *Scherzo à la Russe*, the swing bands of the *Praeludium*, and *Ebony Concerto* to "the outer dress of Americanism."[12] Craft, perhaps the least harsh of these critics, regarded these compositions as "little masterpieces-for-money," "at least genial," and "inventive," evaluations both honest and realistic. As he wrote subsequently, "In the 1940s . . . the[ir] extravagant variety . . . bewildered even his most faithful followers," and most recently, "jolly in mood . . . amazingly varied and fresh."[13] Cross argues that these works cannot "be so easily dismissed," that Stravinsky was seeking "to assimilate himself into American musical culture," and that "he found that his 'journeyman' work seeped into his 'art' work too."[14]

Yet, around the same time as Craft, Walsh discerned in these works "a succession of parodies of commercial style . . . because a popular style was called for by the commission."[15] Eventually, however, Walsh fretted that by late spring of 1944, "it might have struck him that he was in danger of sliding into a creative trough, dragged down by the commercial world's seemingly unquenchable thirst for the credit attached to his artistic fame." Walsh reveals his ambivalence. While characterizing works of this period as "an island of naive charm," he simultaneously denigrates them as "semi-potboilers," "soft-centered commercial potboilers," and "candid commercialism."[16] Charles Joseph adds that Stravinsky "was constantly under attack during the 1940s for writing trifling works."[17] Even the usually sympathetic David Schiff wants to reimagine Stravinsky's output in the 1940s as a "Zarathustrian descent (*untergehen*) from the cloister of academia into the American cultural marketplace."[18] But a persevering reader will discover that these dour evaluations are contradicted by some contemporaries, including that diligent, sharp-eared, highly experienced and often mordant composer-critic Virgil Thomson.

Scholars who complain about the quantity and quality of Stravinsky's production in this period fail to take several factors into account. Chief among these factors are the difficulties attendant on an émigré's relocation (in Stravinsky's case, relocation to relatively unsophisticated California) and the problems of a man who enjoyed money and whose prewar income, if not actually diminished, became more and more uncertain. The substantial amounts of time between 1941 and mid-1943 that he devoted to working with Earnest Andersson and revising hundreds of pages of his works may have been a contributing factor. Critics also seem to forget that even an "immortal's" path is fraught with the torments attendant on mortality.

The composer's dental problems could have sufficed by themselves. There were numerous trips to dentists while still in Boston, then one in Los Angeles, two in New York, and one extraction on 31 March 1941 in Los Angeles.[19] Andersson entered in his notebook on 8 April 1941 that Stravinsky "had 8 teeth out of upper jaw and was ill. Got out of bed to work with me." Just the previous day, Stravinsky recorded a mere "four teeth extracted from the upper jaw."[20] Misery enough, but more was to follow. On 18 April Andersson noted that the Stravinskys' "dentist bill will be $1000," no small sum in 1941. Six days later, Stravinsky recorded in his own diary not only Andersson's twenty-fourth lesson—his student's fifty-dollar fees minimally helpful for such bills—but also a laconic "new denture (2nd one)."[21] On 26 May Vera's diary reads, "Took Igor to the dentist, who extracted a tooth—unexpectedly." Around the same time, Andersson noted that "he must spend 2 hours at dentist to drill for bridge."[22] More visits are recorded on 10 June, 2 and 7 July, 21 August, and 20 October, and then, just two days later, heroically (but fortunately inaccurately) enough by the composer—"Two new jaws." There were still more visits at the close of the year: on 13, 19, 24, 28 November, on 1, 5, 11 December, and then on 17, 24 April 1942 and a broken tooth on 12 July 1943, two weeks after Andersson's death. Stravinsky seems to have been spared only during 1944. Later years saw further visits to dentists on 18 January 1945 and 29 May 1946.[23] As if these ailments were not sufficiently debilitating, still others loomed. For example, in the midst of these oral reconstructions, both Andersson and Vera cite the composer's joint problems. Days after Andersson began lessons, his very first entry in his notebook (about 6 March 1941) captures Stravinsky's colorful English: "Knee not so glad," with Vera's confirmation that "Igor stays home with a pain in the knee."[24]

Shortly after war's end, Stravinsky had to endure a different kind of malaise, hostile European criticism of his music composed during the war. He and his works were embroiled in the same kind of musico-literary wars he had previously endured in the 1920s and 1930s.[25] Two of the attackers were ardent Schoenbergians: René Leibowitz in 1947 and Theodore Adorno in 1948.

Leibowitz can be dismissed because of his evident bias and sheer nastiness. After visiting Stravinsky late in 1947, Leibowitz repaid the Russian composer's hospitality and willingness to be interviewed with a vituperative summation in the decidedly left-wing *Partisan Review,* a journal much favored by US intellectuals. He wrote in part about "works brilliantly made but behind these frozen and sometimes readymade patterns . . . there is nothing except perhaps the illusion of music."[26] Later, Nabokov, a longtime acquaintance of Stravinsky's and a composer himself, rebuked Leibowitz in the same journal.[27] It was said, however, to have "displeased Stravinsky with the superficial arguments," and Leibowitz eventually had the last word.[28]

Adorno had such an obvious anti-Stravinskian bias that Schoenberg was moved to say, "Disgusting, by the way, how he treats Stravinsky, . . . one should not write like that."[29] Although Adorno had studied composition for several months with Schoenberg's pupil Alban Berg, his methods have been described as "inadequate for analyzing musical scores and interpreting a composer's intentions."[30] Schoenberg called Adorno's writings "blathering jargon."[31] Sir Isaiah Berlin characterized Adorno as "a marvelously comic figure" about whose proposed lecture "not a word will be understood."[32] Craft's 1974 essay "A Bell for Adorno" offers an effective coup de grâce.[33] But Milan Kundera best summarizes Adorno's Schoenberg-Stravinsky dialectic:

> [Adorno] depicts the situation in music as if it were a political battle: Schoenberg the positive hero, the representative of progress (though a progress that might be termed tragic, at a time when progress is over), and Stravinsky the negative hero, the representative of restoration. The Stravinskian refusal to see subjective confession as music's raison d'être becomes one target of the Adorno critique.[34]

Even so, readers here will soon encounter a sample of this rhetorical genre (several years before either Adorno or Leibowitz). It was trotted out in July of 1941 by Jorge Santana, a Marxist-Freudian critic in Mexico City who was then reviewing several works led there by Stravinsky, including his premiere of Symphony in C.

More objective are several essays offered during the war: by Nicolas Nabokov;[35] by a more recent intimate, fellow-composer Ingolf Dahl, who first met Stravinsky on 21 September 1941;[36] and by Los Angeles critic Lawrence Morton, who encountered Stravinsky just three weeks later, in October of 1941, but rarely conversed with him again until war's end.[37] These men were sympathetic to and knowledgeable about his music.

A substantive review of many Stravinsky works from wartime (1940–44) by this same Nabokov (cousin of the writer, Vladimir) was slated for *Harper's Magazine*. He was apparently the only person (save perhaps Andersson) who ever overheard Stravinsky actually composing.[38] Nabokov's essay was rejected by *Harper's* for being "too technical,"[39] a restriction rarely, if ever, imposed on critics of literature in that journal. Fortunately for our purposes, Nabokov told Stravinsky (even if vaguely) the general thesis of his article: "Your music . . . brings technique and artistic meaning together again, after the estrangement caused by the hubris of the nineteenth century." According to Stravinsky's letters in September and October of 1943 and early January of 1944, Nabokov's article would have discussed Symphony in C, *Danses concertantes, Four Norwegian Moods, Circus Polka, Dumbarton Oaks Concerto,* and Ode.[40] Yet all was not lost: *Partisan Review* published parts of Nabokov's essay, although neither *Four Norwegian Moods* nor *Circus Polka* finds mention.[41] Succeeding chapters here will cite some of Nabokov's observations, as well as those by Dahl and Morton.

That every work a great musician writes must be accordingly great is manifestly supererogatory. There is no reason why composers should not suffer less creative or even fallow periods when they produce secondary works. We are not particularly disturbed that, during the War of 1812, Beethoven should have written a Battle Symphony ("Wellington's Victory"), nor are we upset by Tchaikovsky's later evocation of the same conflict.

So it was with Stravinsky: he had relatively unproductive periods in both world wars. During the first, except for both the astonishing *Renard* and *Les Noces,* he produced minor but attractive works bounded chronologically by two important compositions: *Pribaoutki* in September of 1914, *L'Histoire* in 1918. In December of 1939 he told a San Francisco newspaper interviewer that "war can never be good for the arts. . . . Life is deranged." Writing composer Carlos Chávez in May of 1940, he expressed himself more personally: "The terrible events in Europe have made me ill and unable to work."[42] True as that surely was, his record of compositional activity during the tense days of World War II is impressive. In several respects it is astonishing: although it comprises such minor but beguiling creations as Tango, *Circus Polka, Four Norwegian Moods,* and the *Scherzo à la Russe,* it also embraces the *Danses concertantes,* Ode, *Babel,* Elegy, Sonata for Two Pianos, and the *Scènes de ballet.*

6

EXCURSIONS (1940–1941)

CONCERT APPEARANCES

26, 28 July: Mexico City, Orquesta Sinfónica

2, 4 August: Mexico City, Orquesta Sinfónica

26, 28 August: Hollywood Bowl

7, 8, 12 November: Chicago Symphony

22, 23 November: Cincinnati Orchestra

20 December: Minneapolis Orchestra

7 January: Baltimore, National Symphony

8 January: Washington, National Symphony

16 January: Cambridge, Boston Symphony

17, 18 January: Boston Symphony

22, 24, 26 January: New York (Balustrade)

13, 14 February: Los Angeles Philharmonic

18 February: San Diego, Los Angeles Philharmonic

18, 20 July: Mexico City, Orquesta Sinfónica

19 July: Mexico City, Orquesta Sinfónica (recording Divertimento)

14 October: WPA Orchestra (I. S. cancelled plans to speak)

19–20 December: St. Louis Symphony

ANGELENO "ASSOCIATES"

"Except for the peculiar case of Mr. Ernest [sic] Anderson," Craft declared himself to be, in the 1940s, "Stravinsky's only monolingual native-born American associate." Later, perhaps seeking to guarantee his own exclusivity, even "the peculiar case" was eliminated: "I was the only born-and-bred American among both his California and New York friends."[1]

Although I am unable to offer names of native-born, non-multilingual East Coasters, I must nevertheless contest these assertions. In addition to Andersson, several California residents in 1940 and 1941 were "American associates," albeit less influential and for far briefer periods than Craft: Los Angeles–born Adele Marcus, the McQuoids and their children, Andersson's daughter Ernestine; and especially his son-in-law, James Sample—all of them "born and bred" in the good old USA.

Mrs. McQuoid and her son, Cary Ellis, having already been introduced in Tour 5, a few words are in order about the late and irrepressible Dorothy Ellis McQuoid Hopper. Knowing considerable French, Mrs. McQuoid could rightfully claim her place among the elect from having occasionally wined and dined the Stravinskys in her garden after their arrival in California on 23 May 1940, that June, and later into the fall. Few of these occasions are cited in the published version of Vera's diary.[2]

Owing to the shoddy state of Kall's house, the Stravinskys moved into an apartment for a week or so. While ascending the outside stairs of some small apartment building, Mrs. McQuoid remembered being in the lead. Followed by Stravinsky with Vera behind him, she heard him whisper "Dorothee, vous avez un bel Popo."[3] Understanding and much amused, rather than in the slightest offended, by his German slang for her *derrière*, she burst out laughing. Vera asked what was so funny and when Dorothy informed her, all three laughed heartily together.[4] On 31 May they drove around (with Dorothy McQuoid or the Adolph Bolms) "all day looking for a house."[5] Notwithstanding a growing housing shortage, the Stravinskys rather quickly, on 3 June 1940, leased a residence at 124 South Swall Drive, just outside of Beverly Hills.[6] Dorothy helped them move in three days later.

Probably notified before he left Boston, Stravinsky had been elected a "Foreign Honorary Member" of the American Academy of Arts and Sciences. For obvious reasons of personal prestige, and even though by then he had moved definitively to California, he used stationery headed "Harvard University" that he had purloined. Typing over the page's "Department of Music," and typing below it "Los Angeles, Calif.," Stravinsky responded graciously the day before he signed the lease at South Swall: "I shall be proud of belonging to such an outstanding institution."[7] This letter was probably typed either by Beata Bolm (wife of the celebrated dancer-choreographer) or by Dorothy herself.

Traveling south of the border to renew their temporary visitor visas, the Stravinskys were met in Mexico City on 22 July 1940 by composer-conductor Carlos Chávez, who would, almost twenty years later, hold Stravinsky's former post as the Charles Eliot Norton Lecturer.[8] About 2 August the Stravinskys mailed a postcard from Mexico City to the McQuoids: Vera greeted them in English as "Dear friends," as did Stravinsky, who anticipated a speedy "return in one week with good news (we hope)" (fig. 6.1), his last four words referring to their expectations of new US visas, which would allow them to apply for US citizenship.[9] Their visas were received on 8 August at the Mexican-American border town of Nogales, although not without considerable wrangling "with a 'very suspicious' U.S. border guard."[10]

At their return the next day from Mexico with the precious visas, Dorothy photographed the pair being helped off the train by Adolph Bolm (whom she also knew), an image run the same day in the *Hollywood Citizen News*.[11] Two days later, she may also have been involved when Stravinsky gave "his first extemporaneous talk in English" on 11 August 1940 "for a women's organization [unidentified]" in Beverly Hills.[12]

That same day, an interview by Isabel Morse Jones was printed in the *Los Angeles Times*:

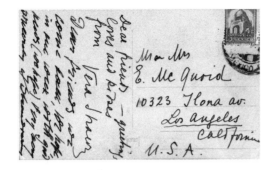

FIGURE 6.1

1940 Mexico postcard (back) to both McQuoids. UBC Stravinsky Collection, no. 70

Igor Stravinsky finding himself at home in a Beverly Hills bungalow ... [his] new work [Symphony in C], which he is now finishing, will be conducted in Chicago.... He will prepare his [Hollywood] Bowl program as he lives: with religious zeal. There will be rehearsals of surpassing earnestness. He has come to Southern California in chaos and turmoil and found quiet. Of this he will produce his music, Russian music always; not of America, not of California, not of Paris but of Russia, that complex and fascinating and nervous people who are individually and collectively artists of the world-theater. He was trained for the law. His study of logic bore fruit in his music.... I can testify that his conversational logic is of the same directness. To logic he has added his own peculiar mysticism.[13]

This stilted and secondhand-sounding report does not resemble Jones's normal prose, even in her most awkward moments. It does not represent Stravinsky's English at this period, either. It has the ring of translation, possibly from French, or more probably from Russian, made with the help of someone whose native tongue was not English. Perhaps it was Dr. Kall, whom Jones knew well and greatly admired and who had just served as translator for Stravinsky at Harvard.

Mrs. McQuoid also remembered playing the newly completed finale of the Symphony in C (finished 17 August) four-hands with the composer. Perhaps this was on 4 September 1940, for she appears that day in Vera's diary.[14] In respect to the new symphony's title, months before it was complete, he told a musicologist in Boston that "all notes gravitate towards a single note."[15]

Probably in the summer or early fall of 1940, Stravinsky inscribed a cropped photograph of himself (fig. 6.2). It came from the series taken by Hoyningen-Huené on 16 May 1934 in Paris.[16] The growing intimacy between the Stravinskys and McQuoids—predictable from the Farmer's Market photograph—is evident in the Stravinskys entertaining on 23 October 1940 "for dinner McQuoids, Mrs. Smith"[17] (perhaps a neighbor) and by actions taken the following week by Edwin McQuoid. The inscribed Hoyningen-Huené photograph to Dorothy inspired him; he imitated the Frenchman's shadow at the right of Stravinsky's head when he made at least three studies of the composer on 28–29 October 1940, noted by Vera as "McQuoid photos" and "McQuoid"[18] (henceforth

FIGURE 6.2
Hoyningen-Huené portrait of
Stravinsky (cropped) inscribed
"Dorothy Dorothy . . . . . / for you / I
Stravinsky / 1940." UBC
Stravinsky Collection no. 72.

McQuoid a, McQuoid b, and McQuoid c). "Edwin McQuoid" is stamped at its lower right side (fig. 6.3) and "PHOTO BY EDWIN McQUOID 10323 Ilona Ave., L.A." stamped on its obverse. Stravinsky frequently used these photos over the next few years, for example, an exemplar of McQuoid *a* inscribed to Mrs. Armsby of the San Francisco Symphony Association. But Stravinsky also continued to use photos from the Hoyningen-Huené sessions, including one for Mrs. Koshland, his hostess in San Francisco, in which areas of light and shadow are strangely reversed (see below, fig. 6.8).

Though hardly the sort of "associates" Craft had in mind, both of Dorothy's boys frequently rough-housed on the floor with Stravinsky, and, undeniably, their conversations were in English. Having already posed on 18 December 1939 in front of Kall's house with Mrs. McQuoid's younger son, Cary Ellis, at some point in the following year the composer sought to enlighten the elder son, Ronald Richard, apropos of a 1932 essay that had appeared in *Minute Sketches of Great Composers*. He inscribed the boy's copy: "It is / perfectly / idiotic / Yes / I Str" (fig. 6.4).[19]

Dorothy's rival, Angeleno Adele Marcus, likewise qualifies as an "associate"; Stravinsky would have talked to her in English, and perhaps also in pidgin German-Italian, as

FIGURE 6.3
Stravinsky posing for Edwin
McQuoid. UBC Stravinsky
Collection, no. 73.

with his "ohne espressione" request in early 1940 at a rehearsal of the Concerto for Two Solo Pianos, mentioned above. No term for "expressive" (let alone "nonexpressive") appears in his Concerto; perhaps he was correcting her overly enthusiastic interpretation of the four cantabile passages or the single dolce that appear only in piano 1, the part she played.[20] She also performed the Capriccio under him in Los Angeles in February of 1941.

The last "associate," US-born Earnest Andersson did indeed speak only English, except for a few Swedish words he learned from his immigrant parents and, much later, from Swedish friends in Los Angeles and perhaps even from Vera Stravinsky, who, from infancy, might have remembered some words from her Swedish-born mother. He became acquainted with the composer in mid-February of 1941, just after Igor and Vera returned to the Château Marmont ("cosy, in good taste")[21] in Hollywood, back from a performance with the Los Angeles Philharmonic in San Diego (the supposed "last" stop on what Vera had called their "concert tour"). Andersson's notebook hints at the deep, serious discussions they had in English about music, belying Craft's description of Andersson's almost two-year association with Stravinsky as a "peculiar case."

THE FIRST EXCURSION

The first concert engagement was for late July of 1940 in Mexico City. After cocktails on 17 July at Kall's house on the eve of their departure, the Stravinskys set out by train on 18 July, arriving five days later in Mexico City. They were met by Carlos Chávez, the widely respected chief conductor (1928–48) of the Orquesta Sinfónica de México, who had invited Stravinsky the previous February.[22]

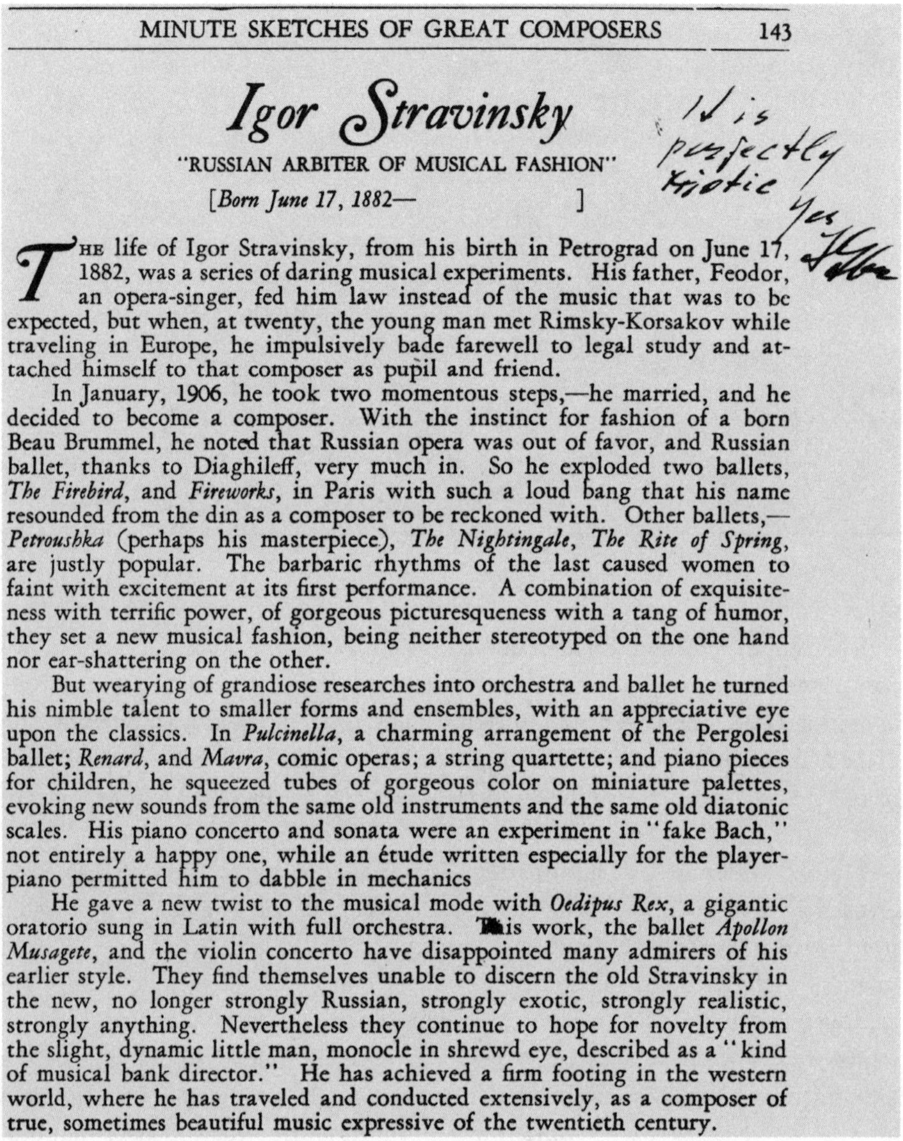

Igor Stravinsky

"RUSSIAN ARBITER OF MUSICAL FASHION"

[*Born June 17, 1882—*   ]

*It is
perfectly
idiotic
yes*

THE life of Igor Stravinsky, from his birth in Petrograd on June 17, 1882, was a series of daring musical experiments. His father, Feodor, an opera-singer, fed him law instead of the music that was to be expected, but when, at twenty, the young man met Rimsky-Korsakov while traveling in Europe, he impulsively bade farewell to legal study and attached himself to that composer as pupil and friend.

In January, 1906, he took two momentous steps,—he married, and he decided to become a composer. With the instinct for fashion of a born Beau Brummel, he noted that Russian opera was out of favor, and Russian ballet, thanks to Diaghileff, very much in. So he exploded two ballets, *The Firebird*, and *Fireworks*, in Paris with such a loud bang that his name resounded from the din as a composer to be reckoned with. Other ballets,— *Petroushka* (perhaps his masterpiece), *The Nightingale*, *The Rite of Spring*, are justly popular. The barbaric rhythms of the last caused women to faint with excitement at its first performance. A combination of exquisiteness with terrific power, of gorgeous picturesqueness with a tang of humor, they set a new musical fashion, being neither stereotyped on the one hand nor ear-shattering on the other.

But wearying of grandiose researches into orchestra and ballet he turned his nimble talent to smaller forms and ensembles, with an appreciative eye upon the classics. In *Pulcinella*, a charming arrangement of the Pergolesi ballet; *Renard*, and *Mavra*, comic operas; a string quartette; and piano pieces for children, he squeezed tubes of gorgeous color on miniature palettes, evoking new sounds from the same old instruments and the same old diatonic scales. His piano concerto and sonata were an experiment in "fake Bach," not entirely a happy one, while an étude written especially for the player-piano permitted him to dabble in mechanics

He gave a new twist to the musical mode with *Oedipus Rex*, a gigantic oratorio sung in Latin with full orchestra. This work, the ballet *Apollon Musagete*, and the violin concerto have disappointed many admirers of his earlier style. They find themselves unable to discern the old Stravinsky in the new, no longer strongly Russian, strongly exotic, strongly realistic, strongly anything. Nevertheless they continue to hope for novelty from the slight, dynamic little man, monocle in shrewd eye, described as a "kind of musical bank director." He has achieved a firm footing in the western world, where he has traveled and conducted extensively, as a composer of true, sometimes beautiful music expressive of the twentieth century.

FIGURE 6.4

Inscription "Perfectly idiotic" in *Minute Sketches*, 1932. Author's photo.

Stravinsky led four highly successful concerts with the Orquesta, on 26 and 28 July and on 2 and 4 August,[23] and was "accorded one of the greatest ovations ever given by the music-loving Mexican public" (fig. 6.5).[24] Between the last pair of concerts, he tried recording his 1934 Divertimento with the Orquesta, but owing to extraneous noise, this attempt failed.[25]

FIGURE 6.5
Conducting the Orquesta Sinfónica de México. *Boletin de la Orquesta Sinfónica de Mexico,* Nov. 1940.

Nine days later, Stravinsky was back in Los Angeles, occupied with finishing his Symphony in C, completing its last movement on 17 August (a work he would program during his next trip to Mexico). That same day, and on 23 and 26 August, he rehearsed his 1919 *Firebird Suite,* Tchaikovsky's Second Symphony, and the *Nutcracker Suite* for the following evening's performance in the Hollywood Bowl. He frequently programmed this particular Tchaikovsky symphony. In the United States he had first performed it on his final transatlantic tour in 1939 in mid-December concerts with the San Francisco Orchestra, then in January of 1940 with the New York Philharmonic, the latter reading preserved on a compact disc. By the time of the Hollywood Bowl spectacular, he was fresh from having just led it in Mexico City.

Among the audience at the Bowl that evening of 27 August were Mr. and Mrs. Edwin McQuoid. At the close of the program they heard and saw a spectacular balletic production of *The Firebird Suite* staged and choreographed by Adolph Bolm,[26] whom they also knew.

One account of the *Firebird* production at the Bowl mentions a "scintillating performance. . . . Changes were made in the story to fit necessary changes in the music."[27] The nature of the changes was unspecified but hinted at in another review as stemming from the music having been "confined to that of the [1919] concert suite, therefore, somewhat restructured."[28] Another review describes the story's changes at the end of the ballet: "the

FIGURE 6.6
Hollywood *Firebird,* 1940. Courtesy of Hollywood Bowl Archives.

orchestra was concealed in the shell behind the dance stage and also behind the opu-
lently fantastic décor ingeniously conceived by Nicolas [Vladimirovich] Remisoff, so that
conductor and dancers were invisible to each other."[29] The end of the balletic narrative is
partly described in still another review: "Remisoff had designed a screen of brightly
painted and brilliantly lit shrubbery to conceal the orchestra. At the end of *The Firebird*
the bushes slid sideways 'to reveal a fairy-tale city that reached into a rainbow' and the
Firebird 'mounted the topmost tower in triumph.' "[30] Remisoff was a friend of both
Stravinsky and Bolm. A photograph of his stage-set confirms the separation of dancers
and musicians and demonstrates the scope of the Bowl's presentation (fig. 6.6).[31]

   After that evening's performance the McQuoids sent Stravinsky a night letter, containing just the single word "Bravo," repeated fifty times. Vera noted it the next day in her
diary as a "telegram / 50 times Bravo / from Dorothy McQuoid."[32]

   Stravinsky, however, responded both verbally and musically: his thank-you letter was
written in English, again on stationery purloined from Harvard's music department (fig.
6.7). This time he simply stroked out its headings in brown ink, adding: "Beverly
Hills / August 28th / 40." He inscribed two short pieces of music on this sheet, both drawn

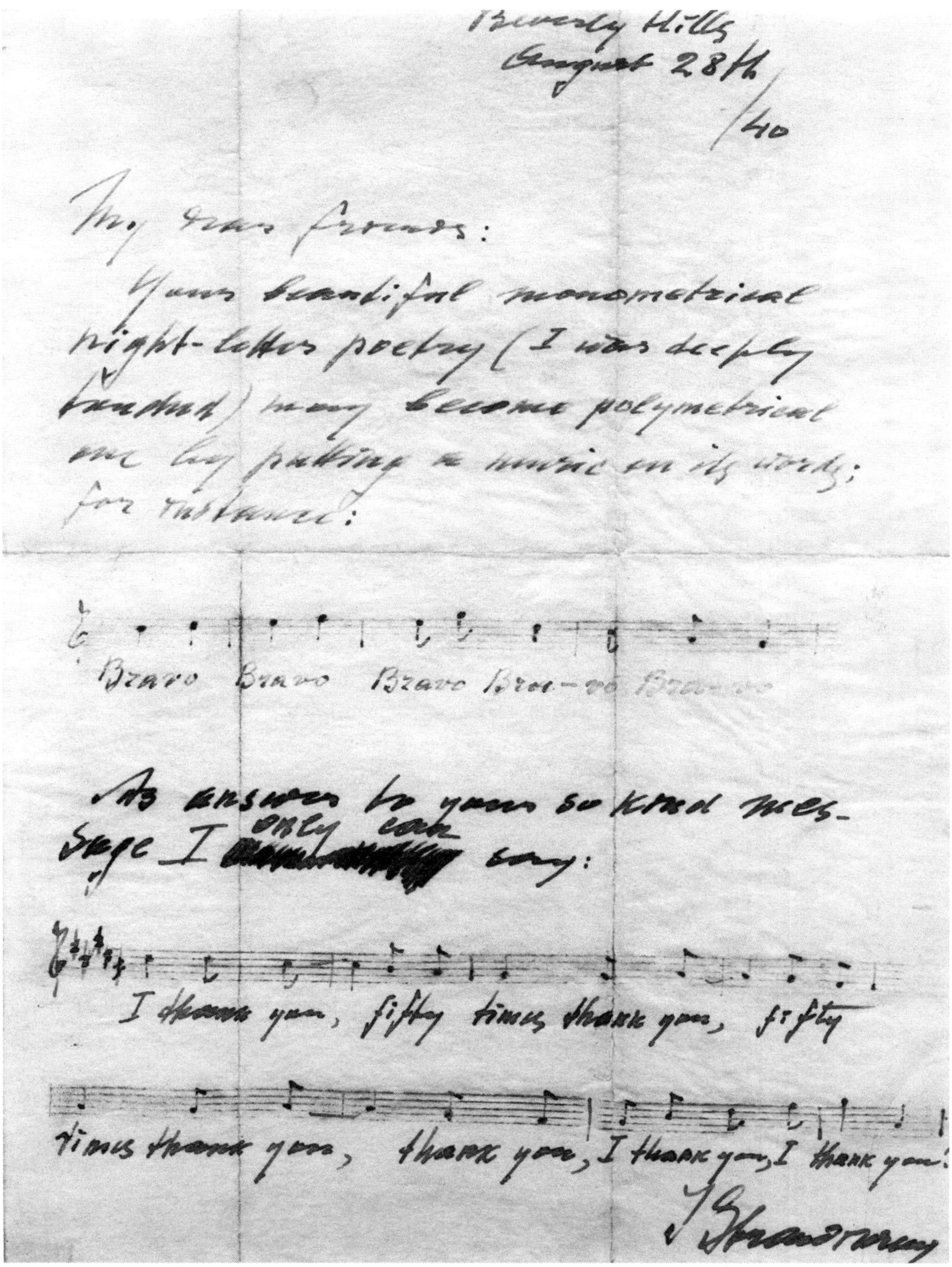

Beverly Hills
August 28th/40

My dear friends:

Your beautiful monometrical night-letter poetry (I was deeply touched) may become polymetrical one by putting a music on its words; for instance:

Bravo Bravo Bravo Bra-vo Bravo

As answer to your so kind message I only can say:

I thank you, fifty times thank you, fifty times thank you, thank you, I thank you, I thank you!

I Strawinsky

FIGURE 6.7

Fragment, Tchaikovsky, "I thank you." UBC Stravinsky Collection, no. 71.

EXAMPLE 6.1

"Bravo, bravo."

Bra - vo Bra - vo Bra - vo Bra - vo Bra - vo

from a work he conducted the previous evening: Tchaikovsky's Second Symphony. Stravinsky's upper quotation consists of four measures of the first theme from Tchaikovsky's finale; his lower one is the antecedent phrase of the second theme from the same finale.

As Stravinsky indicated in his thank-you letter, the first piece of music was as "monometric" (meaning, in uniform time values) as the original congratulatory message: "Bravo, Bravo . . ." Its first two monometric measures, followed by a different monometric pair, thus fulfill his message's promise to "become polymetrical." Normal pronunciation would stress its initial syllable: Brávo. Inhibited perhaps by Tchaikovsky's too-frequent repetition of the Ukrainian folk tune "The Crane" that opens the final movement, Stravinsky utilizes the word just five times: [²⁄₄] "Brá-vo | Brá-vo | Brá-vo Bra- | vó Bra-vó |." Later, in 1944, Nabokov (surely unaware of this message to the McQuoids) would discuss Stravinsky's term *monometric,* apropos of the Symphony in C (see Excursion 4).

The last half of the penultimate measure and the entire closing measure of this four-bar inscription merit attention (see ex. 6.1). Stravinsky transforms "Bravo" from a trochee into an iamb, the latter's effect strengthened in the final measure by the tune's arrival at the lower dominant, even though it falls on the weaker half of the measure.

Much more intriguing is the other piece, his third setting of an English text: a full sentence of his own devising with a pertinent numerical reference to their night-letter: "I thank you, fifty times . . . I thank you!" He uses the eight-measure antecedent phrase of Tchaikovsky's second theme (again in duple meter) from the finale of the "Little Russian" Symphony, a tune stated first in A-flat major and later in C major. Stravinsky omitted all of Tchaikovsky's eighth-note rests and transposed the tune to B major. This transposition was not just to avoid tonal monotony with his previously inscribed "Bravo" and, perhaps, to emphasize its first letter. Rather, except for a brief contrast in G major (reh. 18–19), the "Final" [*sic*] of the *Firebird Suite* (reh. 11 to its close) stays in B major right to its triumphal close. That ultimate, sustained, and shattering full-orchestral B, spanning many octaves, is thus the last pitch that would have rung in the McQuoid's ears at the end of that evening's Bowl concert.

A native English speaker would stress "thánk you" and "fífty." Imposing Stravinsky's English text on Tchaikovsky's music causes several mild deformations. At its initial A-flat major appearance in the first violins, Tchaikovsky gently underlined the stresses resulting from his slightly syncopated tune by accenting sustained half notes every alternate measure in the slower-moving second violins. This effects a kind of mild gulp, reinforcing the

EXAMPLE 6.2

Rebarring of "I thank you."

gentle bump that had resulted from each preceding syncopation in the first violins. When, later on in the movement, the tune returns in C major, this echo-accent increases a little, because this time Tchaikovsky also accents the violas in the same manner as he had the second violins. According to the music alone, then, stresses would fall as shown in example 6.2, with the opening first violin appoggiatura adding a slight emphasis to the first note.

Sixty years ago at Harvard, the revered and brilliant Hungarian scholar Professor Otto Gombosi[33] taught his graduate students in musicology to consider rebarring passages like those in example 6.2 in order to discover their true rhythmic structures. Alas, from 1953 to 1955 I was only briefly the recipient of his inspired instruction, but his longtime student Professor Emeritus Daniel Heartz kindly suggested one rebarring of the tune, which, as he observed, lies in the transposed Dorian mode. His suggestion of triplicity within the melody leads me to propose a still different rebarring from his, wherein Stravinsky opens with three isometric measures ($\frac{3}{8} + \frac{5}{8}$) and concludes with two cadential duple measures. The two-measure isorhythmic formation ($\frac{3}{8} + \frac{5}{8}$), continuing for a third time over the tune's initial six measures, creates iambs rather than trochees. And the syncopations across Tchaikovsky's bar lines cause repeated short-longs at *thank you* and a stress on both statements of *times.*

Rebarring also shows that, whatever verbal emphases Stravinsky may have intended, gentle—but incorrect—iambic stresses will fall on *you* in the isometric measures and perhaps create unwanted stresses on *times* (barred here in $\frac{3}{8}$). A correct trochee occurs only on Stravinsky's final "thánk you," set appropriately to the highest note (the concluding bar of $\frac{2}{4}$), with a lesser stress on the first *I.* This analysis can be confirmed in the recording of Stravinsky's 7 January 1940 performance with the New York Philharmonic, wherein the first violins add a slight vibrato on notes tied across the bar lines, that is, on *you* in Stravinsky's setting (see ex. 6.3).

In setting his own English words to Tchaikovsky's tune, Stravinsky thus produces a minor anomaly:

[$\frac{2}{4}$] I thank yó | u, fífty | tímes thank yó | u, fífty | tímes thank yó | u, thank you, | I thank you, I thánk you! ||

EXAMPLE 6.3

Tchaikovsky, Symphony No. 2, theme 2, initial mm. 1–24.

Still, even his single repetition of *fifty* helps a little to conceptualize a number of considerable and unusual magnitude. Peculiar as it seems, and slightly awkward to sing as its conclusion indisputably is, the stresses on *you* that Stravinsky imposes on his English sentence convey a message of genuine appreciation to the McQuoids for their ingenious telegram.

A BRIEF HOLIDAY UP CALIFORNIA'S COAST

After the Bowl presentations, and a visit to Edward G. Robinson's ranch on 6 September 1940, the Stravinskys embarked on a brief nonmusical adventure: a one-week road trip to San Francisco and back. The previous 28 June, after several extremely necessary remedial driving lessons given by Dorothy McQuoid,[34] Vera had passed the California driver's test and obtained her license. She was probably glad to escape the invitations they were receiving from Angelenos, having written a friend in Europe on 26 August (the last rehearsal for the Bowl extravaganza) that she spent much of her time "fighting off invitations; we have several for each day."[35]

On their way north, accompanied by both Bolms, they motored up the scenic coast to Monterey and Carmel, then inland to Los Gatos,[36] and then on to San Francisco, where they stayed with a wealthy socialite. For her, the thrifty Stravinsky inscribed an image of himself, 11 × 16.5 cm, a somewhat decrepit remnant from the 1934 Hoyningen-Huené photo sessions, but, peculiarly, in reverse, with the message "Pour Madame / Marcus / Koshland son admirateur / Igor Stravinsky / 1940" (fig. 6.8).[37] After visiting the Darius Milhauds in Oakland, they headed northeast to Yosemite and arrived back in Hollywood on 13 September.[38]

During October of 1940, Stravinsky, Gregory Stone (Stravinsky's agent), and Gregory Golubev (Kall's friend and housemate) tried several times to set English words to Stravinsky's tiny Tango, just composed.[39] Preceding a third staff line directly above the piano part, Stravinsky had marked *golos* (voice) in his prerevolutionary Russian hand for an ensuing melody only slightly independent of the piano.[40] The tangled tale of this work stretches well into the following year and beyond, involving New York publisher Feist, Dorothy McQuoid, African American singer-dancer Katherine Dunham, duo-pianists Vronsky and Babin, student Andersson, colleague Dushkin and his accompanist Henry Kaufman, Benny Goodman, pianist-conductor Iturbi, the entire Philadelphia Orchestra, and, eventually, in April of 1942, Leopold Stokowski in Los Angeles. A discussion appears in Excursion 2.

By September of 1940 Sol Babitz had reintroduced himself to Stravinsky, trading on their 1935 orchestral meeting, memorialized with an affectionately inscribed newspaper photograph of the composer in rehearsal. On 13 October 1940 Stravinsky rehearsed his Violin Concerto with Babitz in the auditorium of Hollywood High School with a group called the "Hollywood Rehearsal Orchestra." Perhaps Stravinsky and Babitz envisaged a public concert, because Stravinsky also rehearsed Tchaikovsky's "Little Russian"

FIGURE 6.8

Stravinsky Hoyningen-Huené portrait (flipped) inscribed to Madame Marcus Koshland, 1940. Author's private collection.

Symphony, a work he had just conducted in Mexico and at the Bowl. Seated that day in the auditorium, Vera Stravinsky described the group as "wonderful young people who sightread his Violin Concerto played by Sol Babitz."[41] Ingolf Dahl was at the rehearsal and wrote in his diary that Stravinsky "conducts like a dancing demon."[42] This was not Babitz's initial encounter with the Violin Concerto. He had heard Dushkin premiere it in Berlin on 23 October 1931 with Stravinsky conducting.[43] Nor was Babitz sight-reading such a difficult work, even if the orchestra members were: he had played it for Stravinsky a month earlier, with Dahl at the piano.[44]

Vera's mention of "young people" is only slightly challenged by a large photograph, taken at this orchestral rehearsal, *Hollywood Rehearsal Orchestra,* for it shows at Stravinsky's right a balding second violinist, although the woman next to him and the violinists seated behind Babitz seem youthful enough.

Though he looks too heavy, was this, perhaps, the twenty-eight-year-old Ingolf Dahl?[45] Later, the composer inscribed this photograph for Babitz when Babitz visited the Stravinskys on 27 October 1940 at their rented house on South Swall Drive. In a blank white space (visible below the stage level), the composer wrote a jumbled "Sol Babitz / with my 'kindnest' [sic] / souvenirs / Igor Strawinsky / Oct 27 / 40" and added a line circling back to "Sol Babitz." Vera described this visit as "Igor works with Sol Babitz on the Violin Concerto and is furious because of mistakes in the score."[46] The mistakes were presumably rectified by the time Stravinsky wrote to Babitz on 30 December 1940 from New York, referring to his Concerto, "wich [sic] I conduct in January here (S. Dushkin is playing) at [performances of George Balanchine's ballet, *Balustrade* by] the Ballet-Russe of [Colonel de] Basil.[47] From then on, Babitz and his family were close to the Stravinskys. Craft later reported that in 1948 Babitz was among the first people to whom Stravinsky introduced him.[48]

TWO LECTURES IN BEVERLY HILLS

On 16 October 1940 Kall and Golubev lectured in the Palm Room of the Beverly Hills Hotel. Both Stravinskys attended.[49] Kall contributed his 1937 talk, "Igor Stravinsky as I Know Him," which he had already given in San Francisco and which was, perhaps, still based on those notes he had made on the backs of the Pushkin flyers. This time his talk was "illustrated by Stravinsky's own recordings new and unreleased." They were likely the four April 1940 recordings Stravinsky had made with the New York Philharmonic of the *Rite* and *Petrushka*,[50] or perhaps even the recent spoiled recording of the Divertimento in Mexico City:[51] Golubev's topic was "Stravinsky and Pushkin," based on his recent translation of the essay ghostwritten for Stravinsky by his son-in-law for the 1937 Pushkin celebration. Golubev published his translation ("from the French") in New York and Hollywood in 1940 as *Pushkin: Poetry and Music*.[52] It contains some maladroit—and suspicious—tailorings of the year 1937 into 1940 by means of such clumsy phrases as "Only three years ago . . . during the Centennial Commemoration of Alexander Pushkin's death," and "one hundred and three years after his death . . ."[53] Perhaps Golubev also worked, without much input from Stravinsky, from the 1937 Kavenoki typescript discussed in Tour IV.

Nevertheless, Stravinsky had a genuine, lifelong interest in Pushkin, and he respected Golubev's translation, even though he would surely have wanted to keep secret the true author of the pamphlet; the printed invitation for the dual lecture quotes Stravinsky, in part: "As one reads Pushkin's poetry in Gregory Golubeff's translations, the first thing that comes to one's mind is his extraordinary success in revealing the self-same 'Pushkin' music, the music of his syllables, vowels and phrases. One reads (in English) and wonders at the charm of the original text."[54]

The composer's regard for Pushkin can be traced as far back as the 1902 song "Storm Cloud" and the 1922 *Mavra*, with its libretto "à la mémoire de *Pouchkine*." And later, in July of 1941, when Kall gave the Stravinskys a present of books for their long train-ride at the beginning of Stravinsky's second concert visit to Mexico, the couple mailed a postcard to Kall from El Paso, just before crossing the border. Vera thanked him in Russian for poems by Akhmatova, Blok, and Alfred Musset, then noted that "Igor took [Pushkin's *Eugene*] *Onegin* and did not release his hold on it." Stravinsky added (also in Russian):

I am reading *Onegin* avidly. Its verses and [songs?] are composed in such a way that music is composed—by measures, by musical sentences, [illegible]. This striking similarity to the problems of musical compositional technique arrests my attention to such an extent that

I am struggling not to miss another kind of values. You, an old Romantic, might be shocked by this. But it was you who reminded me [yesterday]: [that] for the ancient Greeks, *cosmos* meant order and beauty. Kisses, I. Strav.[55]

Near the end of Stravinsky's life, on 19 January 1970 his admirer the novelist and essayist Paul Horgan observed Stravinsky reading Henri Troyat's biography, *Pouchkine* (1946; repr. 1970), about which Stravinsky told him that "a biography of Pushkin is no ordinary affair."[56]

Stravinsky's squinting image graces the cover of the 20 November 1940 issue of *Overture,* the house organ of Local 47 (Los Angeles) of the American Federation of Musicians. This curious photograph, taken by one Jack Barsby, depicts the composer in a raincoat. Surely Local 47 would not have countenanced this photograph on the front page of its own magazine were he not then a member. Possibly he had joined the previous summer apropos of his engagement with the Los Angeles Philharmonic at Hollywood Bowl or, more recently, in preparation for the November performances in Chicago and Cincinnati, and December in Minneapolis, pursuant to the federation's legal victories in 1940–41, forcing even conductors to join.

When did Stravinsky join the union? Local 47 advises that its records for this period are no longer available, but other sources offer a couple of hints. First, on 10 December 1941, following one of Andersson's lessons, Stravinsky wrote in his diary of a visit at 4:30 p.m. from "representatives of the local musicians' union."[57] Second, Andersson's son-in-law, the Los Angeles conductor James Sample, who had been a member since 1939, recalled late in life that he had arranged for John te Groen, the local's vice president, to visit Stravinsky and make arrangements for the composer's induction because Stravinsky was now conducting a good deal in the United States. According to Sample, Stravinsky told him that te Groen and the composer each told the other about how honored they were—the former to have enrolled Stravinsky in Local 47, the latter to be a member of it—and that both men knew they were lying! Beguiling as is this tale, te Groen's succession to the Local's presidency in 1946 casts a shadow on the accuracy of Sample's memory or, at least, his chronology.

OFF TO THE MIDWEST, EAST COAST, AND BACK

On 2 November 1940, Mrs. McQuoid, Golubev, and Kall saw the Stravinskys off at the Los Angeles train station for their trip to Chicago on the Southwest Chief.[58] Stravinsky's most important musical event in 1940 was surely the world premiere on 7 November in Chicago of his four-movement Symphony in C, "composed to the Glory of God, . . . [and] dedicated to the Chicago Symphony Orchestra." He led the premiere, as well as local premieres in major US cities and Mexico. Yet "order and beauty" were seriously threatened (though presumably not *within* the cosmos) by mistakes in the orchestra parts that plagued the rehearsals. Vera's diary for 5 November records that in Chicago "an old German, Handke, sits up with [Stravinsky] until midnight correcting the parts."[59] During these rehearsals Stravinsky was introduced to the actor and diseur Paul Leyssac, whom he was to encounter again in Los Angeles in 1943.[60]

All three Chicago performances (7, 8, and 12 November) were well received, even though one critic found that its "immediate appeal undoubtedly lessens as it goes on"; he also thought that on a first hearing its fugue in the third movement (rehs. 127–28) was not easy for a listener and that the finale was decidedly the most "recondite" of the four.[61] Among other Chicago critics, the later notoriously caustic Claudia Cassidy was sufficiently moved to declare it "both contemporary and timeless, autobiographical and impersonal . . . this symphony is more than important, it is extraordinarily beautiful."[62]

Writing for a broader readership, and featuring a 1935 Weston portrait of Stravinsky (no. 3), one national music journal ventured:

> The new symphony is not nearly as puzzling as some people expected it would be. It seems perfectly straightforward in many passages. . . . The second movement in particular . . . has many qualities that seem warmly human, instead of coldly abstract. . . . [The symphony was] impressive in performance and should prove a valuable contribution to symphonic literature.[63]

Because the third movement poses especially tricky rhythmic problems, Stravinsky was understandably cautious about programming it, especially in the absence of sufficient rehearsal time. For the remainder of 1940 he conducted it only in Cincinnati, preceded by five rehearsals, the final one on Thanksgiving Day. He omitted it at Minneapolis, and the 1941 concerts in Washington, DC, and Baltimore, then led it again at Cambridge, Boston, Los Angeles, Mexico City, and St. Louis.

Cincinnati's generous number of rehearsals allowed him to precede the local premiere by *Jeu de cartes* and even, after intermission, to perform *Le Sacre*. One reviewer, Frederick Yeiser, disagreed with Sol Babitz's accompanying program notes for the Symphony in C and anticipated Nabokov's later assessment of the work's solemn closing chords:

> The Symphony in C gives us some notion of his greatness, . . . [and] will mark another high point in his career. Stravinsky sometimes conceals the thematic material. I should not consider the minuet in the third movement as one too promptly to be identified as such. Yet nothing could be more clearly stated than the captivating main subject of the first movement . . . a tune that sticks. If it [the third movement] does not disrupt, it remains . . . less well balanced than the other three, . . . [including] the passepied [rehs. 113–22, which Stravinsky] calls "white" music. The fugue [IV: reh 165–74] would seem to be a vestige of the composer's neo-classical period. . . . There is nothing finer than the stark, gothic chords which expire so gradually at the close. . . . Far from being a mere compendium [of] Stravinsky's styles, the symphony is one in which he has integrated them all into one finished work of art.[64]

Stravinsky's arrival in Minneapolis, late in the afternoon on 15 December for his matinee concert on the eighteenth, was eagerly awaited. It prompted three preconcert notices in the city's *Morning Tribune,* underscoring the visitor's "modernist" credentials; an interview in the *Minneapolis Star Journal;* and one with Vera in the same paper. The first notice, by the *Tribune*'s Francophile poet and music critic Johan S. Egilsrud, appeared on 15 December. Titled "Friday to Be Symphony's Stravinsky Day" and accompanied by a photograph of the composer, it noted that Stravinsky was the first of three visiting conductors to take over during Mitropoulos's absence. The *Tribune*'s second notice of 16 December—on the front page no less—opened with a provocative statement: Stravinsky would be composing a work based on an American subject. (It was not his arrangement of "The Star-Spangled Banner," but was perhaps Tango, in progress since the beginning of October 1940.):

> Igor Stravinsky, world famous conductor, who wrote a ballet about a poker game, is looking around for more characteristic American themes. The Russian modernist confided last night that he already has one subject that he's going to set to music—but its identity is a secret. . . . "It's the spirit of America," he explained. "I hope some day to translate that into a musical composition. For the spirit of America is something quite different from that of Europe. It's something one senses as soon as he arrives in this country. It is the fresh air—boundless and beautiful." As a modernist, Stravinsky has turned many a surprising object to his purpose. His latest opus, Symphony in G [*sic*], revolved about the golden jubilee of [the Chicago Symphony Orchestra].

This teaser, though lacking any reference to America, reappeared the same evening in an anonymous interview in the *Minneapolis Star Journal:*

> The composer, who has spent most of his life in Paris, is devoting his time now exclusively to conducting and composing. 'I used to play the piano in concert, but now there is no time to practice. I am composing something now, but it is a secret,' he added.[65]

The *Tribune*'s third notice (likewise unsigned) was on the nineteenth, titled "Stravinsky Puts O.K. on Orchestra":

> After several strenuous rehearsals with the Minneapolis Symphony Orchestra, Igor Stravinsky, noted modernist composer, announced his conviction that the orchestra will do full justice tomorrow night to several Stravinsky works to be played under the composer's direction. He had high praise for the orchestra.[66]

An interview with Vera Stravinsky by staff writer Dorothy Riley, including a photograph, appeared in the *Star Journal.*[67] Vera's aspiration toward a future domesticity in California, featuring a "one-story rambling house with plenty of grounds" and "chickens, dogs, cats, and maybe a cow," was prescient.[68]

On the last afternoon of 1940, following lunch with the Dushkins and Walter Damrosch, the Stravinskys returned to the Barbizon Plaza, their New York hotel where they had been staying since their 22 December arrival from Minneapolis. There, they were visited by George Balanchine, Nicolas Nabokov and his wife, and José Limantour, a young conductor whom they had met the previous July in Mexico.[69] Inexplicably, the partial edition of Vera's diary omits the arrival at 6 p.m. that New Year's Eve of "éditeur Feist."[70] This was Leonard Feist, owner of Mercury Music Corporation, and their meeting three days later eventually led to contracts to publish Stravinsky's Tango for solo piano and his controversial arrangement of "The Star-Spangled Banner."[71]

Just as Symphony in C was the most important musical event in 1940, so Tango was among the least important, notwithstanding its status as his first work entirely conceived, composed and published on US soil. In spite of its tiny dimensions (just fifty-six measures), the interval between Stravinsky's first sketches, including a version for textless voice and piano, and its eventual appearance in print for ensemble, Tango stretched out from 1940 to 1953, even longer than the four-movement Symphony in C, which spanned ten years (1938–48).[72]

The tale of Tango had already begun in the autumn. After two week's work, Stravinsky completed four pages of three-line sketches (probably with an instrumental ensemble in mind) on 14 October. On 2 October, hoping for a profitable "hit song," he had invited an agent, Gregory Stone, to write lyrics. On 14 October Golubev and Stone worked until 1 a.m., trying in vain to set it to words.[73] Toward the close of 1940 another flurry of activity began. On 29 November Stravinsky and Vera, by chance, encountered Vernon Duke (Vladimir Dukelsky). At Balanchine's invitation the Stravinskys attended a musical the following week, *Cabin in the Sky*.[74] Choreographed by Balanchine, with a score by Duke, the show included a *real* hit song, "Taking a Chance on Love." Stravinsky gave a copy of Tango to a member of the cast, the African American dancer and singer Katherine Dunham. In 1991 she recalled:

> And once I think Stravinsky was there. Balanchine wanted Stravinsky to do something for me, . . . [and] he did persuade Stravinsky to give me a tango. Somewhere it's in our music, and I've never done it. I keep thinking I must find it. . . . It's autographed to me by Stravinsky.[75]

Perhaps this was an ozalid copy of Tango, like the one in the Library of Congress,[76] because at that time the solo piano version of Tango was still a full year away from publication.

On 20 December, having learned of Associated Music Publisher's lack of interest in Tango,[77] Mercury Corporation's Feist wrote to Stravinsky, leading to the New Year's Eve meeting in the composer's hotel room. Two days later (2 January 1941), they signed a contract for (among other works) "a concert arrangement for solo piano." The solo-piano version of Tango was already written down in some form or other,[78] because on 31 January Stravinsky played it for Vitya Vronsky and Victor Babin in his hotel room and gave it to them to arrange for two pianos.[79] Moreover, while still in New York, he worked with Dushkin to forge a version for violin and piano, which was premiered there in March of 1941 by Dushkin and Harry Kaufman.[80] At least one critic—and surely composer and

publisher—hoped Tango might enjoy a success matching that of Ravel's *Bolero*,[81] and though Tango provoked a minor scandal that June involving Stravinsky, Iturbi, and Goodman, it never achieved the same level of popularity.

The contract between Stravinsky and Feist was mentioned in a musical journal on 1 February, below a photograph of the pair discussing Tango in Stravinsky's New York hotel room (fig. 6.9). This photograph was accompanied by the intriguing information that "contracts have been signed with Mercury for the publication of all of Stravinsky's light non-symphonic compositions for a period of years."[82] That part of the agreement lay dormant until midway through 1941, when the Stravinskys were back in Los Angeles.

BRIDGING 1940 AND 1941

Among the Stravinskys' other tasks at the end of the old year of 1940 was to write the McQuoids. Igor and Vera folded a single page of their New York hotel stationery and wrote a note in black ink and red crayon that began with greetings in English (fig. 6.10). Their expression of thanks in French for an "excellent photograph" and a "pretty drawing" surely refers to one of the photographs of Stravinsky that Edwin McQuoid had taken late the previous October and to some drawing by Dorothy that the McQuoids had recently sent to the Stravinskys.[83]

Leaving New York temporarily for several days of concerts in Washington and Baltimore, the Stravinskys mailed a letter in Russian to Kall on 4 January 1941 from their Washington hotel, the Hay-Adams House. Stravinsky's playful postscript to Vera's letter strikes a gentle yet ironic tone, mixing affection and tolerance. It softens some of the bad feeling engendered the previous year by Kall's inebriated behavior:

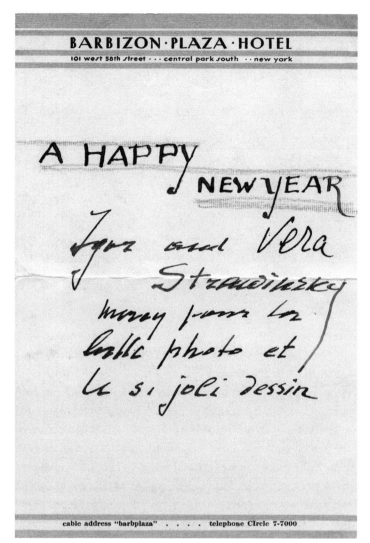

BARBIZON·PLAZA·HOTEL
101 west 58th street · · · central park south · · new york

A HAPPY
NEW YEAR

*Igor and Vera
Stravinsky
merry from la
belle photo et
le si joli dessin*

cable address "barbplaza" . . . . telephone CIrcle 7-7000

FIGURE 6.10
New Year's Greetings to the McQuoids,
1941. UBC Stravinsky Collection, no. 74.

Thank you for the little letter and the fairy story of the ginger kitten. I say "fairy story"
because you never used to have any cats, just as you didn't have any white elephants or
green snakes, thus, [both are] simply a fruit of your imagination. Be careful that you don't
get un-reasonably overheated! (I can hear you saying *pp:* "you bastard").[84]

"Green snakes" alludes to a Russian saying about delirium tremens, similar to the English
locution "pink elephants,"[85] an expression Stravinsky may have heard from tippler Kall
and then misquoted.

As Vera noted in a letter to Boulanger on 4 December, the Boston Symphony and
chorus already knowing *Oedipus Rex* would allow more time for rehearsing the Symphony

FIGURE 6.11
Elliot Forbes (holding McQuoid b) and
the author. Author's collection.

in C that January.[86] Preparation for its rehearsals required a considerable amount of work on the score and parts, just as it had in November of 1940 in Chicago. Vera's diary for 13 January records that "Igor is in despair because of mistakes in the parts." These errors stemmed from difficulties in communication under wartime conditions between Schott, his German publisher, and its representative in the United States, Associated Music Publishers; the Symphony was not printed until 1948. Once again a guest (from 12 January) of the senior Forbes at Gerry's Landing, Stravinsky worked with Nadia Boulanger (then an exile and teaching in Cambridge) to check the orchestra parts.[87] Several photographs of the two working together were taken mid-January of 1941 by Rodman Gilder Jr.: one was later misdated as 1937, another poorly reproduced, and a third misdated to 1943.[88] El Forbes owned four additional photographs of the two working in his father's house: the background of one of them also shows Vera reading.

In gratitude for the Forbes's hospitality and friendship, Stravinsky inscribed probably in January a copy of one of Edwin McQuoid's three surviving photographs (fig. 6.11). In 1995 at Cambridge, the late El Forbes kindly displayed it for me. The message reads:

Pour mes chers / amis Peg et / Edward / Forbes / avec toute / ma fèdile[sic] / affection / I Strawinsky / 1941 (For my dear friends Peg and Edward Forbes with all my loyal affection I Strawinsky 1941)

Stravinsky was fond of this particular McQuoid image. Several years later, in 1943, he was to inscribe yet another copy of it for Klaus Mann, Thomas Mann's eldest and soldier son.

On 16–18 January, Stravinsky led his Symphony in C with the Boston Symphony Orchestra, first in Cambridge and then in Boston, to generally favorable reviews:

> [It] proved one of the most interesting, perhaps the best, of new scores heard here so far this season. . . . While the form of Stravinsky's work appears to be orthodox, apart from a scherzo that involves a minuet, passepied and fugue, a first hearing left me with various impressions of certain pages, rather than a connected idea of the whole. Certainly the Symphony is fascinating, closely-woven, and starts out in a highly original manner. While the harmonic style is peppery, Stravinsky has written more consistently dissonant music than this. Rhythmically it is all quite complex as a whole. At any rate, the Symphony is ponderable and ought to be heard several times more.[89]

Returning to New York on 19 January, Stravinsky rehearsed the next two days, with Dushkin and an orchestra for *Balustrade*, the ballet that Balanchine had made on the composer's Violin Concerto in D. There were three performances: 22, 24, and 26 January, all of them at the Fifty-First Street Theatre. The ballet itself was moderately successful, but the ten-year-old Concerto did not escape disparagement. Irving Kolodin was condescending and offensive: "To be sure, one is hardly so naive as to expect meaning or significance from a ballet, especially one that uses Stravinsky's acidulous and banal violin concerto as a point of departure."[90] Virgil Thomson's review was not so harsh but was less enthusiastic about the Concerto itself than about its performance: "[This concerto] toughly, hard-headedly poetic as music, [lacks] soaring cantilena and sparkling passage work, cadenzas, show-off matter in general. . . . It is tightly woven as a bird-cage. . . . The composer conducted handsomely and Mr. Dushkin executed the violin solo role with accuracy and comprehension."[91] Apropos of the supposed lack of "soaring cantilena" in the Violin Concerto, Thomson could not have known what Mrs. Dushkin did by then (and, perhaps, as postulated above, as early as 1937)—that is, Stravinsky's guilty remorse embedded in the deeply felt, slow-moving, cantabile of "Aria II."

These three ballet performances of the Violin Concerto were to be the last times Stravinsky ever performed with Samuel Dushkin. By June of 1942 he was feeling more and more comfortable with violinist Sol Babitz in Los Angeles. On 28 June 1942 he wrote his publisher that, despite his "personal friendship" with Dushkin, he would prefer a printing of Babitz's transcription of the *Circus Polka* for violin and piano, already finished rather than waiting for one by Dushkin.[92] Thereafter, Dushkin was said to have lost "accuracy" and "began to develop real or imagined problems with his fingers."[93] The final blow to his performing career might well have been a devastating review of a late December 1948 concert in New York with pianist Paul Best:

> His technique—or lack of it—gets into the way of what he has to say. One could overlook occasional falls from technical grace, but last night's playing was so often marred by thin tone, insecurity of pitch, missed notes and other shortcomings that it was impossible to concentrate consistently on the music.[94]

Long before this, there were signs that Stravinsky knew of Dushkin's weaknesses and that he sensed possible negative consequences from Dushkin's long and virtually exclusive association with his Violin Concerto, which they had premiered in 1931 in Berlin and recorded in 1935, as well as with his *Duo concertant,* written for Dushkin in 1931, premiered in 1932 in Berlin, and recorded in 1933, and from the general lack of performance of these works by top-flight violinists. Stravinsky's unease would only have increased had he heard a comment uttered by Jascha Heifetz, who refused to learn the Violin Concerto "because of the 'unviolinistic' first chords" and found it "unplayable from the first bar,"[95] something that would have surely discouraged most other violinists.

Living in California, Stravinsky seems to have embarked on a campaign there to promote his works for violin among local and visiting violinists. On 21 September 1940 Sol Babitz played the Violin Concerto for Stravinsky with Ingolf Dahl at the piano;[96] on 13 October Babitz and the composer rehearsed it with the "Hollywood Rehearsal Orchestra," and two weeks later, on 27 October, Babitz and Stravinsky worked on it together at the North Wetherly house. Even though some of this activity may have been directed toward a first Los Angeles performance, surely most of it was to prepare for Stravinsky's final three performances with Dushkin at the New York presentations of Balanchine's *Balustrade.*

In addition to Babitz, who played the Concerto again late in January of 1943 with Dahl at an "Evening on the Roof" concert,[97] Stravinsky urged it on other violinists in California. In April of 1941 Earnest Andersson noted that Stravinsky "loaned me his violin concerto to have photostated for Erna Rubinstein,"[98] a Russian-born violinist who performed as a child in New York in 1922. In the 1940s she resided in Los Angeles and in 1941 played the Bruch Violin Concerto with Andersson's son-in-law conducting. And in the mid-1940s in Los Angeles, Stravinsky and Szigeti (who had also played the Violin Concerto) recorded the *Duo concertant.* In 1962 Stravinsky wrote in a margin of his copy of Szigeti's memoirs, "Why is my Violin Concerto not mentioned by Szigeti? It is not a bad work."[99]

In the 1940s and 1950s Stravinsky also turned several times to violinist Jeanne Gautier, whom he had known since 1916, when she played his Three Pieces for String Quartet in Paris. In December of 1932 he admired her performance of Prokofiev's Concerto in D,[100] and in 1938 he employed her (in Dushkin's absence) to put bowings and articulation marks in the upper string parts and play first violin for the Paris premiere of *Dumbarton Oaks Concerto.*[101] Significantly, after the war he chose her—instead of Dushkin—to work in Hollywood with him on 25–27 June 1947 (and probably also in mid-July) in order to add one more excerpt, "Ballade," for the publication of his 1932 violin and piano suite drawn from *Le Baiser de la fée.*[102] In 1952 he had planned to conduct his Violin Concerto with her as soloist on 29 May in Brussels, and on 23 April 1954 he actually did so in Turin.[103]

Early in June of 1961 he noted that he would lead his Violin Concerto at UCLA with the Californian Eudice Shapiro, also writing (with some trepidation?) apropos of his recording of it two weeks hence, that soloist Isaac Stern was then still in Australia.[104] Finally, on 29–30 June 1961 in Hollywood studios, Stravinsky achieved his best recording of the Violin Concerto with Stern,[105] although subsequently he complained that the violinist had not even practiced it for their recording and never played it again![106] It would be interesting to have Stern's account of all this and what the virtuoso thought of Stravinsky's November 1966 opinion of him as "still embryonic."[107]

Stravinsky's importunities on fine violinists during the 1940s reveal more than just his wish to promote his violin works. They also validate his decision to concentrate on conducting and to cease playing the piano in public, albeit to continue the instrument as a coaching tool. Both decisions were inextricably linked to creating more time for composing and for making money.

PREMIERING CAPRICCIO AND SYMPHONY IN C IN LOS ANGELES

On 3 February, just before leaving New York for Los Angeles, Stravinsky coached Adele Marcus on his Capriccio in preparation for a pair of concerts he was to lead with the Los Angeles Philharmonic, plus one more with the same orchestra in San Diego.[108] He had also given lessons to Dorothy McQuoid six months earlier on that very work.

Because Marcus's arrival in Los Angeles for February rehearsals was delayed by a day, Mrs. McQuoid substituted for her at Stravinsky's first rehearsal of Capriccio on 10 February 1941.[109] Her frustration at working on it with the composer and rehearsing it with the orchestra, and then not giving the public performance herself, led her, in a minor rage after the 13 February performance, to dismember her copy of that week's Philharmonic program booklet,[110] which contained one of her husband's portraits of Stravinsky (fig. 6.12).

At these same concerts Stravinsky led the Los Angeles premiere of his Symphony in C at Philharmonic Auditorium. Vera noted in her diary "very little [success] for the Symphony in C."[111] The next day, Isabel Morse Jones, in her review of this concert, cautioned readers that "a first hearing [was] quite insufficient to form a clear opinion"; she nonetheless allowed that "it is logical, as complex in its rhythm as Duke Ellington's inspired brevities but Stravinsky's structure is built to last and Ellington's to die." She also noted that "there were lagging tempos" and that "Stravinsky did not ask for enough dynamically." Her second review of the same concert, for a national music journal, did not dispute the value of the Symphony. She did, however, challenge the expertise of its conductor: "Stravinsky is a much better conductor than most composers but he certainly is not the best imaginable conductor of his own works. . . . Symphony in C was written by a genius [but] needed a genius to conduct it."[112] Meanwhile, a local journal in Los Angeles printed a curious negative reaction from the young Lawrence Morton, a staunch admirer of Stravinsky from 1931 to the end of the composer's life. One can only speculate what this brilliant critic might have written about Stravinsky's masterpiece had he completed his book about the composer:

FIGURE 6.12
"McQuoid c" as it appeared in
LA Philharmonic Symphony Magazine,
13–14 Feb 1941. Author's private collection.

There was a time when Stravinsky kept one step ahead of all the gifted young men who struggled valiantly to subject themselves to his influence. They have finally caught up with him, not by their own efforts but by the sterility of the master.

It was a great disappointment.

The Symphony is no culmination but a repetition, a repetition not only of the style which is now a mannerism but also of the very stuff of which Stravinsky makes his music. There is the same muscularity, the same nervousness, and the careful, almost obsessive avoidance of sonority. There are the same rhythmic displacements. As for the tunes, the thematic material, all of it is ascetic in the extreme. Stravinsky calls it "white music." And it is—white as snow, cold and brittle as an icicle.[113]

Presumably "white music" was Stravinsky's way of avoiding the hated term *neo-classicism,*[114] and possibly it refers to "ballet blanc" rather than to the "white" paintings of Mark Tobin, whose work he is not known to have seen, despite their mutual admirer at this period: John Cage.

A week later, an even more negative review followed, this time by Vernon Steele, the recently appointed editor of *Pacific Coast Musician;* he was as opposed to Stravinsky as Morton was favorable:

Among all the great composers living or dead, there are probably half a dozen who are important enough to have orchestral programs devoted exclusively to their compositions. Igor Strawinsky is not one of them. . . . [Excepting the *Firebird,*] this writer doubts that they will be heard again unless the composer conducts them. The music is brittle and even from beginning to end with scarcely ever a restful or grateful moment.[115]

A fine early study and appreciation of the Symphony in C (although restricted to its first movement) is the 1962 essay by Edward T. Cone. A composer himself, Cone was a highly influential theorist and critic, especially during the years he taught at Princeton University (1947–85). His essay is notable for its terse understanding of Stravinsky's so-called neoclassicism, its comparison with Stravinsky's beloved Haydn, and its sympathetic comprehension of Stravinsky's disdain for the academic:

Stravinsky, approaching the Classical [style] as a historically defined manner, superficially follows its conventions more closely than Haydn. The influence of his personal idiom, however, is so strong that the resulting reinterpretation goes far beyond that of the earlier composer. The result is not an extension but a transformation of his model.[116]

After 18 February 1941, when the Los Angeles Philharmonic played in San Diego, Vera noted, "Thank God this San Diego concert is the last one." A day later she wrote of "the end of our concert season."[117] But this was by no means the end of promoting the Symphony in C. In an essay printed after the Los Angeles concert (it was not programmed in San Diego), Sol Babitz discussed and analyzed this work. He must have had access to Stravinsky's autograph, or to its ozalids, since the Symphony itself was not printed until 1948. With Stravinsky's approval, Babitz "carefully examined the score and heard it performed on the piano" (surely by Stravinsky himself). Even with such advantages, Babitz's comments are somewhat disappointing; for example, regarding the second movement, he merely noted that "the composer . . . describes it as 'simple, clear, and tranquil.'"[118]

ANDERSSON'S LESSONS WITH STRAVINSKY

Returning to Hollywood on 19 February 1941, the Stravinskys visited Earnest Andersson, a wealthy, retired inventor to whom they had recently been introduced.[119] On 21 February Andersson offered them one of his three Los Angeles houses. Although initially they accepted the offer, the next day they reserved an apartment in the Chateau Marmont, for which Stravinsky ordered a piano; they remained there for just over a month. Income from lessons given to Andersson during 1941 (just under what Stravinsky was to earn from conducting in all of 1942!) helped the composer achieve single-family home-ownership (the dream of most Americans). In April of 1941 he bought a white house in Hollywood on North Wetherly Drive,[120] a street gently rising off Sunset Boulevard.

Andersson was introduced to Stravinsky in February of 1941 in Los Angeles.[121] When Stravinsky wrote in late April that year to Vittorio Rieti—disciple and, subsequently, New York composer in exile—he mentioned that "Je compose, je travaille avec un monsieur âgé sur ses compositions" (I am composing, I am working with an elderly gentleman on his compositions).[122]

This "monsieur âgé," was only five years older than Stravinsky and apparently his last student.[123] Andersson's notebook shows that Stravinsky had already been working with him on his *Futurama Symphony* for two months.

The wealthy retired inventor also owned an apartment in New York and presumably visited New York in 1939–40 to see the World's Fair. This trip surely prompted the title of his symphony, since one of the exhibits was the immensely popular show, *Futurama*, a fifteen-minute virtual trip across the United States, designed by Norman Bel Geddes for the $8 million exhibit in the General Motors Pavilion: "After waiting an average of two hours in line, visitors took their places in comfortable, high-sided chairs to set out on a simulated airplane-ride twenty years hence over the American landscape of 1960, featuring express highways, radio-controlled cars, massive suspension bridges, and modern high rises."[124] A cultural historian of the Great Depression observes that the General Motors Pavilion "combined capitalist commerce (the auto industry) with public works (a national road network), and the individual family, each in its own conveyance with central planning worthy of Le Corbusier."[125]

There is no evidence that Stravinsky, who stayed in New York for a week early in October of 1939, ever visited the World's Fair or that the Pavilion's "modern" architecture somehow influenced the Symphony in C or, indeed, any of his wartime works, no matter how many times he was deemed a "modernist."

Andersson was a generous patron of the Los Angeles Philharmonic. His and Stravinsky's first meeting probably took place between 10 and 18 February 1941, during rehearsals and concerts with Adele Marcus. The meeting was probably engineered by the formidable Mrs. Florence Leiland Atherton Irish, executive vice president and general manager of the Philharmonic. Andersson's son-in-law also claimed that, for Andersson's orchestration lessons in the mid-1930s, Mrs. Irish had introduced him to another teacher, Max Donner, longtime second violinist in the Philharmonic.[126]

On 21 February 1941 Vera Stravinsky referred to Andersson in her diary as "a future pupil of Igor's."[127] Andersson's first lesson was on 27 February 1941. His last lesson, the 215th (concerning a different work) was on 15 December 1942. He recorded his lessons in a notebook; many of its entries are dated, and those that are not are mostly ascertainable. Unfortunately, his notebook covers only the brief initial period of lessons: some eight months, from February into October of 1941.[128]

Andersson's twelfth and thirteenth lessons on *Futurama* (1 and 5 April 1941) were interrupted by the Stravinskys' move from the elegant Chateau Marmont—"nice rooms, cozy, in good taste . . . very pleasant"[129]—to their newly purchased house—small and

EXAMPLE 6.4

"T-Ra Tor-Ra."

T - Ra   Tor - Ra

unfurnished—on North Wetherly Drive.[130] Dorothy McQuoid recalled transporting the Stravinskys and their luggage there in her car.

By mid-April, Andersson's notebook reveals the two men hard at work on *Futurama*'s third movement, a scherzo. On or about 8 April 1941 Andersson inscribed at the top of page 5 in his notebook on two separate measures four notes bearing the syllables "T-Ra Tor-Ra" below them (ex. 6.4).[131] These four notes, after an introductory diminished-seventh glissando on the harp, are the beginning of *Futurama*'s scherzo. Andersson may or may not have known that these particular four syllables were Stravinsky favorite vocalizations.[132] A dispute about the harp glissando was settled by late May, revealing a notable give and take between the two men: "The glissando at the beginning of Futurama 3 movement took much of S. time. He finally decided to do it as I suggested: i.e., diminished 7ths."[133] This action resulted in the final version of Andersson's now-lost original manuscript score.

In mid-April of 1941, as Mercury Music was readying Tango for its solo piano publication, Dorothy McQuoid alerted Stravinsky to two errors, presumably referring to mistakes in Tango's proofs. Writing on 20 April from North Wetherly and using notepaper purloined from the Chateau Marmont, Stravinsky told Leonard Feist:

> I am sending you in a great hurry the enclosed copy of my TANGO showed to me by Mrs. Dorothy McQuoid. There to my horror I found two absolutely inadmissible mistakes in the main melody I marked with red pencil. Please find some way to correct these errors before publishing the piece in definite form. Kindly notify me immediately as it makes me very uneasy.[134]

JAMES SAMPLE AND THE WPA ORCHESTRA

About this time, Andersson's son-in-law, James Sample, became better acquainted with the Stravinskys. On 22 April Stravinsky wrote in his own diary that, after a lesson with Andersson in the morning and lunch with him at the nearby restaurant on Sunset Boulevard, "Bit of Sweden," the two of them went "to audition James Sample for his music."[135] The occasion was a rehearsal of the Los Angeles WPA Symphony Orchestra. Andersson wrote in this notebook: "Stravinsky and I heard 3rd movement [scherzo] of Futurama play[ed] at rehearsal and conducted by Jimmy. S said J was a good musician. Had mastered much of the art of conducting. Was modest and serious in his work."[136] Such a level of approbation from Stravinsky, notoriously critical of conductors, prompts a few remarks here about the young (and the older) Craft, who first knew Stravinsky at roughly the same age as young Sample, but whose later writings about both Sample and Andersson occasionally have proven inadequate or even inaccurate. Sample's name appears but three times[137] and Sample's wife, Ernestine (Andersson's daughter), whom Stravinsky held dear, never. Remarks about Andersson often need correcting.[138] Craft's "discovery" of *Futurama* was apparently in 1985 rather than, as he claimed, "in the mid-1940s," when he first met Stravinsky. The "Anderson [*sic*] archives" were never "copied by UCLA," although the university library does hold several items pertaining to Andersson as a composer. His final denunciation of *Futurama* is dealt with below in the course of analyzing some of its movements.

Most revelatory was Craft's reaction to scholarly assessment of the five conversation books he wrote with Stravinsky, providing "so much lucrative employment to musicological hacks,"[139] and his strange derision about "the limitations of scholarship based entirely on the almighty document."[140] In respect to the Sample issue, Craft's own diary for 16 December 1967 notes Stravinsky "telling me about a Christmas letter from the conductor James Sample."[141] Regrettably, neither the contents of this letter nor its date are divulged. Such omissions are unfortunate in view of other Christmas letters known to have been exchanged between the Stravinskys and the Samples during the mid-1940s and well into the 1950s.

Like his mentor Pierre Monteux, Sample remained true to Stravinsky, and to his music, until the late serial works, for which he had no empathy. Not only did he program Stravinsky's arrangement of "The Star-Spangled Banner" throughout his conducting career—long after other maestros had abandoned it—but as late as 1953, he lectured publicly in Portland, Oregon (with illustrations at the piano), about its beauties, deriding Damrosch's version. Moreover, in 1950 Sample tried to commission a work from Stravinsky for the Portland Symphony Orchestra, only to be defeated by the composer's obduracy and avarice: Stravinsky's conducting fee, travel expenses, and rental fees for his other works on the program would have far surpassed the dollar amount of the commission itself. Tactfully, Sample ascribed the failure of the proposal to the manager of the Portland Orchestra.[142] A brief reunion of composer and conductor on 8 December 1955 in Cleveland might have related to the failed Portland commission or merely to their decades-long friendship. Sample recalled in 1972 that when Stravinsky conducted in December of 1955 at Cleveland, he and Ernestine sat with Vera.[143] After the concert, when they all went to congratulate Stravinsky, Vera asked whether he remembered them both. Looking directly at Sample, Stravinsky exclaimed, "And *how!*"

In some ways Sample's association with Stravinsky paralleled Craft's own experience. Both men were aspiring young conductors when they first encountered Stravinsky: Sample first met him in 1934, at an afternoon tea *chez* Nadia Boulanger: when her elderly mother Raissa would declaim ribald stories from her illuminated dais. Craft first glimpsed the composer in January of 1946, after writing him in 1944. Several years elapsed before each man actually worked with Stravinsky: almost a decade for Sample, four years for Craft. Sample said that in 1941 Stravinsky had no recollection of their initial 1934–35 meeting in Paris. In both cases Stravinsky sought to have these young men further his own cause through their performance of his music. Sample resisted this task in 1941–42 (Stravinsky's offer being conveyed both directly and through father-in-law Andersson); Craft embraced it from their first meeting until his death in 2015.

Save that he had no appreciation for the late works, Sample remained true to Stravinsky for the remainder of his days, as did Craft. But whereas information about Craft's relationship with Stravinsky abounds, what little survives about Sample's interactions must be mined from interviews taped by family members in 1972 and 1992, documents in his family's archives, and from Andersson's notebook. For example, in the 1972 tapes Sample recalled that Stravinsky attended his 1941–42 rehearsals with the Los Angeles WPA Symphony "a surprising number of times," especially rehearsals with new music by California composers. Stravinsky always sat at the back of the room to avoid being recognized by the orchestra members. If Sample had a spare score of the work being rehearsed, he would pass it on to Stravinsky, who afterward was "very loquacious, very busy talking." This recollection has the ring of truth, even if the secondary sources—not least, Sample's—require vigilance. His "California composers" did not necessarily mean "native-born" but extended to composers then resident in the state, such as Homer Simmons, Charles Wakefield Cadman, Morris Hutchins Ruger, and a still unidentified George Thomas Morgan (active 1942–63 in Los Angeles; not the country singer).[144] Some of Sample's memories may have been influenced or contaminated by Andersson's jottings in his 1941 notebook, to which Sample had access for his 1972 interview and in 1992 after his wife's death, and he sometimes confuses the chronology of events.

To judge from essays in several issues of the Los Angeles–based *Pacific Coast Musician*,[145] its editor, Vernon Steele, should have said more about the Stravinsky-Sample relationship. Steele's abiding animosity toward Stravinsky surely explains why this publication, even while reviewing Sample's performances of Stravinsky's works, never acknowledged the composer's close links with the young conductor. For example, in late April of 1941 Andersson wrote in his notebook, following a party he had just hosted at Santa Monica's Casa del Mar Hotel for the Stravinskys, the Adolph Bolms, the Samples, and several others: "I. S. remarks about Jimmy and Ernestine are most flattering. Bolm said: 'cozy party.' "[146]

COMMERCIAL ENDORSEMENTS

Stravinsky's admiration for Sample's conducting[147] was reciprocated by the young conductor's awe of the composer's business acumen. On 2 May 1941 Stravinsky had written his New York agent, Paul Stoes, that any transaction regarding Stromberg-Carlson should not be less than $1,000.[148] His letter was about endorsing a Stromberg-Carlson radio-record player recently installed in the composer's home.[149] According to Sample, Stravinsky successfully negotiated a $400 increase from the company's original offer of $2,400. Vera then wrote on 8 December 1941 about a radio, and on 24 February 1944 Stravinsky mentions this Stromberg-Carlson machine, having the previous 15 February played records on it for Otto Klemperer.[150] But the sum mentioned by Sample conflicts with Stravinsky's year-end statement for 1941, which notes only $500 from Stromberg-Carlson. Sample probably took into account the cost of the machine itself—said to be $500—presented as a gift to Stravinsky.[151]

Where money and Stravinsky were concerned, Sample had not yet learned that expediency usually triumphed. Stravinsky signed the contract with Stromberg-Carlson in May of 1941.[152] This endorsement was at odds with views he expressed in Washington, DC, only a few months previously. On 7 January, in an article titled "Stravinsky Bares Aversion to Canned Music on Radio," he had declared "I don't care for the radio except for news and lectures." On the same day, in another Washington newspaper, bylined "Stravinsky Here to Conduct, Likes His Music in Person," he confided that "radio [is] all right for some programs but not for symphony," adding that "radio is fine for war news, but it's terrible for music."[153] In fewer than three months he had conveniently shucked his previous aversion to "canned music." His negotiations resulted in this announcement in the 13 August 1941 *New York Times:* "Stromberg-Carlson [will] promote the new line of 1942 radios and radio phonographs. Newspapers throughout the country and national magazines will be used. . . . The Igor Stravinsky autographed model will be featured."[154] By September of 1941 the *Los Angeles Times* could run an advertisement for Stromberg-Carlson's *"The Igor Stravinsky Autograph Model,* a combination FM-AM radio phonograph . . . $400,"[155] followed for months thereafter by similar notices in other news media across the nation.[156] After the Pearl Harbor attack, advertisements became progressively scarcer; in July of 1942 the firm explained that fewer sets were available for home use owing to the needs of the war effort.[157]

Such an endorsement of a commercial product might be regarded as a demonstration of one particular composer's well-known avarice.[158] Yet other famous musicians similarly profited from their reputations. In June of 1942 Yehudi Menuhin even advocated using Johnson Wax on his Stradivarius! Nine months later, Stravinsky's neighbor, Rachmaninoff, endorsed a rival radio-phonograph by Magnavox.[159] Stravinsky—unlike Menuhin, who later endorsed a Capehart Radio[160]—remained faithful to Stromberg-Carlson: in November of 1953 Vera noted in her diary, "Photographs of Igor and me for Stromberg-Carlson."[161] An advertisement the following February excluded Vera but pictured Stravinsky twice. Between the images, the composer was quoted in what was clearly a solicited communication (note his overly casual "thought you might be interested"):

> I have recently replaced my Stromberg-Carlson radio-phonograph, which I acquired in 1940 [*recte:* 1941], with your new "Custom 400" high fidelity equipment. I thought you might be interested in a musician's appraisal of the product.

It is truly superb!

I am perhaps more interested than the average layman in the most subtle nuances of music. In this regard I can best compare your equipment to a fine microscope. Like the latter, your "Custom 400" seeks out the tiniest details of tones, harmony and musical timbre and brings them to life with thrilling clarity. This is indeed home listening as though the artist were in the same room.

I'm so very glad I have brought my equipment up to date, but haven't changed the brand![162]

No further endorsements by Stravinsky appeared during the war years. Nor were there any during the later Red Scare and McCarthyism period. Stromberg-Carlson may have hesitated to use an endorsement by a Russian, even such an avowed anticommunist as Igor Stravinsky.

"THE STAR-SPANGLED BANNER" ARRANGEMENTS

Stravinsky's discussions with Sample about rehearsals and Stromberg-Carlson during the spring of 1941 spilled over into social occasions. One evening, perhaps in May, at a dinner party in Stravinsky's home with Sample's wife and father-in-law, Sample enthused over Stravinsky's 1917 setting of the *Volga Boatmen* for winds and timpani, an arrangement of what had turned out to be a short-lived Russian national anthem. Stravinsky had also arranged *La Marseillaise* for solo violin in 1919. Apparently, this led to a discussion about the US national anthem. The composer asked Sample to supply him with a copy of Damrosch's 1917–18 setting, as well as the setting in Sample's personal copy of *Twice 55 Community Songs* (1919 and also in later editions).[163]

On 17 June 1941 Andersson recorded in his notebook that during lesson 44 Stravinsky "played his choral arrangement of the Star Spangled-Banner made the day before." A day or two later, the composer showed Sample his score of the *Boatmen,* said he would lend it to him, and—most uncharacteristically—offered Sample two *free* performances of it.[164] Yet the original stimulus for Stravinsky's several arrangements of the national anthem came not from Sample but from his father-in-law. This seems incontestable because Stravinsky was later to inscribe his two-page compositional draft for piano: "Souvenir to / Ernest Andersson / for his inspiration / to do this version / of this nobel [*sic*] american [*sic*] / national corale [*sic*] / With my best feelings / Igor Strawinsky / 1941."[165]

His setting may also have been prompted by having had to conduct Walter Damrosch's 1917–18 harmonization in many a US city during his prewar transatlantic tours, including the recent Philharmonic concerts in Los Angeles. He also had to lead the National Symphony through Hans Kindler's equally dull arrangement in Baltimore and Washington. By then, of course, the Damrosch version was well-established in American life: the Daughters of the American Revolution, finding it "generally accepted," had officially adopted it at their Forty-Sixth Congress in 1937 "for use at meetings." Stravinsky's letter of 14 August to Leonard Feist at Mercury Music Corporation, the eventual publisher of the arrangement, discloses his opinion of the "generally accepted" version: "The harmonization of the honorable Dr. Damrosch is no more or less than scholarly conceived academic music which renders it characterless and indifferent as to style."[166] Stravinsky's fulminations about "academic music" stretched back decades: an argumentative letter of 29 March 1912 to his mother about his bête noire, "Glazunov and other academics" in St. Petersburg, asserted that "as far as academicism as a negative phenomenon is concerned, I find no other possibility than still to proclaim constantly, full-throatedly, that [it] is an unavoidable evil either existing or sent from above in order that good should shine more brightly."[167] As recently as March of 1941, he had used the epithet in Andersson's first or second lesson: "whenever Rimsky-Korsakov tries for form he becomes academic."[168]

Andersson's notebook confirms that on 16 June Stravinsky wrote out the piano draft of an orchestra-chorus arrangement. Additional correspondence with Feist in New York and with Charles Cushing in Berkeley, San Francisco newspaper interviews early in 1942, and Sample's recollections all show that by mid-September of 1941, he planned to compose no fewer than *seven* different versions of his arrangement!

Right after Independence Day 1941, Stravinsky surprised and delighted Sample by playing on the piano his brand-spanking-new choral-orchestral setting of "The Star-Spangled Banner." He also offered him its world premiere, which Sample led on 14 October at the Embassy with the Los Angeles WPA Federal Symphony Orchestra and Chorus, and again, exactly two weeks later in the same auditorium. Sample apparently advised Stravinsky to reposition some horn parts and add a few slurs, advice that Stravinsky accepted. He further suggested that Stravinsky compose additional arrangements for band, mixed chorus, piano, etc., several of which he did indeed make.

By virtue of its beauty, one of the three surviving and variant choral harmonizations deserves special mention, because of its availability in a reproduction of the composer's fair copy, and because of Craft's luminous, sensitive, and nuanced recording of it.[169] Like two of Stravinsky's three extant versions for small chorus, it is set for male voices, in this case unaccompanied; the divided first tenors and baritones in this version sometimes produce five-voiced harmonies. Like the other vocal settings, it is transposed from B-flat major to D major so as to best exploit the male vocal ranges. It makes an utterly different sonic impact from the brilliant "July 4" version in B-flat for chorus and large orchestra, and it seems perfectly adapted for private, rather than public, celebration. Nevertheless, harmonically—and even contrapuntally—it differs very little from the massive B-flat choral setting (see exs. 6.5a and 6.5b). Transposition cannot mask the strikingly similar bass lines and even, in some places, the kinship of inner voices.

Stravinsky knew that Francis Scott Key, in 1814, wedded his patriotic text to the contours of an old drinking song, particularly at the line "And the rocket's red glare, the bombs bursting in air." Such words were particularly apt for the song's seesawing melodic sequence at this point. Stravinsky further emphasized this feature in his "July 4" setting

EXAMPLE 6.5a

"The Star-Spangled Banner" orchestra excerpt.

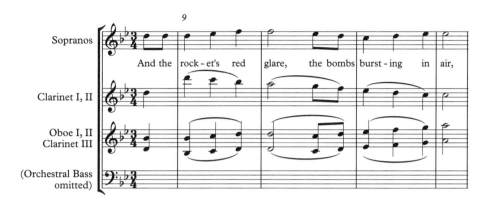

EXAMPLE 6.5b

"The Star-Spangled Banner" male chorus excerpt.

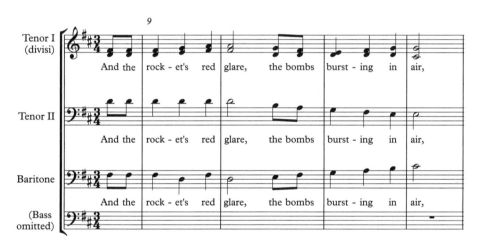

with contrary motion between both clarinets, on the one hand, and the two oboes and third clarinet, on the other hand.

For his unaccompanied male-voice version, Stravinsky retained the same contrapuntal procedure. An inner-voiced and stepwise contrary motion between second tenors and baritones at "glare, the bombs bursting in air" (mm. 10–13/1), successfully replicates the slightly longer contrary motion through an octave assigned to winds and strings in his orchestral-choral version, even though it begins a little earlier, at "rocket's red . . ." (mm. 9–13/1). Such contrary motion could hardly be more transparently purposeful. The rising figure graphically depicts ascents of rockets and bombs, and the descending figure depicts their falling back to Earth. So much, then, for Stravinsky's oft-iterated statements about his music not illustrating text.[170]

It is with these and other contrapuntal features in mind ("voice leading") and with a sly dig at Damrosch ("scholarly conception") that Stravinsky dedicated his gift to Andersson of a photostat of his first compositional draft: "My wish was to mold this music / in the traditions of the most severe / classic voice leading, witch [sic] is / quite diffirent [sic] from the usual / scholarly conception of this kind / of song."[171] Similarly, in his praise for Charles Cushing: "Your band transcription of my version is most successful as well as the general sonority of the instrumental ensemble and also the way you followed so faithfully my voice leading."[172] Three brief, pertinent examples of what Craft called "updating"—a conscious reshaping of Stravinsky's own legacy—may be added here. Regarding the genesis of Stravinsky's arrangements, recent discoveries show Stravinsky copied out the full orchestral-choral score in July of 1941. First, he used Andersson's large specially printed twenty-seven-staved paper, given to him by Andersson on 19 June 1941, but scraped away his student's name, printed at the bottom of each sheet. Second, however patriotic and well-meant, the inscription at the lower-right margin of page 3, "Finished July 4, 1941 / Igor Strawinsky," is a bit deceptive. Andersson's notebook (pp. 41–42) proves that it was completed on or before 1 July: he writes that Stravinsky "showed me his finished orchestration," having already "inked in one of the three pages (over pencil)." Then on Thursday, 3 July—just before that year's long holiday weekend—Stravinsky persuaded his student to have the full-score manuscript photostated. In Andersson's own words, jotted down the same day (p. 45): "7-3-41. S. handed me the finished orchestration of his [Star-Spangled Banner]. I am having it photostated at my expense—one photostat for S., one for Jimmy [Sample], one for me to send to the copyright office, and one for me."

A third example stems from Craft himself. One would be hard-pressed to find a greater concatenation of error in a single sentence (with its footnote) than the one formulated in 2002 as a revision ("updating") of what Stravinsky and his assistant had published (correctly) more than three decades earlier. Asked what had prompted Stravinsky's arrangement, the composer supposedly replied: "I wrote it on July 4 1940, and it was first performed in Hollywood Bowl, 27 August 1940, conducted by me, at the beginning of a staged performance of Firebird that was repeated on the 30th."[173] By now, the hardy reader will know that the date of composition, the locale, the performance date, the place in the program of the other work, the program's supposed date of repetition, and even Craft's footnoted reference to his own edition of Vera Stravinsky's diary as source for the supposed occasion are all incorrect.

USEFUL ANDERSSON

On that same day, 1 July, Andersson had taken forty photographs of Stravinsky with his Leica, "most of them working at the piano on my Futurama 2nd movement." Just a single one survives: the rest are thought to have been destroyed by a fire at one of Andersson's houses. Stravinsky, always with an eye for pretty young women (single or married), and perhaps grateful for Sample's assistance with "The Star-Spangled Banner," inscribed it (far left): "To Ernestine / Sample my / best greetings, for you, on your / birthday with / this picture your father took of me. / I Strawinsky / August 15 / 1941."[174] As is well-known, Stravinsky almost never allowed others to see or hear him when he was composing. The forty photographs thus reveal the scope of his friendship with Andersson and his confidence and trust in him, as do the copies of published works that Stravinsky inscribed to him. For example, on 30 May 1941 (Memorial Day) Andersson wrote in his notebook (p. 30): "S presented me with a [proof?] copy of his Tango for piano. Duly inscribed. He had a jazz arrangement made for orchestra which he edited. He played it for me."[175]

Money was not the only benefit Stravinsky derived from Andersson's lessons; he frequently co-opted his student as secretary and handyman. For instance, Andersson probably composed the letter of 20 April 1941 about printing errors in Tango. And on 24 June, following his lesson 48, Andersson recorded in his notebook that Stravinsky "asked me to mail a letter and cash a 25. check for him. Had to stay at home for phone call from SF, from Milhaud re money sent to his son [Théodore] in Switzerland that didn't get there."[176] After an Andersson lesson late in May of 1941, still another assignment occupied an entire afternoon: "When I drove him down town to buy a safe [for his music manuscripts] and [it was] 'no go' on first visit, he said that anyway he had enjoyed my company for the afternoon."[177] A mission on 2 December followed Andersson's lesson 119. Stravinsky noted in his own diary: "He went to pay our real estate taxes."[178]

Andersson's services as handyman from April 1941 onward were many and varied:

Made him a piano rack, for which he was most thankful. Also a piano top [a cover]; Replaced turnbuckle on his awning; Spent some time trying to find C♯ sympathetic rattle in his study. Didn't; Made a music rack for his muted piano. Later took him a lamp. Then a pencil sharpener. Then a piano cover; I put a compo[sition] rack on his piano and two window bafflers to keep the draughts off.[179]

Andersson's last statement, entered after the Stravinskys departed for their second expedition to Mexico and before his sixtieth lesson on 28 July, suggests that he also installed a rack and bafflers during their absence.

That June witnessed still another example of Andersson's usefulness. While they were working together on *Futurama* and Stravinsky was scoring his piano arrangement of "The Star-Spangled Banner" for chorus and orchestra, a noisy row erupted on the East Coast. It concerned Stravinsky's little Tango and José Iturbi. Stravinsky had known Iturbi since 1919, when, at an all-Stravinsky concert in Lausanne, Iturbi played several works and the two men also played piano four-hands.[180] News of the ruckus hit the New York papers on 27 June 1941, after Iturbi announced his refusal to participate in a program, slated for 10 July by the Philadelphia Orchestra at its summer home in Robin Hood Dell, if bandleader Benny Goodman included the jazz-band arrangement of Tango.[181] Shortly thereafter (probably 3 July), Andersson wrote that Stravinsky's New York manager had wired the composer "asking permission to capatilize [sic] on the Benny Goodman-Iturbi controversy." Although Stravinsky told Andersson at the time that the matter "was too cheap to mix in," obviously at Stravinsky's request he dictated a wire for the composer "for which he thanked me most profusely." It stated that Stravinsky was pleased "to have Goodman premiere my rhumba." Privately to Andersson, Stravinsky "said of Iturbi he is too great to appear on program with Goodman, but S. is not [and] that Iturbi was a strutting stallion."[182] Leonard Feist reported to Stravinsky that the performance (in which Iturbi had not participated) was unsuccessful because Goodman had not studied the score "sufficiently to know what he was doing."[183] The jinx persisted into April of 1942, when Vera Stravinsky in Los Angeles declared that "Stokowski conducts Igor's Tango badly,"[184] and even as late as 1974, when Craft referred to it as Stravinsky's "most spectacular flop," (worse than *Mavra?*) and as his " 'last tango,' mercifully!"[185]

CONCERTS IN MEXICO AND OBTAINING THE VISAS

On 10 July 1941, Andersson wrote: "S. left for two concerts in Mexico City. . . . So sorry I didn't get ready and go with him. It would have been a grand trip and instructive."[186] Stravinsky had told Andersson the previous May about some of the difficulties he and Vera were experiencing in respect to this Mexican visit: Stravinsky "wants to conduct in Mexico City this [July] but is having trouble getting his re-entry permit." Then in July Andersson learned that Stravinsky had to pay his 1941 Federal income tax to date, a requirement for departing aliens. Moreover, there was a "mixup on passports as Mrs. S. is without a country and [has] no passport. Only [a] letter from France identifying her. Mexico vises [sic] received after much ado—wiring, etc."[187] Andersson's precise information in 1941 about these difficulties corresponds to additional details only very recently brought to light.[188]

Had Andersson traveled with the Stravinskys, he would not only have had "a grand trip." He would surely have encountered Dorothy McQuoid. Stravinsky programmed Symphony in C and Capriccio, but not with Adele Marcus. He had told Dorothy that he was uneasy about conducting Capriccio with a Mexican pianist whom he had never heard play. Regarding this as an auspicious gamble, she flew (at her own expense) from Biloxi to Mexico City, just in case he needed her. Vera recorded in her diary on 14 July, "Igor goes to [*recte:* with (Francisco)] Agea to hear a pianist Ochoa who will play the Capriccio."[189] Fortunately for Stravinsky—but not for Mrs. McQuoid—Salvador Ochoa met Stravinsky's standards and on 18 and 20 July they successfully performed Capriccio together.

Mrs. McQuoid's impulse to assist the composer-conductor in Mexico City marked the beginning of a gradual distancing from the Stravinskys. Two young boys and her pregnancy with a third child—a girl born 2 November 1942—limited her availability, as did the sudden death of her husband in 1950, which obliged her to find employment. She recalled to me that she last saw the Stravinskys on 10 September 1948 at the Russian

Orthodox burial service for Kall. In response to the composer's inquiry, she answered that she had last seen Kall just a few days before he died.[190]

A newspaper review of the Mexico City performances of the Symphony in C and Capriccio reveals more about its writer's politics than it does about the performances themselves. The Symphony must have gone well, because on 14 July Vera recorded in her diary that "Igor is pleased with the first rehearsal, having worried about the difficulties of the Symphony." The day after the second concert, the newspaper *Excelsior* printed the review, by Jorge Santana. It would have startled and annoyed Stravinsky, even though he had surely already discovered during the rehearsals—to his certain horror—the political leanings of his piano soloist, "el joven socialista, Salvador Ochoa."

Santana relied heavily on Marxist rhetoric, evident from his first subtitle, "Musica revolucionaria," a particular bugbear of the composer (already elaborated at length in his *Poetics* and later in conversation with Nabokov in December of 1947).[191] Even without the subtitle, the first sentence would have stopped Stravinsky cold with its mention of not only "revolution" but also "expression": "In the most correct meaning of the term, Stravinsky's music must be considered essentially revolutionary; the orchestra in his hands functions to serve as a sole and unique and complete instrument of expression." Santana felt obliged to employ such *terminos marxistas* as "dialectical synthesis" and the "revolutionary destruction of the past by the new." The influence of Adorno and even Trotsky, the latter of whom had been living in Mexico City for some time and had been murdered there the previous summer, is not too far distant. Santana went on to say that the Symphony in C would be viewed not only as a "glorification to God" but also as a "neurosis of the present time." Santana summed up: "Now, we do not excuse the unnerving acidity of the 'Symphony in C'—with its obsessive pauses—rather a constant fantasy; its beginning [is] like the murmuring of the creeks and the caresses of the wind."[192] Was Santana mocking Stravinsky's own remarks in early 1936 about music *not* expressing either the "sighing of the wind" or the "sound of sea?"[193] Fortunately, the reader who wishes to form his or her own judgment of Stravinsky's conducting may now consult a recently released recording: a 19 July 1936 performance of Divertimento with the Orquesta Sinfónica, still marred by a man's shouts.[194]

On 28 July, the day the Stravinskys returned from Mexico, Andersson again proved useful. Stravinsky noted in his diary that his student had sent off the 8 July photostat of "The Star-Spangled Banner" to be copyrighted.[195] And on 23 August Andersson wrote a letter to Mercury Music, advising Feist that Stravinsky did not want any performance fees to be levied for it.[196]

A SANTA BARBARA PROJECT

According to Vera's diary, late the following month, 27–28 August, the Stravinskys were whisked off to Santa Barbara in a limousine belonging to Arthur Sachs, a prominent New York Philharmonic patron. There they visited the Sachs and their house guest Nadia

Boulanger; the four were photographed in a memorable image of Stravinsky "playing dead,"[197] modifying his old party trick chez Ocampo in Buenos Aires. Andersson's notebook reveals a more significant motive for this trip, one not previously considered by historians delving into Stravinsky's relationships with his patrons: "28 August he is [to be] in Santa Barbara. Back Friday. Mrs. [Robert Woods] Bliss is sending car for them. He will feel her out on the possibility of starting an orchestra in Santa B[arbara]." After lesson 75 on 29 August, Andersson made another entry in his notebook: "[Stravinsky] is much interested in Santa Barbara proposed orchestra. Will return there to feel out patronage."[198] The Stravinskys did, in fact, go to Santa Barbara several times: on 20 September, staying with the Sachs at Hope Ranch, and then returning to Hollywood to give lessons 85–87 to Andersson on 22, 24, and 26 September.[199] The next day, the Stravinskys again visited the Sachs, and on 28 September they had tea with Mrs. Bliss and El Forbes. The project, however, came to naught.

This endeavor implies that Stravinsky was contemplating not only establishing, but also conducting, some body of orchestral musicians in Santa Barbara. Andersson's "starting" and "proposed" might have referred to the already-established "small City WPA Orchestra co-sponsored by The Southern California Music Project and the friends of music in Santa Barbara . . . with the help of municipal funds."[200] Stravinsky was probably seeking patronage from Mrs. Robert Woods Bliss—she owned a house in Santa Barbara[201]—as one of "the friends of music" in order to enlarge her small city's WPA orchestra to the level the composer had observed and admired the previous 22 April when, with Andersson, he attended Sample's rehearsals of the Los Angeles WPA Symphony Orchestra.

PREMIERE OF "THE STAR-SPANGLED BANNER"

By the time the Stravinskys returned to Hollywood, Feist had printed a small first run of a twenty-five-cent edition of the piano-vocal score of Stravinsky's arrangement of "The Star-Spangled Banner." He sent six copies to the composer. In a burst of patriotic anticipation—Stravinsky was not yet a US citizen—he colored the anthem's title in red and blue crayon on a blank white cover sheet[202] and inscribed the very first copy to Andersson in red and blue crayon on the white areas of its cover.[203] He disliked the original design of the printed cover, and by 14 September he complained to Feist about "such a lot of red and therefore does not indicate properly the national colors." He demanded that the edition be scrapped and a new one printed, but only after he had read the proofs,[204] remembering perhaps the previous April's errors in Tango. This rebuke prompted Mercury Music Corporation's second edition, printed mid-October, but now raised a nickel, to thirty cents per copy. Dorothy, in this instance not so blessed as Andersson, had to be content with a simple inscription on the second edition, "To Dorothy McQuoid / with all my best / wishes / I Strawinsky / 1941" (fig. 6.13).

Near the end of August (probably by the twenty-sixth), Andersson noted that Stravinsky "has selected [movements] 2 & 3 of Futurama for proposed Sept 9 [premiere] for his Star-Spangled Banner."[205] Though indeed slated for a 9 September "Presentation

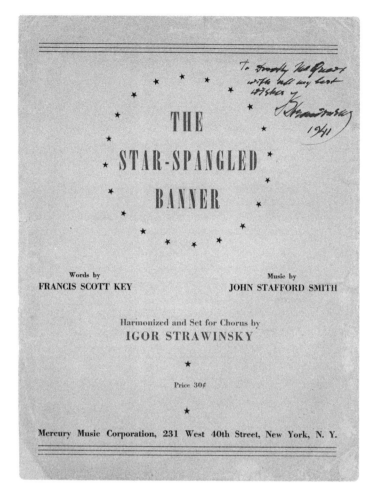

FIGURE 6.13
"The Star-Spangled Banner"
(cover, Dorothy McQuoid's copy).
UBC Stravinsky Collection, no. 75.

Ceremony" of the anthem's autograph full-score to a representative of President Roosevelt, political considerations delayed the actual premiere to 14 October. It took place at the Embassy Auditorium, located in downtown Los Angeles.[206] The "remarks" by Stravinsky promised on the printed program—an extract from a more elaborate dedicatory essay written in August—ended up being delivered by Karl Wecker, presumably at the request of the linguistically challenged composer.[207]

A dedicatory letter to the president, surely written by Andersson or Sample, was copied out by Stravinsky in his own hand (fig. 6.14). It was received at the White House on 23 August and is now at Hyde Park in the Franklin D. Roosevelt Memorial Library. A near duplicate, even to line breaks (save for spelling *California* in full), slightly predates it; this copy is preserved in a private Pennsylvania collection as part of Andersson's legacy.[208] A less carefully copied version (misspelling "through" as "trough") and dated October 1941 is in facsimile in Mercury's printed edition of the score.

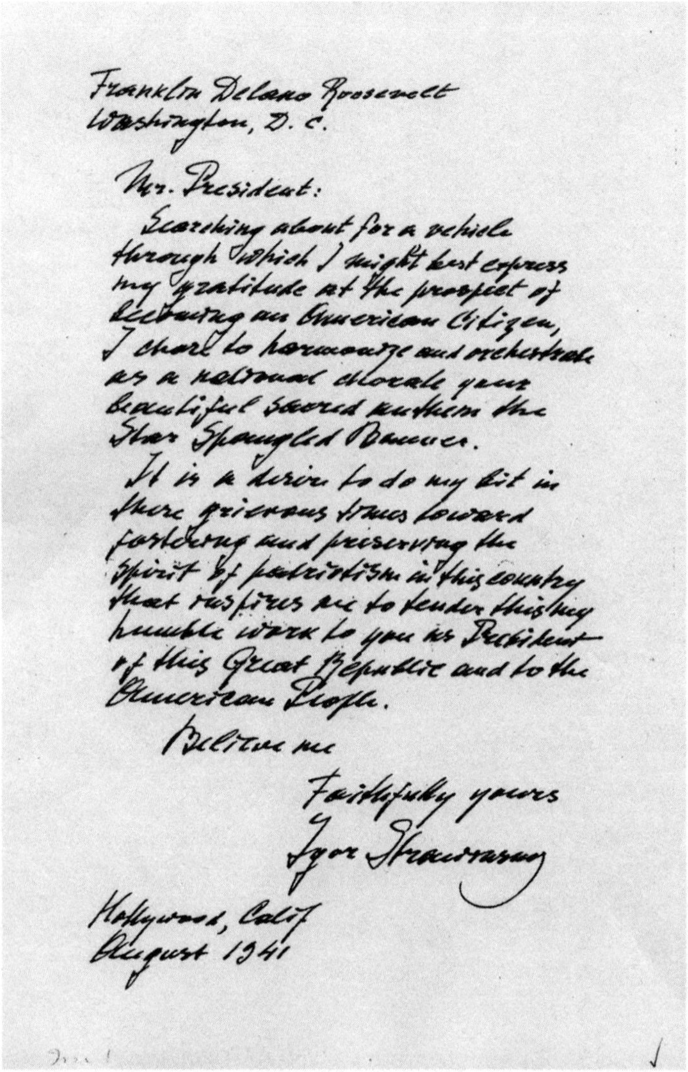

Franklin Delano Roosevelt
Washington, D. C.

Mr. President:

Searching about for a vehicle through which I might best express my gratitude at the prospect of becoming an American Citizen, I chose to harmonize and orchestrate as a national chorale your beautiful sacred anthem the Star Spangled Banner.

It is a desire to do my bit in these grievous times toward fostering and preserving the spirit of patriotism in this country that inspires me to tender this my humble work to you as President of this Great Republic and to the American People.

Believe me

Faithfully yours
Igor Strawinsky

Hollywood, Calif
August 1941

FIGURE 6.14
Stravinskyto Franklin Delano Roosevelt, August 1941. Franklin D. Roosevelt Memorial Library, Hyde Park, New York.

In preparing the presidential gift, it was Sample's turn to serve as Stravinsky's factotum. After the 14 October premiere, Sample took the autograph score and dedication to a Los Angeles binder, Charles L. Malotte. The elegant binding required about two weeks to complete. Sample picked it up, packaged, addressed, and mailed it to the president early in November. Although it arrived safely, the gift was never directly acknowledged. To this day it is displayed in the Jefferson Room at the Library of Congress.

Aware that Stravinsky had inscribed a copy of the (thirty-cent) edition for Mrs. McQuoid, and hoping for an informative reaction to its premiere from such a witness as she,[209] I asked her if she had attended it. She was unable to remember. After her death

I discovered, in the Music Division of the Library of Congress, the night-letter telegram she had sent on the evening of the premiere from Burbank:

> Dearest Igor
> For some unexplained reason we confused the date of your concert thinking it this Saturday [18 October] Ed is judging [a] pictorial solon [*recte:* salon, i.e., a photo competition] I am alone with [my] boys no way to reach concert Cannot tell you what an intense disappointment it is Many bravos and many kisses Our deepest love / Dorothy McQuoid / 8:37 [p.m.]

Her cheeky salutation disproves Craft's later dictum that "no one except the composer's wife was allowed to call him by his first name," Craft apparently forgetting his own citation of the same transgression on 16 April 1940 by Mrs. Charles Goodspeed in Chicago. Stravinsky's displeasure seems to have extended more to men, for example, the composer David Diamond, who plunged himself into hot water in May of 1949.[210]

Critical reaction was mixed following Sample's world premiere and his repeat two weeks later, in marked contrast to the disasters at year's end in St. Louis and in January of 1944 in Boston. Some reviews of the premiere were favorable: "streamlined and yet with added harmonic richness" (Jones); "a reverent orchestration . . . rich tapestry of sound" (Lawrence); "new facets of beauty . . . a rich tapestry of instrumental lines to support the melody and achieving a solemn and profound dignity . . . intrinsic beauty and consistent nobility" (Saunders); and "respectful . . . new harmonies . . . infinitely more interesting than Damrosch" (Morton). Yet negative opinions predominated: summing up eight months of reaction in Los Angeles, Morton noted in June of 1942 that "some of the objections which have been raised are in truth too ridiculous to consider seriously even though they are widespread."[211] Curiously enough, one of these "ridiculous" verdicts came from one of the best of the older generation of the city's critics, Bruno David Ussher, who had been trained at Leipzig. Ussher opined right after the premiere that the arrangement was "not an improvement nor even an enrichment." Ussher dubbed Sample's second performance a "spotty harmonization."[212]

HOLLYWOOD GLITTERATI AND INTIMATIONS OF WAR

During early and late fall of 1941 frenetic partying of a kind often preceding cataclysmic world events took place in Los Angeles and surely elsewhere in the country. It was especially pronounced among the social set courting newly arrived celebrities. Although the McQuoids (who had movie connections) were absent from the premiere of "The Star-Spangled Banner," former silent-movie star Dagmar Godowsky was probably in the audience, since Stravinsky inscribed a printed copy of the piano-vocal score for her.[213] That summer she had leased "a house on North Bedford in Beverly Hills [with] a garden laden with fruit trees." Having visited the Stravinskys on 3 September,[214] she gave a notably drunken party on 9 September, which both Stravinskys attended, along with Mr. and Mrs. Artur Rubinstein, writer-translator Mercedes de Acosta, Mr. and Mrs. Josef Hofmann, Mr. and Mrs. Harry Kaufman, composer Richard Hageman and his wife, author Erich Remarque, Gladys Robinson—wife of actor Edward G., and frequent contributor to *Script's* gossip column "Horrible Hollywood"—and "scores more."[215] According to Los Angeles's most widely read gossip columnist, Hedda Hopper, "Dagmar Godowski's party was more darned fun, with Stravinsky."[216] One can only speculate whether, after that disastrous 1936 dinner in Rio de Janeiro, any conversation took place between the Hofmanns and the Stravinskys.

On 2 October 1941 Dagmar offered a more intimate "little dinner" in her garden, with just eight guests. The day before, Hedda Hopper announced: "Greta's gone musical again and will attend a dinner this week given by Dagmar Godowsky at which Stravinsky and Rubinstein will be guests."[217] At the dinner: " 'Geegee' [Greta Garbo] met 'the great Mr. Stravinsky,' who also was dying to meet the mysterious Garbo. . . . They were both disenchanted.[218] This outcome substantiates a rather dour evaluation of Hollywood actors frequenting the Farmers' Market "who [in the late 1940s] gaped with greater interest at the composer and the writer [Aldous Huxley] than the other way around." In the late 1940s Craft's first (and apparently self-appointed) task was to "cut down on movie people."[219] Yet this effort at reform hardly explains why Stravinsky, who had a lifelong love affair with movies and movie people,[220] still took such visible pleasure in the company of another "Geegee," this time, movie-star Greer Garson.[221]

On 28 October the Stravinskys presumably attended Sample's second performance of "The Star-Spangled Banner," again in the Embassy Auditorium. The rest of the concert, instead of music by Andersson,[222] featured a suite for orchestra, *The Thief of Bagdad*, drawn from a movie of the same title of the previous year with a score by Miklós Rózsa, a Hungarian refugee who had arrived in Hollywood with famed movie producer Alexander Korda at about the same time as had the Stravinskys.

The previous evening, Dagmar had provided dinner for the Stravinskys, after which they all went to Remarque's house, where there was "a lot of drinking." The couple did not return home until 2:30 a.m.[223] Dagmar reported that, not long after her autumn parties, "Vera called and asked if I would help receive at their housewarming."[224] She may have refused this task or simply mixed up the date in her memoir, because her name does not appear among the invitees listed in Vera's diary for "our first American party," given on 1 November at the North Wetherly house. Among the thirty-one guests were such notables as the Edward G. Robinsons, the Hammonds (composer Richard Hammond and his life-partner, George Martin), Mercedes de Acosta,[225] the Adolph Bolms, and Earnest Andersson.[226] Less than a year later, the blessedly affluent Andersson returned the favor.

Just days after the Japanese attack on Pearl Harbor (7 December: "a date which will live in infamy" in Roosevelt's broadcast to the nation), Stravinsky and his wife traveled to St. Louis to introduce the new Symphony in C and his "Star-Spangled Banner" arrangement. Performance of the latter—bizarrely viewed by the orchestra's administration as "unpatriotic"—was blocked. Stravinsky led what he called "the Standard version," presumably Damrosch's harmonization, "with pleasure" (or so he said!). According to one critic, he did it "as a priest on the podium . . . [and] it took on a new meaning to the audience";[227] he probably conducted it at the solemn, slow, almost priestly tempo that he approved in Sample's recording of his own version rather than at the brisk pace that he favored later in life.

Despite the humiliation, the Symphony in C was mostly well-received.[228] Under a heading that was broader than it was accurate, "Analysis of Symphony," one local writer was lavish in his praise:

> It is possible to say . . . after only one hearing that it has a radiant beauty and that its elements are disposed in such a way as to demonstrate a clear and formidable mastery of its materials. . . . This evident mastery invites the formal uses of repetition, transformation and recall, of synthesis and analysis. . . . In no preceding work has he shown a greater virtuosity in solving the problems imposed by a formal design. Yet . . . the melodic invention disclosed in this symphony is considerable. . . . His melodies . . . are functional according to classic usage and are not overshadowed by explosive rhythms, dynamic masses, or brilliant colors. . . . Some of his harmonies are extraordinarily beautiful. . . . This symphony is definitely emotional. The pathos of the second movement, though a bit wry, was sustained and seemingly sincere.[229]

Like the Chicago reviewer at the world premiere and Santana in Mexico City, this reviewer was particularly struck by the slow movement, and his "wry," while still distant from *le mot juste*, is a bit more perceptive than Santana's "acidity."

Another critic, writing for a national music journal, was not so perceptive: "From a structural standpoint, it is undoubtedly one of Mr. Stravinsky's best works, but its tonal vagaries did not create the most pleasant reaction on first hearing."[230]

STRAVINSKY'S CONTRIBUTIONS TO *FUTURAMA*

Notwithstanding the terminus of Andersson's notebook (October 1941) and that Stravinsky's diary entries and markings on *Futurama* sketches are mostly datable to 1941, *Futurama* was not finished until late January of 1942. Stravinsky's diary and the markings by both men on three other Andersson orchestral scores supply precise dates for some but not all of their labors. The title Andersson gave his four-movement symphony prompts a few words. *Pace* Craft's verdict of "disappointing,"[231] the music itself deserves many more words—and receives them near the beginning of Stravinsky's next domestic excursion (1942). Table 6.1 summarizes what is known about the number of lessons taken for *Futurama* and gives beginning and ending dates for each of its four movements during the 143 lessons that Andersson took with Stravinsky between 6 March 1941 and 27 January 1942.

TABLE 6.1 Dates of *Futurama* Manuscript

Movement	Lesson Number	Begun	Finished	References in 1941 *Notebook*
I	68–?	14 August	27 January 1942	none
II	43–67	15 June	8 and 12 August 1941	13, 19, c. 26 June; 1 July
III	1–42	27 February	13 June 1941	8, 22 April; 15 May; 13 June
IV	?–143	unknown	27 January 1942	none

The data in Stravinsky's own diary and Andersson's notebook demolish Stravinsky's preposterous claim, made at a symposium at the Eastman School of Music on 8 March 1966, that "*I* composed it—with his themes," as well as a slightly tempered version a year and a half later to Craft: "[Stravinsky] describes how he wrote much of his pupil's symphony for him."[232] By this time, no one would have dared to challenge the world-famous, elderly Stravinsky's veracity. Loring B. Conant (an undergraduate I knew at Harvard in 1959) was then in medical school at the University of Rochester and traveled across town that Sunday afternoon to attend the symposium. Dr. Conant's prime recollection is of having been overwhelmed by the force of the composer's fame, personality, and authority, thus putting the statement about his role in Andersson's *Futurama* beyond question. Yet Stravinsky seems to have been aware of his own dissembling when Walter Hendl asked: "Are you teaching these days?" Apparently still thinking about his experiences in 1941–42, he prevaricated: "I gave some [hesitating]—it was not—lessons." This answer, despite having painstakingly labeled, in his own diary, each one of Andersson's 215 appointments as "lessons."

Stravinsky's ambivalence about lessons for Andersson and about teaching in general may well be unresolvable. In 1960 he stated that "I have very little gift for teaching and no disposition for it."[233] He said nothing about having taught Nadia Boulanger's composition students in 1935–36, and Harvard undergraduate composition students in 1939–40, nor of giving private lessons to Robert M. Stevenson. Stravinsky concluded his 1966 Eastman interview: "Composing is one thing and to teach somebody music is quite a different thing, you know. I have no pedagogical talent, not at all. I don't feel it. . . . I have no passion [for] teaching."[234]

Futurama's two inner movements (and perhaps the others) existed well before Andersson was introduced to Stravinsky. The slow movement and scherzo were premiered by Sample on 6 April 1941, but their initial composition must have taken much longer than six weeks.[235] Andersson may have begun work on them after Gastone Usigli led the Los Angeles WPA Federal Orchestra on 31 January and 7 February 1939 in the final movement of Andersson's 1937–38 tone poem *The Sun Worshiper*.[236]

An intriguing notion about Stravinsky's and Andersson's work together stems from an observation by Craft, with the qualification that it requires much clearer and more persuasive documentation than he provided. In 1978 he hypothesized a connection between the first movement of Stravinsky's 1942–45 *Symphony in Three Movements* and Andersson's *Futurama*.[237] Stravinsky's "work on it was contemporary with the first movement of his own final symphony, from which Andersson's might have received some residue, or contain vestigial hints."[238] But Stravinsky's short-score drafts for passages in *Futurama* and Andersson's notebook prove just the opposite. Their joint work on *Futurama* was *not* "contemporary" with Stravinsky's labor on his own first movement: the earliest dated sketches for Symphony in Three Movements are marked 4 April 1942, a full year after the *Futurama* partial premiere. Although several undated Stravinsky sketches for his own Symphony may stem from the previous February, they clearly come after the end of his work with Andersson on *Futurama*. Stravinsky's early sketches may have been provoked by Pearl Harbor, but they date from well after the attack.[239]

Several more details may prove useful for future research. Andersson wrote on the folder of Stravinsky's short score for *Futurama*'s first movement, "Rewrite started Aug 14th-41." This rewrite was finished no later than 27 January 1942. For the second movement, variously titled "Notturno," "Nocturno" [*sic*], and "Nocturne" in printed programs and reviews, though not so titled in the manuscript, Andersson wrote: "Finished Orchestration August 12th 1941." He inscribed no specific dates on Stravinsky's short-score suggestions for *Futurama*'s "scherzo," but his notebook shows that they worked on it from late February to mid-May of 1941. The two men finished all revisions to *Futurama* by 27 January 1942, several weeks before Stravinsky's initial sketches for his own Symphony in Three Movements. Although Andersson ordered a fair copy of his entire freshly revised *Futurama* manuscript score from a professional copyist, it was not completed until 9 May 1942. As a result, when Andersson set out on 15 February to hawk his symphony to conductors across the country, he must have carried his own working copy (now lost). He also carried letters of recommendation from Stravinsky to several top-flight conductors: the one to Barbirolli in New York refers to Andersson as "my dear friend."

At least one passage in Andersson's second movement, "Notturno" (13 June 1941), for three chattering French horn triads and ensuing three trumpets over a pizzicato ostinato by the cellos,[240] seems peculiarly akin to a similar passage almost a full year later in the first movement of Stravinsky's Symphony in Three Movements (manuscript version of 15 June 1942). Stravinsky wrote three repeating French horn chords above an arpeggiated ostinato that he had originally assigned to bassoons but later gave to the piano on completing his short score.[241] In this passage at least, the influence would seem to have traveled from the Andersson-Stravinsky *Futurama* to Stravinsky's Symphony.

The private collection of Anderson's papers in Pennsylvania holds Stravinsky's short-score draft pages for *Futurama* and for Andersson's other two orchestral works, as well as numerous mementos of the period between their initial meeting in February of 1941 and Andersson's death in June of 1943. Among them are Andersson's notebook;

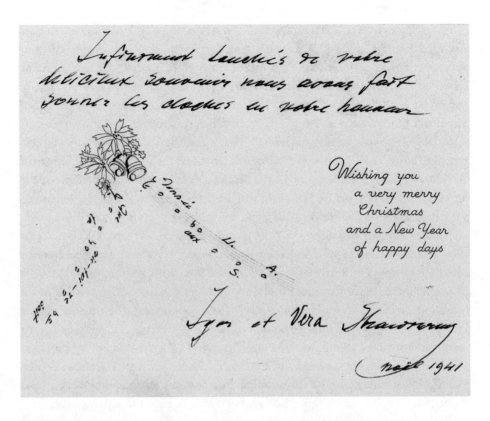

FIGURE 6.15
Christmas card "Bells Ring" (1941), with "Star-Spangled Banner" fragment penned by Stravinsky.
UBC Stravinsky Collection, no. 76.

Stravinsky's inscribed holographs and printed editions of his "Star-Spangled Banner"
arrangements; Stravinsky's inscription on a pencil (c. 16 June 1941) used by him to copy
the anthem; Stravinsky's letters and inscribed *cartes de visite* to orchestra conductors; a
sterling silver money clip Stravinsky gave to celebrate Andersson's sixty-fourth birthday
(10 February 1942); a kitchen apron inscribed with congratulatory messages from
Stravinsky and thirty-six of Andersson's dinner guests on 16 September 1942; and a
remarkable tea-towel embroidered by Vera with Andersson's name for his sixty-fifth—
and last—birthday.[242]

YEAR-END TASKS

Late in the fall of 1941, Serge Koussevitzky offered Stravinsky a teaching appointment for
the summer (5 July through 16 August) at Tanglewood.[243] Perhaps because of his instruc-
tional experience with Andersson, he agreed on 23 November to teach eight "beginner
composers." He would include his "critique and advice while we go over their work" but

wanted it understood that he would give no course in "harmony, counterpoint, orchestration, or other musical disciplines."[244] The appointment was publicly announced on 20 December as "Stravinsky Joins Tanglewood School," accompanied by Weston's 1937 photograph (box 2.1, no. 3).[245] However, on 14 June 1942, he cabled Koussevitzky and cancelled the entire project, pleading "circumstances completedly [*sic*] changed."[246] These "circumstances," detailed in the next chapter, were his initial efforts to write movie music.

At the close of 1941 Stravinsky inscribed dedications for Mrs. McQuoid and for Dagmar Godowsky on the thirty-cent copies of his piano-vocal scores of his arrangement of "The Star-Spangled Banner." On 30 December he did the same for Sample on the anthem's full orchestral score. These three dedications were virtually coeval with a delightfully patriotic Christmas card (its envelope lost) that he and Vera signed and sent to an unknown recipient some two weeks after the attack on Pearl Harbor (fig. 6.15).[247] At the top of the card, Stravinsky wrote in French: "Deeply moved by your / charming memento, we are making the bells ring in your honor." At the bottom, as if emerging out of the bell printed on the card, he drew two staves with his rastrum. He then inscribed a dozen whole notes on the staves, and underlaid a text in French: "May victory be / given to the U.S.A." No reader here will register much surprise that the twelve notes are the opening two phrases of "The Star-Spangled Banner."

7

EXCURSIONS (1942)

CONCERT APPEARANCES

9, 10 January: San Francisco Orchestra

8 February: Los Angeles, Werner Janssen Orchestra (*Danses concertantes* premiere)

28 September: rehearses unidentified [Hollywood] studio orchestra [in Vera's diary]

19 October: Santa Barbara, Four-Hand Piano Sonata with Marcelle Manziarly

Declarations of war by the United States on Japan, 8 December 1941, and on Germany and Italy, 12 December 1941, greatly diminished the Stravinskys' prospects and their appetite for travel. For his pair of concerts early in January of 1942 in San Francisco, a letter written Christmas Day 1941 to Pierre Monteux[1] provides information about Stravinsky's rehearsals in the Bay City. The letter is typed on the reverse side of a piece of the same Department of Music stationery, purloined from Harvard University, that he had used the previous year. In the right margin, the penurious composer excuses his theft of Harvard letterhead by claiming a lack of writing paper in his Hollywood house. He explains in a lengthy handwritten *marginale* that Monteux's letter, dated 10 December, arrived on Christmas Eve, the very day the couple returned home on a train that pulled into the station twelve hours late.

Stravinsky agrees with Monteux that his proposed San Francisco program is a little on the short side, but he sees no way to add any other work because of the Musicians Union limitation to four rehearsals. Previous experience with his new Symphony in C in other cities allows him to predict that rehearsals for it alone will consume between two and a half and three sessions (most of that surely devoted to its complex third movement), leaving what remains for the Divertimento—first time for this orchestra and "not an easy work"—and a run-through for the twenty-minute *Firebird Suite,* which the players know reasonably well. Because of the postal delays, Stravinsky needs to hear from Monteux immediately.

He did not request rehearsal time for his new arrangement of the national anthem but said that he would bring the orchestra parts with him, presumably the set he had used in St. Louis. Not surprisingly, he says nothing of the scandalous suppression of this arrangement in St. Louis. He asks for clarification from Monteux about rehearsal dates, preferring Tuesday afternoon (6 January) and Thursday at 2 p.m., and is adamant that Monteux not schedule a 4 January Sunday rehearsal, claiming that it would consume too much of the time he needs for a project that is subject to a deadline. This unnamed, and still "secret," project was certainly *Danses concertantes,* and the deadline he faced was to complete the score and ready it for photographic reproduction in time for rehearsals early in February in Los Angeles.[2]

Just preceding his signature in the complimentary close to Monteux, Stravinsky's phrase "ce temps d'angoisse" (referring to World War II, and specifically to Pearl Harbor) echoes the "these grievous times" in his August 1941 letter to President Roosevelt accompanying his arrangement of the national anthem. That early venture into formal English (surely assisted by Andersson or Sample) blossomed five years later (without aid from either man) into "arduous time of sharp shifting events, time of despear [sic] and hope, time of continual torments, of tention [sic]" in his letter to the New York Philharmonic for the premiere of the so-called "Victory" Symphony (Symphony in Three Movements, 1943–45).

Between 28 and 31 December 1941, after a Christmas that the Stravinskys celebrated with the Bolms, Mercedes de Acosta, Dagmar Godowsky, and Eugene Berman, Andersson took lessons 129–32 on *Futurama*—on the way to completing its final revisions. During the first week of 1942, two old friends, El Forbes (then teaching at the Cate School in Carpinteria, California) and his mother, Peg (then visiting in Pasadena with his father, Edward), had made an afternoon excursion to the Stravinskys in Hollywood. This visit probably also included El's wife, Kay, because thereafter Stravinsky inscribed a copy of his "Star-Spangled Banner" arrangement: "To Eliott [sic] Forbes, to him and to his beautiful wife I Str / 1942."[3]

On 5 January, after Andersson's lesson 135, Stravinsky and Vera took the night train from Los Angeles to San Francisco. Perhaps Stravinsky had a rehearsal that very afternoon, a Tuesday, with the San Francisco Orchestra; the next day he had two, each followed by a meal with Monteux. A final rehearsal on Thursday evening included his "Star-Spangled Banner." His concerts took place on Friday afternoon, at 2:30 p.m., and Saturday evening.[4]

In San Francisco, where he was esteemed and supported by Monteux, his new arrangement of the national anthem enjoyed approval even at the evening rehearsal on 8 January, as well as at both performances. Its success had been in preparation since October of 1941, when news arrived of the Los Angeles world premiere: "Conductor James Sample predicted that Stravinsky's score eventually will be accepted as standard. 'The music is lofty and full of reverential feeling,' he said. 'One is reminded not of a strictly military air, but a feeling from the bottom of the heart of love and reverence for his country.' "[5] At least one San Francisco critic, Ashley Pettis, disagreed, characterizing its harmonization as "singularly turbid";[6] *turbid* may have been a reference to the reiterated B-flat major arpeggio in low string instruments during the middle section. Just before the performance in January, another San Francisco critic sat on the fence:

> The Star-Spangled Banner, both in its Stravinsky version and in its more or less unelaborated forms, has already been the subject of much controversy all over the country, during which it has been examined in a variety of lights, discussed by every amateur and professional expert on the subject, and generally snatched back and forth by all and sundry. By now the whole argument is worn so threadbare that it seems to require no further comment until San Francisco has actually heard the Stravinsky orchestration and had an opportunity to form an opinion about it at first hand.[7]

Still another critic who had heard from Los Angeles that there was "no question as to its reverence" warned of its "Stravinskian chords" and its "modern dissonances inappropriate and harsh, not to say absurd."[8]

Alfred Frankenstein, dean of West Coast critics, knew better: as usual, he had done his homework. He even consulted with the Music Librarian at the Library of Congress before writing "a rather extensive program note on our national anthem to be published in the program book of the San Francisco Symphony when Stravinsky directs his arrangement of it here."[9] His assiduity and intelligence allowed him, right after the premiere, to declare the new arrangement "sonorous and dignified."

Just before the San Francisco performance, Stravinsky had disclosed to an anonymous interviewer that " 'I like the melody. . . . [It is] just right for a [national] hymn[.] But'—he threw up his hands—'it is so poorly organized.' . . . Not only as a composer but also because of his patriotic spirit, Stravinsky is interested in the 'Star-Spangled Banner.' "[10]

One of the city's critics, Marjorie Fisher, observed that Stravinsky faced the San Francisco audience, obviously expecting them to sing, but not a voice was heard, although the audience clearly was entranced by the arrangement. Fisher wrote that she admired his transformation of the anthem from its "usual rambling musical structure" into a "four-square architectural form." She seems not to have noticed that the new harmonization made no change either to the anthem's melody or to its design. Shortly thereafter, she wrote for a national music magazine that the San Francisco audience "listened attentively and rewarded the arrangement with a considerable applause" and that she regarded it as a "fine straightforward work."[11]

Among major US cities, San Francisco was, that same evening, rather late in premiering the Symphony in C. Frankenstein's enthusiastic review the next morning sharply contrasts with the one Morton had written the previous year in Los Angeles:

> Few of Stravinsky's bigger works are so immediately enjoyable as this one. The symphony is in the vein of objective modern "classicism" Stravinsky has exploited for a long time, but is more mellow in feeling than most of his instrumental works in this idiom. The nervous,

ceaselessly active rhythmic texture is still there, but not the element of the ironic and diabolic that so often manifests itself in this composer's music. It is an eloquent work and a magnificently contrived one. Not the least of its fascinations is the sculpturesque, chamber-like orchestration, which lets space and air play about each instrumental line. It has more than enough learning in its structure to please the most exacting of the doctors, but its ultimate effect suggests that Stravinsky's neo-classicism is now coming close to a kind of new romanticism. At all events, this is certainly one of the most important symphonies of recent years.[12]

Following the first (afternoon) concert in San Francisco, the Stravinskys were driven to Mills College, in Oakland, where the Milhauds held a reception for them. Stravinsky almost certainly encountered Milhaud's protégé, Charles Cushing, the young East Bay enthusiast from the 1935 tour, who, as an assistant professor in 1942, also conducted the University of California Band. Cushing was so taken by the new version of the national anthem that he asked Stravinsky's permission to arrange it for his ensemble. After receiving authorization, Cushing sent him the completed transcription on 6 March. Stravinsky acknowledged it five days later with considerable praise for "the general sonority of the instrumental ensemble and also the way you followed so faithfully my voice leading."[13]

But in mid-January of 1942 in Washington, the arrangement was not so well-favored. Hans Kindler led it to open the second half of his program with the National Symphony Orchestra in Constitution Hall, home of the National Society of the Daughters of the American Revolution. That organization had long favored Damrosch's harmonization. Kindler's purpose was to hold a competition in which the audience could vote for either Stravinsky's or his own arrangement. He had been programming the latter for a decade, so predictably enough, the audience voted about three to two in his favor. Reporting this outcome, a Washington critic also wrote inaccurately about Stravinsky's version: "The harmony is simple, slightly astringent and veers toward the minor mode."[14] When, a month later, Kindler had his orchestra play it in Baltimore, a critic observed much more bluntly that "the Stravinsky arrangement of the Star-Spangled Banner made its first, and last, appearance locally at this concert."[15] *Time* magazine hastily tempered its stance of six weeks earlier: on 2 February 1942 it reported on the Kindler-sponsored competition that "Stravinsky's Russianized version of 'The Star-Spangled Banner' is muscular and musicianly, but audiences don't like it too well."[16]

Early in 1942, probably having heard about the Kindler competition, Koussevitzky contemplated conducting Stravinsky's arrangement. Learning of his interest, Stravinsky wrote to him on 10 February 1942—a trifle deceptively—of the "great success on my recent tour," meaning, of course, just San Francisco. He neglected to mention (as he had with Monteux) his lamentable experience in St. Louis. He hoped that Koussevitzky would program it for the upcoming Boston Symphony Orchestra concerts in New York in the second half of February. The conductor wired Stravinsky that it was too late to give it in New York but that he was thinking of early April in Boston and New York. No such performances ever took place. Stravinsky considered it important for Koussevitzky to establish "the proper attitude towards it." Without mentioning Kindler's name, Stravinsky noted that the Washington competition had generated "adverse and controversial criticisms."[17] Koussevitzky, who was planning an April concert in Washington, probably had second thoughts about programming it to open an all-Russian program attended by Mrs. Roosevelt, diplomats, and government officials. At that time, several months before the German invasion of Soviet Russia (12 June 1941), Stravinsky's and Koussevitzky's homeland was still an ally of the Nazis, resulting from the Soviet-German nonaggression pact (23 August 1939).

STRAVINSKY AND *FUTURAMA*

The Stravinskys returned from San Francisco on 12 January 1942. Andersson took his last seven lessons on *Futurama* between 15 and 27 January. In mid-February he made several visits with his autograph fair copy of all its four movements, finally completed. Unfortunately this manuscript, self-dated "January 21 1942," does not survive. It certainly once existed, however, because in June of 1941 Andersson wrote in his notebook: "Going over my scores [Stravinsky] is very careful that every note is readable for the copyist's sake."[18] In connection with these lessons, or possibly earlier ones, Stravinsky sketched out various passages, often in short score, on various-sized pieces of music paper. And although Andersson's autograph fair copy has been lost (as has the score of the work as it existed prior to the lessons with Stravinsky), Stravinsky's sketches, entirely in his hand, survive in a private archive in Pennsylvania. Those readers wishing to gain an idea of the specific relationship can compare a page of Stravinsky's short-sketch score with its final version in the professional copyist's score of *Futurama*'s second movement in my article about Andersson's lessons with Stravinsky. They are reproduced there through the kindness of its present owner.[19]

On 15 February Stravinsky wrote a series of notes and *cartes de visite* to introduce Andersson and to recommend his symphony to Mitropoulos in Minnesota, Stock in Chicago, Barbirolli in New York,[20] and Koussevitzky in Boston. Andersson then took to the road—or, rather, to the rails—and did not resume lessons with Stravinsky until mid-March.

Although none of the four conductors ever programmed *Futurama*, Stravinsky's advocacy and the work itself deserve evaluation. Five years afterward, in the fall of 1946, he disclosed that he "learned a great deal while doing it." To date, the sole clue about what he meant by this resides in an interview Sample taped in 1992, when he was eighty-two years old. There he revealed that Stravinsky had been fascinated by, and seemingly envious of, Andersson's method of creating themes from the pitches of Chinese words. Sample further observed that Stravinsky had a "very difficult time to find his motives, his melodies." We can only surmise that Andersson also "learned a great deal," the one, of course, not precluding the other.

One of Andersson's prime learning experiences was how to orchestrate effectively. In view of a prohibition by the present owner against reproducing Stravinsky's 1941

Futurama sketches, owing to an intended sale of these manuscripts, I can offer only general comments here. They are based on a comparison of my observations when viewing Stravinsky's sketches at this private Pennsylvania archive with ozalid reproductions of the copyist's full orchestral score there, in Los Angeles, and in Washington.

In respect to *Futurama*'s first movement, quite a few passages in Stravinsky's sketches contain directions for orchestrating. For example, on the first page, Stravinsky wrote "Cmbl" above four circled *X*s, thus indicating that cymbals should sound with each of the four massive opening chords. Yet no indication for cymbals appears on the copyist's manuscript (see ex. 7.1), or indeed, elsewhere in *Futurama*'s first three movements. Perhaps relevant is Stravinsky's remark on 15 May 1941 to Andersson near the end of their work on *Futurama*'s third movement: "Cymbals out. Too much like something fell out of your pocket."[21] Also striking in Stravinsky's *Futurama* sketches is his direction (p. 30) "Score as," referring to a chord for winds. At the very next page—the last of his first-movement suggestions—Stravinsky carefully specifies how Andersson is to distribute French horns and trumpets during the movement's final, sustained, dominant-seventh chord. This chord, inherent in octatonic Collection III, is simultaneously startling and lame at the close, even though the same chord had been heard previously and briefly but not following such an extended period of orchestral writing that emphasizes octatonic Collection II.[22]

The preponderance of whole-tone passages in *Futurama*'s first movement suggests that Andersson had already incorporated some whole-tone writing there before he showed it to Stravinsky and that Stravinsky either refined, or merely tolerated, such passages. It is far less probable that Andersson knew anything previously about octatonic procedures. Sample recalled, in the January 1992 family-taped interview, that in February of 1941 "Stravinsky and [Andersson] agreed that Stravinsky would help him rewrite his music and *open new doors of harmony*" (emphasis added). Certain passages in the completed first movement suggest such knowledge, especially those with successions of dominant sevenths. Stravinsky had probably instructed Andersson in what has been deemed "Rimsky's beloved octave partitions, both whole-tone and octatonic."[23]

Each of the two possible whole-tone scales can furnish only incomplete dominant sevenths in various inversions. Having no more than three of their four required pitches, neither whole-tone scale can form a *complete* dominant seventh chord (let alone one in root position). Octatonic procedures, on the other hand, can generate not only complete root-position dominant sevenths but also considerable numbers of such seventh chords in their several inversions. Four complete dominant-seventh chords in root position can be formed on each scale step of an octatonic scale—1, 3, 5, and 7—using only the pitches (some with enharmonic spellings) of that particular scale. Scale steps 2, 4, 6, and 8 of the three octatonic collections each generate three different dominant-seventh chords, but they are in an inverted form.

It would not be surprising if at this time Stravinsky taught his student these octatonic principles, stemming from his own tuition under Rimsky-Korsakov. Andersson's notebook records Stravinsky mentioning various composers in a haphazard order comprising

EXAMPLE 7.1

Andersson, *Futurama*, first movement, mm. 1–13: "Maestoso."

Debussy, Schoenberg, Rimsky-Korsakov, Wagner, Beethoven, Scriabin, Mendelssohn, Ravel, Tchaikovsky, Anton Rubinstein, Bach, Milhaud, Liszt, Prokofiev, Glazunov, and Haydn. Most of these are single citations, except for Wagner, who receives the usual middle-period Stravinsky fulminations. Rimsky, however—that wizard of octatonicism—claims a full dozen citations, not all that surprising given the 1941 teacher-student relationship, a mirror image of what Stravinsky enjoyed as Rimsky's pupil. The final mention, that the "trouble with Russian music, S[travinsky] says, is too much symmetry (Rimsky etc.),"[24] implies discussion with Andersson of such symmetrical concepts as whole-tone writing and octatonicism.

A frequent (if often partial) use of the three octatonic collections has been brought to light in several works Stravinsky composed during the Andersson years, such as *Danses concertantes* (1940–42) and the Symphony in Three Movements (1942–45).[25] One such collection also appears briefly in the form of an "octatonic-diatonic interaction" in *Scherzo à la Russe* (1943–44).[26] How the octatonicism Stravinsky learned from Rimsky-Korsakov coexisted with whole-tone writing in his early oeuvre (in, for example, the *Scherzo fantastique* of 1907–8 and in the "extremely brainy" *Fireworks* of 1908–9) has also been well demonstrated.[27]

Unfortunately, Andersson's own complete manuscript of the entire *Futurama*, self-dated "January 21 1942," does not survive, although it certainly once existed. Eventually, Andersson sent this score to a professional copyist in Los Angeles.[28] Using Andersson's preprinted twenty-seven-staved manuscript paper (the same kind that he had given Stravinsky in June of 1941 for copying "The Star-Spangled Banner"), this unknown copyist dated his own 145-page labors in ink below the bottom staff of the final page "May 9 1942." That date is well within the second cycle of Andersson's lessons with Stravinsky: those no longer dealing with *Futurama*. At the bottom of every page the copyist also carefully affixed a sticker and, on the final page, "Copyright 1942."[29]

Two smaller and less awkwardly sized photocopies of the copyist's score also survive, each bearing on every page the shadowy imprint of the original sticker.[30] Andersson had *Futurama* copyrighted on 16 May 1942,[31] but his copyright was not renewed by his heirs. Thus *Futurama* is in public domain.

Three passages in the opening movement of *Futurama* merit discussion here. The first is the initial thirteen measures of its introduction. The second is a developmental coda near the movement's close. A third immediately follows it: the brief codetta that ends the movement. The musical examples are my Particell reductions made from one of the photocopies of Andersson's full orchestral score.

In August of 1941 Stravinsky had, of course, no need to relearn either octatonic or whole-tone composition. But this may have been a period when he taught Andersson how to combine and disguise these compositional techniques into fresh, constructive models. A case in point is the *Maestoso*, the introduction to his first movement (ex. 7.1). The passage sets forth a motive of forceful whole-tone writing doubled in octaves, punctuated by eight heavily scored chords (until reh. 2), all on third beats, excepting chords four and eight. The introductory motive is crafted—more accurately, squeezed—into an unusual antecedent-consequent construction, quite unknown to music's "Classical Period" or even to Stravinsky's so-called neoclassicism. This strange construction appears solely in the copyist's score. The disappearance of the score that Andersson gave to his copyist prevents us from knowing what part of it came from Andersson and what from Stravinsky. And it probably represents decisions suggested by the latter to the former.

The idea may have originated with Stravinsky on the first page of his sketches (the one cited above with indications for cymbals, copied out in virtually full score on four-teen-staved paper at the bottom of which he added one more staff to accommodate the harp). At the beginning of his fourth measure (between the third and fourth staves), Stravinsky altered his original opening signature of triple time to $\frac{2}{4}$. In the blank space following m. 4 he then wrote $\frac{3}{4}$ between the third and fourth staves, thus warning of the resumption of triple meter on his next page. Whatever may have been Stravinsky's intent, or however Andersson's missing manuscript may ultimately have read, the copyist amal-gamated (i.e., jammed) Stravinsky's fourth ($\frac{2}{4}$) bar on page 1 into Stravinsky's first ($\frac{3}{4}$) bar on his page 2. The length of the copyist's resulting eight-measure period thus became, with Andersson's and Stravinsky's acquiescence, impeccably "classical" in the eighteenth-century sense: four measures closing in a half-cadence, answered by four measures with a full cadence, a balanced structure.

The consequent phrase (beginning at m. 4) is mostly a repetition of its antecedent, transposed down a whole tone. Yet the novelty of this bizarre compositional period lies not in its whole-tone cast, or its "classical" eight-bar length, but in the forced intimacy—a "wedging"—of its antecedent-consequent phrases. Andersson's-Stravinsky's late inter-vention creates a copulative, rather than a complimentary, relationship. That is, while the traditional antecedent seeks a half-cadence in its fourth measure (finishing here by descending chromatically, in the bass, from F to D-flat through a rapid triplet), the con-sequent quite unexpectedly bursts in, one measure too soon, in that same m. 4. This early appearance grants the consequent more leisure to cadence, which it does, not once but twice: at mm. 7 and 8. Both descents are surely cadences—each one recalling that "dying fall" of Shakespeare's "strain" in the music opening *Twelfth Night*.

All this takes place without compromising the structure of a period's traditional eight-measure length. During the penultimate measure 7, and again in the final measure, the consequent cadences in the same rapid triplet as the antecedent, this time descending to B-flat, but then (at m. 8) as a *slow* triplet (note values doubled), and the final note is sus-tained by woodwinds and piano. Evidently, the consequent now enjoys total approval because after its slightly varied repetition (reh. 2), the slow triplet sounds again, this time thunderously orchestrated in octaves (m. 12). Jamming the antecedent and consequent together in this manner thus constitutes an ironic mediation on an eighteenth-century commonplace, a maneuver almost certainly originating with Stravinsky.

Of the eight massive chords that punctuate this boldly constructed opening period and its extension to thirteen measures, not one chord can be derived from pitches available in either of the two whole-tone scales. Of course, just because some of these chords can be referred to octatonic collections does not prove beyond dispute that they stem from them. But if one assumes that they do, then the first three of these big major chords (mm. 1–3), each a whole step higher than its predecessor, would stem from octatonic Collections III, II, and I, respectively. All five of the dominant-seventh chords that follow (mm. 4–7) would likewise stem from Collections I, II, I, III, and I, respectively.

Following that emphatic repetitive cadence of the consequent, the opening whole-tone melodic motive—slightly varied and now penetrated by semitones—returns *all'unisono* in four French horns (reh. 2). Securely anchored on third beats by a B-flat pedal in trumpets and pizzicato strings and harp in octaves, the motive and its format combine aspects of the consequent more than of the antecedent. They are emphasized (m. 12) by repeating and heavily orchestrating the consequent's slow descending cadential triplet, thus forming a twelve-measure period.

Futurama's introduction closes with a last pair of short, massive chords (reh. 3: –1), evenly punctuating the final three-beat measure. These latter chords could stem from a whole-tone scale, but the first chord also occurs in octatonic Collection II, and the second one, in Collection I. Thus ambiguity is created about the roles of both systems—whole-tone and octatonic—in the introduction.

No more hints of whole-tone or octatonic writing surface until the close of Andersson's first movement. There, at reh. 55–62, an extended passage involving whole tones and dominant seventh chords develops some implications of the introductory measures (see ex. 7.2a). The copyist's score shows, at the beginning of a long passage (rehs. 55–60), a whole-tone series in cellos and basses of segments that gradually descend from C down a tritone to G-flat, utilizing the same whole-tone scale exposed in the introductory *Maestoso*. Descending lower strings in octaves reach their tritone precisely at the moment that the uppermost strings, rising from C in parallel first-inversion dominant-seventh chords by consecutive whole steps, reach the same pitch, spelled as F-sharp (reh. 56: –1). Neither of the two possible whole-tone scales being capable of generating complete dominant sevenths, Stravinsky and Andersson again turn—theoretically at least—to possibilities residing in the three octatonic collections (granted that these sevenths are familiar in common practice). For example, the initial four rising dominant-seventh chords (rehs. 55–56) occur (sometimes enharmonically spelled) in octatonic Collections III, II, I, and III, respectively. In the course of Ex. 9a, rising dominant sevenths and falling whole-tone scales are interrupted (rehs. 56, 59, and 60) by gradually shortening harmonized reminiscences of the introduction.

Here and there, Stravinsky's short-score sketches could show him reminding himself of the available pitch vocabulary. Near the bottom of his p. 27, he wrote a chord in bass clef (reading upward) of F-sharp, A-sharp, C-sharp, E, and in the treble clef (reading upward) of G, B-flat, C, E. It thus might draw on six pitches from Collection III generated from its scale steps 3 and 4. The result would be a version of the famous *Petrushka* chord of long ago. Stravinsky's sketch chord could equally well embody five of the six tones of

EXAMPLE 7.2a

Andersson, *Futurama*, first movement, rehs. 55–62 (= mm. 288–316).

Futurama Symphony: I (mm.288-316)

EXAMPLE 7.2a *(continued)*

the whole-tone scale in contrary motion that he will use on his next sketch page (28: duets between uppermost and lowermost strings) corresponding to reh. 55 in the copyist's score.

The grip of whole-toneism already begins to loosen at reh. 58. Here, the last six notes of Violin I rise in an E-flat major scale, the last beat of which is marked by an unexpectedly violent fortissimo chord, C7 in first inversion. Scored for woodwinds and brasses and highlighted by shrill upward swoops in both flutes and piccolo, this chord could derive from an F-major scale as much as it could from Collection III. The ensuing dissolution becomes increasingly audible at reh. 61. Rising whole-tone scales by high strings in thirds now pair asymmetrically with a syncopated low-string and bassoon figure selected from Collection I.

With added high trilling woodwinds drawing on Collection II as do the low strings, the interlocked, dialoguing upper and lower strings might seem (by continuing in whole tones) merely obstinate (see ex. 7.2b). Yet by including an E-flat in the string dialogue—and an E-flat within the high woodwinds simultaneously reiterating and arpeggiating dominant sevenths—the composer signals that the lower partners (bassoons, cellos, and double basses) might also be drawing on Collection II. Here the upper strings employ pitches from just one whole-tone resource, the very one utilized in the movement's introduction. Yet the genesis of whole-tone pitches for bassoons and lower strings (reh. 62) remains ambiguous because their pitches also occur in Collection II. This opposition continues until the upper strings (fortified by Piccolo, Flute I, and Trumpet I) rise to B-natural (reh. 63), thus clinching Collection II as pervasive for all participants. Moving the note in the upper strings to B-natural, as forecast in halved-note values by Stravinsky (bottom of his p. 29), seems to foreshadow an apparent supremacy for Collection II. The latter's supremacy is only dashed by the truly surprising, and almost simplistic, final lame dominant seventh chord from Collection III, even though

EXAMPLE 7.2b

Futurama, first movement, reh. 62 to end of movement (= mm. 317–25).

Futurama Symphony: I (317-325)

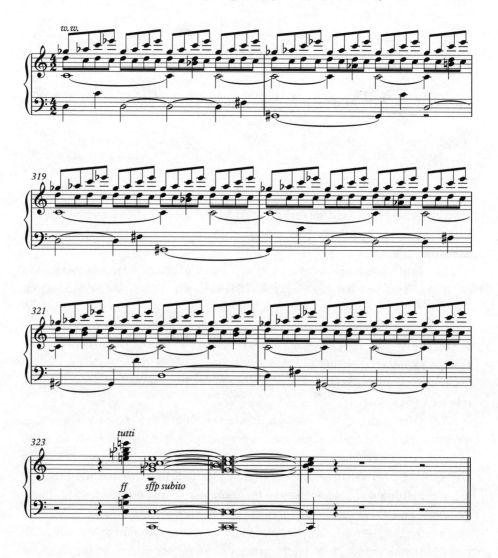

this very same chord had been forecast by the shrill double-forte outburst of woodwinds and brass.

This is a masterful demonstration of whole-tone and octatonic deployment. And just as surely, it is a deliberate exercise in ambiguity. Whether or not either system (whole-toneism or octatonicism) prevails here, there is no escaping that, despite their common parentage within Collection III, C[7] ultimately triumphs over F-sharp[7].

Several entries in Andersson's notebook (pp. 5, 16, 37, and 54) confirm that he and Stravinsky were discussing the *Rite of Spring* during *Futurama* revisions. If only because of Walt Disney's *Fantasia*, the *Rite* was very much *à la page* in the early 1940s. Even Andersson's first-inversion dominant sevenths (reh. 55ff.) recall the *Rite* (reh. 13ff.). Indeed, the boldest (and certainly the most notorious) example of Stravinsky's utilization of whole-tone and octatonic interpenetrations had appeared in the *Rite* almost four decades before Andersson's lessons: near the end of part 1, as shown in sketches for the "Dance of the Earth."[32]

Perhaps it seems odd that Stravinsky was teaching Andersson a compositional methodology of whole-tone and octatonic interpenetration that he had seemingly abandoned so many years before. But he was himself still using it. At a scholarly conference held at Long Beach State University on 4 March 2013, Professor van den Toorn agreed with me that the first movement of *Futurama* manifests some aspects of octatonicism, and he pointed out a resemblance of its ubiquitous dominant sevenths to those employed just a year later in the first movement of Stravinsky's Symphony in Three Movements (1942–45). There (rehs. 8–13), the composer employs two forms of Collection III, built on scale-step 4, over an ostinato constructed from steps 5 and 7. Then at rehs. 88–94, and based on Collection II, its scale-step 6 provides the two dominant sevenths over an ostinato comprising scale steps 7 and 1.

There is a further passage in *Futurama* that foreshadows the first movement of the Symphony in Three Movements: the texture and orchestration of *Futurama*'s second movement (reh. F: −2 mm., and what follows) resemble places in the first movement of Stravinsky's Symphony (reh. 38ff.).[33] Stravinsky's work on Andersson's *Futurama* surely influenced his own compositions of that period.

A "SECRET" COMMISSION: *DANSES CONCERTANTES*

Save for the San Francisco performances early in January of 1942, this first US wartime year saw few concert engagements; the nation's trains were increasingly crowded with troops. Blackouts had been ordered on 10 and 11 December 1941; at least partly in fear of air raids, the Stravinskys made frequent excursions by car to Santa Barbara. Although the sirens sounded even there (in the middle of the night on 25 February 1942), they contemplated, for a while in 1942 and as late as 1943, relocating northward.[34]

Early in February of 1942, just before Andersson's return from points east, and around the time of the world premiere of *Danses concertantes* in Los Angeles, Igor and Vera were twice photographed inspecting a sickly looking tree-shrub. It was described as "one of the many rosebushes thriving" in the steeply sloped garden of their house on North Wetherly.[35] Stravinsky's skills as a gardener had already received some indirect attention from Andersson, who had brought him some homegrown roses and reported in his notebook (p. 18, late May of 1941), "[Stravinsky:] said my roses were so much nicer than his. He 'was jealous.'"

FIGURE 7.1
"Gardening with Vera." Unknown LA
newspaper, c. 1942.

'Bombardier' lead g

IGOR STRAVINSKY, who will be guest conductor of the Werner
Janssen symphony in a concert tomorrow afternoon at the Wilshire
Ebell, discusses a gardening problem with his wife.

And with good reason. The two February photographs of Stravinsky's rosebush were taken the same day by the same unidentified photographer; one image (fig. 7.1) was reproduced in a local newspaper, the other in a national music magazine. To judge by the spindly limbs and dead leaves piled below it, "thriving" better describes the composer's improved health after his last major bout with tuberculosis in 1939 than any horticultural skills. Eventually, with the aid of his Russian-born gardeners, his rosebushes flourished,[36] and his better health led to renewed compositional activity for the concert hall, the ballet, the movies, and even the circus.

Although Sample's recollection in 1972 that he was "involved" with Stravinsky's *Danses concertantes* from the very beginning is plausible, a considerable amount of amplification is required to justify it. That "very beginning" occurred on 19 October 1939.[37] By the time conductor Werner Janssen commissioned it for his newly established chamber orchestra in Los Angeles on 30 September 1941, it was "about half" written, according to Stravinsky; years later, Walsh even said it was "two-thirds written."[38] Andersson discretely referred to it in his notebook: once on 18 April 1941 as "a composition . . . [Stravinsky] says is a secret" and twice in late May. This notion of a "secret" accords with Stravinsky's later request that Janssen keep his commission private.[39] Sample's recollection, preceded by the observation that Stravinsky sometimes showed him works in progress, implies that Stravinsky had also disclosed its progress to him. Vera's diary reports that her husband played it to her on 12 November 1941 and that his orchestral score, photographed on 14 January 1942, was copyrighted two days later. Perhaps this latter task was Sample's, but more probably it was Andersson's. He had a lesson that day and had undertaken copyright applications for Stravinsky in the past.

However involved were conductor Sample and a Polish composer-in-exile, Alexandre Tansman, in the various stages of the *Danses concertantes*,[40] it was Sol Babitz (who played in Janssen's orchestra) who assuredly had the composer's ear as the premiere approached. He wrote the program notes,[41] for which his annotated typescript (derived from conversations with Stravinsky) surfaced just a few years ago at auction.[42] Additional evidence for Stravinsky's trust in Babitz is a note in the printed program of 8 February itself that "the composer has confided his thoughts in writing to his friend, Sol Babitz."

After five rehearsals with the Werner Janssen Chamber Orchestra on 2–3 and 5–7 February, Stravinsky led the premiere of *Danses concertantes* on the eighth, ostensibly as a concert work for orchestra, in the Wilshire Ebell Theatre. A knowledgeable Los Angeles critic concluded that its

> method is one of commentary and allusion. . . . [It] supersedes any program or any literary and choreographic background that the composer may have had in mind. . . . It excels in variety and scope . . . a slow section in which the composer allows himself an unwonted "expressiveness" in melody, and in sonority. . . . He has avoided grotesqueness and has relaxed the severity and acidity that have, for me, marred so much of his "neo-classic" music of recent years.[43]

As usual, the *Pacific Coast Musician* reported negatively a week later:

> [It] can be classed only as sparklingly clever orchestral color. It is almost devoid of melodic or harmonic content . . . interesting only because of cleverly contrived rhythms and incongruous crossing of voices. . . . [It is] not an important contribution to orchestral literature.[44]

Every commentator since its premiere has supposed *Danses concertantes* was conceived independent of an actual ballet. This impression was solidified by Stravinsky himself at the beginning of June of 1944 in a reply to a query from Ben Hymans, a New York radio announcer: "this work was composed without any idea of a dramatic action, be it ballet, or pantomime."[45] Serendipitously, it has since been discovered that on 15 February 1942 Stravinsky telegraphed George Balanchine, wanting him to choreograph it for the Ballet Monte Carlo. Thus, and *pace* Stravinsky, Charles Joseph has hypothesized—surely correctly—that "choreography was envisioned from the first."[46]

Sample stated that he attended the premiere led by Janssen (whereas in reality it was led by the composer) and that, because of attendant festivities and a party, he had neither sufficient nerve nor opportunity to query Stravinsky about Janssen's interpretation. Sample's confusion might stem from his attending a later performance led by Janssen, perhaps even the second performance.

Be this as it may, Sample's conducting at this period so impressed Stravinsky that he wrote a letter of recommendation on 15 February 1942 to Dimitri Mitropoulos, then conducting in Minneapolis, Sample's hometown. It was carried by Andersson along with the four letters regarding *Futurama*. Obviously, Sample had told Stravinsky about the government's plan to disband the WPA Federal Orchestra in May and was seeking future employment. Perhaps Sample had sent Stravinsky reviews or he had read glowing reviews in Los Angeles from October 1941 about Sample's handling of the WPA Southern California Symphony Orchestra; one writer titled his evaluation "Sample in Triumph."[47] Another observed that the "players responded admirably to his baton" and, two weeks later, that "during the last two years, [audiences] have been privileged to see Sample grow from a young leader of promise to a conductor of real achievements. He has firm control of his orchestra and the skill to achieve nicety of balance, enjoyable nuance and shading, and excellent finesse of interpretation."[48] Stravinsky wrote Mitropoulos that he had followed Sample's conducting career "with growing interest" and that Sample had "done wonders" with the Los Angeles Federal Orchestra and "given many first class concerts and operas . . . a veteran of musical knowledge."[49] Like his mentor Monteux, Sample was a calm, Apollonian conductor; Mitropoulos was just the opposite—passionate, often a trembling Dionysian. Not surprisingly, then, the position went to another equally Dionysian, young Leonard Bernstein.[50]

Yet only days after writing the recommendation, Vera noted that her husband decided not to attend Sample's concert the evening of 18 February, on discovering that the latter had programmed his early *Cat's Cradle Songs* (1915).[51] One possible explanation for this odd behavior may lie in Sample's recollection on tape, thirty years later, of a vexing opinion of these songs by a critic in Los Angeles. The critic might have been Florence Lawrence of the *Los Angeles Examiner,* but more probably it was Isabel Morse Jones of the *Los Angeles Times,* who wrote that " 'The Cat' has amusing titles that have nothing to do with the case, tra la! . . . Judging from the music, he must prefer Siamese."[52] The reference was presumably to that breed's distinctive "yow" in place of an ordinary feline's "meow." Stravinsky, who was very fond of cats, might have known what Morse Jones's opinion would be in advance of the concert, since she was friendly with Kall.

A more plausible explanation has Stravinsky not particularly interested in a work Sample programmed that same evening: Theme, Variations and Finale. Led by its composer, Miklós Rózsa, it was described by Morse Jones as going "back beyond the Gypsies. It is Slavic Oriental," certainly not Stravinsky's current taste and, arguably, not so since

Firebird. Perhaps to the older composer's chagrin, Rózsa had been hired by producer Korda and was writing successful and remunerative film scores such as *The Thief of Bagdad* (1940). Moreover, late in October of 1941, having opened his concert with a second performance of Stravinsky's "Star-Spangled Banner," Sample had premiered a suite drawn from *The Thief* with Rózsa seated in the audience.[53] Not only was the *Thief* score acclaimed as "vivid musical silhouettes," its orchestration "of a high order of invention"[54] and "replete with Oriental colors," for which Rózsa "received a long ovation,"[55] but no such praise was recorded for "The Star-Spangled Banner." Perhaps once bitten in October of 1941, Stravinsky was twice shy four months later.

On 29 June 1942, with no appointment forthcoming from Mitropoulos, Stravinsky wrote another letter for Sample, this time a more general to-whom-it-may-concern type, describing him as:

> an outstanding talent. . . . His manner quiet and unassuming, he has complete authority in his work. . . . I have attended rehearsals of his orchestra at which times I have seen him help his players solve their problems in a correct and efficient manner. . . . He is capable of getting the best that can be had from his orchestra. . . . This is done by their cooperation rather than by forced work.[56]

At the time, Sample was a candidate for the conductorship of the Kansas City Symphony Orchestra. Sample later observed that Stravinsky was irked by the failure of the orchestra's management to acknowledge his letter. That October, Stravinsky praised Sample again, in an inscription on another copy of the 1934 Hoyningen-Huené portrait in reverse: "To James Sample my best greetings / and sincere thanks for the / record of my STAR- / -SPAN-GLED— / BANNER / under his baton. / It sounds splendidly / I Strawinsky / Oct / 1942." Sample's recording, probably made late in 1941, survives.[57] Stravinsky's approval of its solemn, slow tempo allows some notion of how he himself might have led it in the 1940s, vastly different from the brisk manner in which he recorded it in Toronto in May of 1964.[58]

STRAVINSKY'S FILM MUSIC

Movie composer Alexandre Tansman claimed that he was shown the *Danses concertantes* in 1941, one year before its premiere. A Polish self-exile, Tansman had known Stravinsky in France; recently arrived in Hollywood, he wrote on commission and had composed some film scores. By 1942, he was sufficiently close to Stravinsky to have had his image drawn by the elder composer, and in June of 1945 he even had discussions with Stravinsky and his lawyer (Tansman's cousin) over performing fees for *Firebird*.[59] Three years later, in 1945, Tansman published a book in French about Stravinsky's music, a book that Stravinsky thoroughly disliked.[60] One letter Tansman later wrote in 1945 from Los Angeles to a European friend relays his pleasure in reacquainting with Stravinsky. On 24 November 1945, to the same friend, Tansman notes that he and his wife are the first

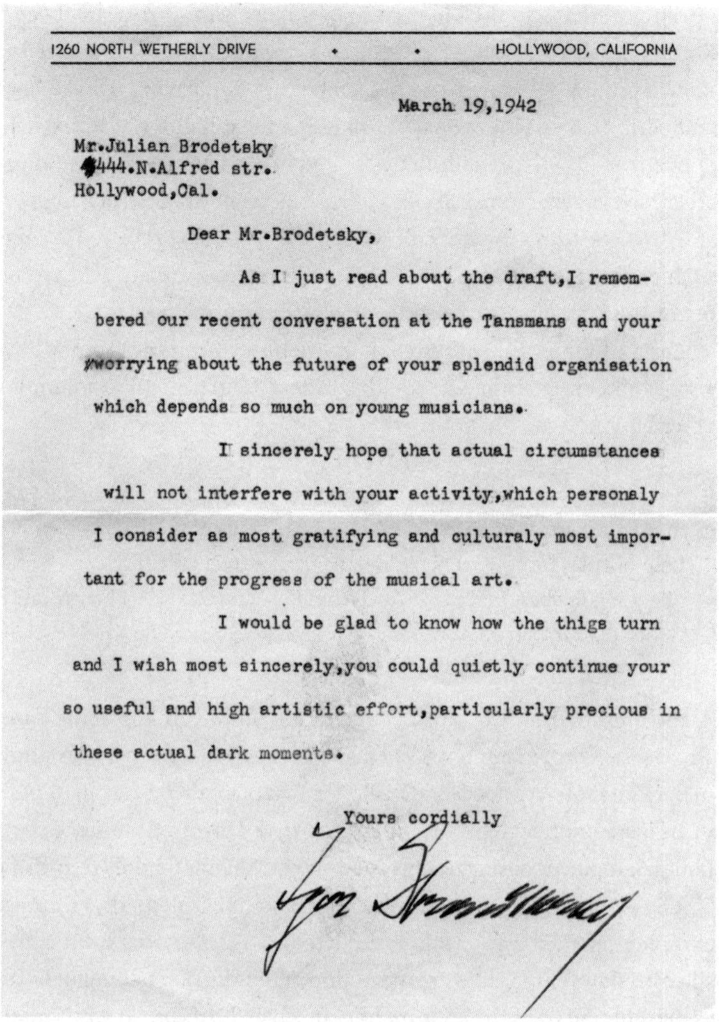

1260 NORTH WETHERLY DRIVE   •   •   HOLLYWOOD, CALIFORNIA

March 19,1942

Mr.Julian Brodetsky
4444.N.Alfred str.
Hollywood,Cal.

Dear Mr.Brodetsky,

As I just read about the draft,I remembered our recent conversation at the Tansmans and your worrying about the future of your splendid organisation which depends so much on young musicians.

I sincerely hope that actual circumstances will not interfere with your activity,which personaly I consider as most gratifying and culturaly most important for the progress of the musical art.

I would be glad to know how the thigs turn and I wish most sincerely,you could quietly continue your so useful and high artistic effort,particularly precious in these actual dark moments.

Yours cordially

FIGURE 7.2
Stravinsky to Brodetsky,
19 March 1942. UBC Stravinsky
Collection, no. 77.

to hear his new works, either played by Stravinsky himself, or six-hands by Stravinsky, Tansman, and wife[61]—neither the same thing, of course, nor nearly as intimate as Sample playing Bach fugues with Stravinsky, each employing two hands.

Tansman first appears in Vera's diary on 19 March 1942—"Tansman for lunch"—although he twice claimed that he knew Stravinsky in Hollywood "from the end of 1941."[62] Following this lunch, Stravinsky wrote to the Los Angeles violin teacher, and conductor, Julian Brodetsky,[63] of "our recent conversation at the Tansmans," documenting a previously unknown and three-pronged relationship of some undetermined length (fig. 7.2).

Stravinsky's still halting English, seemingly unaided by others, is revealed by his deformation of the French *actuel* ("present") into "actual." His intended reference to "present circumstances," concerned the US military draft, which would soon exact a toll on some members of Brodetsky's fine orchestra of young players, made up of "eight string quartets trained to precision and delicacy."[64] Stravinsky may well have read Lawrence Morton's warm printed endorsement to Brodetsky of "The Star-Spangled Banner": Morton, one of its staunchest admirers, had written, just ten days after the premiere, that "I think it is *sine qua non* for a group like the Brodetskys." His fuller evaluation came a year later; and still more detailed recollections eventually appeared in 1986.[65]

As late as autumn of 1942, Brodetsky still had enough string players to contemplate performing Stravinsky's *Apollon musagète*.[66] On 24 October the composer wrote to him again (fig. 7.3), this time in Russian (except for "present" in Russian script and "photostat" in English):[67]

> Sincerely grateful to you, kindest Brodetsky, for the kind present. Your photostat of my *Apollon* came out v[ery] successfully.
>
> With heartfelt greetings to you both,
>
> Yours,
>
> I. Stravinsky

Stravinsky must have lent Brodetsky his 1928 printed score of *Apollon*, from which Brodetsky had one or more photostats made. Such a task would normally have fallen to the ever-obliging Andersson. During Brodetsky's early wartime programs, however, *Apollon* never appears. The photostat that Brodetsky sent to Stravinsky may well be the one that the composer inscribed "photostatic copy of the 1st Koussevitzky édition 1928 orch. score, To Sol Babitz, cordially, I Str."[68]

After returning from his unsuccessful *Futurama* trip, Andersson continued his lessons with Stravinsky. Beginning on 24 March 1942, there was a round of fifty lessons for revisions to his eight-part orchestral suite, *Dreams of Solfomby*, which concluded on 3 August. A twelve-day hiatus ensued during which Stravinsky's calendar was crowded with visitors, including such luminaries as Mercedes de Acosta, Janet Flanner of the *New Yorker*, Sergei and Mrs. Rachmaninoff, Artur Rubinstein, Louis Bromfield, George Balanchine and his wife, the ballet dancer Vera Zorina, and the ubiquitous Dagmar Godowsky.[69] When Stravinsky resumed lessons with Andersson, there was a final group of twenty-two meetings that stretched from 25 August until 22 December during which they reworked Andersson's early four-part orchestral suite *The Sun Worshiper*, the third and fourth movements of which had been performed in 1938 and 1939.[70] Unlike *Futurama*, there are no known Stravinsky sketches for *Dreams of Solfomby* or *The Sun Worshiper*.

But their meetings were not all work. On 16 September Andersson hosted a large party for thirty-seven guests at one of his Los Angeles houses. Each guest autographed his cook's apron. Among the signers was the prolific Hollywood composer of more than one hundred film scores Jenö (Eugene) Zádor, who had emigrated from Hungary in

FIGURE 7.3
Cover and Russian letter from
Stravinsky to Brodetsky, 24 October
1942. UBC Stravinsky Collection,
no. 79.

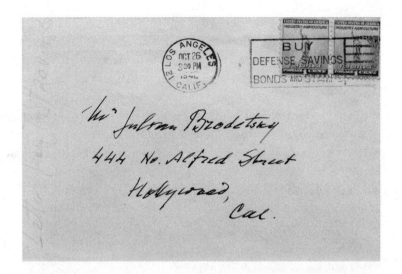

FIGURE 7.3
Cover and Russian letter from
Stravinsky to Brodetsky, 24 October
1942. UBC Stravinsky Collection,
no. 79.

1939. Nothing suggests that his countryman Rózsa was also invited to the party. Other guests included the Stravinskys, the Sample family, and future well-known pianist and pedagogue at USC John Crown and wife. All the signers were highly complimentary toward Andersson. Stravinsky wrote across the seam of his host's apron: "Bravo / for yo|ur GU|LAS! Many thanks / Igor Strawinsky / Sept 16th / 1942."[71]

The total number of lessons that Andersson took in 1941 and 1942 amounted to 215. They were contracted at one hour each, but the majority extended well beyond the stipulated time. They consumed the equivalent of twenty-two days' worth of Stravinsky's precious creative energies. Was this huge investment of Stravinsky's time, in exchange for dollars he did not truly need, worth the result? To date, none of the three Andersson-Stravinsky works has been performed. A definitive answer must await performances, recordings, and the judgment of a knowledgeable and sympathetic public.

Although none of Stravinsky's previous contacts with the film industry had produced a project—visiting MGM with Kall in 1935, the foiled proposals with Chaplin in 1935 and 1937, the disappointment in 1937 with Morros at Paramount, Stravinsky's friendship with Robinson and other Hollywood notables, Disney's unexercised options for film versions of *Firebird, Renard,* and *Fireworks,*[72] and Andersson's "Fox Film Corporation" pencil that Stravinsky inscribed in June 1941—all these contacts merely whetted his appetite.[73] By the spring of 1942, Stravinsky and Tansman were involved in a film project. Tansman wrote relatively little about their joint project in the above-cited 1945 letter to a European friend. He merely records that he and Stravinsky were to have written a score together for an unnamed film and that he had thus had the pleasure of working with Stravinsky for several weeks.[74] The dates might be deduced from two entries in Vera's 1942 diary: "Two men come to see Igor about writing music for a film [unnamed]"; and the other, the aforementioned "Tansman for lunch."[75]

The title of the movie was revealed, two decades later, by Rózsa in his memoir, *Double Life,* dictated in Hungarian in 1981 and published the following year in English:

> One night Tansman and Stravinsky told me that they had been offered a film; since Stravinsky had never written a film score, Tansman had been engaged as his assistant and adviser. It was a war picture called *The Commandos Strike at Dawn,* set in Norway. They asked my advice on all sorts of technical matters.

Produced during 1942 by Columbia Pictures, *The Commandos Strike at Dawn* was released early in 1943. The musical score was not by Stravinsky but rather Ann Ronell and Louis Gruenberg.[76]

Rózsa, much more experienced than either Stravinsky or Tansman, having negotiated with movie producer Korda, among others, showed himself astute when he worried that neither was given a contract for *Commandos.* About mid-April, after a month with no contract, Tansman and Stravinsky showed Rózsa the Russian composer's "Prelude . . . in full score based on Norwegian folk songs," thus supporting Walsh's suspicion twenty-five years later that "Stravinsky probably worked on a score for [*Commandos*]."[77] It was for the sake of this film project that, on 14 June, Stravinsky had recklessly, at the last minute, cancelled his plans to teach that summer at Tanglewood. Only three weeks later, the movie's producer claimed that Stravinsky would demand a huge, costly orchestra, and on these fictitious and flimsy grounds he cancelled any further participation in the project.[78]

The reason for cancellation was thus financial, not because, as recently advanced, Stravinsky's score was "rapidly-written"[79] or "too astringent."[80] In fact, Stravinsky's limping waltz, taken from the middle of the "Wedding Dance" (third movement of his *Four Norwegian Moods*, rehs. 35–41), was dubbed into a few frames of the wedding feast in *Commandos* in a 2014 documentary.[81] It coordinates so beautifully with the waltz steps of the dancers that *Four Norwegian Moods* must have been Stravinsky's original response to the movie's script. Limping, because this ingenious waltz, so effortlessly straddling some twenty-three *duple* measures, would try even a Gombosi to rebar, particularly because of its pair of giddy anacrustic gestures, also in $\frac{2}{4}$ (reh. 37: –1, and reh. 38).

Stravinsky's "Prelude . . . based on Norwegian folk songs" became "Entrada," the first of his *Four Norwegian Moods*. Despite his protestation in 1960 that it contained no music by Grieg, some passages in it were lifted—perhaps unknowingly—from works, owing their presence to an 1881 printed anthology, *The Norway Music Album*, a source Stravinsky is known to have utilized.[82] He completed the entire score of *Four Norwegian Moods* by 25 July.[83]

Not published until 1944, Stravinsky premiered it on 14 January of that year with the Boston Symphony Orchestra in Cambridge and then in Boston proper. Following its New York Philharmonic premiere (also that of the *Circus Polka*) on 1 February 1945, a reviewer, signing himself only as "P.," spoke of *Four Norwegian Moods* as "twaddle sugared *à la* Hollywood" and the *Circus Polka* as "drivel"; the critic also opined that "Mr. Stravinsky is no great conductor."[84] But the same performance prompted an entirely different reaction from Virgil Thomson.

WARTIME ARRANGEMENTS

Rózsa states in his 1982 memoir that he first met Igor and Vera in the fall of 1940 (perhaps in mid-October) at an evening party given by conductor Antal Doráti and choreographer Adolph Bolm and that he often saw the Stravinskys at the Tansmans.[85] He also knew Sample from at least 28 October 1941, when Sample conducted his *Thief of Bagdad* suite.[86] He met Sample again on 18 February 1942, when Sample and the WPA Orchestra presented Rózsa's Theme, Variations and Finale, led by the composer.

Independently of Craft, Rózsa published, in 1980, new information about Andersson, perhaps stemming from his acquaintance with Sample. Rózsa somehow knew that Andersson helped with Stravinsky's correspondence.[87] This has been confirmed through Andersson's notebook, beginning in June of 1941; the virtually identical dedications to

President Roosevelt of "The Star-Spangled Banner"; Stravinsky's letters of introduction for Andersson; and his letter of recommendation for Sample. All are in a refined English quite beyond Stravinsky's competence in the early 1940s.[88]

Rózsa's inside information about Andersson as part-time secretary lends verisimilitude to a provocative tale in his memoirs. He and his wife were invited to a party—probably at the end of 1942, or early 1943, when the Sample family finally left Los Angeles for New York—given by Sample in Andersson's house.[89] The Rózsas were "promised that the Stravinskys would also be there." Andersson apparently had been drinking heavily, "splashing spaghetti into the plates (and faces) of his guests" and became physically abusive to one guest for whom, ultimately, Sample had to call an ambulance. Upstairs during all this commotion, another guest, "a local musician," continually played a tune on his host's piano from *The Thief of Bagdad*. This "local musician" was not Sample, even though he knew that particular score very well, having conducted it in 1941. When Stravinsky asked Rózsa "petulantly" whose music the pianist was playing, its young composer—surely fearing Stravinsky's candid opinion—replied that he did not know! Soon after, the Stravinskys, with some other guests, fled the party.

It is difficult to decide how much credence to give Rózsa's tale about a drunken Andersson. Rózsa certainly knew Sample, and could well have known the Tansmans, but his memoirs are not always internally consistent. For example, some pages state that he never got to know Stravinsky; others claim that he dined with him. Five years after Andersson's death, Rózsa certainly dined on 7 July 1948 with Stravinsky and eleven other composers, including Arnold Schoenberg, in the Crystal Ballroom of the Beverly Hills Hotel. A newspaper photographer took a picture of the diners, showing Rózsa just two places away from Stravinsky.[90]

Beginning in the spring of 1942, Stravinsky and Sol Babitz worked on arrangements for violin and piano, some published, others not. Among the latter was Tango, which was arranged by Dushkin.[91] Among the former were the four movements comprising the composer's Suite No. 2 for Small Orchestra (1921). This was Stravinsky's orchestration of movements he had long ago selected from *Three Easy Pieces* (1914–15) and *Five Easy Pieces* (1917–18), both sets originally written as piano duets. In August of 1921, when Stravinsky orchestrated the "Polka" from *Three Easy Pieces,* he not only gave it a three-bar introduction but also repeated the final strain, adding a new countermelody sounded by a trombone. In 1996 Richard Taruskin reported that the trombone's countermelody quoted the "Katinka" polka, a tune associated with a young blond dancer, Zhenya Nikitina, with whom Stravinsky was smitten just two evenings before Diaghilev introduced him to Vera Soudeikina.[92]

Taruskin's sterling-silver report remains untarnished by Babitz's probably having known of it four decades earlier. This likelihood emerges from Stravinsky's remark about one item in the revision, a remark that Babitz could well have pursued further with the composer. Appended in pencil at the spot where Babitz distributed the trombone melody between piano and violin, Stravinsky wrote "only 2 bars of the gesang."[93] As if to verify Stravinsky's instruction, Babitz recopied it in ink at the bottom of the page, inserting

"8ve" before "gesang." Surely at some point the lively and intelligent Babitz would have asked Stravinsky, "What is this *gesang?*" All four of their arrangements remain unpublished.[94]

BALANCHINE AND THE *CIRCUS POLKA*

On 12 January 1942 in Los Angeles, Stravinsky received a phone call from Balanchine in New York, requesting a polka for ballerinas and elephants that he was choreographing for Ringling Brothers Circus. An excellent case has been made for it being Balanchine himself who suggested Stravinsky's famous inclusion of Schubert's *Marche militaire* tune near its close.[95] On 6 February Stravinsky played his new polka on the piano for his wife. He then offered it to Leonard Feist of Mercury Music in New York, who promptly declined to publish it.[96] Feist's refusal of the one work that in the early 1940s made a truly respectable amount of money for its composer and eventual publisher, Associated Music Publishers—from some four hundred performances![97]—attests to Feist's curious lack of instinct for profit.

On 18 February Vera was charged with mailing a copy (probably an ozalid) of Stravinsky's piano version of the *Circus Polka* to Balanchine. "Hollywood, February 15th, 1942" appears on the last page of music in the piano edition,[98] the same date on the piano autograph, now in the Library of Congress. Probably the mailing fell to Vera only because Andersson was far away in the Midwest, pitching *Futurama.*

By 19 March, when Stravinsky offered *Circus Polka* to AMP, he could explain that it existed "actually"—his favorite faulty English mistranslation of the French *actuel*—not only for piano solo but also for "military band (as used by the circus)."[99] This was an unusual orchestration for circus band by David Raksin. First visiting Stravinsky on 7 March and then employed for this task, Raksin finished it in about a week, and Stravinsky mailed it to New York.[100]

Sixty-six years later, on 15 May 2008, lot 139 of Sotheby's catalogue[101] of items that had belonged to Babitz, offered four items related to *Circus Polka.* Two items concerned business matters with publisher AMP: a letter of 3 July and a contract of 3 September 1942 concerning the publication of arrangements of the *Circus Polka.*[102] The third item was a copy of AMP's first edition (New York, 1942) of the solo piano arrangement, inscribed by the composer as "Un Amical souvenir à l'excellent musicien Sol Babitz de I Stravinsky 1943."[103] Its title page announced two other arrangements: one for violin and piano by Babitz and Stravinsky: plate numbers A.S. 194225–26,[104] and one for two pianos arranged by Victor Babin.[105] In 1948 the same publisher offered the full score and parts of Raksin's arrangement for circus band.

The fourth item offered by Sotheby's is the most intriguing. Their cataloguer erroneously called it a "printed copy of the 'Circus Polka'" and then a "printed reproduction of Stravinsky's autograph piano score."[106] In reality, it is an ozalid copy of Stravinsky's autograph manuscript transparency of the piano arrangement that he wrote out on fourteen pages of three-staff systems, but when printed for solo piano, it was condensed to eight pages of two-staff systems, save for one system of three staves on its final page. Stemming from the collection belonging to Babitz, this fourth item appears at first glance to be another arrangement for violin and piano. However, some paired notes on the uppermost staff are unplayable as double stops, and the E-flat section (bottom triple staff) differs entirely from the Babitz-Stravinsky arrangement. The latter's piano part, with the violin part printed above, occupies ten pages, and the violin part is printed separately. This arrangement was first performed on Sunday evening 21 March 1943 by Babitz and Dahl at a concert attended by both Stravinskys that lasted "until midnight."[107] Perhaps lot 139 was Babitz's reward for participating in the premiere.

Sotheby's lot 139 was also said to have Stravinsky's indications "in red crayon and lead pencil" and of "parts for cornets, saxophones, horns, barytons and bass." The single page illustrated in the auction catalogue bears the composer's pencil and red crayon indications, and added notes (in the following sequence) for "[5] Cornets, Cornet, Fl[ute] & Picc[olo], cl[arinet]s, saxophones," and "Horn pedal" (cf. rehs. 17 to 19). Indications said by the cataloguer to be for "barytons and bass" presumably occur on another page.

The purpose of this "lot 139" version is unclear. Several of the listed instruments—cornets, saxophones, barytons—make no appearance in Stravinsky's own arrangement for symphony orchestra, finished by October of 1942, although they do appear in the circus arrangement by Raksin. Even though that arrangement calls for five cornets, as does lot 139, Raksin's arrangement calls for flute *or* piccolo, not both at once, and Raksin calls for two barytons and two tubas but not for bass. Lot 139 probably contains suggestions that Stravinsky made early in March of 1942 on his own ozalid copy so as to assist Raksin in making the Ringling Brothers score. Alternatively, markings on lot 139 might represent an effort by Stravinsky to orchestrate the *Circus Polka* for band, perhaps to satisfy a request from the US Air Force Band at Bolling Field, Washington, DC. On 15 February 1944 he sent a copy of what he called his "band score" and his "band *orchestration*," to AMP.[108]

Raksin's first appointment with Stravinsky for "orchestrating the *Polka* for military band" was on 7 March 1942, following the composer's lunch with Babitz.[109] Years later, Raksin recalled that in 1942 Ringling Brothers had a "crazy band combination," including a Hammond Organ "to compensate for the lack of certain instruments. . . . So I'd do two pages at a time and [Stravinsky] would look at them, and he never changed a note." According to Raksin, they "met often at Stravinsky's home (over vodka and Russian pastries) going over a few pages at a time."[110] Raksin's arrangement premiered in New York at Madison Square Garden on 9 April 1942.[111] Seventy years later, in 2003, the Stravinsky-Raksin version for Ringling—Hammond organ and all—was reprinted, though neither original nor reprint credits Raksin.[112]

In 1941 Sample had recommended that Stravinsky make his own arrangements of "The Star-Spangled Banner," in order to control copyright and maximize profits. This he did, and in several cases he produced truly beautiful variants; the one for unaccompanied male voices has been examined above. The arrangements of the *Circus Polka* demonstrate a similar effort to control the marketing of his works, but this time, as he ultimately told his publisher on 25 July 1942, "I am in the impossibility to control all the transcriptions of my works as it would take me too much time."[113] The arrangements did not materially alter the musical content of the *Circus Polka;* nor did a two-piano arrangement he farmed out to Vitya Vronsky and Victor Babin. Foreseeing cash possibilities from a symphonic arrangement, he orchestrated it himself for full symphony orchestra, completing it on 5 October 1942.[114] Probably owing to wartime shortages of paper, this was not yet published at the time of its highly successful world concert premiere in mid-January 1944 with the Boston Symphony Orchestra (along with the hotly contested "Star-Spangled Banner").[115]

Reviews were mixed: Virgil Thomson's genial review of Stravinsky's February 1945 New York Philharmonic performance, and Jack Benny's war-effort broadcast of the *Circus Polka* to US troops abroad are reported below. The *Circus Polka,* like the earlier Tango, did not appeal to Charles Joseph, who considered it "sheer musical lunacy," "commercially inspired twaddle," and "bizarre"; later, "a 'gig,' an easy commission to be tossed off effortlessly"; and most recently, "no more than a manufactured score."[116] He thus seems to ally himself with the unidentified "P.," who in 1945 considered it "drivel." But Thomson got it right: Stravinsky's rehearsal of *Circus Polka* in October of 1952 with the Vancouver Symphony Orchestra delighted my distinguished former teacher, Vienna-born ethnomusicologist Dr. Ida Halpern, as it did me, a nascent graduate student. Its charm remains.

Notwithstanding the July 1942 fiasco with *The Commandos Strike at Dawn,* Stravinsky's compulsion to write movie scores endured, resulting in a visit on 30 November of that year from Mitchell Goertz, an MGM agent. Like the *Commandos* film project, this meeting would result in music in 1943 and 1944.

8

EXCURSIONS (1943)

CONCERT APPEARANCES

27 January: *Petrushka* in San Francisco

8 February: *Petrushka* in Shrine Auditorium, Los Angeles

21 March: "Igor's concert lasts to midnight" [presumably in Los Angeles]

2, 12 April: *Petrushka* at the Metropolitan Opera

21–22 April: Golschman coached in *Danses concertantes*

24–25 April: Stravinsky rehearses and conducts *Apollon*, New York

26 April: conducts *Petrushka*, New York

9 May: conducts *Apollon*, New York

18, 21 May: rehearses *Dumbarton Oaks* at First Congregational Church, Los Angeles

13 July: Hollywood Bowl rehearses *Petrushka*

17 July: conducts *Petrushka* at Hollywood Bowl

The year 1943 opened brightly for Stravinsky. On 7 January Samuel Goldwyn offered him a script to read with a view toward composing music for a movie.[1] The script was *The North Star,* by Lillian Hellman, intended for an MGM film about the recent German invasion of Russia. Stravinsky disliked the script and even hoped that a contract would not be signed, perhaps so as not to alienate any possible future employment. Neither man was willing to compromise; the opportunity vanished by 18 January, even though that very day he dated, on studio music paper, a draft of a "Little Children's Chorus" for the movie.[2] This left him with some music which he put to good use later in 1943 and early in 1944 for duo-piano works, one of which had been in process since 1942.[3] On 24 January gas rationing obliged the Stravinskys to entrain for, rather than motor to, San Francisco. Three days later, deploying local musicians, Stravinsky rehearsed and conducted *Petrushka* in San Francisco with the Ballet Theatre of New York, choreographed by Bolm, with Léonide Massine in the title role.[4] Vera's diary noted only that her husband's performance received an ovation. Having arrived in the Bay City on the twenty-fifth, they visited the Milhauds that day in Oakland. There, Stravinsky once again set to music a little family salutation. Presumably in French, it was reminiscent of his friendly relations with the McQuoids and their children earlier in the 1940s. This time it was "To our friends, the dear family Milhaud, Darius, Madeleine and Daniel, their little boy."[5] The Milhauds found Stravinsky "plus gentil et détendu" (kinder and more relaxed) since his arrival on US soil.[6] Perhaps this change was owing to special efforts the Milhauds had made in 1941–42 on behalf of Stravinsky family members. Stravinsky seems to have jettisoned (or temporarily buried) his earlier anti-Semitic feelings.

Back in Los Angeles on 8 February, Stravinsky repeated his 1937 conducting feat of a staged *Petrushka* in the Shrine Auditorium. This time, the dance company was the Ballet Theatre of New York, with Bolm's choreography and starring Massine. The next day, Stravinsky encountered Lester Donahue at a luncheon; nothing more is known of their encounter there than on the occasion of their first meeting in 1925. Yet Vera singled him out in her diary as "Donahue (pianist)," perhaps suggesting that Donahue, born in Los Angeles and resident there for at least the previous decade,[7] had been hired to entertain socially prominent guests. Donahue's papers contain nothing about either meeting, nor did he relate the sort of stories about notable Angelenos in 1943 that he had reported about New York socialites in 1925.

West Coast critics Alfred Frankenstein in San Francisco and Sol Babitz in Los Angeles had reservations about the quality of the orchestra employed by the Ballet Theater for these *Petrushka* performances. The defects were caused, at least in part, by a wartime shortage of experienced musicians. Frankenstein's review of the 27 January performance (confirming Vera's enthusiastic diary entry of "an ovation" on that date) begins thus: "Never before in the history of the San Francisco Opera House has a ballet conductor received the kind of preliminary ovation given Wednesday night to Igor Stravinsky when he stepped into the pit to direct his own 'Petrouchka' with the Ballet Theater."[8] Yet Frankenstein went on to concede that "the San Francisco Symphony gave him brilliant but not letter-perfect support." For professional violinist Babitz in Los Angeles, the situation on 8 February in the Shrine Auditorium was more grave: "in the first place, the orchestra fell short (by about twenty-five men) and not even Stravinsky's masterful conducting could make it sound as it should."[9]

Northern and Southern California had had their premieres of the Symphony in C, but New York, of all places, was slow to have its own. Now it had to endure a flawed radio performance by Leopold Stokowski. On 2 February the flamboyant conductor had visited North Wetherly Drive to discuss his upcoming performance on 21 February with the NBC Symphony, scheduled to be broadcast nationwide. The "difficulties" that Vera mentioned in July of 1941 at Mexico City apparently undid Stokowski. Despite Stravinsky's protest that "I gave him all the necessary directions of performance of my Symphony," Stokowski foundered on the shoals of "metrical and tempo changes . . . the most extreme in the whole inventory of my work," in the third movement. After hearing the radiobroadcast on 21 February, the composer gave vent to strong words about Stokowski's performance of each movement of the Symphony, and "as for the third movement, this was simply beyond his technique, and instead of going to the source of the problem (rhythmic relationships), he plunged the music into a chaos of disordered sounds."[10]

Equally disconcerting was a favorable review by New York's most distinguished and savvy music critic. Acknowledging his access to some ozalid copy of the unpublished Symphony ("any conductor can see from looking at the score"), the normally astute Virgil Thomson declared Stokowski's performance to have been "a rendition marked by such detailed clarity and so much over-all comprehension."[11] Stokowski also flummoxed Dushkin, who telegraphed his approval to the composer.[12]

A different kind of performance took place on 2 March. Granted a brief leave from military service at Camp Roberts (near San Luis Obispo, California), Vladimir Ussachevsky sang—with the priest, a deacon, and one of the elders—a *panikhida* (memorial service) for Stravinsky's first wife, Catherine, in Los Angeles's Russian Orthodox Church on Micheltorena Street. After Stravinsky's confession and absolution, "Stravinsky gave a charming smile of recognition, and we exchanged a few words." Ussachevsky was struck by the inordinate length of Stravinsky's confession. Queried, the priest just laughed: "Well, it all started in a routine enough way, but then he began to argue theology with me!"[13]

Despite reservations of the critics, the January and February performances of the Massine-Bolm *Petrushka* in California were so successful that Sol Hurok booked Stravinsky to lead it on 2, 10, 12, and 26 April with the Ballet Theatre at the Metropolitan Opera. Sample, who was in New York seeking employment after the disbanding of the Los Angeles Federal WPA Orchestra in May of 1942, attended his rehearsals at Stravinsky's telephoned invitation and sat in one of the front-row seats.[14] A photograph taken at one of them shows Stravinsky conferring with their mutual friend, choreographer Bolm, who also danced the role of the Blackamoor.[15]

Sol Babitz's Stravinskyana collection contained at least one 1943 item. While Stravinsky was away in San Francisco that January, Babitz and Ingolf Dahl had played the Violin Concerto at an "Evenings on the Roof" concert; the violinist was acclaimed for his "rhythmic vitality and warmth of tone."[16] On 30 April, while still in New York, the composer wrote in French to thank Babitz for inviting him to conduct his prewar *Dumbarton Oaks Concerto* in Los Angeles and asked Babitz to have Dahl rehearse it before his return.[17] Notwithstanding an initial rehearsal on 18 May led by Stravinsky himself in the Los Angeles "First Congregational Church with a pick-up ensemble," and another rehearsal there three days later led by Dahl in the presence of Otto Klemperer, Alexander Smallens, Aaron Copland, and George Antheil, that second rehearsal was a disaster.[18] The problem was neither too many conductors nor too many composers but too few regular players. Poor Dahl had to cope not only with some musicians for the first time but also with other players (previously rehearsed by Stravinsky and Dahl) simply not showing up. Predictably, Stravinsky fled the rehearsal and sulked for the remainder of the day. For all of Babitz's Hollywood connections—after leaving the Los Angeles Philharmonic, he himself played violin in Hollywood studios from 1942 into the 1960s—Babitz could not muster even the small number of musicians required for *Dumbarton Oaks*. Los Angeles had to wait one more year for its premiere, the chief reasons being the wartime dearth of experienced Southern California musicians and gas rationing for those who remained.[19]

By late May of 1943, the Stravinskys' two-year residency at 1260 North Wetherly was no longer fulfilling the dreams of pastoral domesticity that Vera had confided to the Minneapolis reporter. She had envisioned a white California ranch house with dogs, cats, chickens, and even a cow. On 6 October 1941 she noted the arrival at 1260 of a "marmalade[-colored] cat" and on 19 January 1942 their adoption of "a nice dog." On 30 January there was a present of "parrots for me," although one promptly flew away, and another died the following year. At the beginning of January of 1943, the Stravinskys returned from Santa Barbara to find their hen-coop finished and "the parrots well," though by mid-February only six chickens survived. But on returning from New York in mid-May, there was a welcome turnaround: fifteen chickens and a hen. Ten days later, Vera lamented that their roosters' crowing in the early mornings disturbed them and their neighbors, portending swift removal.[20] Accordingly, on 5 June the Stravinskys took some of their poultry to Santa Barbara: a photograph shows the composer, hat in hand, triumphantly holding aloft a mesh bag full of live chickens.[21] Still, as late as January of 1945, Vera reported that two of their loudest roosters had to be taken away.[22] Situated as was their Hollywood dwelling just above Sunset Boulevard, the introduction of animals and chickens—no cow is reported—provoked a conflict between rural and urban values, inevitably resolved in favor of the latter.

Perhaps nothing more domestic might be imagined than the tea towel Vera affectionately hand-embroidered for Andersson's sixty-fifth birthday in February of 1943. It was destined to be his last: he died suddenly on 23 June,[23] only months after he witnessed Sample conducting two of his works in Salt Lake City on 30 March. Perhaps it was the cachet of having revised both works so recently with Stravinsky that caused Andersson to be acclaimed there—astonishingly—as "America's foremost living composer."[24] A month later, Andersson received an honorary doctorate from the New York College of Music. Both Stravinskys were in New York for Metropolitan Opera performances of *Petrushka* and *Apollon* with Lucia Chase's company, so perhaps they attended the ceremony on 1 May. This honor might have resulted from admiration by Sample and by their mutual friend, film composer Zádor, who, along with Stravinsky and thirty-six others, had inscribed Andersson's apron in the fall of 1942.[25] Sample and his wife, Ernestine, quickly returned from New York for Andersson's funeral on 30 June, where Sample observed both Stravinskys weeping openly.[26] Soon afterward, Stravinsky reportedly wrote superstitiously and, perhaps, insensitively to Soulima, then in occupied Paris: "All this is very sad, and just shows that I shouldn't teach."[27]

Vera's diary for 14 August has a laconic entry regarding cocktails at Lady Mendl's; she was the wife of the British consul in Los Angeles. Four days later, Hedda Hopper offered an equally sketchy notion of what transpired: "Stravinsky, Artur Rubinstein, and Sir Thomas Beecham had a talkfest in Sir Charles Mendl's garden with Rise Stevens."[28] We shall probably never know what they discussed.

On 28 August, just before leaving for Santa Barbara, the Stravinskys dined again with Thomas Mann and his wife, Katia, at the home of fellow novelist and playwright Franz Werfel, latest husband of Alma Mahler.[29] Many years later, Stravinsky disclosed that in the spring of 1943, Werfel had wanted him to write a score for 20th Century–Fox's production of *The Song of Bernadette* and that "I actually did compose music for the 'Apparition of the Virgin' scene, however, and this music became the second movement of my Symphony in Three Movements."[30] Indeed, this movement is dated by its composer 15 February–17 March 1943.[31] Its possible relevance—via Rossini—to the "Apparition" scene in *Song of Bernadette* did not become known to the public until a Boston review of the Symphony in 1946.

A CONTRIBUTION TO THE WAR EFFORT

That fall witnessed a notable event—an auction, including music manuscripts by Stravinsky and Schoenberg, in support of US War Bonds. At the Werfels, Stravinsky had just missed meeting Sergeant Klaus Mann, who, after spending leave with his parents in Pacific Palisades, had returned to his army base in Missouri.[32] On 9 October Sergeant Mann auctioned the manuscript of Stravinsky's solo-piano reduction of his "Star-Spangled Banner." Stravinsky recalled sending a "manuscript to Mrs. F. D. Roosevelt for a war-fund auction" (i.e., in support of the sale of US War Bonds), but "my score was returned with an apology."[33] Precisely when Stravinsky had sent his "manuscript" or "score" to Mrs. Roosevelt is difficult to decide, for there were war-loan drives in December of 1942 and April through June of 1943.[34] After its return, he "gave it to Klaus Mann, who soon succeeded in selling it for a similar purpose."

A good deal of the problem here lies in Stravinsky's use of the terms *score* and *manuscript*.[35] *Score* can mean any autograph or printed music, or music notated in score format, say for chorus, string quartet, or orchestra, or music notated for some combination of either, or even for one instrument or a singer. Thus, exactly what he sent Mrs. Roosevelt is debatable because by early fall of 1941 Stravinsky had made an unknown number of such "scorings," perhaps as many as seven, of his arrangement of the anthem. Only three survive.

The composer was entirely accurate about having given an arrangement of his first version of the anthem to Klaus Mann.[36] Then a brand-new US citizen, Sergeant Mann was back in Camp Crowder (in Joplin, Missouri) by 22 August. There is no evidence that Klaus met Stravinsky in Pacific Palisades.[37]

Supported at Camp Crowder by his commanding officer, white-haired Colonel E. I. Pratt, and later by Colonel George Teachout, Sergeant Mann prepared to hold a giant auction for the benefit of the Third War Bond Drive. By 1 August, plans for this drive were being made, and the drive itself officially got under way during an 8 September radio broadcast by President Roosevelt.[38] On 25 August Klaus wrote his twin sister, Erika, then a war correspondent in Cairo, about his plans. The auction would have "signed books, manuscripts (including those of music), and photographs of film-stars with authentic signatures. . . . I am scrounging MSS and portraits from my 'prominent' circle of friends."[39]

Two days later, he wrote Clarence R. Decker, president of the University of Kansas City about the possibility of holding his auction in Kansas City under the university's auspices: "My father has promised me a few things and I can also count on [nine authors, plus] Albert Einstein, John Steinbeck, Igor Stravinsky, Arnold Schoenberg, Lotte Lehman, etc." President and Mrs. Decker responded enthusiastically, ultimately inviting Klaus to Kansas City to stay with them over the weekend of 8–11 October so as to hold his auction in their house.[40]

Sergeant Mann first wrote to Schoenberg in German on 1 September and then, three days later, to Stravinsky in English:

> Dear Mr. Stravinsky:
> This is to ask you a favour which, I hope, will not be too much of a nuisance to you. What I want is an autographed copy of your biography, or (which might be even better) a fragment of a musical manuscript, or an autographed photography.
> Of course, I would not have the nerve to bother you with such a request if it were not for a serious purpose.
> The point of the matter is that I have volunteered to appear, as a representative of this [Army] Post, at a few War-Bond-Drive meetings to be held in this part of the country, and to auction, as a special attraction, autographed books and pictures, or manuscripts, of well-known authors, musicians, and actors. Some chairmen of some committees here seem to think that this might prove a fairly effective device to stimulate sale of bonds.
> May I count on your kindness? Your contribution—almost needless to say—will mean a considerable asset to our little collection.
> And: the sooner, the better! As usual in the Army, everything has to be arranged at the very last moment, in a mad kind of rush. . . .
>
> Merci mille fois
> In faithful admiration
> Yours Klaus Mann
>
> P.S. My mother wrote me about a delightful evening she and my father were having with you and Madame Stravinsky at the [Franz] Werfels. What would I not have given to be with them on that occasion.[41]

Klaus's request for an "autographed copy of your biography" refers to Stravinsky's *Chroniques de ma vie.* Just then, his father was reading the 1937 German translation and had probably already communicated this fact to his son.[42] Around this time Thomas Mann saw a good deal of Stravinsky.[43] Away in Santa Barbara when Mann's letter arrived, and returning to Hollywood on 7 September, the composer did not grant Sergeant Mann's request for a copy of *Chroniques.* Instead, he wrote on 13 September:

Dear Klaus Mann:

Thank you for your note. This—with pleasure, sending you the manuscript of my version of the National Anthem and my photograph, wishing you success for your WAR-BOND-DRIVE and sale.

We too spoke the other night of your most interesting study on André Gide with your parents—a delighteful [sic] occasion.

Until we meet, perhaps

Yours

Igor Strawinsky.[44]

The photograph that Stravinsky enclosed was one of the three surviving portraits that Edwin McQuoid had taken in 1940 (McQuoid *b*.) He inscribed it (probably with the coming auction in mind) simply "Igor Strawinsky / Hollywood, 1943."[45]

What Stravinsky sent Mann with the photograph was far more precious than the requested "fragment of a musical manuscript." He donated his own reduction for solo piano of his arrangement of the US national anthem. This 11 3/4 × 17 inch manuscript is folded in half, vertically, with the title and Stravinsky's signature on the front. It comprises three double rastrum-inscribed staves extending across a folded two-page opening. At the bottom of the second page, the composer wrote "Harmonized by / Igor Strawinsky / 1941." On the cover page, he wrote: "The Star Spangled Banner / manuscript / of my version (piano / -arrangement) / Igor Strawinsky / 1941." Whether he sent Mann a solo piano version copied in 1941 or copied it out anew in 1943 cannot now be determined, though normally he dated his manuscripts at the time he finished the composition in question. Consequently, this might be the very manuscript from which he played for the astonished and delighted James Sample in July of 1941.

Stravinsky's source that generated the Klaus Mann manuscript was his own compositional pencil draft, signed in late June 1941, also for solo piano. He had given this draft to Andersson on 9 July 1941 (a photostat of it is in the Library of Congress) along with the pencil with which he had copied it provided by Andersson (later the property of his heirs). The yellow six-sided pencil, with attached eraser, is stamped on three sides "FOX FILM CORPORATION MADE IN USA No. 2." On the remaining three sides, Stravinsky wrote by hand "STAR-SPANGLED BANNER / JUNE 16–1941 / Igor STRAWINSKY."[46]

Though not nearly as spectacular as the Andersson manuscript and pencil, the Mann manuscript is unique and remains unpublished. It has no text and is virtually identical to the thirty-cent piano version republished by Feist in 1941, in which the piano part was set out below the chorus of sopranos, altos, tenors, and basses. Three tiny pitch deviations (at mm. 3/2, 3/3, and 18/2) are probably just slips of the pen.

The only hint of any pre-Klaus history for this Kansas City manuscript is Stravinsky's recollection in 1960 that, having sent his setting of the anthem after its October 1941 premiere to Mrs. Roosevelt for some war-bond drive, it was returned with an apology, apparently from "some high official," before he sent it to Klaus Mann. When he sent it to the First

Lady thus depends on which "war-bond drive" he had in mind. This was obviously not the Third Bond Drive of late summer 1943, the very one that Klaus Mann's auction was supporting: Stravinsky must have sent his manuscript of the anthem to Mrs. Roosevelt either for the nation's first or for its second Bond Drive (1941 and 1942 respectively), most probably for the second one. He was astute about War Bonds. During 1941 he earned $361.75 from what he listed as "3/1/2 percent War Bonds," the amount of the compounded interest meaning that he had held these particular bonds since or near the beginning of 1941.[47]

But why did Mrs. Roosevelt's return of Stravinsky's gift need an apology? Neither the National Archives nor the Presidential Library at Hyde Park records its receipt, so perhaps someone in the US Government objected to the anthem's harmonization. Stravinsky later speculated to this effect: "my major seventh in the second strain . . . must have embarrassed some high official." There are actually two "major sevenths"—at "glare" and "air"—and both are on strong beats. But these momentary "discords" pale in comparison with much longer and stronger dissonances so common in popular music of the day— for example, in such hits as *Moonlight Serenade* or *I'll Never Smile Again* (both 1939), or *I Don't Want to Set the World on Fire* (1941). In recollecting these early war years, neither I, my teenage friends, nor our elders winced from dissonances in such songs or expressed "embarrassment" about them. (In the language of the period, we "jived" on them.)

Stravinsky was on the right track about "some high official" rejecting his version. Federal officials no less elevated than two colonels—the one, secretary of the War Department's General Staff, and the other, secretary to the president—had conveyed to President Roosevelt late in August of 1941 the "inappropriateness" of the president receiving "any particular version or arrangement of the anthem as a gift to the people of the country," the phrase "version or arrangement" surely including harmonization.[48] This admonition must have reached Mrs. Roosevelt's ears. Perhaps the president and First Lady were embarrassed at having to deal again, so soon after receiving the first elegantly bound full score, with such a famous émigré and his enthusiastic display of patriotism.

On Saturday afternoon, 9 October, Klaus Mann's auction took place in the Deckers' living room: from 4 p.m. until midnight "the public was invited to make sealed bids in liberty bond purchases." The lead bidder for both score and photograph was one William Thomas Grant, then president and a director of the Business Men's Assurance Company of Kansas City. Just six months previously, on 25 April, Grant had successfully bid $1 million in war bonds at the War Bond concert of the NBC Symphony for the manuscript of Arturo Toscanini's arrangement of "The Star-Spangled Banner."[49] At Mann's auction, and on behalf of the Assurance Company that Grant had founded in 1909, he bid at least another $1 million in war bonds; some sources state the amount at $1.3 million or $1.5 million for war bonds.

In 1943 these were truly enormous sums (raising a question about the present-day value of Stravinsky's bound volume of the full-orchestra version displayed in the Library of Congress!). Grant, one of the founders of the University of Kansas City, promptly donated the entire collection that he had purchased at the auction—some 150 items—to the university's library, then called the Linda Hall Library. To this day, the since-renamed University of Missouri at Kansas City holds most of these items, including the Stravinsky manuscript and inscribed McQuoid photograph. Initially, this collection was of too easy access to readers: some of the autographed photographs of film stars and—of much greater importance to music historians—two Schoenberg manuscripts, fragments from the Second Chamber Symphony and from *Kol Nidre,* have disappeared.[50]

Reporting the auction the next day, the *Kansas City Star* described the Russian composer's donation as "an original score of an arrangement of the 'Star-Spangled Banner' by Igor Stravinsky."[51] On 11 October Klaus wrote Stravinsky from Camp Crowder:

> This is to thank you, most cordially and warmly, for your generous and appropriate contribution to my personal little War Bond-drive. I was proud to have you represented (for you are undoubt[e]dly the composer whose work has meant more to me than that of any other contemporary musician) and I was particularly pleased to have your version of our national anthem (I have a right to say, 'our'; for I have been made a citizen, a couple of months ago . . .). Your manuscript was indeed one of the most attractive and most valuable pieces in my little collection.[52]

Klaus did not tell him, however, what he had written the same day to Schoenberg in another thank-you note:

> Your skepticism concerning the popular attractiveness of your manuscripts turned out to be completely wrong. The truth is that there were more individual bids on your musical fragments than we had on any other single article (including Strawinsky's manuscript of his version of the "Star-Spangled Banner").[53]

Could the smaller number of individual bids on Stravinsky's manuscript have resulted simply from the lack of text underlay? For a certainty (as Sergeant Mann's letters attest), Stravinsky's music was then, as it still is, admired more highly in the popular mind than Schoenberg's, but the anthem's tune itself *and* its words remain honored by US citizens far above any musical work by either composer.[54]

ODE: ELEGIACAL CHANT IN THREE PARTS

On the Friday afternoon, 8 October, just before Sergeant Mann's auction, attendees at the Boston Symphony Orchestra heard the world premiere of Stravinsky's Ode: Elegiacal Chant in Three Parts, commissioned the previous April in memory of Natalie Koussevitzky (née: Natalia Konstantinova Ushkova). However "secondary" and "cerebral" a work Ode might be for some,[55] its compositional circumstances and devices merit examination. Stravinsky's disclosures about the genesis of Ode postdate Serge Koussevitzky's death in 1951 by more than a decade.[56] The publication of further observations over ensuing decades about its central movement, "Eclogue,"[57] have engaged scholars, one of whom uncovered its octatonic content and procedures.[58]

While the tale about the gestation of the outer sections of "Eclogue" is well known, the textual relationship of the central section to its poetic antecedent remains unexplored. The outer sections came from Stravinsky's music for an English hunt scene in the 1944 movie *Jane Eyre,* starring Orson Welles. But on a sketch dated 12 February 1943,[59] he headed the central core of Ode's middle movement (only later called "Eclogue") as "Song for Bessie," a rubric taken from the third chapter of Charlotte Brontë's novel.[60] The history of the score's initial connection to film can serve to illustrate several aspects of Stravinsky's creativity and character.

Much ink has been spilt over the "Russianness" of the Ode; the present author doubts that Stravinsky could ever have regarded the *entire* work as nostalgia for Old Russia. That was the fantasy of a young scholar of Russian music who wrote about Stravinsky's performances of Ode in Moscow on 26 and 28 September 1962, which were recorded there by Melodiya. Despite quoting the composer's clear statement that "my journey to Russia has nothing to do with nostalgia," the critic still claimed that he had programmed Ode "to remind people of the many Russian emigrants like the Koussevitzkys . . . who made Russian music their cause. . . . The audience understood the message fully, as the frenetic applause proves."[61] This critic's opinion was immediately challenged by Israel Nestyev, another Soviet critic, who found Ode (and perhaps also the earlier critic's "message") to be "a deadly kind of musical Esperanto,"[62] meaning perhaps an overly simplified mixture of national character, or, more likely, an idiom denatured as to nationality. Even Stravinsky's niece, Xenia, though present at both Moscow concerts, wrote precious little about either performance of Ode.[63]

A recent brief for the Russian qualities of Ode's outer movements is not to be denied, but what is termed there as a "jaunty" central "Eclogue," cannot be sustained, especially for its innermost core.[64] What its proponent deems "an idealized pastoral . . ." in "bucolic horn calls" that Stravinsky scored in the outer sections of the "Eclogue" was, in truth, necessitated because the screenwriter had added a new hunt scene—a quintessential "British" feature—aimed straight at American moviegoers. So much for the "Russianness" of Ode's second movement. Even if there can be no agreement that Ode "speaks of exile" in its outer movements, it was heard as such.

At its world premiere, on 8 October in Boston's Symphony Hall, an audience member could read Stravinsky's own words on page 22 of the program: "I was asked by the Koussevitzky Music Foundation to compose a symphonic piece which I have called Ode. The Ode is a chant in three parts for orchestra. It is an appreciation of Natalie Koussevitzky's spiritual contribution to the art of the eminent conductor, her husband, Dr. Serge Koussevitzky." Reading on about its middle movement, the attendee would discover: "Part II. Eclogue, a piece in lively mode, a kind of *concert champêtre,* suggesting out-of-door music, an idea cherished by Natalie Koussevitzky and brilliantly materialized at Tanglewood by her husband." This description closely follows what Stravinsky had written the previous 9 July in Russian to Koussevitzky: "Second [song]: of more lively, scherzo-like character—Eclogue or Concert champêtre. That is, music in the open air, the principle which Natalia Konstantinova defended with such passion and which you realized so brilliantly in Tanglewood."[65]

For at least the early years of its performances and its recordings, Ode's "Eclogue" continued to bear this deceptive description. Yet knowledge of its cinematic roots was available early in the 1960s to anyone who cared to read *Expositions and Developments* or to consult Eric Walter White's 1966 biography.[66] The composer himself at first pretended that "Eclogue" was conceived to describe Tanglewood's pastoral atmosphere and open-air music shed. Both "The Shed," built in 1938, and Stravinsky's 1943 commission did in fact stem from the recently departed Natalie, whose inherited wealth also supported the Édition russe de musique in Berlin and later in Paris, and still later, the Galaxy Music Corporation in New York. The composer managed to pull the wool over even Koussevitzky's eyes with flattering references: "eminent conductor" and "brilliantly realized." That Koussevitzky believed him is all too evident in a telegram in English and in letters in Russian that the conductor, after receiving the completed score, sent Stravinsky in Los Angeles before its premiere. On 21 July 1943, Koussevitzky wired "your work so beautifully conceived so wonderfully in memory of Natalie"; eight days later, he wrote, "deeply touched by the insightful idea and music, by their spiritual truth and simplicity."[67] The more mundane truth he probably never knew.

Furthermore, the innermost core of "Eclogue" (especially, rehs. 20–24) derives from a nineteenth-century American collection of songs from the British Isles. Stravinsky's designation "Song for Bessie" on an orchestral sketch for this core thus represents a double borrowing. Preparing to compose the film score, Stravinsky copied out several melodies (not in the order they appear in their source) and headed his page: "from the MELODIST,"[68] a reference to an early nineteenth-century American anthology by G. S. Thornton: *The Melodist; Comprising a Selection of the most Favorite English, Scotch and Irish Songs, Arranged for the Voice, Flute or Violin.* Craft stated—erroneously—that Stravinsky chose from "model dances." Not one of the songs Stravinsky copied could be classified as a "model dance" piece, nor does the title page of *The Melodist* suggest this. Although Craft identified this source in 1985, not much has been made of it: no one has investigated which melody Stravinsky chose or how he used it.

For eight tunes from *The Melodist* that Stravinsky copied out on his sheet of paper (all of them in a treble clef), he obligingly furnished page numbers (not in this order): 16[-17], 19, 42, 49, 75, 85, 88–89, and 90–91; and in some cases he provided titles. For two songs, he gave page numbers and metric indications (pp. 88–89: 6/8; and 90–91: C). In these two instances, Stravinsky neither copied music nor cited titles. The tunes on these pages resemble nothing in Ode. In addition, he copied music for a "Scotch Song," which appears in *The Melodist* (pp. 25–26) as "Bruce's Address to his Army / A favorite Scotch Song, sung by Mr. Incledon."

Directly to the right of his references to pp. 88–89 and 90–91, Stravinsky wrote seemingly pertinent (but ultimately deceptive) indications: "for Bessie's song" and "my feet

EXAMPLE 8.1a

Stravinsky: sketch "For Bessie's Song" (for *Jane Eyre* movie).

my   feet   they   are   sore   and   my   limbs   they   are   we - a - ry

they are sore, & my limbs they are weary." These lines do not appear in *The Melodist,* and the tunes on pp. 88–91 do not appear in "Bessie's Song." They are not even from the first song in *Jane Eyre,* whose author designated them for Bessie Lee, Jane's servant. Brontë had appropriated Bessie's initial song-text—"In the days when we went gipsying / A long time ago"—from an 1837 verse by Edwin Ransford.[69] Her own verse for Bessie, "My feet they are sore, etc." appears a few lines later.

Stravinsky added faint strokes to his two-bar "for Bessie's Song," following the words *my, limbs,* and *weary.* They probably sprang from his extension upward of bar lines that he had added to thirteen eighth notes below the words, inscribed on an extremely faint five-line staff; but extending these strokes downward from the text is equally conceivable for a necessarily speculative transcription (see ex. 8.1a).

The prosody is faulty: if Stravinsky had help from some native English speaker, he paid little attention. The anacrusis at *my* is fine, but the concluding half-measure is poor (splitting the two-syllable *weary* over three notes), unless he meant to slur pitches four and five over *wea-* and reserve the final pitch for -*ry.* Something similar occurred a decade later in setting Auden's libretto for *The Rake's Progress:* "when there were not enough notes to cover the final syllable . . . he added rhythmic stems in parentheses."[70]

One of his orchestral sketches for the second movement of Ode, marked "Song for Bessie,"[71] bears no relationship to the music he called "for Bessie's song" on his *Melodist* page. In addition, the jiggling 6/8 tune he composed for oboes in thirds and sixths in the central part of "Eclogue" does not match the verbal stresses of Brontë's song text. This discrepancy between text and music might signify that, for the "Bessie" section of "Eclogue" Stravinsky wrote newly composed music and did not draw on any *Melodist* tune. There is no obvious match in *The Melodist.*

But there *is* a well-concealed match, although each one of its three elements is tiny. Taken together, they reveal the methods of a composer already notorious as the boldest thieving magpie of his generation.[72] The clue to Stravinsky's source in his Ode manuscript sketch "Song for Bessie" lies in his next-to-last selection from *The Melodist* (pp. 16–18): his un-named G-major tune of twenty-four measures, "O, Nanny, wilt thou gang with me" (see ex. 8.1b). He did not copy "O, Nanny's" opening seven measures, but he did copy its music from its pickup to measure 8 through measure 12, slightly altering this last measure. Melodic connections to "O, Nanny" occur in two distinct places within "Song for Bessie" (rehs. 20–27). These tiny isomelisms (resemblances) may seem fortuitous, but they stem from a period when the composer was using similar procedures on a larger

EXAMPLE 8.1b
"O Nanny," mm.7–12.

Tho love - ly cot and rus - set - gown? No long - er drest in

silk - en sheer, No long - er deck'd with jew - els rare,

scale. For example, in 1943–44 he drew on a nineteenth-century collection of Russian folk songs for considerable sections of *Scherzo à la Russe* and Sonata for Two Pianos.[73]

These melodic connections are important, out of proportion to their size, for three reasons. First, both "O, Nanny" and the orchestral "Song for Bessie" are in G major. More important, Stravinsky used the first half of "O Nanny's" m. 8 (with its pickup) for Oboe 1 at the pickup to reh. 20. Then on the way from there to the close of m. 12 of "O, Nanny," he continued, slightly rewriting to accommodate this instrument. Finally, from what little he had copied of "O, Nanny," he used the part from its pickup at m. 11 to the first note of m. 12. In "Eclogue" (reh. 22) he assigned this material to Violin 1 and then continued it to Flute 1 (reh. 22: +3). Stravinsky simply took apart "O, Nanny." He divested it of its text, most of its tune, and even its rhythms, refashioning his new orchestral music from snippets of vocal melody. In truth, his selections from "O, Nanny" are exceedingly sparse, but they are perceptible to an attentive ear. This core central section of "Eclogue" lacks any connection to the "open air" concept that Stravinsky described to Koussevitzky and in his program notes. That connection arises solely from the outer sections of the movement, which recycle music that Stravinsky had previously composed. It is these outer sections that correspond to what he would later call "music in the open air." Buried thus in Ode is Stravinsky's last known attempt to compose film music.

The world premiere by Serge Koussevitzky was a disaster. Vera observed in her diary: "Igor sad because the Ode was badly played." Just two weeks before the Ode's premiere, Stravinsky advised Koussevitzky on 27 September that he had sent the "corrected masters or orchestra parts for reproduction with revised orchestra score" to his publishers. In a second letter of the same day, he mentioned "orchestra parts *carefully corrected* by me. . . . I have also *revised and corrected some mistakes* on the photostatic copy of my manuscript orchestral score."[74] Somehow, the *matériel* used at the premiere of Ode on 8 October was not corrected; after its embarrassing national broadcast the next evening, Stravinsky apologized to the conductor in two letters (11 and 12 October). The first one was in English, typewritten by himself, the other, handwritten in Russian.[75] Conceding that the disaster was owing to his own mistakes in the score, he wrote "Errare humanum est," and "It is very, very unpleasant for me, my dear."

STRAVINSKY AND KOUSSEVITZKY: THE BLAME GAME

Stravinsky never publicly acknowledged any culpability.[76] Instead, thirteen years after Koussevitzky was safely dead, he ungenerously blamed others for two of his own errors: "the trumpet player misread the key of his instrument," and "two systems of score from the final page had been copied erroneously as one."[77] Nevertheless, it was Stravinsky himself who had written the trumpet parts in B-flat for BSO's C-trumpets and neglected to proofread diligently the copy of the score that he sent to Koussevitzky. His praise for Koussevitzky's good qualities was fainter than it could have been: Koussevitzky "was a generous man who did more than any conductor to help composers financially," but he did not tell the rest of the story: Koussevitzky's many years of lucrative employment for him and his patronage— between 1925 and 1949 Stravinsky played in or conducted BSO concerts no less than nineteen times, and there was also the 1930 commission for *Symphony of Psalms*. Although Stravinsky himself can hardly be blamed, when his article was reprinted posthumously in 1972, even the generalized acknowledgment of Koussevitzky's virtues vanished.[78]

Stravinsky's difficulties with Koussevitzky proceeded from three main causes: long-festering resentment about the conductor's botched premiere in June of 1921 of Symphonies of Wind Instruments in London and Koussevitzky's subsequent insulting assessment of the work in an open letter; envy of Koussevitzky's success in Europe and the United States; and pronounced anti-Semitism. Difficulties resulting from the first two causes are well-documented. Having myself led Symphonies in 1961 at the University of Chicago, sympathy flows for the rhythmic and other problems that beset Koussevitzky forty years earlier at its premiere.

Public awareness of Stravinsky's anti-Semitism did not arise until a decade after his death. His prejudice is now well-documented from 1918 to 1948 and probably continued to the end of his life. Early in 1981, his loyal assistant found sections of his papers to be "so shocking that Goebbels might have written some of it";[79] and in 1996 Denise Stravinsky attempted to clear her in-laws: "for Igor and Catherine anti-Semitism never had any place."[80] Craft tried to justify it some years later by reasoning that "Stravinsky used anti-Semitic language in the pre-Revolutionary Russian colloquial tradition,"[81] as if such a "tradition" (real or otherwise) were somehow its own justification. By 1989, many perceived the fallacy: not all pre-Revolutionary Russians were anti-Semitic—for example, Stravinsky's own teacher, Rimsky-Korsakov.[82] The conditional tense of Stravinsky's verb in a suppressed portion of his letter dated 8 October 1948 about dancer-choreographer Serge Lifar in New York tells all: "I would gladly change my mind about Jews."[83]

Several instances of Stravinsky's anti-Semitic prejudice against Koussevitzky, early in their careers, stand out. On 24 July 1921 Koussevitzky responded in the *Sunday Times* (London) to a justified complaint that the composer had lodged in the *Weekly Dispatch*

(12 June 1921) about Koussevitzky's incompetence when conducting the 10 June premiere of the Symphonies of Wind Instruments at Queen's Hall. Not content with simply defending himself, Koussevitzky opined that Symphonies had nothing new either in its scoring or in musical content and that it "represents a stage of decline in Stravinsky's art." That very day (or the next), Diaghilev—himself an anti-Semite—wrote Stravinsky:

> I am sending you an article [Koussevitzky's] written by one of your Jewish friends. . . . I advise you to beware of the services of all these musical Jews, since you are beginning to see what this friendship is worth. I shook with rage as I read the piece by this swine.[84]

Stravinsky's reply on 27 July not only exceeded Diaghilev's in viciousness but also broadened the issue: any public answer should not merely address Koussevitzky's "malicious idiocies and banalities" but should be directed "to what comprises the essence of that whole Jewish (as you say) German mentality."[85] Writing again to Diaghilev on 29 July,[86] he three times penned in Russian "g . . . a" (genitive form of *govno,* i.e., "shit"). The first time, he referred to any conceivable Russian peace in 1921 as "not once, but three times shit"; the second time was to Koussevitzky's criticisms as "a pile of shit"; and a third time he "was not writing it as shit." Earlier in the letter he referred to Koussevitzky as a "venomous beast," and he concluded by stating that he had learned well from the conductor (whom he had recently seen) "car il en tire le profit de juive" (for he makes a Jewish profit from it)—that is, from any reply sent to the press.

Two years later, Koussevitzky visited Stravinsky, then living in Biarritz. Stravinsky, learning from the conductor's Jewish secretary, Zederbaum, about a new chamber-music organization in Paris with Koussevitzky as its president, wrote on 9 September 1923 to Ernest Ansermet: "These Jews, as you well know, seeking my Octet [for performance (and for publication?)], thus wish to invite me to conduct it."[87] Scorning Koussevitzky here as one of "these Jews" is doubly repugnant: he knew of Koussevitzky's conversion in 1888 to his own faith and marriage in 1905 to the Russian Orthodox Natalya Konstantinova Uskov. Her fortune propelled both her husband's career and the publication of much of Stravinsky's music and that of many others.[88] The publishing enterprise she financed, Édition russe, allowed for a long line of Stravinsky's works in print, beginning in 1912 with the *Two Poems of Balmont* and *Petrushka,* and by 1924, it would include his Octet.[89] On 21 September, Stravinsky again wrote Ansermet, this time revealing his real motive, money: "There is still this business of the Octet. Koussevitzky had invited me to lead it. . . . They will pay me an amount so significant that I could [hardly] refuse."[90]

A quarter century later, Stravinsky was still excoriating Koussevitzky and indulging in scabrous language, beginning with the letter to Diaghilev. Annoyed that Koussevitzky had not programmed Nabokov's *Elegia* (Pushkin's *Return*), he wrote in Russian to Nabokov: "What a lot of sh[it] this is anyway, all of this K. [double-entendre on 'kaká' (turd in baby talk)]. Neither him, nor a mother with a hundred asses, nor the French word *con* can describe him in Russian any other way than with K."[91] Most people will have difficulty squaring this kind of talk in 1948 with Craft's recent assertions that "they remained on good terms for the rest of Koussevitzky's life," and "Stravinsky was personally very fond of Koussevitzky."[92] Stravinsky's peculiar interest in the body's excretory functions, bordering on scatophilia, did not go unremarked by his chronicler, who twice noted it during a trip to Tokyo in April of 1959 and again, in greater detail, in September of 1963 at Rio de Janeiro,[93] with the facile observation that such talk "indicates a traumatic toilet training." Still, it cannot excuse Stravinsky's attitude toward Jews in general or Koussevitzky in particular: he had it both ways with Koussevitzky, using and abusing him.

In turn, Koussevitzky had no illusions about Stravinsky. Two New Year's letters he wrote in 1931 and 1935 to Païchadze at the Édition russe in Paris reveal all. Stravinsky was a "callous egoist who . . . relates to people merely when it is profitable." "If [only] one could forget all of Stravinsky's misdemeanors and his attitude toward people," he mused.[94] Stravinsky was capable of generosity, as documented in a letter of 21 December 1947, requesting "packages [of] foodstuffs or plain wearing apparel" to be sent to needy persons in Europe, even if this was in exchange for donating his *Danses concertantes* manuscript to Stanford University.[95]

A PROJECT, NOT A PUPIL

The year 1943 drew to a close seemingly with a new pupil to fill the void left by Andersson's sudden death. Vera's diary for 17 and 18 December notes that Stravinsky gave "lessons" on these dates to a certain Leyssac. Her editor, identifying him wrongly as a "Los Angeles musician, pupil of Stravinsky for a short time," had apparently forgotten that Leyssac dined in Chicago on 10 November 1940 with the Stravinsky's and some musicians and university people.[96] Which of the innumerable musicians working in Los Angeles could this have been, and how long might he or she have studied with Stravinsky? What of Stravinsky's professed dislike of teaching?

In Stravinsky's own diary that year, no such pair of "lessons" appears for those days, unlike Andersson's lessons, which were carefully tabulated there. I can confirm Howard Pollack's suggestion that this student was Paul Leyssac.[97] As it turns out, Vera's diary (citing him solely by his surname) mentions a lunch with "Leyssac" on 10 November 1940. At that time, there was a Paul Leyssac lecturing in Chicago on just the day he lunched with the Stravinskys.[98] Diseur and actor Paul Leyssac (1881–1946) had narrated *Oedipus Rex* on 28–30 March 1940, with Stravinsky leading the Boston Symphony Orchestra. Years earlier, in February of 1928, he had done the same with the orchestra's first *Oedipus* performances under Koussevitzky.[99] In 1942 Leyssac lived in Hollywood, and that September he "was on the lookout to discover someone who will write a musical score to be used with the delightful [Hans Christian] Andersen stories,"[100] a writer for whom Stravinsky had a special affection. Consequently, Leyssac's two "lessons" in mid-December of 1943 were surely conferences on a possible new project. Sadly, no such project ever came to fruition.

EXCURSIONS (1944)

CONCERT APPEARANCES

13 January: Cambridge, Boston Symphony Orchestra

14, 15 January: Boston, Boston Symphony Orchestra

20 January: Lecture at University of Chicago: "Composing, Performing, Listening"

21 January: University of Chicago, *Duo concertant* with John Weicher; leads *Histoire;* Two-Piano Concerto with Willard MacGregor

23 January: Madison, Wisconsin, Edgewood College (lecture)

12 August: Hollywood Bowl, *Petrushka*

31 August: Hollywood Bowl, *Petrushka*

25 October: Mills College, Oakland; lecture plus *Circus Polka,* Sonata, and *Scherzo à la Russe* with Boulanger

6 December: Los Angeles, *Danses concertantes* ballet, "possible Stravinsky will conduct"

28 December: Palos Verdes, chez Szigeti; rehearsing *Duo concertant*

An event on 14 January 1944 reaffirmed Stravinsky's long-established reputation as a "modernist" and, perhaps in the eyes of some, as a musical terrorist best dealt with by the Boston Police "Radical Squad." It guaranteed an abiding notoriety and, at the same time, a dearth of future performances for Stravinsky's orchestral-choral arrangement of "The Star-Spangled Banner." As announced in the *Boston Globe* the previous day (fig. 9.1), he led the Boston Symphony Orchestra in a performance of his arrangement as a preface to the Symphony in C.[1] Although the previous evening's concert in Cambridge provoked no notable dissent, there was trouble that January afternoon in Boston's Symphony Hall: "At the start, the audience began to sing with the orchestra in customary manner, but soon the odd, somewhat dissonant harmonies . . . became evident. Eyebrows lifted, voices faltered, and before the close practically everyone gave up even trying."[2] The following evening at the beginning of the 8:30 p.m. broadcast of the concert, the announcer said: "Mr. Stravinsky will play the Star-Spangled Banner in its customary version. . . . Unaware the state of Massachusetts had a law forbidding the playing of the national anthem in any but the original version . . . and now informed, he will readily conform to the Massachusetts laws."[3]

STRAVINSKY REVISES NATIONAL ANTHEM—Famous Russian composer looks over score of his new version of "Star Spangled Banner," which Boston Symphony Orchestra will play when he directs it Friday and Saturday.

FIGURE 9.1

"Stravinsky Revises National Anthem." *Boston Daily Globe*, 13 Jan. 1944, 12.

An unsigned report, subheaded "Officers Set to Arrest Boston Conductor If He Repeated His Unorthodox Rendition" in the *New York Journal-American* (datelined "Boston, January 15"), sensationalized the occasion for its readers:

> A squad of 12 police—including a captain, sergeant and members of the Radical Squad . . . had been all set, Police Capt. Harvey disclosed, to arrest the noted composer. . . . Just before the concert got underway, Harvey remarked: "Let him change it just once, and we'll grab him."[4]

But Stravinsky had changed not one note of the old drinking song. Given the late Captain Harvey's devotion to the anthem, it is just as well that he was spared the melismatic indignities that present-day crooners habitually inflict on the melody at athletic events.

What, then, is to be made of this, and of Craft's revisions of his and Stravinsky's earlier remarks about "The Star-Spangled Banner"? In the preface to the 2002 version of their *Memories and Commentaries,* Craft claimed that "updating had been kept to a minimum, as well as corrections of proven errors of text."[5] Unfortunately, not all "proven errors" were rectified, and several are particularly relevant here. The current mischief began in 1980 with Craft's amplification of the 1944 report in the *New York Journal-American* for a documentary film:

> [Stravinsky] even made an arrangement of "The Star-Spangled Banner," not realizing it was illegal to do so, played the piece in Boston and was arrested. But he tried it out in about thirty cities more or less, and got the same hisses and boos. It was all very touching.[6]

Twenty years later, presumably relying on his own statements and on incorrect ones in Joseph's *Stravinsky Inside Out* (in all other respects a fine study from which Craft abruptly withdrew his imprimatur),[7] Craft further embroidered this tall tale. Both he and Joseph wrongly identified a visa photograph of the composer that was taken in 1940 at a Boston police station with the aborted 15 January 1944 performance.

Ignoring the date of 14 April 1940, so conspicuous on the placard hanging on the composer's chest in the visa photograph, both writers then metamorphosed this four-year-old image into a "mug-shot," purportedly taken at his "arrest" in 1944. Facetiously, Craft even called the composer a "criminal," parodying Joseph, who had erroneously judged Stravinsky's "rearrangement" and "refurbishing" of the national anthem in 1941 as "illegal,"[8]—as if Congress or the Commonwealth of Massachusetts had somehow authorized Damrosch's 1917 harmonization or, indeed, any other.

In spite of this criminological-chronological blunder, there was a further error of the composer having led the premiere of his arrangement in 1940 at the Hollywood Bowl.[9] The correct date is 1941, and it was led by Sample at the Embassy Theatre in Los Angeles with Stravinsky present in the audience. Nor was the composer ever arrested in 1944 by the Boston police or by anybody else. In truth, the city's police commissioner merely warned Stravinsky that he had run afoul of a 1917 Massachusetts law and that if he persisted for the Saturday evening performance, the police would remove the parts from the orchestra's music stands and impose a $100 fine. Innate anxiety about money, and the status of his application for US citizenship, deterred him from the third performance.[10] As if to make amends for Stravinsky's distress and embarrassment, the next Boston Symphony program contained an accurate account of, and seemingly apology for, the whole incident, culled from the *Boston Traveler* (20 January 1944).[11]

The radio broadcast (or rebroadcast) of the 15 January Boston Symphony concert heard by Nicolas Nabokov included Stravinsky conducting his three-year-old Symphony in C with the Boston Symphony Orchestra.[12] Stravinsky did not make a commercially available recording of it until late 1952.[13] This delay stemmed from two factors. First, he associated the Symphony with the disastrous receptions in St. Louis and Boston of his arrangement of "The Star-Spangled Banner," which was to have preceded the Symphony in each case. Second, by April and May of 1948 his young assistant was already performing the Symphony: on 11 April 1948 he wrote that "I know the Symphony in C better than Mr. S does." The next month Craft earned the composer's accolade: "a noble and discriminated [*sic*] performance," inscribed on Schott's newly published score.[14] In 1952 Stravinsky complained to Vera that the Cleveland Orchestra "has great difficulty in mastering the almost chamber-music quality."[15] This might suggest problems with his own conducting skills, especially in the difficult third movement, given that the virtuoso Cleveland ensemble had been trained by George Szell, a strict disciplinarian. When the Symphony in C was recorded again, in Toronto in 1962, Craft ably prepared the orchestra for Stravinsky to conduct.

Nabokov had access to an ozalid or photocopy of the score of the Symphony in C and as early as November of 1943 had studied it "thoroughly"[16] before he heard the Boston Symphony broadcast, and long before Craft knew it. As a composer himself, he was, by the summer of 1944, able to write more perceptively (and more poetically) than most about the Symphony and its significance. Concerning the finale, he stated:

> This work . . . achieves something . . . never previously done[:] a . . . "perception of timelessness" . . . most clearly in the epilogue. . . . Large, soft, subtly measured chords move slowly on the horizon of vanishing musical time. . . . A broad noble melody . . . slowly returns to its modal center, its root, and the whole body of this ideal musical being acquires a serenity, a motionless beauty.[17]

In the same essay, he also touched on the movement's monometricalism, Stravinsky's term for isochrony:

> One of the principles by which Stravinsky carries out his investigation into the nature of rhythm is in the reduction of every musical measure to one monometrical unit or metrical cell . . . most clearly in the Symphony . . . you will find that it [the cell] is not the measure closed in by bar lines (Mozart, for example) but the monometrical unit of the measure, the single beat which determines the life of his musical organism. . . . Observe . . . the well-balanced lengths of his chords . . . for example, the epilogue of his Symphony, and the frequent and absolutely necessary changes of time . . . caused by the reduction of the metrical tissue to the organic cell.[18]

Nabokov thus illuminates somewhat Stravinsky's own concept of the same term used on 28 August 1940 in responding to the McQuoid telegram just after finishing the Symphony in C on 19 August.

CHICAGO

On 5 March Stravinsky broke two years of silence to write publisher Leonard Feist; their last communication had been a brief inquiry in 1942 about Koussevitzky and a possible performance of the national anthem in Washington, DC.[19] Still irritated by Feist's refusal in 1942 to take on *Circus Polka,* and still upset by the Boston fiasco, Stravinsky wrote that he regretted having entrusted his Tango "to a firm indifferent to its fate and only for the sake of you using my name in your catalogue. Equally the fate of the Star-Spangled Banner." Concerning the anthem, Stravinsky also complained about difficulties musicians were experiencing in discovering even the publisher's name: he continued, "This fact shows the utter absence of publicity and distribution."[20] Truth be told, neither Stravinsky nor Mercury Music Corporation made much money from either arrangement.[21]

Because Stravinsky had been invited to lecture in English at several colleges during 1944 and 1945, he had written in some desperation on 17 October 1943 in French to Professor Edward Waldo Forbes at Gerry's Landing. He asked Forbes to send him Forbes's personal copy of the 1940 Kall-Forbes-Fine translation of his 1939–40 Norton Lectures:

> My first idea had been to address myself to Dr. Kall who has both his English translation and Mr. Fine's corrected version. . . . Poor Doctor Kall for the past two months has been confined to his bed in a Los Angeles hospital with an amputated leg; he had a gangrenous toe, a result of his diabetic condition.[22]

Harvard had still not published an English translation of the *Poétique musicale,* so Stravinsky badly needed Kall's version: his first public lecture was slated for mid-January of 1944 at the University of Chicago, followed by Edgewood College (Madison, Wisconsin: late January); Mills College (Oakland, California: October); and the Art Alliance (Barclay Hotel, Philadelphia: February 1945). The senior Forbes promptly sent him the 1940 Kall-Forbes-Fine translation after gaining permission from Harvard University Press, which held the copyright.

During the closing months of 1943 Stravinsky worked on this talk in Santa Barbara and Hollywood, assisted by Nadia Boulanger in Santa Barbara.[23] They called it "Composing, Performing, and Listening," and Walsh cites a hilarious excerpt from their Franco-Russian attempt at English translation.[24] Their title was sufficient to prevent at least one scholar from recognizing its origin in Kall's previous labors, even from the facsimile pages reproduced from the third Norton lecture of Kall's 1940 typescript. By no means are all the typescript's corrections in Stravinsky's hand.

Less than a week after the Boston contretemps, Stravinsky was at the University of Chicago. On Thursday evening, 20 January 1944, after an introduction by the university's president, Robert Hutchins, he delivered the prestigious William Vaughan Moody Lecture. The title was indeed "Composing, Performing, Listening," and the text had been completed on 8 December 1943, with the help of Boulanger at the Santa Barbara home of their mutual friend Arthur Sachs. Although it was well advertised and well attended—among others present were Arthur Rubinstein and Jacques Maritain (then a professor at the university)—none of the Chicago newspapers reviewed it. That quickly changed.

In Mandel Hall the next evening, Stravinsky played the piano and conducted, notwithstanding his known stated aversion to play and conduct on the same occasion. The concert was organized by the university's assistant professor of music, Remi Gassman. Stravinsky played *Duo concertant* with John Weicher, concertmaster of the Chicago Symphony Orchestra. Then came the Concerto for Two Solo Pianos with Willard MacGregor, the third American pianist after Webster and Marcus with whom he was to perform it—the composer taking, as always, the slightly easier second piano. Finally, with seven players from the Chicago Symphony (including Weicher), he conducted a suite from the *Histoire du soldat*. Favorable reviews appeared the next day by Claudia Cassidy *(Chicago Tribune)* and Gassman himself *(Chicago Times)*. In the *Chicago Sun* Felix Borowski, a minor English composer, violinist, and former dean of the Chicago Musical College (1916–24), criticized Stravinsky for what he deemed a lack of piano technique.[25] Only Gassman evinced any understanding of the *Duo concertant* or of the Double Concerto. Claudia Cassidy, however grudgingly, managed to come up with some good observations on the performances. Both works "belonged to a more sterile period. . . . [The Double Concerto was] an angular, clever, and hard to remember work well played." In the *Duo concertant*, even though for her, Weicher's "violin often sounded like a discouraged banshee wailing over pianistic percussion, [there was] no denying the intelligence back of the work, or the upcropping wit of the gigue and the bucolic design of the whole."[26] As in so many reviews, "pianistic percussion" alludes to Stravinsky's mode of playing the instrument. Except for the lyrical "Eclogue II" and concluding "Dithyramb" of the Duo, his two recordings of it—April 1933 in Paris with Dushkin and October 1945 in Hollywood with Szigeti—do bear her out.[27]

After a brief excursion to Madison to visit Nadia Boulanger and lecture at Edgewood College (22–23 January), Stravinsky was back in Los Angeles on 30 January. He continued sketching his new Sonata for Two Pianos, completing it on 11 February.[28] Afterward, he also worked on the *Scherzo à la Russe* (begun in 1942–43) and completed it in June.

In the mail that accumulated during his absence was a letter from the American-born writer, poetess, playwright, and screenwriter Mercedes de Acosta.[29] He and Vera had met her when she visited Paris early in the 1920s. By 1931 she had moved from her native New York to Los Angeles. The Stravinskys saw a great deal of her there from May of 1941 until she temporarily returned to New York in July of 1942, then settled permanently there in the autumn of 1943.[30] On the East Coast she worked as a magazine writer and assistant editor at, among others, *Victory* and *Tomorrow*. Her several letters in early 1944 invited Stravinsky to write music for her play *The Mother of Christ* for $10,000 plus 30 percent royalties. Having written it in 1928 for Paris, though never staged there, she was revising it for New York under a new title, *The Leader*. No performance ever took place. One reason was surely Stravinsky's objection on religious grounds to portraying the Holy Virgin onstage,[31] the same objection he had raised with Charlie Chaplin in 1935 about portraying Christ,[32] though not one he raised for the *Song of Bernadette*. Nevertheless, he stayed in touch with de Acosta. In January of 1949 he noted her Park Avenue location among addresses of his other luminary New York friends and associates.[33] Eventually, in

1953, her New York publishing connections allowed her translation of his 1937 memoir of Diaghilev to appear in the *Atlantic Monthly*.

Mid-March 1944 saw Stravinsky fulfill a request from the US Office of War Information, inviting him to prepare a message commemorating the centenary of Rimsky-Korsakov's birth on 18 March. Although he owned a copy of the 1923 English translation of Rimsky's *My Life*, he enlisted the aid of a native English speaker and spoke of Rimsky's "loving, unforgettable truly fatherly guidance in the very inception of my creative musical life."[34] In view of the several composers resident in the Soviet Union who had also been nurtured by Rimsky's tuition (Maximilian Steinberg, Michael Gnesin, and Prokofiev),[35] discretion rather than modesty probably restrained Stravinsky from broadcasting Rimsky's extraordinarily high opinion of his talent and of his early works, not to speak of him envying Rimsky's even higher opinion of Steinberg.

Otherwise, March and April 1944 were occupied with composing *Babel*, a cantata for narrator, male chorus, and orchestra. The origins of Stravinsky's contribution are essentially clear. Setting Genesis 11: 1–9, *Babel* is the seventh and concluding movement of the *Genesis Suite*, a work commissioned by Nathaniel Shilkret from seven composers: Stravinsky, Schoenberg, Milhaud, Tansman, Mario Castelnuovo-Tedesco, Ernest Toch, and Shilkret himself.[36] All of them were younger, less gifted, and less famous than Stravinsky and deferred to him, except Schoenberg, who subsequently had some critical remarks about *Babel*. The premiere was projected for 1944 but, in the event, was delayed by a year. Especially ironic, in view of Stravinsky's anti-Semitism, he was the only non-Jew participating in the project.[37]

Shilkret approached Stravinsky by 5 March 1944 about the project. Just over three weeks later, on 29 March, Stravinsky finished his draft score, and on 12 April completed the full score—twenty-three pages of transparencies that were used to make ozalid copies.[38] Six days later Shilkret visited Stravinsky's home, presumably to check on *Babel*'s progress.[39] Strangely enough, a formal contract was apparently not drawn up until 5 May, probably in connection with negotiations surrounding the commission paid to Stravinsky.

Clarity does not obtain about compensation for the *Genesis* composers. Shilkret is said to have offered Stravinsky $1,000. In 1981 he reported that he paid "$1,500 each for Schoenberg and Stravinsky." In 1993 it was announced that each contributor, including Schoenberg, was paid $300 but that Stravinsky was secretly paid $1,000. Then in 2006 Schoenberg was said to have received $1,500 as a flat fee, and Stravinsky, by retaining a royalty on sales, received only $1,000. Shilkret's posthumous (2005) memoirs give the $1,500 figure, and claim that Stravinsky's lawyer outsmarted him in the pages of a revised contract, but give no details. Still other authorities provide more—and sometimes, more confusing—information.[40] Presumably the truth lies in Shilkret's memoirs.

The premiere of the *Genesis Suite* took place on 18 November 1945 in Los Angeles, and the work was recorded for RCA Victor and released that year on an ad hoc label called Artist Records (subsidized by Werner Janssen, the conductor), when RCA exercised its option to decline. Clearly regarded as the most notable participant, Stravinsky was also the only composer who was invited to supply program notes for the premiere. Duly printed as "About My Babel Cantata / By Igor Stravinsky, Hollywood, California. November 5, 1945" and then duplicated for the record album, the notes contain a jab about the lack of performance of some of his major works in his home city:

> For those who are not very familiar with my compositions, knowing my name only by the reputation of my earlier works such as the *Firebird, Petrouchka* or *The Rite of Spring*, my *Babel*—a Cantata for Chorus with Orchestra and a Narrator—will present itself probably as a casual, an isolated work which has little to do with my present compositions, with my actual features as a composer. This feature presents itself in an entirely different aspect to those who know my musical mind and my symphonic work, especially such as the *Symphony of Psalms*, the Melodrama *Persephone* or the Opera Oratorio *Oedipus Rex*, to mention only those capital compositions of my catalogue, compositions never played in Los Angeles. Yet the acquaintance with but these compositions could easily explain my bent toward musical forms cultivated by the best musical brains of all times. Therefore the approaching performance of my Cantata among other compositions of the Bible collected of Mr Nathaniel Shilkret by the brilliant company of Werner Janssen Symphony seems to me most opportune and I welcome it.[41]

Stravinsky's remark about "the best musical brains of all times" surely refers as much to J. S. Bach's brain as to his own. Indeed, Tansman (one of the contributing composers) was "present at the conversation between the composer [Stravinsky] and our patron [Shilkret]." Tansman thus felt "qualified" to remark that "the construction of the [Babel] tower corresponds chronologically to a fugal fragment," referring here to "fugue itself."[42]

A decade after its composition, *Babel* was pronounced among Stravinsky's "religious pieces for concert use" and hence, "thoroughly contrapuntal,"[43] although there are plenty of splendid homophonic works for church services. For his own recording of *Babel* in November of 1962, Stravinsky merely wrote that it "includes several types of movement, an orchestral introduction, a choral prologue, an instrumental fugato and a postlude."[44]

Tansman also noted how Stravinsky, by having God's words sung by male voices rather than spoken by the narrator, thereby "avoided any suspicion of imitation of the divine voice by the human [spoken] voice," the former remaining, "so to speak, in quotes," or as White so nicely put it later, Stravinsky "avoided the anthropomorphic solution."[45] Tansman pointed out that in discussion with Shilkret, the composer forcefully iterated his credo that neither the divine word nor the Deity should be suggested by anything in the music: "music should illustrate nothing whatsoever. Such is not its function,"[46] maintaining the dictum about "expression" in *Chroniques de ma vie*. Nevertheless, the *Babel* music clearly intends to depict its text in several places, although restricted to words uttered by the narrator and the Deity: "scattered" and "left off to build" (verse 8), and then "scatter" (verse 9).

A fascinating glimpse—readily accessible without a trip to Basel—into this aspect of Stravinsky's creative process is afforded by a color plate of the first page of Stravinsky's five-page sketch score for *Babel*[47] (that is, up to the first entrance of the men's chorus). Save for one small group of inscriptions at the top, the page is devoted to *Babel*'s opening section. It involves a five-measure introduction in low strings and the ensuing five verses from *Genesis* 11, spoken by the narrator (until reh. 8).

On this 9-by-11¾-inch sheet, Stravinsky used his rastrum to draw staves of varying length. A dozen staves begin near the page's left margin (numbered by me as 1–12). Several shorter staves are drawn above and below them. There can be certainty neither about the order in which Stravinsky drew his staves nor about the order in which he notated them, but a hypothesis can be ventured. Because of their regularity in length and Stravinsky's own initiative in bracketing staff pairs, staves 5–6, 7–8, and 9–10 were probably the first to be inscribed.

Staves 5–6, bracketed together, include a metronome sign: eighth note = 84 (later published as quarter note = 42). They do not offer the version of the opening printed in the 1953 score but rather commence at its fifth measure (reh. 1: –1). They continue, with additional staves drawn above and below, through reh. 4: +1, and include the Narrator's verses 1–3.

Staves 7–8 and 9–10, all four united under a single bracket, with additional staves drawn above and below, lead from reh. 4 to the entrance of the Men's Chorus (reh. 8) and thus include the Narrator's verses (from Genesis 11: 4–5).

Staves 11–12, also bracketed, were probably drawn last. Extending the furthest toward the left margin, they offer *Babel*'s initial four measures, precisely those "missing" from staves 5–6. They also contain notations (reh. 1) lacking at the same place on staves 5–6, namely, the oboe solo (rehs. 1–2), inserted (later?) in green ink, just above the Narrator's verse 1 (which Stravinsky reinscribed).

The editorial annotations to this facsimile neglect to mention what Stravinsky wrote on staves 1–4, the second of which he left blank. Likewise drawn from near the left margin of the page, these unbracketed four staves extend but a short distance across the page. Stravinsky notated a treble clef on staff 1, followed by "4" (i.e., 4/4 meter) and a syncopated order of pitches descending from G: C-sharp, B-flat, F-sharp (perhaps an octatonic fragment from Collection III). Staves 3 and 4 are occupied with accompanying triads reiterated in a succession of G minor, G minor seventh, and E minor, the last triad in first inversion.

Staves 1, 3, and 4 surely memorialize a sudden inspiration during his sketching of the introduction. They adumbrate a motive that does not appear until a later sketch page (reh. 17: –3), scored for flute, oboe, and trumpet 1, accompanied by triadic French horns (reh. 17: –3 to reh. 18). Soon thereafter, the same instruments set the motive completely (rehs. 18: –2 to 19). For this inspiration Stravinsky drew his melodic pitches from octatonic Collection III and his harmonic ones from Collection I. Indeed, it has been remarked how much of *Babel* derives from the opposition of octatonic collections, though here, this chiefly involves opposing Collection I (e.g., the low-string introduction and the entire orchestral fabric at reh. 19) to Collection II (French horn 1, reh. 23: –1; and trombone, reh. 25).[48]

EXAMPLE 9.1
Babel: openings of verses 6 and 7.

Stravinsky, Babel (1944): rehs. 8-10, 13-15

White's brief analysis of *Babel* discerned a closeness between the cantata's opening low strings and a passage Stravinsky conceived shortly thereafter for strings (uppermost and lowest) in the finale (reh. 152) of his Symphony in Three Movements.[49] But White omitted the Symphony's ensuing D-flats. The true relevance of *Babel*'s introduction to the brief passage from the Symphony can only be demonstrated convincingly by including those D-flats (pizzicato inner strings and piano, harp) from its third measure, also at reh. 153–54. Having noted the extent of octatonic writing in *Babel,* van den Toorn analyzed this very passage from the Symphony,[50] showing that D-flats demonstrate that both *Babel* and the Symphony's finale are related because both passages draw on similar pitches in octatonic Collection I.

In respect to setting God's words, Stravinsky simultaneously faced challenges and exploited opportunities. One problem was the uneven lengths of His words in the King James translation. Genesis 11:6 has thirty-one words, comprising thirty-nine syllables, whereas verse 7 has nineteen words, with twenty-four syllables (see ex. 9.1). Recognizing the grammatical similarity of verbal imperatives in "Behold," "Go to," and "their language," Stravinsky opted for very similar settings, continuing in the same manner for much of each verse.

Superimposed, these partial transcriptions demonstrate his considerable pains to unify verse 6 with verse 7, especially their beginnings. Though they are of unequal lengths, he understood verses 6 and 7 as two similar pronouncements in both grammar

EXAMPLE 9.2

Babel: continuation of verse 6, matched against my rebarring.

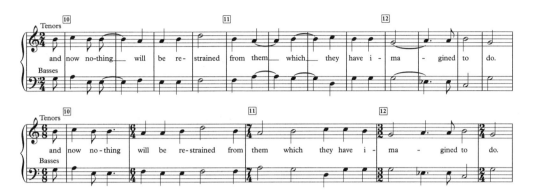

and content. Stravinsky correctly perceived that their initial imperatives were virtually identical. Thus, for "Behold" in verse 6 and for "Go to" in verse 7, he set each command with the same pitches in parallel tenths. For the next seventeen words of verse 6 and the next fourteen of verse 7, he found plenty of opportunities for creating similarities. Several are audible (and even visible) in such a simple connection as the *and* in verse 6 (m. 4) and the *-stand* (of *understand*) in verse 7 (just preceding reh. 15: –3 and –4). Particularly felicitous and economical in verse 7 is the halving of some note values used in verse 6. This occurs initially at *down* (verse 7) compared to *one* (verse 6) and especially the halved note values on the same pitches in verse 7: "that they may not understand," as compared to those in verse 6: "this they begin to do: and." The latter procedure seems to reveal a trait Stravinsky disclosed to Auden, probably 4 January 1970, about his "habit of translating syllables to note values before any real notes were composed."[51] The result in *Babel* is a homophonic and pseudo-strophic variety of hymn, redolent of the genre sung by the bleaker evangelical congregations.

Below the continuation of verse 6, as Stravinsky barred it, is my rebarring (see ex. 9.2). It demonstrates a certain metrical flexibility, moving between 6/8, 6/4, 7/4, and 3/2, and it allows a ready grasp of Stravinsky's macro-rhythms. At rehearsal 10, rebarring also discloses that he probably believed that "noth-ing" was the same as "no thing." (Here Andersson's observation in 1941 about Stravinsky's difficulty with the word *thing*, pronounced "ding," might be pertinent.) Rebarring, however, does not reveal much more about Stravinsky's sense of stress in English. Even so, Stravinsky's accentuation in *Babel* seems more sophisticated than naive, more deliberate than uncomprehending. Above all, it reflects the composer's "rejoicing discovery," circa 1914, concerning prosody.[52]

Beyond the mere felicities of accentuation shown in example 9.1, sustaining the second syllable of "Be-hóld" seems to open up a kind of aural vista in much the same way as that spatial command, "Go tó." Likewise, each ensuing elongated *and* urges careful consideration from the listener of what might follow. Although tonic accents on *language* are correct, dwelling on its second syllable is not, but perhaps the latter is meant to signify a continuing quandary. Transforming and contracting the rather solemn "they begin to do" into a negative, by halving the note values (reh 15: –2) of "that they may not," is surely a stroke of inspiration and ingenuity. At reh. 12 (in ex. 9.2) Stravinsky emphasizes the temerity of *imagined* by Babel's inhabitants by means of elongation (the penultimate 3/2 in the rebarred version) with a suggestion of G major in the tenors, opposed by the C-minor descent in the basses. In 1954 Craft noted that for Stravinsky "words must serve the musical use he finds for them, whether or not this use violates the common practice with regard to stress, syllable groupings, metrics, etc. . . . Differences of language do not change his principles."[53]

Believing that *Babel* was Stravinsky's first venture into setting a text in English, Leonard Stein, whose job as pianist in 1944 was to play all the composers' settings at chorus rehearsals, noted that the sole adjustment Stravinsky made was to correct a wrongful elision into just two syllables of God's third and fourth words: "people is" (in verse 6), to give them their proper three syllables.[54] The need for this adjustment is perhaps a little surprising in view of Stravinsky's previous settings of our language, especially the one four years earlier in which he had navigated far more complex verbal rhythms when he composed his thank-you note on a Tchaikovsky melody in response to the McQuoids' fifty-bravo telegram.

Neither fully chromatic nor octatonic, Stravinsky's Deity in *Babel* communicates diatonically and in C major by means of steadily paced and two-voiced homophony assigned to tenors and basses. In setting the first of two verses, chromaticism is endorsed just once, near its close, with an E-flat (reh. 12: +1), and with occasional F-sharps by upper strings and winds (reh. 11: –1, and after reh. 12: +2). The choral harmonization for God's words in verse 7 (rehs. 13–15) has many parallels to verse 6, but from the outset of verse 7 the orchestral accompaniment becomes increasingly tense, depicting God's growing anger. This anger is also signaled by C-sharps in the tenors at the presumption of building a tower to heaven, hardening into exile for Babel's inhabitants and thus aborting their tower's completion. Low strings close God's words with a chromatic descent to F-sharp, harmonized by a descending F-sharp major arpeggio in the upper strings (reh. 16: –1). Simultaneously, the upper winds, bassoon 1, French horn 1, and trumpet 1 sound an angry dominant seventh of F at God's final word, *speech*, thus producing, yet again, a pepped-up *Petrushka* chord.

Although both these chords appear in Collection III, their "authentic" resolutions point to B and to F, respectively—that is, two pitches found together only in Collection I. And in fact, at the brief *(con moto)* orchestral introduction to the narrator's description of the Deity's actions that follows, both chords resolve deceptively—signaling God's change of mind. Furthermore, they resolve into Stravinsky's long-favored simultaneous bitonality (here G minor plus G major), both triads afforded by Collection I.[55]

Despite the composer's strictures about not illustrating text in music, repeated for Tansman and Shilkret with respect to this very piece, Stravinsky, stimulated by the Narrator's report in the *con moto* section that "the Lord scattered them" (reh. 16ff.) so that Babel's inhabitants "left off to build the city" (reh. 18), composed music that graphically illustrates the verbs *scatter* and *build*.[56] Two composer-theorists have complained about the ensuing orchestral duet between winds and upper strings (rehs. 19–21): considering it canonic, they speak of "a twice-as-fast traditional diminution" at the unison, and they scorn the duet as "voices that run themselves ragged."[57] Although both melodic lines at reh. 19 derive from the low string introduction (and each could belong to Collection I), they are not identical; thus, there can be no true diminution, let alone canon. As for Stravinsky expressing the text, the operative words here continue to be not only the business of building but *also* the biblical "one language" and "scattered," uttered by the narrator as early as verses 4, 5, 8, and 9: both verbal quotations take on added significance with slightly different dueting but widely spaced melodies in winds and strings at reh. 19. Moreover, Stravinsky's ensuing fugue-like exposition employing brass doubled by agitated strings (reh. 23: –1 to reh. 27) highlights, by negation, the tale in the Narrator's verse 9 about the Lord's reaction to Babel as it simultaneously documents scattering its denizens across the earth. "By negation," for what could be more positive in the sense of building than the exposition of a fugue? Here Stravinsky forms his subject (French horn 1), its answer (trumpets), and its reiterated subject (trombones) perhaps by drawing on pitches from Collections II, III, and II, respectively. The fugue's brief concluding stretto (rehs. 26–27) among piccolo and flutes, trumpet, cellos and double basses, and trombone 3 joined by timpani, might also employ fragments from those same two collections.

An affecting moment in this little cantata occurs in what Stravinsky called its "instrumental postlude." Presumably, this epithet encompasses the Narrator's final verse and especially the closing ten measures. Therein most of the strife inherent in opposing chords of G major-minor and E major-minor (all four chords referable to Collection I) gradually resolves into a tonal calm. The postlude has a very clear tripartite structure, each section shorter than its predecessor (rehs. 27–29, 29–30, and 30–31), followed by a definitive cadence (reh. 31–end). The first section features a solo bassoon with a conjunct melody drawn from Collection II. Stravinsky marked it, of all things, *espressivo*. The section half cadences with a solemn, protracted, E-minor wind chord, inflected with F-natural (reh. 28), followed by a G-major/minor chord. All pitches of both chords occur in Collection I. In the second section of the postlude, the bassoon's pitches that sounded in the first section disperse (reh. 29) into a kind of contrary motion between oboe 1 and trumpet 1, marked *dolce* (a frequent ally or substitute for *espressivo* in Stravinsky scores). Once again, there follows the same half-cadence of two chords of inflected E minor and G major-minor (the first one of much shorter duration).

The third section assigns to cellos and basses in octaves the final limb of that bassoon melody from section one. This time, the drawn-out pitches of these low strings stem exclusively from Collection I, and, wonder of wonders, Stravinsky marked them *espressivo*. They sound below an even longer chord sustained by French horns, comprising notes stemming also from Collection I, except for an E-flat drawn from Collection II. Yet a pair of instruments dropping a fifth, from F-sharp to low B (bassoon 1 and, briefly, trombone 3), imply a strong, calming root-movement of dominant to tonic, resolving into the B major of Collection II, suggesting more a tonal than an octatonic framework. In addition, B major's leading tone (an A-sharp from Collection I in violas and cellos) never rises the final half-step. The cantata thus closes on a beautifully spaced major-seventh chord above the low, soft, sustained B in the bassoon. This seventh-chord, not octatonically referable, symbolizes the ambiguity of this work. The question remains. Was, or was not, *Babel* octatonically conceived?

Critical reaction to *Babel* arose as early as the rehearsals of the *Genesis Suite*. Rehearsals and the premiere, slated for 1944, were delayed until November 1945 because of Hindemith's withdrawal the preceding July from his commitment to compose the prelude.[58] The premiere was to garner comment from composers and critics alike.

On 17 July 1944 the Stravinskys celebrated Kall's name day; he had been out of the hospital for some time and had been fitted with a prosthesis for his amputated leg. They sent him greetings embodying the composer's characteristically Russian strain of black humor.[59]

At the top of a sheet of paper, Vera wrote "Dear Woof / I am writing you congratulations / on rosy paper so that everything will look rosy and cheerful / around you / Vera S." Stravinsky's message, below, read "On your name day / (of ALEXIS, man of God) I kiss you and / wish all happiness to / dear WOOF on / the wooden stump." At the bottom of the page is a musical quotation from Stravinsky's 1916 *Song of the Bear on a Wooden Stump*, slightly altered in rhythm at the second measure. Above the music Stravinsky took special pains to place the song's original text, "Creak on leg, creak on lime-wood," so that his tiny rhythmic alteration gave an added accentuation to that second "creak." Just the thing for a recent amputee.[60] That Kall retained the greeting from the Stravinskys in his papers shows how well he understood its Russian humor and how deeply he treasured their friendship.[61]

A STRAVINSKY-DAHL COLLABORATION: *SCÈNES DE BALLET*

Since 11 April, Stravinsky had been occupied by a commission from Paul Whiteman to convert *Scherzo à la Russe* from its original 1943 two-piano version to a new combination of instruments—some unfamiliar to him.[62] He was also working for several weeks on a commission from Billy Rose. First broached early in June, it offers a rare example of Stravinsky being bested financially: he asked for $15,000 initially, but ultimately accepted $5,000. Completed by the end of August, *Scènes de ballet*, inspired by *Giselle*, and said to be "the major work of 1944,"[63] was part of Rose's then-current stage review "The Seven Lively Arts." Its first performances took place from 24 November in Philadelphia and others ensued from 7 December in New York by various orchestras led by Maurice Abravanel. Although Stravinsky's scoring suffered cuts and reorchestrations for the revue, the wily composer prearranged with Rose and Abravanel that his music should always be billed as "excerpts" from the complete score.[64] This enabled him to program his original score in New York early in February 1945 as a "world premiere."

By August, he was also rehearsing and leading *Petrushka* at the Hollywood Bowl, as well as attending several Bowl concerts led by others. For all these reasons, he turned that summer to Ingolf Dahl for assistance in orchestrating some portions of *Scènes de ballet*.

That Dahl made an excellent piano reduction of *Scènes,* so that it could be recorded in September and used by Billy Rose's choreographer to rehearse dancers, has long been known. Recent research, based on a 2008 study of Dahl by his stepson, has disclosed that Dahl later told his University of Southern California music students (in 1968 and in strictest confidence) that he went to "Stravinsky's house every day or so, to pick up the piano sketches, and take them home and orchestrate them."[65] Stravinsky would presumably then incorporate such labors into his autograph score.

Scholars do not seem aware that this particular cat has been out of the bag for a half-century: in 1966, the information appeared in a footnote in Eric Walter White's last book on Stravinsky. According to the author's preface, Stravinsky had "encouraged" the book, and even White's footnotes were "based on information supplied by Mr. Stravinsky." This, despite the composer's previous harsh words for the redoubtable author (on 1 February 1948 Stravinsky wrote that even before he had read White's 1947 article in *Horizon* about him, it "causes me nausea").[66] After White's 1966 book appeared, Stravinsky called him "an incompetent writer of my music, which he discovered very recently."[67] These thoughts did not, however, deter Stravinsky from inscribing shortly thereafter a shabby secondhand-looking 1921 photograph of himself: "To / Eric W. White / best wishes. I Stravinsky / 1966."[68]

Whatever confidence Stravinsky might have had in White in 1966, his footnote about Dahl orchestrating *Scènes de ballet* was probably not supplied by Stravinsky himself. White's footnote relates that an unnamed pupil of Schoenberg wrote in his diary on 16 September 1944 that he told Schoenberg the same day that Dahl had orchestrated some portion of "a piece that Stravinsky had written for Billy Rose." This revelation took Schoenberg by surprise, for he quite logically did not understand why Stravinsky would ever need help in orchestrating.[69] Significantly perhaps, Stravinsky never contested this particular allegation.

If the student's allegation and Dahl's claim are accurate, then the assistance was probably provided during July of 1944. Several entries in Vera's diary seem relevant. For 24 July she wrote, "Ingolf Dahl in the afternoon"; the next day, "Igor locks himself in his room and works"; and on 30 July, "Dahl works with Igor." Much of the composition itself was probably finished by 11 August, when Vera wrote, "[Anton] Dolin and [Alicia] Markova [choreographer and dancer] for lunch and to hear Igor's Scènes de ballet." On 23 August Stravinsky wrote in French on his score's final page that "Paris is no longer occupied by the Germans," and he finished his "Introduction" to the full score of *Scènes* on 29 August.[70] On 11 and 12 September, two sessions were allotted for Dahl to record his piano transcription. On 14 September Dahl brought the recordings to Stravinsky. Two days later, the composer sent copies of the full score and Dahl's piano reduction to New York.[71] Dahl's contribution seems undeniable: the New York Public Library, Lincoln Center, Music Division, owns an ozalid copy of the full orchestra score, half in Dahl's hand, the other half in Stravinsky's.[72] Moreover, in a letter drafted to Leopold Stokowski, Dahl averred that "Stravinsky engaged me to help on orchestration of the *Scènes de ballet*."[73]

Early in October at Featherhill Ranch—the Arthur Sachs's home in Montecito—the Canadian composer Jean Papineau-Couture turned the pages for his former teacher, Nadia Boulanger and Stravinsky. They were playing four-hands from the orchestral manuscript of *Scènes*. Papineau-Couture and his wife Isabelle reported:

> Stravinsky, leaning toward the music rack, literally, had his head buried in the score, whereas Boulanger, straight as an arrow, . . . would perceive in advance what Stravinsky could not physically accomplish with two hands and from his *sol-fa-mi*-ing, and she would supplement this with notes high in the upper register of the keyboard.[74]

At its first concert performance (the real premiere) led by the composer on 3 February 1945 with the New York Philharmonic, *Scènes de ballet* was rightly esteemed as the "work of a master . . . superbly orchestrated and harmonically supersophisticated, they [*Scènes*] retain an ultimate simplicity of effect, like all of Mr. Stravinsky's later works. Their nervous, spasmodic rhythms, their startling changes of sonority, their touches of ironic banality are an integral part of this style."[75] Thankfully, the anonymous reviewer well comprehended that "simplicity" and "ironic banality," rather than "neoclassicism," were "integral" to, as well as true and valid signifiers of, this era of Stravinsky's compositional life.

While Nadia Boulanger was visiting the Stravinskys, *Dumbarton Oaks Concerto* finally achieved its Los Angeles premiere, with Werner Janssen leading his own chamber orchestra. In May of 1943 Stravinsky had labored in vain with a Los Angeles pickup orchestra over this score. On 22 October Stravinsky, Vera, and surely Boulanger (their houseguest that evening) attended Janssen's concert, where the composer was "given warm plaudits."[76] The next day, the *Los Angeles Times* offered a fuller account, calling *Dumbarton Oaks*

> a musical treat of the highest order, and in addition to the pleasure it gave the audience it must have given conductor Janssen and his players a feeling of tremendous satisfaction to see the composer pounding his palms red with appreciation and approval from the audience—as Igor Stravinsky did last night.[77]

Lawrence Morton's review was broader and more thoughtful:

> All three [movements] are genial and optimistic and not adequately described either by the stock adjectives of Stravinsky's detractors—frigid, uninspired, mechanical, contrived—nor by the equally extravagant panegyrics of his admirers. . . . Stravinsky is contemporary even

when he is going back to Bach for ideas, even when he transforms these ideas with his own original notions about dissonant counterpoint, fragmentary melodies, non-symmetrical rhythms, and spatial arrangements. Behind these devices and behind the legends about him the spirit of the man is not at all lacking in geniality and warmth and humor.[78]

Unfortunately, Stravinsky's reaction to another work on Janssen's program is unrecorded: excerpts from Shostakovich's *Lady Macbeth of the Mtsensk District.* It might easily be conjectured: after attending the US premiere in 1935 in New York, probably with Dagmar Godowsky, he thoroughly excoriated both the opera and its Soviet composer.

THE MILLS COLLEGE LECTURE-RECITAL WITH BOULANGER

Stravinsky's third public lecture in English took place at Mills College with Nadia Boulanger on 25 October 1944 and was followed by a fourth on 21 February 1945 with pianist Vincent Persichetti for the Arts Alliance in the Barclay Hotel in Philadelphia. At Mills he and his copianist performed his Sonata for Two Pianos (1942–44) and his new *Scherzo à la Russe* (i.e., the 1943–44 version for two pianos), and perhaps the *Circus Polka,*[79] and in Philadelphia the Sonata and perhaps also the *Scherzo.*

That fall, Boulanger and Stravinsky practiced together a great deal: on the Sonata and especially the more difficult *Scherzo.* Vera's diary for 22 October mentions that "Nadia and Igor work together the whole day," although they probably spent some of that time practicing his lecture. A photograph, taken on 24 October at the Milhaud home near the Mills College campus, shows the Milhauds, Stravinsky, and Boulanger (holding a telephone) lunching together.[80] Years later (c. 1991–96), Madame Milhaud recalled that day, or perhaps the next one: "I attended the rehearsal. [Boulanger] was very severe and at one point slapped Igor's hand, saying 'No, Igor, it isn't right. Count!' "[81] She told the tale again, c. 1997—she lived well beyond her hundredth year—and revealed that, at that moment, they were not practicing the *Scherzo* or the *Polka* but instead, "une sonata à quatre mains," i.e., the Sonata for Two Pianos: "Nadia tapait sur les doigts d'Igor en lui disant: Vous n'allez pas en mesure!"[82] Milhaud himself remembered this performance as Stravinsky's "new and admirable Sonata and *Scherzo à la Russe* (very *Petrushka* 1944),"[83] his parenthesis referring to the *Scherzo.*

Albert Frankenstein, who attended the Mills lecture-recital, seems to have been the first auditor of "Composing, Performing and Listening" to identify the source of its lecture: "This was, one suspects, one of the famous series of lectures Stravinsky prepared for Harvard some years ago, lectures which through an incredible lapse, have never been published in English and have gone out of print in the French edition."[84] He also described Boulanger's playing as "profound and fluent" and Stravinsky's "with his customary mordant virtuosity." The adjectival *mordant* refers to Stravinsky's percussive playing, not audible in the gentle Sonata but clear in the boisterous *Scherzo à la Russe,* which Frankenstein judged "vigorously tuneful, . . . all open and airy." Chronologically, his perception of the

Scherzo's "reminiscences of the Bellini period in Russian music" was not far off from the real source of its tunes: an anthology of Russian folk melodies first published in 1847. The thorough Russianness of both the *Scherzo* and the Sonata and the relationship of the *Scherzo* to moviemaking was not firmly established until four decades later.[85]

Nabokov knew the Sonata as early as mid-May of 1944, when he heard fellow composer Marcelle de Manziarly play it in New York. She was using an ozalid copy that Stravinsky had sent to her, made from his autograph transparencies, which are now in New York's Morgan Library.[86] Stravinsky had already tried out some portions of the Sonata with Manziarly at Santa Barbara as early as 1942.[87] Even this was preceded by Boulanger's attempt early that July to play a portion of it with one of her students in Bloomington, Indiana: the projected performance was foiled by her student's unauthorized publicity stunt for the event.[88] After the Sonata was finished, Manziarly and Harold Shapero played it privately on 21 March for Balanchine in New York.[89] Ultimately, Boulanger and Canadian pianist Richard Johnston gave the Sonata's formal world premiere, albeit a very private one, on 2 August, at Edgewood College in Madison. Stravinsky was unable to attend because he was working with Dahl on *Scènes de ballet*. Eight days later, Boulanger and Robert Stone Tangeman gave a more public premiere at Indiana University in Bloomington. Duo-pianists Celius Dougherty and Vincent Ruzicka were wrongly credited with a "first performance" on 29 October 1944 in Washington, DC."[90]

Stravinsky hoodwinked not only his reviewers and fellow composers but even his publisher's agent, regarding Russian folk songs in the Sonata. Frankenstein, for example, thought that, unlike the *Scherzo*, he heard nothing Russian in the Sonata: it had "a kind of unpretentious elegance" and its "purling counterpoint challenged the intellect and soothed the ear." Poor Nabokov was fooled as well, having already observed in print that "sometime in the twenties Stravinsky ceased using Russian themes in his music."[91] And Stravinsky hoodwinked his editor at Associated Music Publishers by prevaricating that even his *Scherzo à la Russe* (1943–44) was composed "without use of a special folktune."[92]

Variously deemed "an amusing skit," a "little potboiler," "lightweight," "frivolous big band swing style," "frothy," "folk fluff," and even as "amusing, confessedly unimportant,"[93] the *Scherzo à la Russe* is a peppy miniature with two trios. It deftly conceals its thematic origins, its artistry, artifice, performance techniques, and even its date. It was Taruskin who uncovered the source for its themes and, guided by previous research by Morton, the source for the tunes in the Sonata for Two Pianos as well.[94] Melodies for both Stravinsky works came from an 1886 reprint of an 1847 anthology, *Pesni russkogo naroda (Songs of the Russian People)*. Stravinsky purchased his copy in Los Angeles, probably early in November of 1942,[95] and, soon after, began work on the Sonata.

As to artistry in the "Scherzo" section proper, Stravinsky deftly spins a little tune of just seven bars into a convincing and attractive thirty-seven bar period.[96] Although harnessed there to a doggedly triadic opening section, his relentless diatonicism seems to continue even in the first trio; with a delicate canon at the octave (later deliciously scored for harp and piano at the octave), the composer briefly reverts to a familiar technique. To transition to the main scherzo section at the close of the trio (reh. 16: –2), he employs octatonicism (Collections II and III), a skill he learned from his teacher. Rimsky-Korsakov was surely "the source not only of Stravinsky's knowledge of the scale but also of his technique for manipulating it."[97] These technicalities are artistically concealed near the close of the trio, for octatonicism appears in such a diatonic context that the hearer scarcely experiences these two brief excursions as much more than slightly dissonant dominant sevenths.

The evolution of this little opus also furnishes valuable information about how Stravinsky himself fingered and performed the second piano part when he played it with various pianists. One of the ozalid copies (no. 3b, now in the Library of Congress) was made from his original manuscript transparencies of the *Scherzo à la Russe* and was his own performance copy.[98] This ozalid's fourteen pages are bound together with brown paper and Scotch tape folded accordion-style, so that the pages can gradually be extended along the piano's music rack; it contains many autograph fingerings and additional slurrings for piano 2 (fig. 9.2). He also used liquid paper to make extensive alterations and deletions in "Trio 2," simplifying its original rapid and quite difficult double- and triple-note passages, which were apparently too much even for his large hands (see, e.g., fig. 9.3). The Library of Congress ozalid is all the more precious because no recording of him performing the *Scherzo* is known.

Even though Stravinsky almost always dated his fair copies according to their compositional completion, rather than the date he actually copied them out,[99] the *Scherzo* poses chronological problems.[100] On its first complete manifestation in a two-piano version (at UBC) he wrote "1943" on its first page and "June 1944" on its final page. The explanation lies in the work's complex origin and evolution. It began life as music for a film score for *The North Star* (a movie released in 1943). Stravinsky started this project late in 1942 but abandoned it by mid-January of 1943; the movie's score was eventually composed by Aaron Copland.[101] He rapidly turned its materials into a work for two pianos (the *Scherzo à la Russe*) and later, in mid-April of 1944, orchestrated it on commission for Paul Whiteman's jazz band; the terms of the commission were set out in a contract, signed on 13 July 1944 (see figs. 9.4a–c). Finally, in May of 1945, he arranged it for full symphony orchestra. Although 1945 saw both this and the two-piano arrangement in print, publication of the jazz-band version was delayed until 1949 and then did not see the light of day again for almost a half-century, in 1996.

The metamorphosis of the two-piano *Scherzo* into the dance-band version is readily perceptible on an ozalid copy in the Paul Sacher Stiftung, Basel, of the arrangement for Whiteman's band, made from the first page of Stravinsky's original transparencies. He began the task simply enough, penciling indications for jazz-band orchestration into the

FIGURE 9.2
Scherzo à la Russe, p. 1. UBC Stravinsky Collection, no. 80.

ozalid copy made from the first page of his original (UBC) transparency of the two-piano *Scherzo*. This reveals him changing his mind about the details: for example, in measure 4 of the Stiftung ozalid copy, he had contemplated reinforcing the sustained three-trumpet triads with one oboe and two saxophones in eighth-notes (fig. 9.5). The printed version reveals that he abandoned this strategy.

FIGURE 9.3
Scherzo à la Russe, p. 13. UBC Stravinsky Collection, no. 80.

The name "Severine," written in Stravinsky's hand, appears in the upper left of the initial page of the Stiftung ozalid containing indications for the jazz-band version. This is certainly Severin E. Kavenoki, Stravinsky's New York agent in 1936–37. Kavenoki's papers in the New York Public Library show that he remained in touch with Stravinsky at least through 1940. Unfortunately, the reason Stravinsky wrote his name on the

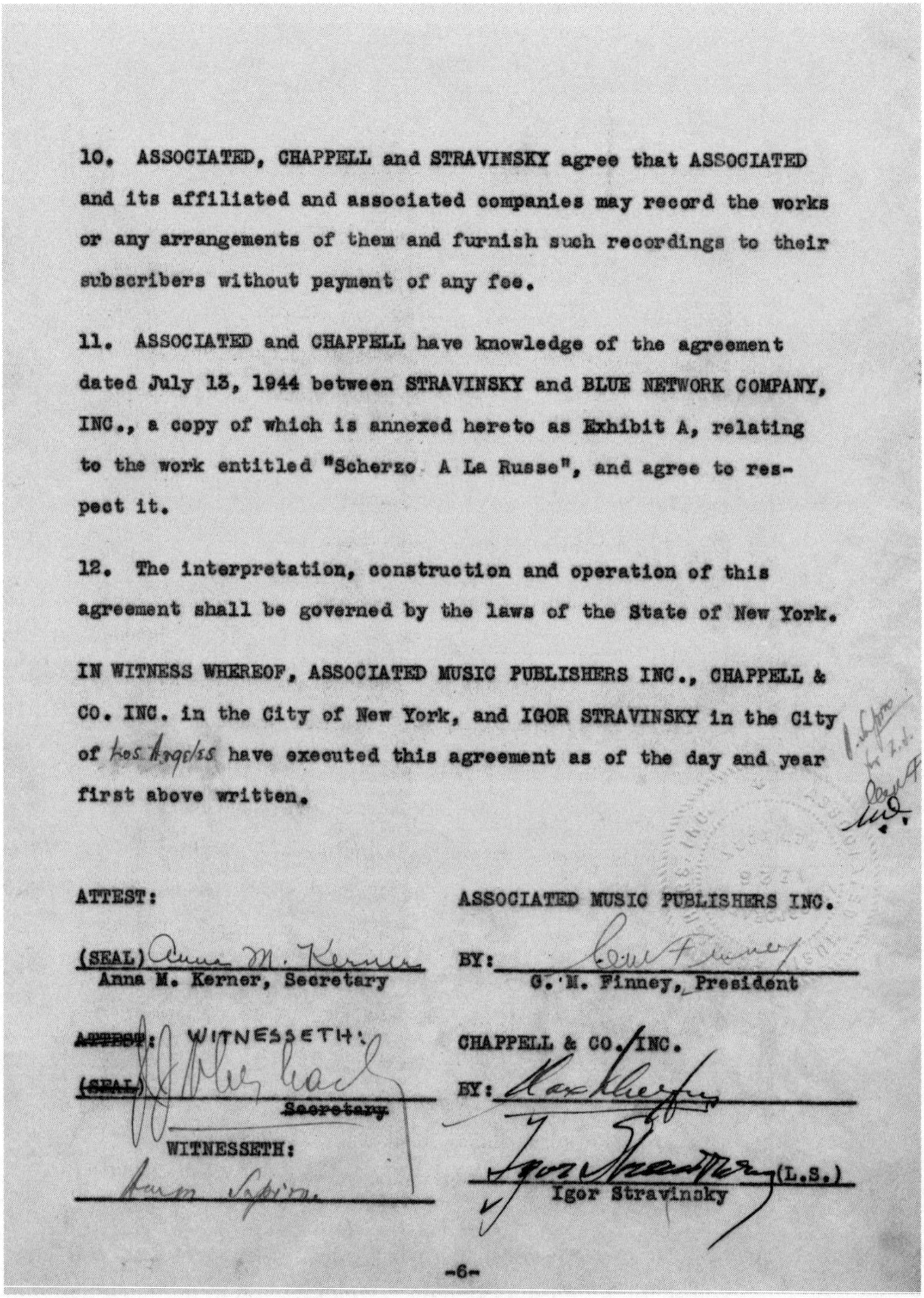

10. ASSOCIATED, CHAPPELL and STRAVINSKY agree that ASSOCIATED and its affiliated and associated companies may record the works or any arrangements of them and furnish such recordings to their subscribers without payment of any fee.

11. ASSOCIATED and CHAPPELL have knowledge of the agreement dated July 13, 1944 between STRAVINSKY and BLUE NETWORK COMPANY, INC., a copy of which is annexed hereto as Exhibit A, relating to the work entitled "Scherzo A La Russe", and agree to respect it.

12. The interpretation, construction and operation of this agreement shall be governed by the laws of the State of New York.

IN WITNESS WHEREOF, ASSOCIATED MUSIC PUBLISHERS INC., CHAPPELL & CO. INC. in the City of New York, and IGOR STRAVINSKY in the City of Los Angeles have executed this agreement as of the day and year first above written.

ATTEST: ASSOCIATED MUSIC PUBLISHERS INC.

(SEAL) *Anna M. Kerner*   BY: *C. M. Finney*
Anna M. Kerner, Secretary   G. M. Finney, President

ATTEST: WITNESSETH: CHAPPELL & CO. INC.

(SEAL)   BY: *Max Dreyfus*
         Secretary

        WITNESSETH:
                                       Igor Stravinsky (L.S.)
                                       Igor Stravinsky

-6-

FIGURE 9.4a
Page 6 of a seven-sheet agreement between Stravinsky in Los Angeles and Associated Music Publishers Inc. and Chappell and Co. Inc. in New York, signed below on the right. UBC Stravinsky Collection, no. 81, item 2.

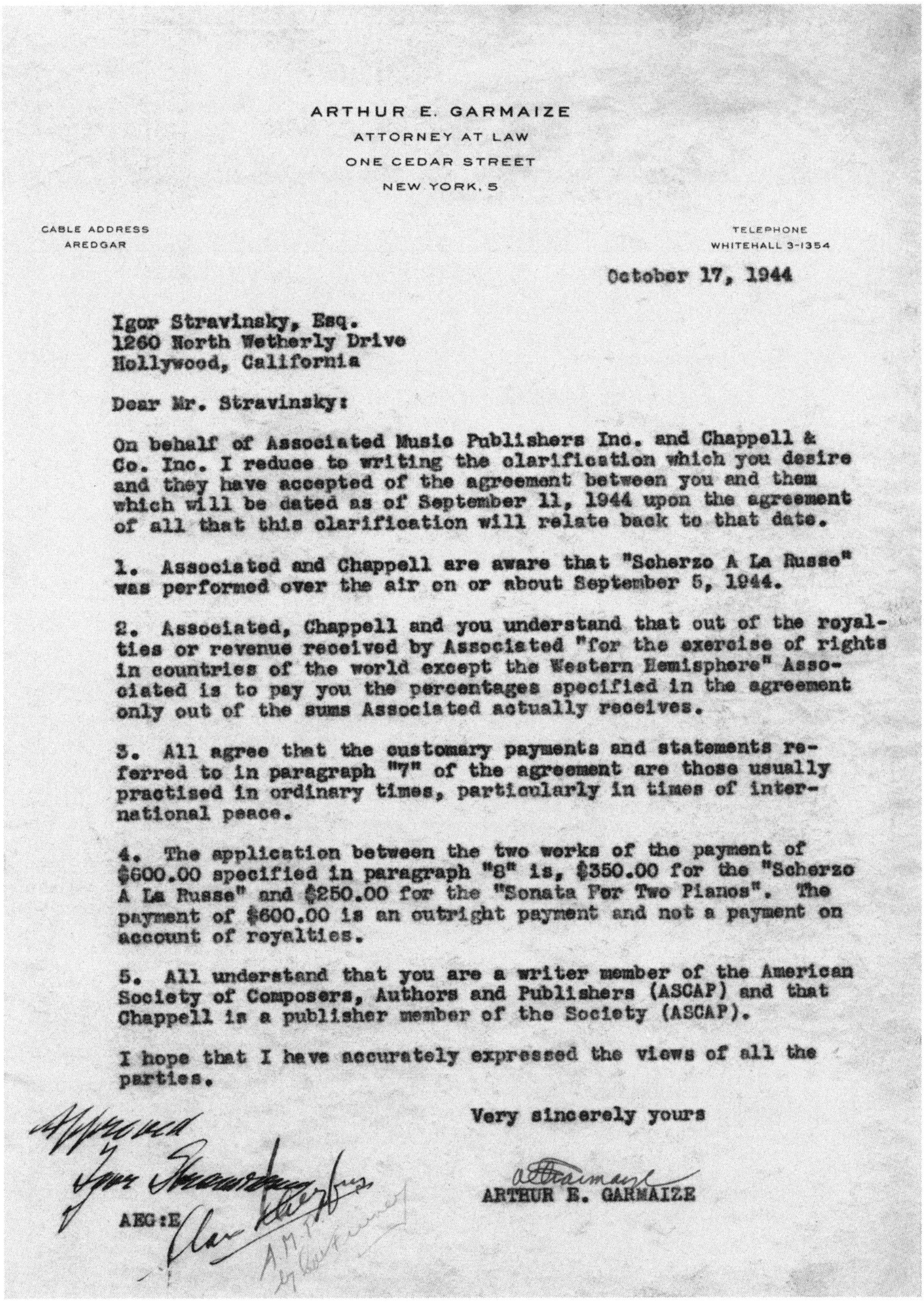

ARTHUR E. GARMAIZE
ATTORNEY AT LAW
ONE CEDAR STREET
NEW YORK, 5

CABLE ADDRESS
AREDGAR

TELEPHONE
WHITEHALL 3-1354

October 17, 1944

Igor Stravinsky, Esq.
1260 North Wetherly Drive
Hollywood, California

Dear Mr. Stravinsky:

On behalf of Associated Music Publishers Inc. and Chappell &
Co. Inc. I reduce to writing the clarification which you desire
and they have accepted of the agreement between you and them
which will be dated as of September 11, 1944 upon the agreement
of all that this clarification will relate back to that date.

1. Associated and Chappell are aware that "Scherzo A La Russe"
was performed over the air on or about September 5, 1944.

2. Associated, Chappell and you understand that out of the royalties or revenue received by Associated "for the exercise of rights
in countries of the world except the Western Hemisphere" Associated is to pay you the percentages specified in the agreement
only out of the sums Associated actually receives.

3. All agree that the customary payments and statements referred to in paragraph "7" of the agreement are those usually
practised in ordinary times, particularly in times of international peace.

4. The application between the two works of the payment of
$600.00 specified in paragraph "8" is, $350.00 for the "Scherzo
A La Russe" and $250.00 for the "Sonata For Two Pianos". The
payment of $600.00 is an outright payment and not a payment on
account of royalties.

5. All understand that you are a writer member of the American
Society of Composers, Authors and Publishers (ASCAP) and that
Chappell is a publisher member of the Society (ASCAP).

I hope that I have accurately expressed the views of all the
parties.

Very sincerely yours

ARTHUR E. GARMAIZE

AEG:E

FIGURE 9.4b
Single sheet of clarification among all parties of 17 October 1944. UBC Stravinsky Collection, no. 81, item 3.

THE BLUE NETWORK
BLUE NETWORK COMPANY, INC.
30 Rockefeller Plaza - Tel. CIrcle 7-5700
New York 20, N.Y.

July 13, 1944

Mr. Igor Stravinsky
c/o Miss Gretl Urban
c/o Associated Music Publishers Inc.
25 West 45th Street
New York, N.Y.

Dear Mr. Stravinsky:

This letter will confirm our mutual understanding as follows:

1. You agree to compose an original orchestral composition for an orchestra of approximately thirty-five pieces of our selection within the period hereinafter set forth for broadcasting over our facilities in a series of programs designed to present original compositions of outstanding composers.

2. You agree to submit your completed score within two months following the date of your acceptance of this agreement as indicated below. It is understood and agreed that commencing with the date of the delivery of your composition we shall have: (a) the right to broadcast the first radio performance of your composition within a period of three months after its delivery to us, (b) the right to give the first and only one public concert performance during the ensuing year, (c) the right to photostat your composition and copy the parts at our expense, and (d) the right to designate the orchestra to make the first recording of your composition and to have the composition identified with Blue Network on the labels of the recordings.

3. For all the rights in your composition granted to us in paragraph 2 hereof we agree to pay you and you agree to accept the sum of $500 on the day this agreement is executed by you. In addition, we agree to advance $500 to you at the time of the first radio performance of your composition which we agree shall be performed within a period of three months following the delivery of the score, and you hereby agree to pay over to us all royalties you receive from the publishers of your composition until such time as the aforesaid $500 advance has been repaid. It is understood and agreed that the advance of $500 is not to be repaid except insofar as that amount is forthcoming from royalties mentioned above.

EXHIBIT A, P. 1

FIGURE 9.4c

First page of a two-sheet agreement with The Blue Network, UBC Stravinsky Collection, no. 81, item 1.

FIGURE 9.5

Ozalid copy of *Scherzo à la Russe*. Igor Strawinsky Collection, Paul Sacher Foundation, Basel.

Stiftung ozalid for the Paul Whiteman version, four years after their last documented contact, will probably never be ascertained.

While scoring *Scherzo à la Russe* for Whiteman's band, Stravinsky sought help with unfamiliar instruments. Tansman later wrote that "often he would telephone me asking, for example: 'is the baritone sax written an octave higher or at the same octave it sounds?' "[102] Perhaps as a result of this reply, Stravinsky used the octave higher.

Tansman also observed that "the Russian quality of this short *Scherzo* . . . is amiable and placid, and recalls by its infectiousness certain turns of the airs in *Mavra*."[103] "Amiable" certainly, but on the whole this *Scherzo* is more rambunctious than Tansman's "placid," an adjective really suitable only for the first trio. Taruskin, however, shows that Tansman's intuition was correct regarding its Russian origin.

STRAVINSKY'S FAMILY IN WARTIME EUROPE

Stravinsky's method for communicating through Milhaud with his children in wartime Europe was already described by Andersson in his notebook entry for 24 June 1941. It was dangerous for Milhaud's parents in France and illegal for their son, Darius, in the United States.

Stravinsky also communicated with his children from early January of 1944 well into November of 1944 through Dr. Walter Adolphe de Bourg—a member of the Swiss delegation in Washington, DC, from about 1941—and on 26 April 1944 Stravinsky met him in Los Angeles.[104] Three letters to de Bourg in French from Stravinsky and references in sales catalogues to three other letters to him from Stravinsky (all six mailed to Washington in 1944) are known. Recently acquired, the first letter, of 5 January 1944 (like the next four), is available in the Stravinsky collection at UBC (fig. 9.6):

> 1260 N. Wetherly Drive
> Hollywood, 46, Cal.
> 5 January, 1944

Dear Monsieur de Bourg:

We were deeply moved by my son's [Theodore's] letter that you so kindly passed on to me. I thank you very much. I should like to use this occasion to send him word from me about us which you would be so good as to send on to him.

So here is the message:

1) Received his letter of 2 November,* [penciled here and in ink bottom right of page] the only one received since his letter of Jan 25. 43 as well as the one of 30 December.

2) I am leaving for concert tours and will be back at the end of January.

3) I have requested several times (since October) that the Swiss Bank Corporation of New York send my son Theodore dollars instead of Swiss francs, as granted by the license I obtained. Since my request has not been honored for reasons unknown to me, I have ordered the transfers be stopped (the free francs rate becoming an utter disaster). However, I am still working on it, and I have not lost hope that I can arrange a transfer of dollars for him, and not in Swiss fr.

4) By contrast, I just obtained a license to send monthly payments of $100 for my daughter-in-law, Denise, and the first transfer at the official rate went out on Dec. 29.

5) When I return, I shall try to arrange help through the Red Cross for my sick daughter [Milène], or at least to let her sanatorium [at Sancellemoz] know that I am good for any expenses that her state of health necessitates.

6) We are in good health. We are awaiting anxiously to hear news about our sick daughter's state of health and about everybody else. I expect to write again after my return.

I hope I am not taking too much advantage of your kindness, dear Monsieur de Bourg, and it is with that hope that I send you my sincere best wishes and gratitude.

[Signed] Igor Strawinsky

Walter de Bourg, Esq.

Legation de Suisse

Washington, D.C.

[handwritten in ink:] P.S. The current address of my son is: 40, rue du Marché, Genève.[105]

Vera Stravinsky's diary reveals that de Bourg and Stravinsky met in Los Angeles on 28 April 1944.

Knowledge of Stravinsky's second and third letters of 16 September and 22 October, respectively, comes solely from excerpts translated from the French in two US or British sales' catalogues,[106] both from the same and as yet unidentified dealer:

I am very surprised to learn of your upcoming departure for Switzerland, and greatly regret that I did not have a chance to get together with you this year. I am very touched by your proposition to transmit to my son news of us upon your arrival in Switzerland, and I thank you sincerely. . . . Since my son has been without news of us for so many months, would it be possible for you to send him a brief message now . . .

His third letter reads:

How kind you are to send me a copy of *The Swiss* with those remembrances, so dear to me, of my stay in your country which I love and will continue to love profoundly. Thank you, thank you a thousand times. I am going to San Francisco for three days and upon my return I will send you a final little note before you depart for Europe. I hope it will arrive in time.

Stravinsky kept his word. Returning to Hollywood on 27 October, he wrote de Bourg the next day (fig. 9.7). This fourth letter, 28 October 1944, was also in my collection. Significantly, perhaps, in view of the large (now empty) mailing envelope that concludes the present series, this letter is unfolded and lacks any envelope. Sent from Hollywood on 28 October, its first words relate to the two preceding letters:

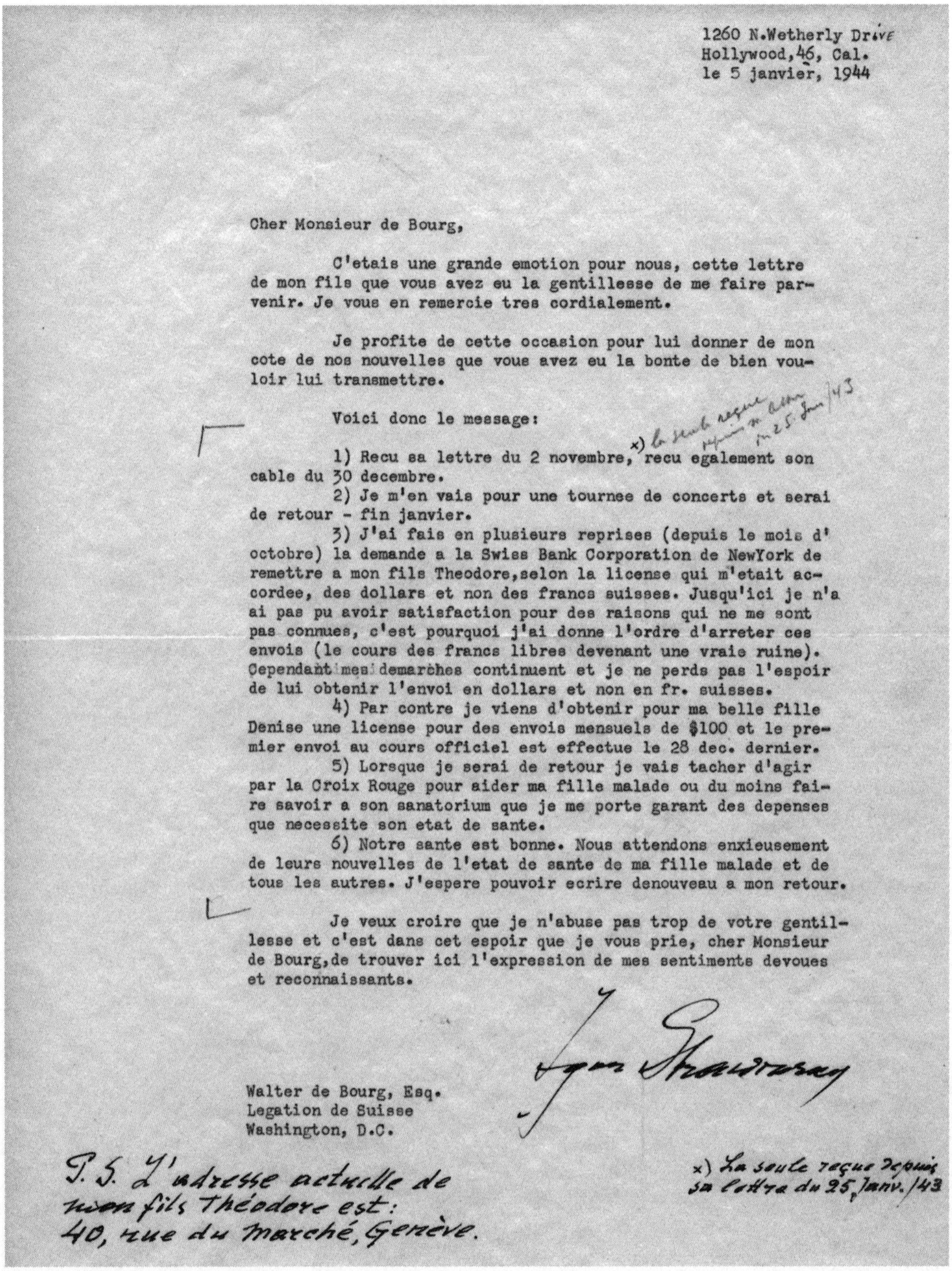

1260 N.Wetherly Drive
Hollywood, 46, Cal.
le 5 janvier, 1944

Cher Monsieur de Bourg,

C'etais une grande emotion pour nous, cette lettre de mon fils que vous avez eu la gentillesse de me faire parvenir. Je vous en remercie tres cordialement.

Je profite de cette occasion pour lui donner de mon cote de nos nouvelles que vous avez eu la bonte de bien vouloir lui transmettre.

Voici donc le message:

1) Recu sa lettre du 2 novembre, x) recu egalement son cable du 30 decembre.
2) Je m'en vais pour une tournee de concerts et serai de retour - fin janvier.
3) J'ai fais en plusieurs reprises (depuis le mois d'octobre) la demande a la Swiss Bank Corporation de NewYork de remettre a mon fils Theodore, selon la license qui m'etait accordee, des dollars et non des francs suisses. Jusqu'ici je n'a ai pas pu avoir satisfaction pour des raisons qui ne me sont pas connues, c'est pourquoi j'ai donne l'ordre d'arreter ces envois (le cours des francs libres devenant une vraie ruine). Cependant mes demarches continuent et je ne perds pas l'espoir de lui obtenir l'envoi en dollars et non en fr. suisses.
4) Par contre je viens d'obtenir pour ma belle fille Denise une license pour des envois mensuels de $100 et le premier envoi au cours officiel est effectue le 28 dec. dernier.
5) Lorsque je serai de retour je vais tacher d'agir par la Croix Rouge pour aider ma fille malade ou du moins faire savoir a son sanatorium que je me porte garant des depenses que necessite son etat de sante.
6) Notre sante est bonne. Nous attendons enxieusement de leurs nouvelles de l'etat de sante de ma fille malade et de tous les autres. J'espere pouvoir ecrire denouveau a mon retour.

Je veux croire que je n'abuse pas trop de votre gentillesse et c'est dans cet espoir que je vous prie, cher Monsieur de Bourg, de trouver ici l'expression de mes sentiments devoues et reconnaissants.

Walter de Bourg, Esq.
Legation de Suisse
Washington, D.C.

P.S. L'adresse actuelle de mon fils Théodore est: 40, rue du marché, Genève.

x) La seule reçue depuis sa lettre du 25. Janv./43

FIGURE 9.6
First Letter to Monsieur de Bourg, 5 Jan. 1944. Author's private collection.

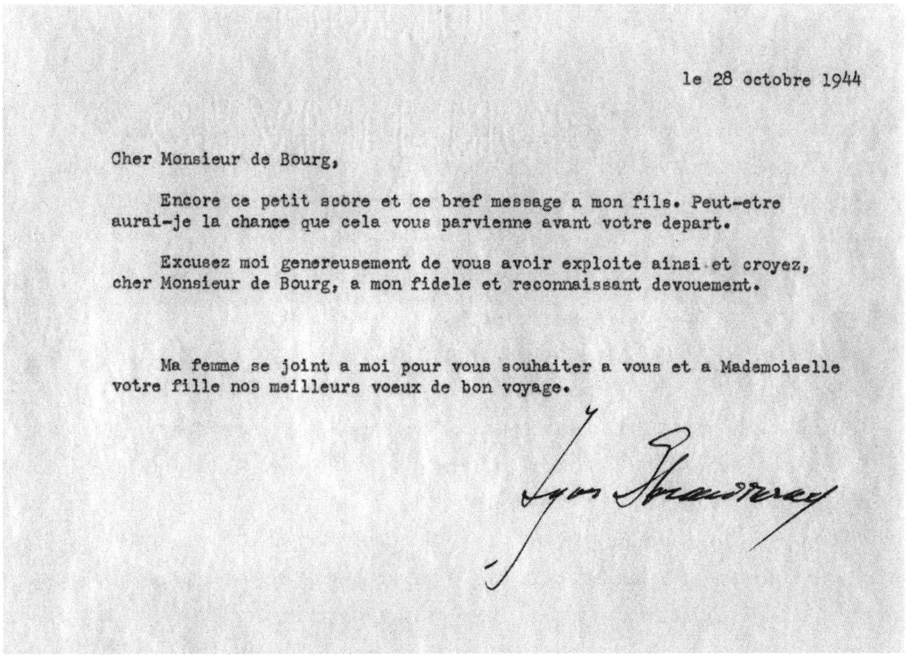

le 28 octobre 1944

Cher Monsieur de Bourg,

Encore ce petit score et ce bref message a mon fils. Peut-etre aurai-je la chance que cela vous parvienne avant votre depart.

Excusez moi genereusement de vous avoir exploite ainsi et croyez, cher Monsieur de Bourg, a mon fidele et reconnaissant devouement.

Ma femme se joint a moi pour vous souhaiter a vous et a Mademoiselle votre fille nos meilleurs voeux de bon voyage.

Igor Strawinsky

FIGURE 9.7
Fourth Letter to Monsieur de Bourg, 28 Oct. 1944. UBC Stravinsky Collection, no. 82.

Dear Mr. de Bourg:

In addition, this miniature score and this brief message for my son. Perhaps I shall be lucky enough for it to arrive before your departure.

Kindly forgive me for having thus exploited you, and please accept, dear Mr. de Bourg, my sincere gratitude.

My wife joins me in sending you and your daughter our best wishes for a good trip.

Igor Strawinsky.[107]

A fifth communication I acquired recently: a special-delivery envelope hand-addressed by Stravinsky with a red, white, and blue sticker: "VIA AIR MAIL." This large and now empty envelope, 8.5 × 10.5 in, could easily have contained a note, a miniature score, a postcard, or a photograph. Its contents are lost or perhaps were just dispersed among various dealers. He mailed this envelope from Hollywood on 15 November 1944 to Washington, DC, where it arrived two days later and was dispatched to de Bourg via the State Department. He sent still another letter (no. 6 in the present listing) to de Bourg on the address side of a photograph of himself, dating it simply as November, though surely in 1944. Its present location is unknown. The aforesaid large envelope may well have included this letter-photograph:

For Mr / Walter de Bourg / with all my / prayers for a good / and happy / return to Switzerland. / I Strawinsky / Hollywood, / Nov. 1944.[108]

Stravinsky's fourth letter reveals he was sending one of his sons a message and a
pocket score, presumably one of his most recently printed works. De Bourg could either
have delivered it personally or through the diplomatic pouch. He would have encountered little difficulty in sending it through occupied Europe by means of neutral Swiss
channels. But for which son? Because Stravinsky mentions a "petit score," I blithely
assumed in a previous study (well before acquaintance with these letters) that the "fils"
in question was his pianist son, Soulima, in occupied Paris, rather than the "fils ainé,"
his artist son Théodore, in Switzerland.

Yet the fourth letter was certainly intended for Théodore. Despite a career in painting,
Théodore was sufficiently qualified, and just then uniquely positioned, to appreciate
receiving a miniature score of one of his father's works. Like all his siblings, he first
studied piano with his father, playing the Three Easy Pieces and Five Easy Pieces, four-
hands.[109] Both sets were published in 1917,[110] when Théodore was ten years old, though
presumably he played them even earlier from handwritten copies. He continued his
study with various teachers; for example, when the family moved to Nice in 1924, he
worked with Alexander Nápravník.[111] Théodore's cousin, Tanya, visiting the family in
Nice, wrote home to Leningrad at the beginning of 1926: "Fedya [Théodore] has given
up music lessons, as he's taking painting so seriously. But he understands music very
well; he's musically educated, and he seems to me very talented."[112]

By November of 1944, when de Bourg left for Switzerland, Théodore was probably
already at work on the little book Le Message d'Igor Strawinsky, which he ultimately
signed "Summer 1948." Containing a photograph of his father dated that September, it
was printed in November. In respect to Stravinsky's letter of 28 October 1944 to de
Bourg, the "miniature score" was not the Mass: Stravinsky was still composing the Kyrie
and Gloria, not finishing them until just before Christmas, and the entire work was
completed only on 15 March 1948. Those two movements were not performed until 26
February 1947, by the Harvard University Music Club in Paine Hall, from which occasion, forty-one years later, the former graduate student El Forbes still recalled "the
excitement."[113]

Even though Théodore's book occasionally quotes Tansman's Igor Strawinsky, published just a few months earlier in Paris, Théodore was the more up-to-date, because he
mentions the Mass as "just composed" (undoubtedly thus informed by his father).[114] In
a letter to Théodore, dated 7 January 1949, the composer called Tansman's study "a bore,
unintelligent and unconvincing." In the same letter he praised his son's book as "the first
one about my music that entirely satisfies me."[115]

The value of Théodore's little book is sometimes underestimated. Commissioned for
its English translation by Stravinsky himself in January of 1952, one of its translators
called it a "small exercise in hagiography," and one of its publisher's referees deemed it

"not only worthless but detrimental."[116] These critics undervalue some acute observations by Théodore about his father when composing. For example, Théodore describes how his father always needed physical contact with the sonorous material at the piano. He would "re-éprouver en quelque sorte par l'ouie chaque accord, chaque intervalle, chaque sequence de notes, etc." (108). This particular observation was picked up by several others, including Théodore's younger brother. Years later, Soulima paraphrased it for one of his piano students. Soulima remembered "hearing him at the piano for hours, intently testing one chord after another, sometimes altering the spacing of a chord slightly."[117]

When de Bourg departed in November of 1944, the most recent works published in miniature score were *Danses concertantes* and *Circus Polka*, both advertised in June of 1944.[118] *Four Norwegian Moods*, extolled at Christmas that year as "music [of] exquisite delicacy," was perhaps ready as well, because Stravinsky had received proofs the previous June.[119] Since Théodore (unlike Tansman) mentions in his book only the *Danses concertantes*, in print since June,[120] the *Danses* may well have been the "petit score" transported by de Bourg.

Premiering the two-piano version of *Scherzo à la Russe* with Nadia Boulanger at Mills College just three days before his letter to de Bourg would surely have brought back memories of playing his two-piano music during the late 1930s with Soulima in France, Germany, and South America. It would also have rekindled Boulanger's own memories of having taught Soulima theory in prewar France: happier and more propitious times for this second son than what befell him during World War II. Although not a French citizen, Soulima was quickly conscripted into that country's army. Demobilized during the German occupation, he was said by tattlers Souvtchinsky, Nabokov, and Poulenc to have collaborated by giving piano recitals for Germans in Paris in 1941 and even *wishing* to do so in Germany. Yet, at one of the Paris concerts late in the spring of 1941 featuring *Les Noces* led by Charles Munch, not only Soulima but also Poulenc himself played one of the pianos.[121] Obviously, neither Munch nor Poulenc were collaborationists. Soulima was also accused of having published two articles in German newspapers in 1941.[122] Craft, who *said* he liked Soulima, first became acquainted when he and his family arrived in New York on 17 June 1948.[123]

Nijinsky famously remarked in 1916 that Stravinsky often acted "like an emperor, and his wife and children are his servants and soldiers."[124] Craft wrote massively on the subject, although one wonders whether in 1956 Stravinsky really said to Morton that "[Soulima] is very stupid,"[125] particularly since the insufficiently identified source remains unlocated.[126] Though hotly contested by Stravinsky's late assistant, Walsh's essays about both sons display perception and compassion. For those interested in the symbiosis of genius and male offspring, Joseph's moving portrait of Soulima, his piano-teacher during 1968–70 at the University of Illinois (Urbana), and their continuing friendship until Soulima's death in 1994, set out in his chapter "Fathers and Sons: Remembering Sviatoslav Soulima," is engrossing reading, as is Levitz's recent discussion.[127]

ÉLÉGIE

The pleasure that Stravinsky took in the early 1940s when he played Bach fugues "quite a few times" with James Sample—one man taking the upper staff, the other the lower—was recalled late in life by Sample. Often asking to replay some passage or other, Stravinsky was both incredulous at and humbled by Bach's skills and facility in composition. In truth, good contrapuntal writing and fugue were never far from Stravinsky's mind. In the World War II period he often employed fugue. It appears in the third movement (composed at Harvard in 1939) of the Symphony in C; in "Eulogy," the first movement of the 1943 Ode; in the second movement of the 1942–44 Sonata for Two Pianos; in his 1944 cantata, *Babel;* and preceding the coda to the finale of the Symphony in Three Movements; but most ingeniously perhaps in his 1944 *Élégie.*

By mid-November 1944, encouraged by Nadia Boulanger, Stravinsky finished composing the central section of *Élégie* for solo viola for Germain Prévost in New York.[128] *Élégie* is no exemplum of the Gallicized "neoclassicism" dear to the hearts of Stravinsky's Russo-Parisian critics in the 1920s and 1930s. Had Sample (who played viola) still been living in New York, Stravinsky might have shown his fellow Bach enthusiast *Élégie's* deliberate evocation of the fugal movements in the solo violin sonatas and partitas. Instead, late in December of 1948, he asked another relatively new Californian, Michael Mann, youngest of Thomas Mann's four sons, to perform *Élégie,* coaching Mann on it in his study at home.[129]

Prévost gave the world premiere at the Library of Congress on 26 January 1945, the day before Stravinsky arrived with Vera by train in New York. Prévost then played it for him privately on 7 February.[130] Stravinsky had created a miraculous two-voice fugue, complete with opening subject and answer, episode and middle entry, a C-pedal, and a final pair of entries in inversion and stretto. Even if, as noted by Balanchine, *Élégie* does not really exhibit "all the possibilities of a two-voiced fugue"—its subject lacks augmentation and diminution—the great choreographer revealed the scope of his own musical training and his profound musicality[131] in detailed remarks. He choreographed *Élégie* in 1945 and again in later years.[132]

The year ended with a cancelled conducting opportunity late in November. After the 10 September premiere in New York of Balanchine's staging of *Danses concertantes* for Serge Denham's Ballet Russe de Monte Carlo, conducted by the company's Emanuel Balaban, Denham telephoned Stravinsky on 2 November and invited him to rehearse and conduct *Danses* when the Ballet Russe was in San Francisco.[133] Scheduled for 28 November, the company's final evening at the Opera House,[134] the performance of *Danses* was cancelled,[135] but Denham and company staged it in Los Angeles, 1 and 6 December. Walsh states that Stravinsky conducted the first performance, but Vera reports only that he was "pleased" at its first rehearsal on 1 December. One Los Angeles reviewer, looking forward to the 6 December performance, wrote confusingly: "it is possible that Stravinsky will conduct one performance of 'Dances [*sic*] Concertantes' next week,"[136] perhaps indicating that Balaban had been the conductor on 1 December. Vera's diary for 6 December reports that she and her husband attended a performance of *Danses*, without indicating any conducting.

A final excursion, on 28 December, was with Vera driving the composer to Szigeti's house at nearby Palos Verdes. Its significance for Stravinsky's career is discussed in the next chapter.

10

EXCURSIONS (1945–EARLY 1946)

CONCERT APPEARANCES

1–4 February: New York Philharmonic

5 February: Philharmonic (recording)

8 February: rehearses Two-Piano Sonata with Persichetti

14 February: New York Philharmonic, recording *Apollon*

21 February: Philadelphia, Lecture and Two-Piano Sonata with Persichetti

1 March: Rochester Philharmonic

5 March: Montreal Orchestre Philharmonique with cellist Marcel Hubert

8 April: Beverly Hills chez Atwater Kent with Szigeti

15 May: Los Angeles Philharmonic, Shrine (half-concert with Klemperer)

11 October: Records *Duo concertant* with Szigeti in Los Angeles

18 November: Janssen rehearses and premieres *Babel* in Stravinsky's and Schoenberg's presence

24, 25–27 January 1946: New York Philharmonic premiere: Symphony in Three Movements

28 January: Philharmonic recording: 1945 *Firebird Suite*, *Fireworks*, Symphony in Three Movements

30 January: Philharmonic CBS Broadcast: *Symphony of Psalms*, *Apollon*, and 1945 *Firebird Suite*

The ultimate defeat of Japanese forces became increasingly certain during the first months of 1945, and Hitler committed suicide on 30 April. After the relatively calm and comfortable domestic home life in Los Angeles of the war years, Stravinsky began to realize renewed opportunities for concert activity with the approaching end of the European conflict. On 10 December 1944 he wrote Vittorio Rieti in New York that he was trying to substitute the newly completed *Scènes de ballet* for the *Danses concertantes* with the New York Philharmonic at the beginning of February but added that "the few rehearsals available deprive me of the possibility of performing my Symphony [in C],"[1] doubtlessly remembering the rhythmic difficulties of its third movement and Stokowski's disastrous broadcast. From early February through March he had concerts and broadcasts in New York City and Rochester, a lecture and piano performance in Philadelphia, and a radio address plus concert in Montreal; the latter was a first venture beyond US borders since the war began.

Following rehearsals on 30 and 31 January, Stravinsky led the New York Philharmonic in several concerts. Each featured *Scènes de ballet,* Ode, *Four Norwegian Moods, Circus Polka,* and the 1923–24 Piano Concerto with Beveridge Webster as soloist. Seated in a box in Carnegie Hall for the first of these concerts were, among others, Vera, Rieti, Haieff, and banker-financier Arthur Sachs. As if to celebrate in advance Stravinsky's American citizenship conferred near the end of December of 1945, Arthur Sachs, on behalf of the New York Philharmonic Society, commissioned a "Victory Symphony."[2] It was to be fulfilled with a work he was already composing: the Symphony in Three Movements, his first large-scale work entirely conceived in the United States.[3] He had already finished two movements, and the finale saw revision and completion between 7 August and 14 October.[4] It premiered early in 1946.

Also attending Stravinsky's New York winter concerts was Virgil Thomson. On 2 February a surprisingly genial Thomson allowed that Ode "retains its elegance on rehearing and gains intellectual interest"; that *Four Norwegian Moods* was "not distant at all" but "warm and picturesque and cheerful, wonderfully melodious and impeccably tailored"; and that *Circus Polka* was "a lively picture . . . of the sawdust ring."[5] The latter was recorded at the 4 February Sunday-afternoon concert broadcast from Carnegie Hall, its national radio premiere. Before long, US troops deployed abroad also heard it, with an introduction by a well-known comedian: "This is Jack Benny talking. I'd like to say hello again this month and introduce a very unusual record: Eyegor [thus pronounced!] Stravinsky conducting the New York Philharmonic Orchestra in his own work entitled Circus Polka. Here it is on V[ictory]-Discs, so let's all listen."[6]

After rehearsing with Vincent Persichetti in New York on 8 February, and repeating his Mills College lecture at Philadelphia on the twenty-first—performing there his Two-Piano Sonata with Persichetti for an arts organization—Stravinsky returned to New York. Entraining on 26 February with Vera for Rochester ("very provincial"), he rehearsed the Rochester Philharmonic from the twenty-seventh. Vera's verdict was confirmed by one Rochester newspaper that failed even to mention Stravinsky's presence in that upstate outpost.[7] After the concert they took the night train to Montreal.[8]

Arriving in Montreal's Windsor train station on 2 March for several rehearsals with the city's Orchestre Philharmonique, Stravinsky was interviewed at the station by Thomas Archer, the savvy music critic for the *Gazette:* "The Circus Polka, he stressed, is not a contribution to the 'American Scene.' Rather, is it an aural approach to the art of Toulouse-Lautrec, the great French painter, 'the caustic recorder of the dance halls of Montmartre.' "[9] Two days later, when interviewed by Archer for the Canadian Broadcasting Corporation, Stravinsky expanded this a little: "It is a musical equivalent of a painting by Toulouse-Lautrec, a satire on a familiar subject. Just as Toulouse-Lautrec depicted a Montmartre scene in terms of visual objects, so the Circus Polka suggests a typical circus scene in terms of sound."[10] Stravinsky's insistence that *Circus Polka* was really a tribute to the grand tradition of late nineteenth-century French painters, rather than a mere commission from

Ringling Brothers, flies in the face of his earlier positions since 1934 about music being unable to express anything other than itself, reemphasized in 1946 to Dahl: "My music expresses nothing of a *realistic* character."[11] He neglected to explain how or to what degree.

After a rehearsal at which he was photographed rehearsing the Orchestre Philharmonique (fig. 10.1), on the evening of 5 March Stravinsky led a program of old and new favorites: the 1919 *Firebird Suite*, Tchaikovsky's Second ("Little Russian") Symphony, *Scènes de ballet,* and the *Circus Polka.* Unusually for him this late in his conducting life, he also led the 1877 Concerto in D Minor by Edouard Lalo with the visiting French cellist Marcel Hubert, with whom Stravinsky had conferred in New York on 18 February. Vera Stravinsky reported the concert "a tremendous success"; after it, "many young people following him to his car."[12] Her opinion is buttressed by further details found in Archer's review (see below).

Later that March, back in Hollywood, Stravinsky offered some coaching to pianist Harry Kaufman, who had been Dushkin's accompanist in 1941 for Tango, and subsequently for Josef Szigeti. A photograph of Szigeti, Stravinsky, and Kaufman survives.[13] Szigeti and Stravinsky performed his *Duo concertant* on the afternoon of 8 April. That evening, the three musicians and their wives were honored at the Beverly Hills mansion of the wealthy inventor and music-lover A. Atwater Kent.

Several events about this time foreshadowed the end of Stravinsky's role as a pianist in public life, already predictable from his 1939 letters to Kall. On the evening of 28 December 1944 at Szigeti's house in Palos Verde, Stravinsky and Szigeti had rehearsed for no less than seven hours.[14] The result of their intense practice was captured in a recording and photograph in a Hollywood studio almost ten months later, on 11 (or 13) October;[15] it depicts them "relaxing after recording Stravinsky's *Duo concertant.*" The recording was released well after the two musicians had performed the *Duo* again, this time in New York on 8 February 1946 for a Philharmonic pension concert. It was heard by young Robert Craft.[16]

This pension concert was Stravinsky's last public appearance as a pianist. The reason for his retirement seems clear. Practicing and rehearsing for single concert events and recording did not greatly remunerate him and took away precious hours from composing. Conducting was more lucrative and coaching more efficient. The role change is evident enough in the March 1945 Kaufman photograph but even more so in one taken on 7 February 1946, where Stravinsky is seen coaching Claudio Arrau in his *Serenade en la* for the pension concert.[17] Years later, Arrau gratefully but tersely acknowledged this tutoring: "Serenade in A, . . . studied with the composer."[18]

While revising and arranging *Scherzo à la Russe* for full symphony orchestra during the summer of 1945 and devoting hours and hours to his exceptionally beautiful chirography on ozalid transparencies,[19] Stravinsky had by no means forgotten his last student, Andersson, not yet two years deceased. Andersson had given him, in September of 1941, a stock of that very large preprinted paper that so delighted him and on which he was

STRAVINSKY HERE

Igor Stravinsky was photographed for The Gazette in rehearsal for tonight's concert at the St. Denis. The celebrated Russian composer conducts the Montreal Philharmonic Orchestra in his own Fire-Bird Suite, Circus Polka and his Ballet Music written for Billy Rose's The Seven Lively Arts.

Caroline Harder Photo.

FIGURE 10.1
Stravinsky in rehearsal.
Montreal Gazette, 5 March 1945, 2.

now laboring. The difference between Stravinsky—composer-musician and self-styled "inventor of music"—and Andersson—composer-industrialist whom Stravinsky in 1966 called "an inventor of gadgets"—could not be more precisely formulated than in their dissimilar observations concerning this particular custom-printed music paper. About 9 September 1941, Andersson had written in his notebook: "S[travinsky] liked my paper. Said 'it had solidity and honor'" (54). The pedestrian and objective Andersson then added: "I told him the proportions come from the standard 28 × 34 sheets." Proof of the recollection lies in two orchestral works. Stravinsky had already used several sheets of Andersson's paper for his 1943 revision of the "Danse sacrale" from the *Rite*.[20] But in his orchestral arrangement of "Trio 2" from the *Scherzo à la Russe* he superstitiously inked out Andersson's name, printed at the bottom.[21]

On 18 November 1945 in downtown Los Angeles, Werner Janssen led the world premiere of the *Genesis Suite*. The *Los Angeles Times* was perceptive neither in expectation nor evaluation: "We expected a Mass from Stravinsky's 'Babel,' but it proved to be one with the others in its use of the chorus and the modern idiom."[22] Although Lawrence Morton found Schoenberg's Prelude to be the most successful movement, he believed that the "*Genesis [Suite]* was, from the very birth of the idea, doomed to be a hopelessly insoluble mixture of styles, techniques and attitudes." In *Babel* he found references to the *Symphony of Psalms*, the latter of "far greater nobility and propulsion."[23] "I wish it were possible to say that 'Genesis' is a great and important work. Unfortunately that can not be said. Only Schoenberg's piece seemed to me to be equal to the occasion."[24] The editor of *Pacific Coast Musician*, Stravinsky's perpetual adversary, offered a far more blunt assessment: "Toch's *The Covenant* . . . would have served vastly better as a closing to the entire suite than Stravinsky's *Babel*. This section of the work vindicated this writer's belief that except where Stravinsky uses borrowed material, he has not composed anything of real value since *The Firebird*."[25] Perhaps Steele's irritation stemmed from what he considered presumption on the part of the composer. Stravinsky's comments about *Babel* were the only ones by a contributing composer to be included in the program notes for the concert and subsequent recording. Notes for the other works were written by Steele's editorial colleague and Los Angeles newspaper critic Richard Drake Saunders.

On 16, 17, and 18 November Stravinsky attended Janssen's three rehearsals for the world premiere, the latter two in the afternoon. Apparently, Schoenberg went only to the final dress rehearsal on the afternoon of the eighteenth for his own contribution to the *Genesis Suite*. The two composers sat on opposite sides of the hall, just as they did at the premiere.[26] Schoenberg famously quipped after *Babel*'s dress rehearsal that "it didn't end; it just stopped."[27] The explanation may well lie in that final low B-natural for the bassoon. At the dress rehearsal it may not have materialized. The extreme rarity in Stravinsky's works of any soft, sustained, and unprepared low B for the bassoon where it is not doubled by some other instrument is owing to the bassoon's characteristic tendency toward sharpness for this pitch, plus a concomitant difficulty in sounding it softly.[28] The single, identical low B sounded so briefly and softly by trombone 3 at the close of *Babel* provides no real cover. Perhaps, since the other two instances where Stravinsky ventures this same soft note for bassoon concern death, this one signals, if not death, the desertion of the Babel tower and dispersal of its inhabitants.

COMPOSING THE SYMPHONY IN THREE MOVEMENTS

The Symphony in Three Movements, finished in 1945, Stravinsky's last work composed during World War II, and also his last symphony, was not premiered until 1946. It has been thoroughly searched for octatonic writing, particularly in its finale. The composer's reliance on Collection I is regarded as a "triumph of the octatonic imagination."[29] Recent analysis of its outer movements, under headings of "Generative Cells" and "Metric Shifts,"[30] discloses other features. Yet still another aspect of this symphony merits investigation here—namely, the question of whether Stravinsky intended to write a programmatic work. Although we may never know, octatonicism, generative cells, metric shifts, and program might be connected.

A decade after these analyses, Craft was the first to note a compositional alteration Stravinsky made on 7 August 1945 in the symphony's full draft-score for the close of the finale.[31] His sketch-score had originally closed this movement at the end of rehearsal number 195: +2 (page 96 in the 1946 edition) with three measures that included E-flats from Collection II (also in Collection III), thus continuing their presence from the preceding three measures (p. 95).

By removing those E-flats in his full draft-score from the three measures that now precede the final sustained chord, Stravinsky could have been restricting himself to pitches solely in Collection I. These pitches at reh. 195: −1 now comprise what might be loosely described as reiterations of a first-inversion minor-seventh chord built on B-flat. The last half-dozen iterations alternate the lowest pitch of seventh chords between D-natural and D-flat (in trombone 1, for example), all six notes of this chord perhaps drawn from Collection I.

Perhaps recalling that his commission the previous mid-February from the New York Philharmonic was for a "Victory Symphony,"[32] and surely affected by news about the bomb dropped on Hiroshima on 6 August, Stravinsky changed the ending in his full draft-score the very next day.[33]

The Symphony in Three Movements now ends on a D-flat major chord with an added sixth, all these pitches also derivable from Collection I, plus a much more weakly placed E-flat, perhaps drawn from Collection II (also in Collection III).[34] Yet Stravinsky's designation in 1961 of this chord as a "rather too commercial, D-flat sixth chord—instead of the expected C" suggests that he derived it from tonal practice. With these alterations he thus avoided closing on any "expected C," as Stravinsky told his assistant, c. 1962.[35] Any "expected" pitch of C would inevitably have pointed to Collection II (or III). On the full

EXAMPLE 10.1

Stravinsky, Symphony in Three Movements, third movement, reh. 194–95.

draft-score, at the lower edge of this pair of newly added measures, Stravinsky wrote "August 7, 1945."

Having made such important observations, their discoverer did not run very far with them. Perhaps such reticence stemmed from a remark he uttered late in February of 1997: "I found the vogue of octatonic analysis tiresome."[36] Be this as it may, notice should also be taken of Stravinsky's compelling and masterful series of sustained wind chords in gradual diminutions from the second bar after rehearsal 194 (p. 95: reh. 194: +2) right up to the penultimate and unmetered chord, marked *lunga* (p. 96) (see ex. 10.1). Flanked at each end by a silent 1/4 measure, itself a standard big band effect, these eight chords provide an inscribed—assuredly, an inspired—series of shorter and shorter hammer blows. Clearly defined by brief silences: they can be re-grouped into diminishing lengths as: $\frac{12}{8} + \frac{12}{8} + \frac{6}{8} + \frac{5}{8} + \frac{4}{8} + \frac{3}{8} + \frac{3}{8} + \frac{3}{8}$. (See box 10.1.)

At first (reh. 194: +1), these chords are joined by the timpani (during the above-cited $\frac{12}{8} + \frac{12}{8}$), their player alternately striking C and E-natural. These two pitches could emanate from the sole instrument still demanding an ending on the C from Collection III, and ultimately with that Collection's E-natural sounding up to the *lunga*. Thereafter, by means of the timpanist's final roll during the *lunga* on an A-flat, perhaps drawn from Collection I, its previous strokes on C and E stemming from Collection III give pride of place to nearly all the other instruments during the newly added ending solidly grounded over a D-flat.

Convincingly for some listeners, it was argued in 1966 that Stravinsky's new ending and added date signaled victory over the Japanese and the approaching close of World War II. In this respect consideration might also be given to a gradually reducing number of rhythmic groupings of an eighth-note ostinato in the piano and low strings: reductions from fours to threes (beginning at reh. 194: +2). During those three measures from which Stravinsky eventually removed the E-flats (from reh. 195: –1), this rather erratic ostinato settles down to precisely *eight* final groups of melodically identical threes: successions on D, B-flat, and D-flat, these three pitches found in octatonic Collection I. The quantity of *eight* in this ostinato, as well as the *eight* durationally shrinking chords shown, might signal the month of August. Most people believed that the war would end shortly, and Stravinsky certainly knew that he would complete his Symphony in Three Movements in August.

A settling on pitches of C, E-flat, B-flat, and E-natural (from reh. 194) for the beginning of rapid eighth notes in bass instruments could point to Collection III. Yet the sustained D-flats and A-flats elsewhere, reinforced by a move upward (reh. 195: –1) to D-natural by French horn 2, trumpet 3, and second violin—first trombone seemingly unable to decide between D-flat or D-natural—could occur only in Collection I. Thus Stravinsky's early introduction of D-natural (reh. 194: +3) into the quickly moving eighth notes, plus D-natural into the above-mentioned sustained wind chords (see ex. 10.1), might already seem to point to an eventual, long-planned supremacy of this Collection I. Even the ostinato's ultimate compression (reh. 194: +3 and continuing) into eight constant metrically shifting repetitions of just three eighth-note pitches—D-natural, B-flat, and D-flat (reh 195: –1)—makes the utilization of Collection I conceivable, though hardly definitive.

Stravinsky's added pair of closing measures firmly move D-natural from the three-note ostinato down one-half step to a final sustained D-flat. It serves as the bass of an added-sixth chord, though this chord also incorporates an E-flat. Any "expected C" would have had to belong to Collection II or III, as does this E-flat, whereas D-flat belongs to Collections I and III. Although E-flat not only occurs in the beginning of and during the ostinato itself (reh. 194: +2 to 4), it had also once appeared (in the sketch-score) during the ostinato's concluding three measures. Stravinsky's elimination of this E-flat pitch during the last three measures of the full draft-score (reh. 195: –1), plus its ultimate reappearance during his new ending could show his intention to resolve all octatonic collisions—van den Toorn's "clashes"—in the entire movement. Such collisions would be mainly between Collections I and II. Stravinsky might have accomplished this goal by firmly grounding the tonality of his final chord around the added-sixth chord (also found in Collection I: D-flat, F, A-flat, B-flat), plus a comparatively weak E-flat, perhaps drawn from Collection II or III.

Despite this "foreign" E-flat, one might theorize that the weight of his final diatonic settling onto a D-flat added-sixth chord assures an ultimate triumph of Collection I over Collection II because Stravinsky scores his E-flat much less strongly in respect to other pitches in his final chord. The E-flat sounds solely in clarinet 3, trumpet 2, more faintly as the middle note of a triple stop in violin 2, and even less audibly within a chord for harp. At least five recordings survive with the composer himself conducting Symphony in Three Movements. Although two of them are unavailable (2 October 1956 with the Berlin Radio Symphony Orchestra, and 19 December 1958 with the BBC Symphony), the other three recordings—28 January 1946, with the New York Philharmonic, following its premiere (heard by Craft); 21 May 1954, with the Radio Symphony Orchestra of the Südwestfunk at Baden-Baden; and early in February of 1961, with the Columbia Symphony Orchestra in Hollywood—make the rogue E-flat audible, if a little subdued.[37]

Thus, the internal compositional logic of Stravinsky's new ending on 7 August 1945, possibly resolving a conflict between competing octatonic Collections I and II in favor of the former, is at least as—and for the present writer, more—convincing than his new ending's possible relevance to a historical event. This is something more than the moment earlier in the war when Stravinsky added words to the final page of *Scènes de ballet* concerning the liberation of Paris from the Germans.

Stravinsky might even have buried more than just the month of that historically significant date in the finale of the Symphony in Three Movements: the numbers seven (seventh day) in the symphony's newly sketched diatonic conclusion, and eight (August) in the movement's striking amount of octatonicism (however conflicted its several Collections). Yet both of these hypothetical constructions seem all too facile. Such analyses could well deflect listener and scholar from the real *coup de théâtre* of the Symphony's finale and its new ending—namely, "that the finale was not an expression of the excitement of the end of the war but the solution to a formal problem: how to unite two movements: one of them [I] violent with a percussive piano solo, the other [II] delicate and bardic, with a solo for harp."[38]

RECEPTION OF THE SYMPHONY IN THREE MOVEMENTS

Matters of a possible program associated with this symphony call for discussion of selected reactions after its premiere. For the 24 January 1946 world premiere in New York, Stravinsky (all too patently on his own hook) wrote the following notice (see fig. 10.2), first denying any program and then temporizing about it:

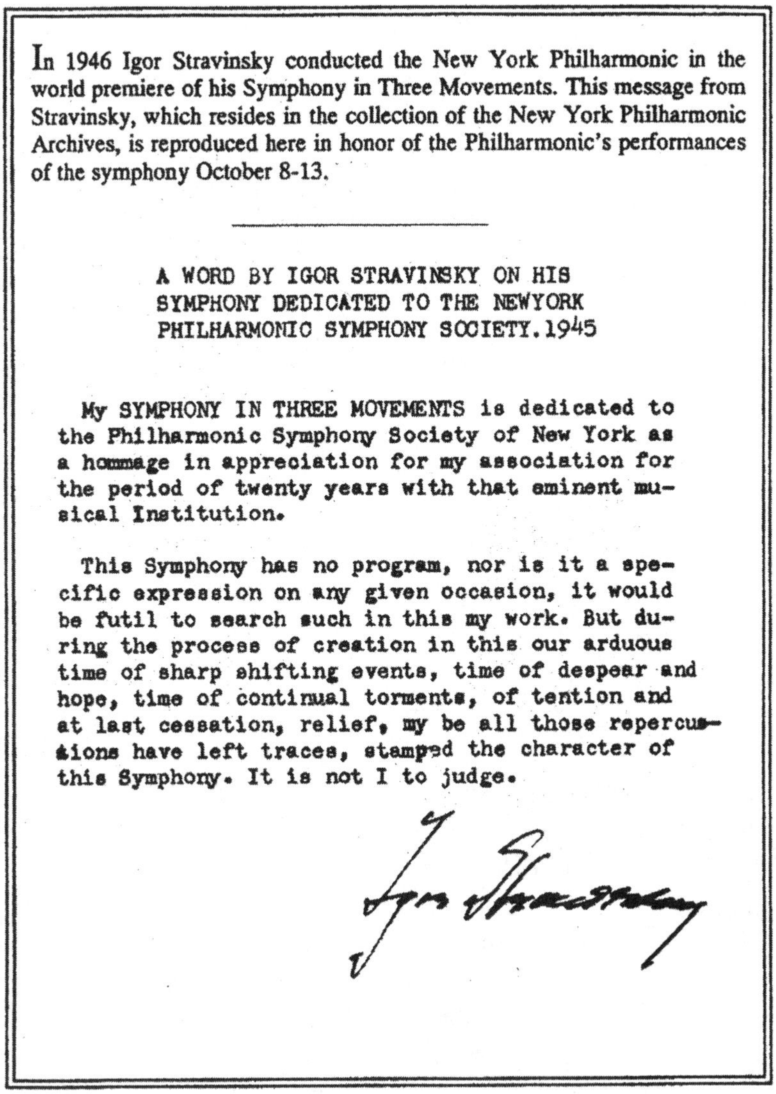

In 1946 Igor Stravinsky conducted the New York Philharmonic in the world premiere of his Symphony in Three Movements. This message from Stravinsky, which resides in the collection of the New York Philharmonic Archives, is reproduced here in honor of the Philharmonic's performances of the symphony October 8-13.

```
          A WORD BY IGOR STRAVINSKY ON HIS
          SYMPHONY DEDICATED TO THE NEWYORK
          PHILHARMONIC SYMPHONY SOCIETY.1945


      My SYMPHONY IN THREE MOVEMENTS is dedicated to
   the Philharmonic Symphony Society of New York as
   a hommage in appreciation for my association for
   the period of twenty years with that eminent mu-
   sical Institution.

      This Symphony has no program, nor is it a spe-
   cific expression on any given occasion, it would
   be futil to search such in this my work. But du-
   ring the process of creation in this our arduous
   time of sharp shifting events, time of despear and
   hope, time of continual torments, of tention and
   at last cessation, relief, my be all those repercus-
   sions have left traces, stamped the character of
   this Symphony. It is not I to judge.
```

FIGURE 10.2

Photo of Stravinsky's notice as printed in the New York Philharmonic Program of 24 January 1946. New York Philharmonic Archives.

A WORD BY IGOR STRAVINSKY ON HIS / SYMPHONY DEDICATED TO THE NEWYORK / PHILHARMONIC SYMPHONY SOCIETY. 1945

My SYMPHONY IN THREE MOVEMENTS is dedicated to the Philharmonic Symphony Society of New York as a homage in appreciation for my association for the period of twenty years with that eminent musical Institution.

This Symphony has no program, nor is it a specific expression on any given occasion, it would be futil to search such in this my work. But during the process of creation in this our arduous time of sharp shifting events, time of despear and hope, time of continual torments, of tention and at last cessation, relief, my be all those repercussions have left traces, stamped the character of this Symphony. It is not I to judge.

[signed:] Igor Stravinsky.[39]

That he wrote and then typed it himself is abundantly clear.

This notice was typed in Los Angeles on the same machine on which Stravinsky had written a response on 15 December 1945 to the M. Nizon in France who had inquired about "expression" (see chapter 2 and fig. 2.3). The Philharmonic's notice is the source for program notes in many later concert programs and commentary on record jackets.[40]

Dahl—with Stravinsky—had written extensive program notes in 1945 for the world premiere.[41] They thus enjoyed the composer's full approval and make no mention of any "expected C," merely of a "sonorous ending":

> Harmonically, too, the new Symphony speaks a language which its composer has not spoken for a long time. His immediately preceding diatonicism is widened immensely, and an integral part is played by many of the intervals which give the period of *Sacre* to *Symphonies of Winds* its character. . . . It cannot be coincidental that simultaneously . . . Stravinsky undertook a revision and reorchestration of parts of the "Sacre" and "Petrouchka."

These Stravinsky-Dahl program notes were frequently reprinted, either in part (e.g., the Boston Symphony premiere led by Stravinsky on 22 February 1946) or in whole (e.g., the Los Angeles Philharmonic premiere on 6 January 1947, led by Otto Klemperer).

Stravinsky's own phrase, "instead of the expected C," first appears late in the summer of 1962 in jacket notes for his fifth and last recording, made early in February of 1961. In 1963 these jacket notes, lightly edited, appeared in the fourth volume of Stravinsky-Craft conversations, *Dialogues and a Diary*, where they include "instead of the expected C" and appeared, further revised, almost four decades later in the posthumous omnibus, *Memories and Commentaries*.[42] That Stravinsky said nothing to Dahl in 1945–46 about his symphony's altered ending is, of course, entirely consistent with his previous failures to alert Nabokov and Urban to the "folk-song influence" in the Sonata for Two Pianos or in the *Scherzo à la Russe*.

Reviews of the world premiere of his final symphony were in general laudatory, if not uniformly perceptive.[43] Leading it on 24 January in the same city where two decades earlier he had first set foot in the United States elicited harsh criticism similar to what he had endured with the same orchestra in January of 1925 and some of it from the same "old famous ass," Olin Downes. Stravinsky's forty-one-year-antagonist pounced on what he believed was a major Stravinskian anomaly in respect to "expression":

It is sterile stuff, at best a reworking of ideas expressed much more vitally in preceding scores. Singular claims are made for this symphony in the program book. [Stravinsky's above letter is then repeated]

Isn't this just a little coy? The mere suggestion by Stravinsky himself, that his music might mean something apropos of the times we live in, is a contradiction of his long and oft repeated doctrine. . . .

But this music is inorganic in its effect. It does not convey the impression of a unified form, but of fragmentary and short-breathed ideas, alternated and in places monotonously repeated. War is one of these ideas, in itself of significance. Any of the movements could stop at various places, and the listener be neither surprised nor worse off for the cessation. The symphony does not add to Stravinsky's reputation.[44]

To be sure, Stravinsky was more than "a little coy." Nonetheless, Downes received a posthumous comeuppance in 1955. Having referred to him as cited above, and then in 1949 to him as "the old fool,"[45] Stravinsky refused to have Leopold Stokowski perform his Mass (1944–48) in Downes's memory, observing that "it would be an unkind irony."[46] Downes has rightfully been dubbed (by Walsh) "not a serious critic," but Stravinsky certainly read his reviews, no matter how much they upset him. Downes's phrase "war is one of these ideas," based on Dahl's "close to the core of a world at war" in his own program note, merits some pondering. Either or both might be a possible source for the detailed and highly descriptive wartime scenario for this symphony that Stravinsky put forward in the 1960s.

Because Stravinsky had the only score, neither Downes nor, apparently, anyone else had noticed a "dreadful error" by the solo cellist in the middle of the Symphony's second movement: he played "in the bass rather than the tenor clef," necessitating a rerecording session.[47] The sharp-eared Craft, then just twenty-three years old, and with his relationship with Stravinsky still in the future, noticed this while attending several rehearsals for the world premiere.[48] This raises an interesting question, never mentioned then or later by either of them: why didn't Stravinsky correct this fault in rehearsal? Presumably the cellist would have made the same error during rehearsals and not just at the performance. The mistake was then rectified at the recording made on Monday afternoon, 28 January.

For its sophisticated readership, the *New Yorker* ran an amusing interview with Stravinsky on the morning of the premiere. It reported him still having difficulties with English, and declaring "Bravo for the Construction" (corrected by Vera to "Constitution"). Perhaps thinking of his ill-received arrangement, Stravinsky then "backed up this statement by humming a few bars of 'The Star-Spangled Banner.' "[49] The *New Yorker* also ran a substantial review of the premiere; the Symphony in Three Movements was

no casual souvenir presented in passing. It is serious, finely wrought music, marked by the characteristic emotional reticence of many of the recent Stravinsky works. The composer conducted with a sort of modest studiousness that drew hearty cooperation from the orchestra and a hearty ovation from the listeners, although parts of the work may have been a bit difficult for some members of both groups . . . excellent performances under the visiting director, whose conducting becomes more impressive every year.[50]

With similar praise, a brief essay in *Modern Music* judged the new symphony "Stravinsky's real masterpiece. . . . Now we can see that his excursions in varied directions were not merely attempts to shock, indicated no failure at stylistic orientation. They were probing drives toward completion, part of the whole that the rich yet completely integrated manner of this symphony represents."[51]

The work did not fare as well in the nation's two most widely subscribed popular music journals. Initially, an "H. C. S." complained about Dahl's printed program notes and that "some of the ideas seem labored," although later he conceded that "nevertheless, through the involved texture and crabbed style, there often emerged a feeling of intensity far removed from the slick writing of other recent works . . . and the orchestra responded as though it enjoyed playing under him.[52]

The other major national music journal printed a hopelessly biased review. Identified again solely as "P.," its author considerably outdistanced Stravinsky's longtime New York nemesis, even replicating that critic's "inorganic." Although it never found a place in Slonimsky's 1952 *Lexicon of Musical Invective*, it surely deserves one:

> To the woes of the world Igor Stravinsky has added a symphony. A monotonous and noisily repetitive play of scraps and fragments, of rhythmic splinters, choppy syncopations, bits of sawdust from the workshop of the composer's earlier days—all these and other mouldy remnants from the Stravinskyan rag-bag, thrown together in a shapeless heap, suffice, presumably, to make up a symphony according to Stravinsky's latest lights. Possibly this is what is meant by "additive construction." In any case, it has little in common with any discernible organic effect.[53]

P.'s quotation of "additive construction" refers to a comment in the program notes by Stravinsky and Dahl.[54]

P.'s diatribe apparently prompted the journal's editor to offer a conciliatory postscript by another staff reviewer, "S.," who had also heard the work. It demonstrates that neither opinion was shared by the audience: "At the Saturday evening and Sunday afternoon concerts, Mr. Stravinsky again conducted his Symphony. . . . The performances were superb in every respect and the audience applauded the eminent composer and the orchestra with might and main."[55]

Interviewed late in February of 1946, the day before the Boston premiere, and responding to a remark about the work from a reporter to whom he must have shown his score, the miffed composer snapped: "I am never the old Stravinsky."[56] After the premiere on 20 February, another writer took a jab at Dahl's program notes, observed that "fortunately, the music is clearer than the explanation," and then, echoing his colleague, declared, "I detected nothing new in it." He ended by noting that "the audience rewarded him with prolonged applause after the symphony,"[57] just as Deems Taylor had had to concede in 1925 about a New York audience's innate intelligence in vindicating Stravinsky's Piano Concerto.

In respect to both the new Symphony and *Scènes de ballet,* still another Boston reviewer, Cyrus Durgin, wondered "if Stravinsky had not passed his creative peak."[58] In *Scènes,* this writer "simply couldn't find a tune anywhere." He went on: "There is more juice in the Symphony in Three Movements than in Stravinsky's last Symphony, the one in C major." Having also mocked Dahl's program notes, Durgin allowed that "the new Symphony is strong and vigorous, rhythmic from start to finish, mostly of a rough-woolen texture in regard to dissonance." But, expanding one observation in Dahl's notes, Durgin purported to hear in the second movement a "melodic fragment associated with the impersonation of Don Basilio by Count Almaviva in Rossini's *The Barber of Seville.*" This intriguing idea has not yet been addressed in the scholarly literature about the Symphony in Three Movements. The reason is perhaps twofold: (1) perhaps in part because of its obscurity in Boston's *Daily Globe* but (2) also because Durgin's citation is slightly misleading. He meant not Almaviva impersonating Don Basilio, *maestro di musica,* but rather Almaviva impersonating Basilio's *pupil,* Don Alonzo, at the beginning of act 2. Durgin's "melodic fragment" thus refers to Stravinsky's second violins, harmonized a sixth lower by the violas, that open his second movement (rehs. 112–17), Durgin comparing them to the first violins introducing and accompanying the opera's B-flat duet and the beginning of the duet itself sung by Almaviva as "Don Alonzo": "Pace e gioia sia con voi."

Such an appropriation was entirely consistent with Stravinsky's past record. His 1936 *Jeu de cartes,* quoted from *Il Barbiere* amongst borrowings from several other composers,[59] and his notation of 3 March 1937, made on Orrington Hotel stationery in Evanston, Illinois, during his fourth tour, quotes from Rossini's overture as a first sketch for the opening movement of his Symphony in C.[60] From his youth in St. Petersburg, he enjoyed an intimate familiarity with Rossini's opera: he would have heard it there frequently—even prenatally. His father, Fyodor, first sang the role of Don Basilio in February of 1873 and January of 1874, switched to Don Bartolo in October of 1882 and continued this role into 1891 with his own wonderful signed drawing of himself in the latter role dated: "Pechisky 1891. / 7 August."[61] During his son's early years, Igor was a "favorite mascot" at the Maryinsky.[62] In 1922 he had even considered composing "an updated Barber of Seville."[63] Given Stravinsky's methods with the opera's overture in *Jeu de cartes,* Durgin's suggestion seems tenable: quoting "Pace e gioia sia con voi" would not be a mere egregious larceny. As a homily, Don Alonzo's "Peace and joy be with you" becomes extraordinarily relevant for the "Apparition of the Virgin" scene in the 1944 movie *Song of Bernadette*, in light of Stravinsky's disclosure in 1962 that originally he had composed the music for the second movement of his Symphony in Three Movements for that very scene in the movie.[64]

A more substantive review of Symphony in Three Movements by a knowledgeable, gifted, but regrettably short-lived, young Boston composer soon appeared:

> While in many ways this score can be characterized as an uncommonly successful regression (perhaps that is why it has met with a more cordial reception than has been the case with the composer's more recent works), Stravinsky achieves in the synthesis of old and more recent idioms something that is new.[65]

The following month, on Thursday afternoon, 22 March 1946, Stravinsky led the West Coast premiere in San Francisco. Regarding him as "the most important musical influence to appear on the scene since the death of Wagner," Alfred Frankenstein felt that because "this is his era, a work that sums him up is therefore a document of the highest importance." The Symphony stands "forth with special dignity, monumentality and power." At a first hearing, the main impression

> is of its colossal compacted force. . . . The famous rhythmic energy, the kinetic drive and nervous tension . . . build up structures and shape themes of exceptional nobility and breadth. . . . The timing of contrasts (as differentiated from their mere presentation) is something which only composers of great experience and exceptional creative instinct know anything about.[66]

If one Washington, DC, reviewer is to be trusted, Stravinsky's premiere on Sunday afternoon, 4 April 1948, of the Symphony with Hans Kindler's National Symphony Orchestra did not elicit much enthusiasm from its audience. Having misinformed readers that it differed little from the *Firebird*, the *Washington Post* then noted optimistically that the new Symphony "simply failed to register for most listeners because it was a first hearing. In time, this symphony should become recognized and accepted as one of Stravinsky's most significant works."[67]

Advertised as a first performance of the Symphony in Three Movements not led by Stravinsky, the program notes for the Los Angeles Philharmonic's concert on 6 January 1947, conducted by Otto Klemperer, were credited to Dahl though excluding all of Stravinsky's own words he had written with him for New York.[68] The work was favorably noticed, if a little confusingly, in the *Los Angeles Times* as

> difficult to tone down to an audience. Its planes are vast and it takes a musical giant to relate them. . . . [It is] impossible to accustom one's ears to the sound immediately, but the rhythm of silences and sound takes shape in patterns that are powerful and impressive . . . music for an atomic age . . . strange and stormy musical elements.[69]

In good part relying on Dahl's program notes, Mary Jeannette Brown, the reviewer of a regional newspaper was impressed by "Stravinsky's exploration into new symphonic structures . . . a sharply arresting and demanding work, insistently stern in purpose, relentlessly making its point." The "atavistic force . . . biting accents and motor rhythms . . . solid blocks of dissonance" of the first movement reminded her of the *Rite* and of the "exceedingly varied textures" in the third movement of *Petrushka*. She found tenderness only near the middle of the first movement and during the second movement's flute and harp passages in "some pungently impressionistic utterances of violin and harp. For the rest, the concern is over the harder emotions, the less affable aspects of the great human endeavour . . . a provocative score by one of the most provocative composers of our time."[70]

But ten days later, the *Pacific Coast Musician* once again displayed its editor's ignorance and hostility:

> The new Strawinsky Symphony . . . proved to be a succession of unpleasant noises apparently having neither purpose nor direction. The work is wholly without form in the generally accepted meaning of that term and ambles its weary but noisy way for some twenty or more minutes beginning nowhere and arriving nowhere. . . . There was no way to tell whether [the orchestra] played well in the Strawinsky.[71]

The same day, Lawrence Morton reviewed the Los Angeles premiere,[72] almost as if to atone for both his ignorant colleague, Steele, and for his own and peculiar notice a half-dozen years earlier about the Symphony in C. The appearance of these two opposing reviews on the same day may not be sheer coincidence. Just the previous year, the pair had tangled over Steele's review of the Los Angeles premiere of Bartók's 1932 Sonata for Two Pianos and Percussion, when Steele had deemed that great work "utterly inane, puerile and, in some instances, almost offensive."[73] Whether or not the simultaneous appearance of the two Stravinsky reviews was planned, Morton demonstrated his own greater familiarity with, and access to, Stravinsky's new symphony—an access not seized on by some of his less diligent colleagues. Morton had already heard it on two broadcasts: late in January from New York and again on 4 January 1947 from Cleveland. Morton thought Klemperer's account superior to both of Stravinsky's because it was characterized by "a more deliberate pace that gave the sparsely orchestrated music more time to sound, and by a consequent increase of weight . . . appropriate to the thematic material."[74] He felt that the first movement was one of "high seriousness which compels earnest attention and contemplation. . . . [It was] an occasion . . . for strong musical talk . . . never equaled . . . in drama and life-like intensity, forceful and expressive in a way that the composer has seldom felt it necessary to speak."

Morton did not care as much for the final two movements. The second had "many marvellous moments, but developed out of nostalgia and preciousness." The last movement was "somewhat spotty, episodic," although its opening and closing sections "return to the grandeur and intensity of the first movement." Like some of his colleagues, Morton was "puzzled" by part of this movement (reh. 170: –2): "the fugue with its almost grotesque coupling of the trombone and piano." In this respect Craft subsequently observed even as late as 22 May 1952, in a Paris performance of the Symphony in Three Movements led by its composer, that "the paradiddle for two bassoons in the finale [reh. 148ff.] went unnoticed as well as its connection to the fugal piano-trombone exposition near the end of the movement [reh. 170: –2]."[75] Not once mentioning Dahl's program notes that were incorporated into the booklet for the Los Angeles Philharmonic's performance, let alone writing of any "expected C," Morton did later acknowledge that Dahl was the "official annotator of Stravinsky's Symphony."[76]

In fact, even Dahl's study, "developed out of an interview with Mr. Stravinsky late in June [1946]," had merely asserted that "the seemingly surprising ending of the symphony in the tonality of D-flat is prepared far in advance."[77] Nor do either of the sleeve-notes to Stravinsky's first two recordings—the one made on 28 January 1946 (New York), the other on 21 May 1954 (Baden-Baden)—mention any "expected C." Notes for the former were certainly approved by Stravinsky and those for the latter probably also.

A "PROGRAM" FOR THE SYMPHONY IN THREE MOVEMENTS?

Recently, new light has been shed on the Symphony in Three Movements and its allusions to Beethoven's Symphony No. 5, and even overt connections of the first movement to that of the *Eroica*.[78] These deserve consideration. Obviously, a "Victory Symphony," commissioned during World War II, would have to engage with the so-called Victory motto, used by both the Allies and the Axis, that opens Beethoven's Fifth Symphony.

These proposed links are further supported by Stravinsky's lifelong interest in, and high regard in maturity for, Beethoven. In December of 1948 Eric Walter White was told that Stravinsky *does* like Beethoven[79] and that Symphonies Two, Four, and Eight—note the *Eroica*'s and the Fifth's absence—were "sometimes wholly fresh and delightful."[80] Further observations in the early 1960s regarding four Beethoven symphonies again excluded the *Eroica*.[81] Then there was Stravinsky's 1966 Halloween exchange with the young Michael Tilson Thomas about the late piano sonatas,[82] and a discerning 1968 review by Craft (though attributed to, and probably approved by, Stravinsky) of Joseph Kerman's book, *The Beethoven Quartets*.[83] In his final years Stravinsky reaffirmed such opinions a half dozen times; though Craft asserted that only after he "stopped composing did he embrace Beethoven fully."[84] Very late in life, on 19 January 1970 in New York, he was observed with Craft listening intently to recordings of Beethoven's string quartet "op. 125" (perhaps op. 135) and the last piano sonata, op. 111.[85] Craft's longest discussion about Beethoven's symphonies and quartets was embedded in a 2002 omnibus, thirty years after Stravinsky's death.[86]

Other events raised the possibility of a radically different and descriptive program for Stravinsky's new symphony. Just a few months after Craft's arrival on the Los Angeles scene in the late 1940s, poor Dahl and also his program notes fell out of favor. Initially, Stravinsky's trust in Dahl was not in question. Dahl must have known the Symphony in Three Movements very well. For example, he was called out to the Stravinsky home one Thanksgiving afternoon (probably 29 November 1945) "to hear it,"[87] meaning, to play it four hands with the composer.[88] In the summer of 1946, Dahl published a more detailed study, developed "out of an interview with Mr. Stravinsky late in June."[89] Substantial portions of this study appeared on jacket notes for the first pressing of the late January 1946 recording of the Symphony by Columbia Records, issued around May of 1947. That very month, Stravinsky called Dahl a "distinguished annotator" and cited "his competent analysis of my Symphony in Three Movements."[90]

Nevertheless, on 9 February 1948 Stravinsky wrote Dahl about these program notes, disclaiming any "extramusical connotations" for his symphony, none of which Dahl had formulated, save for the symphony's closeness to "the core of a world at war."[91] Much later, David Raksin, who knew both Stravinsky and Dahl, verified in conversation that "Stravinsky endorsed the [so-called] descriptive program notes that Dahl had written for the Symphony in Three Movements." Joseph editorialized that "although Stravinsky always adamantly denied this, in fact Raksin's memory is accurate."[92] Perhaps Stravinsky's sudden disaffection with Dahl stemmed from learning about Dahl's 1944 indiscretion in leaking to his USC students news of their professor orchestrating portions of *Scènes de ballet*.

The first hints of any potential program for the Symphony in Three Movements followed a morning rehearsal of its first movement on 1 April 1948 with the National Symphony in Washington. Stravinsky remarked that the bass clarinet at rehearsal 111 was "a kind of laughing or nose-thumbing."[93] But at what or at whom? Perhaps this was the opening salvo for a (re-)visualization of the entire work, accomplished more vividly and in greater precision and detail by the close of the ensuing decade. In 1961 Stravinsky replaced Dahl's serious rhetoric with an anecdotal and descriptive account for the 1962 record jacket of his February 1961 recording—"written under impression of world events. I will not say that it expresses my feelings about them."[94] This remark and several others were slightly revised and even expanded in one of his conversation books and published in 1963. Like the 1962 record jacket, it contained similar phrases: "written under the sign of world events"; "visual impressions of world events were derived largely from films"; "genesis of a war plot"; "goose-stepping soldiers"; "rise of the Allies"; "movements of war machines"; and even "scorched-earth tactics in China."[95] All these statements are utterly at odds with Stravinsky's previous avowal in September of 1946 that "good music must be heard by and for itself, and not with the crutch of any visual medium."[96]

Both the derivation and the authenticity of this replacement program have repeatedly been questioned by British scholars.[97] For one of them:

it represents a complete denial of the neoclassical credo. . . . His admission to having written the *Symphony* in response to such stimuli compromises Stravinsky's whole neoclassical creed, that music is by its very nature powerless to express anything at all (*Chroniques* 1935). His misdemeanour is hardly exonerated by his belated attempt to portray the earlier comments as "simply a way of saying that music was supra-personal and supra-real."[98]

But perhaps this work might not be a "denial of the neoclassical credo" or does not "compromise Stravinsky's whole neoclassical creed"; it might not be a "neoclassical" composition at all.[99] Stravinsky's contempt for both term and concept is well-known (see the Appendix).

Not without some wryness, Schiff urges "a little caution . . . in equating the music with a program that remained hidden from sight for almost twenty years." In *Expositions and Developments* (p. 66) written with Craft and completed in 1961, Stravinsky merely acknowledged that the second movement stemmed from music written in 1942 for the film *Song of Bernadette*. Coming from a composer who so disdained description, and who denied "expression" as applied to music, his remarks about Symphony in Three Movements do seem utterly at odds, even though in both 1961 and 1963 he catches himself by saying, "In spite of what I have said,[100] the Symphony is not programmatic. Composers combine notes. That is all."[101]

Even this caveat has not prevented a recent and baffling assertion, the most extreme in its visualization. First citing the posthumous version of Stravinsky's 1963 remarks, its author then declares that "Stravinsky's pictorial narrative for the finale works splendidly—I happen to know, because (with the video artist Peter Bogdanoff, for California's Pacific Symphony) I've tried it out, with actual Second World War newsreel clips."[102] Assuredly, such dubbing of the Symphony's finale into selectively chosen newsreels does work; and so does Disney's dubbing of the *Sacre*'s "Glorification of the Chosen Victim" fit galumphing dinosaurs in *Fantasia*. But, of course, neither dubbing enjoyed the composer's endorsement.

Flowery descriptions such as "war plot," "goose-stepping," "war machines," and "scorched-earth" smack of commerce. They did not appear on sleeve-notes for Stravinsky's first recording in 1946 but only sixteen years later. Stravinsky (publicly at least) actively resisted commercial mandates; he once lauded Goddard Lieberson (president of Columbia Records and his producer since April 1940),[103] as one who "keeps his Sales Department from dictating to his Artist and Repertory Department."[104] According to Lieberson on its jacket, the 1961 recording was made "in the eightieth year of his life." Such a major anniversary was an ideal vehicle for commercial exploitation. Had someone in Columbia Records pried these comments out of Stravinsky in 1961 or 1962? Did Stravinsky himself create such extravagant prose—by 1963 reprinted in *Dialogues and a Diary*—and then exclude it from the "Programme Notes" in Stravinsky's own (and posthumously edited) 1972 volume, *Themes and Conclusions,* only to have it reappear in the one-volume Craft omnibus, the 2002 *Memories and Commentaries?*

In respect to any suggestion of commercial exploitation, one scholar is surely on the right track. David Schiff proposes a "re-brand" (i.e., repackaging a product, often a failing one):

> Nowhere in these sketches do we find any notations about current events . . . [as] in the score of *Scènes de Ballet*. . . . It is possible that in 1963 he hoped to re-brand his symphony, which had yet to attain a firm place in the repertory in terms that would place it among other wartime works: Schoenberg's *Survivor from Warsaw* (1947); Bartok's *Concerto for Orchestra* (1943–45); Strauss's *Metamorphosen* (1944–45).[105]

Perhaps recalling its initial healthy sales of 7,237 copies within the first month of its release in May of 1947,[106] rebrand it Stravinsky did. With his eventual full approval, in December of 1966 United Airlines used portions of the Symphony in Three Movements "assembled and edited by Robert [Craft]" for the "Manhattan" segment of United's promotional film *Discover America*. Even though Craft recalled that Stravinsky was "interested in the reasons for mating certain sections of his music with certain scenery,"[107] he did not disclose any of these reasons. Seven photographs taken by Arnold Newman in mid-December of 1966 show Craft's recording sessions in Los Angeles with Stravinsky present, one of them showing Lillian Libman and both Stravinskys watching the United Airlines film with Craft in the background discussing it with two men.[108]

As late as 1968, the Symphony in Three Movements, conducted by Craft with the Oakland Symphony with Stravinsky present, could still elicit incomprehension as "polytonal . . . [and] represent[ing] the drier, more structurally oriented aspects of Stravinsky's art."[109] Directly after having led the first of those three Oakland performances, 13–15 February 1968, Craft related (in two different publications) that Stravinsky told him "the *Symphony in Three Movements* is naive in construction."[110] What could he have meant? Was he employing *naive* not in any disapproving or condescending sense, such as "artless," but within the broader French (and English) resonance of "ingenuous," "unaffected," "simple," "natural"? Or was he referring in some way to a putative program? It would seem that by "naive in construction," he was—with hindsight—contrasting his twenty-three-year-old Symphony with recent serial works, such as *Variations: Aldous Huxley in Memoriam* (1964) and the *Requiem Canticles* (1966). This might be so, because by then his "tonal" music was embarrassing to him.

Even though uncertainty will always cloud any piece of "program music," it seems especially so when evaluating any viable "program" for the Symphony in Three Movements. Late in life, his comments about it made on camera give no hint: "My Symphony in Three Movements celebrated, as it were, my arrival in the United States of America."[111] An obfuscation of course, because his earliest sketches for it date from 6 February 1942,[112] several years after his arrival in the United States, and much closer in time to the Japanese attack. The "war" word occurs only by implication in Stravinsky's initial note for the 1946 New York Philharmonic premiere, only once in Stravinsky's and Dahl's joint program notes for the same occasion, and not at all in Dahl's summer 1946 essay for *Modern Music*. Perhaps in disowning Dahl's writings, and responding to a demand for descriptive prose from Columbia Records, Stravinsky dissembled yet again. He slyly appropriated the one word, *war*, that Dahl had used least. His views changed from one time and place to another, and we do not really know how he regarded his last symphony. As late as 1968 in Oakland, did he still "like eet myzelf," as he had recounted to me about his Symphony in C backstage two years before in Los Angeles?[113]

WARTIME AND POSTWAR CONDUCTOR

Stravinsky's concept of an ideal conductor may have resided in the letter of recommendation that he wrote for James Sample on 29 June 1942: "getting the best that can be had from [an] orchestra . . . done by their cooperation rather than by forced work." He articulated another tenet to Andersson at his first lesson in March of 1941: "My music and rehearsals are all hand made." And fifty-one years later, Sample recalled that Stravinsky was "anxious that music have a hand-made feeling."[114]

"I have a strong conducting technique," said Stravinsky modestly to a *New York Times* reporter (probably early in the 1940s), and in January 1949 he informed the *Houston Post* that "all conductors hate me. . . . They cannot play my music correctly [because they] are more interested in expressing themselves than the music before them. My music will not take glamour: it must speak for itself."[115] In light of these declarations (not to speak of him letting down his guard at Houston about "expressing . . . the music"), his extensive conducting during wartime deserves a closer look.[116]

An essay about Stravinsky's concerts in Mexico City, published on 4 August 1940, included two photographs of him leading the country's national orchestra. It noted that "the world-famous composer of The Firebird has conducted the Orquesta Sinfónica de México with resounding success, without any of the ridiculous poses favored by other conductors."[117]

Morning and evening reviews of Stravinsky's concert with the Minneapolis Symphony on 20 December 1940, which included suites from *Jeu de cartes*, *Fairy's Kiss*, *Firebird*, and *Petrushka*, stressed his conducting abilities. Their authors were struck by the difference between his calm style—cited above by New York reviewers in 1937 and 1940—and that of the orchestra's resident conductor, Dimitri Mitropoulos. One reviewer of Stravinsky, Johan S. Egilsrud, observed "the great economy of means through which he produced his effects, never exaggerating any dynamics or tempos and relying on the tone quality of the various instruments and the rhythmic impulses for variety."[118] The evening paper, while calling the composer "the wild man of modern music," praised the conductor's

> calm, measured beat and a self-possessed, entirely unferocious manner, . . . all business on the platform, and he gets what he wants from the orchestra with a kind of pedagogical

determination that hasn't a tinge of showmanship or display. . . . A real achievement for a man whose life has been given largely to composition to draw from an orchestra such clear purposes and such clear statement.[119]

In the privacy of rehearsals it was sometimes another matter: for example, returning on 19 January 1941 from Boston to New York, Stravinsky rehearsed the next two days for *Balustrade,* the ballet that Balanchine had made on the Violin Concerto in D, and, according to Stravinsky: "one of the most visually satisfying of any of my works."[120] Years later, Boris Schwarz, who had been the concertmaster, recalled that during the first rehearsal (20 January), Stravinsky lost his way at a perilous change of meter in the first movement, vainly waving his hands and muttering in French under his breath: "But what's going on? But what are they doing?"[121]

Clearly, Stravinsky's conducting had improved by the early 1940s and was often mentioned favorably in newspaper reviews: "San Francisco's ballet history gained a brilliant memory Wednesday evening at the Opera House. Igor Stravinsky was acclaimed as conductor of the Ballet Theater in his own *Petrouchka.* . . . Under the composer's refreshing command, both his dancers and the San Francisco Symphony gave a gripping performance."[122]

In April of 1943, his four New York performances of *Petrushka* were particularly lauded by the rigorous dance critic John Martin:

Igor Stravinsky and quite the most brilliant aggregation of ballerinas to be found in any single company shared the rather copious honors of last night's performance at the Metropolitan Opera House. . . . It was his particular mission to conduct his own now classic *Petrushka.* The standard he set was a high one, for he made the music sound as it has not sounded in a ballet performance in many a season. Always one of the greatest of theatre scores, it took on an extra crispness and clarity and many tonal colors that are generally missing.[123]

Isabelle Papineau-Couture observed Stravinsky conducting *Apollon musagète* in New York. Hearing him rehearse it on 24 or 25 April 1943, she wrote about his

very special technique, a very angular beat that gained in precision what it lost in suppleness or in nuance. . . . Ever afterward, when I saw Stravinsky conduct, I recognized these same characteristics of his beat, no matter what the style of the work. His explanations and remarks to the performers were made with equal amounts of courtesy and command. Never any uncertainty about his wishes. Always respect for the work just as it emerged from the pages of the score.[124]

In a provocative but difficult-to-date conversation with Bronislava Nijinska (retired in Los Angeles since 1940) about an unidentified though popular ballet—perhaps a Los

Angeles performance early in December of 1944 of *Danses concertantes* by the Ballet Russes de Monte Carlo—impresario Serge Denham told Nijinska that "Stravinsky liked it [but] he never saw it. . . . Throughout the entire ballet he kept his head down, watching the orchestra. Stravinsky directed but never saw it."[125]

After a first rehearsal on 30 January 1945 with the New York Philharmonic, while under the care of Dr. Garbat for a fever,[126] the undaunted composer led four concerts. Reviewing the first of these (1 February), Virgil Thomson noted:

> Mr. Stravinsky's conducting of his own works was, as always, a delight. . . . His rhythm was precise, his tonal texture dry, the expressivity complete. . . . His [conducting] is a poetry of exactitude, a theater of delicate adjustments and relentless march. His scores are correctly indited, and the composer's reading of them is the way they go. It is also the way they go best.[127]

A month later, on 5 March in Montreal, reviewers for the city's two chief newspapers expressed utterly different opinions. In the English edition of *Le Devoir Montreal,* a French-language newspaper, Roman-Octave Pelletier (unrelated to the conductor of the same surname) wrote, "As with many great composers, Stravinsky does not have a great reputation as an orchestral conductor, but he is certainly not as bad as some have said him to be." Yet for *Firebird,* Pelletier had to concede that Montreal had rarely heard a better performance. He regarded *Circus Polka* as "une boutade amusante" and correctly identified its quotation from Schubert's *Marche militaire,* but faith in his critical acumen is shaken by him having imagined he also heard Sousa's *Stars and Stripes Forever* quoted in it.[128]

The *Gazette* reviewer, Thomas Archer, commented:

> Mr. Stravinsky's conducting of the [Tchaikovsky second] symphony was remarkable for its sound scholarship, consistent tempi and, as far as could be judged, strict adherence to the score. He made Tchaikovsky sound as clear as Mozart. Never once did he let go. Every detail was taken care of, every nuance faithfully marked. . . . As a conductor, Mr. Stravinsky has a style all his own. The gestures are decisive and characteristic of a man who throws himself completely into the task at hand. He knows exactly what he wants. He is not in the least interested in his appearance from the point of view of the audience. He is much too absorbed for that. Yet in spite of this absorption, he is visually as lively a figure as the majority of his colleagues, although a good deal more true to music than most of them are. There is scholarly cerebration in the results he obtains. There is also a mastery and a superb command of formal pattern, [and] clear method.[129]

The accompanying photograph of his rehearsal with the Montreal Philharmonic (see fig. 10.1) depicts Stravinsky giving the attentive players the benefit of his "sound scholarship" and "scholarly cerebration."

But orchestra members did not always respect his rehearsal methods. For example, in 1940 Vera hinted at some "bad behavior of the New York Philharmonic Orchestra when Igor conducted them" and "mocking the dissonances and the difficulties of the changing metres" in the *Rite of Spring*.[130] Lukas Foss, when he was pianist for the Boston Symphony Orchestra, was even more specific in 1946. He remembered Stravinsky's rehearsals in the latter half of February for the Boston premiere of the Symphony in Three Movements:

> They would imitate [his] "uck, uck" [for articulation]. Orchestral musicians could not understand that little black bird, that hovering beat, that man without any kind of allures of a great man, none. . . . The kind of authority that emanated from him was only his knowledge and love for the [music]. So he stood almost like an innocent child in front of all those naughty boys; it was really a kind of tragic scene, because the rehearsal deteriorated completely.[131]

A reviewer for the *Boston Daily Globe* observed the day following the concert that "Mr. Stravinsky's conducting is smoother than it used to be, but it still concentrates on rhythm rather than on the quality of sonorities."[132]

Early in April of 1948, after reviewing Stravinsky's concert with the National Symphony Orchestra, a critic for the *Washington Post* observed:

> On the podium, Stravinsky achieved greater results with less fuss and ostentation than the majority of men who devote themselves entirely to conducting. He is clear and concise in indicating the beat and giving cues, and he literally radiates a spontaneous vitality that calls forth the best from every individual.[133]

To date, the best general survey of Stravinsky's entire conducting career is a brief essay by Maroth. He bases his evaluations chiefly on his own recorded interviews, and those by an associate, with five US composers and one career conductor. His informants are Virgil Thomson and Elliot Carter, both observing Stravinsky in Paris during the 1920s and 1930s; Roger Sessions at Princeton in 1937; Lukas Foss in Boston in the mid-1940s and Los Angeles in the mid-1950s; Claudio Spies at Harvard, New York, and Princeton from the 1940s to the composer's death; and of course, Robert Craft.[134] In addition, conductor Michael Tilson Thomas often observed Stravinsky working during the 1960s with top-flight studio musicians in Los Angeles. In 1996 he memorably recalled that Stravinsky "had such energy. He was like an old bird of prey—a bit feeble but still dangerous."[135]

Craft maintained that Stravinsky was at his conductorial peak at age eighty, that is, during the 1960s. He may well have been right, though I am inclined to disagree. My recollections from attending a final rehearsal on 5 October 1952 in Vancouver and then singing under him in Los Angeles rehearsals and concerts in January of 1966 tell a different story from Craft's. In October of 1952, rehearsing his own works and those by Glinka and Tchaikovsky with the Vancouver Symphony Orchestra, I saw and heard the seventy-year-old exert extraordinary control over what was really a midlevel orchestra, especially for rhythmic articulation, balance, and subtle effects of *rubato*. I discerned no disrespect, such as occurred during the 1940s in New York and Boston and would again occur in August of 1963 at Santa Fe, but rather the most acute and rapt attention to his every word and gesture.

Confirmation of this 1952 recollection comes from the late Dr. Ida Halpern, the highly respected ethnomusicologist and music critic, and a former teacher of mine.[136] Having by her renowned charm evaded Stravinsky's refusals to other observers (even those on the Symphony's Board of Directors), she attended his first rehearsal on 2 October:

> His manner of conducting is concise. . . . His movements are swift, precise and always well-controlled, like the movements of an accomplished dancer or acrobat: but at the same time quick, electric and nervous. He is not using a baton and his expressive hands interpret the music clearly. To give certain effects he sometimes claps his hands and snaps his fingers. His manner towards the orchestra is very kind. I did not notice any of his famous sarcasms, but only eagerness to be of help.

She went on to observe:

> One player [John Avison] did not seem to get along too well and Stravinsky asked him to come up with his score [she means his part]. Then the famous composer understood. "There are mistakes," he exclaimed, taking a pen and starting to correct the faulty score. What a manuscript to have, what a collector's item![137]

Reviewing the Sunday concert itself, she commented: "Noteworthy is Stravinsky's special emphasis of the accentuation of the music. As he explained to the musicians at rehearsals: 'Make a comma between your notes.' "[138]

On 12 July 1962 Vera wrote alarmingly of "big mistakes quarrels, fights and offenses . . . during and after the four-hour rehearsal" at New York's Lewisohn Stadium. Apparently these only concerned managerial matters.[139] The collection at UBC houses a dozen photographs Fred Fehl took of Stravinsky, then in his eighty-first year, rehearsing the orchestra of mostly New York Philharmonic players.[140] The next day's review in the *New York Times* by Raymond Ericson about this concert, delivered via loudspeakers to an "audience of 11,000," observed that

> with his slight bent figure, he gave the impression of keeping his nose in the score all the time, but his beat and cues were always exact and clear. Moreover, he got the Stadium Symphony to play with the kind of precision and clarity of ensemble that give the music an unaccustomed dryness that points up all the beautiful details of the scoring.[141]

FIGURE 10.3
Stravinsky rehearsing at Lewisohn
Stadium, 1962. UBC Stravinsky
Collection.

The above remarks concern the *Firebird Suite*. Among other works performed was his
symphonic arrangement of *Scherzo à la Russe,* shown in rehearsal in another of Fehl's
images (fig. 10.3). Extraordinary patience must have been required for achieving balance
in an outdoor acoustic, but apparently he managed the gossamer-like, spider-webbed
canon at the octave between piano and harp in the *Scherzo.*

In January of 1966, at eighty-four, when he shared a half-concert with Craft, leading
the Los Angeles Philharmonic, I—in the guise of a very temporary member of the Roger
Wagner Chorale—saw Stravinsky lose his way at least once. By miscuing the woodwinds,
he caused some serious (although momentary) confusion during the second variation in
his own transcription of Bach's chorale-variations on *Von Himmel Hoch.* That mishap

may have been just a momentary loss of concentration, in the context of a less-than-attentive orchestra.

Over a considerable time, many photographs were taken of Stravinsky in rehearsal and show this vigor. Lesser-known ones from his later years are equally informative, for example, three of him in July of 1960 rehearsing the Santa Fe Opera orchestra, taken by an unidentified photographer.[142] On 23 July 1966 in New York, Paul Horgan heard the eighty-five-year-old Stravinsky lead the *Symphony of Psalms* with the Philharmonic. He was struck by "his extraordinary vigor, his orchestral and auditory conception more acute than I had ever found it."[143] Craft may well have been right. Each of Fehl's 1972 images affirms such vitality.

STRAVINSKY AND "NEOCLASSICISM"

Stravinsky's works written from 1920 to 1945 are often burdened, in my judgment, and increasingly in the opinions of others, with the term *neoclassic*.[1] Even though repudiating this term in 1943, Bartók praised Stravinsky for "creating works of a new individual style."[2]

Invented by Boris de Schloesser, a Russian expatriate in Paris, the term stems from French and Italian composers and French literary critics dedicated not only to anti-Debussyism but also to anti-Schoenbergism.[3] De Schloesser first applied it to Stravinsky in two reviews in 1923, though quite inaccurately.[4] Stravinsky disliked this term intensely, complaining about it in 1924, frequently thereafter, and as late as 1966.[5]

In 1948 Alfredo Casella, Stravinsky's close composer-friend and confidant in Paris during World War I and the 1920s and 1930s, justly recalled the history of "neo-classica" as a series of "malintesi" (misunderstandings). Three decades earlier, Casella had explained Stravinsky's motives in writing works so-labeled: "from 1911 Stravinsky was reacting against *l'arte io* [self-expression] that always starts with *confesssione* [personal statement] by the artist and turns into *espressione* or even into *impressione*."[6]

Two reviews by Olin Downes underscore this term's failings. In 1935 he found in *Perséphone* "a kind of synthetic classicism, not always 100 per cent," predicting "serene vistas of order, beauty, truth that defy the passing of time. The refuge will be in the direction of classicism—or so Stravinsky implies."[7] Just seven years later, he was calling Stravinsky's later-period works "plain fake classicism, sterile, feeble, melodically commonplace," imitating "this and that master."[8] So much for [neo-]classicism's "serene vistas," "refuge," and "direction"!

A more useful substitute for *neoclassicism* might be the term *irony*, as it is sometimes understood—and in a positive sense—in literary studies: "a form of utterance that postulates a double audience, consisting of one party that hearing shall hear & shall not understand,

& another party that, when more is meant than meets the ear, is aware both of that more & of the outsider's incomprehension."[9] In music this would signify an inner meaning directed to a musically sophisticated audience, not necessarily entailing any sacrifice of sincerity or profundity.[10] An example of this type of irony occurs in the finale of Stravinsky's Violin Concerto. Soloist joined by concertmaster (rehs. 117–19) forge a clear recall of Bach's Concerto in D minor for Two Violins (BMV 1043).[11] A second example is Stravinsky's rethinking of a "classical" phrase-structure in his student Andersson's 1941–42 *Futurama Symphony:* squeezing and jamming antecedent-consequent during the introduction to *Futurama*'s first movement—that is, the "wedging" in example 7.1.

NOTES

PREFACE

1. Walsh, *The New Grove Stravinsky*, 34.

2. "Not a Very Happy Choice," in Cantoni, *The Language of Stravinsky*, 3.

3. One example is a correspondence during much of 1944 between Stravinsky and a member of the Swiss legation in Washington, DC (which I donated recently to UBC). It included a mailing of several of Stravinsky's newly published miniature scores to his son in Switzerland. Another example is Stravinsky's own signed copy of the reprinted 1912 orchestral score of *Petroushka* (London: Boosey and Hawkes, no. 574 [c. 1945]), auctioned (New York: Bonhams, *Fine Books and Manuscripts*, 9 Dec. 2015, lot 159), also now at UBC. He annotated seventy-two pages in red, blue, and green pencil and in ink. Many, but not all, of these changes appear in his revised full score manuscript of 1946–47 and in the revised edition (London: Boosey and Hawkes, no. 16236 [c. 1948]). His alterations extend beyond the present study's chronological boundaries.

4. Craft, *Stravinsky: Discoveries and Memories*, 48.

5. See Morton, review of *Stravinsky*, by Eric Walter White.

6. In Joseph, *Stravinsky Inside Out*, 265.

7. Cropping and other problems when working from photographs are examined in Slim, "Lute Ladies and Old Men," esp. figs. 18a, b, c and 19a, b.

8. Vigilance regarding names of ocean vessels and their arrivals and departures stems from my early seven-summers career as a ship's assistant purser on Canada's West Coast (including thirteen trips to Alaska).

9. Joseph, *Stravinsky Inside Out*, 10–11.

10. Quoted in Huxtable, "Mies van der Rohe."

11. Thirlwell, *The Delighted States*, 87; quoted and discussed in Oates, "Sex, Farce & Futility," wherein the last sentence is attributed to Vladimir Nabokov, though it does not follow directly in Thirlwell's book (Nabokov being quoted there at p. 26).

12. Morton, "Los Angeles to Hear Resident Composers."

13. See Paddison, "Stravinsky as Devil." Cantoni, *The Language of Stravinsky*, 1–2, discusses important modern-day repercussions of Adorno's attacks on Stravinsky.

14. DeLibero, "Rabbit Redux."

INTRODUCTION

1. Craft, *Igor and Vera Stravinsky*, 63, pl. 73, citing the *Philadelphia Inquirer*, 29 March 1925, 2.

2. Oja, *Making Music Modern*, 448n17, citing Bauer, "Ultra-Modern Concerto."

3. Gunn, [Reviewing the CSO]; cited in Wagner, "A Stravinsky Scrapbook," 18.

4. *Coco Chanel et Igor Stravinsky*; see Buch, "The Scandal of the Score," including pl. at 64 and color pl. 33 at 435.

5. See Taruskin, *Russian Music at Home*, 366–83, 395–427.

6. *Seattle Post-Intelligencer*, 28 March 1937, 4; *Minneapolis Morning Tribune*, 19 Dec. 1940, 10.

7. *Globe and Mail* (Toronto), 2 Jan. 1937, 5.

8. Slim, "Stravinsky's Four Star-Spangled Banners," 333–38.

9. Rhodes, "Prospect of Citizenship." Though not citing Rhodes, this fib supports Stephen Walsh's "Remembering the *Rite of Spring*": "By temperament, Stravinsky was a revisionist. . . . He told untruths about his music and about himself" (157).

10. Craft, *Dearest Bubushkin*, 12 October 1940.

11. Rhodes, "Prospect of Citizenship," 2.

12. Rhodes, "Prospect of Citizenship," 2; Craft, *Dearest Bubushkin*, 23 October 1940, cites a (business) discussion of *Renard* "with two Disney directors."

13. Liebling, "Variations."

14. W., "Stravinsky Opens Engagement."

15. Craft, *Dearest Bubushkin*, 13 February 1941.

16. Eyer, "Our Orchestra vs. The Modern Composer"; Eyer and Sabin, "Repertoire of Orchestras Is Surveyed"; and Sabin, "A Survey of Our Orchestral Repertoire."

17. Smith, "Stravinsky Meets the Boston Censor."

18. See, e.g., Watkins, *Pyramids at the Louvre*, 229–74.

19. Davis, *Classic Chic*, passim.

20. See Stuart, *Igor Stravinsky*, 70, no. L2; now on Pearl Records: GEMM CDS 92, track 24.

21. Addressed to the fifteen-year-old Ferdinand Hiller (1811–85), as recalled in Hiller, *Aus dem Tonleben unserer Zeit*, 169–70; quoted in Forbes, *Thayer's Life of Beethoven*, 2:1046.

22. Craft, *Stravinsky: Glimpses*, 65; Stravinsky and Craft, *Memories and Commentaries* (2002), xvii. Schoenberg felt similarly; see his letters of 1945 and 1947, cited in Feisst, *Schoenberg's New World*, 154.

23. Joseph, *Stravinsky Inside Out*, 1–34.

24. Morton, "Los Angeles to Hear Resident Composer."

25. Craft, "An Interview," 34; see also Craft, "Igor, Catherine and God"; and Craft, "Sufferings and Humiliations of Catherine Stravinsky."

26. "Music: Master Mechanic," *Time,* 26 July 1948, 26–29.

27. *Pace* Francis, *Teaching Stravinsky:* "1962—the only time Boulanger returned to North America after the war" (238). In the spring of 1958 at Harvard University I had the great good fortune to hear her lecture in Adams House about Hindemith's piano sonatas.

28. A balanced and sympathetic view of the Stravinsky-Craft interaction is in Stuart, *Igor Stravinsky,* 14–16. See also Joseph, *Stravinsky Inside Out,* 302n33.

29. See Stravinsky, *Selected Correspondence,* 1:331n8; Craft, *An Improbable Life,* 62; and Craft, *Stravinsky: Glimpses,* 24–25. For its sobriquet see Craft, *Dearest Bubushkin,* 15 February 1945.

30. Craft, *An Improbable Life,* 63; first reported in V. Stravinsky and Craft, *Stravinsky in Pictures,* 651n101.

31. Stravinsky, *Selected Correspondence,* 1:327.

32. Nabokov, *Igor Strawinsky,* 89–90.

33. Craft's 2013 book, *Stravinsky: Discoveries and Memories,* is accompanied by a 2007 CD of the *Rite.*

34. Craft, *Dearest Bubushkin,* 17–19. Early on, Jann Pasler alerted readers to serious editorial deficiencies in Craft's abbreviated edition of Vera's diaries and in his volumes of Stravinsky's correspondence; see Pasler, "Stravinsky: Insights and Oversights."

35. New information about both Mexico City tours appears in Levitz, "Igor the Angeleno," 141–43, 161–69.

36. Even so, Vera refers to "concert season" (see Craft, *Dearest Bubushkin,* 18 February 1941); and Stravinsky refers to "tournée de concerts" on 5 Jan. 1944, and "concert tour" on 25 Sept. 1946, in letters housed at the H. Colin Slim Stravinsky Collection at the University of British Columbia, Vancouver.

37. Concerning the post–World War II period, the reader might consult Craft, *Stravinsky: Discoveries and Memories,* 188–236.

38. Several amorous escapades with her are cited from documents in the Stravinsky archive at Basel and from Kall's papers at UCLA in Slim, "Chère amie." Peculiarly, given these Basel and UCLA documents, neither Professor Levitz nor her contributors to *Stravinsky and His World* mention either Godowsky or Kall; about the latter see Slim, "Unknown Words and Music."

39. See Dushkin, "1949: Working with Stravinsky." Dushkin wrote that he soon "realized that [Stravinsky] was not only capable of giving tenderness and affection but seemed to be in great need of them himself," sensing "something tense and anguished about him," requiring "comfort and reassurance" (181).

40. See Evans, "Stravinsky's Music in Hitler's Germany," 528–29, Tables I, II, and passim.

41. Fried, "Stravinsky Fears Blow"; and Fried, "Stravinsky Likes Idea," respectively. For composers' work options during the Great Depression see Giroud, *Nicolas Nabokov,* 106–8; and Taruskin's review, "In from the Cold."

42. Walsh, *Stravinsky: A Creative Spring,* 407. Craft, in *Stravinsky: Discoveries and Memories,* upped this estimate in 2013 to "nearly a million dollars" (135).

43. On his passion for clothes see Craft, *Stravinsky: Discoveries and Memories*, 123–24; and Craft, *Stravinsky: Glimpses*, 126–27n30; the revised edition (New York: St. Martin's, 1993) adds one final essay, four plates, and an index, to which henceforth reference is made.

44. The original letter is at the University of British Columbia. Craft's published edition and translation made from Stravinsky's carbon copy of this letter lack his copious, querulous marginalia, quoted below.

45. See Walsh, *Stravinsky: A Creative Spring*, 26; Taruskin, *Stravinsky and the Russian Traditions*, 95–99; and Craft, *Stravinsky: Discoveries and Memories*, 103.

46. Walsh, *Stravinsky: A Creative Spring*, 231.

47. Taruskin, *Stravinsky and the Russian Traditions*, 1456.

48. Walsh, *Stravinsky: A Creative Spring*, 390.

49. Walsh, *Stravinsky: A Creative Spring*, 488, and note 13, Stravinsky's letter of 15 Jan. 1930. Additional examples of Stravinsky's anti-Semitism are cited below.

50. Jonathan Cross, for example, regards Stravinsky's anti-Semitic statements as "sporadic and ultimately more stupid and thoughtless than malevolent." See Cross, *Igor Stravinsky*, 169.

51. Walsh, *Stravinsky: A Creative Spring*, 447.

52. This canon was written in 1951 for Mary Curtis Bok, wife of violinist Efrim Zimbalist; see Stravinsky, *Selected Correspondence*, 3:387–88n40.

53. Craft, *A Stravinsky Scrapbook*, 115, pl. 239 (cropped), and 38, pl. 77, respectively. For the date and an uncropped photograph see Walsh, *Stravinsky: The Second Exile*, 288, and pl. 6, bottom, between pp. 492 and 493.

54. Fox, "Robert Craft, Stravinsky Adviser"; see also a more nuanced notice by Shawn, "The Genius of Robert Craft."

55. Craft's comment apparently stemmed from a conversation of unknown date that Stravinsky had with Sir Isaiah Berlin; see Craft, *Stravinsky: Discoveries and Memories*, 302; Craft, *Dearest Bubushkin*, 29 May 1963; V. Stravinsky and Craft, *Stravinsky in Pictures*, 661n18; and esp. Walsh, *Stravinsky: The Second Exile*, 479–80: "Stravinsky . . . applauding *ostentatiously*" (my emphasis). Craft, in *Stravinsky: Chronicle* (1994 ed.), had observed that Stravinsky was not moved by the occasion and was "loudly critical of the performance" (359; quote is not in the 1972 Vintage edition).

56. Indispensable as they are, Craft's published writings about the composer, their innumerable editions and revisions, even the altering of his own diaries, and his extended bouts of Walsh-bashing, constitute a biobibliographical nightmare for scholars and general readers alike. Most of his books (though not his essays) are listed in Craft, *Stravinsky: Discoveries and Memories*, 360. As good an example as any appears therein (147), when Craft confused *Themes and Episodes* with what he really was referring to in *Themes and Conclusions*. Complaints about Craft's editing appear in Francis, "Nadia Boulanger and Igor Stravinsky," 140n5; in Francis, *Teaching Stravinsky*, where Francis refers to Jeanice Brooks's previous "trenchant criticism" (8n41); and in Cross, *Igor Stravinsky*, 174–75.

57. The lecture, first given in 1993 and "more than two dozen times" thereafter, was first printed as Taruskin, "Stravinsky and Us." Taruskin later disclosed that "Stravinsky's anti-Semitism was not the issue I was addressing this time, anyway." I had followed neither Taruskin's previous writing in the *New Republic* (1988) nor his subsequent quar-

rels with John Rockwell and Robert Craft in the *New York Review of Books,* about both of which now see Taruskin, "The Dark Side of the Moon." See also Taruskin, "Stravinsky and Us: Postscript, 2008," 442, a virtually identical reprint of the earlier "Stravinsky and Us" but lacks the above-quoted statement; and, further, Taruskin, *Russian Music at Home,* 475.

58. Slim, *Annotated Catalogue,* 207–8.

59. Stravinsky and Craft, *Expositions and Developments,* 94–95.

60. Liese, *Elisabeth Schwarzkopf,* 37.

61. Slim, "Unknown Words and Music." In addition, many reports of Professor Kall also being friendly with Prokofiev in St. Petersburg (1913–January 1915) and of Kall and Prokofiev together in Los Angeles (December 1920–January 1921 and February 1930) are in Sergey Prokofiev, *Diaries,* vols. 2 and 3, *1915–1923* and *1924–1933,* indices: s.v. "Kal."

62. Craft, *A Stravinsky Scrapbook,* 5.

63. Spies, review of *Stravinsky: Glimpses,* 409. For the Craft-Spies friendship see Craft, *An Improbable Life,* 52–53.

64. Craft, *An Improbable Life,* 393–95 (perhaps inadvertently) missed an opportunity in 1997 to explore in-depth experiences in the early 1940s of then fledgling composers Arthur Berger, Harold Shapero, and Claudio Spies working with Stravinsky in Cambridge and Boston.

65. On him see V. Stravinsky and Craft, *Stravinsky in Pictures,* 642–43n13 (final paragraph); Craft, *An Improbable Life,* 113–14; and Craft, *Stravinsky: Discoveries and Memories,* 292–93. For him in 1944, as Stravinsky's music copyist and pre-Craft assistant, see Walsh, *Stravinsky: The Second Exile,* 188–89. Two photographs taken in April of 1948 depict him with Stravinsky and Craft; see Craft, *A Stravinsky Scrapbook,* 20, pls. 38 and 39.

66. V. Stravinsky and Craft, *Stravinsky in Pictures,* 352. Preceding this book's title page, the authors state they are preparing *Stravinsky: The American Period.* It did not appear until "The American Years (1939–1971)," in Stravinsky and Craft, *Memories and Commentaries* (2002), in which for Stevenson, see 214.

67. Stevenson, "Comentario del autor."

68. Slim, "Lessons with Stravinsky," 350, and evidence cited there at 341 for the preexistence of *Futurama*'s second movement (then titled "Nocturne"). See also the review by Steele, "WPA Symphony Sample": "Nocturn [*sic*], by Ernest Anderson [*sic*], opened the second half of the [WPA Orchestra's] program [on 9 April] and proved to be more of a noisy and indeterminate improvisation than a nocturne" (8).

69. Joseph, *Stravinsky Inside Out,* 266; his sixth chapter, "Film Documentaries: The Composer On and Off Camera," is a fine survey, several of its documentaries utilized here.

70. For an account of the entire operation see Adaskin, *A Fiddler's Choice,* 132–36. Viktor Varunts mistakenly located this Canadian premiere of *Les Noces* in Montreal. See Varunts, *I. F. Stravinsky,* 3:851, no. 62. Attending a revival of Bronislava Nijinska's choreography of *Les Noces* at Covent Garden on 2 February 1981, I was pleased to hear Milla Andrew sing, as she had at UBC. Further details about the first (Adaskin) invitation for Stravinsky to visit Vancouver are in Slim, *Annotated Catalogue,* 6–7.

71. Craft, *Stravinsky: Chronicle* (1994), 1–6; Craft, *An Improbable Life,* 72–74; and Craft, *Stravinsky: Discoveries and Memories,* iii.

72. "Dossier Stravinsky-Canada," 25.

73. R. M. K., "Stravinsky Conducts His Works."

74. Craft, "Sunday Afternoon Live," 16; see also Craft, *Down a Path*, 111.

75. Craft, "An Interview," 25.

76. A recording of a broadcast by the San Francisco Symphony on 17 December 1950 for *The Standard Hour,* held by the San Francisco Performing Arts Library, Museum of Performance and Design, reveals he had conducted *Firebird*'s "Ronde des princesses" exactly the same way; surprisingly, there was faulty ensemble just before reh. 7: –1m. by the orchestra's undoubtedly finer double bass players. On *The Standard Hour* in San Francisco (and elsewhere) see Marcus, *Musical Metropolis*, 146–53.

77. Craft, *A Stravinsky Scrapbook*, 176n45, omitted listing Stravinsky's Bach arrangement on this program. Taruskin, *Stravinsky and the Russian Traditions*, 780n2, referring to 1949, observed that Craft knew *Zvezdoliki* better than anyone else, though, arguably, Taruskin himself (at 779–91) now bears the palm. See also *"Oedipus Rex, Perséphone, Zvezdoliki,"* in Craft, *Stravinsky: Glimpses* (1993 ed. only), 393–95.

78. I acquired the *Threni* quotation in 1995; see Slim, *Annotated Catalogue*, 310–14, item 106; see also Lowinsky, *Tonality and Atonality;* and Craft, *Stravinsky: Discoveries and Memories*, 69.

79. Perhaps because I had not inscribed it to the composer, *Musica Nova* is not in Craft, "Selected Source Material."

80. Craft, *An Improbable Life*, 260 (my emphasis).

81. Levitz, *Modernist Mysteries*, 530.

82. Lillian Libman offers a slightly different story. See Libman, *And Music at the Close*, 332–33. He can be seen both standing and hoisting his hat on 30 November 1966 at Ohio State University in Newman, Craft, and Steegmuller, *Bravo Stravinsky*, 79 (lower image).

CHAPTER ONE. TOUR I (1925)

1. See Krasovskaya, *Nijinsky*, 302.

2. Yuzefovich, "Chronicle of a Non-friendship," 755.

3. *Ballet Material and Manuscripts from the Serge Lifar Collection*, Sotheby's (London), 9 May 1984, lot 220, letter in Russian.

4. Casella, "Igor Strawinsky e la sua arte"; Slim, *Annotated Catalogue*, items 7–9 further document their friendship.

5. Stravinsky, *Selected Correspondence*, 2:132.

6. Craft, *Dearest Bubushkin*, Vera Soudeikina to Catherine Stravinsky, 28 Dec. 1924.

7. Slim, *Annotated Catalogue*, 120–23, item 27.

8. Whether *Faun* was related in any way to his juvenile song *Le Jeune Faune et la bergère*, which in 1928 he claimed to have composed at age ten, remains unknown. See Stravinsky, "Pourquoi l'on n'aime pas ma musique"; translated as "Why People Dislike My Music." See also Evans, "Stravinsky's Music in Hitler's Germany," 541n68.

9. Slim, *Annotated Catalogue*, 116–20, item 26.

10. Given twice there in 1908; see Walsh, *Stravinsky: A Creative Spring,* 110; again there in 1915, see Taruskin, *Stravinsky and the Russian Traditions,* 1123; and for Barcelona, mid-March 1924, see Walsh, *Stravinsky: A Creative Spring,* 386.

11. Prokofiev, *Diaries,* 2:444 (6 December) and 445n1 (10 December). She sang this work again in 1923 in Paris with Stravinsky in the audience.

12. Serge Diaghilev introduced her to Stravinsky in Montmartre on 21 February 1921. For two autographed love letters late that year from Stravinsky to Vera de Bosset-Soudeikina, see Slim, *Annotated Catalogue,* 76–90, items 18 and 19. On the violent encounter in 1921 between Stravinsky and Soudeikine see the latter's account (on 18 January 1930, New York) in Prokofiev, *Diaries,* 3:907.

13. Craft, "An Interview," 32; and Craft, *Stravinsky: Discoveries and Memories,* 157–58.

14. Craft, "An Interview," 31–32, so asserted, although his date of "May 1940" for the Stravinsky marriage is incorrect. He had it correctly as 9 March 1940 in V. Stravinsky and Craft, *Stravinsky in Pictures,* 366, although Vera's marital and divorce circumstances related in her letters to Stravinsky in the fall of 1939 differ greatly; see Craft, *Dearest Bubushkin,* 95–99, letters 2, 4, 5, 7, and 10; see also Craft, *A Stravinsky Scrapbook,* 9, no. 6 and its plate. Craft, *Stravinsky: Discoveries and Memories,* 199, noted their Russian church wedding as 14 October 1940 in Los Angeles.

15. Craft, *Down a Path,* 267–69; Craft, "An Interview," 34–35; Craft, *Stravinsky: Discoveries and Memories,* 176–77. Craft, *Dearest Bubushkin* for 1 Jan. 1924 has her "married to M. Staal" (certainly him), and Stravinsky's letter to her on 24 August 1924 is thus (correctly) addressed to Vera Staal.

16. Prokofiev, *Diaries,* 2:388, although performers were frequently thus addressed.

17. The Belgian composer Arthur Hoérée in *Le Ménestrel,* cited in Slim, *Annotated Catalogue,* 119.

18. Prokofiev, *Diaries,* vols. 2 and 3, indices, s.v. "Janacopulos," and s.v. "Stahl."

19. "Ce soir," *Le Figaro,* 29 May 1923, 4, cited in Slim, *Annotated Catalogue,* 108–9, item 23 (Stravinsky's letter of 19 April 1923 to her). The date of 29 May 1923 for her performance, cited in Stravinsky, *Selected Correspondence,* 2:163n10, is correct, a date miscopied as 23 May 1923 in McFarland, "Stravinsky and the Pianola," 93n90.

20. "Stravinsky Arrives to Lead Orchestra," *New York World,* 5 Jan. 1925, 16.

21. On their return Sabline attempted to blackmail Stravinsky, an act apparently concerning neither his wife nor Vera; see Craft's remarks in Stravinsky, *Selected Correspondence,* 2:474–81.

22. "Opera and Concerts of the Week," *New York World,* 4 Jan. 1925, sec. M2. Lipnitzki's photograph—part of a series—is in Schaeffner, *Strawinsky,* pl. 63 (wrongly dated); for its date see Kunstmuseum Basel, *Strawinsky: Sein Nachlass,* 13; and this exhibition's accompanying *Katalog der ausgestellten Bildnisse und Entwürfe für die Ausstattung seiner Bühnenwerke,* item 155.

23. Malkiel, "Modernists Have Ruined Modern Music."

24. V. Stravinsky and Craft, *Stravinsky in Pictures,* 254–55, 355; and Walsh, *Stravinsky: A Creative Spring,* 400. Messing, *Neoclassicism in Music,* 141, reproduces various versions of Stravinsky's New York newspaper interviews.

25. *Pace* Cross, *Igor Stravinsky*, 141, who opts for the later Symphony in C.

26. See "Igor Stravinsky," *Musical America*, 24 Jan. 1925, 1. This photo also appears in Wiborg, "Igor Strawinsky," 9; *Strawinsky: Sein Nachlass*, 13; and Rosar, "Stravinsky and MGM," 108.

27. Slim, *Annotated Catalogue*, 127. Craft incorrectly reports "only one . . . verbal exchange"; see Craft, *The Moment of Existence*, 266. Still later, Craft, "An Interview," 27, mentions all three 1925 meetings. Walsh, *Stravinsky: A Creative Spring*, cites only the second meeting that year, his index at page 682 referring the reader to page 408 for "Gershwin," whose name is absent there; there is a reference at 641n34 (this footnote based on a partly erroneous source). Walsh names four "classical" US composers whom Stravinsky did *not* meet (408).

28. Jablonski, *Gershwin*, 92.

29. Craft, *Stravinsky: Discoveries and Memories*, 115n1, called her an "entirely lesbian American." In "An Interview," 27, and *Stravinsky: Discoveries and Memories*, 250, Craft stated that Arthur Sachs was the host "at a private party" that evening. Wiborg reappeared on 22 November 1940 in Cincinnati, detailing to both Stravinskys "the latest gossip from Paris," and she saw them a week later in New York; see Craft, *Dearest Bubushkin*, 117. For more on Wiborg early in 1930 in New York with Prokofiev, see Prokofiev, *Diaries*, 3:898, and note 2.

30. Reported in Stravinsky and Craft, *Memories and Commentaries* (2002), 206, thus fleshing out (posthumously) Stravinsky's much briefer report forty years earlier in Stravinsky and Craft, *Expositions and Developments*, 97. On Sachs and Stravinsky see Craft, *An Improbable Life*, 107.

31. On this instrument see Slim, "Lessons with Stravinsky," 334–35.

32. Saunders, *Music and Dance in California*, 196, 199, with photograph. On 9 February 1943 Donahue met Stravinsky again, this time at lunch with Vera in Los Angeles; see V. Stravinsky and Craft, *Dearest Bubushkin*, 127.

33. Slonimsky, *Baker's Biographical Dictionary of Musicians*, 705–6; Craft, *An Improbable Life*, 66n20; Prokofiev, *Diaries*, 3:956n1.

34. Stravinsky, *Selected Correspondence*, 1:332n13. As future president of Keynote Records, Hammond issued the first recording (New York, 28 April 1947) of Stravinsky leading his 1938 *Dumbarton Oaks Concerto;* see Stuart, *Igor Stravinsky*, 33, no. 46.

35. Armitage, *George Gershwin*, 172–73; paraphrased in Jablonski, *Gershwin*, 92–94.

36. Stravinsky, *Chroniques de ma vie*, 2:166; translated as *Igor Stravinsky: An Autobiography*, 165.

37. Craft, *Dearest Bubushkin*, 5 December 1930.

38. Jablonski, *Gershwin*, 168. On Hammond see also Craft, *An Improbable Life*, 118.

39. Downes, "Hail and Farewell; Career and Position of George Gershwin in American Music," *New York Times*, 18 July 1937, X5, an account printed sub "1937" as by Downes in Armitage, *George Gershwin*, 223–24; partly reprinted in Downes, *Olin Downes on Music*, 236. Craft, *Stravinsky: Discoveries and Memories*, 251–52, adduced another account, from an unidentified New York newspaper, preserved in a Stravinsky scrapbook, titled and cited by V. Stravinsky and Craft, *Stravinsky in Pictures*, 575, as "Olin Downes's Incompetence."

40. Stravinsky, *Selected Correspondence*, 2:256–57n29, is probably referring to 25 Jan. 1946: Downes's horrific review of Stravinsky's New York Philharmonic concert, cited below.

41. Jablonski, *George Gershwin*, 168; and V. Stravinsky and Craft, *Stravinsky in Pictures*, 647n48, the latter mistakenly reporting that the story appears in the *New York Herald Tribune*.

42. Downes, "Stravinsky as Visitor Stirs Various Reactions"; repr. in Downes, *Olin Downes on Music*, 95. Downes's "prophet" was probably Richard Wagner.

43. Olin Downes, "Music: The Philharmonic Concert," *New York Times*, 6 Feb. 1925, 15; repr. in Downes, *Olin Downes on Music*, 98–100.

44. Downes, "Nostalgia of the Neo-Russians."

45. Perhaps reacting to Downes's sentence, Stravinsky back in France noted in 1926, for an article intended for a US music journal, that in the 1923–24 Piano Concerto he had tried to "catch the note of our marvelous present, not the remote past." Quoted in Levitz, *Modernist Mysteries*, 582n28.

46. Howerton, "The Reception of Igor Stravinsky," unpublished paper (2014), especially 1–9; Howerton kindly sent me a copy of her essay.

47. Prokofiev, *Diaries*, 3:76 and 3:905, reports on these Paris and New York meetings.

48. Taylor, "Music: The Stravinsky Concerto"; his vague "anybody at all" might mean of little distinctiveness, poverty of invention, or even of no value.

49. Craft inexplicably scolded Walsh for saying nothing about "Joseph Steinway's dinner party for Stravinsky," whereas, in fact, he mentions it several times. See Craft, *Down a Path*, 261, mentioning neither place nor date; and, Walsh, *Stravinsky: A Creative Spring*, 401, 642n64.

50. "Brilliant Past Recalled."

51. "Flashlight Photograph."

52. See Craft, *Dearest Bubushkin*, pl. 20. A falsification rendered by cropping in Craft, *Dearest Bubushkin*, 108, pl. 87, is cited in Slim, *Annotated Catalogue*, 211–12, item 67.

53. Craft, *Igor and Vera Stravinsky*, 62 (commentary).

54. Stravinsky and Craft, *Memories and Commentaries* (2002), pl. 14.

55. Stravinsky and Craft, *Expositions and Developments*, pl. 10.

56. Stravinsky and Craft, *Expositions and Developments*, pl. 9.

57. Walsh, *Stravinsky: A Creative Spring*, 401, crediting both Craft books at 641n35; see Stravinskaya, *O I. F. Stravinskom*, 50–54; and Varunts, *I. F. Stravinsky: Perepiska*, 3:121–22, no. 1208. See also Craft, *Stravinsky: Discoveries and Memories*, 138. I thank Vera Micznik for several additional details (in square brackets) about the above translation.

58. "Brilliant Past Recalled."

59. Stravinsky and Craft, *Expositions and Developments*, 73, pl. facing.

60. Craft, "An Interview," 26.

61. Ostensibly for lack of rehearsal time, even though the orchestra's manager offered him additional time; see V. Stravinsky and Craft, *Stravinsky in Pictures*, 658–59n54.

62. Malkiel, "The Guest Conductor," 3, 38, with a plate showing Stravinsky at the piano, Furtwängler looking on. Herzfeld, *Wilhelm Furtwängler*, pl. facing 112, misdates it as 1928. The same plate in Craft, *Dearest Bubushkin*, 63, pl. 67, reproduced from its reprint

in *L'Intransigent* (4 June 1934), Stravinsky probably correctly inscribed as taken "en 1924 à Berlin," where he had indeed played his Piano Concerto with Furtwängler on 8 December; also discussed in Walsh, *Stravinsky: A Creative Spring*, 398. Craft, "An Interview," 27, observed that Stravinsky "did not know how to conduct it—and neither did Furtwängler."

63. V. Stravinsky and Craft, *Stravinsky in Pictures*, 359–60; and Craft, *Dearest Bubushkin*, 29 March 1943. Specifically, Rubinstein, *My Many Years*, 490, recalls the two composers early in the 1940s in Hollywood discussing the loss of "the immense fortunes they might have earned" had the Russian Revolution not deprived them of their legitimate royalties.

64. "Stravinsky Plays at Vincent Astor's"; and Stravinsky, *Selected Correspondence*, 2:472–73n2. Torpadie is pictured earlier, rehearsing for the US premiere in February 1923 of Schoenberg's *Pierrot lunaire*, in *Musical America*, 20 Jan. 1923, reproduced in Feisst, *Schoenberg's New World*, 27, fig. 2.3.

65. Walsh, *Stravinsky: A Creative Spring*, 405.

66. Stravinsky, *Selected Correspondence*, 3:242–43, double plate.

67. Craft, *Dearest Bubushkin*, 28, pl. 21; Stravinsky and Craft, *Memories and Commentaries* (2002), pl. 15.

68. V. Stravinsky and Craft, *Stravinsky in Pictures*, 254–55 (source attribution incorrect), quoted in Rosenfeld, *Musical Impressions*, 144–49; partly quoted in Walsh, *Stravinsky: A Creative Spring*, 403.

69. Stein, "Schoenberg and 'Kleine Modernsky,'" 319–24; and see Schmidt, "The Viennese School and Classicism," esp. 358–59 (pl. 212g), and 365. Unknown to Stein, the Berlin opera source of Schoenberg's clipping—N. Roerig, "Igor Stravinsky über seine Musik: Ein Gespräch mit dem russischen Meister"—had been cited in White, *Stravinsky*, 258n1, though incorrectly, as by "S. Roerig." The ensuing translation of Stravinsky's remark is Stein's; that of Schoenberg's comment is mine.

70. See Olin Downes, "Stravinsky's Chamber Music," *New York Times*, 26 Jan. 1925, 15; Thompson, "Stravinsky Leads Chamber Music Forces"; and Stravinsky and Craft, *Memories and Commentaries* (2002), 206.

71. See Lawson, "Stravinsky and the Pianola," 293–94; and Walsh, *Stravinsky: A Creative Spring*, 403, 406.

72. Craft, *Dearest Bubushkin*, 39, pl. 33.

73. Slim, *Annotated Catalogue*, 129–31, item 31.

74. Walsh, *Stravinsky: A Creative Spring*, 401; Stravinskaya, *O I. F. Stravinskom*, 53; Varunts, *I. F. Stravinsky: Perepiska*, 3:122, no. 1208; Craft, *Stravinsky: Discoveries and Memories*, 138.

75. "Stravinsky Is Grateful," *New York Times*, 8 Feb. 1925, 26.

76. Gunn, [Reviewing the CSO]; cited in Wagner, "A Stravinsky Scrapbook," 17–18.

77. Craft, in Stravinsky, *Selected Correspondence*, 2:293n2, suggested that Arthur Rubinstein may have introduced them, but it might equally well have been Kochanski; see the Garbat obituary, *New York Times*, 14 August 1968, 39.

78. V. Stravinsky and Craft, *Stravinsky in Pictures*, 301–2; Walsh, *Stravinsky: A Creative Spring*, 406, both quoting Charles Ludwig in an unidentified Cincinnati newspaper.

79. Darsky, *Tsar Feodor*, 149 (a source to be used cautiously, according to Shengold, *Opera News*, Dec. 2012, 76, although in this case Darsky's information is correct).

80. Oscar Thompson, "Igor Stravinsky Makes N.Y. Debut."

81. Craven, "Russians Descend on Philadelphia." V. Stravinsky and Craft, *Stravinsky in Pictures*, 253, wrongly identified this orchestra as the "Philharmonic." For the famous story of Stravinsky's hand being kissed by eight hundred elderly ladies in Philadelphia, see Walsh, *Stravinsky: A Creative Spring*, 404. A different wording appears in Saavedra, Fiori, and Levitz, "Stravinsky Speaks," 189–90.

82. Stinson, "Stravinsky Leads Chicago Symphony."

83. Gunn, [Reviewing the CSO]; and Rosenfeld [source and date uncited], in Wagner, "A Stravinsky Scrapbook," 18.

84. Barhyte, "Cleveland Hails Local Debut"; and E. D. B., "Cleveland Orchestra Presents Two Visitors."

85. Furney, "Stravinsky Music Entertains Detroit."

86. Craft, *An Improbable Life*, 75, citing the Russo-America benefit concert in the Shrine Auditorium, 15 May 1945, wrongly asserted that this "was only the second time" in the United States that Stravinsky shared conducting.

87. Thompson, "Stravinsky Lionized."

88. Taylor, "Music: At the Metropolitan"; an anonymous, scurrilous—and untrue—story with pictures in the *Philadelphia Inquirer* (29 March 1925) is cited in Craft, *Igor and Vera Stravinsky*, 62–63, pls. 72 and 73.

89. V. Stravinsky and Craft, *Stravinsky in Pictures*, 241; repeated in Craft, *Igor and Vera Stravinsky*, 62.

90. "Stravinsky Sails Home."

91. Walsh, *Stravinsky: A Creative Spring*, 409.

92. Nicolodi, "Casella e la musica di Stravinsky in Italia," 41–42n1; Walsh, *Stravinsky: A Creative Spring*, 413.

93. Charles Ludwig, quoted in Walsh, *Stravinsky: A Creative Spring*, 641–42nn52, 58; and identified as from the *Cincinnati Times-Star*, 4 March 1925, in Levitz, "Igor the Angeleno," 175n72.

94. Stravinsky to Rafael Moragas, 25 March 1925; see Saavedra, Fiori, and Levitz, "Stravinsky Speaks," 189–90. Fearing this would wear out his conducting hand, Stravinsky halted the kissing after the eight-hundredth lady.

95. Varunts, *I. F. Stravinsky: Perepiska*, 3:121, no. 1208 (14 May 1925); translated slightly differently in Craft, *Igor and Vera Stravinsky*, 62; in Walsh, *Stravinsky: A Creative Spring*, 408; and in Craft, *Stravinsky: Discoveries and Memories*, 138, as "lethally boring."

96. Cited in Craft, *Stravinsky: Discoveries and Memories*, 188, and attributed to Jane Heap in *The Little Review* (6 Jan. 1925).

97. "Stravinsky Pays Tribute to Kochanski's Art with Promise of Violin Work," *Musical America*, 18 April 1925, 33, with plate of both. Wiborg, "Notes on Modern Soloists," 40, offers a fine photograph of Kochanski.

98. Stravinsky to Werner Reinhart, 12 August 1925, in Stravinsky, *Selected Correspondence*, 3:157.

99. Craft, *Stravinsky: Discoveries and Memories*, 7n5.

100. Stravinsky, *Selected Correspondence*, 3:162, 164.

101. "Stravinsky at 85." There are two different violin transcriptions of *Pulcinella*.

102. On Moodie, the premiere, and these several suites see Walsh, *Stravinsky: A Creative Spring*, 422–24; and Slim, *Annotated Catalogue*, 140–44, item 35.

103. For Stravinsky's November 1926 autograph of two excerpts, "dédié à Paul Kochanski," see Cahoon, *Mary Flagler Cary Music Collection*, 48, no. 202; and Joseph, *Stravinsky and the Piano*, 195–97, including pl. 15.

104. Slim, *Annotated Catalogue*, 131–35, item 32.

105. See Rubin, "*The Pipes of Pan*," noting at 140 that Picasso made two hundred drawings of her.

106. See V. Stravinsky and Craft, *Stravinsky in Pictures*, 158; Walsh, *Stravinsky: A Creative Spring*, 168; Craft, *An Improbable Life*, 219.

107. Stravinsky's niece, Tanya, met Picasso "recently" at Juan-les-Pins, noted in her letter of 28 September 1925; see Craft, *Stravinsky: Discoveries and Memories*, 140–41.

108. Walsh, *Stravinsky: A Creative Spring*, 330–32, 398.

109. Slim, "Lessons with Stravinsky," 385, 399.

110. See Stravinsky and Craft, *Themes and Episodes*, 145–56; and Stravinsky, *Themes and Conclusions*, 223–31; see also V. Stravinsky and Craft, *Stravinsky in Pictures*, 281–82.

111. Information is drawn from Walsh, *Stravinsky: A Creative Spring*, 231, 260–61, 276, 372; Stravinsky, *Selected Correspondence*, 2:14–15; and V. Stravinsky and Craft, *Stravinsky in Pictures*, 142, 243.

112. Frederick J. Maroth with William L. Malloch, "Stravinsky the Conductor," booklet accompanying *Stravinsky Conducts Stravinsky*, compact disc CD-1184 (2) [AAD] (Kensington, CA: Music and Arts Program of America, 2006), 4; the source of Thomson's remark has not been located, perhaps deriving from, or tinged by, Thomson's subsequent observations of Stravinsky's conducting. See also the oral history by Maroth and Malloch, *Igor Stravinsky: The Man and His Music*. Photographs of him conducting in Paris (1928), Germany (1929), London (1931), and Berlin (1931) are in Lesure, *Igor Stravinsky: La carrière européenne*, 106–7, no. 353, pl. 354 [recte 353], about which see vol. 2 of Stravinsky, *Selected Correspondence*, Appendix A, 423–24n3; in Woitas, "'A Powerful Motor Drive,'" 93 (three images); in Stravinsky, *Selected Correspondence*, 2:338–39, pl. 2 (lower image); and in Craft, *Dearest Bubushkin*, pl. 57. The full photograph, "c. 1928" (location unidentified) in Walsh, *Stravinsky: A Creative Spring*, 364–65, pl. 5 (lowest image) is of 1929. Though cropped, it is the second of the three reproduced by Woitas.

113. Rosenfeld, *Musical Impressions*, 144–45; partially quoted in V. Stravinsky and Craft, *Stravinsky in Pictures*, 254–55; and more partially in Walsh, *Stravinsky: A Creative Spring*, 403.

114. Taylor, "Music: Stravinsky Conducts."

115. Lawrence Gilman, review, *New York Herald Tribune*, 9 Jan. 1925.

116. Osgood, "Stravinsky Conducts an Interview."

117. Thompson, like Taylor and reporter Jorge Mendoza Carrasco in Mexico City (as late as August 1940), mistakenly dubbed the composer a "Muscovite." For Carrasco see Saavedra, Fiori, and Levitz, "Stravinsky Speaks," 206.

118. Thompson, "Igor Stravinsky Makes N.Y. Debut," 6.

119. Cited in Edgerton, " 'Petroushka,' Igor Strawinsky's Famous Ballet," including reproductions in *Arts and Decoration* (at 66 and 79) of Soudeikine's sketches for the coming New York ballet production conducted by Tullio Serafin.

120. Henry Levine, "Stravinsky Plays His Own Piano Concerto in Its American Première in Boston," *Musical America*, 31 Jan. 1925, 8.

121. M. M. C., "Philadelphia Orchestra Gives Stravinsky Program."

122. Craven, "Russians Descend on Philadelphia."

123. E. D. B., "Cleveland Orchestra Presents Two Visitors," *Musical Courier*, 26 March 1925, 9.

124. Stinson, "Stravinsky Leads Chicago Symphony."

125. Furney, "Stravinsky Music Entertains Detroit," 3.

126. J. H., "Stravinsky Directs Cincinnati Orchestra," *Musical Courier*, 26 March 1925, 42 (dateline 10 March). For more on this episode see the Cincinnati critic Charles Ludwig, quoted in V. Stravinsky and Craft, *Stravinsky in Pictures*, 301–2; Hart, *Fritz Reiner;* and Walsh, *Stravinsky: A Creative Spring*, 406, 641nn52 and 53.

127. Walsh, *Stravinsky: A Creative Spring*, 413.

128. On their love-hate relationship see Prokofiev, *Diaries, 1924–1933*, 131, 587–88, 790–91, 796–98, and 854–55; and Craft, *Stravinsky: Discoveries and Memories*, 84n7: "he always spoke badly about Prokofiev's music," wherein at 245–55, "Sergei Prokofiev," Craft vividly analyzed their relationship, without reference to Prokofiev's *Diaries*. On Stravinsky's improved conducting see Prokofiev, *Diaries, 1924–1933*, 176.

129. Prokofiev, *Diaries, 1924–1933*, 592 (2 June 1927).

130. Walsh, *Stravinsky: A Creative Spring*, 447.

131. For some of these remarks in 1928, 1930, and 1932 see Levitz, *Modernist Mysteries*, 231n178.

CHAPTER TWO. TOUR II (1935)

1. Jones, "Condensation Essence of Stravinsky Compositions." See also Stravinsky, "I—As I See Myself": "after writing the Violin Concerto, I became deeply interested in studying the role of the violin in chamber music." Levitz, "Igor the Angeleno," 151–53, offers a survey of their association, her note 57 (at 174) also correcting Craft's mistranslation from the French of 24 October 1937, in Stravinsky, *Selected Correspondence*, 2:308.

2. One opening is illustrated in V. Stravinsky and Craft, *Stravinsky in Pictures*, 320.

3. Malkiel, "Modernists," 9.

4. Affirmed in Walsh, *Stravinsky: The Second Exile*, 4, 578n8; and V. Stravinsky and Craft, *Stravinsky in Pictures*, 258.

5. Schriftgiesser, "Stravinski Brings Dynamic Ego to City."

6. Stravinsky, *Selected Correspondence*, 2:304n43; and Craft, *Dearest Bubushkin*, 62n5. On Merovitch and his management (1927–33) of "The Three Musketeers"—Gregor Piatigorsky, Vladimir Horowitz, and Nathan Milstein—advertising himself grandiloquently as the trio's "General Representative to the World," see Plaskin, *Horowitz*, 118–19 and passim; and King, *Gregor Piatigorsky*, 61 and passim.

7. Walsh, *Stravinsky: The Second Exile*, 5n9. He is pictured as "President of Musical Art Management" in *Musical America*, 10 Feb. 1935, 51.

8. A photograph of Dushkin appears in Sherman, "Twin Cities Hear Russian Composer"; and another, posed with Stravinsky, is in an advertisement for Musical Art Management Corporation / Alexander Merovitch, President, in *Musical America*, 10 Feb. 1935, 177, 97: "Igor Stravinsky playing his own composition in joint recital with Samuel Dushkin."

9. See Milstein and Volkov, *From Russia to the West*, 126–48, esp. 133–34, 142–46. A longer version, "Igor Stravinsky," in King, *Gregor Piatigorsky*, 80–81 (though wrongly dating these incidents as 1933), also describes Stravinsky's risible but sharp business practices in 1935 with the cellist in New York; see also V. Stravinsky and Craft, *Stravinsky in Pictures*, 647–48n48.

10. Joseph, *Stravinsky and Balanchine*, 133, implies that composer and choreographer met in New York during January.

11. Dushkin, "1949: Working with Stravinsky," 191–92; and Schwarz, "Stravinsky, Dushkin, and the Violin." Most of their itinerary is in "Dear Samsky," in Stravinsky, *Selected Correspondence*, 2:301–2; and Craft, *An Improbable Life*, 146.

12. See Smith, *Making Music in Los Angeles*, 208, fig. 26. Stravinsky composed no such work. Although the 16 July Bowl program promises details about it on the 15 July program, they are not there, for which information I thank Stephen Lacoste of the Los Angeles Philharmonic archive. Nor is there any identification of it in the 22 July 1933 edition of *Pacific Coast Musician*, which mentions for the previous week at the Bowl only "several whimsical fanfares, of brilliant brevity, of course" (1–3).

13. "Concert Honors Igor Stravinsky," *New York Times*, 8 Jan. 1935, 26.

14. The entire photograph is in Kunstmuseum Basel, *Strawinsky: Sein Nachlass*, 13; and a signed copy in Lisa Cox Music, *Music Catalogue 44* (1955), item 140; and in Lisa Cox Music, *Music Catalogue 54* (2005), item 116.

15. Rosar, "Stravinsky and MGM," pl. at 108. On 26 February 1935 Stravinsky inscribed another Lipnitzki portrait of himself (seated at the piano in 1929) to Leonid Victor Raab, a Russian-born émigré composer-orchestrator employed by MGM; reproduced in N. William Snedden, "Hollywood Golden Age of Music Orchestration," work in progress, part 3, 23.

16. Steinert, "*Porgy and Bess* and Gershwin," 43–46; and Jablonski, *Gershwin*, 282.

17. See Walsh, *Stravinsky: The Second Exile*, 5.

18. The following year, Kramer, who had more than three hundred works to his credit, was appointed managing editor and vice president of the music publishing firm Galaxy Corporation of New York (see "Joins Music Publishers," *New York Times*, 12 May 1936, 27). See also his obituary, "Walter Kramer, Music Editor, 79," in the *New York Times*, 9 April 1969, 47; Reese and Matthews, "Kramer"; and Von Glahn and Broyles, "Musical Modernism before It Began," 44–45.

19. K[ramer], "Composers' League Honors Stravinsky." Whether Gershwin attended is unknown.

20. Yuzefovich, "Chronicle of a Non-friendship," letters 29, 31, 38–39, 46–49, 51–53, 55–62, 79–80, 82–83, and 85–88.

21. On 12 December 1934. See Stravinsky, *Selected Correspondence*, 2:301; Slim, *Annotated Catalogue*, 171; and a printed copy of Divertimento inscribed 4 July 1935 to Roland-

Manuel, illustrated in Lisa Cox Music, *Music Catalogue 59* (Crediton, Devon, Great Britain: Lisa Cox Music, 2010), item 115.

22. "New York Concerts," *Musical Courier*, 19 Jan. 1935, 14.

23. "With Pen and Pencil," *Musical America*, 10 April 1935, 9. On this drawing see Slim, *Annotated Catalogue*, 152–54, item 39; and ill. in Slim, "From Copenhagen and Paris," 549, fig. 4. When father and son concertized in Denmark in May of 1935, her drawing was reproduced before and after their concert in the Copenhagen newspaper *Dagens nyheder*, 1 May and 27 September 1935.

24. Fruhauf, *Making Faces*, 163, 227–29, 242.

25. "Stravinsky's Tour Includes Midwestern Concert," *Musical Courier*, 2 Feb. 1935, 11.

26. Devries, "Stravinsky Leads His Works."

27. Quoted in Wagner, "A Stravinsky Scrapbook," 18. Craft, *Stravinsky: Discoveries and Memories*, 270, claimed that Stravinsky's later "caustic" responses to Goldberg sent to the *Los Angeles Times* were authored by Lawrence Morton.

28. McC., "Stravinsky Leads Chicago Orchestra."

29. See Varunts, *I. F. Stravinsky: Perepiska*, 3:553–54, 558–559, nos. 1782 and 1785.

30. Moore, "Feuermann Is Cello Soloist at Stock Concert." Taruskin, *Stravinsky and the Russian Traditions*, 171–233, provides illuminating discussion and analysis of this symphony.

31. Lukewarmly reviewed in Huneker, "Russian Symphony Orchestra." "Dossier Stravinsky-Canada," 31, claims Altschuler's concert of the same work on 12 January 1919 in Montreal was the first performance in Canada of any work by Stravinsky. However, on Monday, 15 January 1917, Vancouver's ballet fans had heard Pierre Monteux lead fifty-six musicians at the old C. P. R. Opera House in Stravinsky's 1909 orchestrations of two Chopin works to open and close *Les Sylphides,* danced by the touring Ballet Russes; see *Vancouver Sun*, 10 Jan. 1917, 5; and Meyer, *Settling New Scores*, 70, no. 20.

32. See the advertisement "Hollywood Bowl," *Los Angeles Times*, 2 August 1927, A9; and Morton, "Stravinsky in Los Angeles," 77.

33. Moore, "Earliest Work by Stravinsky Given Ovation."

34. "Dushkin . . . with Stravinsky constituted a flawless ensemble of an artistry superior to any of its kind ever heard here." See Victor Nilsson, "Stravinsky Sets Mark."

35. Burke, "Society Folk Heed Call of Modern Music"; Burke, "Patrons Aren't Sure Who'll Entertain Noted Concert Pianist." Obviously, Stravinsky's thirty-three North American hotel residencies from 1925 to 1945, as cited in standard sources (Craft, Walsh, et al.), are too few.

36. D. J., "Stravinsky, Dushkin Quintet in Toledo" (however misleading this report's running head!).

37. H. C. G., "Indiana Ensemble in Third Concert." The quartet was named after Alexander Glazunov, whom Stravinsky despised and who succeeded Rimsky-Korsakov as director of the St. Petersburg Conservatory in 1905.

38. Packenham, [Essay on Stravinsky].

39. "Durant toute la mattinée . . . s'acquitta de cette tâche avec une mauvaise grâce attentive." See Wagner, "Igor Strawinsky und René Auberjonois."

40. "Activities of Musicians Here and Afield," *New York Times*, 3 Feb. 1935, X7. These works were the overture to *Ruslan and Lyudmila* and the *Nutcracker Suite*.

41. According to Craft, in Stravinsky, *Selected Correspondence*, 2:301n32, whose source is unspecified.

42. F., "Stravinsky and Lange Conduct G. M. Programs." Walsh, *Stravinsky: The Second Exile*, 7–8n20, reports, however, that the other conductor was Frank Black.

43. V. Stravinsky and Craft, *Pictures and Documents*, 275; staged and danced by Adolph Bolm at the Library of Congress, commissioned from Elizabeth Sprague Coolidge through Engel, then head of the Library. *Pace* Francis, *Teaching Stravinsky*, 24, he did not conduct its premiere.

44. Walsh, *Stravinsky: The Second Exile*, 8. Neither Walsh, nor Craft, nor Dagmar Godowsky herself furnish its date.

45. Godowsky, *First Person Plural*, 213–14. A fuller version about her ensuing affairs with Stravinsky, 1936–40, including a plate of the postcard he mailed to her on 25 March 1937 is in Slim, "Chère amie," 329–45, at 330–31, 334–35, and 339–42. Craft, *Stravinsky: Discoveries and Memories*, 182–84, detailing (inaccurately) her affairs with Stravinsky, omitted the introductory tea.

46. "Capacity House at Opera," *New York Times*, 6 Feb. 1935, 23. V. Stravinsky and Craft, *Stravinsky in Pictures*, 641–42n5; and Walsh, *Stravinsky: The Second Exile*, 8, give the date incorrectly as 4 February. Stravinsky's opinion of the opera is in Stravinsky, *Selected Correspondence*, 1:224. Heyworth, *Otto Klemperer*, 2:45, cites both the date and the opera's conductor incorrectly.

47. Craft, *An Improbable Life*, 197, documentation not provided. Prokofiev, *Diaries*, 2:389 (16 Feb. 1919), called her a "wild daughter." V. Stravinsky and Craft, *Stravinsky in Pictures*, 387, graphically describe Stravinsky's "sexual utopia"; and Craft, *Stravinsky: Discoveries and Memories*, 179, reported his preference as "zaftik" (i.e., Rubenesque).

48. "Music Notes," *New York Times*, 8 Feb. 1935, 27.

49. *Pace* Walsh, *Stravinsky: The Second Exile*, 8, who speaks of "two weeks of relative inactivity."

50. See Slim, "Unknown Words and Music," 302, with valuable corrections by Walsh, *Stravinsky: The Second Exile*, 579n14. On "Woof," Kall's nickname, see below, Tour V. Information about Kall discovered since 2003 is in the present work's notes.

51. See Yastrebtsev, *N. A. Rimskiy-Korsakov*, 2:294.

52. Taruskin, *Stravinsky and the Russian Traditions*, 166, 171. On the recently found Stravinsky memorial for Rimsky, see Braginskava, "New Light." "Funerary Chant," performed by the Maryinsky Orchestra led by Valery Gergiev and broadcast on 2 December 2016 from St. Petersburg, closes with chiming sounds recalling those in Stravinsky's 1966 *Requiem canticles*. See review by Richard Taruskin, *Times Literary Supplement*, 23 Dec. 2016, 19; Rhein, "Long-Lost Opus by Igor Stravinsky"; and Rhein, "CSO Revives Long-Lost Stravinsky."

53. Taruskin, *Stravinsky and the Russian Traditions*, 166, 171.

54. For Kall see Prokofiev, *Diaries*, 1:553 (with Debussy), 624, 685. Prokofiev on 21 December 1920 in Los Angeles notes that Kall "had fallen desperately in love with Ariadna Nicolskaya (Prokofiev's fellow piano student at the St. Petersburg Conservatory and by July 1914 a married woman) and had followed her to America." See Prokofiev, *Diaries*, 2:559.

55. Burke, "2923 [Donors] Enrich Pension Fund"; and O.C., "Stravinsky Leads St. Louis Players."

56. The program is in Wenborn, *Stravinsky*, 117.

57. Frankenstein, "Stravinsky's Career Epitomizes Century." The portrait was Picasso's third (31 December 1920) but was incorrectly identified there as his first (1917); see Geelhaar, "Strawinsky und Picasso," 289, 301, 303. Frankenstein later corresponded with Stravinsky; see UCLA, Charles E. Young Research Library, Special Collections 601, Kall papers, box 5: Stravinsky, folder 7, letters.

58. Walsh, *Stravinsky: The Second Exile*, 364, 638n41.

59. The same photograph appears in the *Los Angeles Philharmonic Program*, 21–22 Feb. 1935, 230.

60. Fried, "Igor Stravinsky Due Wednesday."

61. Fried, "Stravinsky's Music Needs an Orchestra."

62. Lewando, "Igor Stravinsky Devotes Program."

63. Frankenstein, "Stravinsky Proves Popular."

64. Mason, "Inspiration Is Myth," S7.

65. "Stravinsky, Famed Composer, Conducts His Music Monday: Queer Ideas Are Voiced by Russian," *Milwaukee Journal*, 13 Jan. 1935, 6.

66. In addition to these brief comments see, e.g., Giese, "'Espressivo' versus '(Neue) Sachlichkeit,'" 26–42; and Taruskin, *Russian Music*, 433, 469n59, 473–74, 476–79.

67. Jones, "Condensation Essence of Stravinsky."

68. Taruskin, *Stravinsky and the Russian Traditions*, 995–1003; Taruskin, *Text and Act*, 338.

69. Walsh, "Remembering *The Rite of Spring*"; Walsh, *Stravinsky: A Creative Spring*, 207–9.

70. Including arrangements. See Walsh, *The Music of Stravinsky* (1993), 298–306; and, more fully, Walsh, *The New Grove Stravinsky*, 51–56.

71. Cross, "Stravinsky in Exile," 19n14; see also Cross, *Igor Stravinsky*, 100–104.

72. White, *Stravinsky*, 574–75; Walsh, *Stravinsky: A Creative Spring*, 375, 636n1.

73. See Cross, "Stravinsky in Exile," 6, and Ex. 2b, marked *cantabile,* for alto flute, but in the 1947 version (assigned there to bassoon 1) marked *dolce.* Stravinsky frequently substitutes *dolce* for, and even companions *dolce* with, *espressivo. Espressivo* survives but once in the 1947 edition (at 3 mm. before reh. 40).

74. Tawa, *From Psalm to Symphony*, 432n15, recounts an anecdote told to the late Tawa by a BSO player. Several other passages also thus marked *accompany* the piano: for English horn and clarinet (reh. 47–48) and English horn, French horn I, and oboe I (reh. 80).

75. Joseph, *Stravinsky and the Piano*, 201.

76. Holland, "Adele Marcus Is Dead."

77. Craft, "Dix années avec Stravinsky," 76.

78. Taruskin, *Stravinsky and the Russian Traditions*, 1206n137; Taruskin, *Text and Act*, 338.

79. During his fourth tour (1937), such instructions did not deter Stravinsky from altering "many of the expression marks in the printed score" when rehearsing the Toronto Symphony Orchestra; see Bridle, "Stravinsky Thrills Orchestral Audience."

80. Slim, *Annotated Catalogue*, 254–56, item 83.

81. Saavedra, Fiori, and Levitz, "Stravinsky Speaks," 209 (his bracketed words refer to Shostakovich's views, previously cited by the interviewer).

82. Slim, *Annotated Catalogue*, 76–83, item 18.

83. See Craft, *Dearest Bubushkin*, 8–16 April 1963; Craft, *The Moment of Existence*, 270; and Craft, *Stravinsky: Discoveries and Memories*, 160. On 2 February 1933 he had declared to an interviewer in Munich that "in art, emotion is understood. . . . Emotion is for the audience" (quoted in Craft, *Stravinsky: Discoveries and Memories*, 50–51).

84. Szymborska, as quoted in Charles Simic, "Late-Night Whispers from Poland," 30.

85. Letters dated 17 January, 2 April, 10 September, 1 and 10 October 1935, and 3 June 1936, two of them with Kavenoki's annotations on their envelopes, all part of the collection of Kavenoki's papers donated in 1974 by his widow. Professor Janet Neary kindly examined them for me. I am grateful to Dr. Robert Kosovsky of the Music Division at the New York Public Library for the Performing Arts, Lincoln Center, for further details. The six letters supplement information in Robert Craft, "A Chronology of *Chroniques de ma vie*," in Stravinsky, *Selected Correspondence*, 2:494–99.

86. See Stravinsky, *Selected Correspondence*, 2:494.

87. The Oscar W. Koch photograph collection (1944–45), no. 48905580, US Army Military Historical Institute, Carlisle, PA. (A companion photograph, plate 29, below, is wrongly dated 1935 on its reverse side.) A fire in July of 1973 destroyed Kaven's military service records for 1944 and 1945.

88. Stravinsky, *Selected Correspondence*, 2:496.

89. Slim, *Annotated Catalogue*, 163–65, item 43.

90. Emil Hilb to Severin Kavenoki, 1 May 1936; see Stravinsky, *Selected Correspondence*, 2:498–99.

91. Stravinsky, *Selected Correspondence*, 2:499.

92. One high opinion in 1943 of by then Associate Professor Cushing was proffered in Milhaud, "Through My California Window," 94; and another by Milhaud (concerning 1947) in his *Notes without Music*, 299–300. In April of 1947 Cushing led a well-regarded performance of *L'Histoire du soldat* at the University of California, Berkeley; see Cushing, "Precede [*sic*] to Strawinsky Music," a concert reviewed by Frankenstein in the *San Francisco Chronicle*, 21 April 1947, 14.

93. See *Thanks to Berkeley*, 32, pl., a detail of page 1 of *Orpheus* (Hargrove Music Library). The full page is reproduced in Dahl, "The New Orpheus," 286; repr. in Lederman, *Stravinsky in the Theatre*, 72; the latter itself reprinted (New York: Da Capo, 1975). Slim, *Annotated Catalogue*, 298–301, item 101, discusses Stravinsky's handwritten letter of 1957, purchased from Cushing's widow.

94. Lynott, "Composers Igor Stravinsky and Prof. Cushing," 19; slightly cropped on all sides in Fried, "Stravinsky's Role in S. F."

95. Craft, *A Stravinsky Scrapbook*, 139, pl. 280.

96. *San Francisco Chronicle*, 12 Feb. 1935, 1; and *San Francisco Examiner*, 12 Feb. 1935, CCC.

97. "Stravinsky Plays Tonight," *San Francisco Chronicle*, 13 Feb. 1935, 7.

98. Craft, *Stravinsky: Glimpses*, 188n20. Craft's statement summarizes an account in the city's Russian-language *Novaya zarya* (New dawn).

99. *Novaya zarya*, 14 Feb. 1935, 3, translation courtesy of Professor Emeritus Robert Hughes.

100. Armitage, *Accent on Life*, 176–77, explains the origin of "Woof," Kall's nickname.

101. "[Stravinsky] Juggles Baton and Languages," *Los Angeles Illustrated Daily News*, 21 Feb. 1935, 4; see the copy in UCLA, Charles E. Young Research Library, Special Collections 601, Kall papers, box 5: Stravinsky, folder 8, clippings.

102. Armitage, *Igor Strawinsky*.

103. See V. Stravinsky and Craft, *Stravinsky in Pictures*, 325, for the photograph credited to Edward Weston; and Varunts, *I. F. Stravinsky: Perepiska*, 3:432–33, pl. 12.

104. Armitage, *Accent on Life*, pl. 13, lower image. The date was read incorrectly as "le II 35" in Slim, *Annotated Catalogue*, 261.

105. Armitage, *Accent on Life*, 179.

106. Armitage, *Igor Strawinsky*, preceding page 1.

107. V. Stravinsky and Craft, *Stravinsky in Pictures*, 325, caption to plate.

108. Van Patten, *A Memorial Library*, 257, pl. Regarding the charitable circumstances of his earlier donation of the manuscript score of *Danses concertantes* (1941–42) to Stanford University on 9 January 1948, see the 21 December 1947 letter, transcribed in Slim, *Annotated Catalogue*, 258–60, item 85.

109. Kunstmuseum Basel, *Strawinsky: Sein Nachlass*, 129.

110. Louis and Stooss, *Igor Strawinsky*, 50–51.

111. Craft, *Dearest Bubushkin*, 73–74, pls. 72–76, crediting them to Weston.

112. Stravinsky, *Selected Correspondence*, 3:521, Appendix D, a text slightly revised in Craft, *Stravinsky: Glimpses*, 329–30.

113. Weston, "Thirty-Five Years of Portraiture," 453 (reproducing no. 7, above) and 458.

114. Wilson and Madar, *Through another Lens*, 78.

115. Thompson, *Edward Weston Omnibus*, 133. Conger, *Edward Weston*, fig. 864/1935, provides the date, but her same study (fig. 864/1935) mentions only "Nine poses." See also Stark, *Edward Weston Papers*, 47 (Stravinsky correspondence, 1935 cc.).

116. Stravinsky, *Selected Correspondence*, 2:498.

117. Stutsman, "Stravinsky Leads Boston Symphony"; and Stutsman, "Stravinsky Joins Tanglewood School."

118. Jones, "Contemporary Composers Flocking to Los Angeles"; see also Walsh, *Stravinsky: The Second Exile*, 9–10.

119. Lee Shippey, "The Lee Side o' LA"; Rosar, "Stravinsky and MGM," 117n4, cites August and September of 1934 announcements for Stravinsky's arrival in 1935.

120. Slim, "Lessons with Stravinsky," 384.

121. Marcus, *Musical Metropolis*, 153, 196–97. Rodriguez edited *Music and Dance in California* (Hollywood: William J. Perlman, 1940).

122. Jones, "Merle Armitage Book Reveals Stravinsky."

123. Rodriguez, "Drama and Music."

124. C. R., "Stravinsky-Dushkin Recital," *Pacific Coast Musician*, 2 March 1935, 10.

125. Varunts, *I. F. Stravinsky: Perepiska*, 3:571, no. 1801, translated in Slim, "Unknown Words and Music," 306.

126. V. Stravinsky and Craft, *Stravinsky in Pictures*, 324: "Oh, how delicious is California!"

127. Varunts, *I. F. Stravinsky: Perepiska*, 3:562–63, no. 1791, partly translated in Walsh, *Stravinsky: The Second Exile*, 10–11.

128. See Rosar, "Stravinsky and MGM," 113, and 110 for the photograph taken during the visit.

129. V. Stravinsky and Craft, *Stravinsky in Pictures*, 324–25; its anonymous source—"Propositi di Strawinsky," *Gazetta del popolo*, 31 May 1935—is cited in Walsh, *Stravinsky: The Second Exile*, 580n34.

130. Thus incorrectly as two years later: "I met Chaplin in Hollywood in 1937," in Stravinsky and Craft, *Memories and Commentaries* (1960), 103; and "shortly before Gershwin's death [1937]" (174, in the 2002 edition).

131. Jablonski, *Gershwin*, 313; Walsh, *Stravinsky: The Second Exile*, 62n33.

132. See Stravinsky and Craft, *Memories and Commentaries* (1960), pl. 3, between 120–21, from "Two Celebrities Roll a Hoop," *Life*, 26 April 1937, 60, one of these photographs reproduced in V. Stravinsky and Craft, *Stravinsky in Pictures*, 335; and in Craft, *Stravinsky: Discoveries and Memories*, pl. 22, between 176–77, neither identifying its source.

133. For the composer and Chaplin see Stravinsky, *Selected Correspondence*, 2:307–9; and Walsh, *Stravinsky: The Second Exile*, 11–12.

134. Details (also unmasking Robinson's illegal immigrant status) appear in Stravinsky and Craft, *Expositions and Developments*, 83; and Craft, *Stravinsky: Discoveries and Memories*, 190.

135. Craft, *Dearest Bubushkin*, 29 December 1945.

136. See the signed and dated carbon typescript in Slim, *Annotated Catalogue*, 329–32, item 113.

137. Walsh, *Stravinsky: The Second Exile*, 494–95, and note 63; and Craft, *An Improbable Life*, 273n30.

138. Stravinsky, "Programme Notes," *London Magazine*, Feb. 1966, 41n1; repr. in Stravinsky and Craft, *Themes and Episodes*, 43n3.

139. Robinson and Spigelgass, *All My Yesterdays*, 152–53, plate, said to include Toscanini's inscription but undetected by me. Gansberg, *Little Caesar*, 257, reports this (by now) historic piano was willed to the University of California, Los Angeles, after the death in 1991 of Robinson's second wife, Jane.

140. Fritz, "Toscanini in Hollywood," 14–15. Toscanini may have heard this from Romain Rolland, to whom Stravinsky had made such a remark on 26 September 1914: "Il n'aime presque aucun des maîtres consacrés: ni Jean-Sébastien Bach, ni Beethoven"; or from Marcel Proust, to whom Stravinsky on 3 June 1922 purportedly said, "I detest Beethoven." See Rolland, *Journal des années de guerre 1914–1919*, 1:60; and Bell, *Old Friends*, 179–80, citing Proust in English, but to whom early in the 1920s Stravinsky presumably uttered something on the order of "Je déteste Beethoven."

141. For Koldofsky and his departure from Vancouver and Klemperer there, 1944–46, see Crawford, *A Windfall of Musicians*, 233; and Becker, *Discord*, 11–13, 165.

142. Craft, *Stravinsky: Chronicle* (1994), 40; and Craft, *Stravinsky: Discoveries and Memories*, 57.

143. Nor did Stravinsky hear its Los Angeles performance on 22 January 1950; see Craft, *Stravinsky: Discoveries and Memories*, 11–12.

144. See Craft, *Dearest Bubushkin*, 147n3; Craft, *Stravinsky: Discoveries and Memories*, 228n1; and the group photograph, July 1949, in Craft, *Stravinsky: Glimpses*, pl. 3, lower image, in which, despite Craft, Stravinsky is not visible.

145. Even so, Soulima Stravinsky recalled attending the premiere with his father; see Walsh, *Stravinsky: The Second Exile*, 251.

146. Walsh, *Stravinsky: The Second Exile*, 251; a photograph of Koldofsky and Schoenberg is in Feisst, *Schoenberg's New World*, 172, fig. 4.6. Koldofsky recorded the Phantasy on Dial, disc no. 14.

147. The diary is housed in the UCLA Charles E. Young Research Library, Special Collections 601, Kall papers, box 5. Perhaps Chaliapin's imminent arrival a month later in Los Angeles (24 March 1935) was already on Kall's mind; see Darsky, *Tsar Feodor*, "Season 1935," 297; and especially Armitage, *Accent on Life*, 70–74.

148. See *Los Angeles Times*, 23 Feb. 1935, 5, for the advertisement for *Merrily We Roll Along*. It had opened just five days earlier after a three-month run in New York.

149. Quoted in Purcell, *Merle Armitage Was Here!* 39.

150. Levitz, "Igor the Angeleno," 158, incorrectly dates the introduction of Stravinsky and José Maria Aguilar to the spring of 1936 in Argentina.

151. Rodicio, "Cuarteto Aguilar," *Diccionario de la música espanola e hispanoamericana*, ed. E. C. Rodicio ([Madrid]: Sociedad general de autores y editores, 1999), 4:232 (pl. of the 1920s). For California see J. B. Muns, *Musical Autographs, List 13–03* (Berkeley: Muns, 2013), item 16; and the *Los Angeles Times*, 27 Jan. 1935, C1, and 18 March 1935, A5.

152. "Aguilar Quartet Will Appear on Pan Piper Series," *Los Angeles Times*, 7 Jan. 1934, A5; and "The Aguilar Lute Quartet," *Musical Courier*, 2 Feb. 1935, inside front cover.

153. UCLA, Charles E. Young Research Library, Special Collections 601, Kall papers, box 4 and box 2: photographs identified, and box 5: Stravinsky, folder 2.

154. UCLA, Charles E. Young Research Library, Special Collections 601, Kall papers, box 5.

155. Stravinsky, *Themes and Conclusions*, 160, facing pl. It also appears in Robinson and Spigelgass, *All My Yesterdays*.

156. Stravinsky and Craft, *Expositions and Developments*, 120, facing pl. no. 13.

157. G. S., "Stravinsky and Dushkin Appear"; and Stravinsky, *Themes and Conclusions*, 145, facing pl.

158. Joseph, *Stravinsky's Ballets*, 144; for the Warburg-Kirstein-Stravinsky initial meeting see Duberman, *The Worlds of Lincoln Kirstein*, 287. Jordan, *Stravinsky Dances*, 159; and Giroud, *Nabokov*. 133, note that soon after 1933, Nabokov, then living in New York, was giving refresher lessons to Balanchine in counterpoint and harmony. In 1935, on Balanchine's behalf, Nabokov had contacted Stravinsky in France but was then in his bad books. Giroud, 128, finds no evidence that Stravinsky responded, referring to his *Selected Correspondence*, 2:364–65, this latter with a useful preface by Craft, 364–68. Probably much is still to be learned from Nabokov's memoir, *Bagázh*; Giroud, 399–401 and passim, notes its several versions and how little of it is published.

159. Stutsman, "American Premiere of Persephone," 1, 4; see also Yuzefovich, "Chronicle of a Non-friendship," 838.

160. Walsh, *Stravinsky: The Second Exile*, 13, 580n41; unconfirmed in Jordan, *Stravinsky Dances*, 513, or in any of Joseph's three most recent Stravinsky books (2001–11). On 20 March 1937 the first conductor in New York to lead *Firebird* in connection with the staged ballet was Antal Dorati for De Basil's Monte Carlo Ballet; see Martin, "Monte Carlo Ballet."

161. Moore, "Stravinsky Is Ill"; Walsh, *Stravinsky: The Second Exile*, 580n42. This 1935 cold and cancelled Chicago engagement went undetected by Craft in Stravinsky, *Selected Correspondence*, 2:302, who at 2:303 reported the 3 and 4 March 1937 concerts at Winnetka.

162. V. Stravinsky and Craft, *Stravinsky in Pictures*, 321; the interviewer was Karl Schriftgiesser, as cited above.

163. Eversman, "Coolidge Festival Held at Library of Congress." Their entire 1935 repertoire is cited in Stravinsky, *Selected Correspondence*, 2:293–95.

164. Godowsky, *First Person Plural*, 212–15.

165. The present translation follows the one in English of 1936 that Stravinsky himself approved; see Stravinsky, *Chroniques de ma vie*, 2:168–69, 502n9. James Laughlin, US poet and founder of *New Directions in Prose and Poetry*, wrote his mentor and Stravinsky admirer, Ezra Pound, on 5 December 1939 that "anti-semitism is contemptible and despicable. . . . I cannot tell you how it grieves me to see you taking up with it" (cited in *New York Review of Books*, 2 April 2015, 38). Neither R. M. Schafer, in *Ezra Pound and Music*, nor Richard Taruskin, in "Ezra Pound: A Slim Sound Claim to Immortality," suggests that Stravinsky and Pound conversed during the 1920s and 1930s in Paris, Venice, or Rapallo about their mutual prejudice. It was not confined to Europe. For example, Dwight Macdonald, US essayist and later editor of *Partisan Review*, wrote bluntly to a friend in 1925: "You are a Jewess, and are rather obviously one. . . . For I dislike rather violently the Jews as a race" (cited in Skinner, *The Story of Ain't*, 41).

166. On their intimacy and collaborations from February of 1931 in France, Germany, Italy, and England, see Craft in Stravinsky, *Selected Correspondence*, 2:293–311 ("Dear Samsky"); Craft, *Stravinsky: Discoveries and Memories*, 12, 143–44, 147; Dushkin, "1949: Working with Stravinsky"; and Schwarz, "Stravinsky, Dushkin, and the Violin."

167. Stravinsky, *Selected Correspondence*, 2:304.

168. Varunts, *I. F. Stravinsky: Perepiska*, 3:571, no. 1801, 2 March 1935, sent from Colorado Springs; partial translation in Slim, "Unknown Words and Music," 306.

169. Slim, *Annotated Catalogue*, items 15, 17, and 64.

170. Nor was any directed against his friend, the Jewish-Italian composer, Vittorio Rieti, to whom on 10 December 1944, Stravinsky expressed his horror at the death the previous year of Rieti's mother, deported from Paris to Auschwitz; see Ricci, *Vittorio Rieti*, 412. Walsh, *Stravinsky: The Second Exile*, 83–84, proves that Stravinsky's stand in June 1938 in Fascist Italy for performing Rieti's Piano Concerto was motivated by stubbornness rather than moral disposition.

171. Taruskin, *Defining Russia Musically*, 465 (in 1916, plus two instances in 1919); 445n90 (in 1930); 458 and note 105 (in 1933, 1935, and 1948); and Prokofiev, *Diaries*, 3:855 (in 1929), 982 (*recte*: 983), and 986 (the latter two 1 December 1930). The 1936 example Taruskin reports (*Defining Russia Musically*, 459n108) was not suppressed by Craft: see Stravinsky, *Selected Correspondence*, 3:239 (27 Jan. 1936). Levitz, *Modernist Mysteries*, 308n57, alludes to a letter of 9 July 1939 wherein Stravinsky calls Boris de Schloezer a "dirty Jew." Botstein, " 'The Precision of Poetry,' " 322, citing Vladimir Nabokov's "ardent" aversion to anti-Semitism, does not mention Stravinsky's prejudice.

172. Prokofiev, *Diaries*, 3:983, i.e., Darius Milhaud. The editor did not identify "Einstein," but surely he is Alfred Einstein, the distinguished scholar and music critic (1927–33) for the *Berliner Tageblatt* who fled Germany in 1933. Evans, "Stravinsky's Music," 569–70, discusses the 1938 Nazi "Degenerate Music" at Düsseldorf that linked Stravinsky and Einstein.

173. Taruskin, *Defining Russia Musically*, 455, and note 90. He discovered—partially cited, translated, and included—a previously suppressed sentence. I have translated this letter differently (including a few more phrases cited above). Walsh, *Stravinsky: A Creative Spring*, 515, translated it from Peter Sulzer, *Zehn Komponisten um Werner Reinhart: Ein Ausschnitt aus dem Wirkungskreis des Musikkollegiums Winterthur (1920–1950)*, 3:74–76, letter 30. Previously (in 1:68), Sulzer had reported this particular letter—mysteriously— as "missing."

174. Compagnon, *Le cas Bernard Faÿ*, 21, 87–89, and Will, *Unlikely Collaboration*, passim, but esp. 31, 101–5, and 187. There is no evidence that either Reinhart or Stravinsky knew Faÿ or his writings. For Stravinsky's relationship with Mussolini and fascism see Taruskin, *Defining Russia Musically*, 451; V. Stravinsky and Craft, *Stravinsky in Pictures*, 551–52; Craft, *Stravinsky: Discoveries and Memories*, 264–67; and Levitz, *Modernist Mysteries*, 334–36.

175. See, e.g., his letter of 2 August 1937 to Willi Strecker in Stravinsky, *Selected Correspondence*, 3:252; and other evidence as late as 1938 with his recording of *Jeu de cartes* in Berlin as cited in Taruskin, *Defining Russia Musically*, 458–59; and in Taruskin, *The Danger of Music*, 404n58.

176. V. Stravinsky and Craft, *Stravinsky in Pictures*, 553. Walsh, *Stravinsky: A Creative Spring*, 661n18, suggests that Stravinsky may have conveniently assumed this "loathing" at a later date. Perhaps this was even true during World War II, when he was safely settled in the United States.

177. About this and the letters, one of them later cited in translation from a secondary source, see Taruskin and Craft, "Jews and Geniuses." Additional items can be found in Taruskin, *Stravinsky and the Russian Traditions*, 1134n39; and especially in Taruskin, *The Danger of Music*, 215–16.

178. Taruskin, *The Danger of Music*, 391n26, citing a translation by Messing, *Neoclassicism in Music*, 124.

179. Tappolet, *Correspondance Ansermet-Stravinsky (1914–1967)*, 2:17–20, no. 191, at 19 (my emphasis).

180. Stravinsky, *Selected Correspondence*, 3:239n35; and Evans, "Stravinsky's Music," passim.

181. Darsky, *Tsar Feodor*, 175.

182. Stravinsky and Craft, *Memories and Commentaries* (1960), 142; phrased differently in its "reprint" (1981), 152; and differently yet again in its one-volume edition (2002), 173. Hindemith's observation cannot be verified because the "Berlin Radio recording [was] lost during World War II" (Stuart, *Igor Stravinsky*, 72, notes).

183. "Vera to Igor," 1 Feb. 1935, in Craft, *Dearest Bubushkin*, 68.

184. Diamond, "Stravinsky Likes His Wine Red," quoted in Walsh, *Stravinsky: The Second Exile*, 579n13; and in Devries, "Stravinsky Leads His Works," 7.

185. *Chicago News,* 23 Jan. 1935, quoted in "Igor Stravinsky Playing His Own Composition in Joint Recital with Samuel Dushkin, Violinist," *Musical America,* 10 Feb. 1935, 97.

186. McC., "Stravinsky Leads Chicago Orchestra."

187. Burke, "2923 [Donors] Enrich Pension Fund."

188. Rodriguez, "Stravinsky," 12.

189. Stutsman, "American Premiere of Persephone," 1 and 4.

190. M. S., "Stravinsky Leads Premiere."

191. Jacobi, "On Hearing Stravinsky's Perséphone," 115, repr. in Oja, *Stravinsky in Modern Music,* 50.

192. Olin Downes, *New York Times* (1935), cited in Armitage, *Igor Strawinsky* (1936), 54–55.

193. Slim, "From Copenhagen and Paris," 544n7, from *Dagens nyheder,* with the original Danish and my translation.

194. V. Stravinsky and Craft, *Stravinsky in Pictures,* 204, 625n83, citing *Excelsior* (Paris), 11 Sept. 1935.

CHAPTER THREE. TOUR III (1936)

1. Some dates in V. Stravinsky and Craft, *Stravinsky in Pictures,* 329–30, conflict with those reported on 25 April 1936 in an unsigned article for *La Nación,* translated in Saavedra, Fiori, and Levitz, "Stravinsky Speaks," 199–200. These conflicts are not resolved either by Walsh, *Stravinsky: The Second Exile,* 49, writing rather vaguely of Ocampo reciting *Perséphone* "two or three times" in the Teatro Municipal in Rio de Janeiro; or by Levitz, in her "Igor the Angeleno," 153–60. When there are conflicts, I have relied on *La Nación.*

2. Advertisements, *Musical America,* 10 Feb. 1935, 35, 51, 97.

3. See I. Stravinsky, *Selected Correspondence,* 2:305–6, which omits Dushkin's New York residence (Hotel Ansonia).

4. H. Colin Slim, private collection (now at UBC), on 11 October 2012 from J & J Lubrano; provenance: Dushkin estate. *Pace* Francis, *Teaching Stravinsky,* 114, Stravinsky's frequent and cramped handwritten additions are not related to "sobriety" but to frugality concerning notepaper and postage.

5. I. Stravinsky, *Selected Correspondence,* 2:304, 3:238.

6. I. Stravinsky, *Selected Correspondence,* 2:314.

7. The 1936 New York premiere of *Perséphone* was instead conducted on 4–5 Feb. by Hugh Ross with his Schola Cantorum, prompting a truly invidious review by Olin Downes, "Schola Cantorum at Carnegie Hall," *New York Times,* 6 Feb. 1936, 15.

8. For this telegram of 4 January 1936 to Dushkin see I. Stravinsky, *Selected Correspondence,* 2:314.

9. I. Stravinsky, *Selected Correspondence,* 2:313; Walsh, *Stravinsky: The Second Exile,* 53–54n62.

10. I. Stravinsky, *Selected Correspondence,* 3:233; and V. Stravinsky and Craft, *Stravinsky in Pictures,* 241.

11. In 1997 Lion Heart Autographs of New York kindly sent me a partial translation of Stravinsky's original letter, which the firm then owned and from which only a few excerpts are in Craft, *Stravinsky: Glimpses,* 197n77.

12. See Lourié, *My Work in Films*, 1–75; Craft, *Dearest Bubushkin*, 147n3; Walsh, *Stravinsky: The Second Exile*, 251; Craft, *Stravinsky: Glimpses*, pl. 3, lower image (July 1949); Craft, *An Improbable Life*, 125, 202; and Craft, *Stravinsky: Discoveries and Memories*, 228n1.

13. I. Stravinsky, *Selected Correspondence*, 3:231 (20 Feb. 1932); Walsh, *Stravinsky: A Creative Spring*, 513.

14. J. A. S. and A. E. G., "Buenos Aires," 2:1393.

15. Walsh, *Stravinsky: The Second Exile*, 43. That year, Lourié was in London, designing and painting scenery for the Ballet Russe de Monte Carlo; and in 1948 he stage-designed *Perséphone* for the San Francisco Ballet Company; see Lourié, *My Work in Films*, 208, 361.

16. V. Stravinsky and Craft, *Stravinsky in Pictures*, 328–31, give a detailed itinerary. Levitz, "Igor the Angeleno," 153–60, cites a photo taken shipboard and reproduces several of both Stravinskys with Victoria Ocampo, although she omits one of the composer photographing Ocampo (for which see Vásquez, *Vitoria Ocampo*, upper pl. 10 [between 128–29]). Joseph, *Stravinsky and Balanchine*, 133, reports incorrectly that in the spring of 1936 Stravinsky was in New York.

17. Slim, "From Copenhagen and Paris," 550. In 1935, of course, there was no idea of my participating in the Canadian premiere, 7 April 1952, of his Concerto for Two Solo Pianos, the program reproduced and discussed in Adaskin, *A Fiddler's Choice*, 94–95 (pl. 16); and in Slim, *Annotated Catalogue*, 269–70, item 90; nor that I would hear Stravinsky on 5 October 1952 rehearse Divertimento with the Vancouver Symphony Orchestra; and still less that I would own an autograph fragment of Divertimento. For the relationship of the suite to its parent ballet see Slim, "A Stravinsky Holograph," 447–58, fig. 27.2, illustrating the autograph fragment.

18. V. Stravinsky and Craft, *Stravinsky in Pictures*, 389; and Walsh, *Stravinsky: The Second Exile*, 42. Craft, *Stravinsky: Discoveries and Memories*, 181–82, hypothesized that Stravinsky had an affair with her.

19. See *Paul J. Jackson Opera Collection*, part VII: R–S (Syosset, NY: J & J Lubrano, 2016): lot 760, Stravinsky's concert program at the Teatro Colón with Soulima, 2 May 1936; this program, autographed by both Stravinskys, is now at UBC, Slim Stravinsky collection.

20. White, "Stravinsky Directs Own Works."

21. Reproduced in Levitz, "Igor the Angeleno," 160, fig. 7, lower left; sharper reproductions of images from Ocampo's own photo collections are in three biographies of her cited in Slim, "A Stravinsky Holograph," nn. 29 and 33.

22. The entire interview in translation is in Saavedra, Fiori, and Levitz, "Stravinsky Speaks," 197–200, which also lists all the performances proposed for Buenos Aires. About this scandal see V. Stravinsky and Craft, *Stravinsky in Pictures*, 193, 200, and 552–53; Walsh, *Stravinsky: The Second Exile*, 46; and especially Corrado, "Stravinsky y la constelación."

23. Levitz, *Modernist Mysteries*, 338.

24. Craft, *Dearest Bubushkin*, 80, pl. 77.

25. She danced at the Colón from 1925 until her retirement in 1938, and as late as 1999 she was still living in Buenos Aires; see Slim, *Annotated Catalogue*, 166–67.

26. Formerly in my collection; see Slim, *Annotated Catalogue*, 169–78, item 45. I first heard this work at Stravinsky's rehearsal with the Vancouver Symphony Orchestra, Sunday morning, 5 October 1952.

27. See Muñoz, "Juan José Castro (1895–1968)"; Corrado, "Stravinsky y la constelación"; and especially Manso, *Juan José Castro*, 180. Manso notes that Castro was dismissed from both his conducting posts in 1946 for signing an antigovernment petition. See also Hess, "Copland in Argentina," 204–5, 209–10, 215–16, 219, 223, and 231.

28. I. Stravinsky, *The Rite of Spring*, 1.

29. See Joseph, "Stravinsky Manuscripts," 337, no. 7; Levitz, *Modernist Mysteries*, 471n264; and Saavedra, Fiori, and Levitz, "Stravinsky Speaks," 214n10. Neither of Levitz's citations gives its present location: New York, Morgan Library, MS Cary 516.

30. I. Stravinsky, *Selected Correspondence*, 1:369–78, with a facsimile of Stravinsky's copy. For the original manuscript see Jans and Handschin, *Igor Strawinsky: Musikmanuskripte*, 42, 54.

31. Libman, *And Music at the Close*, 85, described there as a "holograph" and reproduced in her book's endpapers. Indeed, no holograph of "Ricercar II" is listed in June of 1984 by Shepard, "The Stravinsky *Nachlass*," 728, nor is the Cantata's manuscript cited in 1989 as complete in the Sacher collection at Basel by Jans and Handschin, *Igor Strawinsky: Musikmanuskripte*, 16.

32. Slim, *Annotated Catalogue*, 308.

33. Walsh, *Stravinsky: A Creative Spring*, 529; Joseph, *Stravinsky Inside Out*, 82–83. For a photograph of Castro, Stravinsky, and Soulima taken at this broadcast, see Manso, *Juan José Castro*, pl. 12 (between pp. 96–97), who reports (p. 95) that Soulima performed the 1924–25 Concerto for Piano and Winds. Oddly, Walsh, *Stravinsky: The Second Exile*, never mentions Castro; Walsh (47) notes that in one Teatro Colón concert (9 May) led by Stravinsky, Soulima, who had performed the work since 16 November 1933 at Barcelona, played both the Piano Concerto and Capriccio.

34. Facsimile in Del Carlo, "Dedicado a Juan José Castro," unpaginated: "Carta a Juan José Castro" (journal copy at Stanford University).

35. Manso, *Juan José Castro*, 153 (pl. facing).

36. Mead, "Milwaukee Hears Soprano."

37. V. Stravinsky and Craft, *Stravinsky in Pictures*, 367; Walsh, *Stravinsky: The Second Exile*, 118n45, 131; summed up and expanded in Levitz, "Igor the Angeleno," 141, 164, 176n82.

38. On its sketches see Joseph, *Stravinsky and Balanchine*, 125–26. Angelo Cantoni analyzes the parent ballet; see Cantoni, *The Language of Stravinsky*, 127–50, 178–83.

39. Slim, *Annotated Catalogue*, 169–78, no. 45; Slim, "A Stravinsky Holograph," 447–58.

40. See Levitz, "Igor the Angeleno" (abstract of a paper she delivered 1 December 2011, University of California, Los Angeles); and Levitz, "Igor the Angeleno," 162–66, 162.

41. Craft, *Stravinsky: Glimpses*, 275; a beautiful photograph of Patricia McBride and Helgi Tomasson dancing the Divertimento is in Taper, *Balanchine*, 327.

42. Acocella, "The Fatal Kiss."

43. Levitz, "Igor the Angeleno," 145–46, 165. For the recently employed term *cosmopolitan* in musicology (discussed with four vastly differing degrees of clarity), see Gooley et al., "Colloquy." See, as well, the several references in Levitz, *Stravinsky and His World*, 144–45, 161–63, passim; and, for a more sharply focused discussion, Botstein et al., "Cosmopolitanisms."

44. Slim, "Stravinsky Holograph," 458n45.

45. Godowsky, *First Person Plural*, 216–17.

46. Stravinsky and Craft, *Expositions and Developments* (1962), 98. He had not led Capriccio since 23 May 1936.

47. Godowsky, *First Person Plural*, 217–21. A photograph of Stravinsky and Soulima in black tie, shipboard 16 June 1936, and inscribed "Équateur" by the composer is in Stravinsky and Craft, *Dialogues*, 80, pl. facing. For an inscribed photograph (taken in 1934 by Hoyningen-Huené), cropped on all sides: "A Monsieur / Jantos Baruro / Souvenirs / cordials de / I Stravinsky / Rio," seemingly dated by the composer, 11 June 1926 [*sic*] (presumably the upper bar of "3" in 1936 has faded), see Lisa Cox Music, *Music Catalogue* 59 (2010), item 54.

48. Godowsky, *First Person Plural*, 220–21, 227–28 (my emphasis).

49. Ocampo to Stravinsky, 25 Feb. 1954, recalling 1936, in Walsh, *Stravinsky: The Second Exile*, 49.

50. Correspondence of Dagmar Godowsky and Stravinsky, Basel, Sacher Stiftung, film 95, 827ff; see also Craft, *Dearest Bubushkin*, 92n8 (letter of 16 May 1938).

51. I. Stravinsky, *Selected Correspondence*, 2:508n12; Craft, *Stravinsky: Glimpses*, 102–3n11 (source and date undisclosed in Craft).

52. Lawrence Morton Papers, University of California, Los Angeles, Charles E. Young Research Library, Special Collections, Collection 1522, box 85; and Alexis Kall Papers, University of California, Los Angeles, Charles E. Young Research Library, Special Collections, Collection 601, box 5: Stravinsky, folder 1: 11 July 1939, presumably "this dear Dagmar" of 11 July 1939, cited by Craft, *Stravinsky: Discoveries and Memories*, 150.

53. José Gabriel, "Igor Strawinsky ha venido succionar el tesoro argentino," *Señales*, 6 May 1936, quoted in Walsh, *Stravinsky: The Second Exile*, 46–47.

CHAPTER FOUR. TOUR IV (1937)

1. The ship, unnamed in Levitz, *Stravinsky and His World*, 151, fig. 2, is identified from an illustration of Robert and Gaby Casadesus in the same lounge of the *Normandie* in *Musical America*, 10 Jan. 1937, pl. facing 34, the date and ship for their voyage confirmed in "Ocean Travelers," *New York Times*, 9 Nov. 1936, 15.

2. I. Stravinsky, *Selected Correspondence*, 2:307n51.

3. Walsh, *Stravinsky: The Second Exile*, 578n9; I. Stravinsky, *Selected Correspondence*, 2:304n43, 306n46. The New York Public Library, Performing Arts Library, Lincoln Center: JOG 73–164, owns Copley's "Press Book for Igor Stravinsky," donated by Kavenoki's widow. It contains Copley's thirteen undated press releases he called "articles," with blank spaces for dates for concert managers to send to their local presses, among them one for *Jeu de cartes* (1937). For this information I again thank Bob Kosovsky, Curator, Rare Books and Manuscripts, Music Division, New York Public Library.

4. Kavenoki's correspondence in 1936 with Richard L. Simon, Leon Shimkin, and Emil Bills, New York Public Library: *MNY (Kavenoki), kindly examined for me by Professor Janet Neary. I. Stravinsky, *Selected Correspondence*, 2:494, documents Simon and Schuster's interest (through Clifton Fadiman) as early as 9 December 1934.

5. "Activities of Musicians Here and Abroad," *New York Times,* 2 Oct. 1936, X6, states that Stravinsky would be "guest conductor with the Toronto Orchestra for a fortnight," but this was not to be. If so, then he would have arrived in Toronto shortly after Christmas, an arrival belied by Sir Ernest's letter of 30 Dec. 1936.

6. National Archives of Canada, Ottawa, Ontario, Mus 7, series A, box 22, file 671. Retention of this letter in MacMillan's papers and its several marginal insertions suggest a draft, the letter itself presumably mailed shortly thereafter. See also V. Stravinsky and Craft, *Stravinsky in Pictures,* 333.

7. "Theatre and Concert Hall, Brief Comment," *Toronto Globe and Mail,* 2 Jan. 1937, 5.

8. Mactaggart, "Appreciation of Music Greater in America."

9. "Stravinsky 'Composes' Music but Says He 'Writes' Music."

10. "In order to live, one must grow" (my translation); see Eaton, "Igor Stravinsky, Apostle of Today." The article was illustrated with Weston's 1935 photograph of the composer (no. 3 in box 2.1).

11. The Toronto Country and Hunt Club is situated on the north shore of Lake Ontario. A fire on 12 July 1973 destroyed most of Kavenoki's wartime service records.

12. Walsh, *Stravinsky: The Second Exile,* 57, reverses the order of the program; an advertisement (15 Dec. 1936) for the concert is reproduced in "Dossier Stravinsky-Canada," 20.

13. Mason, "A Brilliant Concert," cited in *Toronto Globe and Mail,* 6 Jan. 1937, as quoted in "Dossier Stravinsky-Canada," 21. Roberts, "Stravinsky Leads Toronto Symphony," confirms that the "ovation continued for nearly a quarter of an hour."

14. Preston, "Toronto Gives Acclaim to Stravinsky."

15. Mason, "Two Orchestra Concerts," *Toronto Globe and Mail,* 9 Jan. 1937, 7.

16. Craft, *Stravinsky: Chronicle* (1994), 452. For more about 1937 see V. Stravinsky and Craft, *Stravinsky in Pictures,* 363, citing the *Toronto Evening Telegram,* 4 Jan. 1937. See also "Dossier Stravinsky-Canada," 23, for illustrations of the two conductors shoulder to shoulder; and similarly in Roberts, "Stravinsky Leads Toronto Symphony"; and Schabas, *Sir Ernest MacMillan,* 30–31, upper plate [15].

17. Q., "Stravinsky Begins Fortnight as Philharmonic Guest," *Musical America,* 25 Jan. 1937, 31. Stravinsky, *Selected Correspondence,* 2:296n18, suggests that Dushkin was really suffering from a case of nerves.

18. These critics were Marcel Valois in *La Presse* and Thomas Archer in *Gazette Montreal,* both quoted in "Dossier Stravinsky-Canada," 21 and 23.

19. Downes, "Igor Stravinsky and Dushkin Play."

20. Duberman, *Worlds of Lincoln Kirstein,* 330–31; Joseph, *Stravinsky and Balanchine,* 141, 146–47 (on Smit); and V. Stravinsky and Craft, *Stravinsky in Pictures,* 337.

21. "Stravinsky Peels Off His Coat." See also Elliott Carter's insightful review (quoted below) of Stravinsky, mid-January, conducting Mozart's G-major piano concerto (K. 543) with Beveridge Webster.

22. I. Stravinsky, *Selected Correspondence,* 1:6n10; and Craft, *Stravinsky: Glimpses,* 122–23n9.

23. Monighetti, "Stravinsky's Russian Library," 67–68; "Ships from Europe Late," *New York Times,* 11 Jan. 1937, 39.

24. New York Public Library for the Performing Arts, Lincoln Center, JOF 73-36, donated by his widow.

25. A copy of the 1940 pamphlet is in the Lawrence Morton Papers, University of California, Los Angeles, Charles E. Young Research Library, Special Collections, Collection 1522, box 18; the pamphlet is reprinted in White, *Stravinsky*, 88–89, appendix A, item 8. For the payment to Stravinsky see Craft, *Dearest Bubushkin*, 124n9 (final page of Stravinsky's diary for 1941).

26. Monighetti, "Stravinsky's Russian Library," 67–68, 75n44, believes Mandelstamm wrote the essay in French, citing a Russian translation by Anatoliy J. Shaykevich; see Varunts, *I. Stravinskiy: Publitsist i sobesednik*, 139–42, and 498, no. 77, dated as 1940.

27. New York Public Library for the Performing Arts, Music Division, Lincoln Center, JOF 73–37.

28. Taruskin, *Stravinsky and the Russian Traditions*, 460–61nn73–74, cites a French translation, "Mars 1937," of Nouvel's Russian original plus a letter of 4 March 1935 (mistakenly dated following Stravinsky, *Selected Correspondence*, 2:492n5) from Stravinsky's wife about the essay's still incomplete state; her letter's date is corrected by Walsh, *Stravinsky: The Second Exile*, 578n4, to "4 March 1937." Zilbershteyn and Samkov, *Sergey Dyagilev i russkoye iskusstvo* (Sergei Diaghilev and Russian art), 2:438, no. 201, also cite an undated but probably Soviet-era publication of the essay; see Nouvel, *Diaghilev*. See also the Russian translation in Varunts, *I. Stravinskiy: Publitsist i sobesednik*, 161–69, no. 66, made from Mercedes de Acosta's English translation published in 1953.

29. V. Stravinsky and Craft, *Stravinsky in Pictures*, 644n25, cite translations by de Acosta into both English and French, whereas Walsh, *Stravinsky: The Second Exile*, 307, 629n28, twice mentions "the original French text," as edited by de Acosta and its subsequent appearance in *Le Figaro littéraire*, 21 Nov. 1953, 1, 8, as "Le Diaghilev que j'ai connu." This latter, however, does not mention de Acosta's name.

30. V. Stravinsky and Craft, *Stravinsky in Pictures*, 373. Without explanation Walsh, *Stravinsky: The Second Exile*, 607n8, qualifies this commission confusingly with "had in fact, supposedly."

31. Presumably on commission; there is a version for piano from 1936.

32. Shepard, "The Stravinsky *Nachlass*," 723, 738; Jans and Handschin, *Strawinsky: Musikmanuskripte*, 23, 54 (Skizzenbuch 10).

33. Library of Congress, *Catalog of Copyright Entries*, pt. 3, *Musical Compositions 1937*, n.s. 32, no. 2, 194, no. 4708: 18 Feb. 1937. A folder in tall format labeled *PRELUDIUM* [sic] and lying horizontally on a bookshelf in Stravinsky's library at 1218 North Wetherly, was photographed in December of 1966; see Newman, Craft, and Steegmuller, *Bravo Stravinsky*, unpaginated (final photograph); and Craft, *Dearest Bubushkin*, 19 Dec. 1966.

34. Its orchestral score is dated 6 December; Stravinsky's sketches for *Jeu de cartes* and its completion are noted in Joseph, *Stravinsky's Ballets*, 146–49, showing Stravinsky carefully working backward with materials from Rossini.

35. Craft, *Dearest Bubushkin*, 84, pl. 79.

36. Stravinsky to Ralph Hawkes, publisher, 17 Oct. 1949, cited in Craft, *An Improbable Life*, 105, although patron Reichman is neither identified there nor mentioned in an excerpted letter of that date to Ralph Hawkes in I. Stravinsky, *Selected Correspondence*, 3:329. Nor is Reichman characterized in Walsh, *Stravinsky: The Second Exile*, 58, 310, 588n13, whose

knowledge of a "radio orchestra" stems from an undated letter from Lawrence Morton to Nicolas Slonimsky.

37. In Craft, *Dearest Bubushkin* (under the same date), Vera Stravinsky also called the concert "Stravinsky jazz." Dorothy Crawford kindly furnished a photocopy of the 19 Oct. 1953 program from her personal collection; see Crawford, *Evenings on and off the Roof*, 105, 320n110. Although the program itself lists Ingolf Dahl and Leonard Stein as pianists, it cites neither as a celesta player.

38. Kinkle, *Complete Encyclopedia*, 3:1621, no. 1504, listing his recordings; and Colin Larkin, *Encyclopedia of Popular Music*, 6:840. Professor Kristine Forney kindly supplied references to Reichman.

39. For these data see "Joe Reichman" in online indices of the *Los Angeles Times* and the *New York Times*.

40. Kinkle, *Complete Encyclopedia*, 3:1622–23, item 1506; and Larkin, *Encyclopedia of Popular Music*, 6:846.

41. See, e.g., "Radio Programs Scheduled for Broadcast," and his photo in "Phil Duey, Baritone, Sings for WEAF Audience on Tuesday Nights at 8 o'clock While Leo Reisman Directs the Orchestra," *New York Times*, 1934, sec. 8, 14–15.

42. Pollack, *George Gershwin*, 560–62.

43. Sailing from New York on 23 June 1937, Reisman and his band played in July at the US pavilion for the Exposition Internationale de Paris; see also advertisements for August in *Le Figaro littéraire*, 17 July 1937, "*Spectacles*"; and in *Femina*, July 1937, 4.

44. Dorothy Crawford (personal communication) notes that several performers came from the Elliott Brothers Jazz Band, "a talented and versatile group who played in the Roof and Monday Evening concerts." Lloyd Ulyate Elliott was one of the trombonists; William Ulyate Elliott played alto saxophone.

45. For other examples see figure 5.7 and Stravinsky's letter of 25 Dec. 1941, in Sotheby's, *The James S. Copley Library: Arts and Sciences. Including the Mark Twain Collection* (New York: Sotheby's, 17 June 2010): lot 427, with illustration. James Neary kindly drew this auction to my attention.

46. Strangely, Craft, "The Stravinsky *Nachlass* in New York and Basel," in I. Stravinsky, *Selected Correspondence*, 3:513–17, Appendix D, referring to Shepard, "The Stravinsky *Nachlass*"; and Craft, *Stravinsky: Discoveries and Memories*, 233, citing archives later acquired for $5,250,000 by the Paul Sacher Stiftung in Basel, never commented on this anomaly of names.

47. Despite a remark in the 1968 publication, Stravinsky originally included these five string parts (three violins, viola, and cello), slightly revised by him in June of 1953. See Walsh, *Stravinsky: The Second Exile*, 58, 588n13. Its sketches, drafts, and full scores are described in Shepard, "Stravinsky *Nachlass*," 738 (citing among them a "Leo Reisman Score" of nine pages, signed and dated 1937); and less fully in White, *Stravinsky*, 399, item 68, and 612–13, items 64b and 65a-b. See also Jans and Handschin, *Strawinsky: Musikmanuskripte*, 29 and 54 (Skizzenbuch 10, formerly J). In 1949 Stravinsky invited Balanchine "to perform the composer's 1937 piano arrangement"; see Joseph, *Stravinsky and Balanchine*, 17.

48. CD cover of "Joe Reichman and His Orchestra, 1941–1942," Circle CCD-84.

49. See www.fadograph.wordpress.com/leo-reisman. Because the image is cropped at the left, there may have been additional players.

50. Piaf, *Au bal de la change*, 94–97.

51. Even more imaginatively, Paul Griffiths regarded it as "a little jazz fossil, with the glittering calcite of a celesta in its interstices"; see Griffiths, *Stravinsky*, 119.

52. Phillip Ramey, jacket notes for M 30579 (New York: CBS Masterworks, 1971), though catalogued as 1970 by the Library of Congress: no. 70–752024), and partly reprinted for LP M 30579: *The Original Jacket Collection: Stravinsky Conducts Stravinsky* (Sony Music Corporation), booklet: 53. See also Craft, *Dearest Bubushkin*, 27 April 1965; and Stuart, *Igor Stravinsky*, 50, item 157.

53. For wide-ranging, spirited, and stimulating discussions of octatonicism by theorists and music historians, see Taruskin, "Symposium: Catching Up with Rimsky-Korsakov"; revised in Taruskin, *Russian Music*, 78–119.

54. Taruskin, "The Golden Age of Kitsch," 255 (referring to *Der Rosenkavalier*: reh. 303–8).

55. L. M., in *Excelsior*, 21 Dec. 1933, quoted in Lesure, *Stravinsky: Études*, 254; partly translated in V. Stravinsky and Craft, *Stravinsky in Pictures*, 203, noting at 355 that Stravinsky's fondness for jazz declined after 1926.

56. Watson, ["Stravinsky quoted"].

57. Levitz, *Modernist Mysteries*, 335.

58. Arnold, "Strawinsky Calls Swing American"; repr. in *San Francisco News*, 3 Jan. 1942, 9; see also V. Stravinsky and Craft, *Stravinsky in Pictures*, 644n28. Walsh's date, *Stravinsky: The Second Exile*, 124 and 601n3, for the New York interview (*recte*: Dec. 1940) is incorrect.

59. Craft, *Igor and Vera Stravinsky*, 98, item 164; and V. Stravinsky and Craft, *Stravinsky in Pictures*, 360.

60. McCombs, "Words and Music," 8b (providing their entire program); and McCombs, "Stravinsky, Pianist, Presents Music," 9b. On 9 February McCombs informed his readers that "the musicians are due to leave for Albany where they will begin an engagement with the Cleveland Orchestra on tour" (9b).

61. H. G. D., "Stravinsky-Dushkin, and St. Louis Orchestra in Columbus," *Musical Courier*, 27 Feb. 1937, 27; the phrase "extreme later style" was not defined.

62. Coward, *The Letters of Noël Coward*, 349 (12 Feb. 1937: letter to Coward's mother).

63. McCombs, "Words and Music," 9b; and V. Stravinsky and Craft, *Stravinsky in Pictures*, 334, 640nn183–84. Choisy, "Cleveland Hears Novelty by Symanowski," 7, reports that the orchestra began its "Eastern tour in Buffalo" and that "Igor Stravinsky joins the orchestra for the two last concerts in Allentown, Pennsylvania, and Princeton, returning with the players to Cleveland, to be one of the four guest conductors during Dr. Rodzinski's absence." See "Igor Stravinsky to Lead Cleveland Orchestra in McCarter Program Tomorrow Night at 8: 30," *Daily Princetonian*, 17 Feb. 1937, 1.

64. Stravinsky and Craft, *Expositions and Developments*, 76–77.

65. Cone, "McCarter Audience Acclaims Stravinsky."

66. "Stravinsky, Guest Here, Tells of His Poker Ballet," *Cleveland Plain Dealer*, 22 Feb. 1937, 8. Widder, in "Igor Stravinsky—Small Body but a Giant Brain," gave his height as "five feet two"; see V. Stravinsky and Craft, *Stravinsky in Pictures*, 335. The composer himself

claimed "five feet three inches" in I. Stravinsky and Craft, *Dialogues and a Diary*, 54. Strangely, one journalist's first impression of him in Mexico City early in August of 1940 was a "tall, regular build," cited in Saavedra, Fiori, and Levitz, "Stravinsky Speaks," 206.

67. Elwell, "Stravinsky Stirs Concert Audience."

68. R. H. W., "Stravinsky Leads in Cleveland."

69. An interview there, published in the *Cleveland News*, 22 Feb. 1937, is in V. Stravinsky and Craft, *Stravinsky in Pictures*, 334.

70. I. Stravinsky, *Selected Correspondence*, 1:223n292, but dated incorrectly; see Varunts, *I. F. Stravinsky: Perepiska*, 3:610–12, no. 1851.

71. I. Stravinsky, *Selected Correspondence*, 2:308 (24 Oct. 1937) and note 55; see an important correction to Craft's translation of this letter in Levitz, "Igor the Angeleno," 153, 174n57.

72. A photograph of Stravinsky, Dushkin, and Webster is in Matter, "Stravinsky Leads Cleveland Forces." On 26 January 1953 the late John Brockington and I had the honor to give the Canadian radio premiere of Stravinsky's 1935 Double Concerto from Vancouver via the CBC, a performance that was recorded.

73. "Composer Here for Premiere," *Los Angeles Times*, 9 March 1937, 11. On Kosloff see Naima Prevols, *Dancing in the Sun*, 119–32, esp. 127; and Cohen, *International Encyclopedia of Dance*, 4:56. Slim, "Chère amie," 336–38, charts Morros's career as a minor child prodigy at St. Petersburg's Imperial Conservatory of Music, conductor of the émigré troupe La Chauve-Souris in Paris, music director for Paramount Films in Hollywood and New York, and both Soviet and US spy.

74. Varunts, *I. F. Stravinsky: Perepiska*, 3:610–12, no. 1851; Stuart, *Igor Stravinsky*, 26, item 6.

75. Jones, "Composer to Conduct 'Petrouchka' Ballet."

76. V. Stravinsky and Craft, *Stravinsky in Pictures*, 337, offers (without source) a severely cropped photograph of Stravinsky rehearsing in the Shrine Auditorium on 11 March, thereby excluding ballerinas and set; the full picture is in the *Los Angeles Evening Herald Express*, 12 March 1937, 1. The program booklet, p. 8, reproduces a 1935 *Los Angeles Illustrated Daily News* photograph of Stravinsky rehearsing *Petrushka*.

77. R. D., "Acclaim Igor Stravinsky."

78. "*Petrouchka* Ballet Due Tonight," *Los Angeles Times*, 12 March 1937, A18.

79. H. K., "Philharmonic Orchestra Attracts Crowds"; V. Stravinsky and Craft, *Stravinsky in Pictures*, 336, called the Shrine a "barn-like hall."

80. Gerald Strang, "Schönberg, Mahler and Others in Los Angeles," *Modern Music* 14 (1937): 224, partly quoted in Crawford, *A Windfall of Musicians*, 226. On Strang's relationship with Schoenberg see Feisst, *Schoenberg's New World*, 206. For an unenthusiastic review by one who had seen Nijinsky in the title role (Dec. 1916, New Orleans), see de Pina, "Stravinsky-Kosloff."

81. Levy, "Society Groups to Attend Ballet."

82. Stravinsky and Craft, *Memories and Commentaries* (2002), 229, as related by Stravinsky, his erroneous date corrected; see also Craft, *Down a Path*, 6; and Craft, *Stravinsky: Discoveries and Memories*, 8.

83. See previous note; and Crain, "Native Music Given." Neither Russian nor exile, of course, Usigli led the Los Angeles Federal WPA Orchestra, including its premiere on 12 May 1937

of *The Sun Worshipper* by Earnest Andersson, Stravinsky's future Los Angeles pupil. Andersson's son-in-law, James Sample, later conducted this orchestra, rehearsals of which Stravinsky visited frequently in 1941; see Slim, "Lessons with Stravinsky," 381 (22 April 1941).

84. Prevols, *Dancing in the Sun*, 127; and Hal D. Crain, "Hollywood Bowl Season Sets New Records," *Musical America*, Sept. 1937, 22, 34: "Kosloff's idea of the 'Petruchka Ballet' . . . met with unstinted approval from Stravinsky himself."

85. Kall, "Slava poetu."

86. Slim, "Unknown Words and Music," 308n34.

87. Alexis Kall Papers, University of California, Los Angeles, Charles E. Young Research Library, Special Collections, Collection 601, box 3, folder: manuscripts Russian, kindly translated by Richard Taruskin and Olga Panteleeva. Though in Russian, its heading strikingly anticipates the title of the first Stravinsky-Craft publication some twenty-two years later.

88. Presumably not the best-known—or fully clothed—portrait of 1905: pastel and charcoal (canvas, 235 × 133 cm.), Moscow, State Tretyakov Gallery, ill. in Lapshin, *Valentin Serov*, 91; in Kodicek, *Diaghilev*, 71, cat. 100; and in Valkenier, *Valentin Serov*, 55, fig. 2.10. Serov was the son of composer Alexander Nikolayevich Serov. On portraits of Chaliapin by Russian painters (including Serov) see Raskin, *Shaliapin i russkie khudozhniki*, passim.

89. This last was an "apparently perfectly acceptable" term, applied as early as 1898 to Diaghilev, though within his "circle of friends," according to Scheijen, *Diaghilev: A Life*, 83.

90. This relatively rare superlative appears in Stravinsky's 1919–20 ballet *Pulcinella*, full score (publ. 1924): solo double bass; in his 1922–23 Octet full score (publ. 1924; rev. 1952): bassoons at no. 9 (lacking in 1952), clarinet and bassoon at 3 and 6 mm. after reh. 18 (both lacking in 1952), bassoon at reh. 64 (*stacc.* in 1952 at 66), and flute at reh. 70 (72 in 1952); in his 1923–24 Concerto for piano and wind instruments (publ. 1924; rev. 1950): Fr. Hn. I at m. 3 after reh. 16, Fls. Obs., Cls., at 4 mm. after reh. 22, and Fr. Hn. I at 4 mm. before reh. 38; in his 1930 *Symphony of Psalms*, full score (Paris, 1931; rev. 1948): first movement, 4 mm. after reh. 10 (solo trombone, but in 1931 marked "bien détaché") and in its third movement, at rehs. 4 (low strings) and 14 (English horn; but as just "marcatissimo" in 1931), and at m. 3 after reh. 15 (low strings); and in *Danses concertantes* (1941–42), reh. 130 (upper strings). Although "staccatissimo" is not printed in the 1912 *Petrushka* score that he used for Los Angeles Philharmonic rehearsals in 1937, Stravinsky added it just once to all the strings in his revised 1947 version, at 4 mm. before reh. 240 *(Più mosso)*. Possibly, then, at his 1937 *Petrushka* rehearsal in Los Angeles he had requested "staccatissimo" from the strings, directing his attention either to the concertmaster or to the leader of one of the string sections or even to a nonstring player elsewhere in that work, now unmarked.

91. See Ussher, "Composer Explains Himself," 238; and Varunts, *I. F. Stravinsky: Perepiska*, 3:268, no. 1424, n. 1, the latter quoting *Rul* (29 Feb. 1928). In 1941 Stravinsky told Earnest Andersson that "Skrjabin is a Mendelsshon [*sic*] dressed up modernly." See my "Lessons with Stravinsky," 379.

92. "He is two inches under five feet," cited in "Stravinsky, Guest Here, Tells of His Poker Ballet," *Cleveland Plain Dealer*, 22 Feb. 1937, 8. He himself claimed five feet three inches (see note 66 above).

93. Partial translation is in V. Stravinsky and Craft, *Stravinsky in Pictures*, 21; the complete letter is in Varunts, *I. F. Stravinsky: Perepiska*, 1:104–5, no. 40; the quotation is from Craft, *Stravinsky: Discoveries and Memories*, 101.

94. Craft, *Stravinsky: Discoveries and Memories*, 166–72; and Craft, "Vision in Music," 14, both times alleged homosexual relationships, c. 1910–24, between Stravinsky and Delage and also with Maurice Ravel, though providing no substantive evidence for such allegations. In Craft's 2015 obituary, Margalit Fox noted the "skepticism from a number of prominent musicologists," among whom add Cross, *Igor Stravinsky*, 85, who is "suspicious of [Craft's] motives"; and equally negative verdicts by Corn, "Ambidexterity of a Musician"; and Taruskin, *Russian Music*, 10–13.

95. See Craft, *Igor and Vera Stravinsky*, 69, pls. 85–88; and one more image from 1925 (a back view) in I. Stravinsky, *Selected Correspondence*, 3: pl. following 242. The 1912 Ustilug photograph is only partly illustrated in Taruskin, *Stravinsky and the Russian Traditions*, 651, fig. 9.5b.

96. Grabar, *Valentin Alexandrovich Serov*, 271. Serov had been drawing naked men and women since 1879; see *Valentin Aleksandrovich Serov, 1865–1911: Paintings, Graphic-Art from the Collection of the State Russian Museum* (St. Petersburg: Palace Editions, 2005), 45, Catalogue, item 88.

97. Ukolov and Ukolov, *Dusha bez maski* [Soul minus mask], 186.

98. Taruskin, *Stravinsky and the Russian Traditions*, 512, fig. 8.6.

99. See Grabar, *Valentin Alexandrovich Serov*, 288–92, 297–300; and Valkenier, *Valentin Serov*, 54–56. For the 1897 Chaliapin portrait see Ernst, *V. A. Serov*, 41 and pl. 2, between 24–25; see also *"Milaya moya, rodnaya Rossiya!"* 12.

100. See Grabar, *Valentin Alexandrovich Serov*, 166; *"Milaya moya, rodnaya Rossiya!"* 64; and *Valentin Aleksandrovich Serov, 1865–1911*, 162, pl. 126 (cat. 268), and 238 (same plate in a smaller format).

101. See, e.g., his letter of 19 January to Serov regarding a free ticket for Anton Rubinstein's opera, *The Demon*, in Chaliapin, *Chaliapin: An Autobiography*, 226, 236 (for later dates).

102. See Grosheva, *Fyodor Ivanovich Shalyapin*, 3:278–80 (dates in New Style); Koteliarov and Garmasha, *Letopis zhizni*, 1:261–77; and Fryer, *A Chronology*, 2:787–91.

103. Buckle, *Diaghilev*, 78.

104. Grabar, *Valentin Alexandrovich Serov*, 164, gives the year as 1903; Kochno, *Diaghilev and the Ballets Russes*, 281, gives 1904; and Valkenier, *Valentin Serov*, 73–74, color pl. 4, also gives 1904.

105. Stravinsky and Craft, *Conversations with Igor Stravinsky*, 66, a tactless remark considering Stravinsky's portrait in color by Feodor's well-known émigré son, Boris, on the cover of *Time*, 26 July 1948; see also the black-and-white illustration in Joseph, *Stravinsky Inside Out*, 15. Substantiation of Stravinsky's (and Rimsky-Korsakov's) complaints is in Haldey, *Mamontov's Private Opera*, 165–70. In 1913 the young Prokofiev felt differently; see Prokofiev, *Diaries, 1907–1914*, 429, 437–38.

106. Stravinsky and Craft, *Expositions and Developments*, 99, a book (except for its Appendix) finished in March of 1961, as noted in Libman, *And Music at the Close*, 239.

107. See Taruskin, *Stravinsky and the Russian Traditions*, 1202, paraphrasing Yastrebtsev, *N. A. Rimskiy-Korsakov*, 2:570; abridged in Yastrebtsev, *Reminiscences of Rimsky-Korsakov*, 379–80.

108. Varunts, *I. F. Stravinsky: Perepiska*, 1:204, no. 163, letter to M. O. Steinberg of 12 May 1909. When (if ever) Stravinsky learned of Chaliapin's role as (the most probable) motivator for these commissions is not known.

109. Walsh, *The Music of Stravinsky*, 299, item 16; Walsh, *Stravinsky: A Creative Spring*, 549; and Taruskin, *Stravinsky and the Russian Traditions*, 334.

110. See Klimovitsky, *Igor Stravinsky: Orchestrations*, part 3, 332, and note 7; and the observation by Taruskin, *Stravinsky and the Russian Traditions*, 414.

111. See Koteliarov and Garmasha, *Letopis zhizni*, 1:357, 28 Nov. 1909; Taruskin, *Stravinsky and the Russian Traditions*, 334, 412–15, with the 11 Dec. 1909 program announcement at 398; Varunts, *I. F. Stravinsky: Perepiska*, 1:492–93, items 18–19; and Walsh, *Stravinsky: A Creative Spring*, 133.

112. Varunts, *I. F. Stravinsky: Perepiska*, 1:321–22, no. 267; see also Taruskin, *Stravinsky and the Russian Traditions*, 971n8; and Klimovitsky, *Igor Stravinsky: Orchestrations*, 267, its note 15 (condensed in Craft, "An Interview," 29–30).

113. Stravinsky and Craft, *Expositions and Developments*, 99.

114. Perhaps Stravinsky was affected by a booklet about his father sent from Russia early in 1961 and published only in 1972; see Taruskin, *Stravinsky and the Russian Traditions*, 78n2. For more about Stravinsky's father and his connections with Borodin and *Prince Igor* see Taruskin, *Stravinsky and the Russian Traditions*, 77–92, esp. 89–92. For Fyodor's remarkable library see Monighetti, "Stravinsky's Russian Library," 61–77.

115. Fryer, *Chronology*, 2:709; see also Taruskin, *Stravinsky and the Russian Traditions*, 81.

116. Koteliarov and Garmasha, *Letopis zhizni*, 1:186; Kutateladze, *Fyodor Stravinskiy*, 169, no. 39.

117. In 1908 Chaliapin drew the elderly Rimsky-Korsakov in profile, the same year that Serov drew Rimsky full-face; see Raskin, *Shaliapin i russkie khudozhniki*, 134; and Grabar, *Valentin Alexandrovich Serov*, 200.

118. Craft, *Places*, 169–70, 173, cites snapshots taken (September 1902) in Berlin of Stravinsky with Rimsky's daughter at the time of his father's treatments there for spinal cancer. Reading from Rimsky's (published) diary, his granddaughter described for Craft the chorus that Stravinsky composed in June of 1904 for Rimsky's sixtieth birthday.

119. Grabar, *Valentin Alexandrovich Serov*, 117, 200.

120. Stravinsky and Craft, *Conversations with Igor Stravinsky*, 108, "conscience" presumably referring to matters of ethics.

121. Valkenier, *Valentin Serov*, 70; Scheijen, *Diaghilev*, 94 and note 24.

122. Stravinsky and Craft, *Expositions and Developments*, 27. In Stravinsky and Craft's omnibus, *Memories and Commentaries* (2002), 15, Craft altered the remark about "sin" in *Expositions and Developments* to "Diaghilev wanted to introduce his own rules." And in the same omnibus Craft added that "even Diaghilev deferred to him [Serov] in some matters" (86).

123. Fryer, *Chronology*, 2:788–90; Koteliarov and Garmasha, *Letopis zhizni*, 1:274; and Oldani, "Musorgsky," give the *Boris* "premiere" as 9–22 Nov. 1904.

124. Varunts, *I. F. Stravinsky: Perepiska*, 1:275–76, no. 221.

125. Cousin of Stravinsky's wife, then in medical school at Rome.

126. Lesure, *Igor Stravinsky: La carrière*, 19, no. 40 (not illustrated), loaned by Théodore Stravinsky.

127. Alexandre Benois, *Reminiscences*, 331–35, as noted in Taruskin, *Stravinsky and the Russian Traditions*, 761–62n184, and fig. 10.10; and in Walsh, *Stravinsky: A Creative Spring*, 161. See also Karsavina, *Theatre Street*, 287; and Stravinsky's letter of 22 May 1911 from Rome to Michel-Dimitri Calvocoressi concerning *Petrushka* in Paris that coming June, in Slim, *Annotated Catalogue*, 22–27, item 1.

128. Ernst, *V. A. Serov*, 113–14, no. 16; Serov, *Perepiska, 1884–1911*, 288–89, letter 178; and Serov, *V perepiske, dokumentakh i interv'iu*, 2:290, no. 772.

129. Anatoly Lunacharsky was the "Soviet People's Commissar of Enlightenment," purged by Stalin in December of 1933. For a photograph c. 1920 of Lunacharsky with Lenin, see Kendall, *Balanchine and the Lost Muse*, 114. Stravinsky might have heard this anecdote in Paris from Arthur Lourié, living there from 1924, who had worked for Lunacharsky from 1917 before fleeing Russia in 1922, or from Prokofiev, who visited the older composer late in August of 1934 at Voreppe; see Móricz, "*Symphonies* and *Funeral Games*," 107; and Walsh, *Stravinsky: The Second Exile*, 3. On Lunacharsky and Prokofiev see Prokofiev, *Diaries, 1915–1923*, 260–72; and Prokofiev, *Diaries, 1924–1933*, 554–55, pl. 7, image 30; and Scheijen, *Diaghilev*, 413–14. Presumably Stravinsky knew Lunacharsky's hostile article in June of 1913 about *Le Sacre*, translated by Svetlana Savenko, "*Vesna svyashchennaya* in Its Homeland," 245–46. Items 1–3 above are kindly translated by Richard Taruskin and Olga Panteleeva from Kall Papers, box 1, correspondence Russian.

130. Aber-Count, "Kastner, Alfred."

131. See, e.g., Merrill-Mirsky, *Exiles in Paradise*, 56 (program of August 1939).

132. Kall Papers, box 3: manuscripts Russian.

133. Slim, in "Unknown Words and Music," 311–13 and 318, cites talks Kall gave in 1937, 1940, 1942, and 1946.

134. Items 1–3 recall concepts that Stravinsky adumbrated in 1935 near the close of *Chroniques de ma vie*, 2:161: "Most people like music because it gives them certain emotions, such as joy. . . . Music would not be worth much were it reduced to such an end." See also Stravinsky, *An Autobiography*, 163.

135. For Stravinsky's changing attitudes toward Beethoven, and for them even between his late 1935 ghostwritten *Chroniques* and my conjectured date of 1937 for this loose page, see Klimovitsky, *Stravinsky: Orchestrations*, 331–34; and Monighetti, "Stravinsky's Russian Library," 68. Relevant pages are in *Chroniques*, 2:63–71; translated in *An Autobiography*, 115–19. For his earlier opinions about Beethoven see Fritz, "Toscanini in Hollywood," 14–15.

136. M. T. Zarotschenzeff, "Fingal's Cave," 2. Kall's longtime piano student and admirer Dorothy Ellis McQuoid wrote (presumably with Kall's authorization) that he studied "music theory with Rimsky-Korsakoff." See McQuoid, "Dr. Alexis Kall," 20; no other source corroborates her statement, although Kall certainly knew Rimsky.

137. Stravinsky probably alludes to this occasion in a letter he wrote to Pierre Souvtchinsky (1892–1985) on 27 February 1963, now at Basel, Sacher Stiftung; see Varunts, *I. F. Stravinsky: Perepiska*, 1:124–26, no. 64n1, and 3:321–22, no. 1489n3, partly translated (though misdated) in I. Stravinsky, *Selected Correspondence*, 1:52n15. Over several months Professor Richard Taruskin and Olga Panteleeva very generously strove to achieve a reading and a translation, faced with Kall's truly dreadful Russian hand. Professor Robert Hughes kindly modified their reading of one word and its translation, and I have very slightly altered the punctuation for smoother reading.

138. Frolova-Walker, "Rimsky-Korsakov."

139. Walsh, *Stravinsky: A Creative Spring*, 69–70; Taruskin, *Stravinsky and the Russian Traditions*, 111, reports that Stravinsky's first-known gathering with Rimsky enthusiasts occurred on 1 November 1902.

140. Taruskin, *Stravinsky and the Russian Traditions*, 359–63; Walsh, *Stravinsky: A Creative Spring*, 82.

141. See Yastrebtsev, *N. A. Rimskiy-Korsakov*, 2:279, 302, 305, 328, 343–44, 363–64, 367–71, 375, 395, 411–12, 419, 421–22, 439–41, 445, 452–53, 455–56, 462–63, 479–80, 483–87; and the abridged English translation (hence citing fewer such occasions), *Reminiscences of Rimsky-Korsakov*, 327–28, 340, 362–63, 377, 408–9, 418–19, 422–23, 433, 443–46.

142. Prokofiev, *Diaries, 1907–1914*, 122.

143. Taruskin, *Stravinsky and the Russian Traditions*, 464–66; Varunts, *I. F. Stravinsky: Perepiska*, 3:319–22, no. 1489.

144. I. Stravinsky, *Selected Correspondence*, 1:52n15, translated from a letter in the Sacher Foundation; cited in Varunts, *I. F. Stravinsky: Perepiska*, 1:125–26n1.

145. Varunts, *I. F. Stravinsky: Perepiska*, 3:319–22, no. 1489, with Rimsky-Korsakov's remark to Bel'sky quoted at 319. I am grateful to Professor Robert Hughes for this translation, differing slightly from the one in I. Stravinsky, *Selected Correspondence*, 1:vii, cited in Joseph, *Stravinsky and the Piano*, 27.

146. Karsavina, *Theatre Street*, 256, quoted in White, *Stravinsky*, 36; and Scheijen, *Diaghilev*, 201n42.

147. Stravinsky and Craft, *Conversations with Igor Stravinsky*, 40; Stravinsky and Craft, *Memories and Commentaries* (1960), 56; altered in the posthumous Stravinsky and Craft, *Memories and Commentaries* (2002): 43, 47.

148. Joseph, *Stravinsky's Ballets*, 115.

149. Yastrebtsev, *N. A. Rimskiy-Korsakov*, 2:294, but not in his *Reminiscences*; see Slim, "Unknown Words and Music," 303.

150. Kahl [*sic*], *Die Philosophie der Musik nach Aristoteles*, 48, "Vita."

151. Slim, *Annotated Catalogue*, 156–57; Slim, "Unknown Words and Music," 301–4.

152. Yastrebtsev, *N. A. Rimskiy-Korsakov*, 2:226; Yastrebtsev, *Reminiscences*, 300.

153. See Kall, "Nationalism in Russian Music," 82.

154. Ada Hanifin, "Voice of Russ in Lecture and Song," *San Francisco Examiner*, 12 June 1934, 13.

155. Mrs. Louise Brace (in Berkeley, CA) to Kall, 23 March 1944, cited in Slim, "Unknown Words and Music," 305n23. Kall's diary for 23 May 1944 records "[indecipherable] Berkeley."

156. Peyser, *Memory of All That*, 277; quoted (with her erroneous date corrected) in Walsh, *Stravinsky: The Second Exile*, 588–89n33.

157. Jablonski, *Gershwin*, 313.

158. Jablonski and Stewart, *The Gershwin Years*, rev. ed., 265 (upper caption), 266.

159. I. Stravinsky, *Selected Correspondence*, 2:308. In 2007 Craft "updated" this to "In Paris, Stravinsky sent a deeply felt cable of condolence to the young man's mother"; see Craft, "An Interview," 27.

160. Stravinsky to Kall, 1 April 1937 from Seattle's Olympic Hotel, in Varunts, *I. F. Stravinsky: Perepiska*, 3:623–24, no. 1868, trans. Stanislav Shvabrin. For a different translation see Walsh, *Stravinsky: The Second Exile*, 63–64.

161. Frankenstein, "Rossini-Stravinsky Program."

162. V. Stravinsky and Craft, *Stravinsky in Pictures*, 338, plate, depicts Monteux introducing him to members of the San Francisco Symphony.

163. Frankenstein, "Just Where Is Stravinsky?"

164. Marie Hicks Davidson, "Stravinsky Scores in 'Psalm Symphony,'" *San Francisco Call-Bulletin*, 24 March 1937, 14. See also Alexander Fried, "Stravinsky Guest Leader," *San Francisco Examiner*, 21 March 1937, B6; Fried, "Stravinsky Likes Idea"; and Alexander Fried, "Stravinsky Chorale," *San Francisco Examiner*, 24 March 1937, 19.

165. Her copy was offered for sale in November of 2013. See Muns, *Musical Autographs*, item 73 (illustrated inside back cover); Armsby, *We Shall Have Music*, 6; and "'Mrs. Music' Dies—Leonora Armsby," *San Francisco Chronicle*, 21 Jan. 1962, 6. She is pictured with Pierre Monteux in the *San Francisco Chronicle*, 2 Dec. 1944, 31; and in the *San Francisco Examiner*, 3 Dec. 1944, 1.

166. V. Stravinsky and Craft, *Stravinsky in Pictures*, 336, plate.

167. Copies of this club's notice are in Kall Papers, box 5: Stravinsky, folder 6, ephemera.

168. V. Stravinsky and Craft, *Stravinsky in Pictures*, 337. Joseph, *Stravinsky's Ballets*, 149, is similarly misled, apparently by Lincoln Kirstein.

169. Stamped: "Phil Stroupe, San Francisco," the photograph is in the Performing Arts Library, Museum of Performance and Design, San Francisco. This photograph long awaited reproduction (although slightly cropped and lacking information as to its date or circumstances) in "SF Symphony Spring Concert Preview," *San Francisco Chronicle*, Sunday, 28 April 2013, Q43.

170. I. Stravinsky, *Selected Correspondence*, 2:303; but 1:8 and Craft, *Stravinsky: Glimpses*, 123n15, give 29 March.

171. Madison, "Stravinsky on Wednesday"; Madison, "Stravinsky Here Tonight."

172. Madison, "Stravinsky and Dushkin Attract Large Audience"; Walsh, *Stravinsky: The Second Exile*, 63–64, writes (incorrectly, I believe) of *three* Tacoma-Seattle recitals, citing a final one on 1 April (Thursday); Varunts, *I. F. Stravinsky: Perepiska*, 3:614, no. 1853, cites but two.

173. Though the late Mrs. Dushkin confided these details c. 1980 to a British film director, Tony Palmer, he excluded them from his 1980–81 documentary television film, *Stravinsky: Once at a Border*, now on DVD (West Long Branch, NJ: Kultur, 2008): chap. 18; yet Palmer included a truncated performance of "Aria II" (rehs. 77–79 and 83 to its conclusion); see Joseph, *Stravinsky Inside Out*, 191–92; and Joseph, *Stravinsky*

and Balanchine, 342–43. Facsimiles of sketch pages and of final fair copies for the close of this movement are in Mosch, "Igor Stravinsky." Presumably from his own participation in the Palmer film, Craft, *Stravinsky: Discoveries and Memories*, 148, hypothesized the "Larghetto" (March-August 1939) from the Symphony in C as an "elegy" for Catherine.

174. Milstein and Volkov, *From Russia to the West*, 117, 146.

175. See Kobal, *People Will Talk*, 61; and Christie's auction catalogue *Illuminated Manuscripts*.

176. Kobal, *People Will Talk*, 61. Stravinsky's active tuberculosis is mentioned in his letter to Kall, mid-April 1937; see Varunts, *I. F. Stravinsky: Perepiska*, 3:626–27, no. 1873.

177. Godowsky, *First Person Plural*, 228.

178. Kolodin, *The Metropolitan Opera, 1883–1966*, 404. *Amelia al Ballo* had just premiered in English translation on 1 April 1937 at Philadelphia under Reiner. Craft, *Stravinsky: Discoveries and Memories*, 182–83, mistakenly dated the New York premiere and this episode to 26 December 1936.

179. Stravinsky, *Themes and Conclusions*, upper pl. facing 161 (without explanation). The *New York Times*, 14 April 1937, 31, reported Reiner's departure for London.

180. Jones, "Composer to Conduct 'Petrouchka' Ballet."

181. Steegmuller, "Stravinsky at Work," 44.

182. Walsh, *Stravinsky: The Second Exile*, 61. On 20 March, Crain, in "Stravinsky to Compose Music for Forthcoming Film," mistakenly reported him as "recently signed by Boris Morros of Paramount to compose and arrange the music in a forthcoming film." The contract was never signed.

183. Varunts, *I. F. Stravinsky: Perepiska*, 3:562–63, no. 1791; Walsh, *Stravinsky: The Second Exile*, 10–11. Among the scenarios was one entitled *The Knights of St. David*; see I. Stravinsky, *Selected Correspondence*, 2:307n52; Joseph, *Stravinsky Inside Out*, 284n18; and Walsh, *Stravinsky: The Second Exile*, 588n28.

184. Walsh, *Stravinsky: The Second Exile*, 61n25. In 1948 Stravinsky gave Armitage an inscribed copy of his *Poetics of Music;* see Slim, *Annotated Catalogue*, item 86.

185. Fried, "Stravinsky Likes Idea."

186. Frankenstein, "Just Where Is Stravinsky?" His tautology "unique new" was repeated the next day; see Frankenstein, "S. F. Will Hear Famed Concert."

187. Hindemith, *Selected Letters*, 103.

188. His photograph at Balanchine's April rehearsal of *Jeu de cartes* is in V. Stravinsky and Craft, *Stravinsky in Pictures*, 472, lower pl. On the two ballets in New York see Joseph, *Stravinsky and Balanchine*, chaps. 5 and 6, especially at 146 for Edward Warburg's amusing tale of Stravinsky's opening night in the pit, though Joseph's book (121) and his *Stravinsky's Ballets* (132) wrongly assign the first New York staging of *Apollo* to March of 1937. Duberman, *Worlds of Lincoln Kirstein* (332) correctly cites its performances as 27–28 April.

189. Hindemith, *Selected Letters*, 105. This evaluation by Hindemith, an excellent conductor, might be supplemented by James Sample's remark in 1972. Having frequently heard Stravinsky conduct between August 1940 and December 1955, he averred that "Stravinsky was a terrible conductor . . . [although] he got better towards later life"; see Slim, "Lessons with Stravinsky," 388n176.

190. Joseph, *Stravinsky Inside Out*, 284n18. Unlocatable, this letter is presumably misfiled in Basel, Sacher Stiftung; see I. Stravinsky, *Selected Correspondence*, 2:307n52; and Walsh, *Stravinsky: The Second Exile*, 588n28, who advises that he has also seen it.

191. Varunts, *I. F. Stravinsky: Perepiska*, 3:626, no. 1873, translation by Stanislav Shvabrin.

192. Walsh, *Stravinsky: The Second Exile*, 61, and note 29, citing *L'Intransigeant*.

193. Stull, "Igor Stravinsky."

194. Fried, "Stravinsky Fears Blow."

195. Craft, *Dearest Bubushkin*, 127, 26 Sept. 1942, and note 4.

196. Craft, "An Interview," 44; Craft, *Stravinsky: Discoveries and Memories*, 281; and Levitz, "Stravinsky's Cold War Letters, 1960–1963," 308n5, reproducing at 226, fig. 1, a photograph of Souvtchinsky with Stravinsky in the 1930s.

197. Provines, "Front Views and Profiles."

198. V. Stravinsky and Craft, *Stravinsky in Pictures*, 348; Giroud, *Nicolas Nabokov*, 168, both quoting from Nabokov, *Bagázh*. See also Taruskin, *Stravinsky and the Russian Traditions*, 1623–24, and especially his "In from the Cold," 4–5, more sensitive and exculpatory toward the ensuing Cold War Nabokov than Giroud.

199. I. Stravinsky, *Selected Correspondence*, 2:320.

200. "During a Rehearsal by the American Ballet," *Musical Courier*, 27 March 1937, 2; and Joseph, *Stravinsky and Balanchine*, 386n45, referring to the photograph in I. Stravinsky, *Selected Correspondence*, 2:338–39, and dated incorrectly as April. A different (and cropped) version is in Craft, *Dearest Bubushkin*, 89, pl. 81.

201. Joseph, *Stravinsky and Balanchine*, 149–50, 153; and his *Stravinsky's Ballets*, 149–50, preceded by some information by Lincoln Kirstein, "Working with Stravinsky," 143.

202. Liebling, "Stravinsky Ballet in New York." The orchestra is confirmed in Thompson, "New Stravinsky Ballet." A different appraisal, in Duberman, *Worlds of Lincoln Kirstein*, 321 and 329–33, has at 330—incorrectly—members of the Philadelphia Orchestra in the pit.

203. Smit, "A Card Game," 91. Perhaps this attack signaled conducting nerves and relates to the one (cited above) that Stravinsky described to a Copenhagen reporter in mid-July of 1935.

204. One such coast-to-coast broadcast took place in late February from Cleveland; see R. H. W., "Stravinsky Leads in Cleveland."

205. Giroud, *Nicolas Nabokov*, 128. Cantoni, *The Language of Stravinsky*, 434–36, offers a compelling structural analysis.

206. Varunts, *I. F. Stravinsky: Perepiska*, 3:626, no. 1873, letter of c. 16 April, trans. Olga Panteleeva.

207. Varunts, *I. F. Stravinsky: Perepiska*, 3:627–28, no. 1875, letter of 2 May, trans. Olga Panteleeva.

208. Varunts, *I. F. Stravinsky: Perepiska*, 3:642–43, no. 1893, letter of 27 Dec., trans. Olga Panteleeva.

209. "Conductors Enjoy Life Aboard Ship," *Musical America*, August 1937, 4. Misidentifying the vessel as the SS *Normandie* (and, later, as the SS *Ile de France*) and giving an incorrect sailing date, Craft offered a severely cropped photograph in *Dearest Bubushkin*, 90, pl. 83, even though the 1978 V. Stravinsky and Craft, *Stravinsky in Pictures*, 337, correctly

named the vessel. Craft, in I. Stravinsky, *Selected Correspondence*, 2:303, again misnamed the ship and again gave an incorrect sailing date. In Stravinsky, *Themes and Conclusions*, 161, lower facing pl., he again misidentified her, this time as the *Ile de France* in a different onboard photograph of Nadia Boulanger, Stravinsky, the Dushkins, and Arthur Rodzinski. Francis, *Teaching Stravinsky*, 92 and 106 [pl.] misidentified the *Paris* as the [*Queen*] *Mary* and as SS *Exambrion* [sic: *Excambion*], respectively. The *New York Times* article "Ocean Travelers" and Walsh, *Stravinsky: The Second Exile*, 66, have it correctly.

210. Rosenstiel, *Nadia Boulanger*, 277, crops both photo and inscription; Spycket, *Nadia Boulanger*, 87; and Francis, *Teaching Stravinsky*, 106, give it inscribed. I am indebted to Professor Robert Hughes for the translation.

211. Walsh, *Stravinsky: The Second Exile*, 66nn52–53; and Spycket, *Nadia Boulanger*, 92–93; analyzed in Cantoni, *The Language of Stravinsky*, 62–63, 203–4.

212. Walsh, *Stravinsky: The Second Exile*, 66, cites part of this letter.

213. See V. Stravinsky and Craft, *Stravinsky in Pictures*, 340; Walsh, *Stravinsky: The Second Exile*, 590n59: "NYPL Kavenoki Archive"; and Nadeaud, *Orosco at Dartmouth*. For more on Kavenoki in 1937 see I. Stravinsky, *Selected Correspondence*, 2:503n4.

214. Bridle, "Stravinsky Thrills Orchestral Audience."

215. *Modern Music* 14, no. 3 (1937), repr. in Stone and Stone, *The Writings of Elliott Carter*, 6. A live recording survives of this Mozart performance in Carnegie Hall, 17 Jan. 1937, cited in Stuart, *Igor Stravinsky*, 73.

216. Q., "Stravinsky Begins Fortnight as [New York] Philharmonic Guest," *Musical America*, 25 Jan. 1937, 31.

217. "New York Concerts," *Musical Courier*, 30 Jan. 1937, 12.

218. Maroth, "Stravinsky the Conductor," CD booklet to *Stravinsky Conducts Stravinsky*, 10, the occasion only cited by Craft, *Stravinsky: Discoveries and Memories*, 268.

219. Louis and Stooss, *Igor Strawinsky*, 52–53; on Schaal see Walsh, *Stravinsky: A Creative Spring*, 518, 660nn6–7; Craft, *Dearest Bubushkin*, 51n4; and Taruskin, *Russian Music*, 475.

220. Saunders, "Los Angeles Critic Decries Stravinsky's Later Music."

221. "Completes Surprise Trip," *New York Times*, 24 April 1938, 35. Craft, *Stravinsky: Discoveries and Memories*, 183, implied the year was 1937 and misnamed the ship SS *Britannia* there and in *Dearest Bubushkin*, 92n8. The passport matter was solved on her arrival in England.

222. *Illuminated Manuscripts.*

223. Godowsky, *First Person Plural*, 230–32.

224. Craft, *Dearest Bubushkin*, 21 and 23 May 1938.

225. Craft, *Dearest Bubushkin*, 92n8, translates her long letter to Stravinsky.

226. I. Stravinsky, *Selected Correspondence*, 2:308.

227. *Musical America*, 25 Dec. 1937, back cover.

228. Joseph, *Stravinsky and Balanchine*, 160.

229. See I. Stravinsky, *Selected Correspondence*, 2:308n56; and Craft, *Igor and Vera Stravinsky*, 28n24.

230. See I. Stravinsky, *Selected Correspondence*, 2:70n25 and 308n54; and Walsh, *Stravinsky: The Second Exile*, 72.

CHAPTER FIVE. TOUR V (OCTOBER 1939–LATE MAY 1940)

1. His letter of 2 August 1939 to the Compagnie Transatlantique, Paris, is cited in Craft, *Stravinsky: Glimpses*, 92. Craft, *Stravinsky: Chronicle* (1994), 93–94, records a confusing conversation on 20 January 1953 with Dushkin, recalling Stravinsky's arrival in 1939: "Dushkin proposed a second [*sic*] U.S. tour with I.S." to an uninterested concert manager Levine, because "he's [Stravinsky] been here."

2. For the following see Walsh, *Stravinsky: The Second Exile*, 91–92, 94, and especially 594n12 and 597n1. Craft, "An Interview," 20, mistakenly called Professor Edward Forbes a "Dean."

3. Varunts, *I. F. Stravinsky: Perepiska*, 3:667–69, no. 1924, and 682–83, no. 1938 (translation) (also translated in Slim, "Unknown Words and Music," 307).

4. I. Stravinsky, *Selected Correspondence*, 1:437 (1 May 1939 to Forbes); Craft, *Stravinsky: Glimpses*, 103n16, stated the lectures were reduced to six in June of 1939; see also Walsh, *Stravinsky: The Second Exile*, 104n1; and Joseph, *Stravinsky Inside Out*, 26.

5. V. Stravinsky and Craft, *Stravinsky in Pictures*, 350–51; Walsh, *Stravinsky: The Second Exile*, 104–5.

6. Ussachevsky, "My Saint Stravinsky," 35.

7. Nabokov, *Igor Strawinsky*, 83–84. In fact, eight lectures were proposed, and these were then reduced to six. Vera Stravinsky records their December meeting in New York in Craft, *Dearest Bubushkin*, 31 December 1940. On Nabokov see Craft, *Stravinsky: Discoveries*, 282–90, "Nicolas Nabokov." Giroud, *Nicolas Nabokov*, 204, notes that during the war years Stravinsky avoided visiting Nabokov at *Voice of America* on West Fifty-Seventh Street for fear of meeting another exiled composer and former friend from Paris, Arthur Lourié.

8. "The Poetry of Music," *New York Times*, 29 Oct. 1939, sec. RP, 6.

9. Craft, *Stravinsky: Discoveries*, 148–51.

10. *Archives Roland-Manuel*, 2 and 69, lot 234, with two plates; one other from June of 1939, cropped in Lesure, *Igor Stravinsky: La carrière*, 102, item 343, appears in full in Taruskin, *Russian Music*, 441, fig. 17.3.

11. Gavriyil Païchadze to Koussevitzky, in Yuzefovich, "Chronicle of a Non-friendship," 782. Païchadze predicted that Stravinsky would "be completely cured by the end of the summer."

12. Varunts, *I. F. Stravinsky: Perepiska*, 3:667–69, no. 1924.

13. Its obverse is a photographic profile of Stravinsky in 1936 taken by Gar Vic of Buenos Aires, the photographer identified in Slim, *Annotated Catalogue*, 198.

14. V. Stravinsky and Craft, *Stravinsky in Pictures*, 378; Craft, "An Interview," 66.

15. Slim, *Annotated Catalogue*, 69–71, item 15 (ill.); Walsh, *Stravinsky: A Creative Spring*, 357.

16. Dufour, "Strawinsky vers Souvtchinsky," 17–23; and Dufour, "La 'Poétique musicale,'" 381. Both essays have been incorporated into Dufour, *Stravinski et ses exégètes*, 211–44; and partly revised in Dufour, "The *Poétique musicale*." Dufour concludes that "Stravinsky's imprint is on every page." In *Stravinski et ses exégètes*, 236–37, she draws on the 2006 edition of I. Stravinsky, *Poétique musicale*, to propose some additional revisions.

See also, and especially, Taruskin, "Stravinsky's *Poetics*," and "Did He Mean It?" in Taruskin, *Russian Music*, 428–71, and 480–81.

17. I. Stravinsky, *Selected Correspondence*, 2:503–17, Appendix L; Craft's partial translation is in V. Stravinsky and Craft, *Stravinsky in Pictures*, 662n12.

18. Paul Sacher Stiftung, Basel, Switzerland, film 95, 827ff., 26 June 1939.

19. Unfortunately, Kall's diary for 1939 is not among his diaries archived in the Kall Papers at UCLA.

20. Walsh, *Stravinsky: The Second Exile*, 63.

21. Varunts, *I. F. Stravinsky: Perepiska*, 3:675, no. 1933.

22. See I. Stravinsky, *Selected Correspondence*, 2:320 (letter of 19 August 1937).

23. Varunts, *I. F. Stravinsky: Perepiska*, 3:682–83, no. 1938.

24. Varunts, *I. F. Stravinsky: Perepiska*, 3:610–12, no. 1851, trans. in I. Stravinsky, *Selected Correspondence*, 1:392n3. For the two recordings see Stuart, *Igor Stravinsky*, nos. 29 and 6.

25. Varunts, *I. F. Stravinsky: Perepiska*, 3:688, no. 1945; re: a lost letter, see Alexis Kall Papers, box 5: Stravinsky, folder 1, correspondence.

26. Kall Papers, box 5: Stravinsky, folder 1, correspondence.

27. Soon, in December, Stravinsky's name appeared at the top of an advertisement for that agency; see "The Copley List."

28. Paul Sacher Stiftung, Basel, Switzerland, film 95, 827ff., Godowsky-Stravinsky correspondence.

29. Lawrence Morton Papers, box 85 (photocopy of a lost Stravinsky letter).

30. Source unidentified (Basel, Sacher Stiftung?), in Craft, *Stravinsky: Discoveries*, 150.

31. Letter lost; see 8 August, below.

32. Kall Papers, box 1: folder 1.

33. V. Stravinsky and Craft, *Stravinsky in Pictures*, 282; and Kall Papers, box 5: Stravinsky, folder 1; photocopy in Morton Papers, box 85: xeroxes from Kall Papers.

34. Kall Papers, box 5: Stravinsky, folder 1, correspondence.

35. Varunts, *I. F. Stravinsky: Perepiska*, 3:703, no. 1964.

36. Kall Papers, box 5: Stravinsky, folder 1, correspondence.

37. Kall Papers, box 5: Stravinsky, folder 1, correspondence. The program planned in 1938 included *Jeu de cartes* and *Petrushka*.

38. "Sharps and Flats," presumably referring to Kosloff's Ballet Company.

39. Joseph, *Stravinsky Inside Out*, 52, 240; and Joseph, *Stravinsky and Balanchine*, 5, 180, 213.

40. Varunts, *I. F. Stravinsky: Perepiska*, 3:706–7, no. 1969, trans. Olga Panteleeva.

41. Kall Papers, box 1: correspondence (English).

42. Kall Papers, box 5: Stravinsky, folder 1, correspondence (translation mine). A partial translation-summary is in V. Stravinsky and Craft, *Stravinsky in Pictures*, 630n38. For the "little lecture" (also in French), see White, *Stravinsky*, Appendix A6.

43. Kall Papers, box 5: Stravinsky, folder 1, correspondence.

44. Varunts, *I. F. Stravinsky: Perepiska*, 3:682–83, no. 1938 (postscript); see also Slim, "Unknown Words and Music," 308.

45. Kall Papers, box 1: folder 1, correspondence.

46. Slim, "Unknown Words and Music," 308.

47. Dagmar, *First Person Plural,* 241, misremembered that it was in her hotel, the Navarro: "his old apartment directly above me." Walsh, "Stravinsky," incorrectly states that he "went straight to Cambridge." A charge leveled by Francis, *Teaching Stravinsky,* 112, that both men had overindulged in alcohol, is perhaps sustained by Dagmar's October letter to Kall, in Walsh, *Stravinsky: The Second Exile,* 114.

48. Walsh, *Stravinsky: The Second Exile,* 108, 110; see also many details in Craft, *Dearest Bubushkin,* 98–110.

49. Kobal, *People Will Talk,* 61.

50. See Craft, *Stravinsky: Discoveries,* 150. Craft wrongly claims that this was the period of the composer's third, not his first, lecture; Stravinsky's "inaugural" Harvard lecture was on 18 October 1939.

51. Summarized from Kall Papers, box 5: Stravinsky, folder 1, correspondence.

52. See Reis, *Composers in America.*

53. Constitution of the United States of America (New York: American Civil Liberties Union, n.d.), 31–32.

54. Craft, *An Improbable Life,* 198, where Alexei Haieff's gossip is supported by Kall Papers, box 1, Godowsky correspondence: letter of 27 October [1939] to Kall. Though not a possible witness, Saint-John Perse (Alexis Leger), the exiled poet-diplomat who arrived in the United States on 14 July 1940, retold this gossip to Craft in Stravinsky's presence on 16 January 1962; see Stravinsky and Craft, *Dialogues and a Diary,* 197, the date supplied in Craft, *Stravinsky: Chronicle* (1972), 149, and (1994), 283.

55. Her photograph appears in "Adele Marcus," *Musical Courier,* 1 Jan. 1940, 25.

56. Slim, "Unknown Words and Music," 308.

57. Mach, *Great Contemporary Pianists Speak,* 1:133.

58. C., "Adele Marcus Returns in Recital." "Donor Evening Here of American Jewish Congress," *Lake Placid News,* 3 August 1945, 1, notes her repetition of the *Études* for a concert at Lake Placid, New York, on 7 August 1945.

59. Bruno of Hollywood, "Photograph of Adele Marcus."

60. Joseph, *Stravinsky and the Piano,* 201.

61. Craft, *An Improbable Life,* 79n51.

62. "J'ai besoin de le savoir surtout pour la Sym. de Tchaikovsky étant donné que c'est moi qui apporte le matériel." Slim, *Annotated Catalogue,* 206. Information there at 207 and in Craft, *Dearest Bubushkin,* 106n1, about Charles Munch's (supposed) "1939 arrival" in the United States is incorrect.

63. Craft, *Dearest Bubushkin,* 97, 105, 109, the exact work unspecified.

64. Holoman, *Charles Munch,* 38, 56.

65. Both photographs are in Performing Arts Library, no. 991.071, Museum of Performance and Design, San Francisco. Armsby is pictured with Pierre Monteux in *Musical America,* 25 April 1942, 19.

66. Dehmel, "Lopez Forecasts 'Swing' to Endure," offers a photograph of Lopez at the piano; see also Lopez, *Lopez Speaking,* 298–300, 320 (the UCLA copy is inscribed, inside front cover: "CHORD-ically / Vin Lopez"); and Slim, "Stravinsky's Four Star-Spangled Banners," 347, 363n171.

67. I. Stravinsky, *Selected Correspondence*, 2: pl. 10, upper image, between 338–39, there untranslated. I thank Richard Taruskin and Lois Marcus for their kind translation.

68. Lopez, *Lopez Speaking*, 338.

69. They are Mary Rose Bradford (née Himler), second wife of the southern novelist Roark Bradford (whom she married in the 1930s), and an M [Michelle? or Maybelle?] Powers. See *Jackson Opera Collection, part VII: R-S*, lot 759, the fragment's provenance unknown previous to Mr. Jackson. It is now in the Slim Stravinsky Collection at UBC.

70. Lopez, *Lopez Speaking*, 306.

71. Kall Papers, box 5: Stravinsky, folder 1, Godowsky correspondence (my translation); see also Slim, "Chère amie," 341.

72. Kall Papers, box 5: Stravinsky, folder 6, ephemera.

73. Godowsky, *First Person Plural*, 238; "professional life before" perhaps referring to Morros in 1937.

74. I. Stravinsky, *Selected Correspondence*, 3:274, but also (translated) as "my agent," in Yuzefovich, "Chronicle of a Non-friendship," 786, letter 29.

75. "Igor Stravinsky," *Musical Courier*, 1 Dec. 1940, 78 and 90 (inside facing back page).

76. Craft, *Stravinsky: Glimpses*, 89.

77. Craft, *Dearest Bubushkin*, 14 January 1940, notes Vera attended this exhibition shortly after her arrival in New York. For her difficult entry into the United States see Craft, *An Improbable Life*, 384.

78. Kall Papers, box 5: Stravinsky, folder 1, correspondence, English.

79. Craft, *Dearest Bubushkin*, 21 March 1940 records that Smith did so.

80. Craft, "Appendix K," in I. Stravinsky, *Selected Correspondence*, 2:493–99.

81. Godowsky, *First Person Plural*, 239, summarized and confirmed by Stravinsky himself in V. Stravinsky and Craft, *Stravinsky in Pictures*, 660n66, though dated incorrectly there as 4 April. Certainly his first rehearsal was on 1 April.

82. Craft, *Stravinsky: Discoveries*, 190.

83. Kall Papers, box 1: Godowsky, English correspondence, 25 March 1940 (her emphases). Bruno Zirato was manager of the New York Philharmonic. On Kall's nickname, "Woof," see below.

84. Craft, *Dearest Bubushkin*, 31 March 1940.

85. Stravinsky and Craft, *Memories and Commentaries* (2002), 209–11.

86. Morgan, "Forbes, Elliot." During the academic year 1958–59, I had the good fortune to serve as El's first assistant conductor for the Harvard Glee Club on the heels of his appointment as professor of music at the university.

87. Additional information comes from Frederick Jacobi Jr., a Harvard freshman in 1939; see his "Harvard Soirée," *Modern Music* 16 (Oct. 1939): 47–48, repr. in Oja, *Stravinsky in Modern Music*, 57.

88. Kall Papers, box 5: Stravinsky, folder 1, correspondence.

89. See also Walsh, *Stravinsky: The Second Exile*, 102, and 597n1.

90. President's Papers, Harvard University Archives, UA I 5.168, J. B. Conant 1933–53, box 18, 1939–40, Norton-Page: Norton Professorship of Poetry; Forbes's Latin phrase is from Vergil's *Aeneid*. See also Stravinsky's letter in the spring of 1939 to Edward Forbes, excerpted in V. Stravinsky and Craft, *Stravinsky in Pictures*, 336.

91. Edward Waldo Forbes Papers, Harvard University Archives, Pusey Library, Boulanger.

92. For wine drinking at a slightly later period see Nabokov, *Old Friends,* 197–98; and, especially, V. Stravinsky and Craft, *Stravinsky in Pictures,* 583–84.

93. Armitage, *Accent on Life,* 176–77; and Craft, *Dearest Bubushkin,* 95n1, communicated to Craft by El.

94. Tryon, "Stravinsky as Lecturer"; although Forbes, *History of Music at Harvard,* 74, implies Stravinsky wore formal dress at all six occasions.

95. Paraphrased in Walsh, *Stravinsky: The Second Exile,* 105.

96. Davidson, "Stravinsky in San Francisco Rehearsal."

97. Selections from this newspaper's narrative are quoted carelessly in V. Stravinsky and Craft, *Stravinsky in Pictures,* 351–52; and in Stravinsky and Craft, *Memories and Commentaries* (2002), 214. The newspaper does not mention Robert U. Nelson (Harvard MA [1937], PhD [1944]), noted in Craft, "Selected Source Material," 357, item 50, as "one of Stravinsky's pupils at Harvard in 1939–1940"; Nelson taught at UCLA from 1938 to 1970.

98. I thank Marian Green LaRue.

99. Ussachevsky, "My Saint Stravinsky," 35.

100. V. Stravinsky and Craft, *Dearest Bubushkin,* 223n2, and 114nn7 and 8.

101. W. F., "Harvard Students Taught Music"; see also V. Stravinsky and Craft, *Stravinsky in Pictures,* 351.

102. Zenck, "Leben und Überleben," 56 (asterisk preceding note 1, referring to 1994), 66–67; and Zenck, "Challenges and Opportunities," 175.

103. Slim, "Lessons with Stravinsky," 350 and note 91. Plates of him conducting and listening at Eastman in March of 1966 are in *Official Bulletin of the University of Rochester . . . School of Music* 63, no. 1 (March 1968): 28; and in Louis Ouzer [photographer], *Eastman School of Music, 1921–71* (Rochester, NY: Eastman, 1971), Sept. and Oct. 1971, respectively.

104. Slim, "Lessons with Stravinsky," 380, 388–89.

105. A facsimile reproduction of Stravinsky's letter to Professor A. Tillman Merritt is in Forbes, *History of Music at Harvard,* 75.

106. Joseph, *Stravinsky Inside Out,* 182–84, and pl. (rehearsing the *Ebony Concerto* in 1965), an image also in *Stravinsky: Once at a Border,* chap. 21; and Craft, *Dearest Bubushkin,* 3 and 27 April 1965. Stravinsky perhaps also coached Goodman in 1946, when Vera Stravinsky was giving him Russian lessons at 1260 N. Wetherly (Craft, *Igor and Vera Stravinsky,* 104–5, pl. 180). See also Slim, "Lessons with Stravinsky," 395.

107. "Eisenberg, Moses Joel," American Biographical Archive [microfiche], ser. 2, Munich: K. G. Saur, 1995, no. 167, entries 369–71; and Craft, *Dearest Bubushkin,* 112n3, and 114. Whether or not Dr. Eisenberg was consulted for Stravinsky's looming dental problems, while there the composer was certainly treated on 11 and 12 March 1940 and on 6 May by a Dr. Fink, whose office was on Boylston Street.

108. Added by Craft to "A Centenary View, Plus Ten," in *Stravinsky: Glimpses,* 5 (not in the 1992 ed.), though omitting the placard's present location (see next note). Craft neither quoted nor analyzed Stravinsky's charming musical setting.

109. Kall Papers, box 5: Stravinsky, folder 5; ill. in *UCLA Librarian,* 10 Feb. 1961, 47; and in Slim, "Unknown Words and Music," 314, pl. 2. V. Stravinsky and Craft, *Stravinsky in*

Pictures, 650n94, were thus incorrect about *Babel* being Stravinsky's first setting of English. However, Carter, "*The Rake's Progress* and Stravinsky's Return," cites no Stravinsky setting in English whatsoever before *The Rake's Progress*.

110. See Craft, *An Improbable Life,* 281; and Craft, *Dearest Bubushkin,* 17 March 1965. Another instance appears in Craft, *Stravinsky: Discoveries,* 184.

111. A biography with her photograph is in Saunders, *Music and Dance,* 198–99.

112. This musical postcard, bearing on one side a frontal portrait photograph of Stravinsky taken in 1936 by Gar Vic of Buenos Aires, is briefly described in Hinch, "Music Was Dorothy [McQuoid] Hopper's Life."

113. Carter, "*The Rake's Progress* and Stravinsky's Return."

114. Stravinsky's fastidiousness in creating thank you notes—his exacting (and at times comic) search for just the right phrase—is documented in Nabokov, *Igor Strawinsky,* 61–63; and in Nabokov, *Bagázh,* 175.

115. Craft, *Dearest Bubushkin,* 108, pl. 87. These errors and the cropping greatly angered the late Mrs. McQuoid.

116. A plate is dated thus in Schiff, "Everyone's *Rite* (1939–1946)," 175, fig. 1. Undated in other reproductions of the seated Disney and Stravinsky holding a huge score, glasses in mouth, pen in right hand, the photograph as dated by Schiff may stem from V. Stravinsky and Craft, *Stravinsky in Pictures,* 353. Perhaps Dorothy McQuoid drove them that Sunday to Disney's studio.

117. Walsh, *Stravinsky: The Second Exile,* 204–5, pl. 4 (upper image). One photograph of Kall in I. Stravinsky, *Selected Correspondence,* 2:338–39, pl. 11, is unsatisfactory; he is also cropped from various other photos, such as the one in Craft, *Dearest Bubushkin,* 113, pl. 89, to be compared with another one in Craft, *Igor and Vera Stravinsky,* 95, pl. 156.

118. Varunts, *I. F. Stravinsky: Perepiska,* 3:601–2, no. 1840; as in Slim, "Unknown Words and Music," 306, translated by Michael Green and Stanislav Shvabrin. For the seated Kall see Rosar, "Stravinsky and MGM," 110.

119. Armitage, *Accent on Life,* 176.

120. Edward Waldo Forbes Papers (formerly HUG), Harvard University Archives, Pusey Library, 4401.4: "Stravinsky." Translation is mine.

121. *Musical America,* 10 Jan. 1940, front cover.

122. Craft, *Dearest Bubushkin,* 24 and 30–31 March, 4 April, and 24 May 1940.

123. Kall Papers, box 4: Diaries (1940). I am indebted for the translation to Professor Robert Hughes. Additional details about late March rehearsals with the Boston Symphony are in Yuzefovich, "Chronicle of a Non-friendship," 784, letter 25.

124. "Drops Incognito," interview in an unidentified Pittsburgh newspaper, cited in Craft, *A Stravinsky Scrapbook,* 8, no. 5. This was the day that Stravinsky wrote Edward Forbes about the fifty-dollar increase in room and board at Gerry's Landing.

125. For Stravinsky's speech at the postconcert reception see Craft, *A Stravinsky Scrapbook,* 8, no. 5.

126. A play, *Candlelight* (author unidentified), opened on 12 July 1939 with the Village Hall Players at nearby Framingham; see "Tales, Twice Told and Even More, for Summer Theatres," *New York Times,* 9 July 1939, sec. 9:1. Advertised in the *Boston Evening Transcript,* 3 Feb. 1940, 6, as "Recommended: 'Candle Light in Cambridge.'" The Forbes-

Street Stock Company Will Open at Odd Fellows Hall, North Cambridge," no opening date was given. If "Forbes" is El Forbes (or his father) and "Streett" is Gorg [*sic*] Street (see fig. 5.10), this would explain Kall's attendance; he was then living with Stravinsky on the top floor of the paternal Forbes's home at Gerry's Landing.

127. Much snow appears in Craft, *Igor and Vera Stravinsky,* 95, pl. 156, a photograph taken in Boston on 17 March 1940.

128. Levitz, "Igor the Angeleno," 172n2.

129. Sponsored by the Women's Republican Club of Massachusetts, Inc., 46 Beacon Street, Boston. On the verso of the club's (purloined) stationery, Stravinsky scribbled for Kall in Russian: "Here is a melody for you!" with a two-measure repetitive three-note tune: "Dearest Woof Where's Your Spirit?" reproduced in Slim, "Unknown Words and Music," 315, plate 3.

130. Kall, a witness for the Stravinsky marriage at the Pickman home in Bedford, is cropped out in Craft, *Dearest Bubushkin,* 113, pl. 89 (far right); see Stravinsky and Craft, *Memories and Commentaries* (2002), 211.

131. Stravinsky and Craft, *Memories and Commentaries* (2002), 211; "Andrey" remains unidentified.

132. Craft, *Dearest Bubushkin,* 30 and 31 March 1940.

133. Craft, "An Interview," 24. Craft, *Down a Path,* 219–20, stated that Stravinsky conducted from his own partly manuscript, partly printed score of 1926 for *Le Sacre,* perhaps thus connecting him the more intimately with his recording of it made the next day.

134. Stravinsky and Craft, *Memories and Commentaries* (2002), 213, misdated both lecture and dinner to 11 April.

135. Kall's UCLA papers contain a fictitious "*New York Star,* Late City Edition, Thursday 25 April 1940," with a huge headline in English—"STRAVINSKY THRASHES DR. ALEXIS KALL IN A FIT OF JEALOUSY"—surely intended as a practical joke; see Slim, "Unknown Words and Music," 310. Details of the Harvard Collegium's performance, originally scheduled for 4 p.m. on 11 April 1940, were arranged by two letters (7 and 21 November 1939) from Harvard's then instructor in music Donald Grout; see Kall Papers, box 5: Stravinsky, folder 1, correspondence.

136. See Stravinsky and Craft, *Memories and Commentaries* (2002), 211–12.

137. Forbes, *History of Music at Harvard,* 74; and Stuart, *Igor Stravinsky,* 73.

138. "Stravinsky Conducts His Concerto," *Musical Courier,* 1 April 1940, 24; and "New York Concert," *Musical America,* 25 March 1940, 35.

139. Joseph, *Stravinsky and the Piano;* partly quoted in Craft, *Stravinsky: Glimpses,* 299, and expanded in Craft, *Stravinsky: Discoveries,* 65. Professor Nina Scolnik, University of California at Irvine, who knew Marcus slightly at Juilliard (where Marcus taught from 1954 to 1990), kindly offered this explanation.

140. Taruskin, *Text and Act,* 365; Taruskin, *Russian Music,* 492–93; and Stuart, *Igor Stravinsky,* 30, no. 27.

141. Craft, *An Improbable Life,* 29n1, incorrectly stated that Craft first saw him conduct "sixteen years later." It was just six years later (in January of 1946); see Craft, *An Improbable Life,* 62.

142. Compare J & J Lubrano, *Catalogue 61* (Lloyd Harbor, NY: J & J Lubrano Music Antiquarians, 2005): lot 178 (ill.), slightly cropped at top; and *Strawinsky: Sein Nachlass*, 127, upper pl.

143. Compare *Strawinsky: Sein Nachlass*, 12–13; and Lisa Cox Music, *Music Catalogue 44* (1955), lot 140 (the same item as Cox, *Music Catalogue 54* [2005], lot 116).

144. Yuzefovich, "Chronicle of a Non-friendship," 815, fig. 1.

145. Compare Slim, *Annotated Catalogue*, 268, item 89, and several autographed programs held in Sacher Stiftung, Basel.

146. Craft, *Stravinsky: Chronicle* (1994), 394.

147. See, e.g., Joseph, *Stravinsky Inside Out*, 25: "Three years after his residency in Cambridge, Harvard sent Stravinsky the only copy of the translation" (its translator unidentified); and also the several authors sub "*Poétique musicale*," 350, "Index."

148. Slim, "Unknown Words and Music," 309, quoted from Forbes Papers; on Fine see Forbes, *History of Music at Harvard*, 68. Unacknowledged as authored by Kall, the synopsis is in Joseph, *Stravinsky Inside Out*, 218–20.

149. Alexis Kall, "Stravinsky in the Chair," 296. For one reason that Kall's translation failed to appear in 1940, see Zenck, "Challenges and Opportunities," 187n16, citing Edward Forbes's letter of 20 May 1941 to Stravinsky concerning wishes for a bilingual edition.

150. Kall Papers, box 5: Stravinsky, folder 9, lectures.

151. Joseph, *Stravinsky Inside Out*, 25–26.

152. Craft, *Dearest Bubushkin*, 15 April 1940: "at police headquarters from 2:30 to 4," and "Mr. and Mrs. Stravinsky Are Fingerprinted," *Lion Heart Autographs, Catalogue 43* (New York, 2005), 68, lot 113, ill. Citizenship was granted in December of 1945.

153. *Boston Evening Transcript*, 20 April 1940, pt. 3:6; and Forbes, *History of Music at Harvard*, 92. On Bartók's 1943 Harvard lecture about Stravinsky see Taruskin, *The Danger of Music*, 134.

154. Somfai, *Béla Bartók*, 23.

155. Craft, *Igor and Vera Stravinsky*, 24 and note 19.

156. I thank Richard E. Rodda, who cites Suchoff, *Béla Bartók*, 180, referring to Becker, "Béla Bartók and His Credo," 7, 35. Becker discusses an interview Bartók gave in Budapest prior to his first US tour, December 1927 to February 1928.

157. Vikárius, "Intimations through Words and Music," 183.

158. Craft, *Stravinsky: Chronicle* (1994), 543.

159. Craft, *Stravinsky: Discoveries*, 199n11.

160. V. Stravinsky and Craft, *Stravinsky in Pictures*, 372, 648n57.

161. Taubman, *Pleasure of Their Company*, 119, a critic derided by Stravinsky and Craft as possessing a "lifelong devotion to the commonplace"; see Stravinsky and Craft, *Memories and Commentaries* (2002), 236n9.

162. Craft, *A Stravinsky Scrapbook*, 9, pl. 7, the image severely cropped (at the left).

163. Craft, *Dearest Bubushkin*, 3 and 17 March 1940; the photograph is in the Forbes's family album VI.

164. *Strawinsky: Sein Nachlass*, 147; and Craft, *Dearest Bubushkin*, 183, pl. 134.

165. For these images see V. Stravinsky and Craft, *Stravinsky in Pictures,* 135; I. Stravinsky, *Selected Correspondence,* 2: pl. 10 (between 146–47); and V. Stravinsky and Craft, *Stravinsky in Pictures,* 322.

166. Davidson, "High Praise Won by Stravinsky."

167. J. W., "Stravinsky Guest Leader."

PART II. INTRODUCTION

1. Craft, *Dearest Bubushkin,* 113, pls. 88–89; *Boston Evening Transcript,* 9 March 1940, 6.

2. Craft omits Kall's statements. See Craft, *Igor and Vera Stravinsky,* 96.

3. Tryon, "Stravinsky Concludes Lectures at Harvard."

4. Craft, *Dearest Bubushkin,* 30 and 31 March 1940.

5. V. Stravinsky and Craft, *Stravinsky in Pictures,* 366.

6. Craft, *Stravinsky: Discoveries and Memories,* 189, claimed they were met in Los Angeles by Dr. Kall, but he could not have gotten from Houston to Los Angeles faster than on the train carrying the rest of the party. For Vera's distress on reaching Kall's house see Craft, *Dearest Bubushkin,* 23–24 May 1940.

7. Stravinsky, *Selected Correspondence,* 3:279; less fully in Craft, *An Improbable Life,* 59n2.

8. Levitz, "Igor the Angeleno," 146. On cosmopolitanism in music see Gooley et al., "Colloquy: Cosmopolitanism"; and Botstein et al., "Cosmopolitanisms."

9. "Stravinsky and Wife Become U.S. Citizens," *Los Angeles Times,* 29 Dec. 1945, I:3. Their principal witness was Edward G. Robinson, whose own illegal citizenship was then discovered; see Craft, *Stravinsky: Discoveries and Memories,* 140. The image is strangely, and wrongly, dated 1941 in the partial edition of Vera's diary, despite her own correct date in Craft, *Dearest Bubushkin,* 120, pl. 92, and 28 December 1945. Couple and occasion are correctly identified from the image's caption in Craft, *Igor and Vera Stravinsky,* 97, pl. 160, though wrongly placed (at 97) among three other images from the early 1940s. Although this (different) image also lacks its source, its caption surely stems from the *Los Angeles Times.* Oliver, *Igor Stravinsky,* 140, upper image (sharper, with left side less cropped, the bottom more so), wrongly dates it 1940. Picked up by the Associated Press, the announcement of their new citizenship was of considerable interest to the American public, appearing as far away as the *Plattsburgh (NY) Press-Republican,* 29 Dec. 1945, 1.

10. See, for example, the listing (though incomplete) for December of 1939 through December of 1940, of Stravinsky's concerts and fees paid him, cited by Zenck, "Leben und Überleben," 69n58, 70. The Sacher Foundation documents also underlie such studies as V. Stravinsky and Craft, *Stravinsky in Pictures;* Craft, "The American Years, 1939–1971" and "The Hollywood Years," in Stravinsky and Craft, *Memories and Commentaries* (2002), 203–55; Craft, *Stravinsky: Discoveries and Memories,* 188–210 (chap. 13); the second volume of Taruskin, *Stravinsky and the Russian Traditions;* Walsh, *Stravinsky: The Second Exile;* the above-cited essays by Zenck; many of the essays edited by Levitz in *Stravinsky and His World;* and several of my own previous studies.

11. Schiff, "Everyone's *Rite* (1939–1946)," 174–97.

12. P. Griffiths, *Stravinsky,* 138.

13. V. Stravinsky and Craft, *Stravinsky in Pictures*, 355–56; Craft, *Present Perspectives*, 216–17; Craft, *Stravinsky: Glimpses* (1993 ed. only), 4–5; and Craft, *Stravinsky: Discoveries and Memories*, 54.

14. Cross, *Igor Stravinsky*, 144.

15. Walsh, *The Music of Stravinsky*, 181. Zenck, "Leben und Überleben," 72, disputes Walsh's evaluation, especially during Stravinsky's initial and less impoverished years, 1939–41.

16. Walsh, *Stravinsky: The Second Exile*, 145, 159, 172, 186 ("soft-centered" remaining undefined); Walsh, "Remembering *The Rite of Spring*," 169.

17. Joseph, *Stravinsky and Balanchine*, 170.

18. Schiff, "Everyone's *Rite* (1939–1946)," 179.

19. For these dates see Craft, *Dearest Bubushkin*, 1940–41.

20. Slim, "Lessons with Stravinsky," 380; Craft, *Dearest Bubushkin*, 7 April 1941.

21. Slim, "Lessons with Stravinsky," 380; Craft, *Dearest Bubushkin*, 24 April 1941.

22. Craft, *Dearest Bubushkin*, 26 May 1941; Slim, "Lessons with Stravinsky," 385.

23. These dates from 1941 to 1943 and 1945 to 1946 appear in Craft, *Dearest Bubushkin*.

24. Slim, "Lessons with Stravinsky," 377–78, fig. 11; Craft, *Dearest Bubushkin*, 6 March 1941.

25. There were "innumerable reviews that would bedevil the second half of Stravinsky's career," cited by Taruskin, *Stravinsky and the Russian Traditions*, 1594.

26. Leibowitz, "Two Composers."

27. Nabokov, "The Atonal Trail."

28. Craft, *Stravinsky: Discoveries and Memories*, 14; Walsh, *Stravinsky: The Second Exile*, 236n5, citing Leibowitz's rejoinder.

29. Walsh, *Stravinsky: The Second Exile*, 238, 618n9. Craft, *Stravinsky: Discoveries and Memories*, 14, confused Leibowitz with Adorno.

30. Levitz, *Modernist Mysteries*, 368. On Adorno see Danese, *Theodor Wiesendgrund Adorno*.

31. Feisst, *Schoenberg's New World*, 65, although Schoenberg had only read "parts of scattered pages."

32. For the Berlin letter, 28 Oct. 1962, see Craft, *An Improbable Life*, 232–33.

33. See "A Bell for Adorno," in Craft, *Prejudices in Disguise*, 91–102.

34. Kundera, "Les Testaments trahis," 2:790, 800, and 808; translated in Kundera, *Testaments Betrayed*, 65, 79, 91. For another comparison of Adorno's thought about both composers see Franklin, "Modernism, Deception, and Musical Others," esp. 146–54.

35. Any wholehearted faith in Nabokov is tempered by Taruskin's complaint, in *Stravinsky and the Russian Traditions*, 1323n14, about Nabokov's astonishing incomprehension in 1978 regarding *Svadebka*, the more peculiar considering his statement about it in 1951 as "musical perfection . . . [among] best works," in Nabokov, *Old Friends*, 84, 86. In addition, Nabokov is sometimes chronologically wayward (as documented several times by Giroud).

36. See Linick, *The Lives of Ingolf Dahl*, 100–101; Craft, *Stravinsky: Discoveries and Memories*, 129.

37. Craft, *Stravinsky: Discoveries and Memories*, 269–72, sub "Lawrence Morton," was unaware of their first meetings.

38. Nabokov, *Igor Strawinsky*, 81–82, although Nabokov, *Bagázh*, 166–70, gives 1930. Slim, "Stravinsky's Four Star-Spangled Banners," 439n229, and below, cites Nabokov

overhearing the *Symphony of Psalms* being finished. Giroud, *Nicolas Nabokov,* 91–92, notes their adjacent studios in the Salle Pleyel in the summer of 1930.

39. Stravinsky, *Selected Correspondence,* 2:370.

40. Stravinsky, *Selected Correspondence,* 2:368–70.

41. Nabokov, "Stravinsky Now."

42. Fried, "Stravinsky Fears Blow"; V. Stravinsky and Craft, *Stravinsky in Pictures,* 555. On the latter translation and its source see Cross, "Stravinsky in Exile," 18n9.

CHAPTER SIX. EXCURSIONS (1940–1941)

1. V. Stravinsky and Craft, *Stravinsky in Pictures,* 355; Craft, *An Improbable Life,* 60.

2. Some occasions omitted from the Paul Sacher Stiftung film 145.1 are pp. 831–32: 28 and 30 May; p. 835: 1, 2, 8, 14, and 17 June; p. 851 (Dorothy's phone number and address); p. 884: 4 and 24 September: "Dorothy (lesson)." Just two occasions, 26 May and 9 June 1940, are cited in Craft, *Dearest Bubushkin.*

3. Gleefully reported to me by Mrs. McQuoid, shortly before her death.

4. Mrs. McQuoid's vivacity and *joie de vivre* are evident from a mid-June 1940 photograph of her, Edwin, and Vera taken by Stravinsky himself at Farmers' Market; see a cropped reproduction in Craft, *Dearest Bubushkin,* 113, pl. 90. For her own—uncropped—copy see Slim, *Annotated Catalogue,* 11; a photograph of her is also in Saunders, *Music and Dance in California,* 198–99.

5. Craft, *Dearest Bubushkin,* 23, 26, and 31 May 1940.

6. Craft, *Dearest Bubushkin,* 3 June; Slim, "Unknown Words and Music," 311; and Craft, *Igor and Vera Stravinsky,* 97, pl. 162, reports incorrectly that they lived there from 23 May.

7. A facsimile of Stravinsky's letter is in *Advancing Knowledge,* 20.

8. See the photograph of them arriving in Mexico City in V. Stravinsky and Craft, *Stravinsky in Pictures,* 367; and of Stravinsky with Chávez in Stravinsky and Craft, *Dialogues and a Diary,* 122, facing pl., fig. 3. On Chávez see Saavedra, *Carlos Chávez and His World.*

9. "Ah, the convenience, the happiness when I discovered I could be in the quota [for a visa]," Stravinsky exclaimed to John F. Rhodes; see Rhodes, "Prospect of Citizenship," with photograph; further details are in Zenck, "Leben und Überleben," 67–68.

10. Levitz, "Igor the Angeleno," 142.

11. Personal communication to me; reproduction in Craft, *Igor and Vera Stravinsky,* 97, pl. 161. Mrs. McQuoid owned a somewhat tattered clipping of it, and there is no reason to doubt her claim to have been the photographer. A month earlier, on 8 July 1940, Bolm had written a letter of support for Stravinsky's permanent US residence; see Joseph, *Stravinsky Inside Out,* 278n24.

12. V. Stravinsky and Craft, *Stravinsky in Pictures,* 642n12 (divulging neither source nor content of this "talk").

13. Jones, "Stravinsky Scans Picasso." Jones, a trained pianist and violinist, also gave violin lessons locally.

14. Paul Sacher Stiftung, film 145.1: p. 884, not published by Craft in *Dearest Bubushkin.* Only one two-piano manuscript dated 1940 survives—for all four movements—in Paris,

Bibliothèque nationale de France, Réserve Vma. MS 1039, cited in Goubault, *Igor Stravinsky*, 252; as for four hands see Francis, "Nadia Boulanger and Igor Stravinsky," 150, Table 4. Speculation about a four-hand performance with Mrs. McQuoid (though placing it in June of 1940) is in Slim, "Stravinsky's *Scherzo à la russe*," 519.

15. A remark passed to Edward Downes, son of the critic, quoted in Walsh, *Stravinsky: The Second Exile*, 122. Craft, *Stravinsky: Discoveries and Memories*, 261–62, notes Stravinsky's sale by 13 April 1940 to the Library of Congress of "a handwritten copy of his as yet incomplete manuscript of Symphony in C." In 1941 Stravinsky also spoke to James Sample about its title (see below).

16. Two of these photographs are in *Strawinsky: Sein Nachlass*, 126–27, the lower one also in Stravinskaya, *O I. F. Stravinskom*, 30.

17. See Paul Sacher Stiftung, film 145.1: p. 910; Mrs. Smith does not appear in Craft, *Dearest Bubushkin*.

18. Paul Sacher Stiftung, Stravinsky manuscripts: Vera's diary. The occasion for the McQuoid photographs is not cited in Craft, *Dearest Bubushkin*; see Slim, *Annotated Catalogue*, 225. In February of 1997 Mrs. McQuoid recalled still more portraits made by her husband but was unable to locate them for me. On them see also Slim, "Stravinsky's Four Star-Spangled Banners," 398.

19. For the photograph of Cary Ellis McQuoid see fig. 5.8; and Slim, *Annotated Catalogue*, item 67; for Stravinsky's annotation on Ronald Richard McQuoid's copy of Hansl and Kaufmann, *Minute Sketches of Great Composers*, 143, see Slim, *Annotated Catalogue*, 11.

20. Stravinsky, *Concerto per due pianoforte soli*, 3, 7, 15, 17, 27.

21. Craft, *Dearest Bubushkin*, 9 February 1941.

22. Levitz, "Igor the Angeleno," 172n2; Craft, *Dearest Bubushkin*, 17 July–9 August 1940.

23. Levitz, "Igor the Angeleno," 141, provides the repertoire for each concert.

24. *Boletin de la Orquesta Sinfónica de México*, Nov. 1940, 78, pl.; Kirjoksky, "Mexico City Players."

25. Levitz, "Igor the Angeleno," 141, 172n3.

26. A photograph of Bolm conferring with prima ballerina Nina Gollner and with Stravinsky appears in the Bowl's program booklet, p. 11.

27. Hal D. Crain, "Hollywood Bowl Concludes Most Successful Year," *Musical America*, Sept. 1940, 8.

28. "Symphony Under the Stars / Igor Stravinsky," *Pacific Coast Musician*, 7 Sept. 1940, 5, 10.

29. Saunders, "Hollywood Bowl."

30. W. E. Oliver, "Bolm Ballet Bowl Event," *Los Angeles Evening Herald and Express*, 28 August 1940, cited in Walsh, *Stravinsky: The Second Exile*, 119–20 and 600n53, which also quotes Fokine's disapproval of this and other changes in his 1909–10 scenario for *Firebird*.

31. Rothschild Collection, no. 36232, reproduced courtesy of the Hollywood Bowl Museum.

32. Paul Sacher Stiftung, film 145.1: p. 884, not published by Craft, *Dearest Bubushkin*. Morton, "Stravinsky in Los Angeles," 76, confused Tchaikovsky's first and second symphonies, the latter the one programmed.

33. See Forbes, *History of Music at Harvard*, 123.

34. Slim, "Stravinsky's Four Star-Spangled Banners," 430n97; Craft, *Stravinsky: Discoveries and Memories,* 191. Isherwood, *Diaries,* 889, observed for "31 July 1960: Dear Vera drives worse than one could think possible."

35. Craft, *Dearest Bubushkin,* 26 August 1940; translated differently in Craft, *Stravinsky: Discoveries and Memories,* 195–96.

36. Craft, *A Stravinsky Scrapbook,* 11, pl. 13, shows all four travelers at Los Gatos on 8 Sept. 1940.

37. H. Colin Slim Stravinsky Collection. For the original format of Hoyningen-Huené's image see also *Stravinsky: Sein Nachlass,* 127, upper plate. On Koshland see Craft, *Dearest Bubushkin,* 8–9 September 1940; "Igor Stravinsky to Be Guest," (the latter also mentioning Mrs. Armsby); and on Mrs. Koshland see Adaskin, *A Fiddler's World,* 260.

38. Craft, *Dearest Bubushkin,* 6–13 September 1940.

39. Craft, *Dearest Bubushkin,* 4 October 1940; Capponi, *Language,* 438, discusses its structure.

40. Professor Richard Taruskin kindly provided the translation and this handwriting information; one page of Stravinsky's manuscript is illustrated in Joseph, *Stravinsky and the Piano,* 214, pl. 16.

41. The violinist had recruited the musicians himself; see Craft, *Dearest Bubushkin,* 13 October 1940; and Craft, *An Improbable Life,* 128.

42. Linick, *Lives of Ingolf Dahl,* 101.

43. V. Stravinsky and Craft, *Stravinsky in Pictures,* 323.

44. Linick, *Lives of Ingolf Dahl,* 100–101.

45. The photograph measures 20.5 × 25 cm., and Stravinsky altered the date from 25 October to 27 October; see Sotheby's, *Auction Catalogue LO8402* (London: Sotheby's, 15 May 2008), 113, lot 140, no. 2, ill. Linick, *Lives of Ingolf Dahl,* does not mention Dahl as a string-instrument player.

46. Sotheby's, *Auction Catalogue LO8402* (15 May 2008), lot 140, ill. at 113; Craft, *Dearest Bubushkin,* 27 October 1940.

47. Sotheby's, *Auction Catalogue LO8402* (15 May 2008), lot 143, no. 2.

48. I. Stravinsky, *Selected Correspondence,* 1:346n45; Craft, *Stravinsky: Discoveries and Memories,* 234.

49. Craft, *Dearest Bubushkin,* 16 October 1940. For citations about Golubev, who supplanted the frequently dipsomaniac Kall, see *Dearest Bubushkin,* 6, 7, and 16 April, 16 May, 11 June, 4, 15, 16, and 28 October 1940.

50. Craft, *Stravinsky: Discoveries and Memories,* 190, cites "test pressings" of *The Rite* in Stravinsky's hands by the end of May 1940.

51. See Stuart, *Igor Stravinsky,* 30–31, items 30–32.

52. Spelling his name "Golubeff"; see Golubev, *Pushkin: Poetry and Music;* and White, *Stravinsky,* 588–89, appendix A, item 8.

53. White, *Stravinsky,* 588.

54. Kall Papers, box 5: Stravinsky, folder 3.

55. Kall Papers, box 1: Russian correspondence [1941]; translation by Olga Panteleeva. Possibly Kall had cited Plato's description of the cosmos in *Timaeus.*

56. Horgan, *Encounters with Stravinsky,* 257.

57. Craft, *Dearest Bubushkin*, 10 December 1941.

58. Paul Sacher Stiftung, film 145.1: p. 918.

59. Craft, *Dearest Bubushkin*, 5 November 1940. Publication of the Symphony in C was delayed until 1948, explained by Craft in I. Stravinsky, *Selected Correspondence*, 1:437–45, App. L; performance dates cited therein at 442 are incomplete.

60. Craft, *Dearest Bubushkin*, 17 December 1943; note 7 wrongly identifies him as a "pupil" of Stravinsky.

61. Barry, "Stravinsky's New Symphony Stirs Acclaim"; more fully quoted in Walsh, *Stravinsky: The Second Exile*, 121.

62. Claudia Cassidy, review, *Journal of Commerce*, 8 Nov. 1940, cited in Wagner, "A Stravinsky Scrapbook," 20; Wagner reproduces the printed program for 7 and 8 November 1940 (22), observing that Stravinsky both changed its order and added *The Firebird Suite*.

63. Quentin, "Stravinsky's New Symphony Played."

64. Yeiser, "Symphony Concert."

65. "Stravinsky, Russ Composer, Will Become U.S. Citizen," *Minneapolis Star Journal*, 16 Dec. 1940, 15.

66. These quotations appear in the *Minneapolis Morning Tribune*, 15 Dec. 1940, 6; 16 Dec. 1940, 1; and 19 Dec. 1940, 10.

67. Riley, "Composer's Wife Rushes"; reproduced with Vera's photograph, but with omissions and repositionings, in Craft, *A Stravinsky Scrapbook*, 11, pl. 14.

68. On 12 July 1965 she told a reporter in Vancouver that, brought up in a country estate near St. Petersburg, she was still "happy to see a cow or a horse," quoted from the *Vancouver Sun* in Craft, *A Stravinsky Scrapbook*, 131, no. 268.

69. On José Limantour see Kirjoksky, "Mexico City Players," which also provides his picture.

70. Paul Sacher Stiftung, film 145.1, and visible in the plate facing the title page of Craft, *Dearest Bubushkin*.

71. Walsh, *Stravinsky: The Second Exile*, 600n61. Tango is not to be confused with its namesake, excerpted from the "Pesante" of *Five Fingers* (1921), a work that Stravinsky extended and arranged in 1961 for chamber orchestra, heading his revision as "Tempo di Tango," about which see Craft, *Down a Path*, 183.

72. For the latter see Craft, "Appendix L," in I. Stravinsky, *Selected Correspondence*, 1:437–45. For manuscript sources of Tango see Shepard, "The Stravinsky *Nachlass*," 745–46; and Jans and Handschin, *Igor Strawinsky: Musikmanuskripte*, 37.

73. Walsh, *Stravinsky: The Second Exile*, 121, 600n61 (the sketch manuscript at Paul Sacher Stiftung, Basel); and Craft, *Dearest Bubushkin*.

74. Craft, *Dearest Bubushkin*, 29 November and 9 December 1940; Joseph, *Stravinsky and Balanchine*, 158, gives 9 December. On Dukelsky as composer see Prokofiev, *Diaries*, 2:282n1, and 3:1094, Index, "Dukelsky, erotic activities."

75. Quoted in Mason, *I Remember Balanchine*, 191.

76. Joseph, *Stravinsky and the Piano*, 214, pl. 16, reproduces a page of the Library of Congress manuscript.

77. Walsh, *Stravinsky: The Second Exile*, 600n61.

78. Joseph, *Stravinsky and the Piano*, 213. In July 1954 Stravinsky referred to "a kind of piano reduction"; see Craft, *Stravinsky: Glimpses*, 17n1.

79. Craft, *Dearest Bubushkin*, 31 January 1941.

80. See the Kaufman obituary in the *Los Angeles Times*, 23 August 1961, B1. On bibliographical problems of the various arrangements of Tango see de Lerma, *Igor Fedorovitch Stravinsky*, 95–96 (T1-T5); Schwarz, "Stravinsky, Dushkin, and the Violin," 307; and Walsh, *Stravinsky: The Second Exile*, 602n37.

81. Taubman, "Dushkin Presents Stravinsky Work," *New York Times*, 1 April 1941, 29.

82. "Igor Stravinsky: Photo by F. Palumbo," *Musical Courier*, 1 Feb. 1941, 133.

83. When I asked in 1995, Mrs. McQuoid could no longer recall exactly what these were. Using the same hotel's stationery, Stravinsky wrote to Nadia Boulanger on 4 December 1940 and to Edward Forbes on 4 and 10 December; all three notes are in the Edward Waldo Forbes Papers at Harvard; see also Slim, *Annotated Catalogue*, 227–28.

84. Slim, "Unknown Words and Music," 312, translated there by Stanislav Shvabrin and Michael Green from Kall Papers, box 5.

85. The heavy drinker Father Damian in Chekov's short story "The Bishop" (April 1902) imagines he sees a green snake (singular in Russian).

86. Francis, *Teaching Stravinsky*, 122–23, though mistranslating Vera's French.

87. Craft, *Dearest Bubushkin*, 13 January 1941; I. Stravinsky, *Selected Correspondence*, 1:238 (3 March 1941).

88. Lesure, *La carrière*, 71, item 210; and Francis, *Teaching Stravinsky*, 124, fig. 5.1; Rosenstiel, *Nadia Boulanger*, 318; and Spycket, *Nadia Boulanger*, 113, lower pl. (mislocated); Craft, *Stravinsky: Glimpses*, 316n5, correctly dated but located only the first of these.

89. Durgin, "Boston."

90. Irving Kolodin, review, *New York Sun*, 23 Jan. 1941, quoted in García-Márquez, *The Ballets Russes*, 277–81, 281; see also Joseph, *Stravinsky and Balanchine*, 161–66.

91. Thomson, *The Musical Scene*, 95–96, repr. from the *New York Herald Tribune*, 23 Jan. 1941, quoted selectively here.

92. I. Stravinsky, *Selected Correspondence*, 3:282–83, letter of 28 June 1942.

93. Craft, *Stravinsky: Discoveries and Memories*, 250n7.

94. Howard Taubman, "Dushkin Presents Program on Violin," *New York Times*, 21 Dec. 1948, 32.

95. Uttered sometime before 1946; see Craft, *Stravinsky: Chronicle* (1994), 87 (18 Oct. 1952); Craft, *An Improbable Life*, 54; and Craft, *Stravinsky: Discoveries and Memories*, 250–51.

96. Crawford, *A Windfall of Musicians*, 214.

97. Morton, "Music Notes," *Rob Wagner's Script*, 6 Feb. 1943; Crawford, *Evenings on and off the Roof*, 61.

98. This refers presumably to the violin-piano reduction; see Slim, "Lessons with Stravinsky," 383 and note 151. She was the grandniece of Russian composer-pianist Anton Rubinstein.

99. V. Stravinsky and Craft, *Stravinsky in Pictures*, 307; Szigeti, *With Strings Attached*; and Joseph, *Stravinsky and Balanchine*, 306. In 1955 Stravinsky conducted his Concerto with Eudice Shapiro at the Ojai Music Festival (east of Santa Barbara); see Crawford, *A Windfall of Musicians*, 238, 255n12. In 1961 he recorded it with Isaac Stern; see Stuart, *Igor Stravinsky*, 43, no. 107.

100. I. Stravinsky, *Selected Correspondence*, 2:89n10; and Prokofiev, *Diaries*, 2:1038.

101. I. Stravinsky, *Selected Correspondence*, 3:257, 260.

102. Craft, *Dearest Bubushkin*, 141n7.

103. I. Stravinsky, *Selected Correspondence*, 3:359; Craft, *Dearest Bubushkin*, 25 June 1947, note 7; and Stuart, *Igor Stravinsky*, 78, "R.A.I. Auditorium, Turin."

104. Craft, *Stravinsky: Chronicle* (1972 ed. only), 110; I. Stravinsky, *Selected Correspondence*, 3:433.

105. Craft, *Dearest Bubushkin*, 29–30 June 1961.

106. Walsh, *Stravinsky: The Second Exile*, 517.

107. Significantly, perhaps, in November of 1966 when Stravinsky conducted *Firebird* in Honolulu with the "worst orchestra we've had," Craft led the Violin Concerto with the twenty-one-year-old Itzhak Perlman (1945–), whose rehearsal of it "pleases the composer as much as any performance of his music for a long time"; see Craft, *Dearest Bubushkin*, 222n12; and Craft, *Stravinsky: Chronicle* (1972 ed. only), 299. Stravinsky's ambiguous opinion, 14 November 1966, of Stern (published three years later in Craft's diary), appears in I. Stravinsky and Craft, *Retrospectives and Conclusions*, 233.

108. Craft, *Dearest Bubushkin*, 3 February 1941.

109. Personal communication, Feb. 1997. In her mid-eighties, she could still play Capriccio quite well, also recalling for me the composer's instructions to her about it. Despite enquiries to the—very few—surviving Los Angeles Philharmonic players of that era (with a subsequent lack of response), I have been unable to verify her claim. There seems no reason to doubt her veracity.

110. *Symphony Magazine*, 13–14 Feb. 1941. This issue contains her husband's 1940 photograph of Stravinsky (facing p. 145). Furious, she tore out the table of contents (p. 143) that bore Marcus's name. After preserving the program for some fifty-one years, she generously gave it to me in 1997, when she also recounted an equally frustrating story about her subsequent involvement with the Capriccio (discussed below).

111. Craft, *Dearest Bubushkin*, 13 February 1941. Sample probably heard this concert, recalling in 1972 and in 1992 two answers by Stravinsky as "just a tonal center" and "the center of a wheel," to Sample's (later) question about "in C" as to major or minor. Both answers resemble Stravinsky's explanation during the symphony's gestation: "all [its] notes gravitate towards a single note." See Downes, "Igor Stravinsky: Plans and Views"; quoted more fully in Walsh, *Stravinsky: The Second Exile*, 122n66.

112. Jones, "Stravinsky Conducts Fine Concert"; Jones "Los Angeles," *Musical America*, 25 Feb. 1941, 24. Stravinsky never met Ellington; see Craft, *The Moment of Existence*, 265.

113. Morton, "Music Notes," *Rob Wagner's Script*, 22 Feb. 1941.

114. Essential here are Messing, *Neoclassicism in Music*; and Taruskin, "Back to Whom?"

115. V. S. [R. Vernon Steele], "Strawinsky—Philharmonic."

116. Cone, "The Uses of Convention" (1963), 29. Lucid essays and analyses (stimulated by Cone) are in Joseph, *Stravinsky and the Piano*, 174–75; Straus, "Sonata Form in Stravinsky," 148–55; Kielian-Gilbert, "Stravinsky's Contrasts," 465, fig. 2; Boulanger's lecture notes (1941), cited in Francis, *Teaching Stravinsky*, 120–21, and 256; Cross, *The Stravinsky Legacy*, 198–211; Cross, *Igor Stravinsky*, 141–43; and, above all, Cantoni, *The Language of Stravinsky*, 67–72, 234–48.

117. Craft, *Dearest Bubushkin*, 18 and 19 February 1941.

118. Babitz, "Stravinsky's Symphony in C." Babitz does not quote the composer on "white music," as alleged by White, *Stravinsky*, 407n1. Stravinsky's own description of "white" occurs in Morton's review, "Music Notes," *Rob Wagner's Script*, 22 Feb. 1941.

119. Craft, *Stravinsky: Discoveries and Memories*, 201; and Craft, "An Interview," 60–61, state mistakenly that Sol Hurok introduced them in January of 1941 in New York and that Andersson's first lesson was on 27 January 1941, *recte* 27 February, as in Craft, *Dearest Bubushkin*. For further details see my "Lessons with Stravinsky," 341–42.

120. Craft, *Dearest Bubushkin*, 1, 6, 21, 24 March; 2, 4–5 April; and 31 December1941 (mistotaled).

121. Craft, *Dearest Bubushkin*, 21–22 February and 1 March 1941.

122. Ricci, *Vittorio Rieti*, 406. See also I. Stravinsky, *Selected Correspondence*, 2:311; and V. Stravinsky and Craft, *Stravinsky in Pictures*, 359.

123. Stravinsky's first—and far wealthier—composition student was Gerald Tyrwhitt (Lord Berners from 1919). Between 1916 and c. 1936 Tyrwhitt came to Stravinsky "for criticism and advice in his composition." See Stravinsky and Craft, *Memories and Commentaries* (1960), 78–81; I. Stravinsky, *Selected Correspondence*, 2:135–59; and Craft, *Stravinsky: Discoveries and Memories*, 175.

124. For photographs of "Futurama" see Cohen, Heller, and Chwast, *Trylon and Perisphere*, 45, plate.

125. Dickstein, *Dancing in the Dark*, 528.

126. Slim, "Lessons with Stravinsky," 337, 342. Crawford, *A Windfall of Musicians*, 45; and Slim, "Stravinsky's Four Star-Spangled Banners," 425n18, briefly discuss Mrs. Irish.

127. Her entry thus refutes Craft's claim in *Stravinsky: Discoveries and Memories*, 201, that an initial lesson took place "on 27 January at Andersson's home." Such a claim is impossible, because all during January the Stravinskys were still on the East Coast.

128. These and any subsequent nonfootnoted references concerning Andersson's lessons and his notebook stem from my essay "Lessons with Stravinsky," 323–412. Unknowingly for sure, Stravinsky charged Andersson just half of Schoenberg's fifty-dollar fee; see Feisst, *Schoenberg's New World*, 208, concerning lessons for Hugh Hodgson in 1936.

129. Craft, *Dearest Bubushkin*, 9 February 1941.

130. Craft, *Dearest Bubushkin*, 2 and 4 April 1941.

131. Slim, "Lessons with Stravinsky," 353, fig. 6, and 380.

132. These syllables of Stravinsky, orally instructing the solo violinist at a recorded rehearsal on 29 January 1963 of *Apollon Musagète*, are clearly audible; see Stuart, *Igor Stravinsky*, 66, no. 74048.

133. Slim, "Lessons with Stravinsky," 386.

134. Paul Sacher Stiftung, film 82, box 17–18: p. 0810, cited in Slim, "Stravinsky's Four Star-Spangled Banners," 399 and 442n284. Mrs. McQuoid remained in touch with the Stravinskys until at least after the birth of her third child, in November of 1942, when Vera sent her a note of congratulation; see Slim, *Annotated Catalogue*, 11. She recalled last seeing the Stravinskys in 1948, at Kall's funeral. See "Dr. Kall Passes": "a resident of Los Angeles for 30 years . . . a leader in the White Russia Colony . . . one of its most highly respected and best loved members."

135. Craft, *Dearest Bubushkin,* 22 April, meaning: "to evaluate James Sample's music-making abilities."

136. Slim, "Lessons with Stravinsky," 381.

137. Craft, *Dearest Bubushkin,* 22 April 1941 and 8 December 1955; Stravinsky and Craft, *Retrospectives and Conclusions,* 284.

138. Andersson added the second *s* to his family name not only "while studying music" but sometimes in his business practice—for example, on his 1922 letterhead. This usage was communicated not by Andersson's daughter, Ernestine (now long dead), but by a descendant who wishes to remain anonymous.

139. Craft, *An Improbable Life,* 180. Taruskin, *Stravinsky and the Russian Traditions,* 302n46, places little trust in the memoirs and interviews of Stravinsky's last period for general biographical purposes.

140. Reprinted in Craft, "Jews and Geniuses," 276. See also Taruskin, *The Danger of Music,* 442 and 446n41.

141. Stravinsky and Craft, *Retrospectives and Conclusions,* 284.

142. Stravinsky's response of 15 September to Sample's letter of 5 September 1950 is in a private Pennsylvania collection, as are the Christmas letters cited above.

143. Craft, *Dearest Bubushkin,* 8 December 1955.

144. Half a dozen years later, appearing on its cover, Stravinsky was telling *Time* magazine (July 1948) that he would like to be known as a "California composer"; cited in Cross, *Igor Stravinsky,* 156, 178.

145. See, e.g., *Pacific Coast Musician,* 16 August 1947, 6; a picture of Sample appeared on the cover of this issue.

146. Slim, "Lessons with Stravinsky," 383.

147. Stravinsky's remarks about Sample's 22 April *Futurama* rehearsal; and Slim, "Stravinsky's Four Star-Spangled Banners," 353, on the composer's remark in October of 1942 apropos of Sample's recording of Stravinsky's "Star-Spangled Banner" arrangement that Sample had just recently sent to him. This recording from a broadcast by Sample—including works by American composers with announcer Kenneth Del Mar, a voice omnipresent during the Great Depression and World War II—survives at the Library of Congress.

148. Zenck, "Leben und Überleben," 70.

149. Sample's 1972 interview mistakenly identifies it as either a "Capehard [*sic*] or Magnavox" and in his 1992 interview as a "Motorola."

150. Craft, *Dearest Bubushkin,* 8 December 1941; I. Stravinsky, *Selected Correspondence,* 3:291; and *Dearest Bubushkin,* 13 and 15 February 1944.

151. Craft, *Dearest Bubushkin,* 124; Zenck, "Leben und Überleben," 70n62.

152. Walsh, *Stravinsky: The Second Exile,* 131.

153. "Stravinsky Bares Aversion to Canned Music on Radio," *Washington Times Herald,* 7 Jan. 1941, n.p.; "Stravinsky Here to Conduct, Likes His Music in Person," *Washington Post,* 7 Jan. 1941, 28.

154. "Stromberg Campaign Expanded," *New York Times,* 13 August 1941, 31.

155. See anonymous advertisements, "What makes a radio-phonograph worth $400?" and "How to buy a radio that will give you *all* of FM," *Los Angeles Times,* 11 Sept. 1941, 15,

and 11 Dec. 1941, 4, the latter pricing the instrument at $415. (These prices conflict with the value assigned to the radio in Zenck, "Leben und Überleben," note 62.)

156. *Life,* 15 and 29 Sept. 1941, 17 and 1; 20 Oct. 1941, 119; 17 Nov. 1941, 21; 1 Dec. 1941, 86; *Time,* 22 Sept. 1941, 31; 6 Oct. 1941, 37; 24 Nov. 1941, 5; and 15 Dec. 1941, 15; and *New Yorker,* 4 and 25 Oct., both at 7.

157. Advertisements for "The Autograph Model" and "Stromberg-Carlson," in *Life,* 23 Feb. 1942, 55, and 6 July 1942, 77.

158. This is not to deny his generosity. See, e.g., his 1947 gift of his autographed score of *Danses concertantes* to Stanford University in exchange for donations of "foodstoffs [*sic*] or plain wearing apparel" to "unfortunate people" in Europe, cited in Slim, *Annotated Catalogue,* 258–60, item 85.

159. "Care of 'Stradivarius' Points Up Lessons in Wartime Conservation," *Life,* 1 June 1942, 12; *Musical America,* 10 Feb. 1943, back cover.

160. "The New High Fidelity Capehart," *Saturday Review of Literature,* 29 May 1954, 39.

161. Craft, *Dearest Bubushkin,* 27 November 1953.

162. Advertisement for Stromberg-Carlson, *Saturday Review of Literature,* 27 Feb. 1954, 46.

163. Slim, "Stravinsky's Four Star-Spangled Banners," 327.

164. Slim, "Lessons with Stravinsky," 390, 391–92.

165. Slim, "Stravinsky's Four Star-Spangled Banners," 328, fig. 1.

166. Paul Sacher Stiftung, Stravinsky manuscripts, film no. 82, box 1, p. 0836, partly quoted in V. Stravinsky and Craft, *Stravinsky in Pictures,* 556.

167. Varunts, *I. F. Stravinsky: Perepiska,* 1:323–24, no. 271, kindly translated by Professor Robert Hughes. Its translation in V. Stravinsky and Craft, *Stravinsky in Pictures,* 201— deeming the academic "shapeless" and "unformed"—was invented, confirming (in this instance) Walsh's complaint in "Letters," *Areté* 25 (2008): 152, about "gross textual manipulations that characterize Craft's editorial and translating work."

168. Slim, "Lessons with Stravinsky," 377, fig. 11.

169. Craft, *A Stravinsky Scrapbook,* 12–13, pls. 16–17; and Craft, *American Stravinsky: The Composer,* Vol. 4 (Ocean, NJ: Music Masters Classics, 1993), CD track 2, and especially Craft's fastidious attention in the latter to the ravishing downward—and Bachian—leap of a minor seventh and subsequent whole-step recovery upward in the basses (m. 14).

170. Statements in 1923, 1932, 1946, and 1958. See Stravinsky, "Some Ideas about My Octuor"; V. Stravinsky and Craft, *Stravinsky in Pictures,* 358 (with the French text); Dahl, "Igor Stravinsky on Film Music," 35, repr. in Cooke, *The Hollywood Film Music Reader,* 277; and Joseph, *Stravinsky Inside Out,* 128.

171. Slim, "Stravinsky's Four Star-Spangled Banners," 420, item no. 6b; spelling errors are Stravinsky's.

172. Stravinsky to Cushing, 11 March 1942, in Slim, "Stravinsky's Four Star-Spangled Banners," 434n155.

173. Stravinsky and Craft, *Memories and Commentaries* (2002), 234, and note 7; see also the different (correct) reading in the original edition (1960), 93.

174. For Andersson on 1 July 1941 see Slim, "Lessons with Stravinsky," 394, and for his 1 July photograph: 346, fig. 5.

175. Slim, "Lessons with Stravinsky," 389 (Andersson's copy of Tango now lost). The jazz arrangement, made by Dr. Felix Guenther, employed by Feist at Mercury Music Corporation, had received Stravinsky's approval. Printed copies of the piano version were not advertised until December of 1941 (in *Musical America*). However valid Charles Joseph's negative opinions in his *Stravinsky and the Piano*, 212–13, 215, Stravinsky valued Tango sufficiently to present a printed copy in 1941 to Mrs. McQuoid (now lost) and in 1941 to inscribe another copy (surviving in a private Pennsylvania collection) to James Sample.

176. Slim, "Lessons with Stravinsky," 392. Explanations of how Stravinsky exploited Milhaud and his mother in France during World War II to send funds (illegally from the United States) to his children in Europe are in Craft, *Dearest Bubushkin*, 24 June 1941; Craft, *Stravinsky: Glimpses*, 142; and especially in Walsh, *Stravinsky: The Second Exile*, 130–31, where Walsh also observes that Stravinsky, "on terms somewhat generous to himself," eventually repaid Milhaud.

177. Slim, "Lessons with Stravinsky," 387.

178. Craft, *Dearest Bubushkin*, 2 December 1941.

179. Slim, "Lessons with Stravinsky," 383, 388, 398. Piano rack and window bafflers appear in photographs of Stravinsky's study at 1260 N. Wetherly in Tansman, *Igor Stravinsky*, frontispiece; I. Stravinsky, *Selected Correspondence*, 2:338–39, pl. 12; Craft, *Igor and Vera Stravinsky*, pl. 199; and Craft, *A Stravinsky Scrapbook*, pl. 241. These photographs belie Craft's contention in *Stravinsky: Once at a Border*, chap. 22, that Stravinsky invented the piano rack.

180. The 1919 program is printed in V. Stravinsky and Craft, *Stravinsky in Pictures*, 173, though the performance itself is doubted by Walsh, *Stravinsky: A Creative Spring*, 308.

181. "José Iturbi in Rage over Benny Goodman," *New York Times*, 27 June 1941, 15 (dated 26 June, Philadelphia); other sources are cited in Slim, "Lessons with Stravinsky," 395n208.

182. Slim, "Lessons with Stravinsky," 395.

183. V. Stravinsky and Craft, *Stravinsky in Pictures*, 368.

184. Craft, *Dearest Bubushkin*, 21 April 1942.

185. Craft, *Prejudices in Disguise*, 273; repr. in Craft, *Stravinsky: Glimpses*, 278.

186. Slim, "Lessons with Stravinsky," 397; the year is mistaken in Craft, *Stravinsky: Discoveries and Memories*, 206, as 1942.

187. Slim, "Lessons with Stravinsky," 389, 394.

188. Levitz, "Igor the Angeleno," 142, cites Stravinsky's complaints of "red tape," a letter to a former Mexican president, and a "very suspicious border guard."

189. Craft, *Dearest Bubushkin*, 14 July 1941. Agea, who wrote program notes and essays for *Boletin de la Orquesta Sinfónica de México*, was Ochoa's teacher. Levitz, "Igor the Angeleno," 141, cites the works that Stravinsky led during his concerts and notes that "Chávez chose Salvador Ochoa" (who was then unknown to Stravinsky).

190. Slim, "Unknown Words and Music," 319.

191. See Stravinsky's introduction quoting G. K. Chesterton, and the long discussion formulated for him by Souvtchinsky in the *Poetics of Music* (1947): 10, 98–116; and Nabokov, *Old Friends*, 199.

192. Santana, "Cronica Musical" (my translation). No reviews of Stravinsky's 1940 and 1941 performances in Mexico—as opposed to interviews with him—appear in Levitz, *Stravinsky and His World*.

193. Diolé, "Stravinsky in Interview," 7–9.

194. Levitz, "Igor the Angeleno," 164, 176n82, citing *Stravinsky and Prokofiev Conduct Their Works*.

195. Craft, *Dearest Bubushkin*, 28 July 1941.

196. Slim, "Stravinsky's Four Star-Spangled Banners," 336, 427nn47 and 52; Slim, "Lessons with Stravinsky," 399n277.

197. Craft, *Dearest Bubushkin*, 27 August 1941; and Spycket, *Nadia Boulanger*, 110. Arthur Sachs as patron is discussed in Francis, *Teaching Stravinsky*, 130–31.

198. See Slim, "Lessons with Stravinsky," 398–99, on patronage of Mrs. Bliss and perhaps of others (Sachs?), as well.

199. These dates are referenced in Craft, *Dearest Bubushkin*.

200. Jones, "Santa Barbara" (with her word order altered).

201. He is pictured by George F. Wern, 9–11 May 1942, dining at her home there; see Craft, *Dearest Bubushkin*, 126, pl. 96; reproduced (though misdated) with photographer identified in Lesure, *La carrière*, 12, no. 13.

202. Meyer, *Settling New Scores*, 159, no. 84.

203. Joseph, *Stravinsky and the Piano*, 147–48, notes Stravinsky's habit of adding red and blue markings to his scores as conducting cues.

204. Slim, "Stravinsky's Four Star-Spangled Banners," 338–39 and 419, item 5d.

205. Slim, "Lessons with Stravinsky," 398.

206. Slim, "Stravinsky's Four Star-Spangled Banners," 332–42.

207. Slim, "Stravinsky's Four Star-Spangled Banners," 342–47.

208. Further details are in Slim, "Stravinsky's Four Star-Spangled Banners," 335, fig. 3, and 334, 336, 343.

209. Slim, *Annotated Catalogue*, 228–33, item 75.

210. I. Stravinsky, *Selected Correspondence*, 1:440, 16 April 1940; Craft, "A Modest [eleven-page!] Confutation," 4; Craft, "An Interview," 62; and Craft, *Stravinsky: Discoveries and Memories*, iii. Stravinsky's own explanation of his distaste in 1962 at Santa Fe appears in Horgan, *Encounters with Stravinsky*, 220.

211. Some of these negative reviews are in Slim, "Stravinsky's Four Star-Spangled Banners," 409.

212. Ussher, "Sounding Board." Further details about these and other reviews are in Slim, "Stravinsky's Four Star-Spangled Banners," 349–52.

213. See *Illuminated Manuscripts*.

214. Craft, *Dearest Bubushkin*, 9 September 1941. Here, Walsh, *Stravinsky: The Second Exile*, 129, forgets their earlier 1938 encounters in Paris, cited above.

215. Craft, *Dearest Bubushkin*, 9 September 1941, "no [movie-]stars"; and (perhaps authored by Gladys Robinson) "Horrible Hollywood," *Rob Wagner's Script*, 27 Sept. 1941, 18.

216. Hopper, "Hedda Hopper's Hollywood," *Los Angeles Times*, 15 Sept. 1941, A16.

217. Hopper, "Hedda Hopper's Hollywood," *Los Angeles Times*, 1 Oct. 1941, 12.

218. Godowsky, *First Person Plural*, 246; Craft, *Dearest Bubushkin*, 2 October, lists still other guests there.

219. Craft, *An Improbable Life*, 114–15n1; *Stravinsky: Discoveries and Memories*, 204. Strangely, Craft, "An Interview," 46, faulted Walsh, *Stravinsky: The Second Exile*, for "not including Stravinsky at a Hollywood movie-star party." Joseph, *Stravinsky Inside Out*, 17, offers a handy alphabetical list of Stravinsky's movie associates (culled from Vera's diary, *Dearest Bubushkin*).

220. His long friendship with Lourié, art director and production designer, comes immediately to mind. Another example, from Paris, 1936: "I go almost nowhere. . . . But I go to the movies," is in V. Stravinsky and Craft, *Stravinsky in Pictures*, 327; and at 357: "an incurable movie addict."

221. Newman, Craft, and Steegmuller, *Bravo Stravinsky*, 46, upper pl. (probably 16 Dec. 1966); Libman, *And Music*, 298.

222. Sample's complete program is in "Mischa Violin Again to Aid W.P.A. Group," *Los Angeles Times*, 26 Oct. 1941, D5.

223. Craft, *Dearest Bubushkin*, 27 October 1941.

224. Godowsky, *First Person Plural*, 245.

225. A photograph of Stravinsky, Martin, Dagmar, and Mercedes in Walsh, *Stravinsky: The Second Exile*, 204–5, pl. 4, was perhaps taken by Vera or Hammond on 6 November 1941, Hammond having recently bought property in Los Angeles. Craft, *An Improbable Life*, 118; and *Stravinsky: Discoveries and Memories*, 203, cited Hammond and Martin. Photographs of 1958 autographed by Stravinsky to them appear in Lisa Cox Music, *Music Catalogue* (c. 2000), lot 129; and *Autographs* (New York: Gary E. Combs, 2009), 11.

226. The guest list in Craft, *Dearest Bubushkin* differs from the one of just fifteen persons in Craft, *Stravinsky: Discoveries and Memories*, 202–3, omitting (among others) the Bolms, de Acosta, and Andersson.

227. Slim, "Stravinsky's Four Star-Spangled Banners," 354–57, also noting the orchestra's regular conductor, Vladimir Golschmann, subsequently promising Stravinsky to lead it himself on 26 December in St. Louis, although he never did. *Time*, 22 Dec. 1941, 56, with its heading, "Stravinsky's Bit," endorsed "its slightly Russian accent," which it described as "genuinely spacious and stirring," proclaiming that it "should be welcomed by conductors."

228. "National Anthem Played, Not Stravinsky Version," *St. Louis Post-Dispatch*, 19 Dec. 1941, 12C; and Burke, "Stravinsky Gets Warm Ovation Here."

229. Thomas B. Sherman, "Stravinsky Conducts His Second Symphony," *St. Louis Post-Dispatch*, 20 Dec. 1941, 5A. However, an anonymous reviewer for *Musical America*, 15 Jan. 1942, 11, complained that "tonal vagaries did not create the most pleasant reception on first hearing."

230. Cost, "Stravinsky Leads St. Louis Symphony."

231. Craft, *Stravinsky: Discoveries and Memories*, 201. For *Futurama*'s first movement see below.

232. Slim, "Lessons with Stravinsky," 350; and Stravinsky and Craft, *Retrospectives and Conclusions*, 284. The recorded Eastman interview betrays a whistling hiss, a by-product of ill-fitted dentures.

233. Stravinsky and Craft, *Memories and Commentaries* (1960), 104; (2002), 261.

234. Partly quoted in Joseph, *Stravinsky Inside Out*, 298n15; and fully so in Slim, "Lessons with Stravinsky," 350.

235. Slim, "Lessons with Stravinsky," 343, 344n72. Even earlier premieres had taken place for two other Andersson works that the pair worked on in 1942: *Dreams of Solfomby* and *The Sun Worshiper*.

236. Slim, "Lessons with Stravinsky," esp. 339 and 378n131.

237. About the third movement of the Symphony in Three Movements, see the chapter on excursion 5 (1945).

238. V. Stravinsky and Craft, *Stravinsky in Pictures*, 359.

239. Walsh, *Stravinsky: The Second Exile*, 139, dates its first sketches as 4 April 1942 (as do V. Stravinsky and Craft, *Stravinsky in Pictures*, 370), and pl. 12 reproduces the 15 June 1942 version, including Stravinsky's still different series of measure numbers. Craft, *Stravinsky: Discoveries and Memories*, 54, confessing that "the chronology of the work is bewildering," then dated this movement from 6 February 1942 and confused some (not all) "bars" with rehearsal numbers in the 1946 printed edition. A sketch and a final draft for the close of the first movement, both dated 15 October 1942, are reproduced in Kunstmuseum Basel, *Strawinsky: Sein Nachlass*, 132.

240. Slim, "Lessons with Stravinsky," 366–70, fig. 10 and ex. 4.

241. See V. Stravinsky and Craft, *Stravinsky in Pictures*, 370–71, color plate 11 (bottom right quadrant) and Stravinsky, Symphony in C, first movement, reh. 38ff.

242. Details in this paragraph are excerpted from "Stravinsky's Four Star-Spangled Banners" and "Lessons with Stravinsky."

243. Craft, *Dearest Bubushkin*, 23 November 1941.

244. Yuzefovich, "Chronicle of a Non-friendship," 788 (letter 35) and 792 (letter 41).

245. Stutsman, "Stravinsky Joins Tanglewood School."

246. Yuzefovich, "Chronicle of a Non-friendship," 799 (letter 54).

247. Facsimile in Slim, *Annotated Catalogue*, 233, item 76.

CHAPTER SEVEN. EXCURSIONS (1942)

1. Stravinsky's letter of 25 Dec. 1941, in Sotheby's, *James S. Copley Library* (New York: Sotheby's, 2010), lot 427 with ill.

2. Vera documented the reproduction ten days later in her diary for Wednesday, 14 January 1942. In late April of 1941, Andersson had described Stravinsky: "working on a composition but what it is he [Stravinsky] says is a secret," this "it" being the *Danses concertantes*; see Slim, "Lessons with Stravinsky," 181.

3. This was the newly printed "thirty-cent" piano-vocal score. My knowledge of this item is from a conversation in 1995 with the late Professor Elliot Forbes at his home in Cambridge.

4. Rehearsals and concerts are documented in Vera's diary, *Dearest Bubushkin*.

5. Sample, "L.A. to Hear New National Anthem," *San Francisco Chronicle*, 13 Oct. 1941, 6. See also Clague, "Singing the Self into Citizenship," 148.

6. Pettis's review, 21 Nov. 1941, is quoted in Slim, "Stravinsky's Four Star-Spangled Banners," 433n146, with other San Francisco critics there at 357–59. See also Pettis, "The

WPA and the Composer's Forum." About Pettis see Oscar Thompson, *The International Cyclopedia of Music and Musicians*, 10th and 11th eds., ed. Bruce Bohle (New York: Dodd, Mead, 1985), 1657.

7. Christopher Stull, "A New Territory for the Critic," *San Francisco Chronicle*, 4 Jan. 1942, supplement, "This World," 13.

8. Alexander Fried, "Stravinsky Arrives for Symphony's Concerts: Composer to Offer Arrangement of Anthem at Opening Friday," *San Francisco Examiner*, 7 Jan. 1942, 26; and Fried, "Own Classics Directed Here by Stravinsky," *San Francisco Examiner*, 10 Jan. 1942, 13.

9. Frankenstein, "Stand Up"; and Frankenstein, "Stravinsky Presents His Symphony."

10. Unsigned review, *San Francisco Chronicle*, 7 Jan. 1942, 11. By "organized" Stravinsky means "harmonized."

11. Fisher, "Strawinsky Is Best-Seller"; and Fisher, "San Francisco Men Led."

12. Frankenstein, "Stravinsky Presents His Symphony."

13. See Slim, "Stravinsky's Four Star-Spangled Banners," 360.

14. Brown, "Audience Divided"; and Jay Walz, "Capitol Hears Concert."

15. Gustav Klemm, "Kindler Forces Invade Baltimore," *Musical Courier*, 20 Feb. 1942, 13.

16. See *Time*, 21 Dec. 1941, 56; and "Music: Not Even Stravinsky." An informed view appears in McPhee, "Records and Scores," 125, repr. in Oja, *Stravinsky in Modern Music*, 125.

17. See Slim, "Stravinsky's Four Star-Spangled Banners," 361–62.

18. Slim, "Lessons with Stravinsky," 387–88.

19. Slim, "Lessons with Stravinsky," 366–67, fig. 10 and ex. 4 (facsimile and transcription).

20. This letter refers to Andersson as "my dear friend."

21. Slim, "Lessons with Stravinsky," 384 (lesson 29).

22. Informative charts of all three octatonic collections, plus the "dom. 7ths" derivable from them, are in van den Toorn, *Stravinsky and "The Rite of Spring*," 147–48, exs. 63–64.

23. Taruskin, *Stravinsky and the Russian Traditions*, 598.

24. Slim, "Lessons with Stravinsky," 401 (Andersson's notebook, p. 58).

25. Van den Toorn, *The Music of Igor Stravinsky*, 288–90, 354–66, and passim.

26. Slim, "Stravinsky's *Scherzo à la russe*," 524–25. The *Scherzo* is thus wrongly described in P. Griffiths, *Stravinsky*, 138, as stemming from American "swing bands." Strangely, it finds no mention whatever in G. Griffiths, *Stravinsky's Piano*.

27. Taruskin, *Stravinsky and the Russian Traditions*, 335–38, esp. ex. 5.9a.

28. David Gilbert, a music librarian at UCLA, kindly suggested one Earl Lowry, but comparison of his work elsewhere does not sustain this identification.

29. This—the original—copy of *Futurama*'s full orchestral score resides in Special Collections, Music Library, University of California at Los Angeles (M1001.A61 F8 1942).

30. One is in a private Pennsylvania collection; the other is in the Library of Congress (M1001.A5 F8 1942), the latter's photostat copy the very one that Andersson himself had originally submitted for copyright.

31. Slim, "Lessons with Stravinsky," 343n69.

32. Van den Toorn, *Stravinsky and "The Rite of Spring*," 164, ex. 65; Taruskin, *Stravinsky and the Russian Traditions*, 923–33. See also Chua, "Rioting with Stravinsky."

33. See the comparison in Slim, "Lessons with Stravinsky," 366–70.

34. Craft, *Dearest Bubushkin*, 31 October 1943.

35. "Personalities: Igor Stravinsky Tends One of the Many Rosebushes Thriving in the Terraced Gardens of His Newly Purchased Hollywood Home," *Musical America*, 25 Feb. 1942, 16; the photograph of Stravinsky and Vera is from an unidentified Los Angeles newspaper.

36. Photographs of 1946 are in V. Stravinsky and Craft, *Stravinsky in Pictures*, 376 (bottom, far left); and Craft, *Igor and Vera Stravinsky*, 103, pl. 178.

37. Its conception at Harvard in October of 1939 and work on it in Hollywood a year later are described in V. Stravinsky and Craft, *Stravinsky in Pictures*, 368.

38. Stravinsky, *Themes and Conclusions*, 51; Walsh, *Stravinsky: The Second Exile*, 130.

39. Zenck, "Leben und Überleben," 73n73. Andersson's remarks should dispel Zenck's doubts that *Danses concertantes* was already half-written.

40. "When I [Tansman] arrived [in Los Angeles] in late 1941, the first of his works that he [Stravinsky] showed me was *Danses concertantes*," quoted in Timmons and Frémaux, "Alexandre Tansman," 11.

41. Excerpts from Babitz's notes are in Walsh, *Stravinsky: The Second Exile*, 133–34; Joseph, *Stravinsky and Balanchine*, 170; Frankenstein, "Stravinsky in Beverly Hills," 179–80; and "Stravinsky, as Told to Sol Babitz," in Saunders, *Music and Dance*, 12, 152.

42. Sotheby's, *Auction Catalogue LO8402* (15 May 2008), lot 143, no. 7.

43. Lawrence Morton, "Music Notes," *Rob Wagner's Script*, 14 Feb. 1942, 24. A negative opinion of the music by John Martin, prompted by the score's premiere as a ballet on 10 September 1944 in New York conducted by Golschmann, is in Joseph, *Stravinsky's Ballets*: 153.

44. [Steele?], "Janssen Symphony—Stravinsky," *Pacific Coast Musician*, 21 Feb. 1942, 5.

45. Stravinsky, *Selected Correspondence*, 3:295.

46. Joseph, *Stravinsky and Balanchine*, 171–73; Joseph, *Stravinsky's Ballets*, 152. A choreographic plan in May of 1944 is in Walsh, *Stravinsky: The Second Exile*, 160n21. My former collection has a typed, signed letter of 21 December 1947 from Stravinsky to Stanford University, offering the manuscript score of *Danses concertantes* to Stanford, where its score now resides; see Slim, *Annotated Catalogue*, item 85.

47. Bronson, "Sample in Triumph."

48. Richard D. Saunders, "Varied Fare Presented at Concert," *Hollywood Citizen News*, 15 Oct. 1941, n.p.; Richard D. Saunders, "Mischa Violin Applauded at WPA's Concert," *Hollywood Citizen News*, 29 Oct. 1941, n.p.

49. Slim, "Lessons with Stravinsky," 347–48, gives the complete letter.

50. See Trotter, *Priest of Music*, 82–88, 117–18, 128–29, 208; Burton, *Leonard Bernstein*, 69–71; Simeone, *The Leonard Bernstein Letters*, 581, 583; and the review by Robert Gottlieb, "Lenny!" *New York Review of Books*, 19 Dec. 2013, 24–28, esp. 24–26, quoting a letter from Mitropoulos to Bernstein.

51. "W.P.A. Plans Symphony," *Los Angeles Times*, 15 Feb. 1942, C4—featuring a photograph of "Dr. Miklos Rozsa [sic]"—lists the entire program.

52. Craft, *Dearest Bubushkin*, 18 February 1942; and Jones, "Contralto Gains Spotlight." But Jones's "case" is Ko-Ko San in *The Mikado*.

53. "Mischa Violin Again to Aid W.P.A. Group."

54. Bronson, "Sample in Triumph."

55. Saunders, "Mischa Violin Applauded."

56. Slim, "Lessons with Stravinsky," 381n147.

57. For it (which includes George Thomas Morgan's *Suite*) and the photograph see Slim, "Stravinsky's Four Star-Spangled Banners," 353nn123–24. The recording is of a broadcast by the Southern California WPA Symphony Orchestra, ser. 42, program no. 18 (1942), but it may have been made late in 1941 because its intermission speaker on defense industries, Fred R. Rauch (mispronounced "Reich" and identified as "Assistant Commissioner WPA"), resigned on 1 January 1942 as the WPA's deputy administrator.

58. Stuart, *Igor Stravinsky*, 58, no. 141.

59. White, *Stravinsky*, 141; Craft, in Stravinsky, *Selected Correspondence*, 2:254. In November of 1940 Stravinsky told a Cincinnati reporter that "he has signed a two-year contract to collaborate [with Disney] on film versions of some of his other ballets"; see Rhodes, "Prospect of Citizenship."

60. Tansman, *Igor Stravinsky*; Walsh, *Stravinsky: The Second Exile*, 238–39. Stravinsky's dislike is expressed in a letter of 7 Jan. 1949 to his son Théodore.

61. Kokoreva, "Alexandre Tansman et Igor Stravinsky," 95nn16–17. Timmons and Frémaux, "Alexandre Tansman," 11, mention all three playing Bach cantatas, six hands; and Nabokov, *Igor Strawinsky*, 77, reports playing in 1927–28 Bach's Passions, cantatas, and the B-minor Mass four-hands with Stravinsky. On Stravinsky's later—brutal—treatment of Tansman see Taruskin, *The Danger of Music*, 443.

62. Tansman, *Igor Stravinsky*, 239; Timmons and Frémaux, "Alexandre Tansman," 11.

63. On Brodetsky see Saunders, *Music and Dance in California* (1948), 323 (with photograph); Rodriguez, "Our Cover Boy"; and Morton, "Music Notes," *Rob Wagner's Script*, 5 Oct. 1940, 11, 26.

64. Jones, "Los Angeles," *Musical America*, 10 Feb. 1941, 298.

65. See Lawrence Morton, "Music Notes," *Rob Wagner's Script*, 25 Oct. 1941, 28–29; Lawrence Morton, "Music Notes," *Rob Wagner's Script*, 30 June 1942, 26–27; Morton, "Stravinsky in Los Angeles," 66n1; and Morton, "Stravinsky at Home," 332.

66. Varying numbers of young musicians available to Brodetsky occur in reports by Jones, "Los Angeles Sees Ballet Theatre" ("23 players"); and Jones, "Los Angeles Hears Local Artists" ("30 players").

67. Translated by Michael Green.

68. Sotheby's, *Auction Catalogue LO8402* (15 May 2008), lot 142.

69. Craft, *Dearest Bubushkin*, 4–16 August 1942.

70. Slim, "Lessons with Stravinsky," 339. There is no evidence that Stravinsky worked on Andersson's last composition, a one-movement string quartet (1943).

71. Private collection.

72. Noted in November of 1940 by Rhodes, "Prospect of Citizenship"; and in greater detail by Walsh, *Stravinsky: The Second Exile*, 120n58.

73. This pencil is discussed in Slim, "Stravinsky's Four Star-Spangled Banners," 418n4a; and "Lessons with Stravinsky," 404. It might just suggest Andersson's contact, on Stravinsky's behalf, with 20th Century–Fox. Other such projects continued to abort, the last in 1964 with Dino de Laurentiis. See Slim, "Lessons with Stravinsky," 404 ("*Realia*"); and Slim, *Annotated Catalogue*, 329–32, item 113.

74. Kokoreva, "Alexandre Tansman," 95n16.

75. Craft, *Dearest Bubushkin*, 6 and 19 March 1942.

76. Rózsa, *Double Life*, 97–98; and an advertisement in the *Los Angeles Times*, 1 Feb. 1943, 12. Rózsa's account thus nullifies Zenck's contention, in "Leben und Überleben," 74–75, that Stravinsky wrote no music for this film. According to Craft, "The Stravinsky 'Nachlass' in New York and Basel," 521, Tansman owned Stravinsky's autograph score of *Four Norwegian Moods*.

77. Walsh, *Stravinsky: The Second Exile*, 139.

78. Vera wrote, "The film business has fallen through"; quoted in Craft, *Dearest Bubushkin*, 8 July 1942.

79. Zenck, "Leben und Überleben," 75n82, citing Stravinsky's letter of 28 June 1942 to Associated Music Publishers.

80. See Walsh, *The Music of Stravinsky*, 181, an opinion endorsed by Zenck, "Leben und Überleben," 66.

81. *Stravinsky in Hollywood*, dir. Marco Capalbo (Berlin: C major Entertainment GmbH, 2014), DVD, chap. 2.

82. Stravinsky and Craft, *Memories and Commentaries* (1960), 93; Walsh, *Stravinsky: The Second Exile*, 139; and Morton, "Stravinsky at Home," 337–41. Craft, *Stravinsky: Discoveries and Memories*, 207, rightly retitled this work "Norwegian Melodies."

83. The date is given as 25 July 1942 in Stravinsky, *Selected Correspondence*, 3:283, that is, "recently composed"; but it is recorded as 18 August (according to Vera's unpublished diary) in V. Stravinsky and Craft, *Stravinsky in Pictures*, 370.

84. P., "Stravinsky Conducts Philharmonic Symphony," *Musical America*, 10 Feb. 1945, 243. This still unidentified "P." may be Francis D. Perkins, former music critic of the *New York Herald-Tribune*, who had rejoined the *Tribune*'s editorial staff in 1945 after US Army service. Other possibilities are Ashley Pettis, director of the "Composer's Forum Laboratory" in New York, writing, for example, on 15 and 16 December 1945 for the *New York Times*; Herbert F. Peyser; Warren Potter; or Ross Parmenter (even though all four normally sign their full names).

85. Rózsa, *Double Life*, 97. Dorati with the Stravinskys is cited in Craft, *Dearest Bubushkin*, 15–17 October 1940. Rózsa could not have met the Tansmans before late 1941.

86. Saunders, "Mischa Violin Applauded"; Bronson, "Sample in Triumph." Sample also programmed Stravinsky's "Star-Spangled Banner" at this concert; Saunders noted that the arrangement was "strange to conventional ears, yet cuts new facets of beauty in the gem of a noble melody."

87. Rózsa, *Életem Történeteiből*, 141, quoted here from Rózsa's 1981 memoir, *Double Life*, 98–99.

88. After Andersson's death (in June of 1943) Stravinsky benefited from linguistic assistance by Beata Bolm, wife of the celebrated dancer-choreographer; see Craft, *An Improbable Life*, 115; and Craft, *Stravinsky: Discoveries and Memories*, 190.

89. Rózsa, *Double Life*, 99.

90. Rózsa, *Double Life*, 114, pl., captioned: "Hollywood Composers Honor Widow of Gustave Mahler"; also reproduced in Merrill-Mirsky, *Exiles in Paradise*, 62, upper pl. (eleven composers only, not including Schoenberg). "Music Group Honors Widow of Com-

poser," *Los Angeles Times,* 8 July 1948, 17, lists but does not illustrate any of the twelve composers; see also Craft, *Stravinsky: Discoveries and Memories,* 9. Among other dinner guests were Lester Donahue and Thomas Mann, both cited previously.

91. Schwarz, "Stravinsky, Dushkin, and the Violin," 307, contradicting Craft, *An Improbable Life,* 128.

92. Taruskin, *Stravinsky and the Russian Traditions,* 1541–47, with example 19.9a–b. His discussion, documentation, and find (this last known earlier by Craft, in V. Stravinsky, *Stravinsky in Pictures,* 627n15) were unacknowledged in Craft's "An Interview," 31, or in his *Stravinsky: Discoveries and Memories,* 157 and 180. V. Stravinsky and Craft, *Stravinsky in Pictures,* 240; and Walsh, *Stravinsky: A Creative Spring,* 324, wrongly give the Igor-Vera meeting as a Friday; but Craft, "An Interview," 31; and Craft, *Stravinsky: Discoveries and Memories,* 156, have it correctly: Monday, 21 February 1921. I recall puzzling over the addition, having often played the four-hand piano version of the "Polka." On 1 February 1956 I conducted the Suite with the Concord Massachusetts Orchestra and then again on 9 December 1960 with the University of Chicago Symphony Orchestra, both times without recognizing the Katinka addition.

93. Sotheby's, *Auction Catalogue LO8402* (15 May 2008), lot 138, with ill. at III, without a trace of Tango in these Babitz papers.

94. Craft, *Stravinsky: Glimpses,* 306, mentions two arrangements but identifies neither one as "the best of the musical collaborations with Babitz," although these are just two of the four arrangements they made.

95. *Pace* Walsh, *Stravinsky: The Second Exile,* 603n62; see now Joseph, *Stravinsky and Balanchine,* 167–68.

96. Craft, *Dearest Bubushkin,* 6 February 1942; and a mid-February 1942 letter in the Paul Sacher Stiftung at Basel, cited in Slim, "Stravinsky's Four Star-Spangled Banners," 444n326.

97. Slim, "Stravinsky's Four Star-Spangled Banners," 444n327.

98. Stravinsky, *Circus Polka,* pl. no. 194219.

99. Stravinsky, *Selected Correspondence,* 3:280–81.

100. See Craft, *Dearest Bubushkin,* 7 March 1942; and Raksin, "Composer in Paradise," 93–94.

101. Sotheby's, *Auction Catalogue LO8402* (15 May 2008), lot 139.

102. Neither item appears in Stravinsky, *Selected Correspondence,* although two letters there (in 3:283 of 28 June and 25 July 1942) refer to Babitz and the violin and piano arrangement.

103. This edition, dated "Hollywood, February 15th 1942" on the last of eight pages (only this final page necessitating three staves), was printed with plate number A.S. 194219 by AMP in New York and Schott in London and was available for purchase by December of 1942.

104. Finished and revised by 25 July 1942; see Stravinsky, *Selected Correspondence,* 3:282–83.

105. Completed around the same time; plate number A.S. 19422512.

106. Sotheby's, *Auction Catalogue LO8402* (15 May 2008), lot 139, and p. 8 ill. at 112.

107. Crawford, *Evenings on and off the Roof,* 61, "returned in March [1943]"; and Craft, *Dearest Bubushkin,* 21 March 1943.

108. Stravinsky, *Selected Correspondence*, 3:291, letter of 15 Feb. 1944 (Stravinsky's emphasis). On 30 January 1947 he led the United States Army Air Force Band at Randolph Field, San Antonio, TX; see Craft, *Dearest Bubushkin*, 139n5; and Craft, *Igor and Vera Stravinsky*, 105, pl. 181 (not citing works that Stravinsky conducted).

109. Craft, *Dearest Bubushkin*, 7 March 1942.

110. As recalled even later by Raksin to Joseph, *Stravinsky and Balanchine*, 389n19. Joseph, *Stravinsky Inside Out*, 129 and 286n31, cites a Raksin-Stravinsky disagreement in 1948.

111. Merrill-Mirsky, *Exiles in Paradise*, Appendix, 93–94; Stravinsky, *Selected Correspondence*, 3:281; and Walsh, *Stravinsky: The Second Exile*, 135–36.

112. See Stravinsky, *Circus Polka: For Band*, Harmonie serie (Mainz: Schott, 2003).

113. Stravinsky, *Selected Correspondence*, 3:283.

114. V. Stravinsky and Craft, *Stravinsky in Pictures*, 369; Stravinsky, *Selected Correspondence*, 3:281–84; and Craft, *Dearest Bubushkin*, 15 October and 13 December 1942.

115. Ringling Brothers full circus program: "Display No. 18 'The Ballet of the Elephants,'" is printed in the Boston Symphony Orchestra's *Program* (14–15 Jan. 1944), 740. AMP issued the score three months later.

116. Joseph, *Stravinsky and the Piano*, 215n8; Joseph, *Stravinsky Inside Out*, 20; and Joseph, *Stravinsky's Ballets*, 279n15.

CHAPTER EIGHT. EXCURSIONS (1943)

1. Craft, *Dearest Bubushkin*, 30 November 1942, and 7 January 1943. Schiff, "Everyone's *Rite*," 178, misdates the Whiteman commission as 1945 (see Slim, *Annotated Catalogue*, item 81), *The North Star* and *Jane Eyre* as 1942, and omits citing the former's sketches as also used in *Scherzo à la russe*.

2. Craft, *Dearest Bubushkin*, 18 January 1943; Taruskin, *Stravinsky and the Russian Traditions*, 1624 and 1625, ex. E.5.

3. On this latter see the next chapter; and Slim, "Stravinsky's *Scherzo à la russe*," 518–37.

4. Craft, *Stravinsky: Discoveries and Memories*, 8, wrongly dated this to the "last week of [December] 1943."

5. Craft, *Dearest Bubushkin*, 25 January 1943 and 127n12, provided neither Stravinsky's setting nor its location nor whether Craft was translating from French.

6. Milhaud et al., *Conversation*, 244–45.

7. Craft, *Dearest Bubushkin*, 9 February 1943; Ussher, *Who's Who in Music*, 344.

8. Alfred Frankenstein, "Stravinsky Given Ovation at 'Petrouchka' Ballet," *San Francisco Chronicle*, 29 Jan. 1943, 7. Stravinsky did not lead the second performance on 29 January.

9. Babitz, "Ballet Notes." Perhaps these criticisms and Stravinsky's need for regaining copyright led to his revised edition of *Petrushka*, made during 1945 and 1946 for smaller orchestra and published c. 1948.

10. Stravinsky, *Selected Correspondence*, 1:333n15, 442–43; Stravinsky and Craft, *Themes and Episodes*, 43; and Craft, *An Improbable Life*, 67n23. Basing his opinion on an air-check recording, Craft verified Stokowski's problems in a letter to Stravinsky of 24 October 1947.

11. See Thomson, *The Musical Scene*, 97–99; repr. from the *New York Herald Tribune*.

12. Lamented by Craft, *Stravinsky: Discoveries and Memories*, 207.

13. Ussachevsky, "My Saint Stravinsky," 36.

14. When Sample related this story in 1972 and 1992, he was mistaken about the date on both occasions.

15. Lederman, *Stravinsky in the Theatre* (1975), 145, reproduces a photograph said to be taken in New York by Eileen Darby, although not appearing in *Dance Index* 6 (1947), the source for much of Lederman's book. Joseph, *Stravinsky Inside Out*, 51, locates it as taken in Hollywood in 1943, probably correctly: Stravinsky led the Ballet Theatre on 13 July at the Hollywood Bowl with Bolm dancing the Blackamoor; see *Musical Courier*, August 1943, 12. Louis and Stooss, *Igor Stravinsky*, 26–27 (double plate) and 113, col. 1, wrongly date it 1957 and misidentify Bolm as Balanchine.

16. Morton, "Music Notes," *Rob Wagner's Script*, 6 Feb. 1943, 30.

17. On Dahl see Craft, *An Improbable Life*, 130, and passim. Linick, *Lives of Ingolf Dahl*, 283; and Crawford, *A Windfall of Musicians*, 290n38, cite only Dahl's 1957 performance of *Dumbarton Oaks*.

18. Craft, *Dearest Bubushkin*, 18 and 21 May 1943.

19. Stravinsky, *Selected Correspondence*, 3:185, the gas rationing mentioned in Stravinsky's letter of 12 December 1942.

20. Craft, *Dearest Bubushkin*, 6 October 1941; 19 and 30 January 1942; 24 February 1943; 6 January, 16 February, 13 and 23 May 1943.

21. Craft, *Dearest Bubushkin*, 5 June 1943; Craft, *A Stravinsky Scrapbook*, 15, pl. 23.

22. Craft, *Dearest Bubushkin*, 9 January 1945. Vera's postwar account of an initial twelve chickens, then twenty-four hens and two roosters, resulting in forty chicks, is in V. Stravinsky and Craft, *Stravinsky in Pictures*, 647n47.

23. Not on 24 June, as reported in Craft, *Dearest Bubushkin*, 128. The towel is in a private collection.

24. "Concert Lures Well Known U.S. Composer," *Salt Lake Tribune*, 29 March 1943, 9. Sample apparently concurred in this opinion, his taped 1972 interview considering Andersson a better composer than Charles Ives.

25. Zádor had already recommended Rózsa in 1940 and Sample in 1942 for the same honors to Carl Hein, president of the New York College of Music; see Crawford, *A Windfall of Musicians*, 188–89, 281n83.

26. Craft, *Dearest Bubushkin*, 30 June 1943, documented the Stravinskys' attendance at Andersson's funeral.

27. Walsh, *Stravinsky: The Second Exile*, 128, reporting recollections, c. 1960–65.

28. Hopper, "Looking at Hollywood."

29. Craft, *Dearest Bubushkin*, 28 August 1943. The Stravinskys had first seen Werfel on 7 February 1942 at Max Reinhart's following a rehearsal of *Danses concertantes*, and they first dined with him on 28 January 1943, as noted in *Dearest Bubushkin*, 7 February 1942; and Craft, *Stravinsky: Discoveries and Memories*, 309.

30. Stravinsky and Craft, *Expositions and Developments* (1962), 66.

31. Walsh, *Stravinsky: The Second Exile*, 144; and Walsh, *The Music of Stravinsky*, 304n92, provide its beginning and ending dates. Shepard, "The Stravinsky *Nachlass*," 745, with the same ending date, notes its appearance on every page of its draft.

32. On Klaus Mann at this period see Weiss, *In the Shadow*, 192–97.

33. See Stravinsky and Craft, *Memories and Commentaries* (1960), 93, and (2002), 234.

34. Condlon, "Money Circulation Nears 18 Billion."

35. See Stravinsky and Craft, *Memories and Commentaries* (2002), 234.

36. The ensuing draws on and expands observations in my "Stravinsky's Four Star-Spangled Banners," 382–83, 401, 421, item 8, and 440nn232–38.

37. Mann, "How Not to Spend Furlough"; and Craft, *Dearest Bubushkin*, 28 August 1943. Prewar Stravinsky and the Thomas Manns are discussed in Craft, "An Interview," 17. A recent conjecture by Imogen van Tannenberg, cited (perhaps incorrectly) in Mostrom, "Dissonance among the Exiles," mentioning Fritz Lang, Thomas Mann, Arnold Schoenberg, and Stravinsky often meeting for breakfast at Third and Fairfax (in West Hollywood), is, at least concerning Stravinsky, erroneous.

38. "City 'Jumps Gun' in War Bond Drive," *New York Times*, 9 Sept. 1943, 1. Such drives had already taken place early in 1942. Among many other sources of information are programs for the Los Angeles Philharmonic, 8–9 January, 92, especially for 12–13 February, 141, announcing a "Defense Stamp and Bond Concert," to be led by Bruno Walter on 23 February 1942.

39. Klaus Mann to Erika Mann, 25 August 1943, Klaus Mann Papers, University of Missouri at Kansas City, Archives, cited in Slim, "Stravinsky's Four Star-Spangled Banners," 440n235.

40. Decker and Decker, *A Place of Light*, 233–34. Decker was president from 1933 to 1945.

41. Paul Sacher Stiftung, film 98: pp. 1053–54.

42. Mann, *Tagebücher, 1940–1943*, 5:564–65, perhaps the (unmentioned) source for Craft, *Stravinsky: Discoveries and Memories*, 309.

43. Craft, *Dearest Bubushkin*, 28 August 1943, note 16; Stravinsky and Craft, *Memories and Commentaries* (2002), 224–25.

44. Klaus Mann Papers, University of Missouri at Kansas City, Archives, cited in Slim, "Stravinsky's Four Star-Spangled Banners," 440n235.

45. Western Historical Manuscript Collection, University of Missouri at Kansas City, musical manuscript, letter, and photograph.

46. Slim, "Stravinsky's Four Star-Spangled Banners," 328, fig. 1, and 418, item 4a.

47. Craft, *Dearest Bubushkin*, 124.

48. Slim, "Stravinsky's Four Star-Spangled Banners," 337n55.

49. The anonymous, untitled essay with facsimile of Toscanini's first page is in *Musical America*, May 1943, 23. (He is not the same W. T. Grant, well-known to present-day listeners of National Public Radio as a philanthropist through his trust "supporting research to improve the lives of young people.")

50. See Shoaf, "Satellite Collections," 85, U9 (University of Missouri, Kansas City).

51. "Sells Out for Million," *Kansas City Star*, 10 Oct. 1943, 2A.

52. Paul Sacher Stiftung, film 98: p. 1059.

53. Humanities Collections, University of Michigan, Special Collections Library, Harlan Hatcher Graduate Library, Ann Arbor, cited in Slim, "Stravinsky's Four Star-Spangled Banners," 383 and note 238; also cited in Shoaf, "Satellite Collections," 85, U8.

54. A complete inventory of Mann's auction, which was to reach 150 items, remains elusive. Mann's correspondence undertaken to obtain items for it helps (to a limited degree) to establish a list of items still at the University of Missouri. Additionally, Dr. Decker was to write thank-you letters to Schoenberg and Stravinsky. I have been greatly aided by Marilyn Burlingame, senior archivist of the University of Missouri at Kansas City.

55. See Joseph, *Stravinsky Inside Out*, 120–21; and Jules Wolffers, "Boston Hears New Stravinsky Ode," *Musical Courier*, 20 Oct. 1943, 1, 16. Levitz, "In the Shadow of the Zoot Suit Riots," cites the Ode as relevant to her topic, though her lecture did not mention it. On the Ode's possible temporal connection to a Mexican journalist's essays, published 4 August 1940 and 31 December 1942, see Saavedra, Fiori, and Levitz, "Stravinsky Speaks," 206–7, 221n113.

56. Stravinsky and Craft, *Expositions and Developments* (1962), 66n10.

57. V. Stravinsky and Craft, *Stravinsky in Pictures*, 357, 645n34; Stravinsky, *Selected Correspondence*, 3:520–21; Craft, "Selected Source Material," 351, item 12.

58. Joseph, *Stravinsky Inside Out*, 122; Walsh, *Stravinsky: The Second Exile*, 148–49; van den Toorn, *The Music of Igor Stravinsky*, 44 (no. 22), 46 (no. 22), and 294.

59. Zenck, "Leben und Überleben," 76n86, believes the second movement probably dates from the end of 1942.

60. An excerpt from this scene with Stravinsky's music, "Eclogue," dubbed into *Stravinsky in Hollywood*, chap. 2, is not particularly successful owing to the overwhelming volume of the actors' dialogue.

61. Neef, *Stravinsky in Moscow*, 1962, 7, 9.

62. Walsh, *Stravinsky: The Second Exile*, 474, paraphrasing Nestyev, "Vechera Igoiya Stravinskovo," 94.

63. Stravinskaya, *O I. F. Stravinskom*, 117–18, 121.

64. For this view see Cross, "Stravinsky in Exile," 4–9, 17.

65. Yuzefovich, "Chronicle of a Non-friendship," 806, letter 63, for which I have preferred "music in the open air," exactly translating this Russian phrase: "muzika nafone pirodi," as in Walsh, *Stravinsky: The Second Exile*, 605n27. See the *Oxford Russian Dictionary*, rev. ed. (Oxford: Oxford University Press, 1997), 224, col. 1.

66. Stravinsky and Craft, *Expositions and Developments* (1962), 66n10; and Stuart, *Igor Stravinsky*, item 35, LP Columbia ML 4398 (1951, with notes by Morris Hastings made for LP 2758 [LP 27], recorded on 5 Feb. 1945). The movie project itself was mentioned in White, *Stravinsky* (1966), 376–77; followed by Routh, *Stravinsky: The Three Symphonies and Ode*, 3–4.

67. Yuzefovich, "Chronicle of a Non-friendship," 807, letters 64 and 65.

68. Stravinsky, *Selected Correspondence*, 3:520–21, with plate of excerpts; and Craft, "Selected Source Material," 351, item 12 (without plate), embodying some conflicts between Craft's pair of citations. Professor Nancy van Deusen very kindly obtained photocopies of these pages from an 1820 copy of *The Melodist* in the Robert Guy McCutchan Collection of Hymnology, Special Collections, Claremont College Library.

69. Brontë, *Jane Eyre*, 462, notes to pp. 21–22; there is no evidence that Stravinsky tried to set Ransford's verse.

70. Craft, "A Personal Preface," 9, amplified in Craft, *The Moment of Existence,* 16; and esp. Craft, *Down a Path,* 145.

71. V. Stravinsky and Craft, *Stravinsky in Pictures,* 645nn34 and 35, identifying her "Song" at reh. 20 (the oboe duet) in the 1947 printed score, an identification seconded by Walsh, *Stravinsky: The Second Exile,* 144. Shepard, "The Stravinsky *Nachlass,*" 736, does not mention this "Song."

72. To expand an image: "the very magpie," expressed in Bernstein, *The Unanswered Question,* 385, and in Cross, *Igor Stravinsky,* 182, "this greatest of all musical magpies," citing the composer's appropriation in late scores of even the printing style of Universal Edition. Identifications of some of Stravinsky's borrowings from himself, Rossini, Johann Strauss, Ravel, and perhaps others as well are in White, *Stravinsky,* 396–97; Joseph, *Stravinsky and Balanchine,* 344–45; and Joseph, *Stravinsky's Ballets,* 147–49.

73. Taruskin, *Stravinsky and the Russian Traditions,* 1624–41, 1637n48, acknowledging Morton's earlier identification of two Russian melodies used in the Sonata. On this Sonata see Joseph, *Stravinsky and the Piano,* 216–27; Kramer, "Discontinuity and Proportion," 184–87; and Walsh, *The Music of Stravinsky,* 189–90. Wrongly asserting that the Sonata "is based on themes from the *Four Norwegian Moods,*" Francis, "Nadia Boulanger and Igor Stravinsky," 151, misreads Walsh, *Stravinsky: The Second Exile,* 141–54, as does Francis, *Teaching Stravinsky,* 141, who at 150 and 152 cites but does not identify the source of bad reviews from the Midwest of the Sonata.

74. Yuzefovich, "Chronicle of a Non-friendship," 811, letter 69 (all emphases mine).

75. Yuzefovich, "Chronicle of a Non-friendship," 813–14, letters 72 and 73; see also V. Stravinsky and Craft, *Stravinsky in Pictures,* 645–46n37.

76. Privately, he acknowledged in 1944 that Koussevitzky "was a good man, but lacked taste"; see Craft, *Stravinsky: Discoveries and Memories,* 209, translating the French of Isabelle Papineau-Couture. Her "Souvenirs," 61, omits naming Koussevitzky out of "respect for Stravinsky."

77. Stravinsky, "On Conductors and Conducting," 28 and 108; partially reprinted in Stravinsky and Craft, *Themes and Episodes,* 152; and more fully in the posthumous Stravinsky, *Themes and Conclusions* (1972), 228–29. Craft, in *Stravinsky: Discoveries and Memories,* 209n23, offered an explanation about the key of the trumpet part(s) at the Ode's premiere, but the one in Walsh, *Stravinsky: The Second Exile,* 149, best accords with Stravinsky's own statements.

78. Stravinsky, *Themes and Conclusions,* 228–29.

79. Craft, as quoted in Walsh, *Stravinsky: The Second Exile,* 568.

80. Strawinsky and Strawinsky, *Au cœur du foyer,* 142.

81. Craft, "An Interview," 67; a view somewhat akin to Walsh, *New Grove Stravinsky,* 30. According to Scheijen, *Diaghilev,* 231, "Anti-Semitism was a fact of life in tsarist Russia, and Diaghilev's circle was no exception."

82. Taruskin, *Defining Russia Musically,* 454–55; Taruskin, *The Danger of Music,* 21, 215–16. Additional examples of Stravinsky's anti-Semitic remarks about Pierre Monteux and Adolf Bolm in 1918 at the Metropolitan Opera are in Taruskin, *Defining Russia Musically,* 457nn99–100; and Walsh, *Stravinsky: A Creative Spring,* 300, respectively.

83. Taruskin, *Defining Russia Musically*, 457–58, and note 102; see also Taruskin, *The Danger of Music*, 439 and 445n34, reporting that Craft twice suppressed this portion of the 8 October 1948 letter addressed to Stravinsky. Charles Joseph brought the suppressed portion to light.

84. Varunts, *I. F. Stravinsky: Perepiska*, 2:492–93, no. 986, trans. in Stravinsky, *Selected Correspondence*, 2:39–40; and in Walsh, *Stravinsky: A Creative Spring*, 332.

85. Varunts, *I. F. Stravinsky: Perepiska*, 2:494–95, no. 987; partial trans. in Walsh, *Stravinsky: A Creative Spring*, 332–33.

86. Varunts, *I. F. Stravinsky: Perepiska*, 2:496, no. 989, trans. Olga Panteleeva; see also Walsh, *Stravinsky: A Creative Spring*, 372, 636n92.

87. Stravinsky, *Selected Correspondence*, 1:170–73; Tappolet, *Correspondance Ernest Ansermet–Igor Strawinsky*, 2:68, no. 225, 9 Sept. 1923.

88. Even Natalya Konstantinova was capable of anti-Semitic remarks: in the late 1920s in the presence of her husband and Nicolas Slonimsky, she called the latter "a dirty Odessa Jew"; see Slonimsky, *Perfect Pitch*, 95, precisely as Walsh, *Stravinsky: The Second Exile*, 148, noted from Oxford's 1988 edition of *Perfect Pitch*, 105.

89. Yuzefovich, "Chronicle of a Non-friendship," 832–35, "Appendix I: Works by Stravinsky Published [1909–47] by ERM."

90. Stravinsky, *Selected Correspondence*, 1:176; Tappolet, *Correspondance*, 2:77, no. 230. Walsh, *Stravinsky: A Creative Spring*, 372 and note 89, calls Craft's translation here "defective."

91. Stravinsky, *Selected Correspondence*, 2:373–74, 2 January 1948.

92. Craft, *Stravinsky: Discoveries and Memories*, 149, 209n23.

93. Craft, *Stravinsky: Chronicle* (1994), 197–98, 371.

94. Yuzefovich, "Chronicle of a Non-friendship," 778, 856nn7–8.

95. Slim, *Annotated Catalogue*, 258–60, item 85.

96. Craft, *Dearest Bubushkin*, 130n7 and 117, respectively.

97. Pollack, *Skyscraper Lullaby*, 313.

98. Cass, "Program Dance Tonight."

99. Stutsman, "Stravinsky Leads Boston Symphony"; Yuzefovich, "Chronicle of a Non-friendship," 784, no. 25 (19 Feb. 1940), and 836.

100. Walters, "Actor's Life," with photograph. Several other photographs of Leyssac are in Saunders, "Hollywood," *Musical Courier*, 1 Nov. 1942; and Saunders, "Hollywood," *Musical Courier*, 5 March 1943.

CHAPTER NINE. EXCURSIONS (1944)

1. The (autographed) printed program, 14 and 15 Jan. 1944, is in Yuzefovich, "Chronicle of a Non-friendship," 818, fig. 1.

2. "'Star-Spangled Banner' Version of Stravinsky Startles Audiences," *New York Herald Tribune*, 15 Jan. 1944, 7; shortened in Slim, "Stravinsky's Four Star-Spangled Banners," 364.

3. "Anthem," *Boston Sunday Globe*, 16 Jan. 1944, 19.

4. "Police Leave as Igor Plays True Anthem," a report lacking in Slim, "Stravinsky's Four Star-Spangled Banners."

5. Craft, *Memories and Commentaries* (2002), xxii; confusingly enough, this book bears the same title as one of their earlier joint ventures, published in 1960, and is called a "one-volume edition." In fact, it consists of selections, many of them slightly revised, from five of the Stravinsky-Craft books. Strangely, this 2002 omnibus is not listed among Craft's publications at the close of his final book, *Stravinsky: Discoveries and Memories*, 360.

6. Stravinsky, *Once at a Border*, chap. 21.

7. Joseph, *Stravinsky Inside Out*, xx, 19 (photograph); the same error is also in Joseph, *Stravinsky and Balanchine*, 175. An earlier perpetrator of this erroneous connection is Steinberg, "Stravinsky Festival," 15.

8. Stravinsky and Craft, *Memories and Commentaries* (2002), 216; Joseph, *Stravinsky Inside Out*, 18, 21. Unfooled himself, Walsh, *Stravinsky: The Second Exile*, 606n4, cites Tony Palmer, deceived by Craft's erroneous narrative (1980–81) in the television film *Once at a Border*, DVD, chap. 21. Joseph, *Stravinsky Inside Out*, 189, cites some observations (22 Nov. 1982) by Craft, *Present Perspectives*, 410–15, on Palmer's film. Slim, "Stravinsky's Four Star-Spangled Banners," 368nn195–96; and Taruskin, *Russian Music*, 437, correct Craft's narrative, the latter reproducing the "mug-shot."

9. Stravinsky and Craft, *Memories and Commentaries* (2002), 234.

10. Slim, "Stravinsky's Four Star-Spangled Banners," 363–67, gives further details about this incident.

11. Bennison, "Symphoniana," a report lacking in Slim, "Stravinsky's Four Star-Spangled Banners."

12. Stravinsky, *Selected Correspondence*, 2:368–71. Nabokov was then living in Washington, DC.

13. Stuart, *Igor Stravinsky*, 74 and 36, no. 68. A (damaged) copy of a recording made in 1944 from the BSO performance broadcast that January, and transmitted from San Francisco radio station KGO, is in the Hargrove Music Library, University of California, Berkeley.

14. Craft, *Stravinsky: Chronicle* (1994), 6 (7 April 1948) and pl. 2 (upper left) between pp. 142–43.

15. Craft, *Dearest Bubushkin*, 10 December 1952.

16. Stravinsky, *Selected Correspondence*, 2:369 and note 16.

17. Nabokov, "Stravinsky Now," 333–34.

18. Nabokov, "Stravinsky Now," 332–33; more briefly quoted in Taruskin, *Stravinsky and the Russian Traditions*, 1601n150, and noting the term in a sketchbook (1919–22); see also Shepard, "The Stravinsky *Nachlass*," 722; Jans and Handschin, *Strawinsky: Musik-manuskripte*, 42, 54 (Skizzenbuch 7); and Carr, *After the Rite*, 249–52, and her Music Example 7.1. On this term see Jordan, "Stravinsky as Co-choreographer." The term should not be confused with "chronométrique" and "chrono-amétrique," used by Pierre Souvtchinsky, "La Notion du temps," about which see Dufour, *Stravinski et ses exégètes*, 65; and Levitz, *Modernist Mysteries*, 155–59. Responding to Souvtchinsky in the *Nouvelle Revue française* 28 (May 1940), Charles-Albert Cingria stated that "these divisions correspond to those established in distinctions [drawn] between Stravinsky's art and dithyrambic, descriptive art, or ecstatic, discursive, modern [art]." See Cingria, *Œuvres complètes*, 6:142.

19. See Slim, "Stravinsky's Four Star-Spangled Banners," 361–62.

20. Stravinsky's complaints are in his letter held at the Paul Sacher Stiftung; the advertisement is in *Musical Courier,* 15 April 1941, 30. See my "Stravinsky's Four Star-Spangled Banners," 405–6 and 444n328.

21. Still, having purchased the rights to Tango, Feist was hardly "indifferent to its fate." Mercury had advertised it in April of 1941. In 1953 Stravinsky illegally attempted to keep his own instrumentation of it secret from legal owner Feist, but Feist prevailed. That year Mercury published the only instrumental arrangement of it made by Stravinsky. It was premiered on 19 October 1953 at a Los Angeles "Evenings on the Roof" concert, led by Craft; in Craft, *Dearest Bubushkin,* 19 October, Vera called the concert (also premiering the 1937 *Praeludium*) "Stravinsky jazz," quoting the printed program's title for its second half. Stravinsky had newly scored Tango for four clarinets, bass clarinet, four trumpets, three trombones, guitar, three violins, single viola, cello, and double bass.

22. Slim, "Unknown Words and Music," 309, 313–14, citing the Edward Waldo Forbes Papers, Harvard University.

23. "Igor Finishes His Chicago Lecture with Nadia's Help," in Craft, *Dearest Bubushkin,* 8 December 1943.

24. Baltensperger, "Strawinskys 'Chicago Lecture' (1944)"; and Walsh, *Stravinsky: The Second Exile,* 153, respectively.

25. These reviews are assembled in a scrapbook belonging to the university's Department of Music.

26. Cassidy, "Stravinsky and Symphony Aids."

27. Stuart, *Igor Stravinsky,* 28, nos. 17 and 32, no. 38, respectively.

28. See Stravinsky and Craft, *Memories and Commentaries* (2002 only), 233; and Taruskin, *Stravinsky and the Russian Traditions,* 1637.

29. Walsh, *Stravinsky: The Second Exile,* 156.

30. She appears with Stravinsky in 1941 and 1943 group photographs in Walsh, *Stravinsky: The Second Exile,* between 204–5, pl. 4; and in Craft, *Dearest Bubushkin,* 129, pl. 98. The 1943 *Bubushkin* photograph with Stravinsky, shirtless and in shorts, was probably taken the same day as another one wherein he and she are seated with arms over each other's shoulders; see Cohen, *All We Know,* 182, reproduced from de Acosta, *Here Lies the Heart,* between 20–21, pl. 8 (lower image), an image now in the Rosenbach Museum and Library, Philadelphia, as is "an autographed [printed?] score by Igor Stravinsky," cited in Cohen, *All We Know,* 179. She is also identifiable from her striped trousers (far left) with Vera, Stravinsky, and Balanchine in a cropped 1944 image reproduced in Cross, *Igor Stravinsky,* 133.

31. See Walsh, *Stravinsky: The Second Exile,* 156; and, esp., Schanke, *"That Furious Lesbian,"* 147–48, quoting from letters of 16 January and 22 February 1944, the first of which must have been preceded by another one from her to Stravinsky. About his religious objections to Diaghilev's proposed *Liturgie* (1915–16), see V. Stravinsky and Craft, *Stravinsky in Pictures,* 150–51; Stravinsky, *Selected Correspondence,* 2:394 (Nabokov to Stravinsky: "Like you . . ."); and Craft, *Stravinsky: Discoveries and Memories,* 115–21.

32. Walsh, *Stravinsky: The Second Exile,* 12.

33. These included Auden, Balanchine, Dagmar Godowsky, Nicolas Nabokov, and Virgil Thomson, as cited in Stravinsky, *Selected Correspondence,* 3:326.

34. V. Stravinsky and Craft, *Stravinsky in Pictures*, 48; Taruskin, *Stravinsky and the Russian Traditions*, 1624, provides the entire statement. Craft, *Dearest Bubushkin*, 212, pl. 164 (on lower shelf, far right), reveals a copy of Rimsky's *My Life* at 1260 N. Wetherly.

35. A 1904 photograph of them and other students, but not Prokofiev, with Rimsky-Korsakov and Glazunov is in Taruskin, *Stravinsky and the Russian Traditions*, 370, fig. 6.1. Prokofiev studied only briefly with Rimsky in 1907–8, as he notes in *Diaries, 1907–14*, 51–52.

36. Stravinsky, *Selected Correspondence*, 3:291–93 (as before 5 March 1944); and Craft, *Stravinsky: Discoveries and Memories*, 8–9, who reported Shilkret's commission (i.e., payment?) as on 30 September 1945. Zenck, "Leben und Überleben," 72n69, cites relevant letters of 5 and 9 March 1944, suggesting plausibly that such a late date as "18 April 1944" in Craft, *Dearest Bubushkin*, must have been Vera Stravinsky's misunderstanding.

37. Recent claims of German Jewish ancestry for him raise the question as to whether Stravinsky himself knew about these supposed progenitors, a question that may never be answered; see Craft, *Stravinsky: Discoveries and Memories*, 104–5: "evidence exists" (without providing its source); and Stravinsky, *Selected Correspondence*, 3:235–36.

38. White, *Stravinsky*, 615, no. 80.

39. Craft, *Dearest Bubushkin*, 18 April 1944: "Shilkret at 5 to ask Igor to compose Babel."

40. See Zenck, "Leben und Überleben," 71–72n68; and Zenck, "Challenges and Opportunities," 190–91n68; Salzman, "Concert Notes," 30, citing Shilkret, *Nathaniel Shilkret: Sixty Years*, 197; Westby, *Genesis Suite (1945)*, 5; Walsh, *Stravinsky: The Second Exile*, 607n4; and Feisst, *Schoenberg's New World*, 103.

41. Facsimile from the 1945 RCA Victor 78 rpm record album in Merrill-Mirsky, *Exiles in Paradise*, pl. at 51, "About My Babel Cantata / By Igor Stravinsky, Hollywood, California. November 5, 1945." Brief selections from Stravinsky's text are in Westby, *Genesis Suite (1945)*, 5.

42. Tansman, *Igor Stravinsky*, 129–30, 253.

43. Craft, "Music and Words," 100.

44. Stuart, *Igor Stravinsky*, 45, no. 121; this disc, *Stravinsky Conducts Stravinsky: Choral Music*, was released in December of 1964.

45. White, *Stravinsky*, 518.

46. These and the preceding Tansman quotations are cited in Tansman, *Igor Stravinsky*, 130–31. Just a year later, in a radio broadcast from Montreal, Stravinsky was to argue precisely the opposite; see next chapter.

47. *Strawinsky: Sein Nachlass*, 130–31; White, *Stravinsky*, 615, no. 80.

48. Van den Toorn, *The Music of Igor Stravinsky*, 290–94.

49. White, *Stravinsky*, 434–35, ex. 118.

50. Van den Toorn, *The Music of Igor Stravinsky*, 364–65, ex. 75b.

51. Stravinsky, *Themes and Conclusions*, 289; its date found in Craft, *Stravinsky: Chronicle (1994)*, 509 (first line). Reference has been made to his procedure in "For Bessie's Song."

52. Taruskin, "Stravinsky's 'Rejoicing Discovery.'"

53. Craft, "Reflections," 27.

54. Stein, "Schoenberg and 'Kleine Modernsky,'" 315. Craft, "Music and Words," 101, rightly pointed to Stravinsky's "predatory lengthening" of the words *imagined* and *another's*.

55. Van den Toorn, *The Music of Igor Stravinsky*, 291, ex. 61a (at reh. 16). Taruskin, *The Danger of Music*, 111, calls this "during the 1940s . . . a certain cold technical device." Cold or hot, said "device" dates back at least to the A major-minor ostinato in pianos 2 and 4 in *Svadebka* (1914–23), closing its second scene (rehs. 59–64).

56. Walsh, *The Music of Stravinsky*, 191, cites "graphic spiccato string writing" at these words (rehs. 17: –2, 18: –2, and 19); and in *Stravinsky: The Second Exile*, 157, he writes: "broadly descriptive" and "the music scurries about in suitably bewildered figuration."

57. Schönberger and Andriessen, "The Utopian Unison," 209–10.

58. Walsh, *Stravinsky: The Second Exile*, 607n4. White, *Stravinsky*, 12, notes that Bartók and Prokofiev were also invited to contribute to this suite.

59. Reproduced in Slim, "Unknown Words and Music," 317, pl. 4; translation by Michael Green.

60. After entering "End of the War" in his diary for 15 August 1945, Kall valiantly attended an all-Russian concert at the Shrine Auditorium the next day, conducted by Klemperer and Stravinsky (who patriotically led his 1919 *Firebird Suite* without fee), also featuring a speech by their mutual friend Edward G. Robinson.

61. Further testimonies to this friendship until Kall's burial on 10 September 1948 are in Slim, "Unknown Words and Music," 318–19.

62. A legal contract of mid-July 1944, signed by Stravinsky concerning Whiteman's coming broadcast of this version over the "Blue Network," is in Slim, *Annotated Catalogue*, 249–51, item 81.

63. See V. Stravinsky and Craft, *Stravinsky in Pictures*, 374–76; the composer's program notes in Stravinsky and Craft, *Dialogues and a Diary*, 81–83; and (slightly revised) in Stravinsky and Craft, *Memories and Commentaries* (2002), 231–33; Joseph, *Stravinsky's Ballets*, 153–55; Craft, *The Moment of Existence*, 276; and Craft, *Stravinsky: Discoveries and Memories*, 55–56.

64. Schuster-Craig, "Stravinsky's *Scènes de ballet*," 288.

65. Crawford, *A Windfall of Musicians*, 215n50; and Linick, *Lives of Ingolf Dahl*, 102.

66. Craft, *An Improbable Life*, 70. Stravinsky's attitude toward White is in Stravinsky, *Selected Correspondence*, 1:353 and 413n6; and esp. Joseph, *Stravinsky Inside Out*, 6–7.

67. Cited in Joseph, *Stravinsky Inside Out*, 299n21, i.e., from Stravinsky's own copy (now at Paul Sacher Stiftung) of *Tempo* 81 (1967).

68. White, *Stravinsky* (1979 only), 76, pl.

69. White, *Stravinsky* (1966), 382n1 (item 74); White, *Stravinsky* (1979), 421n1 (item 79).

70. Craft, *The Moment of Existence*, 276.

71. V. Stravinsky and Craft, *Stravinsky in Pictures*, 375.

72. New York Public Library, Lincoln Center, Music Division: MS JOB 79–1. I am indebted to John Shepard, Hargrove Music Library, University of California, Berkeley, for this information.

73. Linick, *Lives of Ingolf Dahl*, 102.

74. Papineau-Couture and Papineau-Couture, "Souvenirs," 59–60 (plate) and 61–63, my composite translation from their two slightly varying accounts. Not conservatory-trained, Stravinsky might have learned solmization from Boulanger in 1935; see Walsh, *Stravinsky: The Second Exile*, 32. Craft, *Stravinsky: Discoveries and Memories*, 209,

translated a seemingly related but briefer passage from what he called "Isabelle's diary," his source otherwise unidentified. A group photograph taken in Santa Barbara—to which Stravinsky (for unknown reasons) strenuously objected, as reported in Craft, *Dearest Bubushkin*, 3 October 1944—is best illustrated in Milot, *Jean Papineau-Couture*, 29; and less clearly in Forney, "From Santa Barbara to Xanadu," 405, pl. 4.

75. S[aunders?], "Stravinsky Heard Again," *Musical America*, Feb. 1945, 243. For reviews of the initial ballet performances in November and December of 1944, see Walsh, *Stravinsky: The Second Exile*, 164–65. Craft, *Stravinsky: Discoveries and Memories*, 55–56, offers exemplary analysis and appreciation of *Scènes de ballet*.

76. Saunders, "Los Angeles Orchestra Opening"; Craft, *Dearest Bubushkin*, 22 October 1944. Predictably, *Pacific Coast Musician*, 4 Nov. 1944, 10, slammed it.

77. C. S. H., "'Dumbarton Oaks' Played as Concerto."

78. Morton, "Los Angeles to Hear Resident Composer," 52.

79. Walsh, *Stravinsky: The Second Exile*, 162, states they performed the Sonata and *Circus Polka* (arr. Victor Babin) at Mills; see Stravinsky, *Selected Correspondence*, 3:282 (28 June 1942). V. Stravinsky and Craft, *Stravinsky in Pictures*, 642n12, implied that only the Sonata was performed in Philadelphia. Francis, "Nadia Boulanger and Igor Stravinsky," 150, notes this sonata's score as "missing," even though referenced elsewhere. Stravinsky's transparencies (prepared for making ozalid copies) survive in the Pierpont Morgan Library, New York. On the Sonata's transparencies see Slim, *Annotated Catalogue*, 250; and Slim, "Stravinsky's *Scherzo*," 528–29.

80. Spycket, *Nadia Boulanger*, 115 (upper plate), a photograph sometimes wrongly dated as 1947; Vera's absence from the photograph suggests she took it.

81. Craft, *Dearest Bubushkin*, 22 October 1945; and Nichols, *Conversations with Madeleine Milhaud*, 28, the latter also quoted in Fauser, *Sounds of War*, 188.

82. Milhaud, *Mon XXème siècle*, 11 (note) and 98: "Nadia whacked Igor's fingers while telling him: 'You are not keeping time'" (my translation).

83. In mid-February of 1945, surely referring to triadic passages in *Petrushka* (rehs. 2, 5, 11, 20, 33, etc.); see V. Stravinsky and Craft, *Stravinsky in Pictures*, 645n30. Milhaud does not mention the *Circus Polka*.

84. Frankenstein, "Stravinsky Recital at Mills College."

85. See Taruskin, *Stravinsky and the Russian Traditions*, 1623–48.

86. Stravinsky, *Selected Correspondence*, 2:371n19; Lisa Cox Music, *Music Catalogue 48*, lot 83, thus answering the query about the Sonata's location in Francis, "Boulanger and Stravinsky," 151n33. On Manziarly as composer see P. Griffith, "Manziarly."

87. Craft, *Dearest Bubushkin*, 19 October 1942; Walsh, *Stravinsky: The Second Exile*, 145.

88. Walsh, *Stravinsky: The Second Exile*, 142.

89. Walsh, *Stravinsky: The Second Exile*, 156; V. Stravinsky and Craft, *Stravinsky in Pictures*, 373.

90. Stravinsky had warned them that it could not "be considered a world premiere"; see Barlow, "Mrs. Coolidge's Birthday Party," 40; and Stravinsky, *Selected Correspondence*, 3:300. Craft, *An Improbable Life*, 139, cites a notable later performance of the Sonata on 1 April 1945 in Minneapolis by Ernst Krenek and Mitropoulos.

91. Frankenstein, "Stravinsky Recital at Mills College"; Nabokov, "Stravinsky Now," 331.

92. Stravinsky, *Selected Correspondence*, 3:298, 22 April, to Gretel Urban. See also the analysis—lacking any mention whatever of Russian folksong—of this sonata as "a typical neoclassical work," in Kramer, "Discontinuity."

93. Joseph, *Stravinsky Inside Out*, 21, 119; Frankenstein, "Stravinsky Introduces a Major Work," in its later arrangement for symphony orchestra; many such critics are cited in Slim, "Stravinsky's *Scherzo*," 536.

94. Taruskin, *Stravinsky and the Russian Traditions*, 1623–47; Morton, "Stravinsky at Home," 335–36. Zenck, "Leben und Überleben," 74, 76, and 78, when discussing the *Scherzo* and the Sonata, seems unaware of the items cited in this and the next two notes.

95. Craft, *Dearest Bubushkin*, 4 November 1942, citing Vera Stravinsky: "Downtown with Igor to a music store."

96. See Slim, "Stravinsky's *Scherzo*," 522, ex. 1.

97. Taruskin, "Just How Russian Was Stravinsky?"; repr. in Taruskin, *Russian Music*, 361–65.

98. This L. of C. ozalid and its two predecessors are described in Slim, "Stravinsky's *Scherzo*," 530–31.

99. Walsh, *Stravinsky: A Creative Spring*, 612n61.

100. Slim, "Stravinsky's *Scherzo*." Admittedly, this essay on the keyboard origins of the *Scherzo à la russe* makes for difficult reading, hampered as it was by unanswered requests for permission to include musical examples.

101. For Stravinsky's ensuing (sour) opinion about movie music see Dahl, "Igor Stravinsky on Film Music," 4–5; repr. in Cooke, *The Hollywood Film Music Reader*, 276–80.

102. Timmons and Frémaux, "Alexandre Tansman," 11.

103. Tansman, *Igor Stravinsky*, 252.

104. Craft, *Dearest Bubushkin*, 26 April 1944; Slim, *Annotated Catalogue*, 253–54, with incorrect date of his death.

105. Acquired 7 May 2015 from Lion Heart Autographs Inc., New York (my translation).

106. Both unidentified catalogue excerpts were included in lot 758 from *Jackson Opera Collection*, part VII: R–S.

107. Slim, *Annotated Catalogue*, 252–54, item 82.

108. *Autographen Katalog 916*, 86–87, lot 191.

109. T. Stravinsky, *Catherine and Igor Stravinsky*, unpaginated.

110. Stravinsky's correspondence concerning their original publisher, Adolphe Henn is in Slim, *Annotated Catalogue*, 63–66, item 13.

111. On Alexander Nápravník, son of the longtime conductor at the Maryinsky Theater, Eduard Nápravník, see V. Stravinsky and Craft, *Stravinsky in Pictures*, 32; Strawinsky and Strawinsky, *Au cœur du foyer*, 124; Craft, *Stravinsky: Discoveries and Memories*, 137; and, esp., Stravinskaya, *O I. F. Stravinskom*, 47n1 and 49, pl., depicting Alexander in 1925 with Igor Stravinsky at Nice.

112. Walsh, *Stravinsky: A Creative Spring*, 410. Craft, *Stravinsky: Discoveries and Memories*, 134–42, posits incestuous desires between niece Tanya and composer-uncle Igor, but letters from Catherine and Arthur Lourié reveal a love interest between Tanya and Théodore rather than his father (information kindly furnished by Richard Taruskin); see also Walsh, *Stravinsky: A Creative Spring*, 410–13n4, 418.

113. Forbes, *History of Music at Harvard*, 101–2; Craft, *Stravinsky: Discoveries and Memories*, 113n28. Summaries of previous analyses and discussion, new analyses of the various movements, Stravinsky's sketches, and his corrections are in Schneider, "Tradition und Neuorientierung."

114. T. Strawinsky, *Le Message d'Igor Strawinsky*, 96n1. On 27 October 1948 Ansermet premiered the complete Mass in Milan on the stage of La Scala, thereby earning the composer's disapproval for what he considered an operatic performance; see Walsh, *Stravinsky: The Second Exile*, 231.

115. Translated in Walsh, *Stravinsky: The Second Exile*, 238–39, from Stravinsky's letter of 7 January 1949, now at Paul Sacher Stiftung. Some of Stravinsky's French in this letter appears in Strawinsky and Strawinsky, *Au cœur du foyer*, 172–73; Walsh, *Stravinsky: The Second Exile*, 680, in "*Sfam*," expresses some misgivings.

116. Craft, *An Improbable Life*, 153–54; additional negative opinions by Craft (and others) are in Craft, *Stravinsky: Discoveries and Memories*, 126. The translators were Craft and André Marion, Stravinsky's son-in-law.

117. Joseph, *Stravinsky and Balanchine*, 18, who studied with Soulima, 1968–70. Many of Théodore's and Soulima's recollections, however, stem from Perrin, "Strawinsky dans une classe de composition"; trans. as "Stravinsky in a Composition Class," *The Score and I.M.A. Magazine*, June 1957, 44–46; and as "Lehrer Strawinsky," *Musik der Zeit*, n.s., 1 (1958): 86–87.

118. Advertisement, "AMP," *Musical America*, June 1944, 21.

119. S[aunders?], "Orchestra"; Stravinsky, *Selected Correspondence*, 3:295 (15 January 1944).

120. Stravinsky, *Selected Correspondence*, 3:296.

121. Walsh, *Stravinsky: The Second Exile*, 178–79; Holoman, *Charles Munch*, 59–62.

122. Walsh, *Stravinsky: The Second Exile*, 610n26, cites two letters in private hands and mentions, at 570, Craft's dastardly suppression of would-be-Stravinsky biographer John Kobler—as cited in Craft, *Small Craft Advisories*, 154–55. For more on Soulima see Craft, "Cher père, Chère Vera," in *Stravinsky: Glimpses*, 142; Craft, *An Improbable Life*, 76–77n45; Craft, *Stravinsky: Chronicle* (1994), 152–53; Craft, *Stravinsky: Discoveries and Memories*, 203; Walsh, *Stravinsky: The Second Exile*, 130, 352; and Joseph, *Stravinsky Inside Out*, 281–82n20.

123. Craft, "A Modest Confutation," 2; Craft, "An Interview," 39; and Craft, *Stravinsky: Discoveries and Memories*, 130.

124. Walsh, *Stravinsky: A Creative Spring*, 264n42.

125. For location of the dramatis personae see Craft, *Dearest Bubushkin*, 3 August 1956; Craft, *A Stravinsky Scrapbook*, 53, pl. 112; Craft, *Stravinsky: Chronicle* (1994), 144–45; Craft, "A Modest Confutation," 1; Craft, "An Interview," 38; and Craft, *Stravinsky: Discoveries and Memories*, 130. Said to have taken place in Venice, the incident would date from early August of 1956.

126. Joseph, *Stravinsky Inside Out*, 281n15, is not the first to remark on Craft's "ellipsis."

127. Joseph, *Stravinsky Inside Out*, 64–99; Levitz, *Modernist Mysteries*, 352–56.

128. Walsh, *Stravinsky: The Second Exile*, 162, decrying, at 608n33, Craft's attempts to date *Élégie*'s three movements. Prévost was a Belgian exile living in New York. Francis, *Teaching Stravinsky*, 152, provides Boulanger's letter to Stravinsky of 19 August 1944, concerning Prévost's request.

129. V. Stravinsky and Craft, *Stravinsky in Pictures*, 648n56; Craft, *Stravinsky: Discoveries and Memories*, 309; and Craft, *Dearest Bubushkin*, 28 December 1948. I later knew Michael Mann (Klaus's youngest brother) slightly from his friendship with his Berkeley colleague Professor Daniel Heartz.

130. Craft, *Dearest Bubushkin*, 7 February 1945.

131. On his musical training in 1920 at the Petrograd Conservatory in difficult piano works by Bach, Beethoven, Chopin, and Schumann (among others), and as an improviser, see Kendall, *Balanchine and the Lost Muse*, 138–39; and, more fully, Joseph, *Stravinsky and Balanchine*, 15–21.

132. Balanchine, "The Dance Element," 252; repr. in Lederman, *Stravinsky in the Theatre*, 77 (the latter itself reprinted in 1975); and Joseph, *Stravinsky and Balanchine*, 301, 351, 401n30; and Joseph, *Stravinsky's Ballets*, 239.

133. Craft, *Dearest Bubushkin*, 2 November 1944, without comment.

134. "Pictorial Review," *San Francisco Examiner*, 26 Nov. 1944, unpaginated; "Season Ends Tuesday Evening [28 November]," *San Francisco Examiner*, 27 Nov. 1944, CC16.

135. Frankenstein, "Ballet Rings Down Curtain," describing the company's final program, 28 November.

136. "Next week" would have meant 6 December 1944. See Walsh, *Stravinsky: The Second Exile*, 162; Craft, *Dearest Bubushkin*, 1 December 1944; and Jones, "Ballet Russe Impresses in Return." Jordan, *Stravinsky Dances*, 515, states that Stravinsky led it on 6 December in Los Angeles.

CHAPTER TEN. EXCURSIONS (1945–EARLY 1946)

1. Stravinski to Rieti, 10 Dec. 1944, in Ricci, *Vittorio Rieti*, 412–13.

2. Craft, *Dearest Bubushkin*, 30 January–4 February, and 15 February 1945; see also Walsh, *Stravinsky: The Second Exile*, 173.

3. Cross, *Igor Stravinsky*, 14.

4. Craft, *The Moment of Existence*, 272 (a "full draft-score") and 276; Craft, *Stravinsky: Discoveries and Memories*, 55.

5. Thomson, *Music Reviewed, 1940–1954*, 141–42; repr. from the *New York Herald Tribune*, 2 Feb. 1945.

6. See Sears, *V-Discs*, 687, item NEW-15; Stravinsky, *Selected Correspondence*, 3:292; and Stuart, *Igor Stravinsky*, 70, no. L2, now on Pearl Records: GEMM CDS 9292, track 24, including the Benny introduction. The commercial recording made the next day, 5 February 1945 (lacking Mr. Benny), is on Columbia's "Meet the Composer," ML 4398, and also on compact disc in Sony's *The Original Jacket Collection: Stravinsky Conducts Stravinsky*.

7. The *Rochester Daily Record*, though carrying advertisements for broadcast concerts by the Rochester Civic Orchestra (sponsored by Stromberg-Carlson), never mentions Stravinsky's presence in Rochester.

8. Craft, *Dearest Bubushkin*, 8, 21, 26 February and 1 March 1945.

9. Archer, "Igor Stravinsky Here to Conduct."

10. Joseph, *Stravinsky Inside Out*, 20, quoting from Stravinsky's notes in Paul Sacher Stiftung, Basel.

11. Dahl, "Igor Stravinsky on Film Music," 35; quoted in Joseph, *Stravinsky Inside Out*, 128; and partly in V. Stravinsky and Craft, *Stravinsky in Pictures*, 358 (my emphasis).

12. Craft, *Dearest Bubushkin*, 18 February and 2–5 March 1945; and "Dossier Stravinsky-Canada," 23.

13. Craft, *Dearest Bubushkin*, 8 April 1945; Fox, "Bel-Air Fete." A photograph at Kent's reception after the Szigeti-Kaufman performance depicts (left to right): Szigeti, Stravinsky, and Kaufman, with Stravinsky's left hand on Kaufman's shoulder, in "Salutes and Salaams: Guests of Honor," *Musical Courier*, July 1945, 2.

14. Craft, *Dearest Bubushkin*, 28 December 1944.

15. Szigeti, *With Strings Attached*, 273, plate facing. The photograph's date(s) is in Stuart, *Igor Stravinsky*, 32, no. 38.

16. Craft, *Stravinsky: Glimpses*, 24–25; Craft, *Dearest Bubushkin*, 7–8 February 1946; Walsh, *Stravinsky: The Second Exile*, 188; and Taubman: "3 Artists Heard."

17. Routh, *Stravinsky: The Master*, pl. 3, between 86–87; Craft, *Dearest Bubushkin*, 7–8 February 1946.

18. Horowitz, *Conversations with Arrau*, 115; repr. in Horowitz, *Arrau on Music*, 115.

19. His own opinion and those of others about this calligraphic talent appear in Slim, *Annotated Catalogue*, 15; and Horgan, *Encounters with Stravinsky*, 257.

20. Monighetti, "Working on *The Rite of Spring*," 133; "Danse sacrale" was first published by Associated Music Publisher in 1945, not by Boosey and Hawkes in 1943 as Monighetti claims.

21. These sheets are likewise in the Paul Sacher Stiftung, Basel; see Slim, "Stravinsky's *Scherzo*," 526.

22. Jones, "Music Event Conducted by Janssen."

23. Westby, *Genesis Suite (1945)*, 7, the source of Morton's remarks not disclosed.

24. Morton, "Music Notes," *Rob Wagner's Script*, 1 Dec. 1945, 20.

25. Steele, "Janssen Symphony Orchestra." On Steele's background see Saunders, *Music and Dance in California*, 260.

26. Craft, *Dearest Bubushkin*, 16–18 November; Stravinsky and Craft, *Dialogues and a Diary*, 55; Craft, *Down a Path*, 5, states that one of these occasions was a recording session.

27. Stein, "Schoenberg and 'Kleine Modernsky,'" 315; Craft, *Stravinsky: Discoveries and Memories*, 9, retranslated from the German as "It lacks an ending; it simply stops."

28. Slim, "A Stravinsky Holograph," 458, since confirmed by two additional fine bassoon players.

29. Van den Toorn, *The Music of Igor Stravinsky*, 45–46n25, 47, and 351–66, esp. 364–66; van den Toorn, "Octatonic Pitch Structure in Stravinsky," esp. 155, ex. 8.21. See also, Cross, *The Stravinsky Legacy*, 211–26, though Cross was unaware of Craft's discovery of Stravinsky's new ending.

30. Cantoni, *The Language of Stravinsky*, 73–77 and 205–6, respectively, though not citing the finale's new ending. Cone, in "Stravinsky: The Progress," discussing its first movement only, wrote of a "principle of stratification" and of "sub-stratification."

31. Craft, *The Moment of Existence*, 272; Craft, *Stravinsky: Discoveries and Memories*, 55, dates the rewriting of the finale as 7 August–14 October 1945. Stravinsky's fair copy of this score is in the New York Public Library. Craft first disclosed his discovery in a letter of

17 November 1993, responding to an inquiry of 18 October from Michael Pettersen in Chicago, whom I thank for this information.

32. Craft, *Dearest Bubushkin*, 15 February 1945; but Craft, *The Moment of Existence*, 272, gave 16 February 1945.

33. Shepard, "The Stravinsky *Nachlass*," 745, cites thirteen draft pages dated 7 August 1945. On 20 August he noted his Symphony's completion; see Stravinsky, *Selected Correspondence*, 3:302–3.

34. Years later, composer-teacher Paul Des Marais drolly called this revised, concluding sonority a "Harry James chord," after the celebrated 1940s dance-band leader; cited in Craft, *The Moment of Existence*, 272.

35. Stravinsky's "The final, rather too commercial, D-flat sixth chord—instead of the expected C" first appears in 1962: Columbia ML 5731 record-jacket notes; then in Stravinsky and Craft, *Dialogues and a Diary*, 84; and, slightly revised, in Stravinsky and Craft, *Memories and Commentaries* (2002), 220. Routh, *Stravinsky: The Master Musicians Series*, 99, appropriates "expected," claiming (dubiously enough) that the third movement's final D-flat springs "from the Phrygian D-flat of the second bar" (in the first movement).

36. Craft, *An Improbable Life*, 393.

37. These three are cited in Stuart, *Igor Stravinsky*, nos. 41, 102, and App. C (79); the two unavailable (Berlin and London) are cited on 81–82.

38. Walsh, *Stravinsky: The Second Exile*, 186. Walsh, *The Music of Stravinsky*, 196–97, perceives similarities between the first movement of the Symphony (rehs. 7 and 88) and the first movement of the Concerto for Two Solo Pianos, pp. 10–11 and pp. 15–16 (both in $\frac{12}{16}$) and variation 4 of its third movement. Yet variation 4 has not just one ostinato in piano 2, as Walsh claims, but very frequently another—and a melodic—ostinato in piano 1 that becomes the fugue subject of the Concerto's fourth movement.

39. Stravinsky's spelling is preserved as in this facsimile in a New York Philharmonic stage bill for October 1991 in the New York Public Library, Lincoln Center, Music Division, made from his original letter, New York Philharmonic archives.

40. See Stuart, *Igor Stravinsky*, no. 41 (1946); Stravinsky leading the Baden-Baden orchestra (21 May 1954), partly cited in the booklet to the compact disc: "Stravinsky Conducts Stravinsky" (Music and Arts Program of America), issued in 2006 (but not cited in Stuart, *Igor Stravinsky*, no. 102 [1961]); and see, to a lesser extent, Georg Solti's 1993 recording with the Chicago Symphony Orchestra, issued in 1999 on Decca.

41. V. Stravinsky and Craft, *Stravinsky in Pictures*, 378; a copy of this program is in Kall Papers, box 5: Stravinsky, folder 3, programs.

42. Stravinsky and Craft, *Dialogues and a Diary*, 83–85; *Memories and Commentaries* (2002): 220–21. Stravinsky refers to an envisaged book, entitled simply *Dialogues*, in two letters—30 January and 3 February 1958—to Deborah Ishlon, publicity director for Columbia Records. One letter is cited in Slim, *Annotated Catalogue*, item 104; the other is owned by Professor Emeritus Steven Chatman (UBC), who kindly so informed me; see also "Publisher's Note," in Stravinsky and Craft, *Dialogues*, 7.

43. Clippings of reviews by Irving Kolodin (25 Jan. 1946) and Robert A. Hague (27 Jan. 1946) are in the New York Public Library, Lincoln Center, Music Division. Crawford,

A Windfall of Musicians, 231, dates the premiere incorrectly as 28 December 1945. A half dozen years after the New York premiere, Vera Stravinsky believed that the Symphony in Three Movements suffered in Paris from being programmed with *Scènes de ballet*, just as it had similarly suffered in 1946; see Craft, *Stravinsky: Discoveries and Memories*, 159–60.

44. Downes, "Stravinsky Leads the Philharmonic."

45. Cited in Armitage, *Accent on Life*, 177–78: 14 December 1946; and Stravinsky, *Selected Correspondence*, 1:358–59: 16 March 1949, respectively. Stravinsky's outburst, despite Downes having written a favorable review of *Le Sacre* in 1924, is cited in Taruskin, *Russian Music*, 410.

46. Walsh, *Stravinsky: The Second Exile*, 189; Stravinsky, *Selected Correspondence*, 2:257n29.

47. Craft, "Sunday Afternoon Live," review of CD recordings: *The New York Philharmonic: The Historic Broadcasts, 1923 to 1987*. The passage in question occurs for three measures at reh. 130.

48. Stravinsky, *Selected Correspondence*, 1:331n8; Craft, *An Improbable Life*, 63.

49. "The Talk of the Town," *New Yorker*, 2 Feb. 1946, 13–14; Craft, *Dearest Bubushkin*, 24 January 1946.

50. Simon, "Musical Events."

51. Fuller, "Stravinsky Full-Length Portrait."

52. H[arold] C. S[chonberg], "Stravinsky Leads His New Symphony." Not related to this "H. C. S.," I first heard it in Vancouver the following Sunday from New York by delayed broadcast.

53. P., "Stravinsky Conducts His Own Symphony," 282, 284.

54. See V. Stravinsky and Craft, *Stravinsky in Pictures*, 378, letter of 8 December 1945 to Bruno Zirato; and Stravinsky, *Selected Correspondence*, 2:487n2.

55. S. [Robert Sabin?], Postscript, *Musical America* 66 (February 1946): 284; and confirmed by Vera Stravinsky in *Dearest Bubushkin*, 24 January 1946, who wrote of the Symphony's premiere: "unexpectedly . . . a great success."

56. Tryon, "Stravinsky Returning with New Symphony."

57. Sloper, "Stravinsky at Symphony Hall." A vicious review by Sloper in 1944 is cited in Slim, "Stravinsky's Four Star-Spangled Banners," 364n177.

58. Durgin, "Music: Symphony Hall."

59. Joseph, *Stravinsky's Ballets*, 146–47; Cantoni, *The Language of Stravinsky*, 262, cites a borrowing from Verdi, *Falstaff*.

60. V. Stravinsky and Craft, *Stravinsky in Pictures*, 334; but the connection, "an obvious precursor," is made in Walsh, *Stravinsky: The Second Exile*, 60.

61. Klinko, "Osnovnïye datï," 176–80 and 189–90, respectively, with a photograph of him as Don Basilio on pl. 3, no. 5, and the 1891 drawing as Don Bartolo on pl. 4, between pp. 80–81, translation courtesy of Professor Richard Taruskin. Klinko discusses these roles at p. 70 and at p. 197 notes Fyodor at Pechisky (Ukraine) in May–August of 1891.

62. Taruskin, *Stravinsky and the Russian Traditions*, 92.

63. Stravinsky and Craft, *Expositions and Developments* (1962), 87; Joseph, *Stravinsky Inside Out*, 191.

64. Stravinsky and Craft, *Expositions and Developments* (1962), 66.

65. Irving Fine, "English in Boston; Stravinsky's Symphony," *Modern Music* 23 (Summer 1946): 210.

66. Frankenstein, "Igor Stravinsky Introduces a Major Work."

67. Eagle, "Symphony Season Ends Beautifully."

68. I thank Steven LaCoste, archivist of the Los Angeles Philharmonic Association, for this information.

69. Jones, "Klemperer Conducts Slav Works."

70. Brown, review [of Symphony in Three Movements], a clipping from the Los Angeles Philharmonic Association Archive, courtesy Steven LaCoste.

71. [Steele], "Pension Fund Concert."

72. Morton, "Stravinsky's New Symphony."

73. See Steele, "Evenings on the Roof"; see also his barbed response to Morton's long letter in "One Critic to Another," *Pacific Coast Musician,* 4 May 1946, 10–11. Steele's snap verdict is repudiated not least by the present writer's familiarity stemming from many rehearsals of Bartók's Sonata with the late John Brockington and then with two Vancouver Symphony percussionists for its Canadian premiere, 11 March 1951, at UBC; a rehearsal publicity photograph of the four of us is in the *Vancouver Sun,* 10 March 1951, 10; and *News-Herald* (Vancouver), 10 March 1951, 12. Assuredly, Steele would have ridiculed Hindemith's accurate evaluation of both composers quoted above.

74. Morton, "Stravinsky's New Symphony."

75. Craft, *Stravinsky: Discoveries and Memories,* 160. Stravinsky also led his Symphony in C and Capriccio at this concert; see Giroud, *Nicolas Nabokov,* 262.

76. Morton, "Music Notes," *Rob Wagner's Script,* 15 Feb. 1947.

77. Dahl, "Stravinsky in 1946."

78. Schiff, "Everyone's *Rite,*" 188, 190, and 194: exs. a and b. A connection to the *Eroica*'s first movement is at least questionable because Stravinsky certainly knew that its original dedication to Napoleon was almost immediately renounced by its disillusioned composer, who considered Napoleon's self-elevation to emperor an act of tyranny, about which see Forbes, *Thayer's Life of Beethoven,* 1:348–50. Moreover, Stravinsky consistently omits the *Eroica* from among his four favorite Beethoven symphonies.

79. Stravinsky, *Selected Correspondence,* 1:353.

80. Stravinsky and Craft, *Conversations with Igor Stravinsky,* 145–46; these remarks were first made public in 1959.

81. Stravinsky and Craft, *Dialogues and a Diary,* 62–63.

82. Crawford, *Evenings on and off the Roof,* 228.

83. Stravinsky and Craft, *Retrospectives and Conclusions,* 130–42; repr. from the *New York Review of Books,* 26 Sept. 1968.

84. Craft, *Stravinsky: Discoveries and Memories,* 235; see also Stravinsky and Craft, *Dialogues,* 112–16.

85. Horgan, *Encounters with Stravinsky,* 260.

86. Stravinsky and Craft, *Memories and Commentaries* (2002), 271, 281–89.

87. Linick, *Lives of Ingolf Dahl,* 102. Stravinsky had completed the full score on 15 October 1945; Thanksgiving followed on 29 November.

88. The same method by which Stravinsky had "heard" the last movement of his Symphony in C in the summer of 1940 with Mrs. McQuoid.

89. Dahl, "Stravinsky in 1946."

90. Stravinsky to John Hammond of Keynote [Record] Distributors, New York, 14 May 1947, offered in Lubrano, *Catalogue 63*, 22, lot 195.

91. Stravinsky, *Selected Correspondence*, 2:487n12; Walsh, *Stravinsky: The Second Exile*, 603–4n71.

92. Joseph, *Stravinsky Inside Out*, 286n31.

93. Craft, *Stravinsky: Chronicle* (1994), 5.

94. Jacket notes for Columbia MS 6331 (ML 5731), as cited in Stuart, *Igor Stravinsky*, item 102; additional details are in North and Tierney, "The Columbia Symphony Orchestra," 167; the Symphony was recorded at American Legion Hall, Hollywood, on 1, 10, and 13 February 1961.

95. Stravinsky and Craft, *Dialogues and a Diary*, 83–85, slightly revised in *Memories and Commentaries* (2002), 220–21.

96. Dahl, "Stravinsky on Film Music," 5; repr. in Cooke, *Hollywood Film Music Reader*, 279.

97. See Walsh, *The Music of Stravinsky*, 195; P. Griffiths, *Stravinsky*, 133: "wholly extraordinary and uncharacteristic"; Walsh, *Stravinsky: The Second Exile*, 138, 421–23, 603n71; Walsh, "Remembering *The Rite of Spring*," 169: "We can safely dismiss the nonsense in *Dialogues* . . . about . . . scorched-earth tactics in China"; and Cross, *Igor Stravinsky*, 145: "his attempt swiftly [self-]contradicted."

98. G. Griffiths, *Stravinsky's Piano*, 219 (who closes this quotation with "Expositions and Developments, 1962"); and Walsh, *The Music of Stravinsky*, 198.

99. Walsh goes so far as to note that the "Russian strain in the Symphony . . . takes it out of the ambit of neo-classicism" (*The Music of Stravinsky*, 198).

100. Almost forty years later, Craft changed the word *said* to a perhaps more revelatory *admitted* in Stravinsky and Craft, *Memories and Commentaries* (2002), 221.

101. 1961–62 record jacket notes and Stravinsky and Craft, *Dialogues and a Diary*, 85.

102. Horowitz, "Sorrow on the Prairie," 15; and (more provisionally) in Taruskin, *Russian Music*, 474.

103. Stuart, *Igor Stravinsky*, 10; and esp. Joseph, *Stravinsky Inside Out*, 214–16, and plate at 217. As Stuart notes (18), Lieberson was succeeded by David Oppenheim in 1950 as director of the Masterworks division of Columbia Records, who was succeeded by John McClure in 1959. Lieberson wrote a tribute in 1962, "Igor Stravinsky at Eighty," for Columbia's jacket notes (see Stuart, *Igor Stravinsky*, nos. 102, 107); and McClure wrote a longer one: "Igor Stravinsky at Eighty," *Gramophone* 40, no. 469 (June 1962): 1–3, noting, "We [i.e., Columbia Records] have added the *increasingly popular* Symphony in Three Movements" (2; my emphasis).

104. Stravinsky and Craft, *Expositions and Developments* (1962), 126.

105. Schiff, "Everyone's *Rite*," 191; I have reversed the order of his sentences.

106. Craft, *Stravinsky: Glimpses*, 18n5.

107. Craft, *Stravinsky: Chronicle* (1994), 444.

108. See Newman, *Bravo Stravinsky*, 44–45; Libman, *Music at the Close*, 177, and pl. 5 (lower image); V. Stravinsky and Craft, *Stravinsky in Pictures*, 587, Appendix E; and Craft, *Dearest Bubushkin*, 15 December 1966.

109. Hertelendy, "Symphony Audience Hails Stravinsky."

110. Stravinsky and Craft, *Retrospectives and Conclusions,* 293–94; Craft, *Stravinsky: Chronicle* (1972), 346 (13 Feb. 1968), omitted in the latter's 1994 "revised and expanded" edition. Of course, nothing of this appears in Mrs. Evan Whallon, *Oakland Symphony, Program Notes,* 346; although written expressly for the occasion, her notes just quote Stravinsky's remarks from *Dialogues and a Diary,* 83–84.

111. *Stravinsky: Once at a Border,* chap. 20, a misstatement accepted in Cross, *Igor Stravinsky,* 144–45.

112. Craft, *Stravinsky: Discoveries and Memories,* 54; although Walsh, *Stravinsky: The Second Exile,* 138, gives them as 4 April 1942.

113. That very February of 1966 Stravinsky had written about the "episodic effect" of the ostinatos and the "heavy" emphasis on key centers in Symphony in C; see the *London Magazine,* Feb. 1966, 42, cited in Stravinsky and Craft, *Themes and Episodes,* 44; these comments are variously—and posthumously—redacted in Stravinsky, *Themes and Conclusions,* 50; and in Stravinsky and Craft, *Memories and Commentaries* (2002), 190.

114. Slim, "Lessons with Stravinsky," 377, fig. 11, and 178n127.

115. Taubman, *The Pleasure of Their Company,* 199; Craft, *Igor and Vera,* 77, item 108.

116. Conclusions drawn mostly from Stravinsky's recorded legacy are in Cook, "Stravinsky Conducts Stravinsky," noting Craft's assistance in preparation (170); he last conducted in 1967, in Toronto. There is virtually no discussion of Stravinsky's technique or of its development. All of these matters occupy Craft's fine essay, "On Conducting," in his *Stravinsky: Discoveries and Memories,* 56–57. I add here my own few observations from 1952 and 1966.

117. Saavedra, Fiori, and Levitz, "Stravinsky Speaks," 221n113. This is not to deny that Stravinsky had his own mannerisms.

118. Egilsrud, "Music: Symphony Orchestra."

119. Sherman, "Music: Stravinsky Conducts."

120. Stravinsky and Craft, *Dialogues and a Diary,* 80; Stravinsky and Craft, *Conversations with Igor Stravinsky,* 114.

121. Schwarz. "Stravinsky, Dushkin, and the Violin," 308.

122. Fried, "Stravinsky Conducts for 'Petrouchka' Here."

123. Martin, "Stravinsky Leads Own 'Petrushka.'" On Martin see Duberman, *The Worlds of Lincoln Kirstein,* 713, index.

124. Papineau-Couture, "Souvenirs," 61–62 (my translation). Craft, *Stravinsky: Discoveries and Memories,* 209, offered a different (and longer) translation from what he identified as Isabelle's "diary."

125. Lyons, "Broadway Gazette." Lyons's unidentified "popular" ballet might also have been *Balustrade,* danced by Denham's company in New York in January of 1941, although Nijinska's presence is not documented either at it or at *Danses concertantes.* During 1942 and 1943 she worked with Denham in New York, but she might also have been with him in Los Angeles in December of 1944.

126. Craft, *Dearest Bubushkin,* 30 January 1945.

127. Thomson, *Music Reviewed, 1940–1954,* 142.

128. Pelletier, "Les concerts: Stravinsky."

129. Archer, "Igor Stravinsky Is Given Ovation."

130. Craft, *Dearest Bubushkin*, 16 July and 9 August 1940; Craft, *Stravinsky: Discoveries and Memories*, 190 (referring to sessions on 1–3, 6, and 7 April 1940).

131. Cited in Maroth, "Stravinsky the Conductor," 7; Horgan, *Encounters with Stravinsky*, 234–36, mentions instances of orchestra players mocking his conducting at Santa Fe in mid-August of 1963 during rehearsals for his Mass.

132. Durgin, "Music: Symphony Hall."

133. Eagle, "Symphony Season Ends Beautifully."

134. Maroth, "Stravinsky the Conductor" (see note 131 above), 4–19.

135. Thomas, "On Stravinsky."

136. Borden, "Halpern, Ida," cites four sets of Native Canadian musics that she collected and recorded on the Pacific Northwest Coast. See also "Remembering Dr. Halpern," *Vancouver Sun*, 17 Nov. 2011, "Entertainment" section.

137. Halpern, "Rehearsals Start"; partly quoted in "Dossier Stravinsky-Canada," 25. These "mistakes" may have been slight differences between Stravinsky's 1919 *Firebird Suite* and his revised 1945 edition—that is, confusion between piano and celesta at reh. 149: –2 and reh. 155: –2 of the latter edition, but chiefly at reh. 172 ("Doppio valore"), where the piano doubles the harp an octave higher. Evelyn Barbirolli, *Life with Glorious John*, 84–85, recounts Stravinsky earlier in Hollywood correcting the *Firebird Suite* on a table-cloth for conductor Barbirolli: "[a] misprint in the score and in one of the parts." When Stravinsky led the VSO in *Firebird* in July of 1965, Robert Rogers played piano and celesta; at a rehearsal "Stravinsky called the pianist to the podium and [thus, a second time] wrote him the missing passage." Remarks in the *Vancouver Sun* about *Firebird* rehearsals, 10–11 July 1965, are in V. Stravinsky and Craft, *Stravinsky in Pictures*, 481. "Dossier Stravinsky-Canada," 28, has a photograph of Stravinsky conducting the VSO, 12 or 13 July 1965.

138. Halpern, "Expectations Fulfilled." By "accentuation" I believe she misspoke and meant "articulation," more logically deducible from his request about "commas," the latter which I also heard him express on 5 October 1952 as "make holes in the music."

139. Craft, *Dearest Bubushkin*, 12 July 1963 and note 10.

140. Slim, *Annotated Catalogue*, 324–29, with one pl. at 324. All twelve photographs are reproduced in Dykk, "Legacy of a Musical Giant."

141. Ericson, "Stravinsky at the Stadium."

142. Horgan, *Encounters with Stravinsky*, plates facing 174 and 182. Photographs of him conducting the Leningrad Philharmonic in October of 1972, the Vancouver Symphony in July of 1965, and at the Hollywood Bowl in September of 1965 are in Craft, *Dearest Bubushkin*, plate 163; *Cahiers canadiens*, 28; and Libman, *And Music*, plate facing 208, respectively.

143. Horgan, *Encounters with Stravinsky*, 245.

APPENDIX

1. See Whittall, "Neo-classical"; Levitz, "Who Owns *Mavra*?" 21; Cantoni, *The Language of Stravinsky*, 236, 246; Cross, *Igor Stravinsky*, 100; and Cross, *The Stravinsky Legacy*, 198ff. Much earlier, Casella, *Stravinsky*, 198, stated that "*neo-classica* led to a long series of

misunderstandings." Though citing few instances of Stravinsky's early dissatisfaction with this term, Messing, *Neoclassicism in Music,* 154, notes previous attempts to abandon its use.

2. Bartók, *Essays,* 360.

3. Wheeldon, "Anti-Debussyism" (not mentioning Casella).

4. Taruskin, *Stravinsky and the Russian Traditions,* 1486.

5. See Stravinsky, *Selected Correspondence,* 3:83, 23 July 1924 (my emphasis); Stravinsky and Craft, *Memories and Commentaries* (1960), 89; and Stravinsky, "Programme Notes," *London Magazine,* Feb. 1966, 41; repr. in Stravinsky and Craft, *Themes and Episodes,* 43.

6. Casella, *Strawinsky,* 198, citing his own "La nuova musicalità italiana," 4, as quoted by Nicolodi, "Casella e la musica di Stravinsky," 56–57. Dr. Michael Walensky kindly assisted me in translating Casella's Italian.

7. Olin Downes's essay (repr. from the *New York Times* 1935 review), in Armitage, *Igor Strawinsky,* 57, but excluded by friend Armitage (at Stravinsky's behest?) from the 1949 edition. The Armitage-Stravinsky friendship is cited in Slim, *Annotated Catalogue,* 260–63, item 86.

8. Downes, "Neo-Classicism," adding "it has served bright boys"; repr. in Downes, *Olin Downes on Music,* 306–8. Stravinsky's reaction in December of 1946 to Downes as "the old famous ass" is cited above (chap. 10).

9. Fowler, *Dictionary of Modern English Usage,* s.v. "irony." Taruskin, *Russian Music,* calls irony "a prime 'neoclassic' marker" (85). As early as January of 1925, Oscar Thompson, "Stravinsky Leads Chamber Music Forces," though pillorying the Octet, could "regard it as an ironical travesty." Lesley Hughes, "Irony through Instrumentation," mentions "the problematic use of neoclassicism as a stylistic indicator."

10. Without reference to Fowler the veteran scholar emeritus Theodore Ziolkowski, *Classicism of the Twenties,* utilizes "irony" to some degree in respect to Stravinsky (82, 91, 191–92).

11. Cantoni, *La référence à Bach,* 240, ex. 32, seeks—in vain—to identify some of Stravinsky's (ostinato) pitches in the 1935 Violin Concerto with "B-a-c-h," but these solmized letters of Bach's name never appear in their proper order.

BIBLIOGRAPHY

ARCHIVAL SOURCES

American Biographical Archive, microfiche, ser. 2, Munich: K. G. Saur, 1995.

Forbes, Edward Waldo. Papers. Harvard University Archives, Pusey Library, Cambridge, MA.

H. Colin Slim Stravinsky Collection. Irving K. Barber Learning Centre, Special Collections, University of British Columbia, Vancouver.

Harvard University Archives.

Humanities Collections, University of Michigan, Special Collections Library, Harlan Hatcher Graduate Library, Ann Arbor.

Kall, Alexis. Papers. University of California, Los Angeles, Charles E. Young Research Library, Special Collections, Collection 601.

Kavenoki, Severin. Papers. New York Public Library, Library for the Performing Arts, Lincoln Center.

Koch, Oscar W. Photograph Collection. US Army Military Historical Institute, Carlisle, PA.

Mann, Klaus. Papers. University of Missouri at Kansas City, MO.

McCutchan Collection of Hymnology. Claremont Colleges, Special Collections, Honnold/ Mudd Library. Claremont, CA.

Morton, Lawrence. Papers. University of California, Los Angeles, Charles E. Young Research Library, Special Collections, Collection 1522.

Museum of Performance and Design, San Francisco.

National Archives of Canada, Ottawa, ONT.

New York Public Library.

Paul Sacher Stiftung, Basel, Switzerland.

Pierpont Morgan Library, New York.

Rothschild Collection. Hollywood Bowl Museum.

Schoenberg, Arnold, Collection. Humanities Collections, Special Collections Library, Harlan Hatcher Graduate Library, University of Michigan, Ann Arbor.

Stravinsky, Igor. Music and Papers. Paul Sacher Stiftung, Basel.

AUDIO AND VISUAL MEDIA

American Stravinsky: The Composer, Vol. 4. Conducted and with comments by Robert Craft. Ocean, NJ: Music Masters Classics, 1993.

Coco Chanel et Igor Stravinsky. Directed by Jan Kounen. Paris: Eurowide Film Production, 2009.

Genesis Suite (1945). Program notes by James Westby. American Classics no. 8.559442. Canada: Naxos, c. 2004.

Joe Reichman and His Orchestra, 1941–1942. Circle CCD-84.

Meet the Composer. Columbia ML-4398.

Otto Rothschild Photographic Archive, 1930–1981. University of California, Los Angeles, Charles E. Young Research Library, Special Collections.

Robert Stevenson: Obras para clarinete y piano. Madrid: A/B Master Disc Natural, CD 06–11, 2006.

Stravinsky and Prokofiev Conduct Their Works. Woodstock, NY: Parnassus, 2000. CD, PACD 96023.

"Stravinsky at 85." Telecast. Toronto: Canadian Broadcasting Corporation, 18 May 1967.

Stravinsky Conducts Stravinsky. CD-1184. Kensington, CA: Music and Arts Program of America, 2006.

Stravinsky Conducts Stravinsky. LPM-30579 (Sony Music Corporation); M-30579 (CBS Masterworks, 1971).

Stravinsky Conducts Stravinsky: The Mono Years, 1952–1955. Columbia Masterworks Heritage, Sony: MH2K 63325, 1998.

Stravinsky in America. New York: RCA Victor, BMG Classics, 1997.

Stravinsky in Hollywood. Directed by Marco Capalbo. DVD. Berlin: C major Entertainment GmbH, 2014.

Stravinsky in Moscow, 1962. CD. Melodiya, 1962; BMG, 1996.

Stravinsky: Once at a Border. Telecast documentary directed by Tony Palmer, 1980–81; DVD, West Long Branch, NJ: Kultur, 2008.

Stravinsky: The Three Symphonies and Ode. Booklet notes by Francis Routh. London: Chandos Records, 1982. CD 8345.

BOOKS AND ARTICLES

Aber-Count, Alice Lawson. "Kastner, Alfred." In Sadie, *The New Grove Dictionary* (2001), 13:304.

Acocella, Joan. "The Fatal Kiss." *New Yorker,* 17 Sept. 2012, 15.

Adaskin, Harry. *A Fiddler's Choice: Memoirs, 1938 to 1980.* Vancouver: November House, 1982.

———. *A Fiddler's World: Memoirs to 1938.* Vancouver: November House, 1977.

Advancing Knowledge: Selections from the Archives of the American Academy of Arts and Sciences. Cambridge, MA: American Academy, 2015.

Archer, Thomas. "Igor Stravinsky Here to Conduct: Famous Composer of 'Firebird' Talks of Music and Musicians." *Gazette Montreal,* 3 March 1945, 6.

———. "Igor Stravinsky Is Given Ovation." *Gazette Montreal,* 6 March 1945, 6.

Archives Roland-Manuel. Edited by Paul Renaud. Paris: Thierry Bodin, 24 March 2000.

Armitage, Merle. *Accent on Life.* 2nd ed. Ames: Iowa State University Press, 1965.

———, ed. *George Gershwin.* New York: Longmans, Green, 1938.

———. *Igor Stravinsky.* Edited by Edwin Corle. New York: Duell, Sloan, and Pearce, 1949.

———, ed. *Igor Strawinsky.* New York: Schirmer, 1936.

Armsby, Leonora Wood. *We Shall Have Music.* San Francisco: Pisani, 1960.

Arnold, Elliott. "Strawinsky Calls Swing American Folk Music." *New York World-Telegram,* 15 Jan. 1941.

Autographen Katalog 916. Basel: Erasmushaus, May 2003.

Babitz, Sol. "Ballet Notes." *Rob Wagner's Script,* 20 Feb. 1943, 22.

———. "Stravinsky's Symphony in C (1940): A Short Analysis and Commentary." *Musical Quarterly* 27, no. 1 (1941): 20–25.

Balanchine, George. "The Dance Element in Stravinsky's Music." *Dance Index* 6 (1947): 250–56.

Baltensperger, André. "Strawinskys 'Chicago Lecture' (1944)." *Mitteilungen der Paul Sacher Stiftung* 5 (1992): 19–23.

Bandur, Markus. "Neoklassizismus." In *Handwörterbuch der musikalischen Terminologie.* 22nd installment, IV: M–O, 1–21. Stuttgart: Steiner, 1994.

Barbirolli, Evelyn. *Life with Glorious John.* London: Robson, 2002.

Barhyte, Florence M. "Cleveland Hails Local Debut of Stravinsky." *Musical America,* 21 Feb. 1925, 36.

Barlow, S. L. M. "Mrs. Coolidge's Birthday Party." *Modern Music* 22 (Nov.-Dec. 1944): 40–43.

Barry, Edward. "Stravinsky's New Symphony Stirs Acclaim." *Chicago Daily Tribune,* 8 Nov. 1940, 23.

Bartók, Béla. *Essays.* Edited by Benjamin Suchoff. New York: St. Martin's, 1976.

Bauer, Emilie Frances. "Ultra-Modern Concerto Disgusts New York Audience." *Musical Leader,* 12 Feb. 1925, 152.

Becker, Harry Cassin. "Béla Bartók and his Credo." *Musical America,* 17 Dec. 1927, 7–35.

Becker, John. *Discord: The Story of the Vancouver Symphony Orchestra.* Vancouver: Brighouse, 1989.

Bell, Clive. *Old Friends.* London: Chatto and Windus, 1956.

Bennison, Harold. "Symphoniana." *Boston Symphony Orchestra Program,* 28–29 Jan. 1944, 819–21.

Benois, Alexandre. *Reminiscences of the Russian Ballet.* Translated by Mary Britnieva. London: Putnam, 1941.

Bernstein, Leonard. *The Unanswered Question.* Cambridge, MA: Harvard University Press, 1976.

Berry, Edward. "Stravinsky's New Symphony Stirs Acclaim." *Chicago Daily Tribune*, 8 Nov. 1940, 23.

Boehm, Gottfried, Ulrich Mosch, and Katharina Schmidt, eds. *Canto d'Amore: Classicism in Modern Art and Music, 1914–1935*. Basel: Kunstmuseum and Paul Sacher Foundation, 1996.

Bonhams. *Fine Books and Manuscripts*. New York: Bonhams, 9 Dec. 2015.

Borden, Charles E. "Halpern, Ida." In *Encyclopedia of Music in Canada*, edited by Helmut Kallmann, Gilles Potvin, and Kenneth Winters, 571. Toronto: University of Toronto Press, 1992.

Botstein, Leon. "'The Precision of Poetry and the Exactness of Pure Science': Nabokov, Stravinsky, and the Reader as Listener." In Levitz, *Stravinsky and His World*, 319–48.

Botstein, Leon, et al. "Cosmopolitanisms." *Musical Quarterly* 99, no. 2 (2016): 135–279.

Boulez, Pierre. "Stravinsky and the Century: Style and Idea." Translated by David Noales. *Saturday Review*. 29 May 1971, 39–41, 58–59.

Braginskava, Natalia. "New Light on the Fate of Some Early Works of Stravinsky: The *Funeral Song* Rediscovery." *Acta Musicologica* 87, no. 2 (2015): 133–51.

Bridle, August. "Stravinsky Thrills Orchestral Audience." *Toronto Daily Star*, 6 Jan. 1937, 7.

"Brilliant Past Recalled at Gathering in Steinway Hall." *Musical America*, 17 Jan. 1925, 40.

Bronson, Carl. "Sample in Triumph." *Los Angeles Evening Herald and Express*, 29 Oct. 1941, n.p.

Brontë, Charlotte. *Jane Eyre*. Edited by Margaret Smith, with introduction and revised notes by Sally Shuttleworth. New York: Oxford University Press, 2000.

Brown, Mary Jeannette. Review [of Symphony in Three Movements], *Westwood Hills (CA) Press*, 7–8 Jan. 1947, 9, 11.

Brown, Ray C. "Audience Divided on Stravinsky Arrangement of Anthem." *Washington Post*, 19 Jan. 1942, 13.

Bruno of Hollywood. "Photograph of Adele Marcus." *Musical Courier*, 1 March 1940, 60.

Buch, Esteban. "The Scandal of the Score, Games of Distinction." In Danuser and Zimmermann, *Avatar of Modernity*, 59–78, 435.

Buckle, Richard. *Diaghilev*. New York: Atheneum, 1979.

Burke, Evelyn. "Patrons Aren't Sure Who'll Entertain Noted Concert Pianist." *Pittsburgh Press*, 23 Jan. 1935, 18.

———. "Society Folk Heed Call of Modern Music." *Pittsburgh Press*, 26 Jan. 1935, 5.

Burke, Harry R. "Stravinsky Gets Warm Ovation Here." *St. Louis Globe-Democrat*, 20 Dec. 1941, pt. 3, 1C.

———. "2923 [Donors] Enrich Pension Fund of Symphony Orchestra by $6000." *St. Louis Daily Globe-Democrat*, 11 Feb. 1935, 2C.

Burton, Humphrey. *Leonard Bernstein*. New York: Doubleday, 1994.

C. "Adele Marcus Returns in Recital." *Musical America*, 10 April 1937, 22.

Cahoon, Herbert, ed. *The Mary Flagler Cary Music Collection*. New York: Pierpont Morgan Library, 1970.

Cantoni, Angelo. *La référence à Bach dans les œuvres néo-classiques de Stravinsky*. Hildesheim: Olms, 1998.

———. *The Language of Stravinsky*. Hildesheim: Olms, 2014.

Carr, Maureen. *After the Rite: Stravinsky's Path to Neoclassicism, 1914–25*. New York: Oxford University Press, 2014.

———. *Multiple Masks: Neoclassicism in Stravinsky's Works on Greek Subjects*. Lincoln: University of Nebraska Press, 2002.

Carter, Chandler. "*The Rake's Progress* and Stravinsky's Return: The Composer's Evolving Approach to Setting Text." *Journal of the American Musicological Society* 63, no. 3 (2010): 553–640.

Casella, Alfredo. "Igor Strawinsky e la sua arte." *La riforma musicale* 3, nos. 10–11 (1915): 1–2.

———. "La nuova musicalità italiana." *Ars nova* 2 (January 1918): 1–4.

———. *Music in My Time*. Translated by Spencer Norton. Norman: University of Oklahoma Press, 1995.

———. *Strawinsky*. Brescia: La Scuola, 1947.

Cass, Judith. "Program Dance Tonight to Turn Back the Clock." *Chicago Daily Tribune*, 8 Nov. 1940, 21.

Cassidy, Claudia. "Stravinsky and Symphony Aids Work Musical Magic at U of C." *Chicago Daily Tribune*, 22 Jan. 1941, 7.

Chaliapin, Feodor. *Chaliapin: An Autobiography as Told to Maxim Gorky*. Translated, compiled, and edited by Nina Froud and James Hanley. New York: Stein and Day, 1967.

Choisy, Frank. "Cleveland Hears Novelty by Symanowski—Orchestra Tour." *Musical Courier*, 27 Feb. 1937, 7.

Chua, Daniel K. L. "Rioting with Stravinsky: A Particular Analysis of the *Rite of Spring*." *Music Analysis* 26, no. 1–2 (2007): 59–109; https://onlinelibrary.wiley.com/doi/full/10.1111/j.1468-2249.2007.00250.x.

Cingria, Charles-Albert. *Œuvres complètes*. 11 vols. Lausanne: Éditions l'Age Homme, 1968.

Clague, Mark. "Singing the Self into Citizenship: How Performance Transformed a Star-Spangled Song into the U.S. National Anthem." Abstract. *Abstracts of Papers Read*, American Musicological Society, Eighteenth Annual Meeting, 6–9 Nov. 2014, 148.

Cohen, Barbara, Steven Heller, and Seymour Chwast. *Trylon and Perisphere: The 1939 New York World's Fair*. New York: Abrams, 1989.

Cohen, Lisa. *All We Know: Three Lives*. New York: Farrar, Straus and Giroux, 2012.

Cohen, Selma Jean, ed. *International Encyclopedia of Dance*. New York: Oxford University Press, 1998.

Compagnon, Antoine. *Le cas Bernard Faÿ: Du Collège de France à l'indignité nationale*. Paris: Gallimard, 2009.

Condlon, Edward J. "Money Circulation Nears 18 Billion." *New York Times*, 1 August 1943, S7.

Cone, Edward T. "McCarter Audience Acclaims Stravinsky, Who Led Cleveland Orchestra." *Daily Princetonian*, 19 Feb. 1937, 1, 3.

———. "Stravinsky: The Progress of a Method." *Perspectives of New Music* 1, no. 1 (1962): 18–26.

———. "The Uses of Convention: Stravinsky and his Models." *Musical Quarterly* 48, no. 3 (1962): 287–99. Reprinted in *Stravinsky: A New Appraisal of His Work*, edited by Paul Henry Lang, 21–23. New York: Norton, 1963.

Conger, Amy. *Edward Weston: Photographs from the Collection of the Center for Creative Photography*. Tucson: University of Arizona Center for Creative Photography, 1992.

Cook, Nicholas. "Stravinsky Conducts Stravinsky." In Cross, *The Cambridge Companion*, 176–91.

Cooke, Mervyn, ed. *The Hollywood Film Music Reader*. New York: Oxford University Press, 2010.

"The Copley List." *Musical Courier*, 1 Dec. 1939, 38.

Corn, Alfred. "The Ambidexterity of a Musician." *Gay and Lesbian Review Worldwide* 21, no. 1 (2014): 40–41.

Corrado, Omar. "Stravinsky y la constelación ideológica argentina en 1936." *Revista de música latinoamericana* [Latin American Music Review] 26, no. 1 (2005): 88–101.

Cost, Herbert W. "Stravinsky Leads St. Louis Symphony." *Musical America*, 25 Jan. 1942, 11.

Coward, Noël. *The Letters of Noël Coward*. Edited by Barry Day. New York: Knopf, 2007.

Craft, Robert, ed. *Avec Stravinsky*. Monaco: Éditions de Rocher, 1958.

———, ed. *Dearest Bubushkin: The Correspondence of Vera and Igor Stravinsky, 1921–1954, with Excerpts from Vera Stravinsky's Diaries, 1922–1971*. Translated from the Russian by Lucia Davidova. New York: Thames and Hudson, 1985.

———. "Dix années avec Stravinsky." In Craft, *Avec Stravinsky*, 73–84.

———. *Down a Path of Wonder*. Great Britain: Naxos, 2006.

———, ed. *Igor and Vera Stravinsky: A Photograph Album, 1921 to 1971*. London: Thames and Hudson, 1982.

———. "Igor, Catherine and God." In Stravinsky, *Selected Correspondence*, 1:13–19.

———. *An Improbable Life: Memoirs*. Nashville, TN: Vanderbilt University Press, 2002.

———. "An Interview with Robert Craft: Restoring Stravinsky." *Areté* 24 (Winter 2007): 5–80.

———. "Jews and Geniuses." In Craft, *Small Craft Advisories*, 274–81.

———. "A Modest Confutation." *Naxos News*, Oct. 2005, 1–11.

———. *The Moment of Existence: Music, Literature, and the Arts, 1990–1995*. Nashville, TN: Vanderbilt University Press, 1996.

———. "Music and Words." In Lederman, *Stravinsky in the Theatre*, 85–103.

———. "A Personal Preface." *The Score*, June 1957, 7–13.

———. *Places: A Travel Companion for Music and Art Lovers*. New York: Thames and Hudson, 2000.

———. *Prejudices in Disguise: Articles, Essays, Reviews*. New York: Knopf, 1974.

———. *Present Perspectives: Critical Writings*. New York: Knopf, 1984.

———. "Reflections on 'The Rake's Progress.'" *The Score*, Sept. 1954, 24–30.

——— "Selected Source Material from 'A Catalogue of Books and Music Inscribed to and/or Authored and Annotated by Igor Stravinsky.'" In Pasler, *Confronting Stravinsky*, 349–57.

———. *Small Craft Advisories: Articles, 1984–1988: Art, Ballet, Music, Literature, Film*. New York: Thames and Hudson, 1989.

———. *Stravinsky: Chronicle of a Friendship*. Rev. ed. Nashville, TN: Vanderbilt University Press, 1994. First published New York: Vintage, 1972.

———. *Stravinsky: Discoveries and Memories*. Great Britain: Naxos, 2013.

———. *Stravinsky: Glimpses of a Life*. London: Lime Tree, 1992. Rev. ed. New York: St. Martin's, 1993.

———. "The Stravinsky 'Nachlass' in New York and Basel." In Stravinsky, *Selected Correspondence*, 3:513–21.

———. *A Stravinsky Scrapbook, 1940–1971*. New York: Thames and Hudson, 1983.

———. "Sufferings and Humiliations of Catherine Stravinsky." In Craft, *Stravinsky: Glimpses*, 104–29.

———. "Sunday Afternoon Live." *New York Review of Books*, 28 May 1998, 15–16.

———. "Vision in Music: Igor Stravinsky's Own Instructions for Dancing *The Rite of Spring*." *Times Literary Supplement*, 21 June 2013, 13–15.

Crain, Hal D. "Native Music Given in Los Angeles." *Musical America*, June 1937, 29.

———. "Stravinsky to Compose Music for Forthcoming Film." *Musical America*, 25 March 1937, 8.

Craven, H. T. "Russians Descend on Philadelphia." *Musical America*, 14 Feb. 1925, 13.

Crawford, Dorothy Lamb. *Evenings on and off the Roof: Pioneering Concerts in Los Angeles, 1939–1971*. Berkeley: University of California Press, 1995.

———. *A Windfall of Musicians: Hitler's Émigrés and Exiles in Southern California*. New Haven, CT: Yale University Press, 2009.

Cross, Jonathan, ed. *The Cambridge Companion to Stravinsky*. Cambridge: Cambridge University Press, 2003.

———. *Igor Stravinsky*. London: Reaktion, 2015.

———. "Stravinsky in Exile." In Levitz, *Stravinsky and His World*, 3–19.

———. *The Stravinsky Legacy*. Cambridge: Cambridge University Press, 1998.

C. S. H. "Dumbarton Oaks Played as Concerto." *Los Angeles Times*, 23 Oct. 1944, 10.

Cushing, Charles. "Precede [*sic*] to Stravinsky Music." *San Francisco Chronicle*, supplement: "This World," 13 April 1947, 28–29.

D. J. "Stravinsky, Dushkin Quintet in Toledo." *Musical Courier*, 16 Feb. 1935, 25.

Dahl, Ingolf. "Igor Stravinsky on Film Music." *Musical Digest* 28 (Sept. 1946): 4–5, 35–36. Reprinted in Cooke, *The Hollywood Film Music Reader*, 273–80.

———. "The New Orpheus." In *Stravinsky in the Theatre*, edited by Minna Lederman, 72–74. Previously published in *Dance Index* 6 (1947): 284–87.

———. "Stravinsky in 1946." *Modern Music* 23 (Summer 1946): 159–65.

Danese, Giacomo. *Theodor Wiesendgrund Adorno: Il compositore dialettico*. Soveria Manelli: Rubbettino, 2008.

Danuser, Hermann, and Heidy Zimmermann, eds. *Avatar of Modernity: "The Rite of Spring" Reconsidered*. London: Boosey and Hawkes, for the Paul Sacher Foundation, 2013.

Darsky, Joseph. *Tsar Feodor: Chaliapin in America*. Edited by Elena Svitavsky. New York: Nova, 2012.

Davidson, Marie Hicks. "High Praise Won by Stravinsky." *San Francisco Call-Bulletin*, 16 Dec. 1939, 70.

———. "Stravinsky in San Francisco Rehearsal." *San Francisco Call-Bulletin*, 13 Dec. 1939, 4F.

Davis, Mary E. *Classic Chic: Music, Fashion, and Modernism*. Berkeley: University of California Press, 2006.

Day, Barry, ed. *The Letters of Noel Coward*. New York: Knopf, 2007.

de Acosta, Mercedes. *Here Lies the Heart*. New York: Reynal, 1960.

Dean, Winton. *Bizet*. Rev. ed. London: Dent, 1975.

Decker, Clarence R., and Mary Bell Decker. *A Place of Light: The Story of a University Presidency*. New York: Hermitage House, 1954.

Dehmel, Victor. "Lopez Forecasts 'Swing' to Endure for 6 More Years." *New-Orleans Times-Picayune*, 6 Feb. 1938, 22.

Del Carlo, Omar. "Dedicado a Juan José Castro." Special issue, *ARS: Revista de arte* 29, no. 109. Buenos Aires: R. Peña, 1969.

de Lerma, Dominique-René. *Igor Fedorovitch Stravinsky, 1882–1971: A Practical Guide to Publications of His Music*. Kent State, OH: Kent State University Press, 1974.

DeLibero, Linda. "Rabbit Redux." *Bookforum*, April/May 2011, 35.

de Pina, Albert. "Stravinsky-Kosloff." *Rob Wagner's Script*, 20 March 1937, 10.

de Schloezer, Boris. *Igor Strawinsky*. Paris: Édition Claude Aveline, 1929.

Devries, René. "Stravinsky Leads His Works in Concert with Chicago Orchestra." *Musical Courier*, 26 Jan. 1935, 7.

Diamond, Jack. "Stravinsky Likes His Wine Red, Talks to Orchestra." *Chicago News*, 12 Jan. 1935.

Dickstein, Morris. *Dancing in the Dark: A Cultural History of the Great Depression*. New York: Norton, 2009.

Diolé, Phillipe. "Stravinsky in Interview." Translated by Eric Walter White. *Tempo* 97 (1971): 6–9. Previously published in *Beaux Arts* (Paris), 28 Feb. 1936.

"Dossier Stravinsky-Canada, 1937–1967: Regards en arrière" [Looking back]. *Les Cahiers canadiens de musique / The Canada Music Book*, nos. 4–5 (Spring/Summer 1972): 17–81.

Downes, Edward. "Igor Stravinsky: Plans and Views of a Tonal Giant." *Boston Evening Transcript*, 21 Oct. 1939, pt. 3, 5.

Downes, Olin. "Igor Stravinsky and Dushkin Play." *New York Times*, 28 Jan. 1937, 22.

———. "Neo-Classicism." *New York Times*, 8 Feb. 1942, X7.

———. "Nostalgia of the Neo-Russians." *New York Times*, 8 Feb. 1925, X6.

———. *Olin Downes on Music: A Selection from His Writings during the Half-Century 1906–1955*. Edited by Irene Downes. New York: Simon and Schuster, 1957.

———. "Schola Cantorum at Carnegie Hall." *New York Times*, 6 Feb. 1936, 15.

———. "Stravinsky as Visitor Stirs Various Reactions." *New York Times*, 1 Feb. 1925, X6.

———. "Stravinsky Leads the Philharmonic." *New York Times*, 25 Jan. 1946, 26.

Duberman, Martin. *The Worlds of Lincoln Kirstein*. New York: Knopf, 2007.

Dufour, Valérie. "La 'Poétique musicale' de Stravinsky: Un manuscrit inédit de Souvtchinsky." *Revue de musicologie* 89, 2003, 373–392.

———. "The *Poétique musicale*: A Counterpoint in Three Voices." Translated by Bridget Behrmann and Tamara Levitz. In Levitz, *Stravinsky and His World*, 225–54.

———. *Stravinski et ses exégètes, 1910–1940*. Brussels: Université de Bruxelles, 2006.

———. "Strawinsky vers Souvtchinsky: Thème et variations sur la *Poétique musicale*." *Mitteilungen der Paul Sacher Stiftung* 17 (March 2004): 17–23.

Durgin, Cyrus. "Boston." *Musical Courier*, 1 Feb. 1941, 102.

———. "Music: Symphony Hall, Boston Symphony Orchestra." *Boston Daily Globe*, 23 Feb. 1946, 8.

Dushkin, Samuel. "1949: Working with Stravinsky." In Armitage, *Igor Stravinsky*, 179–92.

Dykk, Lloyd. "Legacy of a Musical Giant." *Vancouver Sun,* 30 March 2002, A6.

E. D. B. "Cleveland Orchestra Presents Two Visitors." *Musical Courier Weekly Review,* 26 March 1925, 9.

E. K. "Mexico City Players." *Musical America,* August 1940, 32.

Eagle, Donald. "Symphony Season Ends Beautifully." *Washington Post,* 5 April 1948, 2B.

Eastman School of Music, 1921–1971. Rochester, NY: Eastman School of Music, 1971.

Eastman School of Music. *Official Bulletin 63,* 1968.

Eaton, Quaintance. "Igor Stravinsky, Apostle of Today." *Musical America,* 10 Jan. 1937, 1.

Edgerton, Giles. " 'Petroushka,' Igor Strawinsky's Famous Ballet." *Arts and Decoration,* Feb. 1925, 17–18, 66, 79.

Egilsrud, Johan S. "Friday to Be Symphony Stravinsky's Day." *Minneapolis Morning Tribune,* 15 Dec. 1940, 4.

———. "Music: Symphony Orchestra." *Minneapolis Morning Tribune,* 21 Dec. 1940, 16.

Elwell, Herbert. "Stravinsky Stirs Concert Audience." *Cleveland Plain Dealer,* 26 Feb. 1937, 18.

Ericson, Raymond. "Stravinsky at the Stadium." *New York Times,* 13 July 1962, 13.

Ernst, Sergei. *V. A. Serov.* St. Petersburg: n.p., 1921.

Evans, Joan. "Stravinsky's Music in Hitler's Germany." *Journal of the American Musicological Society* 56, no. 3 (2003): 525–94.

Eversman, Alice. "Coolidge Festival Held at Library of Congress." *Musical America,* 25 April 1935, 18.

Eyer, Ronald F. "Our Orchestra vs. The Modern Composer." *Musical America,* June 1943, 7.

Eyer, Ronald F., and Robert Sabin. "Repertoire of Orchestras Is Surveyed." *Musical America,* July 1944, 6.

F. "Stravinsky and Lange Conduct G. M. Programs." *Musical America,* 10 Feb. 1935, 172.

Fauser, Annegret. *Sounds of War: Music in the United States during World War II.* New York: Oxford University Press, 2013.

Feisst, Sabine. *Schoenberg's New World: The American Years.* New York: Oxford University Press, 2011.

Finscher, Ludwig. "The Old in the New." In Boehm, Mosch, and Schmidt, *Canto d'Amore,* 63–73.

Fisher, Marjorie M. "San Francisco Men Led by Igor Stravinsky, Conducts Own Arrangement of National Anthem, and His Third Symphony." *Musical America,* 25 Jan. 1942, 11.

———. "Stravinsky Is Best-Seller." *San Francisco News,* 10 Jan. 1942, 5.

"Flashlight Photograph." *Musical Courier Weekly Review,* 15 Jan. 1925, 22.

Forbes, Elliot. *A History of Music at Harvard to 1972.* Cambridge, MA: Harvard Music Department, 1972.

———, ed. *Thayer's Life of Beethoven.* 2 vols. Princeton, NJ: Princeton University Press, 1967.

Forney, Kristine K. "From Santa Barbara to Xanadu: Mildred Couper as West Coast Ultramodernist." In Forney and Smith, *Sleuthing the Muse,* 389–420.

Forney, Kristine K., and Jeremy L. Smith, eds. *Sleuthing the Muse: Essays in Honor of William F. Prizer.* Hillsdale, NY: Pendragon, 2012.

Fowler, H. W. *A Dictionary of Modern English Usage.* Oxford: Clarendon, 1926.

Fox, Christy. "Bel-Air Fete to Honor Trio of Musicians: Postconcert Reception Will Be Held in Home of A. Atwater Kent." *Los Angeles Times,* 2 April 1945, A5.

Fox, Margalit. "Robert Craft, Stravinsky Adviser and Steward, Dies at 92." *New York Times*, 14 Nov. 2015, 28.

Francis, Kimberly A. "Nadia Boulanger and Igor Stravinsky: Documents of the Bibliothèque nationale de France." *Revue de musicologie* 95, no. 1 (2009): 137–56.

———. *Teaching Stravinsky: Nadia Boulanger and the Consecration of a Modernist Icon.* New York: Oxford University Press, 2015.

Frankenstein, Alfred. "Ballet Rings Down Curtain of Long Successful Season with Last Night's Performance." *San Francisco Chronicle*, 29 Nov. 1944, 34.

———. "Igor Stravinsky Introduces a Major Work to S. F." *San Francisco Chronicle*, 23 March 1946, 4H.

———. "Just Where Is Stravinsky?" *San Francisco Chronicle*, 22 March 1937, 11.

———. "Rossini-Stravinsky Program an Effective Contrast of Periods." *San Francisco Chronicle*, 21 March 1937, D5.

———. "S. F. Will Hear Famed Concert by Stravinsky." *San Francisco Chronicle*, 23 March 1937, 34.

———. "Stand Up When You Read This Story." *San Francisco Chronicle*, 28 Dec. 1941, supplement, "This World," 13.

———. "Stravinsky in Beverly Hills." *Modern Music* 19 (March-April 1942): 178–81. Reprinted in Oja, *Stravinsky in Modern Music*, 69–71.

———. "Stravinsky Presents His Symphony." *San Francisco Chronicle*, 10 Jan. 1942, 19.

———. "Stravinsky Proves Popular in Dual Concert at S. F." *San Francisco Chronicle*, 14 Feb. 1935, 13.

———. "Stravinsky Recital at Mills College." *San Francisco Chronicle*, 27 Oct. 1944, 3H.

———. "Stravinsky's Career Epitomizes Century of Musical Development." *San Francisco Chronicle*, 10 Feb. 1935, D5.

Franklin, Peter. "Modernism, Deception, and Musical Others: Los Angeles circa 1940." In *Western Music and Its Others: Difference, Representation, and Appropriation in Music*, edited by Georgina Born and David Hesmondhalgh, 143–62. Berkeley: University of California Press, 2000.

Fried, Alexander. "Igor Stravinsky Due Wednesday." *San Francisco Examiner*, 10 Feb. 1935, B11.

———. "Stravinsky Conducts for 'Petrouchka' Here." *San Francisco Examiner*, 29 Jan. 1943, 26.

———. "Stravinsky Chorale." *San Francisco Examiner*, 24 March 1937, 19.

———. "Stravinsky Fears Blow to Music." *San Francisco Examiner*, 12 Dec. 1939, 36.

———. "Stravinsky Likes Idea of Writing for Movies." *San Francisco Examiner*, 22 March 1937, 8.

———. "Stravinsky's Music Needs an Orchestra." *San Francisco Examiner*, 14 Feb. 1935, 9.

———. "Stravinsky's Role in S. F." *San Francisco Examiner*, 6 April 1971, 4.

Fritz, Bernardine Szold. "Toscanini in Hollywood." *Rob Wagner's Script*, 16 Dec. 1939, 14–15.

Frolova-Walker, Marina. "Rimsky-Korsakov." In Sadie, *The New Grove Dictionary* (2001), 21:411–12.

Fruhauf, Aline. *Making Faces: Memoirs of a Caricaturist.* Edited by Erwin Vollmer. Cabin John, MD: Seven Locks, 1987.

Fryer, Paul. *A Chronology of Opera Performances at the Mariinsky Theatre in St. Petersburg, 1860–1917.* 2 vols. Lewiston, NY: Edwin Mellen, 2009.

Furney, Mabel McDonough. "Stravinsky Music Entertains Detroit." *Musical America,* 14 March 1925, 3.

Fuller, Donald. "Stravinsky Full-Length Portrait." *Modern Music* 23 (Winter 1946): 45–46.

G. S. "Stravinsky and Dushkin Appear in Denver." *Musical Courier,* 6 April 1935, 8.

Gansberg, Alan L. *Little Caesar: A Biography of Edward G. Robinson.* Lanham, MD: Scarecrow, 2004.

García-Márquez, Vicente. *The Ballets Russes: Colonel de Basil's Ballets Russes de Monte Carlo, 1932–1952.* New York: Knopf, 1990.

Geelhaar, Christian. "Stravinsky und Picasso—zwei ebenbürtige Genies." In *Strawinsky: Sein Nachlass, sein Bild,* 289, 301, 303.

Giese, Detlef. " 'Espressivo' versus '(Neue) Sachlichkeit.' " In *Studien zu Aesthetik und Geschichte der musikalischen Interpretation.* Berlin: Dissertationen.de-Verlag im Internet, 2006.

Giroud, Vincent. *Nicolas Nabokov: A Life in Freedom and Music.* New York: Oxford University Press, 2015.

Godowsky, Dagmar. *First Person Plural: The Lives of Dagmar Godowsky.* New York: Viking, 1958.

Golubev, Gregory. *Pushkin: Poetry and Music.* New York: Harvey Taylor, 1940.

Gooley, Dana, Ryan Minor, Katherine K. Preston, and Jann Pasler. "Colloquy: Cosmopolitanism in the Age of Nationalism, 1848–1914." *Journal of the American Musicological Society* 66, no. 2 (2013): 523–49.

Goubault, Christian. *Igor Stravinsky.* Paris: H. Champion, 1991.

Grabar, Igor. *Valentin Alexandrovich Serov.* Moscow: Kenjebel, 1913.

Griffiths, Graham. *Stravinsky's Piano: Genesis of a Musical Language.* Cambridge: Cambridge University Press, 2013.

Griffiths, Paul. "Manziarly." In Sadie, *The New Grove Dictionary* (1980), 11:636–37.

———. *Stravinsky.* New York: Schirmer, 1993.

Grosheva, Yelena Andreyevna, ed. *Fyodor Ivanovich Shalyapin.* 3rd ed. 3 vols. Moscow: Iskusstvo, 1979.

Gunn, Glen Dillard. [Reviewing the CSO]. *Chicago Herald and Examiner,* 15 Feb. 1925.

H. C. G. "Indiana Ensemble in Third Concert." *Musical Courier,* 16 Feb. 1935, 9.

H. G. D. "Stravinsky, Dushkin, and St. Louis Orchestra in Columbus." *Musical Courier,* 27 Feb. 1937, 27.

H. K. "Philharmonic Orchestra Attracts Crowds." *Pacific Coast Musician,* 20 March 1937, 6.

Haimo, Ethan, and Paul Johnson, eds. *Stravinsky Retrospectives.* Lincoln: University of Nebraska Press, 1987.

Haldey, Olga. *Mamontov's Private Opera: The Search for Modernism in Russian Theater.* Bloomington: Indiana University Press, 2010.

Halpern, Ida. "Expectations Fulfilled: Stravinsky, Orchestra in Great Concert." *Vancouver Province,* 6 Oct. 1952, sec. 2, 15.

———. "Rehearsals Start: Stravinsky, Orchestra 'Happy.' " *Vancouver Province,* 3 Oct. 1952, sec. 2, 23.

Hart, Philip. *Fritz Reiner: A Biography*. Evanston, IL: Northeastern University Press, 1994.

Hertelendy, Paul. "Symphony Audience Hails Stravinsky." *Oakland Tribune*, 14 Feb. 1968, X.

Herzfeld, Friedrich. *Wilhelm Furtwängler: Weg und Leben*. Munich: Wilhelm Goldman, 1950.

Hess, Carol A. "Copland in Argentina: Pan American Politics, Folklore, and the Crisis in Modern Music." *Journal of the American Musicological Society* 66, no. 1 (2013): 191–250.

Heyworth, Peter. *Otto Klemperer*. Cambridge: Cambridge University Press, 1983.

Hiller, Ferdinand. *Aus dem Tonleben unserer Zeit: Neue Folge*. Leipzig: F. E. C. Leuckart, 1871.

Hinch, Robin. "Music Was Dorothy [McQuoid] Hopper's Life." Obituary. *Orange County Register*, 28 Feb. 1988, Metro section, 7.

Hindemith, Paul. *Selected Letters of Paul Hindemith*. Edited by Geoffrey Skelton. New Haven: Yale University Press, 1995.

Holland, Bernard. "Adele Marcus Is Dead at 89." *New York Times*, 5 May 1995, B7.

Holoman, D. Kern. *Charles Munch*. New York: Oxford University Press, 2011.

Hopper, Hedda. "Hedda Hopper's Hollywood." *Los Angeles Times*, 15 Sept. 1941, A16.

———. "Hedda Hopper's Hollywood." *Los Angeles Times*, 1 Oct. 1941, 12.

———. "Looking at Hollywood." *Los Angeles Times*, 18 August 1943, sec. 1, 4.

Horgan, Paul. *Encounters with Stravinsky: A Personal Record*. New York: Farrar, Straus and Giroux, 1972.

Horowitz, Joseph. *Arrau on Music and Performance*. Mineola, NY: Dover, 1999.

———. *Conversations with Arrau*. New York: Knopf, 1982.

———. "Sorrow on the Prairie: Hiawatha and Dvořák's New World Symphony." *Times Literary Supplement*, 1 August 2014, 14–15.

Howerton, Rachel. "The Reception of Igor Stravinsky and His Music in Great Britain." Unpublished manuscript, 2014.

Hughes, Lesley. "Irony through Instrumentation: Hindemith's Quintet for Clarinet and String Quartet and the Great War." Abstract. *Abstracts of Papers Read*, American Musicological Society, Eighteenth Annual Meeting, 6–9 Nov. 2014, 59.

Huneker, James Gibbon. "Russian Symphony Orchestra." *New York Times*, 30 Jan. 1918, 9.

Huxtable, Ada Louise. "Mies van der Rohe." *New York Times*, 24 August 1969, D24.

"Igor Stravinsky to Be Guest of Mills President." *San Francisco Chronicle*, 24 Oct. 1944, 6.

Illuminated Manuscripts, Illustrated Books, Autograph Letters and Music. London: Christie's, 29 June 1994, lot 124.

Isherwood, Christopher. *Diaries, Volume One: 1939–1960*. Edited by Katherine Bucknell. New York: Michael di Capua and Harper Flamingo, 1997.

J. A. S. and A. E. C. "Buenos Aires." *Enciclopedia del spettacolo*. Florence-Rome: Sansoni, 1935.

J. W. "Stravinsky Guest Leader in N.Y. Orchestral Fortnight." *Musical Courier*, 15 Jan. 1940, 16.

Jablonski, Edward. *Gershwin*. New York: Doubleday, 1987.

Jablonski, Edward, and Lawrence D. Stewart. *The Gershwin Years: George and Ira*. Rev. ed. New York: Da Capo, 1996. First published 1973 by Doubleday.

Jacobi, Frederick. "On Hearing Stravinsky's Perséphone." *Modern Music* 12 (March-April 1935): 112–15.

Jans, Hans Jörg, and Lukas Handschin. *Igor Strawinsky: Musikmanuskripte.* Winterthur, Switzerland: Amadeus, 1989.

Jones, Isabel Morse. "Ballet Russe Impresses in Return." *Los Angeles Times,* 2 Dec. 1944, 5.

———. "Composer to Conduct 'Petrouchka' Ballet." *Los Angeles Times,* 7 March 1937, C5.

———. "Condensation Essence of Stravinsky Compositions: Musical Forms Compressed into Small, Clear-Cut, Concentrated Patterns; Dushkin His Perfect Exponent." *Los Angeles Times,* 24 Feb. 1935, A6.

———. "Contemporary Composers Flocking to Los Angeles." *Los Angeles Times,* 10 Feb. 1935, A6.

———. "Contralto Gains Spotlight in W. P. A. Concert at Embassy." *Los Angeles Times,* 19 Feb. 1942, A11.

———. "Klemperer Conducts Slav Works." *Los Angeles Times,* 7 Jan. 1947, A2.

———. "Los Angeles." *Musical America,* 10 Feb. 1941, 298.

———. "Los Angeles." *Musical America,* 25 Feb. 1941, 24.

———. "Los Angeles Hears Local Artists." *Musical America,* 10 Feb. 1944, 273.

———. "Los Angeles Sees Ballet Theatre." *Musical America,* 25 March 1943, 34.

———. "Merle Armitage Book Reveals Stravinsky, New Volume Is Fascinating Story of Composer's Effect on Musical Men." *Los Angeles Times,* 6 Sept. 1936, C4.

———. "Music Event Conducted by Janssen." *Los Angeles Times,* 20 Nov. 1945, sec. I, 11.

———. "Santa Barbara." *Musical America,* 10 Feb. 1941, 305.

———. "Stravinsky Conducts Fine Concert at Philharmonic." *Los Angeles Times,* 14 Feb. 1941, A13.

———. "Stravinsky Scans Picasso as Prelude to New Work." *Los Angeles Times,* 11 August 1940, pt. 23, 5.

———. "Stravinsky's Latest Work Introduced." *Los Angeles Times,* 9 Feb. 1942, sec. 2, p. 7.

———. "Walter Conducts Los Angeles Men." *Musical America,* 25 Feb. 1942, 15.

Jordan, Stephanie. "Stravinsky as Co-choreographer." In Woitas and Hartmann, *Strawinskys "Motor Drive,"* 264–65.

———. *Stravinsky Dances: Re-visions across a Century.* Alton, GB: Dance Books, 2007.

Joseph, Charles M. *Stravinsky and Balanchine: A Journey of Invention.* New Haven, CT: Yale University Press, 2002.

———. *Stravinsky and the Piano.* Ann Arbor: UMI Research Press, 1983.

———. *Stravinsky Inside Out.* New Haven, CT: Yale University Press, 2001.

———. "Stravinsky Manuscripts in the Library of Congress and the Pierpont Morgan Library." *Journal of Musicology* 1, no. 3 (1982): 327–37.

———. *Stravinsky's Ballets.* New Haven, CT: Yale University Press, 2011.

Kahl [sic], Alexis F. *Die Philosophie der Musik nach Aristoteles: Inaugural-Dissertation.* Leipzig: Breitkopf and Härtel, 1902.

Kall, Alexis F. "Nationalism in Russian Music." *Art and Archaeology* 13, no. 2 (1922): 78–82.

———. "Slava poetu." *Novaya zarya,* 1 Feb. 1937, 3.

———. "Stravinsky in the Chair of Poetry." *Musical Quarterly* 26, no. 3 (1940): 283–96.

Kallmann, Helmut, and Giles Potvin, eds. *Encyclopedia of Music in Canada.* Toronto: University of Toronto Press, 1997.

Karsavina, Tamara. *Theatre Street.* London: Heinemann, 1930.

Kendall, Elizabeth. *Balanchine and the Lost Muse: Revolution and the Making of a Choreographer.* New York: Oxford University Press, 2013.

Kielian-Gilbert, Marianne. "Stravinsky's Contrasts: Contradiction and Discontinuity in His Neoclassic Music." *Journal of Musicology* 9, no. 4 (1991): 448–80.

King, Terry. *Gregor Piatigorsky: The Life and Career of the Virtuoso Cellist.* Jefferson, NC: McFarland, 2006.

Kinkle, Roger D., ed. *The Complete Encyclopedia of Popular Music and Song, 1920–1950.* 4 vols. New Rochelle, NY: Arlington House. 1974.

Kirchmeyer, Helmut. "Über Geschichte und Bedeutung von Druckfehlern und Korrekturen bei Igor Strawinsky." *Archiv für Musikwissenschaft* 70, no. 4 (2013): 255–75.

Kirjoksky, Elisabeth. "Mexico City Players Led by Stravinsky." *Musical America,* August 1940, 32.

Kirstein, Lincoln. "Working with Stravinsky." *Modern Music* 14 (March-April 1936–37): 143–46.

Klimovitsky, Arkady, ed. *Igor Stravinsky: Orchestrations of "The Song of the Flea" by Modest Mussorgsky; "The Song of the Flea" by Ludwig van Beethoven.* Translated by Paul Williams. St. Petersburg: School of Music Publishing House / Russian Institute for the History of the Arts, 2003.

Klinko, T. V. "Osnovnïye datï" [Basic dates]. In Kutateladze and Gozenpud, *F. Stravinsky.*

Kobal, John. *People Will Talk.* New York: Knopf, 1985.

Kochno, Boris. *Diaghilev and the Ballets Russes.* Translated by Adrienne Foulke. New York: Harper and Row, 1970.

Kodicek, Ann, ed. *Diaghilev, Creator of the Ballet Russes: Art, Music, Dance.* London: Lund Humphries, 1996.

Kokoreva, Ludmila. "Alexandre Tansman et Igor Stravinsky." In *Hommage au compositeur Alexandre Tansman (1897–1986),* edited by Pierre Guillot, 91–103. Paris: University of Paris-Sorbonne, 2000.

Kolodin, Irving. *The Metropolitan Opera, 1883–1966.* New York: Knopf, 1967.

Koteliarov, J., and V. Garmasha. *Letopis zhizni i tvorchestva F. I. Shaliapina* [Annals of the life and works of F. I. Chaliapin]. 2 vols. Leningrad: Muzïka, 1988–89.

Kounen, Jan, dir. *Coco Chanel et Igor Stravinsky.* Paris: Worldwide Film, 2000.

K[ramer] A. W. "Composers' League Honors Stravinsky." *Musical America,* 10 Jan. 1935, 23.

Kramer, Jonathan D. "Discontinuity and Proportion in the Music of Stravinsky." In Pasler, *Confronting Stravinsky,* 174–94.

Krasovskaya, Vera. *Nijinsky.* Translated by John E. Bowlt. New York: Schirmer, 1979.

Kundera, Milan. "Les Testaments trahis." In *Œuvre: Édition définitive,* 2:n.p.

———. *Œuvre: Édition définitive.* 2 vols. Paris: Gallimard, 2011.

———. *Testaments Betrayed: An Essay in Nine Parts.* Translated by Linda Asher. New York: HarperCollins, 1995.

Kutateladze, Larisa, and A. Gozenpud, eds. *F. Stravinsky: Stat'i, pis'ma, vospominaniya* [Articles, letters, memoirs]. Leningrad: Muzïka, 1972.

Lang, Paul Henry, ed. *Stravinsky: A New Appraisal of His Work.* New York: Norton, 1963.

Lapshin, V. P. *Valentin Serov.* Moscow: Galarte, 1995.

Larkin, Colin, ed. *The Encyclopedia of Popular Music*. 4th ed. 10 vols. New York: Oxford University Press, 2006.

Lawson, Rex. "Stravinsky and the Pianola." In Pasler, *Confronting Stravinsky*, 284–301.

Lederman, Minna, ed. *Stravinsky in the Theatre*. New York: Pellegrini and Cudahy, 1949; repr. New York: Da Capo, 1975.

Leibowitz, René. "Two Composers: Schönberg and Stravinsky: A Letter from Hollywood." *Partisan Review* 15 (1948): 361–65.

Lesure, François. *Igor Stravinsky: La carrière européenne*. Paris: Musée d'art moderne, 1980.

———. *Stravinsky: Études et témoignages présentés et réunis*. Paris: Lattès, 1982.

Levitz, Tamara. "Igor the Angeleno: The Mexican Connection." In Levitz, *Stravinsky and His World*, 141–76.

———. "In the Shadow of the Zoot Suit Riots: Racial Exclusion and the Foundations of Music History." Abstract. *Abstracts of Papers Read*, American Musicological Society, Eighteenth Annual Meeting, 6–9 Nov. 2014, 68.

———. *Modernist Mysteries: Perséphone*. New York: Oxford University Press, 2013.

———, ed. *Stravinsky and His World*. Princeton, NJ: Princeton University Press, 2013.

———. "Stravinsky's Cold War Letters, 1960–1963." In Levitz, *Stravinsky and His World*, 273–317.

———. "Who Owns *Mavra*? A Transnational Dispute." in Levitz, *Stravinsky and His World*, 21–59.

Levy, Juana Neel. "Society Groups to Attend Ballet." *Los Angeles Times*, 12 March 1937, A7.

Lewando, Ralph. "Igor Stravinsky Devotes Program to Own Works." *Pittsburgh Press*, 26 Jan. 1935, 12.

Libman, Lillian. *And Music at the Close: Stravinsky's Last Years; A Personal Memoir*. New York: Norton, 1972.

Library of Congress. *Catalog of Copyright Entries*. Part 3, *Musical Compositions, 1937*. Washington, DC: Government Printing Office, 1937.

Liebling, Leonard. "Stravinsky Ballet in New York Premiere." *Musical Courier*, 8 Jan. 1937, 15.

———. "Variations." *Musical Courier*, 15 Nov. 1939, 21.

Liese, Kirsten. *Elisabeth Schwarzkopf: From Flower Maiden to Marschallin*. New York: Amadeus, 2009.

Lindlar, Heinrich. *Strawinsky in Amerika: Das kompositorische Werk von 1939 bis 1955*. Bonn: Boosey and Hawkes, 1955.

———. "Strawinskys Ebony Concerto." *Melos* 21 (1954): 284–85.

Linick, Anthony. *The Lives of Ingolf Dahl*. Bloomington, IN: Author House, 2008.

Lopez, Vincent. *Lopez Speaking: An Autobiography*. New York: Citadel Press, 1960.

Louis, Eleonora, and Toni Stooss, eds. *Igor Strawinsky: Ich muss die Kunst anfassen; Zum 125 Geburtstag von Igor Strawinsky*. Salzburg: Museum der Moderne, 2007.

Lourié, Eugene. *My Work in Films*. San Diego: Harcourt Brace Jovanovich, 1985.

Lowinsky, Edward E. *Tonality and Atonality in Sixteenth-Century Music*. Berkeley: University of California Press, 1961.

Lubrano, J & J. *Catalogue 63*. Lloyd Harbor, New York: J & J Lubrano Music Antiquarians, 2013.

Ludwig, Charles. "'I Love America,' Composer Declares," *Cincinnati Times-Star,* 4 March, 1925.

Lynott, Walt. "Composers Igor Stravinsky and Prof. Cushing." *San Francisco Examiner,* 22 May 1968, 19; 6 April 1971, 4.

Lyons, Leonard. "Broadway Gazette." *Washington Post,* 5 Feb. 1945, 5.

M.M.C. "Philadelphia Orchestra Gives Stravinsky Program." *Musical Courier Weekly Review,* 19 Feb. 1925, 6.

M.S. "Stravinsky Leads Premiere of His Persephone in Hub City." *Musical Courier,* 23 March 1935, 7.

Mach, Elyse. *Great Contemporary Pianists Speak for Themselves.* 2nd rev. ed. 2 vols. New York: Dover, 1991.

Mactaggart, Jessie E. "Appreciation of Music Greater in America." *Globe and Mail* (Toronto), 5 Jan. 1937, 36.

Madison, Dolly. "Stravinsky and Dushkin Attract Large Audience." *Seattle Post-Intelligencer,* 1 April 1937, 11.

————. "Stravinsky Here Tonight." *Seattle Post-Intelligencer,* 31 March 1937, 6.

————. "Stravinsky on Wednesday." *Seattle Post-Intelligencer,* 28 March 1937, 4.

Malkiel, Henrietta. "The Guest Conductor Faces the Music: Preparing 'Le Sacre.'" *Musical America,* 24 Jan. 1925, 3, 38.

————. "Modernists Have Ruined Modern Music, Stravinsky Says." *Musical America,* 10 Jan. 1925, 9.

Mann, Klaus. "How Not to Spend Furlough, Told by the Writer after 6,000 Miles Trip." *The Message: Camp Crowder,* 26 August 1943.

Mann, Thomas. *Tagebücher, 1940–1943.* 10 vols. Edited by Peter de Mendelssohn. Frankfurt am Main: S. Fischer, 1982.

Manso, Carlos. *Juan José Castro: Biografía y epistolario.* Buenos Aires: De los cuarto vientos, 2008.

Marcus, Kenneth H. *Musical Metropolis: Los Angeles and the Creation of a Music Culture, 1880–1940.* New York: Palgrave-Macmillan, 2004.

Maroth, Frederick J. "Stravinsky the Conductor." In booklet with *Stravinsky Conducts Stravinsky,* 4–19. CD 1184. 2 discs. Kensington, CA: Music and Arts Program of America, 2006.

Maroth, Frederick J., and William L. Malloch. *Igor Stravinsky: The Man and His Music.* Berkeley, CA: Educational Media Associates of America, 1976.

Martin, John. "Monte Carlo Ballet Opens Season Here." *New York Times,* 21 March 1935, 26.

————. "Stravinsky Leads Own 'Petrushka.'" *New York Times,* 3 April 1943, 10.

Mason, Francis. *I Remember Balanchine.* New York: Doubleday, 1991.

Mason, Jack. "Inspiration Is Myth, Says Igor Stravinsky." *Oakland Tribune,* 10 Feb. 1935, 5–7.

Mason, Lawrence. "Two Orchestral Concerts." *Globe and Mail* (Toronto), 9 Jan. 1937, 7.

Matter, Stewart. "Stravinsky Leads Cleveland Forces." *Musical America,* 10 March 1937, 18.

McC, J.E. "Stravinsky Leads Chicago Orchestra in Milwaukee." *Musical Courier,* 2 Feb. 1935, 7.

McClure, John. "Stravinsky at Eighty." *Gramophone* 40, no. 469 (June 1962): 1–3.

McCombs, R.L.F. "Stravinsky Pianist Presents Music of Stravinsky, Composer." *Columbus Citizen,* 8 Feb. 1937, 9b.

———. "Words and Music." *Columbus Citizen,* 6 Feb. 1937, 8–9b.

McFarland, Mark. "Stravinsky and the Pianola: A Relationship Reconsidered." *Revue de musicologie* 97, no. 1 (2011): 85–109.

McPhee, Colin. "Records and Scores." *Modern Music* 19 (Jan.-Feb. 1942): 124–26.

[McQuoid], Dorothy Ellis. "Dr. Alexis Kall, a Gentleman and a Scholar." *Baton of Phi Beta,* March 1939, 19–21.

Mead, C. Pannill. "Milwaukee Hears Soprano and Composer." *Musical America,* 10 Feb. 1935, 117.

Menotti, Gian Carlo. *Amelia Goes to the Ball.* 1936–37.

Merrill-Mirsky, Carol, ed. *Exiles in Paradise: Exhibition Catalog.* Los Angeles: Hollywood Bowl Museum and Philharmonic Association, 1991.

Messing, Scott. *Neoclassicism in Music: From the Genesis of the Concept through the Schoenberg/Stravinsky Polemic.* Ann Arbor, MI: UMI Research Press, 1988.

———. "Polemic as History: The Case of Neoclassicism." *Journal of Musicology* 9, no. 4 (1991): 481–97.

Meyer, Felix, ed. *Settling New Scores: Music Manuscripts from the Paul Sacher Foundation.* Mainz: Schott, 1998.

"Milaya moya, rodnaya Rossiya!" Fedor Shalyapin i russkaya provintsaya [Darling mine, my native Russia! Feodor Chaliapin and the Russian provinces]. Iaroslavl: Upper Volga, 2003.

Milhaud, Darius. *Notes without Music.* New York: Knopf, 1953.

———. "Through My California Window." *Modern Music* 21 (Jan.-Feb. 1943): 89–95.

Milhaud, Madeleine. *Mon XXème siècle.* Edited by Mildred Clary. Paris: France musiques / Bleu nuit, 2002.

Milhaud, Madeleine, Darius Milhaud, Hélène Hoppenot, and Henri Hoppenot. *Conversation: Correspondance, 1918–1974.* Edited by Marie France Mousli. Paris: Gallimard, 2005.

Milot, Louise Bail. *Jean Papineau-Couture: La vie, la carrière et l'œuvre.* LaSalle, PQ: Hurtubise HMH, 1986.

Milstein, Nathan, and Solomon Volkov. *From Russia to the West: The Musical Memoirs and Reminiscences of Nathan Milstein.* Translated by Antonina W. Bouis. New York: Henry Holt, 1990.

"Mischa Violin Again to Aid W.P.A. Group." *Los Angeles Times,* 26 Oct. 1941, D5.

Monighetti, Tatiana Baranova. "Stravinsky's Russian Library." In Levitz, *Stravinsky and His World,* 61–77.

———. "Working on *The Rite of Spring:* Stravinsky's Sketches for the Ballet at the Paul Sacher Stiftung." In *Igor Stravinsky: Sounds and Gestures of Modernism,* edited by Massimiliano Locanto, 101–36. Turnhout: Brepols, 2014.

Moore, Edward. "Earliest Work by Stravinsky Given Ovation." *Chicago Daily Tribune,* 23 Jan. 1935, 11.

———. "Feuermann Is Cello Soloist at Stock Concert." *Chicago Daily Tribune,* 7 Dec. 1934, 25.

———. "Stravinsky Is Ill." *Chicago Daily Tribune,* 27 March 1935, 13.

Morgan, Paula. "Forbes, Elliot." In Sadie, *The New Grove Dictionary* (2001), 9:83.

Móricz, Klára. "*Symphonies* and *Funeral Games:* Lourié's Critique of Stravinsky's Neoclassicism." In Levitz, *Stravinsky and His World,* 105–26.

Morton, Lawrence. "Los Angeles to Hear Resident Composer." *Modern Music* 22 (1944–45): 52.

———. "Music Notes." *Rob Wagner's Script,* 22 Feb. 1941, 18.

———. "Music Notes." *Rob Wagner's Script,* 6 Feb. 1943, 30.

———. "Music Notes." *Rob Wagner's Script,* 1 Dec. 1945, 20–21.

———. "Music Notes." *Rob Wagner's Script,* 15 Feb. 1947, 1–8.

———. Review of *Stravinsky,* by Eric Walter White. *Musical Quarterly* 53, no. 4 (1967): 589–95.

———. "Stravinsky at Home." In Pasler, *Confronting Stravinsky,* 332–48.

———. "Stravinsky in Los Angeles." In *Festival of Music Made in Los Angeles,* compiled and edited by Orrin Howard, 66–85. Los Angeles: Philharmonic Association, 1981.

———. "Stravinsky's New Symphony." *Rob Wagner's Script,* 18 Jan. 1947, 18–19.

Mosch, Ulrich. "Igor Stravinsky: Piano Concerto, Piano Sonata and Violin Concerto." In Boehm, Mosch, and Schmidt, *Canto d'Amore,* 187–88, items 225a–c.

Muñoz, Carmen García. "Juan José Castro (1895–1968)." *Cuadernos de música iberoamericana* 1 (1996): 3–24.

Muns, J. B. *Musical Autographs. List 11–06: Signed Photographs, Letters, Musical Quotations.* Berkeley, CA: J. B. Muns, 2013.

"Music: Not Even Stravinsky." *Time,* 2 Feb. 1942, 60.

Nabokov, Nicolas. "The Atonal Trail: A Communication." *Partisan Review* 15 (1948): 580–85.

———. *Bagázh: Memoirs of a Russian Cosmopolitan.* New York: Atheneum, 1975.

———. *Igor Strawinsky.* Berlin: Colloquium Verlag Otto H. Hess, 1964.

———. *Old Friends and New Music.* Boston: Little, Brown, 1951.

———. "Stravinsky Now." *Partisan Review* 2 (1944): 324–34.

Nadeaud, Nils, ed. *Orosco at Dartmouth: The Epic of American Civilization.* Dartmouth, NH: Trustees of Dartmouth College, 2007.

Neef, Sigrid. *Stravinsky in Moscow, 1962.* Melodiya, 1962; BMG, 1996. CD booklet.

Nestyev, Israel. "Vechera Igoiya Stravinskovo." *Sovetskaya Muzïka,* 26 Dec. 1962, 92–95.

Newman, Arnold, Robert Craft, and Francis Steegmuller. *Bravo Stravinsky.* Cleveland, OH: World Publishing, 1967.

Nichols, Roger. *Conversations with Madeleine Milhaud.* London: Faber and Faber, 1996.

Nicolodi, Fiamma. "Casella e la musica di Stravinsky in Italia: Contributo a un'indagine sul neoclassicismo." *Chigiana* 29–30 (1972–73): 41–67.

Nilsson, Victor. "Stravinsky Sets Mark." *Minneapolis Journal,* 22 Jan. 1935, 5.

North, James H., and Tom Tierney. "The Columbia Symphony Orchestra: An Explanation of the Recording History of a Phantom Orchestra." *ARSC Journal* 45 (2014): 156–78.

Nouvel, W. F. *Diaghilev.* Translated into Russian from the French. Moscow: ZGALI, n.d.

O. C. "Stravinsky Leads St. Louis Players in Benefit Concert for Pension Fund." *Musical Courier,* 2 March 1935, 8.

Oates, Joyce Carol. "Sex, Farce & Futility." *New York Review of Books,* 23 Oct. 2010, 41–42.

"Ocean Travelers." *New York Times,* 4 May 1937, 22.

Oja, Carol J. *Making Music Modern: New York in the 1920s.* New York: Oxford University Press, 2000.

———, ed. *Stravinsky in Modern Music, 1924–1946.* New York: Da Capo, 1982.

Oldani, Robert William. "Musorgsky." In Sadie, *The New Grove Dictionary* (2001), 17:549.

Oliver, Michael. *Igor Stravinsky.* London: Phaidon, 1995.

Osgood, H. O. "Stravinsky Conducts an Interview and a Concert." *Musical Courier Weekly Review,* 15 Jan. 1925, 7.

P. "Stravinsky Conducts His Own Symphony." *Musical America,* Feb. 1946, 282–84.

Packenham, Compton. [Essay on Stravinsky], *New York Times,* 27 Jan. 1935, X8.

Paddison, Max. "Stravinsky as Devil: Adorno's Three Critiques." In Cross, *The Cambridge Companion,* 192–202.

Papineau-Couture, Isabelle, and Jean Papineau-Couture. "Souvenirs." *Cahiers canadiens* 4–5 (1972): 59–63.

Pasler, Jann, ed. *Confronting Stravinsky: Man, Musician, and Modernist.* Berkeley: University of California Press, 1986.

———. "Stravinsky: Insights and Oversights." *Musical Times* 127 (Oct. 1986): 557–59.

———. "Stravinsky and His Craft: Trends in Stravinsky Criticism and Research." *Musical Times* 124 (1983): 605–9.

Paul J. Jackson Opera Collection, part VII: R–S, lots 759, 760. Syosset, NY: J & J Lubrano, 2016.

Pelletier, Roman-Octave. "Les concerts: Stravinsky." *Le Devoir Montreal,* 8 March 1945, 6.

Perrin, Maurice. "Strawinsky dans une classe de composition." *Feuilles musicales et revue suisse du disque,* Dec. 1951, 207–12.

Pettis, Ashley. "The WPA and the Composer's Forum." *Musical Quarterly* 26, no. 1 (1940): 101–12.

Peyser, Joan. *The Memory of All That: The Life of George Gershwin.* New York: Simon and Schuster, 1993.

Piaf, Edith. *Au bal de la change.* Edited by Marc Robine. Paris: l'Arcipel, 2003.

Plaskin, Glenn. *Horowitz: A Biography.* New York: Morrow, 1983.

"Police Leave as Igor Plays True Anthem." *New York Journal American,* 16 Jan. 1944.

Pollack, Howard. *George Gershwin.* Berkeley: University of California Press, 2006.

———. *Skyscraper Lullaby: The Life and Music of John Alden Carpenter.* Washington, DC: Smithsonian Institution Press, 1995.

Preston, Bernard. "Toronto Gives Acclaim to Stravinsky." *Musical Courier,* 16 Jan. 1937, 1.

Prevols, Naima. *Dancing in the Sun: Hollywood Choreographers, 1915–1937.* Ann Arbor, MI: UMI Research Press, 1987.

Prokofiev, Sergey. *Diaries.* Translated and annotated by Anthony Phillips. 3 vols. Ithaca, NY: Cornell University Press, 2006–12.

Provines, June. "Front Views and Profiles." *Chicago Tribune,* 22 Feb. 1940, 23.

Purcell, Robert M. *Merle Armitage Was Here! A Retrospective of a 20th Century Renaissance Man.* Morongo Valley, CA: Sagebrush, 1981.

Quentin, Cyrus. "Stravinsky's New Symphony Played." *Musical America,* 25 Nov. 1940, 3, 6.

R. D. "Acclaim Igor Stravinsky: Guest Conductor for 'Petrouchka' Ballet Will Be Welcomed in Los Angeles." LA Philharmonic Program booklet, 4–5 March 1937, 20.

R. H. W. "Stravinsky Leads in Cleveland." *Musical Courier,* 13 March 1937, 9.

R. M. K. "Stravinsky Conducts His Works." *Musical Courier,* 15 Feb. 1945, 12.

Raksin. David. "Composer in Paradise." In Merrill-Mirsky, *Exiles in Paradise,* 86–95.

Raskin, A. *Shaliapin i russkie khudozhniki*. Leningrad: Art Publisher, 1963.

Reese, Gustave, and Ramona H. Matthews. "Kramer." In Sadie, *The New Grove Dictionary* (1980), 10:239; (2001), 13:869–70.

Reis, Claire. *Composers in America: Biographical Sketches of Living Composers, with a Record of Their Works, 1912–1937*. New York: Macmillan, 1937.

Rhein, John von. "CSO Revives Long-Lost Stravinsky." *Chicago Tribune*, 5 April 2017, sec. 4, 3.

———. "Long-Lost Opus by Igor Stravinsky Gets U.S. Premiere with the CSO." *Chicago Tribune*, 8 April 2017, sec. 1, 11.

Rhodes, John F. "Prospect of Citizenship Charms Stravinsky as He Gets Ready for Cincinnati Concerts." *Cincinnati Enquirer*, 22 Nov. 1940, 2.

Ricci, Franco Carlo. *Vittorio Rieti*. Naples: Edizioni Scientifiche Italiane, 1987.

Riley, Dorothy. "Composer's Wife Rushes to Finish Yule Shopping: Minneapolis Equals Paris in Merchandise, She Claims." *Minneapolis Star Journal*, 20 Dec. 1940, 17.

Roberts, Robert H. "Stravinsky Leads Toronto Symphony." *Musical America*, 25 Jan. 1937, 27.

Robinson, Edward G., and Leonard Spigelgass. *All My Yesterdays: An Autobiography*. New York: Hawthorn Books, 1973.

Robinson, Gladys [?]. "Horrible Hollywood." *Rob Wagner's Script*, 27 Sept. 1941, 18.

Rodicio, Emilio Casares, ed. "Drama and Music." *Diccionario de la música española e hispanoamericana*. Madrid: S Golea y E, 1999.

Rodriguez, José. "Drama and Music." *Rob Wagner's Script*, 9 March 1935, 10.

———. "Our Cover Boy." *Rob Wagner's Script*, 5 Oct. 1940, 11.

———. "Stravinsky." *Rob Wagner's Script*, 2 March 1935, 12.

Roerig, N. "Igor Stravinsky über seine Musik: Ein Gespräch mit dem russischen Meister." In *Blätter des Staatsoper und der Städtischen Oper*. Berlin: Staatsoper, 1927.

Rolland, Romain. *Journal des années de guerre, 1914–1919*. 6 vols. Paris: Albin Michel, 1970.

Rosar, William H. "Stravinsky and MGM." In *Film Music 1*, edited by Clifford McCarty, 108–22. New York: Garland, 1989.

Rosenfeld, Paul. *Musical Impressions: Selections from Paul Rosenfeld's Criticism*. Edited by Herbert A. Leibowitz. New York: Hill and Wang, 1969.

Rosenstiel, Léonie. *Nadia Boulanger: A Life in Music*. New York: Norton, 1982.

Routh, Francis. *Stravinsky: The Master Musicians Series*. London: Dent, 1975.

———. *Stravinsky: The Three Symphonies and Ode*. London: Chandos, 1982.

Rózsa, Miklós. *Double Life: The Autobiography of Miklós Rózsa*. Tunbridge Wells, GB: Midas; New York: Hippocrene, 1982.

———. *Életem Történeteiböl* [Life history]. Edited by György Lehotay-Horváth. Budapest: Zenemükiadó, 1980.

Rubin, William. "*The Pipes of Pan*: Picasso's Aborted Love Song to Sara Murphy." *Art News*, May 1994, 138–47.

Rubinstein, Arthur. *My Many Years*. New York: Knopf, 1980.

Saavedra, Leonora. *Carlos Chávez and His World*. Princeton, NJ: Princeton University Press, 2015.

Saavedra, Leonora, Mariel Fiori, and Tamara Levitz. "Stravinsky Speaks to the Spanish-Speaking World." In Levitz, *Stravinsky and His World*, 177–223.

Sabin, "A Survey of Our Orchestral Repertoire." *Musical America,* July 1945, 8.

Sadie, Stanley, ed. *The New Grove Dictionary of Music and Musicians.* 1st ed. 20 vols. London: Macmillan, 1980; 2nd ed. 29 vols. New York: Grove, 2001.

Salzman, Eric. "Concert Notes." In *Festival of Music Made in Los Angeles,* compiled and edited by Orrin Howard, 30–31. Los Angeles: Los Angeles Philharmonic Association, 1981.

Santana, Jorge. "Cronica Musical: Stravinsky en la OSM." *Excelsior,* 21 July 1941, pt. 2, 2.

Saunders, Richard Drake. "Hollywood." *Musical Courier,* 1 Nov. 1942, 22.

———. "Hollywood." *Musical Courier,* 5 March 1943, 22.

———. "Hollywood Bowl." *Musical Courier,* 15 Sept. 1940, 14.

———. "Los Angeles Critic Decries Stravinsky's Later Music." *Musical Courier,* 27 March 1937, 7.

———. "Los Angeles Orchestra Opening and Opera Delight." *Musical Courier,* 15 Nov. 1944, 24.

———, ed. *Music and Dance in California and the West.* Hollywood: Bureau of Musical Research, 1948.

S[aunders, Richard Drake?]. "Orchestra." *Musical America,* 25 Dec. 1944, 32.

———. "Stravinsky Heard Again." *Musical America,* Feb. 1945, 243.

Savenko, Svetlana. "*Vesna svyashchennaya* in Its Homeland: Reception of *The Rite* in Russia and the Soviet Union." In Danuser and Zimmermann, *Avatar of Modernity,* 240–62.

Schabas, Ezra. *Sir Ernest MacMillan: The Importance of Being Canadian.* Toronto: University of Toronto Press, 1994.

Schaeffner, André. *Strawinsky.* Paris: Rieder, 1931.

Schafer, R. M. *Ezra Pound and Music.* New York: New Directions, 1977.

Schanke, Robert A. *"That Furious Lesbian": The Story of Mercedes de Acosta.* Carbondale, IL: Southern Illinois University Press, 2003.

Scheijen, Sjeng. *Diaghilev: A Life.* Translated by Jane Hedley-Prôle and S. J. Leinbach. New York: Oxford University Press, 2009.

Scherliess, Volker. "Strawinsky in Amerika." In *Biographische Konstellation und künstlerisches Handeln,* edited by Giselher Schubert, 158–75. Mainz: Schott, 1991.

Schiff, David. "Everyone's *Rite* (1939–1946)." In Danuser and Zimmermann, *Avatar of Modernity,* 194–97.

Schmidt, Christian Martin. "The Viennese School and Classicism." In Boehm, Mosch, and Schmidt, *Canto d'Amore,* 358–67.

Schneider, Herbert. "Tradition und Neuorientierung in Igor Stravinskijs Mass." *Acta Musicologica* 80 (2008): 251–87.

S[chonberg], H[arold] C. "Stravinsky Leads His New Symphony." *Musical Courier,* 15 Feb. 1946, 14.

Schönberger, Elmer, and Louis Andriessen. "The Utopian Unison." In Pasler, *Confronting Stravinsky,* 207–14.

Schriftgiesser, Karl. "Stravinski Brings Dynamic Ego to City—And Takes It to Movies." *Washington Post,* 24 March 1935, 10.

Schuster-Craig, John. "Stravinsky's *Scènes de ballet* and Billy Rose's *The Seven Lively Arts.*" In *Music in the Theater, Church, and Villa: Essays in Honor of Robert Lamar Weaver and*

Norma Wright Weaver, edited by Susan Parisi, 285–89. Warren, MI: Harmonie Park Press, 2000.

Schwarz, Boris. "Stravinsky, Dushkin, and the Violin." In Pasler, *Confronting Stravinsky,* 302–9.

Sears, Richard S. *V-Discs: A History and Discography.* Westport, CT: Greenwood, 1980.

Serov, Valentin Aleksandrovich. *Perepiska, 1884–1911.* Leningrad: Iskusstvo, 1937.

———. *V perepiske, dokumentakh i interv'iu.* Edited by I. S. Zil'berstein. Leningrad: Soviet Russian Artist, 1989.

"Sharps and Flats." *Los Angeles Times,* 3 Sept. 1939, C5.

Shawn, Allen. "The Genius of Robert Craft." *New York Review of Books,* 14 Jan. 2016, 35–36.

Shepard, John. "The Stravinsky *Nachlass:* A Provisional Checklist of Music Manuscripts." *Notes* 40 (1983–84): 719–50.

Sherman, John K. "Music: Stravinsky Conducts Seventh Symphony." *Minneapolis Star Journal,* 21 Dec. 1940, 10.

———. "Twin Cities Hear Russian Composers." *Musical America,* 10 Feb. 1935, 77.

Shilkret, Nathaniel. *Nathaniel Shilkret: Sixty Years in the Music Business.* Edited by Niel Shell and Barbara Shilkret. Lanham, MD: Scarecrow, 2005.

Shippey, Lee. "The Lee Side o' LA." *Los Angeles Times,* 28 Feb. 1935, A4.

Shoaf, R. Wayne. "Satellite Collections in the Archive of the Arnold Schoenberg Institute." *Journal of the Arnold Schoenberg Institute* 15, no. 1 (June 1992): 9–110.

Shoaf, R. Wayne, et al. "A Preliminary Inventory of Correspondence to and from Arnold Schoenberg." *Journal of the Arnold Schoenberg Institute* 18–19 [double volume] (1995–1996): 1–776.

Simeone, Nigel, ed. *The Leonard Bernstein Letters.* New Haven, CT: Yale University Press, 2013.

Simic, Charles. "Late-Night Whispers from Poland." *New York Review of Books,* 22 Dec. 2011, 2, 28–32.

Simon, Robert A. "Musical Events: Compliments of Igor Stravinsky." *New Yorker,* 2 Feb. 1946, 69.

Skinner, David. *The Story of Ain't: America, Its Language and the Most Controversial Dictionary Ever Published.* New York: Harper, 2012.

Slim, H. Colin. *Annotated Catalogue of the H. Colin Slim Stravinsky Collection Donated by Him to the University of British Columbia Library.* Vancouver: Benwell-Atkins, 2002.

———. "Chère amie: The Mystery of the Unstamped Postcard." In Forney and Smith, *Sleuthing the Muse,* 329–45.

———. "From Copenhagen and Paris: A Stravinsky Photograph-Autograph at the University of British Columbia." *Notes* 59 (2003): 542–55.

———. "Lessons with Stravinsky: The Notebook of Earnest Andersson (1878–1943)." *Journal of the American Musicological Society* 62, no. 2 (2009): 323–412.

———. "Lute Ladies and Old Men in Early Sixteenth-Century Flemish Paintings: Mirrors, Magdalenes, Mottoes, Moralities, Vanities, Allegories." In *Instruments, Ensembles, and Repertory, 1300–1600: Essays in Honour of Keith Polk,* edited by Timothy J. McGee and Stewart Carte, 57–100. Turnhout: Brepols, 2013.

———, ed. *Musica nova.* Vol. 1 of *Monuments of Renaissance Music,* edited by Edward E. Lowinsky. Chicago: University of Chicago Press, 1964.

———. "A Stravinsky Holograph in 1936 for Juan José Castro in Buenos Aires: 'Maître impeccable de la baguette.'" In *Music Observed: Studies in Memory of William C. Holmes,* edited by Colleen Reardon and Susan Parisi, 447–58. Warren, MI: Harmonie Park Press, 2004.

———. "Stravinsky in Vancouver, 1917–2017: Concerts, Premieres, Collections." *Musical Quarterly* 100, nos. 3/4 (2017): 269–96.

———. "Stravinsky's Four Star-Spangled Banners and His 1941 Christmas Card." *Musical Quarterly* 89, no. 2/3 (2006): 321–447.

———. "Stravinsky's *Scherzo à la Russe* and Its Two-Piano Origins." In *Essays on Music and Culture in Honor of Herbert Kellman,* edited by Barbara Haggh, 518–37. Paris: Minerve, 2001.

———. "Unknown Words and Music, 1939–44, by Stravinsky for His Longtime Friend, Dr. Alexis Kall." In *Words on Music: Essays in Honor of Andrew Porter on the Occasion of His 75th Birthday,* edited by David Rosen and Claire Brook, 300–319. Hillsdale, NY: Pendragon, 2003.

Slonimsky, Nicholas, ed. *Baker's Biographical Dictionary of Musicians.* 8th rev. ed. New York: Schirmer, 1992.

———. *Lexicon of Musical Invective.* 2nd ed. Seattle: University of Washington Press, 1969.

———. *Perfect Pitch: An Autobiography.* Edited by Electra Slonimsky Yourke. New York: Schirmer, 2002. Originally published as *Perfect Pitch: A Life Story* (Oxford: Oxford University Press, 1988).

Sloper, I. S. "Stravinsky at Symphony Hall." *Christian Science Monitor,* 23 Feb. 1946, 13.

Smit, Leo. "A Card Game, a Wedding, and a Passing." *Perspectives of New Music* 9 (1971): 87–92.

Smith, Catherine Parsons. *Making Music in Los Angeles: Transforming the Popular.* Berkeley: University of California Press, 2007.

Smith, Moses. "Stravinsky Meets the Boston Censor." *Modern Music* 21 (March-April 1944): 171–73.

Somfai, László. *Béla Bartók: Composition, Concepts, and Autograph Sources.* Berkeley: University of California Press, 1996.

Sotheby's. *Auction Catalogue LO8402.* London: Sotheby's, 2008. Auction catalogue.

———. *The James S. Copley Library: Arts and Sciences. Including the Mark Twain Collection.* New York: Sotheby's, 2010. Auction catalogue.

Souvtchinsky, Pierre. "La Notion du temps et la musique: Réflexions sur la typologie de la création musicale." In *Souvtchinsky: Un siècle de musique Russe,* edited by Frank Langlois, 239–52. Arles: Actes Sud, 2004. Previously published in *Revue musicale,* May-June 1939, 70–80.

Spies, Claudio. "Conundrums, Conjectures, Construals, or, 5 vs. 3: The Influence of Russian Composers on Stravinsky." In Haimo and Johnson, *Stravinsky Retrospectives,* 76–140.

———. Review of *Stravinsky: Glimpses of a Life,* by Robert Craft. *Notes,* 2nd ser., 50, no. 4 (1994): 1408–11.

Spycket, Jérôme. *Nadia Boulanger.* Stuyvesant, NY: Pendragon, 1992.

Stallings, Stephanie N. Review of Carol A. Hess, *Representing the Good Neighbor. Journal of the American Musicological Society* 70, no. 3 (2017): 871–73.

Stark, Abing, ed. *Edward Weston Papers*. Guide Series 13. Tucson: University of Arizona Center for Creative Photography, 1986.

Steegmuller, Francois. "Stravinsky at Work." *Saturday Review*, 29 May 1971, 44–45.

[Steele, R. Vernon?]. "Dr. Kall Passes." *Pacific Coast Musician*, 18 Sept. 1948, 8.

Steele, R. Vernon. "Evenings on the Roof." *Pacific Coast Musician*, 6 April 1946, 12–13; 4 May 1946, 10–11.

[———]. "Pension Fund Concert." *Pacific Coast Musician*, 18 Jan. 1947, 5.

———. "Strawinsky—Philharmonic." *Pacific Coast Musician*, 1 March 1941, 9.

———. "WPA Symphony Sample—Laura Sanders." *Pacific Coast Musician*, 19 April 1941, 8.

Stein, Leonard. "Schoenberg and 'Kleine Modernsky.'" In Pasler, *Confronting Stravinsky*, 310–24.

Steinberg, Michael. "Stravinsky Festival." San Francisco Symphony Playbill, June 1999, 11–18.

Steinert, Alexander. "*Porgy and Bess* and Gershwin." In Armitage, *George Gershwin*, 43–46.

Stevenson, Robert. "Comentario del autor." In *Robert Stevenson: Obras para clarinete y piano*. Madrid: A/B Master Disc Natural, 2006. CD booklet.

Stinson, Eugene. "Stravinsky Leads Chicago Symphony." *Musical America*, 7 March 1925, 41.

Stone, Else, and Kurt Stone, eds. *The Writings of Elliott Carter: An American Composer Looks at Modern Music*. Bloomington: Indiana University Press, 1977.

Straus, Joseph. "Sonata Form in Stravinsky." In Haimo and Johnson, *Stravinsky Retrospectives*, 141–61.

Stravinskaya, K[Xenia] Yu[rievna]. *O I. F. Stravinskom i evo blizkikh* [Stravinsky and his intimates]. Leningrad: Muzïka, 1978.

Stravinsky, Igor. *Chroniques de ma vie*. 2 vols. Paris: Denoël et Steele, 1935. Translated as *Igor Stravinsky: An Autobiography*. New York: Simon and Schuster, 1936; repr. New York: Norton, 1962.

———. *Circus Polka*. New York: AMP, 1942.

———. *Circus Polka: For Band*. Mainz: Schott, 2003.

———. *Concerto per due pianoforte soli*. Mainz: Schott, 1936.

———. "I—As I See Myself." *Gramophone* 12, no. 135 (August 1934): 85.

———. "On Conductors and Conducting." *Show. The Magazine of the Arts*, July-August 1964, 28, 108.

———. *Orchestrations of "The Song of the Flea" by Modest Mussorgsky; "The Song of the Flea" by Ludwig van Beethoven*. Edited by Arkady Klimovitsky; translated by Paul Williams. St. Petersburg: School of Music Publishing House / Russian Institute for the History of the Arts, 2003.

———. *Poétique musicale sous forme de six leçons*. Edited by Myriam Soumagnac. Paris: Flammarion, 2000. Translated by Arthur Knodel and Ingolf Dahl as *Poetics of Music*. Cambridge, MA: Harvard University Press, 1947 and 2000.

———. "Pourquoi l'on n'aime pas ma musique: Une interview d'Igor Stravinsky." In Lesure, *Stravinsky: Études*, 242–46. Previously published in *Journal de Genève*, 14 Nov. 1928, 2. Translated as "Why People Dislike My Music," *Musical Forecast* (Pittsburgh, PA), 17 Feb. 1930, 1, 12.

———. *The Rite of Spring/Le Sacre du Printemps: Sketches, 1911–1913; Facsimile Reproductions from the Autographs.* London: Boosey and Hawkes, 1969.

———. *Selected Correspondence.* 3 vols. Edited by Robert Craft. New York: Knopf, 1982–85.

———. "Some Ideas about my Octuor." In White, *Stravinsky: The Composer,* Appendix A, no. 2, 574–77. Previously published in *The Arts,* Jan. 1924.

———. "Stravinsky at 85." Toronto: CBC, 18 May 1967.

———. *Themes and Conclusions.* London: Faber and Faber, 1972.

Stravinsky, Igor, and Robert Craft. *Conversations with Igor Stravinsky.* Garden City, NY: Doubleday, 1959.

———. *Dialogues.* London: Faber and Faber, 1982.

———. *Dialogues and a Diary.* Garden City, NY: Doubleday, 1963.

———. *Expositions and Developments.* Garden City, NY: Doubleday, 1962.

———. *Expositions and Developments.* Berkeley: University of California Press, 1981.

———. *Memories and Commentaries.* Garden City, NY: Doubleday, 1960.

———. *Memories and Commentaries.* Berkeley: University of California Press, 1981.

———. *Memories and Commentaries: Igor Stravinsky and Robert Craft.* London: Faber and Faber, 2002.

———. *Retrospectives and Conclusions.* New York: Knopf, 1969.

———. *Themes and Episodes.* New York: Knopf, 1966.

"Stravinsky 'Composes' Music but Says He 'Writes' Music." *Toronto Daily Star,* 4 Jan. 1937, 2.

"Stravinsky Pays Tribute to Kochanski's Art with Promise of Violin Work." *Musical America,* 18 April 1925, 33.

"Stravinsky Peels Off His Coat and Brings Down the House." *Newsweek,* 23 Jan. 1937, 24.

"Stravinsky Plays at Vincent Astor's." *New York Times,* 16 Jan. 1925, 17.

"Stravinsky Sails Home; Mary Garden Leaving, Scouts Foreign Offer." *Musical America,* 21 March 1925, 43.

Stravinsky, Vera, and Robert Craft. *Stravinsky in Pictures and Documents.* New York: Simon and Schuster, 1978.

Strawinsky: Sein Nachlass, sein Bild. Basel: Das Kunstmuseum Basel, 1984.

"Strawinsky in Amerika: Das kompositorische Werk von 1939 bis 1955." *Musik der Zeit* 12 (1955).

Strawinsky, Théodore. *Catherine and Igor Stravinsky: A Family Album.* London: Boosey and Hawkes, 1975.

———. *Le Message d'Igor Strawinsky.* Lausanne: F. Rouge, 1948.

Strawinsky, Théodore, and Denise Strawinsky. *Au cœur du foyer: Catherine et Igor Strawinsky, 1906–1940.* Bourg-la-Reine: Zurfluh, 1998.

Stuart, Philip, comp. *Igor Stravinsky—The Composer in the Recording Studio: A Comprehensive Discography.* New York: Greenwood, 1991.

Stull, Christopher. "Igor Stravinsky: Mozart Was Modern, Too." *San Francisco Chronicle,* 13 Dec. 1939, 8.

Stutsman, Grace May, "American Premiere of Persephone in Boston." *Musical America,* 25 March 1935, 1–4.

———. "Stravinsky Joins Tanglewood School." *Musical America,* 25 Dec. 1941, 40.

—————. "Stravinsky Leads Boston Symphony." *Musical America,* 10 Nov. 1939, 15.

Suchoff, Benjamin. *Béla Bartók: Life and Work.* Lanham, MD: Scarecrow, 2001.

Sulzer, Peter. *Neujahrsblatt der Stadt Bibliothek Winterthur.* 3 vols. Winterthur: Atlantis Musikbuch-Verlag, nos. 309–10 (1979–80) and no. 313 (1983).

—————. *Zehn Komponisten um Werner Reinhart: Ein Ausschnitt aus dem Wirkungskreis des Musikkollegiums Winterthur, 1920–1950.* Winterthur: Stadtbibliothek, 1979–80.

Szigeti, Josef. *With Strings Attached: Reminiscences and Reflections.* New York: Knopf, 1947.

Tansman, Alexandre. *Igor Stravinsky.* Paris: Amiot-Dumont, 1948. Translated by Therese and Charles Bleefield as *Igor Stravinsky: The Man and His Music.* New York: G. P. Putnam's Sons, 1949.

Taper, Bernard. *Balanchine: A Biography.* New York: Times Books, 1984.

Tappolet, Claude, ed. *Correspondance Ernest Ansermet–Igor Strawinsky (1914–1967).* 3 vols. Geneva: Georg, 1990–92.

Taruskin, Richard. "Back to Whom? Neoclassicism as Ideology." *19th-Century Music* 16 (1993): 286–302; and in *The Danger of Music,* 382–405.

—————. *The Danger of Music and Other Anti-utopian Essays.* Berkeley: University of California Press, 2009.

—————. "The Dark Side of the Moon." In Taruskin, *The Danger of Music,* 202–16.

—————. *Defining Russia Musically: Historical and Hermeneutical Essays.* Princeton, NJ: Princeton University Press, 1997.

—————. "Ezra Pound: A Slim Sound Claim to Immortality." In Taruskin, *The Danger of Music,* 181–85.

—————. "The Golden Age of Kitsch." In Taruskin, *The Danger of Music,* 241–60.

—————. "In from the Cold." Review of Giroud, *Nicolas Nabokov. Times Literary Supplement,* 5 August 2016, 3–5.

—————. "Just How Russian Was Stravinsky?" *New York Times,* 18 April 2010, 21, 23.

—————. *The Oxford History of Western Music.* New York: Oxford University Press, 2005.

—————. *Russian Music at Home and Abroad: New Essays.* Oakland: University of California Press, 2016.

—————. *Stravinsky and the Russian Traditions: A Biography of the Works through "Mavra."* Berkeley: University of California Press, 1996.

—————. "Stravinsky and Us." In Cross, *The Cambridge Companion,* 260–84.

—————. "Stravinsky and Us: Postscript, 2008." In Taruskin, *The Danger of Music,* 442–43.

—————. "Stravinsky's 'Rejoicing Discovery' and What It Meant." In Haimo and Johnson, *Stravinsky Retrospectives,* 162–99.

—————. *Text and Act: Essays on Music and Performance.* New York: Oxford University Press, 1995.

Taruskin, Richard, and Robert Craft. "Jews and Geniuses: An Exchange." *New York Review of Books,* 15 June 1989, 57–58.

Taruskin, Richard, and Christopher H. Gibbs. *The Oxford History of Western Music: College Edition.* New York: Oxford University Press, 2013.

Taruskin, Richard, et al. "Symposium: Catching Up with Rimsky-Korsakov." *Music Theory Spectrum* 33, no. 2 (2011): 169–229.

Taubman, Howard. *The Pleasure of Their Company: A Reminiscence.* Portland, OR: Amadeus, 1994.

———. "3 Artists Heard in Pension Concert." *New York Times,* 9 Feb. 1946, 9.

Tawa, Nicolas E. *From Psalm to Symphony: A History of Music in New England.* Boston: Northeastern University Press, 2001.

Taylor, Deems. "Music: At the Metropolitan." *New York World,* 14 March 1925, 11.

———. "Music: Stravinsky Conducts." *New York World,* 9 Jan. 1925, 13.

———. "Music: The Stravinsky Concerto." *New York World,* 6 Feb. 1925, 11.

Thanks to Berkeley. Berkeley: University of California Library, 2011. Exhibition catalogue.

Thirlwell, Adam. *The Delighted States.* New York: Straus and Giroux, 2008.

Thomas, Michael Tilson. "On Stravinsky." In booklet accompanying *Stravinsky in America* CD. New York: RCA Victor, BMG Classics, 1997. 8–9.

Thompson, Dody Weston. *Edward Weston Omnibus: A Critical Anthology.* Edited by Beaumont Newhall and Amy Conger. Salt Lake City, UT: Peregrine Smith, 1984.

Thompson, Oscar. "Igor Stravinsky Makes N.Y. Debut as Conductor of The Philharmonic." *Musical America,* 17 Jan. 1925, 1, 6.

———. "New Stravinsky Ballet Achieves World Premiere." *Musical America,* 10 May 1937, 19.

———. "Stravinsky Leads Chamber Music Forces." *Musical America,* 31 Jan. 1925, 26.

———. "Stravinsky Lionized at Brilliant Revival of 'Petrushka.'" *Musical America,* 21 March 1925, 4.

Thomson, Virgil. *The Musical Scene.* New York: Knopf, 1945.

———. *Music Reviewed, 1940–1954.* New York: Vintage, 1967.

Thornton, G. S. *The Melodist; Comprising a Selection of the Most Favorite English, Scotch and Irish Songs, Arranged for the Voice, Flute or Violin.* New York: G. Singleton, 1820.

Timmons, Jill, and Sylvain Frémaux. "Alexandre Tansman: Diary of a 20th-Century Composer," *Polish Music Journal* 1 (Summer 1998): 1–15.

Tobin, R. James. *Neoclassical Music in America: Voices of Clarity and Restraint.* Lanham, MD: Rowman and Littlefield, 2014.

Tommasini, Anthony. "The Greatest." *New York Times,* 21 Jan 2011, 14.

Trotter, William R. *Priest of Music: The Life of Dimitri Mitropoulos.* Portland, OR: Amadeus, 1995.

Tryon, Winthrop P. "Stravinsky as Lecturer on Music as Poetic Art." *Christian Science Monitor,* 19 Oct. 1939, 16.

———. "Stravinsky Concludes Lectures at Harvard. Composer in Final Lecture. Leaves 1940–41 Concert Tour." *Christian Science Monitor,* 11 April 1940, 16.

———. "Stravinsky Returning with New Symphony." *Christian Science Monitor,* 21 Feb. 1946, 14.

Ukolov, E., and V. Ukolov. *Dusha bez maski* [Soul minus mask]. Moscow: n.p., 2004.

Ussachevsky, Vladimir. "My Secret Stravinsky." *Perspectives of New Music* 9 (1971): 34–38.

Ussher, Bruno David. "Composer Explains Himself." Los Angeles Philharmonic Program, 21–22 Feb. 1935, 33–38.

———. "Sounding Board." *Los Angeles Daily News,* 16 and 29 Oct. 1944, 26.

———, ed. *Who's Who in Music and Dance in Southern California.* Hollywood: Bureau of Musical Research, 1933.

Valentin Aleksandrovich Serov, 1865–1911: Paintings, Graphic-Art from the Collection of the State Russian Museum. St. Petersburg: Palace Editions, 2005.

Valkenier, Elizabeth Kridl. *Valentin Serov: Portraits of Russia's Silver Age.* Evanston, IL: Northwestern University Press, 2006.

van den Toorn, Pieter C. *The Music of Igor Stravinsky.* New Haven, CT: Yale University Press, 1983.

———. "Octatonic Pitch Structure in Stravinsky." In Pasler, *Confronting Stravinsky,* 130–56.

———. *Stravinsky and "The Rite of Spring": The Beginnings of a Musical Language.* Berkeley: University of California Press, 1987.

van Patten, Nathan. *A Memorial Library of Music at Stanford University.* Los Angeles: Ward Ritchie, 1950.

Varunts, Viktor. *I. F. Stravinsky: Perepiska s russkimi korrespondentami; Materiali k biographi* [Letters with Russian correspondents; Materials for biography]. 3 vols. Moscow: Kompositor, 1998–2003.

———, ed. *I. Stravinskiy: Publitsist i sobesednik* [Writer and conversationalist]. Moscow: Sovetskiy Kompozitor, 1988.

Vásquez, Maria Esther. *Vitoria Ocampo.* Buenos Aires: Planeta, 1991.

Vikárius, László. "Intimations through Words and Music: Unique Sources to Béla Bartók's Life and Thought in the Fonds Denijs Dille (B–Br)." *Revue belge de musicologie* 67 (2013): 179–217.

Vom B[aur] Hansl, Eva, and Helen L. Kaufmann. *Minute Sketches of Great Composers.* New York: Grosset and Dunlap, 1932.

Von Glahn, Denis, and Michael Broyles. "Musical Modernism before It Began: Leo Ornstein and a Case for Revisionist History." *Journal of the Society for American Music* 1, no. 1 (2007): 29–55.

W. "Stravinsky Opens Engagement with Philharmonic." *Musical America,* 25 Jan. 1940, 8.

W. F. "Harvard Students Taught Music by Russian Composer." *Christian Science Monitor,* 22 Nov. 1939, 12.

Wagner, Denise. "A Stravinsky Scrapbook from the Chicago Symphony Archives." *Notebook: The Program of the Chicago Symphony Orchestra,* 17–28. Chicago: CSO, 1996.

Wagner, Hugo. "Igor Strawinsky und René Auberjonois." In *Strawinsky: Sein Nachlass, sein Bild,* 369.

Walsh, Stephen. *The Music of Stravinsky.* London: Routledge, 1988; rev. repr. New York: Oxford University Press, 1993.

———. *The New Grove Stravinsky.* New York: Palgrave, 2002.

———. "Remembering *The Rite of Spring,* or 'Ce que je m'ai pas voulu exprimer dans Le Sacre du printemps.'" In Danuser and Zimmermann, *Avatar of Modernity,* 155–73.

———. "Stravinsky." In Sadie, *The New Grove Dictionary* (2001), 24: 528–56.

———. *Stravinsky: A Creative Spring; Russia and France, 1882–1934.* New York: Knopf, 1999.

———. *Stravinsky: The Second Exile: France and America, 1934–1971.* New York: Knopf, 2006.

Walters, Margaret. "Actor's Life Is Not a One-Track Matter, Says Versatile Paul Leyssac of Hollywood." *Musical Courier,* 1 Sept. 1942, 23.

Walz, Jay. "Capitol Hears Concert of Swing and Classics." *Musical America,* 10 Feb. 1942, 23.

Waterhouse, John C. G., and Virgilio Bernardini. "Casella." In Sadie, *The New Grove Dictionary* (2001), 5:232–35.

Watkins, Glenn. *Pyramids at the Louvre*. Cambridge, MA: Harvard University Press, 1994.

Watson, G. W. ["Stravinsky quoted."] *Chicago Defender*, 30 March 1935, 6.

Weiss, Andrea. *In the Shadow of the Magic Mountain: The Erika and Klaus Mann Story*. Chicago: University of Chicago Press, 2008.

Wenborn, Neil. *Stravinsky*. London: Omnibus, 1999.

Westby, James. "Genesis Suite (1945)." Record booklet. American Classics no. 8.559442 (Canada: Naxos, c. 2004).

Weston, Edward. "Thirty-Five Years of Portraiture." Part 2. *Camera Craft* 46, 10 October 1939, 449–60.

Wheeldon, Marianne. "Anti-Debussyism and the Formation of French Neoclassicism." *Journal of the American Musicological Society* 70, no. 2 (2017): 433–74.

White, Eric Walter. *Stravinsky: The Composer and His Works*. Berkeley: University of California Press, 1966; rev. ed. 1979; unless otherwise noted, citations refer to the revised edition.

White, Jorge M. "Stravinsky Directs Own Works at Concert in Buenos Aires." *Musical Courier*, 30 May 1936, 1.

Whittall, Arnold. "Neo-classical." In Sadie, *The New Grove Dictionary* (1980), 13:104–5.

Wiborg, Mary Hoyt. "Igor Stravinsky, One of the Great Russians." *Arts and Decoration*, Jan. 1925, 9–36.

———. "Notes on Modern Soloists and Composers." *Arts and Decoration*, Dec. 1924, 40–41, 90.

Widder, Milton. "Igor Stravinsky—Small Body but a Giant Brain." *Cleveland Press*, 20 Feb. 1937, 3.

Will, Barbara. *Unlikely Collaboration: Gertrude Stein, Bernard Faÿ, and the Vichy Dilemma*. New York: Columbia University Press, 2011.

Wilson, Charis, and Wendy Madar. *Through another Lens: My Years with Edward Weston*. New York: North Point Press, 1998.

Woitas, Monika. "'A Powerful Motor Drive' Strawinsky—Neurowissenschaftlich betrachtet." In Woitas and Hartmann, *Strawinskys "Motor Drive,"* 79–93.

Woitas, Monika, and Annette Hartmann, eds. *Strawinskys "Motor Drive."* Munich: Epodium, 2010.

Yastrebtsev, Vasiliy Vasiliyevich. *N. A. Rimskiy-Korsakov: Vospominaniya, 1886–1908*. 2 vols. Edited by A. V. Ossovsky. Leningrad: Muzgiz, 1959–60. Translated as *Reminiscences of Rimsky-Korsakov*. Edited and translated by Florence Jonas. New York: Columbia University Press, 1985.

Yeiser, Frederick. "Symphony Concert." *Cincinnati Enquirer*, 23 Nov. 1940, 22.

Yuzefovich, Victor. "Chronicle of a Non-friendship: Letters of Stravinsky and Koussevitzky." *Musical Quarterly* 86, no. 4 (2002): 750–885.

Zarotschenzeff, M. T. "Fingal's Cave: For the 70th Anniversary of Professor A. F. Kall." *Novaya zarya*, 28 Jan. 1940, 1–3.

Zenck, Claudia Maurer. "Challenges and Opportunities of Acculturation: Schoenberg, Krenek, and Stravinsky in Exile." In *Driven into Paradise: The Musical Migration from*

Nazi Germany to the United States, edited by Reinhold Brinkmann and Christoph Wolff, 172–93. Berkeley: University of California Press, 1999.

———. "Leben und Überleben als Komponist im Exil: Die ersten Jahre Strawinskys in den USA." In *Exilmusik: Komposition während der NS-Zeit,* edited by Friedrich Geiger and Thomas Schäfer, 56–79. Hamburg: Von Bockel, 1999.

Zilbershteyn, Ilya Samoylovich, and Vladimir Alexeyevich Samkov, eds. *Sergey Dyagilev i russkoye iskusstvo* [Sergei Diaghilev and Russian art]. 2 vols. Moscow: Izobratitel'noye Iskusstvo, 1982.

Ziolkowski, Theodore. *Classicism of the Twenties: Art, Music, and Literature.* Chicago: University of Chicago Press, 2015.

INDEX

Page numbers followed by *fig.* indicate figures; *ex.* indicate musical examples.

Associated Music Publishers Inc., 179, 234, 274*fig.*, 275*fig.*

Atlantic Monthly, 86, 258–59

auction, for war bond drive, 241–45

Austin, William, 136

Babel (Stravinsky, I.), 262*ex.*, 263*ex.;* anti-Semitism and, 259; bassoon in, 290–91; on Excursions, of 1944, 259–66; Schoenberg on dress rehearsal, 290

Babin, Victor, 236

Babitz, Sol, 225; on Ballet Theater, 238; *Circus Polka*, 183, 234–35; *Concerto in D for Violin*, 173–75, 184, 239; Dahl and, 239; Dushkin, S., and, 55; inscription to, 55, 173; on Symphony in C, 177, 187; *Tango* and, 233

Bach, Johann Sebastian, 10, 284, 311

Le Baiser de la fée (Stravinsky, I.), 73, 75–76, 78

Balaban, Emanuel, 284

Balanchine, George: American Ballet choreography, 113, 123–24; Ballet Monte Carlo and, 225–26; *Balustrade* by, 183–84; *Cabin in the Sky* choreography by, 179; *Circus Polka* and, 234–36; *Danses concertantes* staging by, 284; *Divertimento* choreography, 77; *Jeu de cartes* choreography, 84, 110, 112–13; Nabokov and, 64, 335n158

Ballet Monte Carlo, 225–26

Ballet Russe de Monte Carlo, 284, 307–8

Ballet Theater of New York, 238

Baltimore, 180

Balustrade (Balanchine), 183–84

The Barber of Seville (Rossini), 299

Barsby, Jack, 176

Bartók, Béla, 3, 150–51

bassoon, 290–91

Beethoven, Ludwig van, 3, 105, 302, 401n78

The Beethoven Quartets (Kerman), 302

Bel'sky, Vladimir Ivanovich, 103–5

Benny, Jack, 3, 236, 287

Berkeley, California, 53–54

Berlin, Isaiah, 112, 159

Berlin Radio Orchestra, 69

Best, Paul, 183

Beverly Hills, 175–76

Bickford, Clara Gehring, 92–94, 93*fig.*, 94*fig.*

Birkel Music Co., 55

black American music, 89

Bliss, Robert Woods, 114, 200

The Blue Network, 276*fig.*

Bolshevism, 92

Borowski, Felix, 258

Boston: *Firebird Suite* in, 70; Godowsky, D., in, 128–29; *Perséphone* in, 64; Symphony Hall, 246; Symphony in Three Movements premiere, 298–99; on Tour V, 143–48

Boston Daily Globe, 254*fig.*, 309

Boston Globe, 253

Boston Symphony Orchestra: "family" relationship with, 134; *Jeu de cartes* rehearsal, 137–38; Koussevitzky, S., with, 34, 47–48; musicians of, 136–38; *Ode: Elegiacal Chant in Three Parts* premiere, 245; *Oedipus R.*, 252–53; "The Star-Spangled Banner" with, 253–54, 254*fig.;* Stravinsky, I., as pianist with, 34; Symphony in C, 181–83, 255–56

Boulanger, Nadia: *Élégie* and, 284; Forbes, Elliot, and, 135; Mills College lecture series, 268–78; Sample and, 190; in Santa Barbara, 199–200, 257; *Scherzo à la Russe* with, 283

"Bravo" letter, from the McQuoids, 168, 170

Bremen, SS, 48

Britannic, SS, 116

Brodetsky, Julian, 228–29, 228*fig.*, 230*fig.*

Brontë, Charlotte, 246, 248

Brown, Mary Jeannette, 301

Buenos Aires, 73, 75, 79

Cage, John, 186

Caldwell, Sara, 11

California, 4; Berkeley, 53–54; on Excursions, of 1940–1941, 173–75; on Excursions, of 1943, 237–40; Santa Barbara, 106, 199–200, 223, 240–41, 257; UCLA, 184–85, 190. *See also* Hollywood; Los Angeles

Cambridge, 118, 128–30, 134–35

Canada, 81–83, 339n17

Cap Arcona, 73

Cap Arcona, SS, 73

Capriccio (Stravinsky, I.), 185–87, 198, 371n109

Carnegie Hall, 25, 42, 110, 134, 153, 287

Carter, Elliott, 115

Cartier-Bresson, Henri, 151

Casella, Alfredo, 15, 313

Cassidy, Claudia, 177, 258

Los Angeles WPA Orchestra, 189–91, 194, 206

Lourié, Eugène, 61, 73, 112, 350n129, 356n7, 376n220

Lowinsky, Edward E., 10–11

Luening, Otto, 7

MacGregor, Willard, 258

MacMillan, Ernest, 82–83, 82*fig.*, 83*fig.*

Madison, Dolly, 108

Maestoso, from *Futurama Symphony* (Andersson), 216*ex.*, 217–18

Malkiel, Henrietta, 24–25

Malotte, Charles, L., 202

Mandelstamm, Yuri, 85

Manhattan, SS, 128

Mann, Klaus, 182, 241–45

Mann, Michael, 284

Mann, Thomas, 241

manuscript, 241

Marcus, Adele, 48, 129, 149, 161, 164–65, 185, 188

Maritain, Jacques, 257

The Marriage of Figaro (Mozart), 28

La Marseillaise (Stravinsky, I.), 193

Martin, John, 307

Marxism, 199

Mason, Jack, 47, 53

Massachusetts: Boston, 64, 70, 128–29, 143–49, 246–47, 298–99; Cambridge, 118, 128–30, 134–35; Harvard University, 118–21, 119*fig.*, 134–39, 210; marriage in, 149–50; "The Star-Spangled Banner" in, 253–56, 254*fig.* *See also* Boston Symphony Orchestra

the masses, 3

Massey Hall, 83

Mastrazzi, Aida, 74–75, 74*fig.*

Mavra (Stravinsky, I.), 46

McCarter Hall, 91–92

McQuoid, Cary Ellis, 141, 142*fig.*, 164

McQuoid, Dorothy Ellis: drawing by, 180; inscription to, 164*fig.*; at Kall's funeral, 372n134; letters to Stravinsky, I., 203; in Mexico City, 198; *Petrushka* score of, inscribed, 144*fig.*, 145*fig.*; playing *Capriccio,* 185, 198; playing Symphony in C, 163; postcard to, 140–41, 140*fig.*; Soudeikina, V., with, 162; Stravinsky, V., and, 173; on *Tango,* 189

McQuoid, Edwin, 163–64, 165*fig.*, 180, 182

McQuoid family, 161, 163–64, 163*fig.*, 168, 169*fig.*, 170, 173, 181*fig.*, 186*fig.*

The Melodist (Thornton), 247–49

Memories and Commentaries (Craft), 255, 296, 390n5

Menotti, Gian Carlo, 109

Menuhin, Yehudi, 192

Mercury Music Corporation, 179–80, 189, 193–94, 199–200, 234

Merovitch, Alexander Bernardovich, 37–38, 71–72, 80–81

Merrily We Roll Along (Kaufman, G., and Hart), 61–62

Metropolitan Opera, 28, 94, 113

Mexico, 75–76, 163*fig.*, 167*fig.*

Mexico City, 4, 48, 165–66, 198–99, 306

MGM film studio, 110, 142–43, 231, 236

Midwest, 26–28, 41–44, 91–94, 176–80

migraine, 70

Milaud family, 237–38, 278, 375n176

Mills College, 269–78

Milstein, Nathan, 38

Milwaukee, 69

Milwaukee Journal, 47

Minneapolis, 177–78

Minneapolis Star Journal, 178

Minneapolis Symphony Orchestra, 178, 306

Minute Sketches of Great Composers, 164, 166*fig.*

Mitropoulos, Dimitri, 226–27, 306

modernism, 1, 81, 178, 253

Modern Music, 298, 305–6

monometric music, 170, 256

Monteux, Pierre, 106; conducting *The Rite of Spring,* 7–8; *Danses concertantes* and, 211; on NBC broadcast, 107–8; on *Les Noces,* 7; photograph, with Stravinsky, I., 107*fig.*; Sample and, 190, 226; in San Francisco, 210; Tour V, of 1939–1940, 130, 131*fig.*, 132; in Vancouver, 329n31

Montreal, 308, 329n31; *Circus Polka* in, 287–88; rehearsal, 289*fig.*

Montreal Gazette, 289*fig.*

Moodie, Alma, 29–30

Morgan, George Thomas, 191

Morning Tribune, 177–78

Morros, Boris, 60, 109–10, 112, 231, 346n73

Victory Symphony. See Symphony in Three
	Movements (Stravinsky, I.)
Violin Concerto. See Concerto in D for Violin
	(Stravinsky, I.)
vox populi, 3
Vronsky, Vitya, 236

Wade Park Manor, 92
Walsh, Stephen, xxii, 231–32, 283–84, 323n49,
	340n33
war bond drive, 241–45
Warburg, Edward, 64, 72, 353n188
Washington, DC, 64–65, 180, 192, 213–14,
	303
Washington Post, 309
Washington Time Herald, 89
Webster, Beveridge, 115, 287
Wecker, Karl, 201
Weicher, John, 258
the West, American, 45–46, 130, 132–34
west coast, United States, 53–55, 106, 110
Weston, Edward, 54–55, 56–58, 57 box, 177
White, Eric Walter, 247, 267
Whiteman, Paul, 86; Scherzo à la Russe version,
	266, 271, 277–78, 277fig.

white music, 186
whole-tone scale, 215, 217–19, 221–22
Wiborg, Mary Hoyt, 20, 322n29
William Vaughan Moody Lecture, 257
Wilshire Ebell Theatre, 225
Wilson, Charis, 57
Wilson, Dorothy, 61–62
Winnetka, Illinois, 64
women, relationships with, 6, 16
World War I, 160
World War II, 4; communication with family
	during, 278–83; invasion of Russia,
	112–13; Pearl Harbor, 157, 204–5, 207,
	209; Stravinsky, I., as conductor during,
	after, 306–12; Symphony in Three
	Movements composed during, 291–92;
	United States declaration of, 210; war
	bond drive, 241–45; works produced
	during, 160
WPA Federal Orchestra, 189–91, 226
Wyck, Wilfrid van, 117

Yeiser, Frederick, 177

Ziloti, Alexander, 7

CALIFORNIA STUDIES IN 20TH-CENTURY MUSIC

Richard Taruskin, General Editor